T0338230

Labor Economics

Labor Economics
PRINCIPLES IN PRACTICE

SECOND EDITION

KENNETH J. McLAUGHLIN

New York   Oxford
OXFORD UNIVERSITY PRESS

Oxford University Press is a department of the University of Oxford.
It furthers the Universitys objective of excellence in research, scholarship,
and education by publishing worldwide. Oxford is a registered trade mark of
Oxford University Press in the UK and certain other countries.

Published in the United States of America by Oxford University Press
198 Madison Avenue, New York, NY 10016, United States of America.

© 2019 by Oxford University Press

Library of Congress Cataloging-in-Publication Data

CIP data is on file at the Library of Congress
978-0-19-085699-1

Printing number: 9 8 7 6 5 4 3 2 1
Printed by LSC Communications, Inc., United States of America
on acid-free paper

To My Girls

About the Author

Kenneth J. McLaughlin is a graduate of Ohio State University (B.A.) and the University of Chicago (M.A., Ph.D.), where he learned his craft from several of the greatest labor economists of all time. His best research in labor economics has appeared in the *Journal of Labor Economics,* the *Journal of Political Economy,* and the *Journal of Monetary Economics.*

After seven years in the Department of Economics at the University of Rochester, Professor McLaughlin joined the City University of New York (CUNY), where he holds positions at Hunter College and the Graduate Center. He's also held visiting professorships at the University of Chicago, the University of Michigan, and Columbia University. He's taught undergraduate and graduate courses in labor economics to students at Chicago, Rochester, Michigan, CUNY, and Columbia (graduate only).

Professor McLaughlin's personal experience in the labor market hasn't been limited to academia. In the years before he headed to graduate school, he worked as a carhop and a gas station attendant. For a short time, a small firm paid him to fly coach between Dayton and Columbus to collect travel vouchers good for free flights anywhere in the United States. He also learned a bit about data analysis while working in the economics departments at Citibank and General Electric.

Professor McLaughlin lives in Maplewood, New Jersey.

Contents

PART ONE

1   Introduction to Labor Economics   1

4 Labor Demand   126

PART TWO

9 Unions   326

10 Wage Inequality 366

PART THREE

11 Compensation Strategies 402

Preface to the Student

Decades ago, I was doing exactly what you're doing now. I had enrolled in a course in labor economics, and I wondered what I had gotten myself into. A fellow student had asked me what that labor econ course was about. My reply exhausted my knowledge of labor economics: "I think it's about applying micro to labor." Uh-oh. Maybe I could figure out what I had gotten myself into by spending a few minutes with the textbook's preface and table of contents.

And so my exploration of labor economics began. My professor was no entertainer, and the textbook was dull, but the topics fascinated me. I hadn't expected economics to be all that relevant to the world of labor, so discovering the power of economic principles to illuminate labor market issues stunned me. I was hooked.

I hope you'll also be fascinated with the topics and impressed by the power of economics to demystify the world of work and pay.

What will you find in the pages that follow? Chapter 1 introduces you to the issues and data in labor economics and prepares you for the exploration ahead. If you've retained a working knowledge of the basic principles of microeconomics, you'll be in good shape; for those with a foggy memory of microeconomic principles, I develop even the most basic economics concepts (e.g., demand and supply) from scratch. You must also be ready to interpret patterns in labor economics data. Haven't taken a course in statistics? No problem. You'll find everything you'll need to know about empirical methods in chapter 1.

Chapters 2–4 present the core of labor economics. Chapter 2 analyzes labor markets using only demand and supply curves and tackles big questions like whether workers are exploited. The applications to innovations, minimum wages, taxes, wage subsidies, and immigration are compelling, important, and relevant to policy debates. Chapters 3 and 4, which have their own compelling applications, dig deeper to figure out where labor supply and demand curves come from.

The topics of chapters 5–10 are job attributes; schooling; training, turnover, and migration; discrimination; unions; and wage inequality. What unifies these topics? Each chapter identifies one or two factors that influence individual wages—my wage, your wage, the wage of the person who sold you coffee this morning. Chapter by chapter, we expose why wages differ across workers and occupations (e.g., why lawyers make more than sales clerks).

Limited information plays a leading role in the two chapters that close our exploration of labor economics. Chapter 11 explores the consequences of employers not observing workers' effort or ability for the form of compensation (e.g., incentive pay). Chapter 12 shows how unemployment arises naturally from employers searching for workers and workers searching for jobs.

A distinctive feature of the presentation is that it draws evidence directly from the data. Rather than referring to estimates from the vast literature of labor economics, I turn to the data to plot or estimate the key patterns. You won't memorize findings from the scholarly literature; you'll actively interpret and evaluate evidence. Analysis of one important data set builds from chapter to chapter, and other interesting data scts drop in along the way.

One of my goals in writing this book has been to make learning labor economics easier. My job is to make the tough stuff not so tough. Here are some features that should make learning labor economics a bit easier for you.

- *Economic models are presented through meaningful examples.* Workers and their employers have names, and numbers replace variables. Thus "Gregg works 9 hours per day" replaces "the worker works h^* hours."

- *Footnotes are eliminated.* If an idea is important, it's woven into the narrative. If it's not so important, it's not in the book.

- *Practice questions pop up within each chapter.* You can check your progress at every stage of the exploration. Each practice question checks whether you understand the material covered in the previous paragraphs or graph. You should pause to answer each practice question along the way. Don't move on until you can do it. Answers to the practice questions appear at the back of the book, so you can check your answers.

- *Graphs include self-contained descriptions of their content.* Pause to read each graph's description after reading the lengthier presentation in the body of the chapter. Don't move on until you fully understand the graph.

- *Each chapter closes with a checklisted summary.* If you grasp a principle or key finding, check it off. If not, return to the body of the chapter to clarify your understanding of the item. You haven't completed a chapter until you can confidently check off each item in the summary.

- *End-of-chapter problems reinforce the models.* You understand the content of a chapter when you can work out its problems. The typical end-of-chapter problem directly applies a model in the chapter to a new numerical context. You draw the line or curve to find an intersection or point of tangency. Graphs with grid lines accompany most problems.

Most chapters include clearly labeled advanced material. Check with your instructor about whether you're responsible for the advanced material. If not, you can skip over it without any loss of continuity.

How can these features help you succeed in this course? Understanding the graphs inside and out is the key to your success. If you thoroughly understand the graphs, then you'll grasp 90 percent of the material. (Details in the body of the chapters can push that A– to an A.) So study every graph with its paired description, work through the practice questions along the way, and solve the problems at the end of the chapter. If you understand the graphs, the checklisted summary at the end of each chapter should be clear as a bell.

Now let's learn some labor economics.

Preface to the Instructor

Labor Economics: Principles in Practice provides a concise, tightly integrated, and engaging exploration of labor economics for undergraduate students. Improving the presentation can make it easier for students to learn without "dumbing down" the content. Indeed, my aim is for your students to acquire an unrivaled understanding of the field's most important models and applications.

Four distinctive features characterize my approach.

- *Focusing on principles.* This textbook emphasizes the vital and enduring principles of labor economics—the principles that flow from the field's most valuable models. The presentation is decidedly not encyclopedic. Covering too much content and over-referencing the scholarly literature detracts from the core principles of labor economics. So topics are confined to the essentials, and connections to the scholarly literature are purposefully restrained. Focusing on core principles also highlights some big-picture questions: Are labor markets efficient? Are workers paid what they're worth? What factors enhance efficiency and reduce or eliminate exploitation of workers?

- *Bringing the data on board.* Other textbooks on labor economics fill the bottom of almost every page with footnotes that reference estimates in the scholarly literature. Few students read the footnotes; the ones who do don't get any sense of empirical research from lists of names, dates, and point estimates. So I weave the data into the narrative. I display important patterns in the data and interpret simple regressions. I introduce students to the Current Population Survey (CPS) in chapter 1, and the analysis of occupation averages in the CPS unifies chapters 5–10. Once students are familiar with the occupation averages, grouping the CPS data in other ways (e.g., wages by state or wage profiles by cohort) can pay off without long digressions. And students are well prepared to interpret scatter plots and regressions from the disaggregated CPS in the chapters on training, turnover, and migration (7), discrimination (8), and wage inequality (10). I also analyze other interesting data sets along the way.

- *Keeping the models simple and specific.* I keep the economic models as simple as possible to deliver the key predictions and explanations. One theme that guides the modeling is that it's better to work with a specific model to deliver concrete results than to generalize without structure. Sharp predictions from specific models set the foundation for discussions of meaningful extensions.

- *Presenting the models by example.* Presentation of a typical model progresses from a table of numbers to graphs and results. Working with simple numerical exercises makes the models less abstract. Numbers replace symbols, and workers and firms get names. Grounding the analysis in numbers engages students and better prepares them to work out problems.

I'm confident that these features will help your students clearly see the principles of labor economics through its models and empirical methods. I also hope that your students will find my informal and friendly writing style engaging. Science is serious business, but students shouldn't have to suffer through dull prose.

The presentation is almost entirely self-contained. Students will surely benefit from having taken a principles of microeconomics course or even a one-semester introduction to economics course. But *the presentation assumes no prior knowledge of economics*. Even demand and supply curves are carefully explained. I develop the most abstract concepts (e.g., indifference curves, isoquant curves, and iso-profit curves) from scratch with plenty of hand-holding. As for math, students must be able to interpret relationships on graphs. Chapter 1 reviews slopes, percentage changes, elasticities, and other tools. Although I weave the empirical work into the narrative, students need not have any prior knowledge of statistics. A meaningful empirical example in chapter 1 introduces scatter plots, regression analysis, causality, before-and-after comparisons, and difference-in-difference estimation. I briefly explain outcomes, probabilities, distributions, and expected values of random variables in the "For Your Toolbox" section of chapter 1.

Let's aim high. While the entry requirements are low, my presentation of labor economics doesn't shy away from the tough stuff. I favor simple models with tangible results over hand-waving. In the end, your students can acquire an unrivaled understanding of the field's most important models and applications.

What's New in Edition 2?

The additions, extensions, and other improvements in this edition stick to my approach. I bring more data on board to develop students' empirical skills. The new models are simple and specific, and I present them by example. You'll find most of the new content in chapters 2 (Labor Markets), 8 (Discrimination), and 10 (Wage Inequality). Here's what's new by chapter.

- Chapter 2—I've added mechanization of farming as an example of innovations that reduce the demand for labor. The minimum wage gets its own section. Two event plots and associated regressions replace an oversized table and a dense discussion of the estimates in Deere, Murphy, and Welch (1995). I've also added "advanced material" with estimates of employment effects of two rounds of federal minimum-wage hikes on state-year data. New content on wage subsidies and employer mandates find a home with employment taxes in the new section, "Taxes, Subsidies, and Employer Mandates."

- Chapter 5—The application of compensating wage differentials to occupational safety regulation now includes a discussion of the wage premium for dangerous work building the Brooklyn Bridge.

- Chapter 6—The introduction includes a time plot of schooling of 25-year-olds by sex back to 1900.

- Chapter 7—I use January 2016's Job Tenure and Occupational Mobility supplement to the CPS to estimate and interpret log-wage regressions with a quadratic in job tenure. I also analyze Galenson's (1981) data on the period of indenture in contracts from eighteenth-century London with a scatter plot and a contract-length regression.

- Chapter 8—In this chapter, I bring old and new data on board in three ways. First, in a new application of standardizing wage comparisons, I estimate wage discrimination against Muslims in America. In particular, I compare the wage effect of having parents who emigrated from Muslim countries with the wage effect of having parents who emigrated from European countries. Second, I bring Neal and Johnson's (1996) data on board with a scatter plot and regressions with and without the test-score variable. Third, in a new subsection on career wage ratios and family demands, I present Goldin's (2014) case for family demands driving mid-career wage penalties of professional women with children. I essentially replicate Goldin's evidence using cohorts from the outgoing rotation group files of the CPS.

- Chapter 10—This chapter gets a new title, "Wage Inequality," and a new section on the effects of skill-biased innovation in the long run. Increasing wage inequality strengthens the incentives to acquire skills, which reduces wage inequality. I also discuss job polarization in the context of this dynamic process. Another addition to this chapter is in adding the graduate-school wage premium to the presentation of the college wage premium. And I replace a table on *income* inequality around the world with a scatter plot on *earnings* inequality around the world, which prompts a discussion of why some countries have low income inequality but high earnings inequality.

- Chapter 11—The subsection on efficiency wages gets an application on paying a wage premium to reduce quits.

- Chapter 12—A new subsection on job vacancies presents the Beveridge curve in the context of the Great Recession.

This edition also updates all the data through December 2017.

I've put lots of effort into improving the writing as well. In reading the text from start to finish, I searched for passages that weren't clear and sentences and paragraphs that ran too long to communicate effectively. I also activated most instances of passive voice and generously introduced contractions.

Organization and Content

I've organized twelve chapters into three parts. After the introduction in chapter 1, chapters 2–4 on labor markets, labor supply, and labor demand present the core of labor economics. The wage equation unifies the second part—the six chapters on job attributes (5); schooling (6); training, turnover, and migration (7); discrimination (8); unions (9); and wage inequality (10). Each chapter adds a variable or two to the wage equation. This part culminates with the study of wage inequality in chapter 10. Limited information unifies the two chapters in the third part: compensation strategies (11) and unemployment (12).

In Part 1, the chapter on labor markets precedes the chapters on labor supply and labor demand. The course then builds from simple models (e.g., with only demand and supply curves) in chapter 2 to more-formal derivations with indifference curves and budget lines in chapter 3 and isoquants and isocosts in chapter 4. Your students will undoubtedly appreciate covering some interesting applications (e.g., the baby boom and the employment and pay of teachers, slavery and the invention of the cotton gin, minimum wages, taxes on labor, the earned income tax credit, employer mandates, migration, and the reserve clause and collusion in baseball) before you shift to a higher level of abstraction in chapters 3 and 4. This organization also echoes the tried-and-true organization of principles courses: we teach demand, supply, and equilibrium before we derive the supply curve (from the fundamentals of production, cost, and profit maximization) and the demand curve (from indifference curves and the budget line) later in the course.

Topics sort naturally into chapters, although my placement of some topics might surprise you. Minimum wages and labor market monopsony find a home in the labor markets chapter (rather than the more typical placement in a labor demand chapter). Some topics in labor supply and labor demand pop up in later chapters. For instance, the schooling chapter covers the effect of schooling on labor supply. The life-cycle model of labor supply fits naturally in the chapter on career patterns, which is chapter 7 ("Training, Turnover, and Migration") And the firm's interest in the workweek (based on quasi-fixed labor costs and fatigue effects) motivates a nice application of compensating wage differentials to the joint determination of the workweek in chapter 5. In each case, learning something new leads us to revisit and to extend the original model.

Finally, I reorganize the conventional chapters on human capital and mobility into a chapter on schooling (6) and a chapter on training, turnover, and migration (7). My presentation includes models of signaling, job shopping, and job matching, so "Human Capital" isn't the right title for such a chapter. Without human capital as a unifying theme, it's more natural to send on-the-job training to a chapter on turnover and migration: career patterns related to work experience and job tenure unify these topics. Even with the changes to these two chapters, topics appear in the familiar order.

Here's a quick summary of the innovative elements in each chapter.

CHAPTER 1—INTRODUCTION.   This chapter highlights the key elements of scientific method in the context of an important question: "Why do lawyers make so much money?" The presentation of scientific method highlights the role of abstraction and the importance of distinguishing between essential and simplifying assumptions. A data section describes the Current Population Survey and other data sets. I use CPS data on median wages by occupation to gently introduce empirical methods, including scatter plots, regressions, instrumental variables, before-and-after comparisons, and difference-in-differences. The chapter also includes a "For Your Toolbox" section that reviews some important concepts in algebra, statistics, and economics.

CHAPTER 2—LABOR MARKETS.   Our study of labor markets begins with a self-contained and thorough presentation of labor supply and labor demand curves in chapter 2 before the more-formal derivations of labor supply and labor demand in chapters 3 and 4. By including "vertical" interpretations of labor demand (i.e., marginal value) and labor supply curves (i.e., marginal cost of workers' time) early in the text, I address efficiency properties immediately and throughout. The content includes minimum wages, taxes on labor, wage subsidies, employer mandates, equilibrium across locational and occupational labor markets, and monopsony. The chapter contains important issues and interesting applications that motivate students to dig deeper in subsequent chapters.

CHAPTER 3—LABOR SUPPLY.   The supply of labor is derived from preferences and opportunities without relying on any prior knowledge of indifference curves or budget lines. Indifference curves represent preferences without any mention of utility. Why leave out utility? Getting students to think in terms of units of utility doesn't illuminate the economics, and students at this level often fail to distinguish between ordinal and cardinal properties of utility. Furthermore, plenty of well-trained students come to a course in labor economics with a utility-free background because some popular principles textbooks don't cover utility. The chapter also includes many applications and extensions, but the schooling chapter (6) covers the effect of schooling on labor supply, and the life-cycle model of labor supply fits naturally in the chapter on career issues (7).

CHAPTER 4—LABOR DEMAND.   One numerical example with a single underlying production function spans the whole chapter, so short-run and long-run labor demands are fully integrated. I even develop Marshall's rules within the context of the running example. The firm's interest in the workweek is an application of compensating wage differentials in chapter 5.

CHAPTER 5—JOB ATTRIBUTES.   The model of compensating wage differentials with a worker's indifference curves, a firm's iso-profit curves, and a hedonic wage function is difficult for students, and I suspect that's why many instructors skip the topic. That's unfortunate because the model is helpful in presenting other models, especially the model of schooling choice. Indeed, the wage–dirt and wage–risk curves in this chapter are the foundations for wage–hours, wage–schooling, wage–ability, and wage–skill curves that appear later. Can we make it easier to understand compensating wage differentials? Sure. This chapter opens with an introductory model that delivers all the key implications. The model matches four workers to four firms, and I derive labor supply and labor demand curves (in the market for dirty jobs) as step functions from reservation wages. The properties of the equilibrium preview all the implications of the familiar model (with indifference curves and iso-profit curves) that follows. Employers' interest in the length of the workday or workweek is undeniable, so a model of the joint determination of the workday or workweek produces an effective application of compensating wage differentials. The chapter also analyzes the effect of taxes on employee benefits.

CHAPTER 6—SCHOOLING.   An explicit and reasonably simple model with a wage–schooling curve and iso-wealth curves delivers the demand for schooling. I informally extend the model to show how tuition, finite life, unemployment, and taxes reduce the demand for schooling. The empirical effect of schooling on log wages is carefully interpreted in the context of these extensions. The chapter also includes the signaling model, and I present evidence on both sides of the human capital–signaling debate. The relationship between schooling and the workweek is quite strong empirically, so the model of consumption–leisure choice is extended to include schooling.

CHAPTER 7—TRAINING, TURNOVER, AND MIGRATION.   This chapter opens with empirical wage profiles for particular birth cohorts in the CPS. General and firm-specific human capital are introduced to determine whether pay can be front-loaded or back-loaded and who pays for training, and the results are applied to the training of pilots. The chapter also contains a simple simulation of Burdett's model of job shopping with an informal extension to Jovanovic's model of learning of match capital. The life-cycle model of labor supply finds its home in this chapter on career patterns. The chapter closes by analyzing migration as an investment in human capital; the analysis of migration also covers selection on skill and an application to indentured servitude in America's colonial period.

CHAPTER 8—DISCRIMINATION.   I use the 2017 CPS to standardize wage comparisons (i.e., the Oaxaca decomposition) and compute residual wage gaps by sex, race, and ethnicity. Unadjusted and residual wage gaps by sex, race, and ethnicity are plotted annually since 1983. The Asian–white wage premium motivates the need to standardize comparisons. I carefully discuss identification of wage discrimination in the presence of omitted skill variables. On the theory side, the first presentation of employer discrimination echoes the first model of compensating wage differentials: four employers varying in degrees of discrimination choose whether to employ women or men. I emphasize the personal cost of discriminating, and an application to institutionalized racial discrimination in the Jim Crow era compares racists' personal and group incentives to discriminate.

CHAPTER 9—UNIONS.   Union success depends on a nurturing legal and regulatory environment, and changes in laws, court rulings, and regulations are used to explain the rise and decline of private-sector unions (and the rise of public-sector unions) in the United States. Students who believe that unions reduce the exploitation of workers are disappointed by models that ignore this possibility. Union bargaining with a monopsonist to push the wage (and employment) up toward the competitive equilibrium is a serious model, and students appreciate it being treated seriously. The chapter presents the monopoly–union model in two ways. The first way marginalizes the demand curve, which connects well with how students learn the monopoly model in their principles of microeconomics course. The second way recasts the monopoly–union model in terms of union preferences and opportunities, which is the point of departure for the efficient-contracting model. The union is a rent maximizer, so the contract curve is vertical at the competitive level of employment. I briefly discuss the weak form of the efficient-contracting model as optional advanced material.

CHAPTER 10—WAGE INEQUALITY.   I leverage students' experience with the CPS to carefully present the distribution of weekly wages and measures of wage inequality in the outgoing rotation groups of the 2017 CPS. Comparison of the distributions of wages and predicted wages shows how the analysis in the preceding chapters explains a lot of measured inequality. And the key wage determinants from the preceding five chapters capture nearly all of the wage inequality across occupations. What generates wage inequality? We look for increasing convex transformations of ability, skill, and even schooling. Mincer's principle that a symmetric distribution of schooling generates a skewed distribution of wages finds some support in the CPS data. The chapter also contains a simple model of job assignment in a hierarchical firm to show how sorting skews the distribution of wages. The section on increasing wage inequality includes the simple model of the wage premium to skill with a perfectly inelastic relative supply of skilled workers in the short run. The final section ("Technology and Jobs in the Long Run") highlights the role of wage inequality in encouraging people to acquire skills and the consequences of skill acquisition for wage inequality in the long run.

CHAPTER 11—COMPENSATION STRATEGIES.   The treatment of compensation strategies emphasizes the advantages and disadvantages of each form of compensation in terms of effort supply, selection and retention of workers, risk from personal and common shocks, product quality, cost of measurement, team work, sabotage, and marginal incentives. I analyze efficiency wages and performance incentives in the same context, so students can compare the cost of efficiency wages and piece rates directly. The application to executive compensation plots and interprets data from ExecuComp.

CHAPTER 12—UNEMPLOYMENT.   Analysis of the distribution of completed spells of unemployment follows seamlessly from the exit rate from unemployment in the steady-state model. The distribution of spell lengths implied by a constant exit rate from unemployment fails to fit the empirical distribution, and that shortcoming motivates important extensions. One extension shows how mixing two heterogeneous groups fits the empirical distribution of spell lengths quite well. The chapter closes with a compact model of aggregate fluctuations that distinguishes between short-run and long-run aggregate supply functions to deliver the expectations-augmented Phillips curve. Analysis of the Beveridge curve closes the chapter.

Pedagogical Features

To help students understand the world of work and pay, I have written a narrative that is simple, engaging, and focuses on the applications. And these principles also guide the pedagogical features.

- *Motivating Examples.* Each chapter opens with an interesting, nontechnical application from scholarly research, and I use the application to preview the chapter's concepts and models.

- *Explicit Units.* Every axis is labeled explicitly (e.g., workers per week, and dollars per worker). Numbers replace symbols. For instance, "the weekly wage increases from $200 to $300 per worker" replaces "the wage increases from w_0 to w_1."

- *Running Examples.* An example or two runs through each chapter. For instance, we follow Gary's career—training and turnover—in the music business in the chapter on training, turnover, and migration (7). In chapter 11, we study how two preparers of tax returns, Julie and Katie, respond to a variety of forms of compensation. In these examples, workers and firms have names, which perks up the prose by avoiding endless repetitions of "the worker" and "the firm."

- *Practice Along the Way.* Each chapter includes brief and simple practice questions within the narrative for students to check their understanding before moving on. Students are encouraged to pause to practice the concept that was just covered. If a student can't answer the practice question, he or she needs to go back before moving forward. Students can find answers to the practice questions at the back of the book. More challenging problems appear at the end of each chapter.

- *Applications without Boxed Examples.* Applications are essential to the presentation, and they are woven into the narrative.

- *No Footnotes.* If a point is important enough to warrant the student's attention, then it belongs in the narrative. If it's not that important, then it's omitted.

- *Few References.* References to six or seven papers and books per chapter are usually enough to identify the classic contributions and less-influential papers that nevertheless provide great examples. Most references are simply tips of my cap to the greatest hits in labor economics.

- *Optional Advanced Material.* I don't relegate advanced material to footnotes, boxes, or appendices. Advanced material is clearly identified within the narrative, so it's easy to skip without loss of continuity. If you assign advanced material, your students won't have to detour to an appendix and later return to the narrative. A good example of advanced material is the derivation in chapter 2 that marginal labor cost is greater than the wage in a monopsony labor market. The derivation relies on only algebra, and it's brief. But it's definitely more mathematically demanding than anything else in the chapter.

- *Parallel Presentations with the Figures.* Each figure includes a self-contained description of the graph. Understanding the graphs is critical, and each graph's companion description condenses the elements of the graph to essentials. That's just what a student needs going into an exam.

Each chapter also includes a checklisted summary, a list of key concepts, a series of short-answer questions, and a set of problems. Most end-of-chapter problems contain "graph paper," so students can carefully draw the curves and their intersections or tangencies. Students can find answers to practice questions at the end of the book. A glossary at the end of the book defines all the key concepts, which are highlighted in boldface when they first appear.

Supplements

I've written a rich set of supplementary materials to help you and your students. You can access all the instructor resources through the Ancillary Resource Center at www.oup-arc.com/mclaughlin. These resources include:

- *Instructor's Manual.* The instructor's manual contains teaching tips, solutions to the short-answer questions and end-of-chapter problems, and connections to the literature. Since I present models by example in the textbook, the instructor's manual also identifies the functional forms hiding in the background.

- *Presentations.* PowerPoint and Beamer—yes!—slides contain bullet-point summaries, as well as all the tables and graphs from the text. A separate set of slides reproduces only the tables and graphs.

- *Test Bank.* The test bank contains over 1,000 multiple-choice questions (80 or so questions per chapter) and all the short-answer questions from the text. The test bank is packaged with Wimba Diploma 6.

- *Data Set of Occupation Averages from the CPS.* The small data set of occupation averages from the Current Population Survey is available in Excel and Stata formats. Students can use the file to view, sort, plot, and fit the data.

- *Econometrics Excercises.* A series of empirical exercises explores wage-equation estimation and interpretation on two extracts (each with several thousand observations) from the CPS. By engaging students in data analysis, the textbook naturally supports students with econometrics training in analyzing individual-level data. The data sets are available in Stata format.

- *Calculus Supplements*. Although the book isn't pitched for students with strong mathematics backgrounds, you can easily supplement the book with calculus-based derivations. I've written the calculus supplements, one PDF file for each chapter, in a friendly style.

Instructors who use a learning management system (LMS), such as Angel, Blackboard, Moodle, or Sakai, can use a course cartridge to access the test bank, exercises, and data sets. Contact your local OUP sales representative or OUP's customer service (800-445-9714) for more information.

Students will find several valuable resources at the companion website (www.oup.com/us/mclaughlin):

- *Chapter Quizzes*. Students can test their understanding of the chapter's concepts and methods. Feedback directs students to the appropriate section of the text for help.

- *Links*. Links to websites point students to data sources and other useful resources.

- *Suggested Reading*. Suggestions for further reading introduce your students to articles in scholarly journals. The list focuses on readable articles, ones that should be accessible to students who grasp the textbook's principles and methods.

Acknowledgments

I'm grateful to the instructors who carefully reviewed chapters for the first and second editions. Your students will benefit from their insights and suggestions.

The following reviewers supplied valuable advice for the second edition:

- Wei-Chiao Huang, Western Michigan University
- Marta Lachowska, W.E. Upjohn Institute for Employment Research
- Patten Mahler, Centre College
- Arindam Mandal, Siena College
- Nicholas Montgomery, University of Maryland

And I continue to appreciate the suggestions from reviewers of my original manuscript:

- John T. Addison, University of South Carolina
- Michael Brun, Illinois State University
- Geoffrey Carliner, Boston University
- Earl H. Davis III, Nicholls State University
- Ethan Doetsch, Ohio State University

- Fred Foldvary, San Jose State University
- David Fractor, California State University at Northridge
- Deniz Gevrek, Texas A&M University–Corpus Christi
- Dora Gicheva, University of North Carolina at Greensboro
- Kaj Gittings, Louisiana State University
- Wei-Chiao Huang, Western Michigan University
- Mark Killingsworth, Rutgers University
- Jongsung Kim, Bryant University
- Fidan Ana Kurtulus, University of Massachusetts at Amherst
- Gerald Marschke, State University of New York at Albany
- Brian McCall, University of Michigan
- Bruce McClung, Texas State University
- Dimitrios Nikolaou, Illinois State University
- Kevin O'Brien, Bradley University
- Silvio Rendon, Stony Brook University
- Elizabeth Wheaton, Southern Methodist University
- Mehmet Yaya, Eastern Michigan University
- Ben Van Kammen, Purdue University

Mark Killingsworth and Gerald Marschke reviewed the entire manuscript for my last-round revisions. Gerald Marschke also evaluated the test banks. Claire Huene searched the entire manuscript for errors and obfuscations, and she answered practice questions, short-answer questions, and end-of-chapter problems. Claire's knack for exposing passages that would confuse students who have little training in economics means that countless students will sleep better the night before an exam.

For answering my questions and offering suggestions, I thank Rick Hanushek, Siu Fai Leung, Jim Lothian, David Neumark, and my colleagues in the Department of Economics at Hunter College (especially Jonathan Conning and Partha Deb). I thank Orley Ashenfelter, Robert Barro, David Card, Hank Farber, David Galenson, Barry Hirsch, Alan Krueger, Jong-Wha Lee, Bruce Meyer, and Derek Neal for data and estimates that I've woven into my narrative. The publicly available extract of Ashenfelter and Krueger's twins data didn't quite satisfy my needs. Before Alan was able to retrieve the full data set from an outdated storage technology, Terra McKinnish supplied me with an extract that solved my problem. I also thank Randy Shifflett and Shayne Brandon from Virtual Jamestown (virtualjamestown.org) for providing indenture data that enabled me to replicate Galenson's sample.

I've enjoyed working with the team at Oxford University Press. My initial contact at Oxford was with Valerie Ashton, whose enthusiasm for my project was irrepressible. My editor, Ann West, has matched Valerie's enthusiasm. With the help of Maura MacDonald and Emily Mathis, Ann skillfully navigated the project through the twilight zone between the author's vision and the reviewers' concerns. Steve Rigolosi's editing of my manuscript was outstanding. In addition to improving my prose, Steve evaluated every example and economic argument. His relentless pursuit of clarity will turn more than a few C students into B students. Other members of the original Oxford team include Patrick Lynch (Editorial Director, Higher Education), Thom Holmes (Development Manager), Micheline Frederick (Senior Production Editor), Clare Castro (Marketing Manager), Michele Laseau (Art Director), Lisa Grzan (Manager, In-house Production), Bob Golden (copyeditor), and James M. Fraleigh (proofreader). The second edition is the product of the hard work of Jennifer Carpenter (Editor), Patricia Berube (Production Editor), Tony Mathias (Marketing Manager), Jordan Wright (Marketing Assistant), Patrick Keefe (Editorial Assistant), Deanna Hegle (copyeditor), and Wesley Morrison (proofreader).

I also thank my girls—Barb Mace and our daughter Jessie—with whom I shared my excitement (and rare frustration) along the way. I've dedicated the book to them because these two extraordinary people have enriched my life extraordinarily.

Thanks for considering *Labor Economics: Principles in Practice*. I hope the book makes it easier for you to teach and for your students to understand the world of work and pay. Please send your questions and suggestions to me at labor.economics@icloud.com.

Ken McLaughlin
July 2018

Introduction to Labor Economics

1

- Li Liyan applies logos to iPhones at one of Foxconn's assembly plants in China. She works from 8 AM to 7 PM, with 10-minute breaks at 10 AM and 3 PM and a 90-minute lunch break, and overtime begins at 5:30 PM. Li earns about $400 per month before overtime, and she pays $17 per month to live in a Foxconn dormitory.

- A doctor in Santa Clara, Cuba, earns more driving tourists in his off hours than the government pays him to practice medicine.

- Susan Connell's job in North Dakota is a seven-hour drive from her husband and two daughters in Montana. She earns thousands of dollars per week hauling waste water, a byproduct of the region's booming oil business, in an 18-wheeler. North Dakota's unemployment rate is among the lowest in the country.

- An investment banker works 70-hour weeks on Wall Street. He juggles his laptop and smartphone on vacations to keep his team in New York productive. If he doesn't, he's crushed with work when he returns from vacation.

- Frank, an Air Force pilot in World War II, took advantage of the GI Bill to take college courses at night while he worked as a shop foreman at General Electric. He earned a degree in engineering and eventually became the head of quality control in GE's aircraft engine division.

- In 1969, Curt Flood's employer ordered him to report for work with a competitor. Flood refused. His employer was the St. Louis Cardinals, he was traded to the Philadelphia Phillies, and he never played professional baseball again.

- Sandra Day graduated near the top of her class from Stanford Law School in 1952. Law firms at the time didn't employ women as attorneys, and 40 law firms refused even to interview Sandra. She took a job without pay as a deputy county attorney. Decades later she became the first woman on the U.S. Supreme Court.

- While working part-time on secretarial jobs, studying to be a teacher, and raising a child as a single parent, Jo Rowling wrote a novel for children. The book sold well, so well that Rowling has earned over $1 billion on her *Harry Potter* series.

- Stu owns a small garment factory in the Bronx. He pays his workers by the piece and complains that quality problems prevent him from landing big contracts with retailers like JCPenney. He also complains that his undergraduate degree in economics from an Ivy League school hasn't helped him a bit in running his business.

- Janet lost her job in the recession of 2007–2009. She collected unemployment compensation for almost two years before filing to collect Social Security retirement benefits at age 62.

These experiences are the subject of labor economics. They are among the billions of threads from around the world and across the centuries that weave rich patterns in the fabric of work and pay. But the patterns can be lost in the details. We need to step back—to abstract—to see the whole fabric in order to appreciate the rich patterns. And that's what we do in this book.

Let's start with an informal example. Hidden in the simple story of a call to tip busboys is one key principle of labor economics. Once identified, this principle steers us clear of erroneous logic and guides us to meaningful conclusions.

1.1   Tipping Busboys

According to a report in the *New York Post* (May 16, 2011), busboys at Cipriani's flagship Fifth Avenue restaurant in Manhattan were feuding with waiters over a cut in their share of tips. Patrons of Cipriani and other restaurants tip the waitstaff, and the waitstaff passes on some of the tips to the busboys. What if patrons tipped busboys (of both sexes) directly, leaving one tip for the waiter and a second tip for the busboy?

Decades ago, a syndicated columnist from the *Chicago Tribune* reported on a movement to introduce busboy tipping to improve matters for beleaguered and underappreciated busboys. Generous tipping of busboys—more generous than what trickles down from the waitstaff—would increase the earnings (including tips) of busboys to their good fortune, right? Wrong.

TABLE 1.1. TIPPING BUSBOYS

	NO TIPPING	TIP $2/MEAL	TIP $2/MEAL
Busboy Wage Rate:	$6/hour	$2/hour	$2/hour
Meal Price:	$25/meal	$25/meal	$23/meal
Revenue*	1,000	1,000	920
Busboy Wages*	120	40	40
Other Costs*	680	680	680
Profit*	200	280	200

Notes: *Dollars per night. The restaurant employs 20 busboy-hours per night to serve 40 meals per night.

Analyzing the impact of busboy tipping involves a heavy dose of economics. To keep things simple, I have cooked up an example in Table 1.1 that illustrates the issues and highlights the striking conclusion: busboy tipping would have no effect on anyone. Let's consider one restaurant, American Fare, which chef–owner Ed operates. The price of a fixed-price meal is $25. Ed and his crew at American Fare serve 40 meals on a typical night, so the restaurant's nightly revenue is $1,000. The restaurant has the costs of ingredients, cooks, dishwashers, waitstaff, and so on. These costs, excluding the cost of busboys, total $680 per night. Without busboy tipping, Ed pays each busboy the going wage for such work, $6 per hour, and each of the four busboys works a five-hour shift. Thus American Fare's cost of busboys without busboy tipping is $120 (= $6 × 5 × 4) per night. (To keep things simple, let's ignore kickbacks of tips from the waitstaff.) Ed is left with $200 (= $1000 − $680 − $120) per night in profit, which is the reward for his long hours running the show.

Patrons of restaurants eagerly adopt busboy tipping, and they generously tip $2 per meal, which is 8 percent. The $80 in busboy tips enriches each busboy $20 per night or $4 per hour. Happy busboys walk home with $10 (= $6 + $4) per hour in pay including tips.

But there's more to the story. Busboys were paid $6 per hour because that wage cleared the busboy labor market. There was no **surplus** (or **excess supply**) of unemployed busboys applying for one job after another, never landing work setting and clearing tables. And there was no **shortage** of (or **excess demand** for) busboys: at $6 per hour, American Fare wasn't left without anyone to clear its dirty tables. Tipping lines the pockets of busboys with an extra $4 per hour, which surely attracts others to this line of work. Plenty of people sweeping and vacuuming floors in office buildings, folding sweaters at malls, and making change at fast-food restaurants quickly find busing tables more appealing. The quantity supplied of busboys rises. If American Fare and other restaurants continue to pay busboys $6 per hour, a surplus (or excess supply) emerges. For every vacant busboy position, perhaps five qualified people apply. Ed hasn't taken a course in labor economics, but he understands that he doesn't have to pay $6 per hour if job seekers flood American Fare with applications. And a motivated applicant might offer to work for $5.50 per hour to secure the job over the other four applicants.

The payroll wage of busboys falls to eliminate the surplus. If the hourly wage fell from $6 to $5 per hour, busboys would earn $9 per hour with tips, and being a busboy would still be too attractive to eliminate the surplus. The wage American Fare and other restaurants pay busboys must fall enough to leave workers indifferent between busing tables and, say, folding sweaters at the mall. Busboy earnings *including tips* must fall back to $6 per hour, so the wage paid by American Fare must sink to $2 per hour. The restaurant pays each busboy $2 per hour, and each busboy earns $4 per hour in tips. Hourly earnings are $6 per hour because that's the only value of hourly earnings that clears the busboy market.

Patrons tipping $2 per meal doesn't line the pockets of busboys. Busboys are no better off. Rather, tipping busboys seems to enrich chef–owner Ed. In the second column of Table 1.1, we see that busboy costs fall $80 per night, and Ed's profit jumps from $200 to $280 per night. If Ed had been clearing $50,000 annually without busboy tipping, he earns $70,000 per year with busboy tipping. Can that be right?

Many people are capable of running restaurants, but most people do other things when running a restaurant earns $50,000 annually. Some own and operate ice-cream shops or delis; others work as accountants. If operating a restaurant paid $70,000 a year (i.e., with busboy tipping), then many people would go into the restaurant business. Accountants and other professionals would open restaurants; even *Seinfeld*'s "soup Nazi" would grudgingly add table service. That would increase the supply of restaurant food without any change in the demand for restaurant food. Tables would stand empty: another surplus! To clear the market for restaurant food, the price of a meal must fall enough to return American Fare's profit to $200 per night. If the price of a meal at American Fare falls from $25 to $23, its nightly revenue drops from $1,000 to $920, and its nightly profit returns to $200. (See the last column of Table 1.1.)

Neither the busboys at American Fare nor chef–owner Ed gains from busboy tipping. What about patrons of American Fare and other restaurants? The price they pay for a meal falls by $2, but each customer tosses $2 on the table for the busboy. So restaurant patrons continue to pay (including tips to busboys) $25 per meal, and they eat at restaurants no more often and no less often.

No one wins; no one loses. Our analysis of busboy tipping contains no graphs nor any mathematics beyond arithmetic, but it's still chock-a-block full of economics. In particular, an unwavering commitment to the principle of **market clearing** delivers the surprising conclusion. If we ignore the possibility that wages adjust to a change in policy or government regulation, then we risk missing the actual consequences of the change.

☑ **PRACTICE**   If customers at restaurants tip busboys $1 per meal, what happens to the payroll wage that restaurants pay busboys, to busboys' hourly earnings (including tips), to the price of a meal, to restaurant revenue, and to profit?

1.2   Labor Economics

This parable of busboy tipping informally demonstrates labor economics in action. It's about the employment relationship, including how many people want to work as busboys, how many busboys restaurants want to employ, and how much busboys earn. It's a nice example of work and pay.

Labor economics is the field or area of economics that investigates the mysteries of work and pay. The subject matter of labor economics includes whether people work (or stay in school or retire), how much they work (e.g., the 55 hours per week our ancestors worked early in the twentieth century or the 30 or so hours per week a typical person works today), whether workers are paid what they're worth or are exploited, how pay varies with education and work experience, how often people change jobs, and the effects of discrimination on gaps in pay by sex, race, religion, and even height. Labor economists also study the effects of unions on employment and wages; the determinants of the distribution of wages; how the form of compensation influences performance on the job, hiring, and retention; and how unemployment compensation affects the unemployment rate.

The scope of labor economics isn't limited to what people usually call "labor"—organized labor in conflict with management. Labor also includes the middle schooler who shovels snow from my driveway and the CEO of a multinational corporation; a taxi driver and a professional basketball player; a middle-aged high school dropout looking for work for nearly two years and the governor of California campaigning for re-election. It's all work. It's all labor economics.

Key Principles

In the chapters that follow, we sketch the most important models of labor economics, identify the field's most important principles, and illustrate these principles in practice with compelling applications. We derive principles from economic models to explain the world of work.

What will you retain in the months and years after you finish this book, after your relentless effort and piercing focus translate into near-perfect performance on the final exam? I hope the key principles (and a confidence that these principles follow from careful reasoning and data analysis) stay with you long after details of the models slip from your memory.

The most important principles are:

- Wages tend to adjust to eliminate shortages and surpluses. Our analysis of busboy tipping demonstrates that recognizing this principle can lead to surprising conclusions.

- Competitive labor markets are efficient. Interfering with competitive labor markets causes inefficiency.

- Migration of workers and firms across locations enhances efficiency. For instance, migration among states in the United States enables U.S. workers to produce more with less labor.

- Competition among employers for workers reduces or even eliminates exploitation of workers.

- A higher wage increases the reward to working, which draws people into the labor market. But a higher wage could lengthen or shorten the workweek because it also increases the value of leisure time.

- Production in undeveloped parts of the world is very labor-intensive because wages in those places are so low relative to the cost of equipment and other forms of capital.

- Innovations that raise workers' productivity increase employment and wages even though firms don't need as many workers after the innovations.

- Workers gain by having access to dirty, dangerous, and otherwise deplorable jobs.

- Schooling is primarily an investment in cognitive skills, and those skills command a premium in the labor market. The wage premium associated with a college education might also reflect schooling's role in sorting people by innate ability.

- If workers can quit and employers are free to dismiss their workers, then employers must pay workers what they're worth at every point in their careers.

- Measurable differences in skills and related worker characteristics partly explain gaps in wages based on sex and race.

- Discrimination isn't free. Discriminators pay a price to exercise their sexist or racist preferences.

- Unions are more successful where demand for the product of their labor and the supply of other inputs are less elastic. Unions support government policies that reduce these elasticities.

- Wages reflect skills, and differences in worker skills explain almost all the differences in pay across occupations.

- Increasing wage inequality encourages workers to acquire skills, which reduces inequality in the long run.

- How workers are paid (e.g., performance incentives) is important for motivating, recruiting, and retaining workers. Designing compensation to solve one problem tends to create other problems.

- Unemployment isn't primarily a surplus (or excess supply) of labor. Unemployment is a natural consequence of a two-sided search process: a worker searches for a high-wage job, and a firm looks for the best workers to fill its vacant positions.

1.3 Economic Detection

As we embark on a scientific study of labor markets, a quick review of logical reasoning and scientific method might help. Let's distinguish the two types of reasoning (i.e., argument and explanation) and show how the standards for evaluating explanations support scientific method. The presentation draws from Kelley (2013, chapter 15).

Arguments and Explanations

"You can make a lot of money by becoming a lawyer." Although this proposition doesn't inspire bitter debate, it is a logical **argument**. In this simple argument, we reason forward from a known premise ("lawyers make a lot of money") to a conclusion about the prospects for your career. In science, we typically start with premises as empirical patterns and theoretical models; we deduce conclusions from these. The validity of the conclusions depends on the validity of the premises and the methods we use to draw the conclusions. In particular, we must not introduce logical fallacies or factual errors along the way.

Some arguments in economics are free of value judgments; others are normative. In labor economics, the conclusion "the minimum wage reduces employment" is a **positive** (or value-free) **statement**. We can't reach the conclusion that "the government should increase the minimum wage," however, without addressing ethical issues; it's a **normative statement**. A statement that includes "should," "good," or "bad" is probably the conclusion of a normative argument.

The primary business of science is **explanation**. The logical machinery of science in general, and labor economics in particular, usually reasons from what is known to its cause. That is, scientists explain. An explanation answers a question: Why did unions take off in the 1930s and 1940s? Why are lawyers paid so much? What causes the labor market to stagnate? So an explanation identifies the cause of something that is known.

A simple example should help. Why won't the lights in Alicia's kitchen switch on? We know that the switch won't turn on the lights. We must reason backward to the cause of the lighting problem. Here are four hypotheses: "A bulb is out." "Alicia forgot to pay her utility bill, so the electric company cut the juice to her house." "The breaker tripped the kitchen circuit." "A raging hurricane downed utility lines in Alicia's neighborhood."

Standards for Evaluating Hypotheses

One standard for evaluating an explanation is **adequacy**. Does the hypothesis adequately explain why the lights in Alicia's kitchen won't switch on? A hypothesis is adequate if it is *strong*, *complete*, and *informative*. First, the strength of a hypothesis reflects how well it accounts for what is to be explained. For instance, neglecting to pay her electrical bill last week wouldn't cause the electric company to turn off Alicia's electric service without a single warning. That hypothesis is weak. Second, a hypothesis should explain all, not just part, of what is to be explained. For instance, the "bulb is out" hypothesis explains why one or perhaps two lights won't switch on, but it fails to explain why all the lights in Alicia's kitchen, as well as the clock on her oven, remain dark. That hypothesis is incomplete. Third, a hypothesis should be informative. For instance, the hypothesis "there's no power in the kitchen" is superficial. An informative hypothesis digs deeper to explain *why* there is no power in the kitchen. Even the tripped-breaker hypothesis could be more informative by specifying what caused the breaker to trip.

A hypothesis can adequately explain what is known and still be wrong. Without any doubt, a hurricane downing the power lines in Alicia's neighborhood would explain why the lights won't switch on in her kitchen. That hypothesis is strong, complete, informative, and wrong! Today is a beautiful day with a light breeze. For the hurricane hypothesis to be right, the essential assumptions of that hypothesis must be true. We need to confirm (1) that a hurricane is blowing through and (2) that the hurricane, if it exists, has damaged nearby power lines. Hence a hypothesis with essential assumptions that the evidence rejects doesn't satisfy the second standard for evaluating an explanation: **hypothetical truth**.

We also reject a hypothesis if the evidence isn't consistent with its **testable implications**—implications that follow from its essential assumptions. For instance, to determine the validity of the tripped-breaker hypothesis, Alicia finds the circuit-breaker panel, scans for any tripped breaker, and confirms (or rejects) that a tripped breaker controls the circuit that includes the kitchen. That is, she checks the essential assumption of that hypothesis. But if Alicia is a typical homeowner, she tests a few implications of that hypothesis before heading to the circuit-breaker panel in her basement or garage. If the breaker tripped, then other rooms in her house and other houses should have lights. She flips the switch to the light in another room, such as the family room, and she peeks outside to see if the lights are on at other houses in the neighborhood. That is, she tests the tripped-breaker hypothesis against alternative hypotheses.

Scientific Method

Alicia observed that all the lights in her kitchen failed to switch on, she quickly identified several hypotheses that would explain the situation, and she sorted through the competing hypotheses by checking essential assumptions and by testing additional implications. Perhaps without realizing it, we all do this detective work in our daily lives. And scientists do it every day in their professional lives. This is **scientific method**: observe, hypothesize, and test to explain the rich details of our world.

For labor economists, that's the world of work and pay. You might wonder why lawyers make a lot of money. Perhaps the source of your curiosity is a casual observation that lawyers dress well, drive expensive cars, and live in affluent neighborhoods. The labor economist takes the first step of scientific method to the next level by collecting data on wage and salary income in dozens of occupations to compute the earnings of a typical lawyer ($2,253 per week in 2017) and to compare it to average earnings in other occupations ($986 per week in 2017).

What could explain lawyers' high incomes? Let's formulate a few hypotheses. Lawyers make a lot of money because (1) they are very educated, (2) they work long hours, (3) the American Bar Association (ABA) restricts entry into the legal profession, or (4) lawyers are greedy parasites feeding off the hopes (and wallets) of victims. (You can add your own hypothesis.) To flesh out how each hypothesis delivers the implication of high pay for lawyers, we introduce a model that abstracts from the rich details of the world. That is, we adopt assumptions that simplify the analysis without interfering with the explanation. (Science can be complicated enough without confusing everyone with inconsequential details.) For instance, we might assume that all lawyers are identical in terms of skills and that each lawyer sets his or her own workweek. Or that every law student attends law school full-time for three years. We then evaluate each hypothesis (in the form of a model) in terms of adequacy.

Next we test all the plausible hypotheses with an eye to eliminating those with essential assumptions or additional implications that aren't supported by the data. For essential assumptions, we should check how many years of school the typical lawyer gets and how this number compares to average years of schooling in other occupations. Are workers in higher-paying occupations more educated? Similarly, how many hours does a typical lawyer work in a week, and how does this compare to workweeks in other occupations? Answering these questions checks the essential assumptions of the first two hypotheses.

We also test additional implications that follow from the essential (but not simplifying) assumptions. For each hypothesis, we ask: "If this were true, then … what?" Is the pay premium in law consistent with the pattern of pay and education (or pay and the workweek) across occupations, or is lawyers' high pay an outlier? Is lawyer pay consistent with how pay varies with schooling (or hours worked) across workers within occupations? How does lawyer pay vary over time or across countries with ABA-like restrictions on entry to the profession? Without providing specific answers to any of these questions, I'll offer my reading of the evidence: the expense of a law-school education (including foregone income during the three years in law school) and the long hours that lawyers work leave little room for more sinister explanations (e.g., the ABA restricting entry or that lawyers are greedy parasites) to explain lawyers' high pay.

In science, simplicity is a virtue. This is the **principle of parsimony**. Although the correct hypothesis just might be complicated, verifying that it is indeed the correct explanation involves a lot of work. The complicated hypothesis bears a bigger burden because there are more essential assumptions to check and additional implications to test. With enough support in the form of confirming evidence, a complicated hypothesis might be the only hypothesis that adequately resolves the mystery and survives confrontation with the data. But parsimony, as a principle rather than a rule, points to the advantage of a simpler hypothesis because it requires less supporting evidence.

1.4   Data

Armed with scientific method, let's turn to data and their use in labor economics. Scientists use data to document patterns and to sort through competing hypotheses. Here are some of the most important data sets in labor economics.

Current Population Survey (CPS) and Census of Population

At 8:30 AM Eastern time on the first Friday of every month, the Bureau of Labor Statistics (BLS) announces the official unemployment rate from the previous month in its monthly jobs report (known more formally as the *Employment Situation*). The announcement triggers a flurry of media coverage, the stock market jumps up or down, and so on. It's a big thing. The statistics released in the jobs report derive from two sources: a survey of households and a survey of business establishments. The unemployment rate is computed from the household survey.

The **Current Population Survey (CPS)**, the BLS's monthly survey of households, is the most important source of data on the U.S. labor market. During the calendar week that includes the 19th day of the month, surveyors interview nearly 60,000 households on the activities of everyone (age 15 and older) in the household during the prior week (i.e., the week containing the 12th day of the month). In a typical month, the CPS collects data from about 110,000 working-age civilians. (Soldiers on active duty in the U.S. armed forces and residents of prisons, mental institutions, and nursing homes are excluded.) CPS data include information on age, race, sex, schooling, location, and whether the person is working, unemployed (i.e., not employed but looking for work), or not in the labor force (e.g., going to school or retired). For those who work, the CPS data include the number of hours worked, the type of work (i.e., occupation), and the employer's line of business (i.e., its industry).

CPS data on wages and salaries are available from two sources. First, the CPS includes an extra set of questions every March about earnings, hours worked, and weeks worked in the prior calendar year. These questions are part of the March CPS's Annual Social and Economic Supplement. Second, one-fourth of the households in the basic monthly survey answer questions about usual weekly pay and union status for the prior week. Those answering these questions comprise what the BLS calls outgoing rotation groups. We make heavy use of the data from the CPS outgoing rotation groups in the chapters that follow.

The data we use depend on the time period. The basic monthly CPS files back to January 1976 are great for employment status and education. Weekly wage and salary data have been available in the CPS's outgoing rotation group files since January 1979. March CPS data going back to 1962 are useful for employment status, education, and annual earnings and hours worked. To get such data before 1962, we typically turn to the Census of Population's public use microdata series (PUMS) from 1940, 1950, and 1960.

☑ PRACTICE   Find the jobs report for the most recent month at the BLS website. Scroll past the executive summaries and head straight to the tables. What was the unemployment rate in the prior month? What was the employment rate, which is also called the employment–population ratio? Exit the jobs report and find the CPS tables of annual averages. CPS Table 1 (at the BLS site) shows the employment status of the civilian, noninstitutional population annually since the 1940s. Compare changes in the employment and unemployment rates between 2010 and 2017.

Current Employment Survey (CES) and Other Data Sets

The monthly jobs report also draws information from the BLS's monthly survey of business establishments, the Current Employment Survey (CES). In the jobs report, we might learn that the private sector added 155,000 jobs last month, and that number comes from the CES data for the same reference week as the CPS. The CES collects data on employment, paid hours, and earnings (by sex) from approximately 140,000 nonfarm businesses and government agencies with nearly 500,000 work sites (i.e., establishments). CES employment, hours, and earnings data don't cover the unemployed or those not in the labor force, and information on workers is limited to hours paid (rather than hours worked), wages, and sex.

For compensation data that include employee benefits, we turn to the BLS's Employer Cost of Employee Compensation data, which is part of its National Compensation Survey. The National Longitudinal Surveys (NLS) follow individuals through time. For instance, the National Longitudinal Survey of Youth (NLSY79) has collected social and economic data on 12,686 people since they were 14–22 years old in 1979. Topics of other important data sets from the BLS include worker turnover via its Job Openings and Labor Turnover Survey (JOLTS); time use (including work, childcare, housekeeping, and socializing) in the American Time Use Survey (ATUS); and workplace injuries and fatalities through its annual Survey of Occupational Injuries and Illnesses (SOII) and its Census of Fatal Occupational Injuries (CFOI).

Not all publicly collected labor data come from the BLS. For instance, publicly traded corporations submit data on the compensation of their top managers (including chief executive officers) to the Securities and Exchange Commission (SEC), and business periodicals such as *Forbes*, *Fortune*, and *Business Week* publish summary tables each spring.

Rich data in labor economics are available from many other sources, and researchers collect some data themselves. For instance, Card and Krueger (1994) collected data on wage, employment, and hours worked from hundreds of fast-food restaurants in New Jersey and eastern Pennsylvania to assess the impact of New Jersey's minimum-wage hike in 1992. (See section 2.2.) Ashenfelter and Krueger (1994) collected labor data on hundreds of identical twins at an annual festival in Twinsville, Ohio, to address a difficulty in estimating the financial reward to getting an education. (See section 6.2.) Galenson (1981) collected data from thousands of contracts that governed the terms of employment of indentured servants in colonial America. (See section 7.5.)

Occupation Averages in the CPS

Evidence from a variety of data appears throughout our exploration of labor economics, but one data set appears in chapter after chapter to highlight the key determinants of weekly wages. The data set contains all the monthly Current Population Surveys since January 1979 but limits the sample to households in the outgoing rotation groups. (Recall that weekly wages and union status are available each month only for the outgoing rotation groups.) The data set includes weekly pay and hours worked, age, sex, race, location, schooling, occupation, and union status for about 6.7 million wage and salary workers (14,400 monthly records or observations) over the 468 months since January 1979.

Although empirical labor economists routinely analyze millions of data points without blinking, an introduction to labor economics requires simpler methods to connect to the data. Here we group the data by occupation (i.e., type of work) to compute occupation averages in the CPS. By computing averages within each occupation, we can explore how weekly wages vary with the workweek, education, and several other variables across occupations.

Table 1.2 lists four variables from our sample of occupation averages in the CPS. For each of the 43 occupations, we have the median weekly wage w, the natural logarithm of the median weekly wage $\ln w$, the average workweek h, and the average highest grade completed s. (For weekly wages, we compute the median rather than the average because the CPS piles many high-wage workers into a "top code" that understates their pay; unlike the average wage, the median wage in an occupation isn't affected by this practice.) We measure weekly wages in real terms (i.e., 2017 dollars) by using the monthly Consumer Price Index to adjust for inflation.

Weekly wages vary dramatically across occupations, which is probably not surprising. A quick scan of the weekly wage w column of Table 1.2 shows that lawyers and judges (Code 11) are in the highest-wage occupation. Doctors (7) and engineers (4) follow close behind the attorneys. Food-service workers (29) and sales-related workers (e.g., product demonstrators, promotors, and models) (20) are in the two lowest-wage occupations. The gap between the lowest- and highest-wage occupations is enormous, over $1,500 per week. Disparities across occupations in the average workweek and average schooling are large, too. The workweek is short (25–32 hours) in some occupations and long (45–50 hours) in others. Farm workers (44) have little education, but doctors (7), lawyers (11), and teachers in colleges and universities (9) are well educated.

The weekly wage w and the workweek h are positively related across occupations. Figure 1.1 displays the **scatter plot** of the 43 pairs (h, w), one for each occupation. The left axis measures the weekly wage w on a log scale, and we read the log of the weekly wage $\ln w$ on the right axis. (A gentle introduction to logarithms follows in section 1.6.) The cloud of points stretches from the bottom left to the top right of the figure, so occupations with long workweeks also tend to have high weekly wages.

TABLE 1.2. OCCUPATION AVERAGES IN THE CURRENT POPULATION SURVEY, 1979–2017

CODE	OCCUPATION	WEEKLY WAGE w	LOG OF WEEKLY WAGE ln w	WORK-WEEK h	SCHOOLING s
1	Officials & Administrators, Public	1,239	7.12	41.0	15.5
2	Executive, Admin. & Managerial, Private	1,186	7.08	44.1	14.7
3	Management-Related Occupations	1,033	6.94	40.8	15.0
4	Engineers	1,523	7.33	42.7	15.8
5	Mathematical & Computer Scientists	1,395	7.24	41.2	15.6
6	Natural Scientists	1,255	7.13	41.4	16.7
7	Health Diagnosing Occupations	1,671	7.42	49.8	17.7
8	Health Assessment & Treatment Occupations	1,026	6.93	36.8	15.5
9	Teachers, College & University	1,056	6.96	36.4	17.3
10	Teachers, Excluding College & University	918	6.82	38.2	16.3
11	Lawyers & Judges	1,793	7.49	45.0	17.7
12	Other Professional Specialty Occupations	859	6.76	38.5	15.5
13	Health Technologists & Technicians	682	6.53	37.2	13.9
14	Engineering & Science Technicians	921	6.83	40.2	13.7
15	Technicians, Other	1,080	6.99	39.7	14.9
16	Supervisors & Proprietors, Sales Occupations	815	6.70	44.1	13.6
17	Sales Reps, Finance & Business Services	936	6.84	40.8	14.6
18	Sales Reps, Commodities, Excluding Retail	1,063	6.97	43.3	14.3
19	Sales Workers, Retail & Personal Services	332	5.80	31.6	12.6
20	Sales-Related Occupations	261	5.56	24.7	12.7
22	Computer Equipment Operators	676	6.52	38.5	13.3
23	Secretaries, Stenographers, & Typists	598	6.39	36.0	13.1
24	Financial Records Processing	599	6.40	35.9	13.1
25	Mail & Message Distributing	872	6.77	38.4	12.9
26	Other Admin. Support, Including Clerical	567	6.34	36.1	13.2
28	Protective Service	785	6.67	41.7	13.4
29	Food Service	318	5.76	31.1	11.8
30	Health Service	425	6.05	35.3	12.4
31	Cleaning and Building Service	404	6.00	33.7	11.0
32	Personal Service	353	5.87	31.2	12.5
33	Mechanics & Repairers	876	6.78	41.9	12.4
34	Construction Trades	816	6.70	39.9	11.7
35	Other Precision Production, Craft, & Repair	825	6.72	41.9	12.1
36	Machine Operators & Tenders, Excl. Precision	587	6.37	40.0	11.2
37	Fabricators, Assemblers, Inspectors, Samplers	654	6.48	40.6	11.7
38	Motor Vehicle Operators	681	6.52	41.5	12.0
39	Other Transportation & Material Moving Occs.	792	6.67	43.1	11.6
40	Construction Laborers	596	6.39	37.7	10.9
41	Freight, Stock & Materials Handlers	445	6.10	34.7	11.7
42	Other Handlers, Cleaners, Helpers, Laborers	471	6.15	37.4	11.2
43	Farm Operators & Managers	720	6.58	48.0	12.7
44	Farm Workers & Related Occupations	428	6.06	38.1	10.3
45	Forestry & Fishing Occupations	615	6.42	41.3	11.3
–	All Occupations	697	6.55	38.5	13.3

Notes: Wage and salary workers only. Weekly wage w is adjusted for inflation and expressed in 2017 dollars. Workweek h is hours worked last week. Schooling s is highest grade completed. Occupations 21 (Supervisors, Administrative Support) and 27 (Private Household Service Occupations) are missing because workers can't be consistently classified into these occupations over the period since 1979.
Source: Current Population Survey, outgoing rotation group files, monthly 1979–2017.

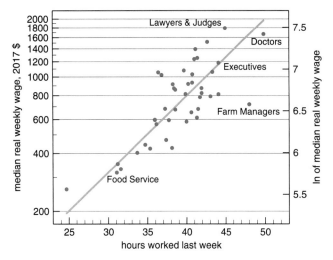

Notes: The left axis measures the wage on a logarithmic scale. The right axis measures the natural logarithm of the wage on the usual arithmetic scale.

Source: Current Population Survey, outgoing rotation group files, monthly 1979–2017.

FIGURE 1.1. Weekly Wage and the Workweek Across Occupations, 1979–2017

✓ **PRACTICE**   In Figure 1.1, which occupation doesn't fit the pattern? That is, which occupation is an *outlier*? Do workers in that occupation earn more or less than the overall pattern of the data suggests?

1.5 Empirical Methods

The scatter plot in Figure 1.1 clearly reveals the positive relationship between weekly wages and weekly hours worked across occupations. Fitting a line to the points in the figure is an application of regression analysis. We use regressions and related empirical methods to evaluate evidence from labor markets. Here's a brief introduction to these methods.

Regression

Regression analysis fits a line to data points, such as the occupation averages of weekly wages and hours worked in Figure 1.1, to quantify the relationship. Methods for estimating regressions are left to courses in statistics or econometrics. Our concern is with interpreting regression estimates. Suppose the log of weekly wages $\ln w$ is linearly related to the workweek h and some other factors: $\ln w = \alpha + \beta h + \epsilon$. In this case, $\ln w$ is the *dependent variable*, h is an *explanatory variable* (or *regressor*), and the Greek letter epsilon ϵ is a random variable that reflects other factors that influence the weekly wage. The Greek letters alpha α and beta β are the true (and unknown) values of the regression coefficients.

Figure 1.1 plots the line that best fits the sample data of weekly wages and the workweek in Table 1.2. The estimated regression line is

(1.1)
$$\ln w = 3.01 + \underset{(.251)}{} .092 \underset{(.007)}{} h$$

with $R^2 = .730$. Our best estimate of the slope coefficient β is the point estimate .092, which is the slope of the estimated regression line in the figure. Along the line, a one-hour-longer workweek translates into a 9.2 percent higher weekly wage. (The .092 increase in $\ln w$ is approximately a 9.2 percent increase in w since the change in the log of a variable is approximately the percentage change in the variable; see section 1.6.)

How precise are the estimates of the regression coefficients? Would increasing or decreasing the estimate of the slope from .092 change the fit of the line by much? Yes, if all the data points are tightly clustered around the regression line. No, if the data points form a loose cloud around the line. For each regression coefficient, the *standard error* measures the precision (or lack of precision) of the point estimate. The slope coefficient in the regression in Equation 1.1 is estimated precisely. Its standard error (i.e., .007) appears in parentheses below the point estimate (i.e., .092). (The method for computing standard errors isn't our concern.) We use the standard error to compute a *confidence interval* around the point estimate. Under normal conditions, we can be confident that the true value of β lies within two standard errors of the point estimate .092. That is, we can be confident that the true value of the slope is between 7.8 ($= 9.2 - (2 \times 0.7)$) and 10.6 ($= 9.2 + (2 \times 0.7)$) percent. Since the confidence interval lies entirely above zero, we conclude that the slope estimate is *significantly different from zero* (or *statistically significant*).

How strongly associated are the workweek and weekly wages across occupations? How well does variation in the workweek predict variation in weekly wages in the occupation data? That is, how much of the variation in $\ln w$ across occupations does the regression line capture, and how much is left unexplained? R^2 is the statistic that answers these questions. (Again, the method for computing this statistic isn't our concern.) Since R^2 is .73 in our case, variation in the workweek across occupations captures almost three-quarters (73 percent) of the variation in weekly wages across occupations; one-fourth of the variation in $\ln w$ across occupations is left unexplained.

These regression methods easily extend to many explanatory variables. Indeed, as we progress from chapter to chapter, we add variables to the regression model. For instance, our analysis of schooling in chapter 6 adds years of schooling s to the weekly wage regression.

(1.2)
$$\ln w = 2.09 + \underset{(.221)}{} .074 \underset{(.006)}{} h + .121 \underset{(.013)}{} s$$

with $R^2 = .923$. If we fix schooling at some value (e.g., $s = 12$), a one-hour-longer workweek translates into a 7.4 percent higher weekly wage across occupations. Since occupations with more-educated workers tend to be longer-workweek occupations, adding schooling to the regression downgrades the importance of the workweek in explaining the weekly wage. If we fix the workweek at some value (e.g., $h = 30$), another grade completed is associated with a 12.1 percent higher wage across occupations. That is, the estimated "rate of return" to a year of schooling is 12.1 percent per grade. The workweek and schooling combine to capture 92 percent of the variation in median weekly wages (in logs) across occupations. Differences across occupations in the workweek and schooling capture almost all of the variation in weekly wages across occupations. We learn why these variables (and a few others) explain so much in the chapters that follow.

 PRACTICE   The point estimate of the effect of schooling s on log wages ln w is .121. What is the standard error of this regression coefficient? Use the point estimate and the standard error to calculate the confidence interval for the rate of return to schooling. Can we be confident that the true rate of return to schooling isn't 10 percent? What about 15 percent?

Causation and Instrumental Variables

The estimated regression line in Equation 1.2 tells us that longer-workweek and more-educated occupations tend to be occupations with higher weekly wages. Should we conclude that lengthening the workweek of every food-service worker by one hour increases the weekly wages of food-service workers by 7.4 percent? Similarly, should we conclude that increasing the education of construction laborers by one grade increases the weekly wages of construction laborers by 12.1 percent? That is, do changes in the workweek and changes in schooling *cause* these changes in the weekly wage? Not necessarily.

Causation might run in reverse, from the weekly wage to the workweek and schooling. Perhaps talented and motivated (i.e., high-wage) workers sort into long-workweek occupations; the higher wage (through talent and motivation) causes a longer workweek rather than vice versa. It is even plausible that paying a higher wage encourages people to work longer hours: Kara worries about losing her job because it pays her so much; to lower her risk of being fired for poor performance, she works long hours. In the context of schooling, innately smarter people surely complete more grades; the higher wage (through innate ability) causes more schooling rather than vice versa. In this case, the dependent variable influences the explanatory variable. It's **endogenous**, and that's a problem.

Endogeneity (or **reverse causation**) biases estimates of the regression coefficients away from their true values. Suppose the true effect of the workweek on the weekly wage across occupations is $\beta = .05$ or 5 percent per hour. But the effect of talented and motivated workers sorting into high-wage occupations is to raise the weekly wage in the long-workweek occupations by 4 percent per hour. Fitting a regression line to these weekly wage and hours observations generates a slope estimate of 9 ($= 5 + 4$) percent. The regression estimate is biased upward from its true value of 5 percent. While a one-hour-longer workweek links to a

9 percent higher weekly wage across occupations, lengthening the workweek by one hour increases the weekly wage by only 5 percent, the causal effect of the workweek on weekly wages. So be cautious interpreting regression estimates: don't declare a causal relationship where only an association is implied.

With better data, we can identify causal relationships. Suppose we are free to run controlled social experiments. In the first experiment, we randomly assign 1,000 workers to jobs with either a 30-hour workweek or a 40-hour workweek. And we calculate how much more, on average, the 500 workers on the 40-hour-workweek job earn. That identifies the causal effect of the workweek on weekly wages. In a second experiment, we direct the education of 1,000 high school students: we send 500 randomly selected students to work immediately after graduating from high school; we sentence the other 500 students to four years of college. Ten years later, we compare the weekly wages of the two groups to identify the causal effect of a college education on weekly wages.

We don't run controlled social experiments of this sort in free societies, but we can take advantage of **exogenous** (i.e., from outside the model) variation in the explanatory variables to identify causal relationships. If we can isolate the variation in schooling that is free of the influence of innate smarts, then we can use *that* variation to estimate the causal effect of schooling on weekly wages. Are there factors that influence schooling but are unrelated to innate smarts?

Several possible factors have come to the minds of labor economists: (1) mandatory schooling laws (when a person can drop out of school varies across states and over time), (2) distances to the nearest two-year and four-year colleges (young people are more likely to go to college if they can commute to one nearby), (3) tuition rates at state colleges (which vary across states and over time), and (4) eligibility for the GI Bills (World War II and Korean War veterans had access to generous educational subsidies). These factors are likely to influence the weekly wage only through their effects on schooling. Using only this exogenous variation to estimate the regression coefficients is, in a nutshell, **instrumental variables estimation**.

Before-and-After Comparison with and without a Control Group

We frequently assess an event's impact by comparing outcomes before and after the event. For instance, we might look at union membership before and after the Wagner Act in 1935 required employers to recognize and to bargain in good faith with labor unions; or look at employment before and after Congress enacted the 25-cent minimum wage in 1938; or look at wages and employment of the native population in Miami before and after an influx of 125,000 Cuban immigrants in 1980; or look at employment in New Jersey's fast-food restaurants before and after that state hiked its minimum wage in 1992; or look at unemployment and employment rates before and after President Obama's stimulus spending package in 2009; or look at weekly wages and the workweek before and after the French government capped the workweek at 35 hours in 2000. In the context of a cap on the workweek, the before-and-after comparison involves computing the change (i.e., "after" minus "before") in the weekly wage Δw. (The Greek letter delta Δ denotes "the change in.") The effect of the cap on the workweek can be expressed as a slope coefficient β by computing the ratio $\Delta w / \Delta h$.

Many things change before and after an event, so the **before-and-after comparison** doesn't isolate the event's effect. We can address this problem with numbers: how does a cap on the workweek affect the weekly wage "wherever and whenever" governments cap the workweek? If the incidental changes aren't common across events, then averaging across events tends to eliminate the effects of the incidental changes on the weekly wage. (We could also estimate a regression line with each event's pair $(\Delta h, \Delta w)$ as a data point.) Unfortunately, not all incidental changes average out. For instance, if weekly wages grow over time for reasons unrelated to the cap on the workweek, then the before-and-after comparison of weekly wages includes this wage trend "wherever and whenever" the workweek is capped. We use a control group to avoid such bias.

Medical researchers compare outcomes of *treatment and control groups* to estimate the effectiveness of a treatment such as a new drug. A before-and-after comparison for the control group (i.e., those who don't get the treatment) identifies the effect of other factors that change during the trial. As an example, consider my daughter Jessie's thinly veiled attempt to increase her candy consumption. She claims that Twizzlers cure the common cold. In our family, such a claim requires supporting evidence. Jessie proposes (1) to eat the twisted strings of licorice twice a day for two weeks (with the first dose starting a few days into the cold) and (2) to determine the effectiveness of the treatment by comparing her cold symptoms *after* the two-week treatment with her symptoms immediately *before* the treatment. Like most people, Jessie would almost surely recover from her cold within two weeks, and she would no doubt celebrate her sweet cure for the cold.

Not so fast. Jessie's test ignores the other factors (the human immune system, in particular) that operate over those two weeks. Treating many sneezing, sniffling, runny-nosed kids with Twizzlers helps average out some other factors but not the common effect of the immune system. Comparison with a control group can identify the actual effect of Twizzlers and resolve our family dispute. One group of runny-nosed kids enjoys a two-week treatment of Twizzlers; another group suffers through their colds without candy. Did the health of the Twizzler-treated group improve more than the health of the candy-denied control group? Proposing the comparison of treatment and control groups thankfully puts to rest my family's debate about Twizzlers as a cure for the common cold.

Economists call the comparison of the change in outcomes between treatment and control groups **difference-in-difference estimation**. The purpose of the control group is to predict the "health" of the treatment group had they not received the treatment. The difference-in-difference estimate subtracts the average change in the control group from the average change in the treatment group. Because we compare *changes* in outcomes between treatment and control groups, persistent differences between the two groups in the level of the outcome don't matter. For instance, more of the Twizzler-treated kids might have allergies.

Difference-in-difference is a powerful and popular method of estimation in labor economics, but it's not infallible. Suppose we want to find the effect of a treatment (e.g., the minimum wage, federal stimulus spending, or a cap on the workweek) on employment. The quality of a difference-in-difference estimate of the employment effect hinges on the quality of the predicted change in employment based on the behavior of the control group. If factors other than the treatment cause employment in the two groups to follow different paths, then the control group's employment change badly predicts the treatment group's employment change without the treatment. Regression analysis can handle this problem if the factors that lead the two groups to follow different paths are measurable. (Let's leave it at that.) But potential pitfalls of difference-in-difference estimation mean that you, the budding evaluator of empirical research in labor economics, must question whether the before-and-after comparison for the control group produces a reasonable prediction for the path of the treatment group if not for the treatment.

Confidence with Caution

Empirical research in labor economics, as well as in economics and science in general, isn't foolproof—it's not even genius proof! First, we estimate effects in samples of data. Estimated effects bounce around from sample to sample, and confidence intervals in samples never shrink to a single number. Sometimes evidence from new samples overturns prior conclusions. Second, there might be deeper problems with the estimates. We might mis-specify the relationship by omitting important explanatory variables (as we did in Equation 1.1 by omitting the schooling variable). Or explanatory variables might be endogenous or measured with error. Fortunately, we have methods to address these problems and improve the estimates. At best, with good data and state-of-the-art empirical methods, we can be confident that the empirical results contribute to our knowledge of work and pay. And as scientists, we are open to new evidence that may overturn our conclusions.

1.6 For Your Toolbox

Our exploration of labor economics is *not* mathematically rigorous, but you need a few tools—mostly simple algebra—to get the most out of the analysis. Read through these tools, "dog ear" this page, and don't hesitate to return to refresh your memory.

Lines

Every college student at least vaguely recalls the equation of a line: $ax + by = c$. The variables are x and y, and the constants are a, b, and c. So, $5c + 50l = 800$ is the equation of a line with variables c and l. (This is an example of a budget line, which is quite important in our study of labor supply in chapter 3.) We can express this line in slope–intercept form by moving $50l$ to the right side and dividing both sides by 5. The result is $c = 160 - 10l$, so the intercept is 160 ($= 800 \div 5$) and the slope is -10 ($= -50 \div 5$).

Slopes, Marginal Changes, and Elasticities

Figure 1.2a plots a fictional relationship between weekly wages w and years of schooling (or grades) s. This wage–schooling curve $w(s)$ is a function like $f(x)$. In your high school or college algebra course, you worked with relationships like $y = f(x)$ where the function $f(x)$ might be a parabola; that is, $f(x) = x^2$. Here we work with the relationship between wages and schooling $w = w(s)$. Two points, A and B, mark combinations of wages and schooling for workers with 12 and 16 grades completed. For instance, at $s = 12$, the wage is $w(12) = 800$; that's $800 per week at point A in panel (a).

Over the four-grade "run" from 12 to 16 years of school, the "rise" in the weekly wage is $400. Let's use the Greek letter delta Δ to indicate the change in a variable. In this case, $\Delta w = \$1200 - \$800 = \$400$ per week, and $\Delta s = 16 - 12 = 4$ grades. The slope of the line segment between A and B is "rise over run," which is $\Delta w / \Delta s = \$400/4$ or $100 per week per grade. So the rate of change of the weekly wage is $100 per grade between A and B.

We can also compute the slope in the neighborhood of any point on the wage–schooling curve $w(s)$. For a marginal change in the schooling variable s in the neighborhood of point A, the slope is $\Delta w / \Delta s = \$80$ per week per grade, and the slope at point B is $\Delta w / \Delta s = \$120$ per week per grade. (The slopes at these two points are derived from the formula that is used to graph the curve $w(s)$; even a careful look at the graph doesn't reveal these numbers.) Since the

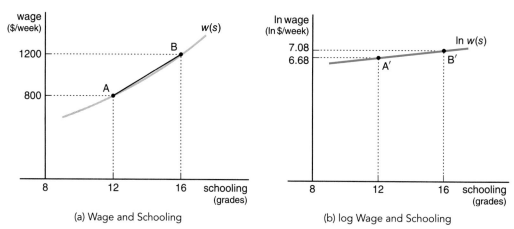

(a) Wage and Schooling

(b) log Wage and Schooling

In panel (a), the wage grows exponentially (i.e., at a constant rate of growth) with schooling, so the relationship between the log of the wage and schooling is linear in panel (b). The slope of the line is the growth rate, which is 10 percent/grade.

FIGURE 1.2. Slopes, Percentage Changes, and Logs

rate of change in the weekly wage is higher at B than at A, $w(s)$ increases at an increasing rate.

We can also recast these slopes in percentage terms. The increase in the weekly wage from $800 to $1,200 is 50 percent as we conventionally measure percentage changes: the difference $1200 − $800 is divided by $800. That's $\Delta w / w(s)$. The problem with the conventional calculation is that a 50 percent increase in the wage followed by a 50 percent decrease in the wage doesn't take us back to the $800 starting wage. The 50 percent wage cut from $1,200 lowers the weekly wage to $600.

One way to avoid this nuisance is by using the wage at the midpoint to calculate the percentage change. In our case, the midpoint is $1,000, halfway between $800 and $1,200 per week, and the increase in the wage is .40 ($= (1200 − 800) \div 1000$) or 40 percent. A second way to calculate a percentage change is by using a marginal change: in the neighborhood of point A, the weekly wage grows 10 percent per grade. That is, $(\Delta w / \Delta s)/w(12) = 80/800 = .10$ or 10 percent per grade at A. And at B, the percentage change in the wage is $(\Delta w / \Delta s)/w(16) = 120/1200 = .10$, which is also 10 percent per grade. Indeed, the rate of growth is constant at 10 percent per grade at every point along $w(s)$.

Elasticity measures the sensitivity (or responsiveness) of one variable to variation in another variable in percentage terms. For instance, how sensitive is employers' quantity demanded of labor L_D to the wage rate w? We could compute the slope of the labor demand curve to measure this sensitivity. Or we could compute the elasticity of demand for labor $\%\Delta L_D / \%\Delta w \equiv (\Delta L_D / \Delta w) \times (w/L_D)$. The advantage of the elasticity is that it doesn't depend on the units of measure. Unlike the slope, the elasticity doesn't depend on whether we measure wages in dollars, pennies, or pesos, or whether we measure labor in workers, worker-hours, or worker-minutes. But using elasticities changes our language: "more elastic" replaces "flatter," and "less elastic" replaces "steeper." These are just more careful terms to describe the sensitivity of the quantity demanded of labor to the wage.

Logarithms

The word *logarithm* scares the dickens out of most students. I would like to purge this book of any reference to logarithms, but I can't. Logarithms are too useful in labor economics. Having even the most basic understanding of logarithms (or logs for short) makes it a lot easier to learn labor economics. So let's give it a try.

Converting ounces to pounds and dimes to dollars are changes in units of measure, and taking the logarithm of a variable is another change in units. This change in units uses a base number. We work with the *natural logarithm* ln, which means the base is the mathematical constant $e = 2.71828\ldots$. For instance, the log of 800 is just the answer to the following question: raising the constant e to what power gives 800? So the logarithm of 800 is the value of x that satisfies $800 = e^x$. I type 800 into my calculator app and press the *ln* key to find that the answer is roughly 6.6846.

Taking the log of a variable (e.g., the wage) also changes the shape of the function on a graph, which is why it's so useful. Figure 1.2b displays how the natural logarithm of the weekly wage $\ln w$ varies with schooling. The wage–schooling curve in panel (a) increases at an increasing rate, but the $\ln w$–schooling curve in panel (b) is a line. Since the rate of growth is constant at 10 percent at every point along $w(s)$, the log of the wage is a linear function of schooling s.

As I stated in interpreting Equation 1.1, the change in the log of a variable is approximately the percentage change in that variable. Figure 1.2b illustrates this property of logarithms. The slope of the line $\Delta \ln w / \Delta s$ is $(7.08 - 6.68)/(16 - 12)$ $= 0.40/4 = .10$ or 10 percent per grade. So the slope of the $\ln w$–schooling relationship reveals the growth rate of the wage for marginal changes in schooling. For bigger changes in schooling (e.g., from high school at A to college at B), the percentage change in the wage (as conventionally measured) is a bit more than 10 percent per grade.

We use another property of logarithms just once: if $w = x^s$, then $\ln w = s \ln x$. No need to memorize this, and no reason to scream with fear when it pops up in chapter 6.

Random Variables and Distributions

Julie must prepare at least 14 tax returns this week to get a $100 bonus. She has plenty of influence on her performance, but some things are out of her control (e.g., the complexity of the tax returns, whether the air conditioning system breaks down, whether the office's computer network goes down). So her performance is random, and whether she gets the $100 bonus is a random variable, too. Similarly, whether J.J., who is unemployed, gets a job offer this week is random, and how long he'll remain unemployed is a random variable.

A *random variable* is characterized by its distribution, which describes the probabilities associated with each outcome. The outcome of flipping a coin is a random variable. The outcomes are head and tail, and the probability associated with each outcome is one-half. Similarly, J.J.'s probability of receiving a job offer this week is .20 or 20 percent, and his probability of not getting an offer (the other outcome) is .80. Based on her skills and effort, the distribution of Julie's preparation of tax returns has six outcomes $\{10, 11, 12, 13, 14, 15\}$, and associated with these outcomes are six probabilities $\{.05, .10, .15, .20, .30, .20\}$. Plotting the pairs of prepared returns (on the horizontal axis) and probabilities (on the vertical axis) gives Julie's distribution of prepared tax returns. (See Problem 1.7.) Notice that Julie has a 50 percent $(= .30 + .20)$ chance of preparing 14 *or* 15 tax returns, so Julie's distribution of bonus pay is $0 with probability .5 and $100 with probability .5.

What happens on average? The *mean* (or expected value) of Julie's performance is 13.2 tax returns. This number comes from weighting the number of tax returns that she prepares by its probability and adding these up: $(.05 \times 10) +$ $(.10 \times 11) + (.15 \times 12) + (.20 \times 13) + (.30 \times 14) + (.20 \times 15) = 13.2$. A second measure of central tendency of a random variable is the *median*: the numerical value such that half the observations are below and half above. Julie's median performance is 13.5 tax returns per week. Half the outcomes are at or below 13, and half are at or above 14. We split the difference and report a median of 13.5.

Adjusting for Inflation

The federal minimum wage in the United States was 25 cents per hour when it first went into effect in 1938. Peanuts. But it wasn't peanuts at the time. Prices of goods and services have risen a lot since 1938. Prices now are roughly 17 times higher than prices in 1938. To get a sense of what that 1938 minimum wage was worth, we should compare it to the prices of bread, newspapers, and many other goods at the time. How much would an hour of work at the minimum wage in 1938 buy? To answer that question, we adjust the minimum wage in 1938 for inflation over three-quarters of a century.

To express the 1938 minimum wage in real terms—in terms of what it could buy—we need to scale 25 cents up to 2017 dollars by comparing the price levels in 1938 and 2017. That is, to express the 1938 minimum wage in 2017 dollars, we multiply 25 cents by the ratio of 2017 prices to 1938 prices.

$$(1.3) \qquad \text{real minimum wage}_{1938} = \text{minimum wage}_{1938} \times \frac{P_{2017}}{P_{1938}}$$

where P_t is the price level in year t.

Table 1.3 reports calculations based on the Consumer Price Index (CPI), a common measure of the price level. The minimum wage in 2017 ($7.25 per hour) was 29 times what it was in 1938 (25 cents per hour), but prices in 2017 were 17.6 times what they were in 1938. So increases in the minimum wage outpaced increases in prices between 1938 and 2017. Indeed, the 1938 minimum wage was $4.40 in real terms (2017 dollars), which means the minimum wage has grown 65 percent in real terms since 1938.

TABLE 1.3. ADJUSTING THE MINIMUM WAGE FOR INFLATION

YEAR	MINIMUM WAGE ($/hour)	CONSUMER PRICE INDEX (P_t)	SCALE FACTOR (P_{2017}/P_t)	REAL MINIMUM WAGE (2017 $/hour)
1938	0.25	14.00	17.6	4.40
1976	2.30	58.20	——	——
2017	7.25	246.52	1.0	7.25

Notes: The Consumer Price Index is the December value for each year. The real minimum wage in 2017 dollars is the minimum wage in the second column times the scale factor in the fourth column. P_t is the price level in year t.

Summary

These are the main points in our introduction to labor economics:

- [ ] Our finding that busboys wouldn't benefit from generous tipping illustrates how an understanding of market clearing can uncover surprising results.

- [ ] Labor economics studies work and pay, including whether people work, how much they work, how they change jobs, and how schooling, work experience, discrimination, and unions affect their wages.

- [ ] Understanding prominent features of labor markets involves comparing many hypotheses. The standards for evaluating hypotheses are adequacy—including strength, completeness, and informativeness—and hypothetical truth.

- [ ] Scientific method, which we apply throughout this book, has three parts: observe, hypothesize, and test. In the context of labor economics, observing is documenting labor market patterns empirically. We hypothesize by constructing models that abstract from inconsequential details to focus on the key features that explain the phenomena. Testing confronts the data to check the model's essential assumptions and additional implications.

- [ ] Two of the most important data sets in labor economics are the sources of the Bureau of Labor Statistics's monthly jobs report. They are the Current Population Survey (CPS), which is a monthly survey of households, and the Current Employment Survey (CES), which is a monthly survey of business establishments.

- [ ] Occupation averages of the CPS's outgoing rotation groups document how the weekly wage varies with the workweek and schooling across occupations. In later chapters, we extend our analysis of occupation averages with variables that measure work experience, sex, race, and union membership.

- [ ] Scatter plots and regression lines often demonstrate association among economic variables (e.g., weekly wages and the workweek). Establishing causal relationships among economic variables is more challenging. Instrumental variables estimation and difference-in-difference estimation help identify causal relationships, such as the causal effect of schooling on weekly wages.

With this preparation, you are ready for an intensive exploration of labor economics. The first stop on our journey is an overview of labor markets and perhaps the biggest question in all of labor economics: Are workers paid what they're worth?

Key Concepts

- surplus vs. shortage, p. 3
- market clearing, p. 4
- argument vs. explanation, p. 7
- positive vs. normative statements, p. 7
- adequacy and hypothetical truth, pp. 7–8
- testable implications, p. 8
- scientific method, p. 8
- principle of parsimony, p. 9
- Current Population Survey (CPS), p. 10

- scatter plot, p. 12
- regression analysis, p. 14
- endogenous variables, p. 16
- reverse causation, p. 16
- exogenous variables, p. 17
- instrumental variables estimation, p. 17
- before-and-after comparison, p. 18
- difference-in-difference estimation, p. 18
- elasticity, p. 21

Short-Answer Questions

1.1 What distinguishes an explanation from an argument?

1.2 What is the role of simplifying assumptions in science? In an economic model, is there any justification for an assumption that is demonstrably false?

1.3 Two parts of the Current Population Survey (CPS) are the outgoing rotation group files (CPS-ORG) and the Annual Social and Economic Supplement (March CPS). What extra information is available on the workers in CPS-ORGs? What extra information is available on the workers in March CPSs?

1.4 In Table 1.2, what are the two highest-wage occupations? What are the two occupations with the most educated workers? How do the wage, workweek, and schooling of the typical food-service worker (code 29) compare to the averages of these variables across all occupations?

1.5 Use Equation 1.2 to predict how much more occupations with a two-hour-longer workweek and one higher grade of education pay per week.

1.6 Critics of the American Recovery and Reinvestment Act of 2009 point out that measures of economic activity (e.g., the unemployment rate) improved little after the government's stimulus spending. Others counter that the unemployment rate would have gone much higher if not for stimulus spending. How can difference-in-difference estimation inform the debate? What is the treatment? Is there a control group? How is the before-and-after comparison of unemployment rates adjusted?

Problems

1.1 Which of the following statements are positive, and which are normative?

    (a) Immigration is inefficient.

    (b) Wages tend to rise with work experience.

    (c) Young people should stay in school to have good careers.

    (d) Federally subsidized student loans increase college-enrollment rates.

    (e) The quit rate falls with years of seniority.

    (f) Women are paid a lot less than men.

    (g) Reducing wage inequality would be an improvement.

1.2 Which of the following statements is part of an argument, and which is an explanation?

    (a) Federal stimulus spending pulled the economy out of the recession.

    (b) Immigration reform will increase the wages of union workers.

    (c) Production in the United States is more capital intensive than production in Haiti because the wage–rental ratio is higher in the United States than in Haiti.

    (d) Young people can increase their lifetime earnings by going to college.

1.3 Visit the website of the Bureau of Labor Statistics, which is part of the U.S. Department of Labor. Find the annual CPS table on employment status by sex. Fill in the labor force participation rate (LFPR), employment rate (ER), and unemployment rate (UR) for women and men in each year in the table below:

Year	WOMEN			MEN		
	LFPR	ER	UR	LFPR	ER	UR
1980						
1990						
2000						
2010						

Compare women's employment status with men's employment status over these years.

1.4 In right-to-work states, a worker can't be compelled to join or to contribute financially to the union with a contract that covers the worker's job. In this fictitious example, two states (A and B) become right-to-work states. Two nearby states (C and D) aren't right-to-work states. The table below lists unionization rates in these states before and after states A and B pass right-to-work legislation:

| State | UNIONIZATION RATE | | |
	Before	After	Difference
A	9.0	5.8	
B	11.8	8.0	
C	17.6	15.8	
D	12.2	11.0	

(a) Compare each state's unionization rate before and after the legal changes in states A and B. Write the changes in unionization rates in the last column.

(b) Average the before-and-after comparison separately for the newly "treated" right-to-work states and the control group of other states. What is the before-and-after estimate of the effect of right-to-work on unionization rates?

(c) What is the difference-in-difference estimate of the effect of right-to-work laws on unionization rates?

(d) Suppose you also have union-membership rates in states that have right-to-work laws before and after states A and B become right-to-work states. How can you use those data to compute a second difference-in-difference estimate of the effect of right-to-work laws?

1.5 Here are several problems to check your toolbox.

(a) The line $3000 = 300L + 200K$ appears in chapter 4. Two points (L, K) on the line are $(6,6)$ and $(8,3)$. Compute the slope $\Delta K / \Delta L$ between these two points.

(b) Express the equation in part (a) in slope–intercept form by solving for capital K. What's the slope $\Delta K / \Delta L$?

(c) Jimbo's hourly wage jumps from $10 to $14. As conventionally measured, how big is his raise in percentage terms? What's the percentage change in his wage using the midpoint formula?

(d) What are the natural logarithms of Jimbo's two wages? (Hint: Start by entering 10 in a calculator app and pressing the *ln* button.) Compute the difference of the two logs. How does the difference in logs of wages compare to the percentage change in the wages?

1.6 With schooling s on the horizontal axis, plot several combinations of the weekly wage w and schooling s from different sections of Table 1.2. On a separate graph, plot the log of the weekly wage $\ln w$ and schooling s for the same occupations. Notice how the transformation to logs reveals a more linear pattern.

1.7 Julie's weekly preparation of tax returns is a random variable with outcomes $\{10, 11, 12, 13, 14, 15\}$. The probabilities (expressed as percentages) associated with these six outcomes are $\{5, 10, 15, 20, 30, 20\}$.

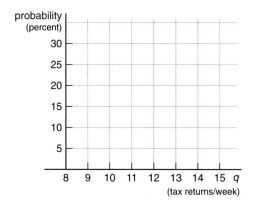

(a) In the graph above, illustrate Julie's distribution of prepared tax returns by plotting the combinations of outcomes and probabilities as a bar chart.

(b) Draw a vertical line at the median number of tax returns.

(c) What is the probability that Julie prepares at least 13 tax returns in a week?

1.8 The federal minimum wage was $2.30 in 1976. In Table 1.3, compute the scale factor (P_{2017}/P_{1976}) and the 1976 minimum wage in real terms (2017 dollars). Was the real minimum wage higher in 1976 or 2017?

References

Ashenfelter, Orley and Alan B. Krueger. 1994. "Estimates of the Economic Return to Schooling from a New Sample of Twins." *American Economic Review* 84(5): 1157–1173.

Card, David and Alan B. Krueger. 1994. "Minimum Wages and Employment: A Case Study of the Fast-Food Industry in New Jersey and Pennsylvania." *American Economic Review* 84(4): 772–793.

Galenson, David W. 1981. "The Market Evaluation of Human Capital: The Case of Indentured Servitude." *Journal of Political Economy* 89(3): 446–467.

Kelley, David. 2013. *The Art of Reasoning: An Introduction to Logic and Critical Thinking*, 4th ed. New York: W.W. Norton.

2 Labor Markets

Over about a quarter of a century, a wave of baby-boom students rolled through elementary and secondary schools. The first baby boomers entered first grade in the early 1950s and graduated from high school in the mid-1960s. The final cohorts of baby boomers started school in the mid-1960s and graduated in the late 1970s. Grade by grade, the 15-year-wide wave squeezed through the school systems.

Schools strained to provide teachers, as well as classrooms and desks, for the baby-boom students (Flyer and Rosen 1997). Driven by intense hiring of new college graduates in the 1960s, the number of teachers grew 55 percent between 1955 and 1970. Almost half the women graduating from college in 1960 became teachers; that number fell to less than 10 percent by 1990. Hiring of new teachers tailed off as the baby-boom wave left elementary school and later high school, and the average age of teachers trended up. Nearly half the teachers in the late 1960s were in their twenties; the fraction of teachers in their twenties fell to 20 percent by the late 1970s and to about 10 percent in 1985.

How do you think the wave of baby-boom students influenced teachers' pay? Chapter by chapter, we study the many factors that influence pay, so the best we can hope to do here is to identify one key factor that captures the essence of the baby boom's influence on teachers' pay. Try this: schools needed more teachers, so they paid a premium to attract people to the classroom. This explanation is surely not shocking, and it might even ring true to you. But those two simple clauses contain a wealth of economics. The first clause suggests that schools respond to increased enrollments by wanting to employ more teachers. The second clause assumes (1) that the need for more teachers translates into schools being willing to pay teachers more money and (2) that paying teachers more attracts more people into the classroom. Our explanation also works in reverse as the wave of baby boomers exited the schools: the wage premium for teachers vanished because schools no longer needed as many teachers.

In this chapter, we apply the concepts of demand and supply to the labor market. In the context of the baby boom and the market for teachers, we model "needing more teachers" as an increase in the demand for teachers. Increases in the demand for labor cause employment and wages to rise, and that's exactly what happened in the market for teachers as baby boomers advanced from grade to grade: employment of teachers rose dramatically, and the pay of teachers rose relative to the pay of other college graduates (Flyer and Rosen 1997). As the baby boomers left school (by the late 1970s), the demand for teachers fell. A fall in the demand for labor decreases employment and wages. Wages of teachers (relative to wages of other college graduates) trended down for 10–15 years beginning in the mid-1970s, and hiring of new teachers ground to a halt by the late 1970s (Flyer and Rosen 1997).

We begin our analysis of labor markets by applying the dual engines of demand and supply to labor in a single competitive market. The model identifies the key factors that determine wages and employment. Next we inject several doses of government to study the effects of minimum-wage law, taxes on labor, wage subsidies, and employer mandates—government requiring employers to provide job benefits. Then we turn to linkages across competitive labor markets to see how differences in wages across locations encourage migration. We close the chapter by studying employment and wages in a monopsonist, a firm that's free from competition from other employers. Comparing competitive and monopsony labor markets identifies the element that drives efficiency and eliminates exploitation of workers: competition among employers.

2.1 Competitive Labor Market

We use the concepts of demand and supply to understand employment and wages in any competitive labor market. Since the typical employer is a firm, firms are the demanders of labor. At some wage w, the amount of labor that these firms want to employ is the quantity demanded of labor L_D. People are the suppliers of labor, so workers populate the supply side of a labor market. At some wage w, the amount of labor people want to supply is the quantity supplied of labor L_S. Each person decides whether to work and how much to work, and those decisions contribute to the supply of labor. For the supply of labor to a location, such as Boston, each person's decision where to work is also important. Each person's decision about the type of work to do is important for the supply of labor to a particular occupation, such as nursing.

	QUANTITY	QUANTITY	EXCESS DEMAND (SUPPLY)
WAGE	**DEMANDED L_D**	**SUPPLIED L_S**	$L_D - L_S$
w ($/nurse)	(mil. nurses/week)	(mil. nurses/week)	(mil. nurses/week)
600	4.0	1.0	3.0
900	3.5	2.0	1.5
1,200	3.0	3.0	0.0
1,500	2.5	4.0	(1.5)
1,800	2.0	5.0	(3.0)

TABLE 2.1. LABOR DEMAND AND LABOR SUPPLY SCHEDULES OF NURSES

Let's explore the market for nurses. Table 2.1 lists demand and supply schedules in the nursing market. Doctors' offices, medical labs, home health-care services, schools, and other organizations employ nurses, and they comprise the demand side of the nursing market. The supply side of the nursing market derives from people choosing to work as nurses (rather than as physical therapists, teachers, web designers, or carpenters, for instance) and how much to work (full-time or part-time, for instance). The interaction of these two sides of the nursing market determines wages and employment in nursing.

Demand for Nurses

The number of nurses that hospitals and other employers want to employ depends on the wage of nurses. Combinations of wages w and quantity demanded of nurses L_D in the first two columns of Table 2.1 are points on the downward-sloping labor demand curve in Figure 2.1. A lower weekly wage of nurses increases the quantity demanded of labor by hospitals and other employers. The quantity demanded of

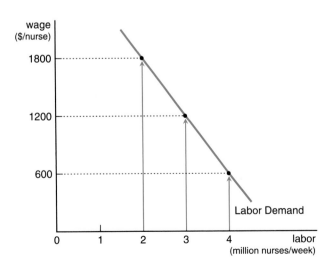

The demand for nurses slopes down. Here the quantity demanded increases from 2 million to 3 million nurses/week as the weekly wage falls from $1,800 to $1,200/nurse. The height of the nursing demand curve reveals the marginal value of nurses in health care.

With more nurses employed, the value of an additional nurse's contribution to health care is lower. Raising employment from 2 million to 3 million nurses/week lowers the weekly marginal value of nurses from $1,800 to $1,200/nurse.

FIGURE 2.1. Demand for Nurses

nurses is 2 million nurses per week if the weekly wage in nursing is $1,800. If, however, the weekly wage is $1,200 per nurse, then the quantity demanded of nurses is 3 million nurses per week. Lowering the weekly wage from $1,800 to $1,200 increases the number of nurses that hospitals and other employers want to employ from 2 to 3 million nurses per week. The lower wage encourages firms to increase employment.

One key to understanding the downward-sloping demand for labor is the diminishing marginal value of labor. Employing an additional nurse produces more health care, which raises a hospital's revenue. "How much does an employer's revenue increase by employing one more worker?" The answer to this question is the **marginal value of labor** MV_L, which is very important because it tells us the hospital's willingness to pay for nurses. Labor's marginal value typically falls as employment rises. Although more nurses produce more health care in total, each additional nurse tends to add less to health care than the one before. There are more eyes and hands to care for patients, but there's less for each nurse to do.

Labor demand and the marginal value of labor are two sides of the same coin. With 2 million nurses employed per week at a weekly wage of $1,800, hospitals and other employers don't want to employ even one more nurse. That implies that the marginal value of the first nurse beyond the 2 millionth isn't as high as $1,800. And since these employers don't stop a few nurses short of 2 million either, the marginal value of those last few nurses must be at least as high as $1,800. Therefore, at 2 million nurses, the marginal value of nurses is squeezed from both sides to $1,800 per nurse. The marginal value at 2 million nurses is $1,800, and the marginal value of nurses declines to $1,200 if employment of nurses increases to 3 million nurses per week. *Thus the height of the labor demand curve at any level of employment L reveals the marginal value of labor at L.*

 PRACTICE If 4 million people are employed as nurses, what's the marginal value of labor in nursing?

Supply of Nurses

The number of people who want to work as nurses depends on the wage of nurses. Combinations of wages w and quantities supplied of nurses L_S in the first and third columns of Table 2.1 are points on the upward-sloping labor supply curve in Figure 2.2. A higher weekly wage of nurses increases the quantity supplied of labor by attracting more people into nursing. (In chapter 3, we investigate the effect of a higher wage on working hours of those already employed as nurses.) The quantity supplied of nurses is 3 million nurses per week if the weekly wage in nursing is $1,200. Raising the wage to $1,800 pulls 2 million more people into nursing, increasing the quantity supplied of nurses to 5 million nurses per week. The higher wage attracts workers to nursing: some trained nurses who aren't

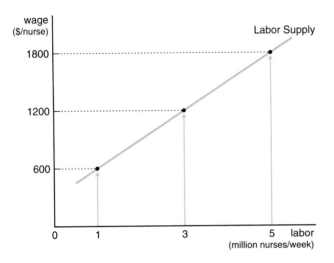

The supply of nurses slopes up. Here the quantity supplied of nurses increases from 3 million to 5 million/week as the weekly wage increases from $1,200 to $1,800/nurse.

The height of the nursing supply curve reveals the marginal cost of nurses' time. With more nurses employed, the opportunity cost of nurses' time in other activities grows. Employment growth from 3 million to 5 million nurses/week increases the weekly marginal cost of nurses' time from $1,200 to $1,800/nurse.

FIGURE 2.2. Supply of Nurses

working or are working in other occupations return to nursing, and some other people begin training to become nurses.

The key to understanding the upward-sloping supply of nurses is the increasing **marginal cost of nurses' time**. "What's the highest value that a person foregoes by working as a nurse?" The answer to this question tells us the opportunity cost of that person's time in nursing (or the marginal cost of nursing time), which also reveals the wage a person requires to work as a nurse. The best alternative use of the nurse's time might be working in another occupation, raising kids and keeping a house, going to college, or fishing and golfing in retirement. The value of the best alternative determines the marginal cost of nursing time, which typically rises as the quantity supplied of nurses rises. The marginal cost of nursing time is low if few people work as nurses: finding another person (without great options outside of nursing) to work as a nurse isn't difficult. However, with millions of people working as nurses, increasing employment draws in nurses with great outside options, so the marginal cost of nursing time is high.

The supply of nurses reflects the marginal cost of nursing time. With 3 million nurses employed per week at a weekly wage of $1,200, not one more person wants to work as a nurse. Therefore, the marginal cost of the first nurse beyond the 3 millionth is greater than $1,200. And since the number of people choosing to work as nurses doesn't stop a few nurses short of 3 million either, the marginal cost of those last few nurses must be less than $1,200. Therefore, at 3 million nurses, the marginal cost of nursing time is squeezed from both sides to $1,200 per nurse. Also, the marginal cost of nurses grows to $1,800 if employment of nurses increases to 5 million nurses per week. *So the height of the labor supply curve at any level of employment L reveals the marginal cost of workers' time at L.*

PRACTICE   What's the marginal cost of nurses' time if 1 million people work as nurses?

Equilibrium in the Market for Nurses

Labor demand and labor supply interact to determine employment and the wage in the labor market equilibrium. The economic concept of **equilibrium** is that no one (e.g., no buyer or seller) has any incentive to do anything different. In the context of the market for nurses, we search for a wage w such that the quantity demanded of labor L_D equals the quantity supplied of labor L_S. Hospitals and other employers employ as many nurses as they want, and everyone who wants to work as a nurse does so.

Let's begin our search for the equilibrium by trying $600 per nurse as the weekly wage (i.e., $w = 600$). Paying nurses a weekly wage of $600 produces a shortage of (or excess demand for) nurses. Hospitals and other firms want to employ 4 million nurses, but only 1 million people want to work as nurses. In response to this huge shortage, hospitals and other firms bid up the wage rather than go without nurses. And nurses gladly accept the higher wage. So the nursing shortage pushes the wage of nurses up from $600. Indeed, any wage below $1,200 causes an excess demand for nurses and lifts their wage.

Key Principle.
Wages tend to adjust to eliminate shortages and surpluses.

Next let's try paying nurses a weekly wage of $1,800. With $w = 1800$, quantity demanded is 2 million nurses per week, and the quantity supplied is 5 million nurses per week, so a huge surplus (or excess supply) of nurses appears. Out-of-work nurses offer to work for less than $1,800, and hospitals gladly pay lower wages while filling all their nursing positions. So the nursing surplus pushes the wage of nurses down from $1,800. In fact, any wage above $1,200 causes an excess supply of nurses and lowers their wage.

We have established that (1) any wage below $1,200 causes a shortage of nurses and (2) any wage above $1,200 causes a surplus of nurses. The only wage that we haven't considered is $1,200. In this market for nurses, the equilibrium wage w^* is $1,200 because that wage produces neither a shortage nor a surplus: the quantity demanded of labor equals the quantity supplied of labor (at $L^* = 3$), and there's no pressure to lower or to raise the wage. In Figure 2.3, the market-clearing equilibrium is $(3, 1200)$, point E at the intersection of the labor demand and labor supply curves.

 PRACTICE   Is there a shortage or surplus of nurses if the wage is $900 per nurse? Carefully mark the size of the shortage or surplus in Figure 2.3.

In a competitive market for nurses (or any other occupation), the market-clearing equilibrium is efficient. That is, a competitive market for labor

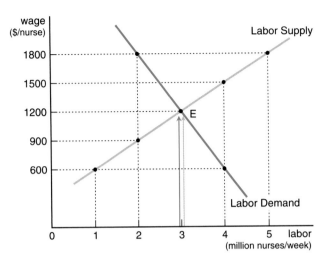

For the nursing market to clear, the quantities demanded and supplied of nurses must be equal. For quantity demanded to equal quantity supplied, the weekly wage must be $1,200/nurse. A nursing shortage (or excess demand) follows from any weekly wage below $1,200/nurse. A higher wage yields a surplus (or excess supply) of nurses.

At the equilibrium point E, the wage equals both the marginal value of labor MV_L and the marginal cost of nurses' time MC_L.

FIGURE 2.3. Market-Clearing Equilibrium in the Market for Nurses

maximizes the *gains from trade*. Let's flesh out several aspects of efficiency with a series of questions.

First, are too few or too many people working as nurses? Nursing employment is too low if the marginal value of nurses exceeds the marginal cost of their time in nursing. At 2 million nurses, marginal value is $1,800 per nurse, and marginal cost of nurses is $900 per nurse. Employing another nurse increases total value by $900: value in health care grows by $1,800 while value in other activities drops by $900. So employing 2 million nurses per week is too low to be efficient. Alternatively, at 4 million nurses, the marginal value of nurses is $600, and the marginal cost of nurses' time is $1,500. Employing another nurse decreases total value by $900 (= $600 − $1500), so employing 4 million nurses per week is too high to be efficient. The equilibrium employment at $L^* = 3$ million nurses is the only level of employment where the height of the demand curve is the same height as the supply curve. Therefore, the marginal value of nurses equals the marginal cost of nurses in the market-clearing equilibrium. And that's efficient.

Second, are those 3 million nurses being put to the best use, or are they being underutilized in low-marginal-value hospitals? With a mix of high-marginal-value and low-marginal-value employers of nurses, it's not efficient to employ nurses in low-marginal-value firms while high-marginal-value firms go without nurses. One of the outstanding properties of the market-clearing equilibrium is that nurses work where they are valued most. Low-marginal-value employers—those further down the labor demand curve—are priced out of the market.

Third, are those 3 million nursing jobs being filled by the lowest-opportunity-cost people? Suppose equally productive nurses differ in their values of other activities. Those with not much else to do have a low marginal cost of nursing time, and they comprise the low end of the labor supply curve in nursing. Other people have great outside opportunities, and the high marginal cost of their time in

Key Principle.
Competitive labor markets are efficient.

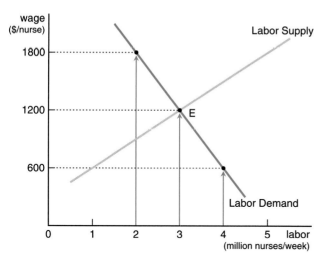

Nurses are paid what they are worth in a competitive labor market. The value of nurses' contribution to health care, which we read off the height of the nursing demand curve, depends on employment of nurses. At the competitive equilibrium level of employment (3 million nurses), the weekly marginal value of nurses is $1,200/nurse, which is exactly the wage of nurses.

At no other level of employment does the marginal value of nurses equal the $1,200 weekly wage.

FIGURE 2.4. Marginal Productivity Theory of Distribution

nursing places them at the high end of nursing's labor supply curve. As Figure 2.3 shows, lower marginal-cost-of-nursing-time people work as nurses; the higher marginal-cost-of-nursing-time people do other things. (People who are passionate about nursing are willing to work as nurses at lower wages, so these people also tend to become nurses.) So another property of the market-clearing equilibrium is that the people who work as nurses are those with the lowest opportunity cost.

Fourth, are nurses paid what they are worth in the market-clearing equilibrium? Yes, they are neither underpaid nor overpaid. "Worth" refers to the value of workers' contribution to production, which we measure by the marginal value of labor. Equilibrium employment is $L^* = 3$ million nurses per week, and the equilibrium marginal value of nurses (i.e., the height of the demand curve at 3.0 million nurses) is $1,200 per nurse, which is exactly the weekly wage of nurses. As Figure 2.4 shows, no other level of employment produces a marginal value of nurses that equals the $1,200 market-clearing wage. The principle that workers are paid a wage equal to their marginal value in a competitive market for their services is the **marginal productivity theory of distribution**. As we see later in the chapter, the conclusion that nurses and other workers are paid what they are worth hinges critically on the assumption of competition.

Shifting the Equilibrium

Increases and decreases in labor demand or labor supply shift the equilibrium, changing the employment and wages of nurses. Increasing the demand for labor increases employment and the wage. Figure 2.5a depicts this case. The equilibrium slides up the labor supply curve, so the number of people employed as nurses and the wage of nurses increase. Increasing the supply of labor increases employment but decreases the wage. In Figure 2.5b, the wage of nurses falls and employment of nurses grows as the equilibrium slides down the labor demand curve.

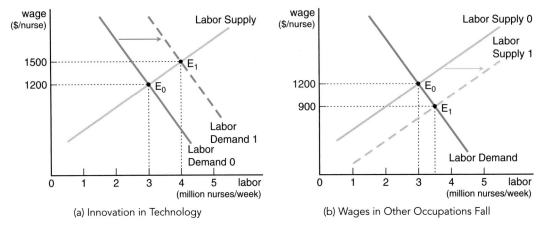

(a) Innovation in Technology

(b) Wages in Other Occupations Fall

(a) An innovation in health-care technology increases the marginal value of nurses, and each nurse is able to care for more patients. The innovation increases the productivity of nurses, so the demand for nurses increases, shifting to the right. A nursing shortage emerges if nurses' weekly wage doesn't rise. Nurses' weekly wage rises to $1,500 to clear the market, and more people are employed as nurses.

(b) Decreasing pay in other occupations makes working as a nurse more attractive and increases the supply of nurses. If nurses' weekly wage remains at $1,200, then a surplus of nurses materializes. To clear the market, the weekly wage falls to $900/nurse, and more people are employed as nurses.

FIGURE 2.5. Increasing the Demand for and the Supply of Nurses

Factors that Shift the Labor Demand Curve.   What factors change the demand for labor, shifting the labor demand curve to the left or right? Let's start by excluding one factor: the wage. To avoid confusing movements along the labor demand curve with shifts in the curve itself, we distinguish increases in the quantity demanded of labor from increases in labor demand. A lower wage raises the quantity demanded of labor *along the labor demand curve* but doesn't shift the position of the curve. So the wage *doesn't* affect the demand for labor.

We explore the factors that influence labor demand in detail in chapter 4, but we can specify the main principle here. Whatever increases the marginal value of labor *at each level of employment* shifts the labor demand curve to the right, increasing the demand for labor. First, increasing the price of health care (i.e., the price of the product) increases the *value* of nurses' contribution to health care. Thus a higher price of health care raises the marginal value of, and increases the demand for, nurses. Second, armed with more medical equipment (i.e., physical capital) to work with, each nurse can care for more patients. So more medical equipment (or a lower price of medical equipment) tends to raise nurses' productivity, increasing the marginal value of and the demand for nurses. Third, innovation in health-care technology (e.g., better medical equipment) also tends to increase the marginal value of and the demand for nurses.

PRACTICE An increase in the wage of nurses [decreases, increases, doesn't change] the demand for nurses and [decreases, increases, doesn't change] the supply of nurses. [Careful!]

That innovations tend to increase labor demand runs counter to conventional wisdom, which focuses on the number of workers needed to produce a fixed quantity of output q_0. An innovation that increases workers' productivity means that a firm needs fewer workers to meet that fixed output q_0. But a firm that pursues profit doesn't limit its output to q_0; it responds to the increase in the marginal value of labor by increasing output and increasing its demand for labor. Thus an innovation that renders labor more productive (in terms of marginal value) increases the demand for labor, shifting the labor demand curve to the right.

The evolution of slavery and cotton production in the South in the wake of Eli Whitney's invention of the cotton gin illustrates this principle. Before Whitney invented the cotton gin in 1793, separating valuable cotton fibers from the nuisance cotton seeds was tedious, cotton was a minor crop, and slavery was in decline. A typical worker could separate one pound of usable cotton fiber in a day. A typical worker using the cotton gin could produce 50 pounds of usable cotton fiber in a day. That means a plantation owner needed far fewer workers to produce the same amount of cotton. Indeed, if 50 workers had been separating fiber from seed before the cotton gin, then a plantation needed only one worker after the cotton gin. Did the cotton gin thus decrease the demand for farm labor in general and slave labor in particular? Did the cotton gin lead to the decline of slavery in the South?

The answer to these questions is No. In fact, Whitney's cotton gin caused the demand for labor, slave or free, on cotton plantations to soar and the supply of cotton to explode. The cotton gin turned cotton into a profitable crop. Cotton production increased 70 percent in the two years after the invention. Nearly 15 times as much cotton was produced in 1805, 12 years after the invention of the cotton gin, than in 1793 (*Historical Statistics of the United States: Colonial Times to 1970, Part 1*, U.S. Department of Commerce, 1975, p. 518). Fewer slaves were needed to meet the old target for cotton production, but cotton production exploded and so did the demand for slave labor on cotton plantations.

 PRACTICE Henry Ford revolutionized the auto industry in the early twentieth century. His assembly line reduced the number of worker-hours required to produce each car. Do you think the assembly line increased or decreased the demand for auto workers? How did the assembly line impact the supply of cars?

Not all innovations increase the demand for labor. The history of farming provides great examples of innovations that have reduced employment on farms. Two hundred years ago, almost everyone worked on farms. Now farms in the

United States employ only 1 in 50 workers. The innovations have propelled a stunning rise in farm output and an equally stunning fall in farm employment.

Mechanization of farming raises the supply of farm products but lowers the demand for farm workers. Innovations in farming combine with inelastic demand for farm products to cut the price of farm products. Farm products become inexpensive, which lowers the marginal value of and the demand for farm workers. So an innovation can lift the productivity of farm workers in terms of output but still cut their marginal value (in dollar terms). In this case, the demand for farm workers falls.

Factors that Shift the Labor Supply Curve.   What factors change the supply of labor, shifting the labor supply curve to the left or right? An increase in the supply of labor is a shift in the labor supply curve to the right. Increasing the wage lifts the quantity supplied of labor *along the labor supply curve* but doesn't shift the labor supply curve. So the wage *doesn't* affect the supply of labor.

We explore the factors that impact labor supply in chapter 3, but we can grasp the main principle here. Anything that increases the value of people's time in other activities (e.g., recreation and other leisure-time activities, child and home care, working in other occupations) decreases the supply of labor. Increasing income from allowances, savings and investments, and other nonlabor sources raises the value of time outside work. So increasing allowances and financial income decreases the supply of labor to any occupation and to the labor market overall. Having more children also decreases labor supply (usually of women) because children increase the value of time at home. More generous pension and government-welfare benefits also decrease labor supply. Finally, higher wages in physical therapy, teaching, web design, and other occupations decrease the supply of nurses.

 PRACTICE   In the mid-twentieth century, women in the United States were having nearly five children on average. Fifty years later, the fertility rate fell to about 2.5 children. How did this drop in the fertility rate affect the supply of labor?

Changes in the population also shift the supply of labor. High fertility rates during the baby boom reduced the supply of labor, but labor supply rose dramatically decades later when the baby boomers entered the labor market. And the supply of labor falls when famine or disease devastates a population.

A striking example from medieval Europe highlights how the dual engines of demand and supply in the labor market illuminate history. The Black Death, the most devastating example of the bubonic plague that periodically ravaged the world for centuries, wiped out one-third to one-half of Europe's population over a few years in the middle of the fourteenth century. The Black Death dramatically reduced the supply of labor throughout Europe, which increased peasants' wages. King and Parliament in England fought for decades to hold the peasants' pay down to pre-plague levels. Try as they did, crown and sword couldn't evade a timeless principle of labor economics: holding a wage down causes a shortage.

The Black Death had a lot to do with the decline of serfdom, under which a peasant was bound to the lord of a medieval manor. Lack of competition was a hallmark of feudalism, but the labor shortage created competitive pressure among the manors. In response to the labor shortage on his lands, a lord offered work as free peasants (rather than as serfs) to lure peasants from towns and other manors. A peasant escaped serfdom on one manor for freedom on another. Serfdom declined for decades and eventually disappeared from Western Europe. Another surprising consequence of the Black Death also followed from a shortage of labor: the shortage of French teachers in England probably contributed to the flowering of English literature in the late 1300s.

2.2 Minimum Wage

Government controls on labor also affect employment and wages. Our introduction to policy analysis starts here with an analysis of the minimum wage.

A week before the federal minimum wage rose from $6.55 to $7.25 per hour on July 24, 2009, CNN news anchor Gerri Willis declared, "No surprise here, experts say higher wages reduce costly turnovers and increase worker productivity. But with unemployment at 9.5 percent, some are wondering if this hike is enough to stimulate job growth" (*Your Bottom Line* on CNN, July 18, 2009). Willis and her unnamed experts seemed to believe that raising the minimum wage—a floor on the price of labor—increases employment and that the 70-cent hike in the minimum wage would be too small to get the army of unemployed back to work. How would a higher minimum wage increase employment? Does raising the price of labor encourage employers to hire more workers?

In the United States, federal minimum-wage law currently requires government and most private employers to pay nonsupervisory workers at least $7.25 per hour. The nominal series in Figure 2.6 presents the federal minimum wage monthly since 1938. The real series in the figure adjusts the minimum wage for inflation and expresses the real minimum wage in 2017 dollars. In real terms, the minimum wage peaked early in 1968 at $11 per hour, and the original 25-cent minimum wage in 1938 is comparable to a $4.40 hourly wage in 2017. Between legislated increases in the minimum wage, inflation erodes its real value. Legislation combines with inflation to produce the conspicuous sawtooth pattern in the figure.

The federal minimum wage binds for few people, mostly teenagers and high school dropouts. In 2017, 57 percent of the wage and salary workers in the United States were paid by the hour, and only 2.3 percent of those hourly workers were paid at or below the federal minimum wage (U.S. Department of Labor, Bureau of Labor Statistics, Current Population Survey, Table 44). Less than a third of those workers—30 percent—report being paid exactly the minimum wage. Therefore, the minimum wage binds for about 0.4 (= .57 × .30 × 2.3) percent of U.S. wage

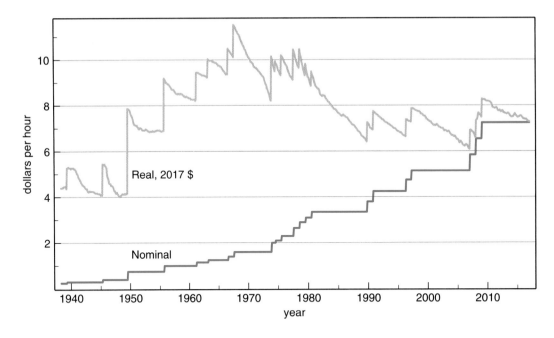

FIGURE 2.6. Minimum Wages in the United States, 1938–2017

Notes: *Nominal* refers to the minimum wage as specified in federal law. *Real* refers to the minimum wage measured in 2017 dollars by adjusting for inflation; that is, in year t, real minimum wage$_t$ = nominal minimum wage$_t$ × (CPI_{2017}/CPI_t).
Source: Bureau of Labor Statistics.

and salary workers, and at most 1.3 ($= .57 \times 2.3$) percent if we include workers who report being paid less than the minimum wage. Our task is to analyze the impact of a binding minimum wage, so let's work in the context of teenagers.

Effect of a Minimum Wage on Employment

A **binding minimum wage** reduces employment. Figure 2.7 illustrates this important principle in the market for teenagers. The market-clearing hourly wage of teenagers is $5.50, and teenagers work in total 150,000 hours each week. Now let's introduce the wage floor, a minimum wage at $7.25 per hour. The quantity demanded of labor falls from 150,000 to 120,000 hours per week (driving the marginal value of labor up to $7.25 per hour), and the quantity supplied of labor rises to 200,000 hours per week: a surplus of 80,000 hours emerges. The drop in employment from 150,000 to 120,000 hours is the **disemployment effect of the minimum wage**. The surplus also reflects the increase in the quantity supplied of labor as more people want to work at $7.25 than at $5.50. The surplus is likely to appear as unemployment: people who want to work at $7.25 can't find jobs.

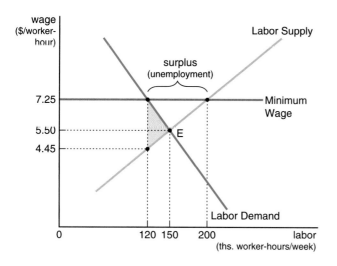

A binding minimum wage raises the quantity supplied and lowers the quantity demanded of labor. Employment falls from 150,000 to 120,000 hours/week, and a surplus of 80,000 hours crops up. The surplus appears as unemployment.

The minimum wage is inefficient. For each hour between 120,000 and 150,000, the marginal value of labor exceeds the marginal cost of workers' time. The deadweight loss from underemployment, the area of the shaded triangle, is $42,000 (= (150,000 − 120,000) × ($7.25 − $4.45) ÷ 2)/week.

FIGURE 2.7. Minimum Wage

 PRACTICE   Increase the minimum wage from $7.25 to $8.00 per hour in Figure 2.7. What happens to employment, the marginal value of labor, and the surplus of labor?

The minimum wage is inefficient. Every one of those 30,000 hours between 120,000 and 150,000 generates a marginal value greater than the marginal cost of workers' time. The potential gains from trade on the extra 30,000 hours are lost or wasted. Workers as a group gain in this example. Each of the 120,000 weekly hours captures an extra $1.75, and that totals $210,000 per week. But 30,000 weekly hours lose the previous gain from employment at $5.50 per hour, which is $15,750 (= 30,000 × ($5.50 − $4.45) ÷ 2) per week. The net gain to workers is about $194,000.

But we shouldn't ignore the loss that employers suffer. Employers lose $1.75 on every one of the 120,000 hours per week. They also fail to capture the previous gain from employment at $5.50 for those 30,000 hours, which is $26,250 (= 30,000 × ($7.25 − $5.50) ÷ 2) per week. The loss to employers totals about $236,000.

For the labor market as a whole, the loss is $42,000 (= $236,000 − $194,000) per week. This **deadweight loss** (or efficiency loss) from underemployment with a minimum wage is the area of the shaded triangle in Figure 2.7. So the minimum wage is inefficient.

Workers who value working the most don't necessarily get the minimum-wage jobs, so the minimum wage causes an additional inefficiency. Suppose that all teenagers are equally productive, but the value of time outside work varies among these workers. (The height of the labor

Key Principle.
Interfering with competitive labor markets causes inefficiency.

supply curve reveals these values of time outside the labor market.) Our minimum-wage equilibrium specifies 120,000 hours per week of employment, but nothing draws those hours from the workers who value working the most, those with little to do outside work. Figure 2.7 does *not* depict this additional deadweight loss.

With our first results in hand, we are ready to evaluate CNN news anchor Gerri Willis's remarks about the consequences of raising the minimum wage in 2009. Our analysis predicts that employment falls. Willis suggests that an even higher minimum wage is necessary to drive up employment enough to make a dent in the unemployment rate. Why would a higher minimum wage stimulate employment? As Willis notes, the unemployment rate was quite high: there was no shortage of labor, so the implied increase in the quantity supplied of labor is irrelevant. Rather, Willis's remark followed from an erroneous idea about stimulating the macroeconomy.

The argument is that a higher minimum wage puts more money in the wallets of the low-wage workers, which stimulates their spending and the macroeconomy, which increases employment. It should be obvious, however, that the extra dollars in the wallets of low-wage workers come from the wallets of others. Spending cuts by those who write the bigger paychecks (or those who pay higher prices for burgers and fries) offset any increase in spending by minimum-wage workers. Moving dollars from one wallet to another wallet in the economy doesn't make us richer and doesn't increase aggregate spending. Thus a higher minimum wage doesn't stimulate the macroeconomy. It *does* raise the price of low-wage workers to employers, so we predict that raising the minimum wage cuts employment.

Preliminary Evidence

Let's consider the evidence. In scores of time-series studies, labor economists have estimated the aggregate relationship between teenage employment (or unemployment) and the minimum wage. In years when the minimum wage is high relative to the wages of all workers, is teenage employment low? Since many teenage workers earn more than the minimum wage, it shouldn't be surprising that the disemployment effects aren't large. Raising the minimum wage 10 percent might decrease teenage employment by 1 percent in the short run and as much as 3 percent within two years.

In Puerto Rico, however, the impact of the minimum wage on employment has been more dramatic. U.S. minimum-wage law applies to Puerto Rico, where the minimum wage "really bites." Puerto Rican workers earn about 40 percent less per hour than workers in the 50 states and the District of Columbia, and perhaps one-third of all Puerto Rican workers are paid at or below the minimum wage. The minimum wage is clearly not just a teenage issue in Puerto Rico.

Figure 2.8 displays the employment rate (i.e., employment divided by population) for Puerto Ricans of all ages and the minimum-wage index. (The index is the coverage rate of the minimum wage times the minimum wage relative

FIGURE 2.8. Minimum Wage and Employment in Puerto Rico, 1950–1987

Notes: Minimum-Wage Index is {coverage rate × minimum wage ÷ average wage} averaged across industries. Employment Rate is employment ÷ population.
Source: Castillo-Freeman, Alida and Richard Freeman. 1992. "When the Minimum Wage Really Bites: The Effect of the U.S.-Level Minimum Wage on Puerto Rico." In *Immigration and the Workforce: Consequences for the United States and Source Areas*, edited by George Borjas and Richard Freeman. Chicago: University of Chicago Press, Table 6A.1.

to the average wage.) Consistent with a disemployment effect of the minimum wage, the two series are inversely related. Indeed, a regression of the employment rate on the minimum-wage index precisely estimates the slope at −.31(.03). The minimum-wage index averages .334, so hiking the minimum wage 10 percent raises the index by 3.34 (= .334 × 10) percent and lowers the employment rate in Puerto Rico by 1.0 (= −.31 × 3.34) percentage point. If every lost job turns into an unemployed worker, then the Puerto Rican unemployment rate jumps by 2.3 percentage points. That's huge.

The original 25-cent-per-hour minimum wage, part of the Fair Labor Standards Act of 1938 (FLSA), went into effect in October 1938, and job losses followed. Although 25 cents was no small amount at the time, the average hourly wage was 60–65 cents. In addition, coverage of the 25-cent minimum was limited to firms involved in interstate commerce, and the law exempted many of those firms. Overall, the minimum wage covered one-fifth of the workforce, and it was binding on only about 300,000 workers, or about 0.5 percent of the workforce. But the law had its effects. The employment rate fell in 1938 and again in 1939. The Department of Labor calculated at the time that 30,000–50,000 jobs were lost. Job losses were concentrated in the South, which might have been by design.

Much of the support for the FLSA came from manufacturers in the North that had been finding it difficult to compete with lower-wage firms in the South.

Seltzer (1997) studied the effects of the original 25-cent-per-hour minimum wage on two of the South's most important manufacturing industries, seamless hosiery and lumber. The minimum wage was binding on many hosiery and lumber producers in the South. Employment in hosiery firms fell from 1938 (before the FLSA) to 1940, and worker-hours fell roughly 20 percent from shortly before the passage of the minimum wage to the summer of 1940. Importantly, employment fell only in hosiery companies that had been paying wages less than the minimum wage. Seltzer also found that hosiery companies shifted from labor-intensive to automated production, and the shift was much faster among companies that had been paying wages below the minimum wage.

In the lumber industry, however, the experience was much different. Overall employment in lumber didn't fall, but production shifted from the low-wage South to the high-wage North. And many small lumber producers in isolated areas simply ignored the law. Other lumber companies stopped shipping across state lines to escape the law. By one report, 300 of 500 Texas sawmills participated in interstate commerce in 1938, and that number fell to 20 by 1941.

Puerto Rico provides an even more dramatic before-and-after illustration of the consequences of the original minimum wage. Congress neglected to exempt Puerto Rico from the 25-cent-per-hour minimum wage. The average wage in Puerto Rico at the time was about half the minimum wage; many of the lowest-wage workers were employed in agriculture (e.g., 6 cents per hour in tobacco and 7 cents per hour in coffee), but even some manufacturing industries paid pennies per hour (e.g., homeworkers in needlework earned up to 4 cents per hour). On the day before the minimum wage took effect, Puerto Rico's labor commissioner declared, "The medicine is too strong for the patient" ("Puerto Rico Hurt by Wage Hour Law," *New York Times*, October 24, 1938, p. 2), and he was right. The results were devastating. Factories closed. The needlework industry almost vanished. Only lax enforcement allowed other industries to survive. Puerto Rico found it couldn't compete in world markets, and its exports plummeted. The 25-cent minimum wage also kicked off an era of emigration from Puerto Rico to the mainland United States. Congress responded to the devastation by amending the FLSA in June 1940 to allow lower minimum wages in Puerto Rico.

New Jersey Raises Its Minimum Wage

In the context of Puerto Rico in the late 1930s, there's really no debate about cause. In other contexts, however, there is a serious concern that before-and-after comparisons ignore other factors that could explain the results. To address this issue, we turn to difference-in-difference methods. (See section 1.5.) Table 2.2 collects difference-in-difference, as well as before-and-after, estimates of the employment effects of New Jersey's minimum-wage hike in 1992.

In a study that sent a shock wave through the economics profession, Card and Krueger (1994) found evidence that raising the minimum wage increases

TABLE 2.2. EMPLOYMENT EFFECTS OF RAISING THE MINIMUM WAGE IN NEW JERSEY IN 1992

Data	Group	EMPLOYMENT		
		Before	After	Difference
Card and Krueger's Survey Data				
Treatment	New Jersey	20.4	21.0	0.6
Control	Eastern Penn.	23.3	21.2	−2.2
Difference		−2.9	−0.1	2.8
Neumark and Wascher's Payroll Data				
Treatment	New Jersey	17.8	17.9	0.1
Control	Eastern Penn.	15.1	16.2	1.1
Difference		2.7	1.7	−1.0

Notes: Employment is the number of workers/store.
Sources: Card and Krueger (1994, Table 3), Neumark and Wascher (2000, Table 3), and calculations on Neumark and Wascher's data.

employment in fast-food restaurants. On April 1, 1992, New Jersey raised its minimum wage from $4.25, the federal minimum wage at the time, to $5.05 per hour. Card and Krueger sampled hundreds of fast-food restaurants before and after New Jersey raised its minimum wage. Employment *increased* from 20.4 workers per store to 21.0 workers per store after the minimum-wage hike, so the before-and-after comparison reveals no evidence of a disemployment effect of raising New Jersey's minimum wage. (See the first row of Table 2.2.)

The economy in 1992 was emerging from the 1990–1991 recession, so the before-and-after comparison of employment in fast-food restaurants doesn't isolate the impact of New Jersey raising its minimum wage. To identify the employment effect, Card and Krueger also sampled fast-food restaurants in eastern Pennsylvania, where the minimum wage remained at $4.25 per hour, as a control group. Employment in the Pennsylvania stores fell from 23.3 to 21.2 workers per store after New Jersey raised its minimum wage. Employment in the treatment group (i.e., New Jersey stores) increased 2.8 workers per store more than employment in the control group (i.e., Pennsylvania stores). So, in Table 2.2, the difference-in-difference estimate of the employment effect of raising the minimum wage in New Jersey is *positive* 2.8 workers per fast-food restaurant.

Card and Krueger (1994) and related studies were subjected to piercing scrutiny. Was seven months long enough for fast-food restaurants to respond to the higher minimum wage? Since New Jersey enacted the $5.05 minimum wage two years before it went into effect, did restaurants reduce employment in advance of the hike? Is eastern Pennsylvania a good control group for New Jersey, or are the two locations subject to different shocks to labor demand? Let's leave these questions unanswered, but another question is worth addressing.

Were Card and Krueger's telephone survey data consistent with payroll records from the fast-food restaurants? Neumark and Wascher (2000) collected data from payroll records of fast-food restaurants in New Jersey and eastern Pennsylvania before and after New Jersey raised its minimum wage in 1992. The payroll data display much less variability of employment responses across restaurants, which suggests that Card and Krueger's employment data contain serious reporting errors. Furthermore, applying Card and Krueger's difference-in-difference method to the payroll data uncovers a sizable disemployment effect of raising New Jersey's minimum wage: fast-food employment growth in New Jersey lagged behind fast-food employment growth in eastern Pennsylvania by nearly one full-time worker per restaurant. (See the lower panel of Table 2.2.)

Two Rounds of Federal Minimum Wage Hikes

Can we uncover the employment effects of hikes in the federal minimum wage, such as the jumps from $3.35 to $3.80 on April 1, 1990, and to $4.25 on April 1, 1991? Let's examine the employment rate of teens (ages 15–19), an important group of low-wage workers, using the basic monthly data from the Current Population Survey. To avoid the complication of a state minimum wage that exceeds the federal minimum wage, we limit the sample to the 33 states with state minimum wages that are at or below the federal minimum wage throughout the sample period.

Figure 2.9a displays teen employment rates annually over an 11-year period before and after the 1990 and 1991 hikes in the minimum wage. In the five years before the 1990 hike, the teen employment rate trended up from 36 percent to nearly 40 percent. Employment of teens dropped dramatically in 1990 and 1991 and trended up again thereafter. The drop in teen employment is telling, but the United States went into a recession a few months after the first hike, so the hit to employment might reflect, at least in part, typical job loss in recessions.

To separate the disemployment effect of the minimum-wage event from the disemployment effect of the recession, we use the employment rate of a control group to predict how the employment rate of teens would have evolved if not for the two minimum wage hikes (Deere, Murphy, and Welch 1995). That is, we create a *counterfactual series* for the teen employment rate. Prime-age high school graduates (i.e., people ages 25–59 with at least a high school diploma) make for a good control group because most of these workers earn well above the minimum wage. In fact, only 6 percent of workers in this group reported earning less than $4.25 per hour in the 12 months before the 1990 hike. One complication, however, is that teen employment fluctuates more than employment of prime-age high school graduates. For instance, if the employment rate in the control group falls two percentage points, the teen employment rate drops about three percentage points. To capture this, a regression equation estimates the relationship between teen and control employment rates, and the estimates generate the counterfactual series. (See the notes to Figure 2.9 for details.)

Figure 2.9a displays the close relationship between the employment rate of teens and the counterfactual employment rate—based on the employment rate of prime-age high school graduates—before the first hike. The counterfactual series

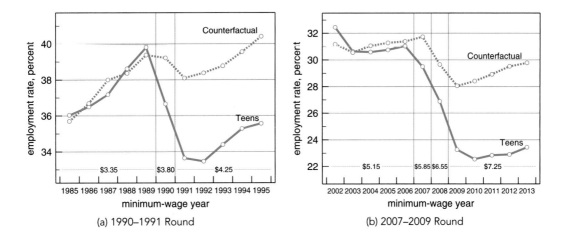

FIGURE 2.9. Employment Rate of Teens Around Two Rounds of Federal Minimum-Wage Hikes

Notes: e_T is the teen employment rate, e_C is the employment rate of prime-age high school graduates, and D_y is a variable that indicates whether a data point is from year y.

In panel (a), each minimum-wage year begins in April of the indicated calendar year and ends in March of the next year. The estimated regression equation is $e_T = -.706 + \underset{(.140)}{1.54} e_C - \underset{(.199)}{.026} D_{90} - \underset{(.005)}{}$

$\underset{(.003)}{.046} D_{91\_}$ with $R^2 = .964$, so the counterfactual series is $\widehat{e_T} = -.706 + 1.54 e_C$.

In panel (b), each minimum-wage year begins in August of the indicated year and ends in July of the next year. The estimated regression equation is
$e_T = -.738 + \underset{(.358)}{1.47} e_C - \underset{(.502)}{.025} C - \underset{(.009)}{.030} D_{07} - \underset{(.012)}{.030} D_{08,09} - \underset{(.010)}{.055} D_{10\_}$ with $R^2 = .976$, so the counterfactual series is $\widehat{e_T} = -.738 + 1.47 e_C$.
Source: Current Population Survey, basic monthly files, panel (a) April 1985–March 1996, and panel (b) August 2002–July 2014.

justifies our concern that the teen employment would have dropped in 1990 and 1991 even without the minimum wage hikes. But the employment rate of teens dropped far more than we predict on the basis of the relationship between teen employment and educated, prime-age employment. The difference between the two series beginning in 1991 provides a difference-in-difference estimate of the effect of the 1990 and 1991 federal minimum wage hikes on the employment rate of teens. The teen employment rate fell from 39.8 percent to 33.5 percent, and the federal minimum wage hikes in 1990 and 1991 account for 4.6 percentage points of the 6.3 percentage-point drop.

Figure 2.9b displays the sharp drop in the teen employment rate following the minimum wage hikes from $5.15 to $5.85 in July 2007, to $6.55 in July 2008, and to $7.25 in July 2009. The U.S. economy peaked just months after the first in the series of three minimum wage hikes, so again we have to deal with recession-driven job loss. The control group of prime-age high school graduates generates a counterfactual employment rate that's closely linked to the teen employment rate over the periods before the first and after the last hike. The counterfactual series again confirms our concern that the recession (rather than the minimum wage) contributed to the sharp drop in teen employment rates in 2007, 2008, and 2009. But the teen employment rate fell much more than we predict on the basis of employment of prime-age high school graduates. The teen employment rate tumbled from 31 percent to 22.5 percent. The recession accounts for 3 percentage points of the 8.5 percentage-point drop. The minimum wage hikes account for the remaining 5.5 percentage-point drop in the teen employment rate—2.5 points in 2007, 3.0 points in 2008 and 2009, and 5.5 points beginning in 2010.

· ·

ADVANCED Let's see if the patterns in Figure 2.9 hold up in regression analysis of state-level data. Instead of the 11 aggregate data points that give us Figure 2.9a, we have 11 annual data points for each of the 33 states with state minimum wages at or below the federal minimum wage over the sample period. Working at the state level gives us more data to sharpen our estimates of the relationship between teen employment and control-group employment and more precisely estimate the employment effects of the minimum wage.

In logs, we regress the teen employment rate e_T on the employment rate of prime-age high school graduates e_C and include a variable (D_{90}) that indicates whether the data point is from 1990 and another variable (D_{91-}) that indicates whether the data point is from 1991 or after. On these 363 ($= 33 \times 11$) state-level data points, the estimated regression equation is

(2.1) $$\ln e_T = -.305 + 2.34 \ \ln e_C - .066 \ D_{90} - .125 \ D_{91-}$$
$$\quad\quad\quad\; (.088) \quad (.213) \quad\quad\quad\quad (.012) \quad\quad\;\; (.009)$$

with $R^2 = .904$. (Each state also gets its own intercept, but we suppress those estimates to save space.) Here we find that, state by state, a 1 percent increase in the employment rate of the control group increases the employment rate of teens 2.34 percent. This relationship shifted down 6.6 percent in 1990 and 12.5 percent in subsequent years. These are the estimated effects of the minimum wage hikes. Since the 12.5 percent drop is from a starting value of about 40 percent, the teen employment rate fell 5 ($= .125 \times 40$) percentage points, half of that in the first year.

The same method produces similar estimates for the 2007–2009 round of federal minimum wage hikes. Only 18 states had state minimum wages at or below the federal minimum wage throughout the sample period. On these 216 ($= 18 \times 12$) state-level data points, the estimated regression equation is

(2.2) $$\ln e_T = -.418 + 2.38 \ \ln e_C - .066 \ D_{07} - .162 \ D_{08,09} - .264 \ D_{10-}$$
$$\quad\quad\quad\;\; (.128) \quad (.399) \quad\quad\quad\quad (.018) \quad\quad\;\;\; (.022) \quad\quad\quad\;\; (.017)$$

with $R^2 = .930$. Fluctuations in the teen employment rate amplify fluctuations in the employment rate of prime-age high school graduates.

This relationship shifted down 6.6 percent in 2007, 16.2 percent in 2008 and 2009, and 26.4 percent thereafter. These are the estimated effects of the minimum wage hikes. The 26.4 percent drop is from a starting value of 31 percent, so the teen employment rate fell about 8 ($\approx .264 \times 31$) percentage points: 2 percentage points in 2007, 5 percentage points in the next two years, and 8 percentage points after that.

The regression analysis on state-level data reveals large employment losses of teens in both rounds of federal minimum wage hikes, and the magnitudes confirm the patterns in Figure 2.9.

. . . .

In the two decades since Card and Krueger's study, it has become common for state minimum wages to surpass the federal minimum wage. And variation in the *effective minimum wage*—the higher of the state or federal minimum wage—across states and time is the new laboratory to assess the employment effects of minimum wages on teens and other low-wage workers. When a state increases its effective minimum wage, what happens to teen employment relative to states where the effective minimum wage hasn't changed? When the federal minimum wage rises, the effective minimum wage rises in some states but not in states with minimum wages above the federal minimum wage. Does employment grow less in states where the effective minimum wage is more sensitive to the federal minimum wage? The preponderance of evidence from analysis of state-level data through time points to a significant disemployment effect for young workers. (See Neumark and Wascher [2008] for a comprehensive evaluation of research on minimum wages.)

The minimum wage is a fiercely debated topic, so it's inevitable that each side of the policy debate cites the research that supports its position. From time to time, a research study reports evidence that challenges the disemployment effect of the minimum wage, and that study captures a lot of attention among labor economists and in the policy debate. But such anomalous evidence should be digested in the context of the wide body of evidence that finds the minimum wage reduces employment of low-wage workers.

2.3 Taxes, Subsidies, and Employer Mandates

The minimum wage is one of many government policies that target the workplace. In this section, we explore the consequences of a few other government policies—a tax on workers, a wage subsidy, and a government-mandated employee benefit.

Employment Taxes

There are two primary ways to tax labor or income from labor. The government can tax workers, which is what the individual income tax in the United States does. (Employers handle tax payments for workers through deductions, but workers are legally responsible for their tax liabilities.) Or the government can place the tax on employers. For instance, a tax on employers funds unemployment insurance in the United States. The payroll tax for Social Security is split 50–50 between workers and their employers, so the mysterious FICA deduction on a worker's pay stub is only half the amount the employer sends to Washington. President Clinton's 1994 proposal for universal health-care coverage would have required employers to fund 80 percent of workers' health-care costs.

It might seem obvious that placing the labor tax on employers protects workers from the tax burden. What appears to be obvious, however, is wrong. The conventional wisdom assumes that the tax is added to a fixed wage. But the wage adjusts to the tax in equilibrium. The tax affects the wage, and that fact delivers a salient principle: *whether the government places the tax on workers or their employers doesn't matter for anything economically important.* In particular, shifting the responsibility for a tax on labor from workers to employers doesn't help workers. We demonstrate the irrelevance of the **legal incidence of a tax** by separately comparing the effects of a tax per worker on employers and a tax per worker on workers.

Employers Pay the Tax.   A tax on employers reduces the demand for labor. To see why, consider the market for labor depicted in Figure 2.10a. In the absence of a tax t, the equilibrium is at point E_0: firms employ 200 people, and each worker earns a $400 weekly wage. Suppose the government levies a $160-per-worker tax on employers. For employers to continue employing 200 workers per week, the wage *plus the tax* must equal $400, the marginal value of labor with 200 workers employed. Therefore, the quantity demanded of labor with this $160-per-worker tax is 200 workers per week only if the wage is $240 (= $400 − $160) per worker.

There's nothing special about 200 workers. For instance, at $L = 150$, the height of the demand curve is $490 without the tax; with the tax, the height of the demand curve is $330 (= $490 − $160) because the wage and the tax must sum to $490, the marginal value of labor at $L = 150$. So generally the demand for labor shifts down by the size of the tax, which is $160 per worker in Figure 2.10a. Since the demand curve with the tax lies left of the demand curve without the tax, the tax on employers reduces the demand for labor.

By reducing the demand for workers, a tax on employers lowers employment, raises the tax-inclusive (or gross) wage employers pay, lowers the after-tax (or net) wage workers receive, and distorts the labor market. Figure 2.10a illustrates the equilibrium with a weekly tax on employers of $160 per worker. Since the labor demand curve shifts down by $160, the equilibrium slides down the supply curve to E_t. Employment falls to 150 workers per week, the weekly wage slips to $330 per worker, and the tax-inclusive wage rises to $490 per worker. The difference between the $490 cost to employers and the $330 wage that workers take home is the $160 tax. With employers taxed $160 per worker for the 150 workers each week, government revenue from the tax on employers is $24,000 (= $160 × 150) per week. The $160-per-worker tax on employers is inefficient because employment shrinks. Indeed, the weekly deadweight loss—the area of the

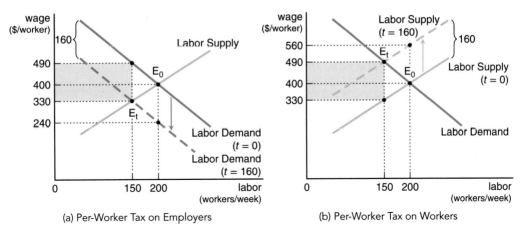

(a) Per-Worker Tax on Employers

(b) Per-Worker Tax on Workers

(a) The government imposes a $160/worker tax on employers. Labor demand falls, which reduces employment and the wage. In the new equilibrium E_t, workers earn $330/week, but the tax-inclusive cost of labor is $490/week. The difference between the wage and the tax-inclusive cost of labor is the $160/worker tax. Workers bear 44% (= 70 ÷ 160) of the tax, and firms bear 56% (= 90 ÷ 160) of the tax. The deadweight loss is $4,000 (= (200 − 150) × $160 ÷ 2) per week.

(b) The government imposes a $160/worker tax on workers. The labor supply curve shifts up, which reduces employment but raises the wage. In the new equilibrium E_t, workers earn $490/week but take home (i.e., after taxes) $330/week. The difference between the wage and the take-home wage is the $160/worker tax. Again, workers bear 44% (= 70 ÷ 160) of the tax, and firms bear 56% (= 90 ÷ 160) of the tax. The deadweight loss is $4,000 (= (200 − 150) × $160 ÷ 2) per week.

FIGURE 2.10. Comparing a Tax on Employers and a Tax on Workers

triangle defined by the three points in Figure 2.10a—is $4,000 (= $160 × (200 − 150) ÷ 2) per week.

 PRACTICE The government places a $160-per-worker tax on employers. Suppose the wage doesn't fall. Mark the size of the resulting [shortage, surplus] with a line segment in Figure 2.10a.

Workers Pay the Tax. A tax on workers reduces the supply of workers. Figure 2.10b displays the case of a $160-per-worker tax. For 200 people to want to work, take-home pay $w − t$ must equal $400, the marginal cost of workers' time. Therefore, the quantity supplied of labor with this $160-per-worker tax is 200 workers per week only if the wage is $560 (= $400 + $160) per worker and take-home pay equals $400 (= $560 − $160) per worker.

Again, there's nothing special about 200 workers. For instance, at $L = 150$, the height of the supply curve is $330 without the tax; with the tax, the height of the supply curve is $490 (= $330 + $160) because the after-tax wage $w − t$ must equal $330, the marginal cost of workers' time at $L = 150$. So generally the supply of labor shifts up by the size of the tax t, which is $160 per worker in Figure 2.10b. Since the supply curve with the tax lies left of the supply curve without the tax, the tax on workers reduces the supply of labor.

By reducing the supply of workers, a tax on workers lowers employment, raises the pre-tax (or gross) wage employers pay, lowers the after-tax (or net) wage workers receive, and distorts the labor market. Panel (b) of Figure 2.10 illustrates the equilibrium with a weekly tax on workers of $160 per worker. Since the labor supply curve shifts up by $160, the equilibrium slides up the labor demand curve to E_t. Employment falls to 150 workers per week, the weekly (gross) wage rises to $490 per worker, and the weekly take-home (net) wage slips to $330 per worker. The difference between the $490 wage that employers pay and the $330 wage that workers take home is the $160 tax. With the 150 workers taxed $160 per worker each week, government revenue from the tax on workers is $24,000 (= $160 × 150) per week. The $160-per-worker tax on workers is inefficient because employment shrinks. Indeed, the weekly deadweight loss—the area of the triangle defined by the three points in Figure 2.10b—is $4,000 (= $160 × (200 − 150) ÷ 2) per week.

"Who Writes the Check" Doesn't Matter.   The consequences of a labor tax in terms of employment, employers' cost of labor, take-home pay, tax revenue, and efficiency are unrelated to "who writes the check." That is, the **economic effects of a tax** on labor are independent of its legal incidence. To see why, let's compare the tax-on-employers equilibrium and the tax-on-workers equilibrium. Employment in each equilibrium is 150 workers per week. If employers pay the tax, the weekly wage is $330; the employer pays each worker $330, but the cost of the worker is $490 (= $330 + $160). If workers pay the tax, the weekly wage is $490; the cost of the worker is $490, but each worker takes home $330 (= $490 − $160). That the transaction wage ($490 or $330) depends on "who writes the check" hides the fact that the employers' cost per worker and the workers' take-home wage don't depend on "who writes the check." Nor do tax revenue and efficiency. Since the two equilibria share the same employment, 150 workers, they also share the same tax revenue ($24,000 per week) and the same deadweight loss ($4,000 per week).

A tax on labor merely drives a wedge between employers' marginal values on the labor demand curve and workers' marginal costs of time on the labor supply curve. Our two labor-tax equilibria in Figure 2.10 define two points, one at $330 on the labor supply curve and the other $160 above it (at $490) on the demand curve. As Figure 2.11 shows, we can find these two points (and fully characterize the economic effects of the labor tax) by sliding a $160-long vertical line segment between the labor demand and labor supply curves *without knowing who writes the check*.

What does determine the economic effects of a tax on labor? The elasticities of labor demand and labor supply. First, if the quantity demanded of labor is quite sensitive to the wage (so the labor demand curve is relatively flat or, more precisely, *elastic*), then workers' take-home pay falls a lot and employers' cost of labor

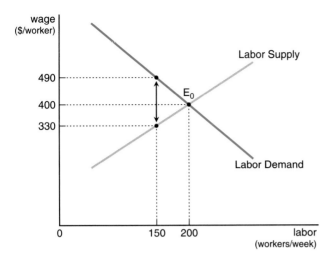

FIGURE 2.11. Driving a Tax Wedge

The \$160/worker tax drives a wedge between employers' marginal values on the labor demand curve and workers' marginal costs of time on the labor supply curve. The tax-inclusive (or gross) wage determines the quantity demanded of labor; the after-tax (or net) wage determines the quantity supplied of labor.

Independent of the tax's legal incidence, the tax-inclusive wage is \$490/worker, the after-tax wage is \$330/worker, employment is 150 workers/week, tax revenue is \$24,000/week, and the deadweight loss is \$4,000/week.

doesn't rise much. Second, if the quantity supplied of labor is quite sensitive to the wage (so the labor supply curve is relatively flat or, more precisely, *elastic*), then take-home pay doesn't fall much and employers' cost of labor rises a lot.

> ☑ **PRACTICE**   Illustrate these two cases by driving a tax wedge between (1) a relatively flat labor demand curve and a steeper labor supply curve and (2) a relatively flat labor supply curve and a steeper labor demand curve.

We are left with three important principles of taxation: the size of the tax matters; elasticities of labor demand and supply matter; who's legally liable for the tax doesn't matter at all.

Wage Subsidy

A tax on labor lowers employment. A government-financed **wage subsidy** raises employment. Paying firms to employ workers encourages them to employ more workers. That bit of wisdom shouldn't surprise you. But you might be surprised to learn that the key principles of a tax on labor carry over to a wage subsidy. In particular, "who (firm or worker) *receives* the check" doesn't matter, and wage subsidies are inefficient.

With a wage subsidy s, either each worker receives s from the government or the government pays the employer s per worker. The Earned Income Tax Credit in the United States is a wage subsidy to low-income workers. For a married couple with two dependent children, the federal government gives a refundable tax

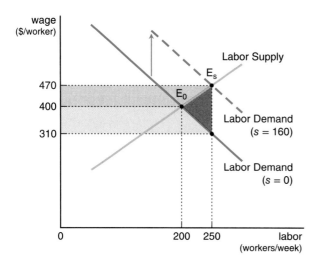

The $160/worker subsidy to employers shifts the labor demand curve up $160, which lifts employment and wages along the labor supply curve. The weekly wage increases from $400 to $470/worker. Employers' labor costs, however, drop to $310/worker.

The wage subsidy costs $40,000/week, which is the area of the rectangle with base 250 workers/week and height $160/worker. The sum of the gains to workers and firms—the areas of the two shaded trapezoids—are less than this. Indeed, the deadweight loss of the subsidy is $4,000/week, the area of the shaded triangle.

FIGURE 2.12. Wage Subsidy

credit of $40 for every $100 earned up to $13,900 in earnings. That's essentially a 40 percent wage subsidy to low-income workers. Alternatively, the government could use a business tax credit to pay the employers of those low-income workers. To explore the effects of a wage subsidy, let's assume that the government pays firms to employ workers. Figure 2.12 shows the effects of a $160 weekly subsidy per worker.

A weekly wage subsidy that pays employers $160 per worker shifts the labor demand curve up $160. If employers are willing to employ exactly 200 workers at weekly wage of $400 per worker without the subsidy, they employ exactly 200 workers at a $560 (= $400+$160) weekly wage with the $160 subsidy. As before, there's nothing special about 200 workers; indeed, at any level of employment, the labor demand curve with the $160 subsidy lies $160 above the labor demand curve without the subsidy.

The wage subsidy slides the equilibrium up the labor supply curve. Employment increases from 200 to 250 workers per week, and the weekly wage rises from $400 to $470 per worker. The government pays the subsidy to employers, but workers benefit from the higher wage. They gain the area of the light-gray-shaded object in Figure 2.12. And firms gain despite the higher wage they pay at E_s. The net cost of employing a worker for a week is $310 (= $470 − $160) with the wage subsidy, which is less than the $400 without the subsidy. The area of the blue-shaded object in the figure measures how much the wage subsidy enriches firms.

So everyone wins. Or do they? Someone funds the wage subsidy, and those someones are the taxpayers. Taxpayers are on the hook for $40,000 (= $160/worker × 250 workers) per week, the area of the rectangle formed by the three shaded objects in Figure 2.12. If we subtract the workers' gains and the firms' gains from the tax burden, we're left with the shaded triangle, the area of which is the deadweight loss. The source of the deadweight loss is the overemployment of workers. Since the original labor demand curve lies below the labor supply curve over the range from 200 to 250 workers per week, the marginal value of each of the additional 50 workers is less than the marginal cost of that worker. The time of those workers is worth more in other activities. So a wage subsidy is inefficient, and the area of the triangle in Figure 2.12 expresses the inefficiency in dollar terms.

 PRACTICE   Apply our principle from employment taxes to show that nothing meaningful depends on "who *receives* the check." That is, analyze what happens when the beneficiary of the wage subsidy shifts from the firm to the worker.

Employer Mandate

Governments require employers to provide some benefits to each worker. Unemployment insurance and paid (or even unpaid) parental leave are two examples. The per-worker cost of the mandated benefit is c. With the **employer mandate**, the weekly cost of a worker is $w + c$, so the cost c is like a labor tax t. Indeed, the labor demand curve shifts down by the cost of the mandated benefit. But the effects of the mandated benefit depend on how workers value the benefit. Let's consider three possibilities.

First, if workers don't value the benefit at all, the mandated benefit resembles a per-worker tax on employers. In fact, our graph of a per-worker tax on employers (i.e., Figure 2.10a) doubles as a graph of an employer mandate that costs $160 per worker. Mandating a benefit shifts the labor demand curve down by the cost of the mandate, and the equilibrium slides down the labor supply curve if workers don't value the benefit. Employment and wages fall, and the equilibrium is inefficient. But this equilibrium differs from the tax equilibrium in one important way: an employer mandate generates no tax revenue. The deadweight loss in this version of an employer mandate includes the shaded tax-revenue rectangle in Figure 2.10a.

Second, if workers value the benefit at cost (i.e., $v = c$), no one wins, no one loses, and the employer mandate is inconsequential. "The government requires every employer to provide its workers with something they really value, and those workers gain nothing" you ask? Absolutely! To unlock this nugget of truth, don't ignore the mandate's effect on the wage. As before, the mandated benefit shifts the labor demand curve down by $c = \$160$, but here the labor supply curve also shifts down by $v = \$160$. Figure 2.13a illustrates the effect of shifting the labor demand and labor supply curves down by the same amount. The equilibrium with the employer mandate lies $160 below the no-mandate equilibrium, so the mandate lowers the wage from $400 to $240. But the cost to employ a worker ($240 + $160) and a worker's value of compensation ($240 + $160) remain at $400. Employment doesn't change either. So if workers fully value the mandated benefit, the employer mandate isn't inefficient. It's just inconsequential.

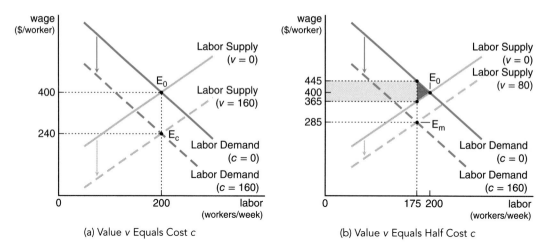

(a) Value v Equals Cost c   (b) Value v Equals Half Cost c

(a) A government mandated benefit that costs $160/worker and workers value at $160/worker shifts the labor demand and labor supply curves down $160 without affecting employment. The wage falls by $160/worker, but employers' cost/worker $w^* + c$ and workers' value of compensation $w^* + v$ remain at $400. In this case, the mandated benefit is efficient, but it doesn't help anyone.

(b) A mandated benefit that costs $160/worker shifts the labor demand curve down $160. Each worker values the benefit at $80, so the labor supply curve shifts down $80. Mandating the benefit reduces employment from 200 to 175 workers/week. The equilibrium wage falls from $400 to $285/worker. Labor cost rises to $445/worker, and workers value their weekly compensation at $365. The deadweight loss from the mandated benefit has two parts. (1) Workers value the benefit less than it costs; this loss is $(c - v)L_m^* = \$80 \times 175 = \$14{,}000$/week. (2) The loss from underemployment is the area of the shaded triangle, which is ($445 − $365) × (200 − 175) ÷ 2 = $80 × 25 ÷ 2 = $1000/week.

FIGURE 2.13. Employer Mandate

Third, if workers value the benefit at half its cost (i.e., $v = c/2$), a mandated benefit reduces employment and is inefficient. Again, the labor demand curve shifts down by $160, but here the labor supply curve shifts down by $c/2 = \$80$. The equilibrium with the employer mandate is point E_m in Figure 2.13b. The weekly wage falls from $400 to $285. Even the worker's valuation of compensation (including the mandated benefit) falls from $400 to $365 (= $285 + $80). And employers suffer, too. The weekly cost per worker rises from $400 without the mandated benefit to $445 (= $285 + $160) with the mandate. So mandating the benefit reduces employment, cuts each worker's value of compensation, and drives up a firm's cost of employing a worker. The deadweight loss includes the area of the shaded rectangle (i.e., the $80-per-worker undervaluation of the benefit times the number of workers) in addition to the inefficiency from underemployment.

Our results depend on how workers value the benefit, but one principle spans the three cases: if we ignore how wages respond to a mandated benefit, we draw the wrong conclusions about who wins and loses from the employer mandate and its overall efficiency or inefficiency.

2.4 Multiple Competitive Labor Markets

The market for nurses isn't isolated from the markets for physical therapists, teachers, and web designers. Like the markets for apples, oranges, and pears, occupational labor markets are distinct but interrelated. A higher price of oranges increases the demand for apples; likewise, a higher wage of physical therapists lowers the supply of nurses.

Occupational and locational (e.g., Chicago and New York, or Mexico and the United States) labor markets are generally linked in the long run. Workers can change occupations or migrate between cities or countries in the long run. Firms can relocate in the long run, too. Equilibrium in the short run requires that each labor market clears—no surpluses, no shortages. But equilibrium in the long run also requires that workers and firms have no incentive to move across labor markets—to change occupations or to move across locations.

Multi-Market Equilibrium and Migration

Let's explore these issues in the context of two locational labor markets: New York and Chicago. Suppose that the labor market in each city clears: there's neither a surplus nor a shortage in either city, so the intersection of each city's labor demand and labor supply curves determines its wage and employment. Figure 2.14

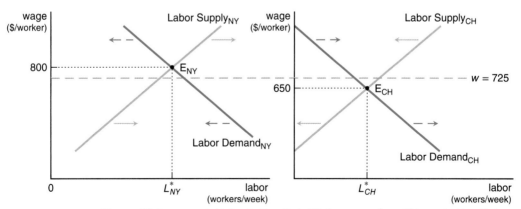

The equilibrium wage is higher in New York. Workers move from Chicago to New York, so labor supply increases (decreases) in New York (Chicago). Firms move from New York to Chicago, so labor demand in Chicago (New York) increases (decreases). The dynamics of migration equalize wages across cities in the long run: wages tend to converge.

FIGURE 2.14. Migration and Equilibrium Across Markets

illustrates this case. In New York, everyone who wants to work is employed at the $800 weekly wage, and every job is filled. The equilibrium weekly wage in Chicago is $650 per worker, and the quantity supplied of labor there equals the quantity demanded of labor there. On the basis of our analysis of equilibrium in section 2.1, we conclude that these labor markets are in equilibrium.

The $150-per-worker gap in the weekly wage across the two cities, however, encourages people to move from low-wage Chicago to high-wage New York. The low wage in Chicago pushes workers from the Windy City, and the high wage in New York pulls workers to the Big Apple. (For simplicity, we abstract from cross-city differences in housing prices, taxes, crime rates, school quality, cultural amenities, and weather, but we could handle these other factors in a more advanced analysis.) **Migration** from Chicago to New York lowers the supply of labor in Chicago and raises the supply of labor in New York. The solid arrows in Figure 2.14 display the directions of the shifts in the labor supply curves. Emigration from Chicago drives the wage up there: the Chicago equilibrium slides up Chicago's labor demand curve. Immigration to New York reduces the wage there as the equilibrium in New York slides down New York's labor demand curve. As an equilibrating process, migration narrows or even eliminates the wage gap between Chicago and New York.

Locational wage differences also encourage firms to relocate. In the long run, firms in high-wage New York move to low-wage Chicago to reduce cost and to increase profit. As a result, labor demand in New York falls, and labor demand in Chicago grows. The dashed arrows in Figure 2.14 illustrate the shifts in labor demand curves. Relocation of firms from New York to Chicago lowers the wage in New York and elevates the wage in Chicago. The relocation process of firms is also equilibrating, narrowing or even eliminating the gap in pay across the two cities.

The result of the relocation processes is **wage convergence**— convergence to a common wage—in the long run. Unless wages equalize across cities—or across labor markets more generally—workers and firms are inclined to move. Hence **multi-market equilibrium** requires that quantity demanded and supplied be equal in each market *and* the market-clearing wage be the same across all markets. Only with a common wage across cities does no person or firm have an incentive to move.

Key Principle.
Migration of workers and firms across locations enhances efficiency.

Migration is efficient. The high wage in New York signals that the marginal value of labor in New York exceeds the marginal value of labor in Chicago. Moving one worker from Chicago to New York decreases the value of production in Chicago by $650 per week and increases the value of production in New York by $800 per week. The net gain in the value of production is $150 per week. As long as labor's marginal value is higher in New York than in Chicago, moving workers from Chicago to New York increases the value of what workers produce. Therefore, an efficient allocation of labor across these cities, as well as across labor markets more generally, equalizes marginal values of labor.

The efficiency property of migration is an important principle, but we shouldn't ignore the fact that migration produces winners and losers. Workers in

New York aren't happy with the influx of immigrants from Chicago and the exodus of employers to Chicago because both factors drive down the New York wage. And employers in Chicago aren't thrilled with competitors relocating to Chicago and the exodus of workers to New York because these factors drive up the Chicago wage. Nevertheless, migration enhances efficiency.

Minimum Wage with Partial Coverage

Minimum-wage law in the United States doesn't cover large segments of the workforce. Executives, administrators, professionals, sales workers, teachers and administrative workers in elementary and secondary schools, skilled computer professionals, fishermen, and farm workers on small farms are exempt from federal minimum wages. The overwhelming majority of the workers in these occupations earn much more than the minimum wage, but the law also exempts small firms (under $500,000 in annual revenue), and these firms employ plenty of low-wage workers. When the Fair Labor Standards Act was passed in 1938, the minimum wage was set at 25 cents per hour and covered few jobs in retail and service industries. In particular, the law exempted public schools, construction, farming, air transport, and much of retail trade. Let's see how a minimum wage in one sector impacts employment and the wage in the uncovered sector.

Workers displaced by the minimum wage in the covered sector **spill over to the uncovered sector**, raising employment and lowering the wage there. The three-panel diagram in Figure 2.15 illustrates these effects for manufacturing and agriculture. Before the manufacturing sector is hit with the minimum wage, employment L and the wage w are determined in one labor market, the total market in Figure 2.15a. The demand for labor, which is the sum of labor demands in manufacturing and agriculture, interacts with the supply of labor to determine the equilibrium wage ($6 per hour) and employment (100 million worker-hours per week): point E in panel (a). Extending the $6 hourly wage to panels (b) and (c) reveals equilibrium employment in the two sectors: 60 million worker-hours per week in manufacturing and 40 million worker-hours per week in agriculture.

Now hit employers in manufacturing with a $7-per-hour minimum wage; employers in agriculture are left uncovered. Employment in manufacturing slides up manufacturing's labor demand curve in panel (b), falling by 10 million worker-hours to 50 million worker-hours per week. And the minimum wage in manufacturing displaces workers. Those 10 million worker-hours spill over into agriculture.

To determine the effect of the spillover into agriculture, we need to derive the supply of labor to agriculture in the presence of the $7 minimum wage in manufacturing. (Without the minimum wage in manufacturing, neither sector has a meaningful labor supply curve; the only relevant labor supply curve without the minimum wage is the labor supply curve to the total market in panel (a).) With the minimum wage in manufacturing, the supply of labor to agriculture is the supply of labor to the total labor market minus employment in manufacturing (up to $7). For instance, if the agriculture wage w_a remains at $6 per hour, then the quantity supplied of labor remains at 100 million worker-hours per week. Fifty million

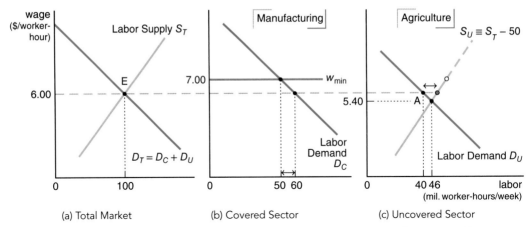

Without a minimum wage, the equilibrium is point E: the $6/hour equilibrium wage yields employment of 60 million and 40 million worker-hours/week in manufacturing and agriculture, respectively. The $7/hour minimum wage in manufacturing displaces 10 million worker-hours to the uncovered agricultural sector. For agriculture wages below $7/hour, labor supply to agriculture is total labor supply S_T minus the 50 million worker-hours/week in manufacturing. Not all the displaced labor is employable in agriculture at $6/hour, so the agriculture wage falls to $5.40/hour.

The minimum wage in manufacturing increases the manufacturing wage, decreases the size of manufacturing, decreases the agriculture wage, increases the size of agriculture, and increases unemployment. The resulting allocation of labor across sectors is inefficient.

FIGURE 2.15. Minimum Wage with Partial Coverage

of those worker-hours are supplied to manufacturing, so the quantity supplied of labor in agriculture at $w_a = 6$ must be 50 million worker-hours per week. Thus one point on agriculture's labor supply curve is 10 million worker-hours per week to the right of point A. And the slope of the labor supply curve in agriculture is the slope of the total labor supply curve (up to $w_a = 7$). Figure 2.15c plots the labor supply curve in agriculture.

The new equilibrium in agriculture slides down agriculture's labor demand curve, increasing employment and decreasing the wage in agriculture. As drawn, agriculture absorbs 6 million of the 10 million worker-hours of labor. The other 4 million worker-hours are from workers who want to work on a minimum-wage job but don't want to work for the lower wage in agriculture; those workers are unemployed. The wage in agriculture falls to $5.40 per hour. The minimum wage increases the wage in manufacturing, shifts employment from manufacturing to agriculture, cuts overall employment, raises unemployment, and decreases the wage in agriculture.

✓ **PRACTICE**   Suppose the government raises the minimum wage in manufacturing from $7 to $8 per hour. What happens to the labor supply curve in agriculture? Illustrate the effect on the wage and employment in agriculture in Figure 2.15.

The minimum wage, with or without an uncovered sector, is inefficient. We found in section 2.2 that underemployment is one source of inefficiency. With an uncovered sector, the minimum wage also causes an inefficient allocation of labor across the two sectors: manufacturing is too small, and agriculture is too big. In the equilibrium with the minimum wage in Figure 2.15, the marginal values of labor are $7 per hour in manufacturing and $5.40 per hour in agriculture. Shifting a worker from agriculture to manufacturing lifts the combined value of production by $1.60 (= $7.00 − $5.40) per hour. The same principle applies to every hour of labor where labor's marginal value in manufacturing exceeds its marginal value in agriculture. Again, efficiency requires that labor's marginal value be equal across all markets.

The employment experience of black teenagers in the South in the 1950s and 1960s provides a vivid application of the minimum wage with an uncovered sector (Cogan 1982). Most young black men in the South worked on farms in 1950, when all of agriculture and most of retail trade and services were not covered by the minimum wage. Innovation in farming technology in the 1950s decreased the demand for young black men in agriculture, and black teenagers moved from agriculture to jobs elsewhere in the uncovered sector, mostly in the retail trade and service industries. In the 1960s, amendments to the FLSA broadened coverage of the minimum wage to include large farms and most of retailing and services, so the uncovered sector shrank. Innovation continued to reduce the demand for black teenagers in agriculture, and they spilled over to the uncovered sector. The smaller uncovered sector couldn't absorb the influx of labor at the going wage. Hence employment of young black men fell, and their unemployment rose in the 1960s.

2.5 Monopsony

In its glory days, about 2,000 people lived in Coalwood, a tiny coal-mining town in rural West Virginia that gained fame through Homer Hickam Jr.'s book *Rocket Boys* (1998) and its big-screen adaptation *October Sky* (1999). The only employer in town was the coal company. A typical family in Coalwood lived in a company-owned house, shopped at a company-owned store (the main one was the "Big Store"), paid for some purchases with company money (i.e., scrip), visited the company doctor and dentist for treatment, worshiped at the company church, and at least one member of the family worked for the coal company in the mines, administrative offices, stores, or even the company-owned hotel. In Coalwood, if you worked, you worked for the coal company.

Coalwood is an example of a one-company town. In the first half of the twentieth century, there were many one-company mining and mill towns in rural America. These towns were simply isolated by poor roads and long distances. Workers lived around the coal mine or textile mill, and the mine or mill rented the housing and sold clothing, food, and other supplies.

The coal company in Coalwood—let's call the company Coalwood because "the company and Coalwood were one in the same" (Hickam 1998, p. 6), and the real name of the coal company changed from time to time—was the only game in town, and that can be a problem. A firm in a competitive labor market can employ as many workers as it wants without driving up the market wage, but Coalwood had to pay higher wages to employ more workers. Increasing employment at Coalwood involved drawing the nonworking folks in town into the mines (e.g., high school students drop out of school) or attracting workers from other towns, and that's costly. But Coalwood can turn this situation to its advantage. Reducing employment at Coalwood drives down the wage. As we'll see, lack of competition for workers allows employers like Coalwood to pay workers less than the value of the workers' contribution to production. Lack of competition breeds exploitation.

Monopsony Model

Coalwood is a **labor market monopsony**, the only employer of labor in the area. The monopsony model mirrors the more-familiar monopoly model. A product market monopoly reduces output to drive its price up along the product-demand curve. A labor market monopsony like Coalwood reduces employment to drive the wage it pays its workers down along the labor supply curve. Marginal labor cost in the monopsony model plays the important role of marginal revenue in the monopoly model. Let's see how this works.

As a monopsony, Coalwood faces an upward-sloping labor supply curve: to attract a larger workforce, it must pay a higher wage. As a profit maximizer, Coalwood chooses the size of its workforce by comparing benefits and costs at the margin, a principle that permeates all of economics. Does a marginal increase in labor (e.g., employing one more worker) increase or decrease profit? To answer this question, we need to know how revenue and cost respond to the marginal increase in employment. The marginal value of labor tells us how much revenue increases from the marginal increase in employment. Now we need to determine how the cost of labor varies with small changes in employment.

For Coalwood and any other employer facing an upward-sloping labor supply curve, **marginal labor cost** is greater than the wage. By employing one more worker, Coalwood's cost of labor rises more than the wage it pays to the extra worker. To see why, let's work with fictional values for Coalwood's employment, wage, labor cost, and marginal labor cost. The first two columns of Table 2.3 display four pairs (L, w) on Coalwood's labor supply curve in Figure 2.16. Labor cost C_L in the third column is the product of employment L and the wage w in the first two columns. In the fourth column, we compute marginal labor cost by comparing labor costs across rows. For instance, labor cost grows by $73,333 as employment expands from 900 to 1,000 workers; marginal labor cost over this range is $\Delta C_L / \Delta L = \$73,333 \div 100 = \$733.33$ per worker. Notice that for any level of employment (i.e., any row in the table) marginal labor cost MLC in column 4 is greater than the wage w in column 2. Plotting pairs of employment L and MLC gives the marginal-labor-cost curve, which lies above the labor supply curve in Figure 2.16.

TABLE 2.3.	LABOR SUPPLY, LABOR COST, AND MARGINAL LABOR COST				
EMPLOYMENT L (workers/week)	WAGE w ($/worker)	LABOR COST C_L ($/week)	MARGINAL LABOR COST MLC ($/worker)	MARGINAL LABOR COST MLC^* ($/worker)
900	400	360,000	733	700
1,000	433	433,333	804	767
1,100	467	513,700	___	833
1,200	500	600,000		900

Notes: MLC in column 4 is computed by comparing labor cost C_L across rows. MLC^* in the final column uses the formula $MLC = 100 + 2L/3$.

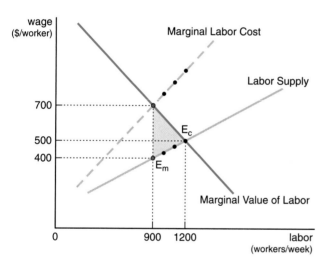

Coalwood faces an upward-sloping labor supply curve, so its marginal-labor-cost curve lies above the labor supply curve.

As a monopsonist, Coalwood chooses labor to equate labor's marginal value to marginal labor cost: 900 workers/week maximizes Coalwood's profit. The monopsony wage is set along the supply curve: the weekly wage is $400/worker, which is $300/worker less than the marginal value of labor. The deadweight loss from underemployment is $45,000 (= (1200 − 900)($700 − $400) ÷ 2) per week.

FIGURE 2.16. Monopsony Labor Market

 PRACTICE   One entry is missing from the fourth column of Table 2.3. Marginal labor cost MLC over the range of employment from 1,100 to 1,200 workers per week is $_____ per worker.

. . . .

ADVANCED   The labor supply curve in Figure 2.16 is linear, and the equation of the line is $w = 100 + L/3$. Let's derive the marginal-labor-cost curve for a linear supply curve with intercept a and slope b.

The cost of labor is $C_L \equiv wL = aL + bL^2$. For those who learned and recall the power rule from a first course in calculus, $MLC = a + 2bL$ is the derivative of C_L with respect to L. The derivation for everyone else uses only algebra.

Let's start with the marginal change in labor $\Delta L = L_1 - L_0$, where L_1 is one unit (i.e., worker) to the right of L and L_0 is one unit to the left of L. Then $\Delta C_L = (aL_1 + bL_1^2) - (aL_0 + bL_0^2)$. As the difference of two squares, $L_1^2 - L_0^2$ factors to $(L_1 + L_0)\Delta L$, so $\Delta C_L = a\Delta L + b(L_0 + L_1)\Delta L = a\Delta L + 2bL\Delta L$. Finally, divide both sides by ΔL to find

$$(2.3) \qquad MLC \equiv \frac{\Delta C_L}{\Delta L} = a + 2bL$$

The marginal-labor-cost curve and the labor supply curve share the same intercept a, but the marginal-labor-cost curve is twice as steep. Thus MLC lies above the labor supply curve for every (positive) level of employment L. Also, marginal labor cost reduces to the wage (a) for a competitive firm ($b = 0$).

In the case of Coalwood, $a = 100$ and $b = 1/3$, so $MLC = 100 + 2L/3$. This formula generates the values for marginal labor cost in the final column of Table 2.3 and in Figure 2.16.

. . . .

To maximize profit, Coalwood chooses the size of its workforce to equate the marginal value of labor to marginal labor cost. Consider the situation in Figure 2.16. If Coalwood employs fewer than 900 workers per week, its marginal value of labor exceeds its marginal labor cost, and expanding employment raises profit. If Coalwood employs more than 900 workers per week, its marginal labor cost exceeds its marginal value of labor, and cutting employment raises profit. Therefore, Coalwood maximizes profit by employing 900 workers per week and paying each worker the lowest wage it can. That wage is $400 per worker because any lower wage doesn't attract 900 workers to Coalwood. Coalwood exploits its monopsony power by reducing the wage below the $500 competitive wage, and it accepts that employment shrinks by 300 workers per week. This monopsony equilibrium is inefficient: the deadweight loss from underemployment is $45,000 ($= (1200 - 900)(\$700 - \$400) \div 2$) per week, the area of the shaded triangle in Figure 2.16.

How does the marginal productivity theory of distribution fare in a monopsony labor market? Not well. The marginal value of labor at Coalwood is $700 per worker, which is $300 greater than the $400 wage Coalwood pays to its workers. Coalwood pays its workers less than the value of their contribution to its production of coal. Call it exploitation.

The monopsony model applies well to the historical experiences in rural mining and mill towns. Medieval manors in Europe provide another fitting historical example. Peasants couldn't own land. The lord of the manor controlled the land. A peasant lived on a manor at the pleasure of its lord and paid the lord to farm parcels of the lord's land. There was no competition within a manor for labor, and mobility across manors was limited. (Indeed, serfs were bound to the lord of the manor.) The absence of competition for labor contributed to poverty among the peasantry. It also explains the evil-villain themes in *Robin Hood* and other books and films about the period.

Key Principle.
Competition among
employers for workers
reduces or even
eliminates exploitation
of workers.

That workers receive less than their marginal value in a monopsony labor market highlights one of the most important principles in all of labor economics: competition among employers pushes the wage up to the marginal value of labor. Remove competition among employers, and workers are paid less than they are worth. The issue of exploitation of workers has been at the center of the intellectual debate between individualism and collectivism since the middle of the nineteenth century and at the center of international conflicts between capitalism and communism during the twentieth century. And it all boils down to whether employers compete for workers.

Most labor markets in the United States are quite competitive. Company towns existed historically, but they never accounted for more than a tiny share of employment. And only a small part of the workforce was employed in labor markets with a small number of employers. Our current society is much more mobile. No one works in Coalwood anymore; the mine closed in the 1980s, and people commute to other towns to work. Some people live in Pennsylvania and commute through New Jersey to work in New York City five days a week. Other people telecommute around the globe. The world is a smaller place, and labor markets are bigger and more competitive.

"More competitive" and "quite competitive" aren't the same as "perfectly competitive." One-company towns aren't empirically important, but the monopsony model of employment applies more widely. Plenty of employers face upward-sloping labor supply curves, which is the key feature facing the monopsony employer. Such a firm attracts more workers with a higher wage and loses some (but not all) workers by paying a lower wage. Facing an upward-sloping—but possibly quite elastic—labor supply curve means that the employer can choose its wage, and the principles of wage setting under monopsony apply.

Low-paying jobs at fast-food restaurants and in retail shops, however, might be the last place to look for the effects of monopsony. A rocket scientist might have few potential employers around the country, but there might be hundreds of local businesses that could hire a teenager to flip burgers, to make change, or to fold sweaters. Nevertheless, some economists argue that applying the monopsony model to teenage employment explains why some studies (e.g., Card and Krueger 1994) find a positive effect of minimum wages on employment. A binding minimum wage eliminates the advantage of reducing employment in a monopsony labor market because the wage can't fall below the minimum wage. Indeed, increasing the minimum wage can increase employment in a monopsony labor market (Robinson 1933, p. 295). (We derive this surprising result in the context of unions in chapter 9.)

Application: Baseball's Reserve System

The market for major league baseball players is a striking application of the principle of competition in the labor market. Baseball clubs didn't compete for players for a very long time, but baseball was injected with a dose of competition for players in the 1970s. What happened is obvious to every baseball fan: salaries in baseball skyrocketed.

For nearly a century (1879–1976), every baseball player's contract included the **reserve clause**: the ball club that employed the player one season reserved the right to employ the player the next season. The reserve clause meant that a player couldn't quit to play for another team. And trading of players—trading one or more players from one team for one or more players from another team—was a consequence of the reserve clause. This common feature of baseball and other sports would be bizarre in other occupations. Imagine a project engineer in Boston learning this morning that Comcast has traded him to Cablevision and instructed him to report to work in Missoula, Montana, tomorrow morning.

By preventing players from quitting to play for other teams, the reserve clause eliminated competition among baseball clubs for player services. Major League Baseball wasn't one employer, but baseball clubs colluded to drive down player salaries by requiring player contracts to include the reserve clause. Without competition among clubs for players, clubs paid players less than they were worth.

The end of the reserve system and the dawn of **free agency** began with the 1977 season. Andy Messersmith and Dave McNally played the 1975 season without signing new contracts. (They were paid on the basis of their 1974 contracts.) Arguing that the reserve clause bound a player for only one year, Messersmith and McNally declared themselves free agents at the end of the 1975 season. Their 1975 teams, the Los Angeles Dodgers and the Montreal Expos, respectively, disputed the players' claim. An arbitrator heard the dispute, sided with the players, and declared Messersmith and McNally free agents. Contracts for the 1976 season included the reserve clause, but 39 players followed the lead of Messersmith and McNally by playing the 1976 season without a contract and declaring themselves free agents for the 1977 season. A collective bargaining agreement in 1976 restored the reserve system for players with less than six years experience in the major leagues, but every baseball season since 1976 has had a crop of more-experienced free agents.

Free agency injected a dose of competition for the services of baseball players. On the basis of the monopsony model, we predict that baseball players' salaries jumped beginning in 1977. (Players also had more bargaining power in 1976 because playing without a contract for the year was a small price to pay to become a free agent at the end of the 1976 season.) The data on baseball salaries since 1969 confirm this prediction. Figure 2.17 plots the average annual salaries and inflation-adjusted (i.e., real) average annual salaries of major league baseball players. The figure also displays the real growth rate of player salaries as a bar graph. In the six years leading up to the demise of the reserve clause in 1976, baseball player salaries grew 4 percent per year above the inflation rate. In 1977, real salaries of baseball players grew 39 percent. In the seven years beginning in 1977, real growth of player salaries averaged 20 percent per year.

In Figure 2.17, salary growth in the years 1987 and 1988 appears to be unusually low for the era of free agency. Since introducing competition explains the explosion of player salaries in the late 1970s and early 1980s, might backtracking on competition explain the stagnation of player salaries in

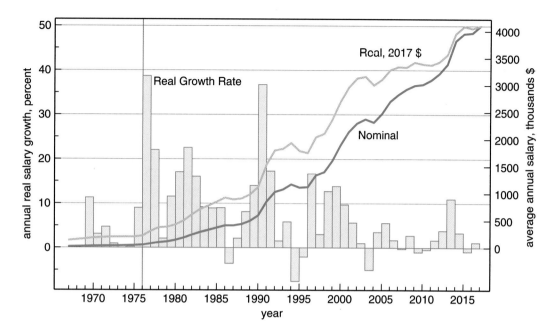

FIGURE 2.17. Average Annual Salaries of Major League Baseball Players, 1967–2017
Source: Major League Baseball Players Association, *Annual Report*, 2017.

the late 1980s? Over the years 1986–1988, baseball clubs conspired to reduce competition for free agents, agreeing not to bid on free agents from other teams and implementing an information bank that helped coordinate offers. The conspiracy was arranged by Peter Ueberroth, the new commissioner of baseball, still basking in the glory of his leadership of the wildly successful 1984 summer Olympics in Los Angeles and his being named *Time*'s "Man of the Year." The players' union accused the ball clubs of colluding in the 1986, 1987, and 1988 seasons. Collusion among ball clubs violated baseball's collective bargaining agreement. (The conspiracy didn't violate U.S. antitrust laws because a 1922 Supreme Court decision granted Major League Baseball an exemption from federal antitrust laws.) Arbitrators ruled in favor of the players and in November 1990 awarded damages of $280 million. The end of collusion injected another dose of competition, and player salaries exploded again in the early 1990s.

These data on the salaries of major league baseball players confirm perhaps the most important principle in labor economics: competition among employers pushes pay up toward the value of workers' contribution to production.

Summary

This chapter introduced the basic machinery of labor economics. We established how employment and the wage are determined. We also identified the importance of competition among employers for the services of workers: competition enhances efficiency and reduces or eliminates exploitation of workers. The key findings are:

☐ The interplay of the demand for labor by firms and the supply of labor from people determine employment and the wage. We read the marginal value of labor off the height of the labor demand curve and the marginal cost of workers' time off the height of the supply curve.

☐ The equilibrium in a competitive labor market is efficient. Employing fewer workers or more workers is wasteful. The competitive equilibrium is also efficient in terms of who employs the workers and who works. The equilibrium delivers the highest value at the lowest cost.

☐ Increasing labor demand increases employment and wages in a competitive labor market. Factors that increase labor demand include a higher price of the product, more physical capital (if more capital increases worker productivity), and innovation that increases worker productivity.

☐ Increasing labor supply increases employment and decreases wages in a competitive labor market. Factors that increase labor supply include lower nonlabor income, less-attractive activities outside work, smaller families, less-generous support from government, and lower wages in other occupations.

☐ A binding minimum wage reduces employment in a competitive labor market. If coverage of the minimum wage isn't complete, then the wage in the uncovered sector falls and the allocation of labor across the covered and uncovered sectors is inefficient.

☐ A tax on labor reduces employment, raises the cost of labor to employers, and lowers the take-home wage. The resulting underemployment of labor is inefficient. Whether the government places the tax on workers or employers is irrelevant.

☐ A wage subsidy increases employment, lowers the cost of labor, and raises workers' pay (including the subsidy). The overemployment of labor is inefficient. Whether the worker or employer receives the subsidy is irrelevant.

☐ Mandating that employers provide an employee benefit depresses the wage. The effects on an employer mandate on employment and efficiency depend on how the workers' value of the benefit compares to the cost of providing the benefit.

☐ Short-run differences in wages across labor markets encourage migration of workers and firms. Wages across labor markets converge to a single long-run equilibrium wage as a result of this dynamic process, and migration is efficient.

☐ A monopsony employer reduces employment to lower the wage. Employment in the monopsony equilibrium is inefficiently low, and workers are paid less than they are worth. A monopsonist, however, responds to a minimum wage by increasing employment.

☐ Free agency injected a dose of competition in the late 1970s, and baseball players' salaries skyrocketed as predicted. Player salaries sagged during a period of owner collusion in the 1980s and shot up again when the conspiracy unraveled.

This chapter demonstrated the importance of the concepts of supply and demand in labor markets. In chapters 3 and 4, we dig deeper to explore how (1) labor supply emerges from workers trading off the value of consumption and the value of time in nonwork activities and (2) labor demand emerges from firms' profit-maximizing production choices.

Key Concepts

- marginal value of labor, p. 33
- marginal cost of workers' time, p. 34
- equilibrium, p. 35
- marginal productivity theory, p. 37
- binding minimum wage, p. 42
- disemployment effect of the minimum wage, p. 42
- deadweight loss, p. 43
- legal incidence of a tax, p. 52
- economic effects of a tax, p. 54
- wage subsidy, p. 55
- employer mandate, p. 57
- migration, p. 60
- locational wage differences, p. 60
- wage convergence, p. 60
- multi-market equilibrium, p. 60
- spillovers to an uncovered sector, p. 61
- labor market monopsony, p. 64
- marginal labor cost, p. 64
- reserve clause and free agency in baseball, p. 68

Short-Answer Questions

2.1 "An influx of immigrants lowers the wage, but it won't last long because the lower wage increases the demand for labor, and increasing the demand for labor raises the wage." The conclusion of this argument might be correct, but the reasoning is faulty. Which one of the clauses is false? Correct the clause, and edit the rest of the argument to reflect the correction.

2.2 Johannes Gutenberg's invention of the printing press in 1440 ushered in the era of mass-produced books. How do you think the printing press affected the marginal value of the monks who copied sacred texts by hand? Your analysis should include the effect of the printing press on the price of books.

2.3 Consider the effect of a tax on labor in the presence of a minimum wage. Assume the minimum wage is the equilibrium wage without the tax. If the government places a $1-per-worker-hour tax on workers, the hourly wage rises by 50 cents. What happens to the hourly wage if the government places the tax on employers? In this case, how do tax-inclusive and after-tax wages depend on "who writes the check"?

2.4 The government mandates that employers provide a benefit to their workers, and the benefit costs $1 per worker per hour. If workers value the benefit at its cost, how does the mandate affect the labor demand curve, the labor supply curve, and the equilibrium? Is mandating the benefit inefficient?

2.5 Hydraulic fracturing (i.e., fracking) increases the demand for labor in North Dakota. What happens to employment and wages in North Dakota in the short run? What happens to labor supply (and wages) in North Dakota in the long run? Some businesses in North Dakota have nothing to do with energy production (e.g., credit-card operations of a major bank). What happens to their demand for labor in the long run?

2.6 Decrease the agricultural demand for labor in Figure 2.15. What happens to the wage and employment in agriculture?

2.7 In our model of minimum wages with an uncovered sector, workers in the covered sector spill over to the uncovered sector. But displaced workers might wait for jobs in the covered sector. These workers would be unemployed. What's the effect of the minimum wage on unemployment? Would the deadweight loss from the minimum wage be bigger or smaller if workers waited rather than spilled over?

2.8 Carefully explain why, in the monopsony context, employing one more worker increases labor costs by more than the wage paid to the extra worker.

2.9 Increasing the demand for labor slides the equilibrium up the labor supply curve in a competitive market. How does an increase in the demand for labor affect the monopsony equilibrium?

Problems

2.1 The figure below displays the market for workers who wash dishes (i.e., dishwashers).

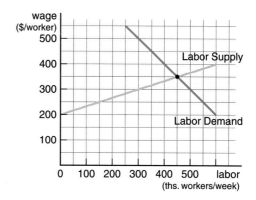

(a) What's the marginal value of dishwashers if 250,000 people wash dishes? [Be sure to specify the units.]

(b) If the weekly wage is $400 per dishwasher, then there's an excess _____ of _____ thousand workers per week?

(c) If the labor market for dishwashers clears, then _____ thousand workers per week work as dishwashers at a weekly wage of $_____ per worker.

(d) What's the marginal value of dishwashers in the market-clearing equilibrium?

2.2 According to the "Assembly Line" entry at Wikipedia.com, Henry Ford's assembly line reduced the labor hours required to produce a single vehicle. That's one way to put it. Another way to put it is that the assembly line increased the productivity of auto workers. More productive workers translate into less labor required to produce each car.

(a) What was the effect of Henry Ford's assembly line on the marginal value of labor in making Ford automobiles?

(b) What does our model of labor demand predict happened to employment of autoworkers at Ford as a result of the assembly line?

2.3 The figure below shows the market for teenage workers in Mississippi. Suppose a minimum wage of $6 per worker-hour applies to the whole labor market.

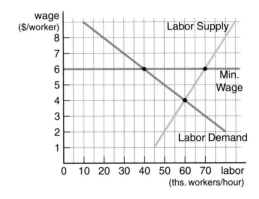

(a)   What are employment and the wage in the market-clearing equilibrium?

(b)   How does the minimum wage affect employment?

(c)   The minimum wage causes an excess _____ of _____ thousand teenage workers per hour.

(d)   Does the $6 minimum wage increase, decrease, or have no effect on the total earnings of teens?

2.4 In Figure 2.9b, the teen employment rate dropped from 31 percent in the 12 months before the minimum-wage increase in July 2007 to about 23 percent for several years after the July 2009 hike. Prime-age high school graduates are our control group. Their employment rate fell from 71.5 percent before the minimum-wage increase in 2007 to about 69 percent after the 2009 hike. But a 1 percentage point change in the employment rate of the control group translates to a 1.5 percentage point change in the employment rate of teens.

(a)   What's the before-and-after estimate of the effect of these minimum-wage hikes on the teen employment rate?

(b)   Use the evidence on the employment rates of the control group to predict how the employment rate of teens would have evolved if not for the minimum-wage hikes. In particular, the teen employment rate would have fallen _____ percentage points without the minimum wage hikes in 2007–2009.

(c) Combine your answers to (a) and (b) to produce a difference-in-difference estimate of the effect of the 2007–2009 minimum-wage hikes on the employment rate.

2.5 The figure below depicts the daily market for labor in the absence of taxes. Suppose the government imposes a daily tax of $30 per worker—that is, $30 for each worker for each day of work.

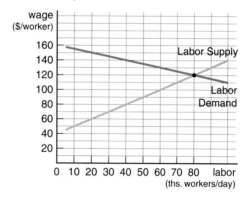

(a) How many people work in the equilibrium with the tax?

(b) In the equilibrium with the tax, what's the employers' tax-inclusive cost of labor per worker?

(c) What's the take-home pay (or after-tax wage) in the equilibrium with the tax?

(d) Illustrate and compute the tax revenue from the $30-per-worker tax.

(e) Illustrate and compute the deadweight loss from the tax.

2.6 The figure below shows a labor market without a wage subsidy. Suppose the government pays a daily $50 wage subsidy to each worker.

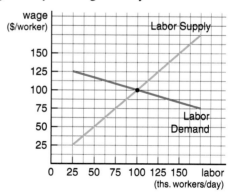

(a) In the figure, shift the appropriate curve(s) to reflect the $50 wage subsidy. Also mark the new equilibrium, and label that point with E$_s$.

(b) How many people work in the equilibrium with the wage subsidy?

(c) How does the wage subsidy influence the equilibrium wage?

(d) How does the wage subsidy influence the a worker's subsidy-inclusive daily wage?

(e) The wage subsidy costs taxpayers _____ per day and reduces total surplus _____ per day.

2.7 The government mandates that employers provide each worker a particular benefit; providing the benefit costs employers $50 per worker per day. Each worker values the benefit at $20 per day. The figure below illustrates the labor market without the mandated benefit.

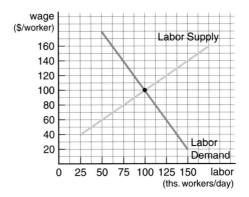

(a) How does the mandated benefit affect the demand for labor? Draw the new demand curve in the figure above.

(b) How does the mandated benefit affect the supply of labor? Draw the new supply curve in the figure above.

(c) Mark the employer-mandate equilibrium with a dot, and label that point with E$_m$. How does the employer mandate affect employment?

(d) In the employer-mandate equilibrium, the daily wage is _____ per worker, and each worker values his or her daily compensation at _____.

(e) Calculate the deadweight loss associated with the employer mandate.

2.8 The figures below illustrate hypothetical short-run labor markets in the United States and Mexico.

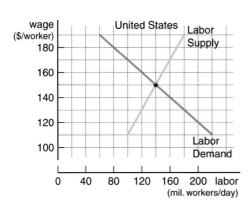 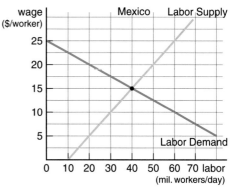

(a) In the short-run equilibrium in the United States, the wage is $_____, and employment is _____.

(b) In Mexico's short-run equilibrium, the wage is $_____, and employment is _____.

(c) As a result of the wage gap across the two countries, workers migrate from _____ to _____.

(d) This migration of workers shifts the labor _____ curve in the United States to the _____.

(e) This migration of workers shifts the labor _____ curve in Mexico to the _____.

(f) Does migration of workers widen or narrow the wage gap across these countries?

2.9 In Mississippi, a $6 minimum wage covers manufacturing jobs, but it doesn't cover agricultural jobs. Suppose that agricultural firms are just like manufacturing firms; in fact, the two sectors have a common demand for labor. The figure below squeezes the three panels of Figure 2.15 into a single figure.

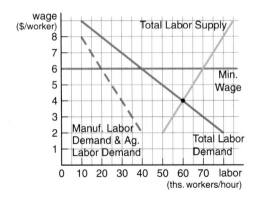

(a) Mark with an A the point that indicates agricultural employment of teens at the market-clearing wage. [This point also indicates manufacturing employment at the market-clearing wage.]

(b) With the $6 minimum wage, manufacturing firms employ how many teens? Mark this point with an M. Calculate and illustrate the disemployment effect of the minimum wage in manufacturing.

(c) If the hourly wage in agriculture remains at $4 per worker, how many teens want to work in agriculture? Mark this point in the figure.

(d) Plot the labor supply curve in agriculture given the $6 minimum wage in manufacturing.

(e) What wage in agriculture clears the market for teen labor in agriculture given the $6 minimum wage in manufacturing?

2.10 The following table summarizes the relationships among employment, wages, labor cost, and the marginal value of labor in a small hospital.

LABOR	WAGE	LABOR COST	MARGINAL LABOR COST	MARGINAL VALUE
0	200	0	____	950
10	225	2,250		850
20	250			750
30	275			650
40	300			550
50	325			450
60	350			350
70	375			250
80	400			150
90	425			50
100	450			−50

The next figure depicts this labor market.

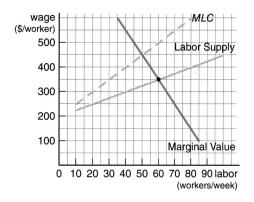

(a) How many workers would the hospital employ if it acted competitively?

(b) What's the marginal value of labor at the competitive employment level?

(c) Fill in the labor cost and marginal labor cost columns in the table. In particular, what's the marginal labor cost associated with increasing the hospital's employment from 40 to 50 workers per week?

(d) In the monopsony equilibrium, the hospital employs how many workers at what wage?

(e) In the monopsony equilibrium, what's the difference between labor's marginal value and the wage?

(f)   Compare the monopsony and competitive labor market equilibria. In the monopsony equilibrium, the hospital employs [fewer, more] workers and pays [lower, higher] wages. And the hospital pays workers [less, more] than they're worth.

(g)   Illustrate and compute the deadweight loss from monopsony employment at the hospital.

References

Card, David and Alan B. Krueger. 1994. "Minimum Wages and Employment: A Case Study of the Fast-Food Industry in New Jersey and Pennsylvania." *American Economic Review* 84(4): 772–793.

Cogan, John. 1982. "The Decline of Black Teenage Employment: 1950–70." *American Economic Review* 72(4): 621–638.

Deere, Donald, Kevin M. Murphy, and Finis Welch. 1995. "Employment and the 1990–1991 Minimum-Wage Hike." *American Economic Review* 85(2): 232–237.

Flyer, Frederick and Sherwin Rosen. 1997. "The New Economics of Teachers and Education." *Journal of Labor Economics* 15(1, part 2): S104–S139.

Neumark, David and William Wascher. 2000. "Minimum Wages and Employment: A Case Study of the Fast-Food Industry in New Jersey and Pennsylvania: Comment." *American Economic Review* 90(5): 1362–1396.

Neumark, David and William L. Wascher. 2008. *Minimum Wages*. Cambridge, MA: MIT Press.

Robinson, Joan. 1933. *The Economics of Imperfect Competition*. London: Macmillan.

Seltzer, Andrew J. 1997. "The Effects of the Fair Labor Standards Act of 1938 on the Southern Seamless Hosiery and Lumber Industries." *Journal of Economic History* 57(2): 396–415.

Labor Supply

3

L
ike bees searching for nectar, yellow taxis swarm about the congested streets of Manhattan searching for riders and delivering those riders to apartment and office buildings, restaurants, theaters, hotels, and airports. The government-dictated fare that riders pay for the service influences taxi drivers' hourly pay, the miles cabbies drive, and the time they spend driving. Regulators hiked New York City taxi fares in 1996 and 2004, and taxi drivers earned more money while working less after the fare hikes. According to evidence presented by Ashenfelter, Doran, and Schaller (2010), these fare hikes raised the revenue per mile of taxi owner/operators by about 20 percent. Taxi drivers responded to the increase in their effective wage by working less: miles driven by taxi drivers fell by about 5 percent (Ashenfelter, Doran, and Schaller 2010, Table 2b). The 5 percent reduction in work amounts to a 20-minute-shorter workday or as much as a two-hour-shorter workweek.

The pattern of hours worked and hourly wages across occupations tells a different story. Across occupations, long workweeks and high hourly wages go together. Doctors, lawyers, engineers, and executives make lots of money and work long hours. They earn even a lot per hour, so the workweek is long in the high *hourly* wage occupations. Hourly wages of clerical workers are much lower, and the workweek in this occupation is much shorter. In fact, comparing real hourly wages and hours worked in engineering and clerical occupations accurately characterizes the relationship between the hourly wage and the workweek in our sample of occupation averages from the Current Population Survey, 1979–2017. (See the data in Table 1.2.) Engineers earn roughly $36 per hour and work

42.7 hours per week. Secretaries, stenographers, and typists earn about $16 per hour and work 36.0 hours per week. The $19 per hour higher wage pairs with a 6.7-hour longer workweek across these two occupations. Across all occupations, an 11-percent-higher hourly wage is associated with an hour-longer workweek.

What about you? Suppose your hourly wage jumped from $10 to $12. How would you respond? If you currently work, would you like to work a shorter or longer workweek? Would you be more or less likely to stop working? If you don't currently work, would the 20 percent increase in hourly pay make working more or less attractive to you?

I've asked undergraduate economics students these questions for years. Answers to the first question ("shorter or longer workweek?") are decidedly mixed. Some students are like NYC taxi drivers; they would use the higher wage to enjoy more free time. Other students fit the pattern across occupations; they would work a longer workweek. The answers to the second and third questions, however, form a consensus: a higher wage doesn't drive anyone away from working, and it entices more people to work.

In this chapter, we explore these issues in labor supply in the context of a model of consumption–leisure choice. Each person's choice of whether to work and how much to work emerges from the interaction of personal opportunities (which depend on the wage rate, nonlabor income, taxes, commuting costs, government welfare programs, etc.) and personal preferences (which depend on personal valuations of consumption goods and leisure time). The model highlights an important tension: to consume more, a person must work more, which leaves less time to enjoy leisure activities.

We also put the model to work. We apply the labor supply model to detect (1) the effects of raising income tax rates, (2) the causes of the shrinking workweek over more than a century, (3) the factors that influence the retirement age, and (4) the consequences of commuting costs and government antipoverty programs. Several of the applications highlight the importance of labor supply for tax policy and government entitlement programs.

3.1 Motivating Evidence

Let's start by exploring how labor force participation, employment, and the workweek have evolved since the dawn of the twentieth century.

Participation and Employment Rates

Early in the twentieth century, 55–56 percent of the working-age population participated in the labor market by working or looking for work. Figure 3.1 shows how the **labor force participation rate** trended up sharply in the post–World War II period. The participation rate grew from 59 percent in the early 1960s to 67 percent at the turn of the century. Since 2000, participation in the labor market has declined to 63 percent.

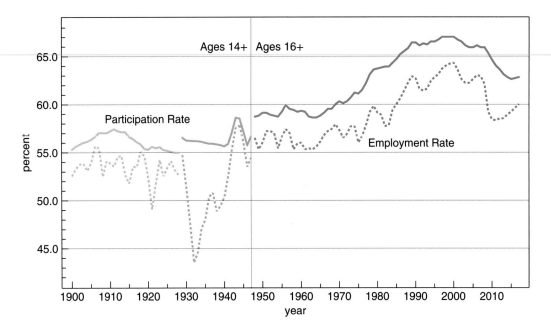

FIGURE 3.1. Participation and Employment Rates, 1900–2017

Sources: 1900–1929: *Historical Statistics of the United States, Colonial Times to 1970*, Series D1–5, p. 126. 1929–1943: BLS Series from Darby, Michael. 1976. "Three-and-a-Half Million U.S. Employees Have Been Mislaid: Or, an Explanation of Unemployment, 1934–1941." *Journal of Political Economy* 84(1): 1–16. 1944–2017: Bureau of Labor Statistics, Current Population Survey, Table A-1.

Not everyone in the labor market works; some people are unemployed. Thus the **employment rate**, which is also known as the *employment–population ratio*, is lower than the participation rate, as Figure 3.1 clearly shows. Trends in the employment rate mimic the trends in the participation rate, but the employment rate fluctuates more than the participation rate. Indeed, in the early years of the Great Depression, the employment rate fell from 55 percent to 44 percent without any change in labor force participation. One-fifth of the workers moved from employment to unemployment. The employment rate recovered to its pre-Depression level during World War II and grew from 55 percent in the early 1960s to 64 percent at the close of the twentieth century. The employment rate slipped to 63 percent before the global recession of 2007–2009 and tumbled to 58.4 percent in 2011. Indeed, the recession drove nearly 5 percent of the working-age population from the ranks of the employed. Through 2017, the employment rate remains 3 percentage points below its pre-recession value.

The sharp trends up in the participation and employment rates in the final four decades of the twentieth century reflect women entering the labor market in large numbers and hide a significant withdrawal of men from the labor market. Figure 3.2 illustrates the explosive growth of female participation in the second half of the twentieth century, from 34 percent in 1950 to 60 percent at the close of the century. (Over the same period, the employment rate of women grew from

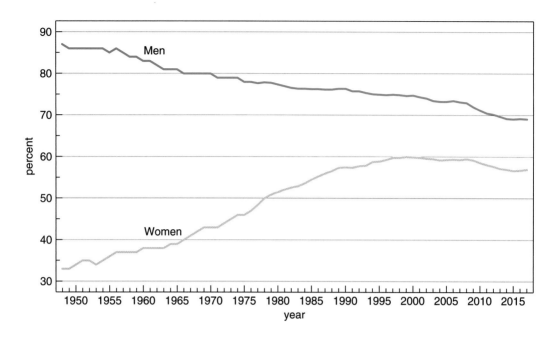

FIGURE 3.2. Participation Rate by Sex, 1948–2017

Source: Bureau of Labor Statistics, Current Population Survey, Table A-1.

32 percent to 57 percent.) Participation of women remained steady at 60 percent before declining slightly after the 2007–2009 recession. For men, however, the participation rate has declined steadily from 86 percent in the middle of the twentieth century to 69 percent in 2017.

Differences in the evolution of participation rates across age groups are also striking. Figure 3.3 presents the patterns. As women entered the labor market in the second half of the twentieth century, the participation rate of prime-aged adults (i.e., ages 25–54) increased from 65 percent in the late 1940s to over 80 percent since the mid-1980s. Older workers (i.e., those ages 65+) began retiring earlier, and the participation rate of workers ages 65+ declined sharply from 27 percent in the late 1940s to 11 percent in 1985. Over the past two decades, however, the participation rate of these older workers has rebounded to 19 percent. For many people, retirement now includes part-time work. Another striking pattern is the vanishing teenage workforce. Teenage participation in the labor market peaked in the late 1970s at 58 percent. Over the next two decades, teenage participation sank to 52 percent and has plummeted to about 35 percent since 2010. The decline in the teenage employment rate is even more striking: nearly half of the teens in the late 1970s were employed; now only 30 percent of teens work.

Weekly Hours of Work

One of the most compelling patterns in labor economics is the decline in the workweek since 1900. Figure 3.4 pieces together data from historical and contemporary sources on the workweek. Data on working hours of production

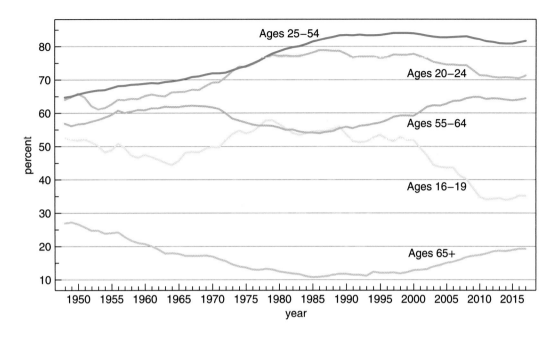

FIGURE 3.3. Participation Rate by Age, 1948–2017

Source: Bureau of Labor Statistics, Current Population Survey, Table A-9.

workers in manufacturing industries document the sharp decline in the workweek from 55 hours at the turn of the century to under 40 hours in the years immediately after World War II. In the Depression years of the 1930s, the weekly hours worked by manufacturing production workers plummeted from 48 hours in 1929 to 34 hours just five years later. The workweek rebounded to 42–44 hours in the war years.

Figure 3.4 documents that hours *paid* of production workers in manufacturing has fluctuated around 40 hours per week since World War II. (The difference between hours *paid* and hours *worked* is paid leave, which includes holidays, vacations, sick time, and personal time.) That is, the dramatic decline in the workweek over the first half of the twentieth century appears to have stalled at the mid-century mark. But the paid workweek of a broader group of workers—production workers in goods-producing industries and nonsupervisory workers in service industries—has fallen from about 40 hours in the late 1940s to under 34 hours in recent years. Only recently has the Bureau of Labor Statistics (BLS) collected hours data from employers for workers in management and other supervisory positions. The paid workweek of all workers in private nonfarm industries has averaged a bit less than 35 hours since the BLS began collecting the data in 2006.

The decline in the workweek from 55 hours to roughly 35 hours probably understates the actual decline. The difference between hours paid and hours worked was negligible in the early 1900s because paid leave was rare. But not anymore. Data on the cost of paying for nonworking time (i.e., holidays, vacations, sick time, and personal time) allow us to estimate nonworking hours per week.

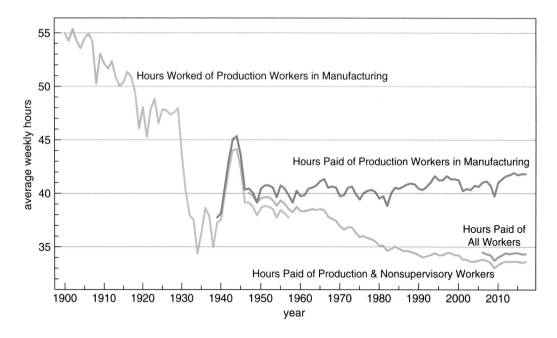

FIGURE 3.4. Average Workweek in Private Nonfarm Businesses, 1900–2017

Notes: Hours paid include paid holidays, vacations, sick time, and personal time. Production and nonsupervisory workers are production workers in goods-producing industries and nonsupervisory workers in service industries.
Sources: 1900–1957: Jones, Ethel. 1963. "New Estimates of Hours of Work Per Week and Hourly Earnings, 1900–1957." *Review of Economics and Statistics* 45(4): 374–385. 1939–2017: Bureau of Labor Statistics, Current Employment Statistics, Table B-2.

(The data come from the BLS's Employer Costs for Employee Compensation calculations, which is part of its National Compensation Survey.) At the end of 2017, private employers' wage and salary costs averaged $23.35 per hour. Of that, 10 percent (i.e., $2.32 per hour) was pay for time not worked. (A similar calculation for 1986, the first year these data were collected, yields 9 percent.) So a reasonable estimate of weekly hours paid but not worked is 10 percent of the paid workweek. By this calculation, the workweek of all workers in the private sector falls from 34.4 paid hours to 31.0 working hours.

Overall, the data point to a sharp decline in the workweek over the first half of the twentieth century and a continued decline over the past 70 years.

3.2   Hours of Work

Human choices, such as what to consume and how much to work, are determined by the interaction of opportunities (i.e., what's available or affordable) and preferences or tastes (i.e., the personal matter of how things are valued). Modeling choice in the context of labor supply proceeds in three steps. First, we derive the budget line, which specifies how opportunities depend on the prices of consumption goods, the wage rate, taxes on earnings, and nonlabor income. Second, we use indifference curves to illustrate how workers value various pairs of consumption and leisure (or nonworking) time. Third, we pull together the budget line from opportunities and indifference curves from preferences to determine the rational choice of how much to consume, how much leisure time to enjoy, and how much work to do. In addition, we explore how such a choice varies with the wage rate. That is, we derive the labor supply curve, how desired hours of work vary with the wage.

Opportunities

The budget line defines opportunities, what's affordable to a consumer. Let's explore Beth's opportunities to consume before we turn to our concern, which is labor supply. In the simplest case of two consumption goods, pizza and beer, the budget line collects all the pairs of pizza and beer that exhaust Beth's budget for Saturday night. Beth's budget for her night out is $30: she will spend no more than $30 on slices of pizza s and bottles of beer b. The prices of pizza and beer are $2 per slice and $3 per bottle, so her expenditures on pizza and beer are $2/slice × s slices/night and $3/bottle × b bottles/night.

If Beth's combined nightly expenditures on pizza and beer exhaust her nightly budget, then her consumption of pizza and beer satisfies $2/slice × s slices/night + $3/bottle × b bottles/night = $30/night, which is her **budget line**. By treating units (i.e., dollars, slices, bottles, and nights) as algebraic variables, we simplify the budget line to

(3.1) $$2s + 3b = 30$$

Figure 3.5a displays this line.

Beth's **budget set** collects all the pairs of pizza and beer on her budget line and all the pairs inside the budget line. (Pairs inside the budget line leave money in her wallet at the end of the night.) The slope of Beth's budget line is –2/3, which means she gives up two-thirds of a beer to enjoy a slice of pizza. Thus the real price of pizza is two-thirds of a beer.

In the context of labor supply, Gregg's opportunities are determined by a budget line that depends on the price of consumption goods, his wage rate, and any income he gets from outside the labor market such as from allowances, inheritances, and financial investments. To get things started, assume that the price of consumption goods p is $1 per unit, Gregg's wage w is $10 per hour, and Gregg has no **nonlabor income** y—no allowance, no lottery jackpot, and no interest on a savings account. And let h denote his daily hours of work. Gregg's expenditures on consumption can't exceed his daily income, which is his labor income or earnings wh. His budget line is $1/unit × c units/day = $10/hour × h hours/day. By eliminating the units, the budget line simplifies to $c = 10h$.

We can also express the budget line in terms of consumption c and leisure l. Gregg sleeps 8 hours per day, and he splits the other 16 hours in his day between

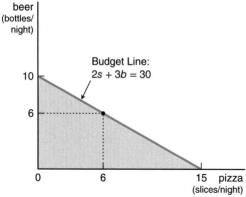

(a) *Beth's Budget Line with Pizza and Beer.* Beth's budget set contains all the pairs of slices of pizza *s* and bottles of beer *b* that she can afford. Points on the budget line exhaust her budget, so they are just affordable.

Since the prices are $2/slice and $3/bottle and Beth's budget is $30/night, her budget line is $2s + 3b = 30$. The slope of her budget line is −2/3, which means the real price of a slice of pizza is 2/3 of a bottle of beer.

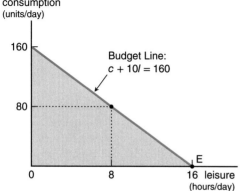

(b) *Gregg's Budget Line with Leisure and Consumption.* Gregg's budget set contains pairs of leisure *l* and consumption *c* that he can afford given the price of consumption *p*, his wage rate *w*, and the 16 nonsleeping hours in every day.

With $p = 1$ and $w = 10$, Gregg's budget line is $c + 10l = 160$. The horizontal intercept (16,0) is Gregg's endowment point E, the leisure and consumption that he enjoys if he doesn't work. The slope of the budget line (in absolute value) is the real wage, which is 10 units of consumption/hour: Gregg can raise his daily consumption 10 units by reducing his daily leisure by one hour. Ten units/hour is also the real price of leisure time.

FIGURE 3.5. Opportunities and Budget Lines

working time *h* and leisure time *l*; that is, $h + l = 16$. Replace *h* in the budget line with $16 − l$ to yield

(3.2)
$$c + 10l = 160$$

which Figure 3.5b displays as Gregg's budget line. The horizontal intercept is his **endowment**—what Gregg can enjoy without working (i.e., 16 hours of leisure without any consumption). If he does work, turning an hour of leisure time into an hour of work time increases Gregg's earnings by his $10 hourly wage and his consumption by 10 units. So his **real wage** is $w/p = 10/1 = 10$ units of consumption per hour. Indeed, the slope of Gregg's budget line (in absolute value) tells us his real wage.

If Gregg's labor income *wh* is taxed at a flat rate *t*, then his take-home pay is (1 − *t*)*wh*. Solve for Gregg's budget line if his wage is $10 per hour and the tax rate is 20 percent. In Figure 3.5b, show how the tax rate influences Gregg's endowment point, budget line, and budget set.

. . . .

ADVANCED Let's think about Gregg's opportunities more generally. Gregg's endowed with T units of time. This time endowment might be hours per day (i.e., $T = 16$), hours per week (i.e., $T = 112$), or weeks per year (i.e., $T = 52$). Gregg also has nonlabor income y; this is equivalent to being endowed with y/p units of consumption if the price of consumption is p. So the pair $(y/p, T)$ is Gregg's endowment point E in Figure 3.6. E represents Gregg's leisure and consumption if he doesn't work. If he does work, working for one hour increases Gregg's earnings by his wage w and his consumption by w/p units; that is, the slope of Gregg's budget line (in absolute value) is his real wage w/p, which we measure in units of consumption per unit of time.

Gregg's budget line is $pc + wl = y + wT$ for all $l \leq T$, and his budget set contains all the points on and inside the budget line. Since Gregg can't enjoy more than T units of leisure time, we remove the section of the budget line that falls to the right of his endowment point. The term $y + wT$ is Gregg's **full income**, the sum of his nonlabor income y and the value of his time endowment wT.

. . . .

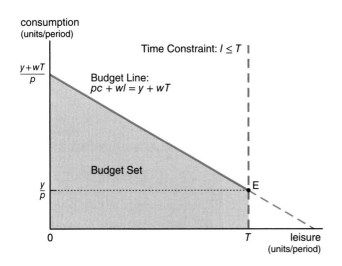

Gregg's budget set contains pairs of leisure and consumption that he can afford and that satisfy the time constraint. One such pair is Gregg's endowment point E, which indicates his consumption if he doesn't work at all. Points on the budget line and northwest of E exhaust Gregg's income and satisfy the time constraint.

The slope of the budget line (in absolute value) is the real wage *w/p*. Gregg must forego *w/p* units of consumption to increase leisure by one hour, so the real wage is the real price of leisure.

FIGURE 3.6. Budget Line and Time Constraint with Consumption and Leisure

Preferences

How does Gregg choose among all the pairs of leisure and consumption that are available to him? To answer this question, we need to investigate Gregg's preferences or tastes, how he values or ranks the various pairs of leisure time and consumption. We use indifference curves to illustrate Gregg's preferences.

Indifference curves on a graph of preferences are analogous to isotherms on a map of surface temperature, isobars on a map of surface pressure, and contour lines on an elevation map. Figure 3.7 depicts isotherms (i.e., curves of equal temperature) across North America on July 4, 2015. Each of the three isotherms for 75° collects locations with a 75° temperature at noon Eastern Daylight Time. Since a single location can't have two or more temperatures at one time, only one isotherm can run through a location; that is, isotherms can't cross. Although we don't clutter the map with scores of isotherms, an isotherm runs through each location. Figure 3.7 shows six isotherms for temperatures from 60° to 85°. Another important feature is that isotherms that are close together, such as in Arizona, reveal that temperature changes rapidly over a short distance.

As isotherms collect locations with equally ranked temperatures, **indifference curves** collect pairs of goods, pizza and beer in the case of Beth, that are equally ranked in preferences. The indifference curves in Figure 3.8a illustrate Beth's preferences over pizza *s* and beer *b*. As with isotherms, Beth has an indifference curve through every pair of pizza and beer (although we depict only a few), and her indifference curves don't cross. But Beth's indifference curves exhibit other features that don't apply to isotherms: her indifference curves slope down and bow toward the origin. Let's explore these properties in the context of Gregg's preferences over his leisure time and consumption.

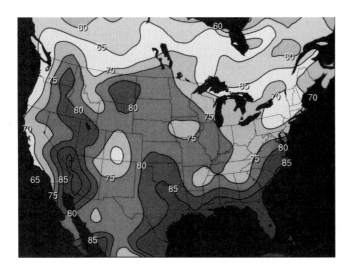

Each curve is an isotherm—a collection of locations with a particular temperature (e.g., 75°), at noon (EDT) on July 4, 2015.

Isotherms don't cross; if they did, a single location would have two temperatures.

Although we could draw an isotherm through any location (e.g., isotherm 72.227° might run through Ann Arbor), the map is easier to read if we limit the number of isotherms.

Isotherms that are close together, such as in Arizona, indicate that temperatures there change sharply over a short distance.

Source: Atmospheric Sciences, University of Illinois at Urbana-Champaign.

FIGURE 3.7. Isotherms on a Surface Map of Temperature

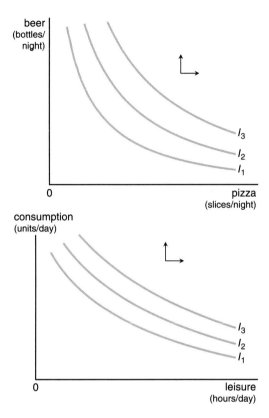

(a) *Beth's Preferences Over Pizza and Beer*. Beth likes pizza and beer, so her preference direction (marked by the two arrows) points to the northeast.

Beth's indifference curves illustrate her preferences. An indifference curve (e.g., l_1) collects pairs of pizza and beer that Beth finds equally satisfying.

Beth's indifference curves slope down, cut through every point, don't cross, and bow toward the origin. Beth prefers pairs of pizza and beer on a higher indifference curve (e.g., l_2) to pairs on any lower indifference curve (e.g., l_1).

(b) *Gregg's Preferences Over Leisure and Consumption*. Gregg likes leisure time and consumption goods; two arrows point northeast to mark his preference direction.

Indifference curves (l_1, l_2, l_3) illustrate Gregg's preferences. Each indifference curve collects pairs of leisure and consumption that Gregg finds equally satisfying.

Gregg's indifference curves slope down, cut through every point, don't cross, and bow toward the origin. Gregg prefers pairs of leisure and consumption on a higher indifference curve (e.g., l_2) to pairs on a lower indifference curve (e.g., l_1).

FIGURE 3.8. Preferences and Indifference Curves

The indifference curves in Figure 3.8b illustrate Gregg's preferences over his consumption c and leisure time l. Gregg's indifference curves exhibit four important properties.

First, *indifference curves slope down*. Figure 3.9a depicts a proof of this property. Since Gregg prefers more leisure time to less leisure time and more consumption to less consumption, the direction of his preferences is to the northeast. (The arrows in the figure indicate his **preference direction**.) Point A is some pair of leisure l and consumption c. The preference direction tells us that Gregg prefers any pair (l, c) in the shaded blue set northeast of point A to point A itself. He also prefers point A to any point in the shaded gray set southwest of point A. He isn't indifferent between any point in the blue set and A or between any point in the gray set and A. Thus the indifference curve through A runs from the area northwest of A through A and into the area southeast of A. That is, the indifference curve through A slopes down. There's nothing special about point A. For instance, we can use "crosshairs" through point B or any other point on Gregg's graph of leisure and consumption to repeat the same argument. Since the indifference curve through any point slopes down, indifference curves slope down.

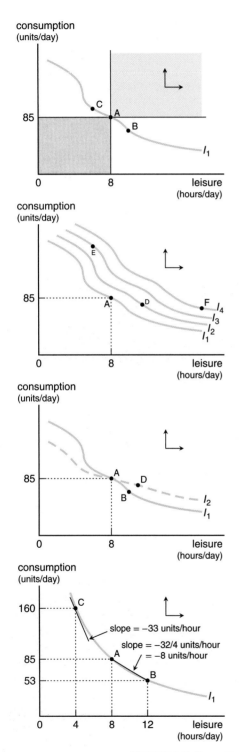

(a) *Indifference Curves Slope Down.* Gregg prefers more leisure and consumption to less, so he prefers any point northeast of point A to the pair of leisure and consumption at A.

Gregg's indifference curve through any point A must slope down because he can't be indifferent between A and any point northeast or southwest of A.

There's nothing special about A. Repeat this argument for any point on the graph to conclude that every indifference curve slopes down everywhere.

(b) *An Indifference Curve Cuts Through Every Point.* This graph displays four of Gregg's downward-sloping indifference curves, but Gregg has an indifference curve through every pair of leisure and consumption.

Higher indifference curves contain "better" combinations of leisure and consumption. For instance, Gregg prefers the pair of leisure and consumption at point F to the pair at point E, pair E to pair D, and pair D to pair A.

(c) *Indifference Curves Don't Cross.* Suppose two indifference curves cross at point A. Along I_1, Gregg's indifferent between A and B. Along I_2, Gregg's indifferent between A and D. Since Gregg certainly prefers D to B, he both prefers D to A (along I_1) and is indifferent between A and D (along I_2). Both can't be true.

Crossing indifference curves would, therefore, imply a contradiction, so indifference curves don't cross.

(d) *Indifference Curves Bow Toward the Origin.* Gregg's willingness to pay for leisure in terms of consumption is measured by his marginal rate of substitution *MRS*.

Between points A and B, Gregg's rate of substitution is 8 units per hour. For a marginal change in leisure around C, Gregg's marginal rate of substitution is 33 units per hour since the slope of the line that is tangent to I_1 at C is −33.

Gregg's marginal rate of substitution of leisure for consumption *MRS* falls as leisure rises and consumption falls along an indifference curve.

FIGURE 3.9. Properties of Indifference Curves

Second, *an indifference curve cuts through every pair of consumption and leisure*, although we display only a few of Gregg's indifference curves on any graph. Figure 3.9b displays four pairs of leisure and consumption, as well as the four indifference curves ($I_1, \ldots, I_4$) that cut through these points. (For practice, pick another point on the graph, and draw an indifference curve through it.) Points on higher indifference curves are preferred to those on lower indifference curves, so Gregg prefers F to E, E to D, and D to A. Of course, Gregg also prefers F to A.

Third, *indifference curves don't cross*. To see why, let's assume that two of Gregg's indifference curves do cross at some point and show that crossing implies a contradiction. Here goes. Two of Gregg's indifference curves intersect at point A in Figure 3.9c. Since points A and B are along indifference curve I_1, he's indifferent between A and B. Since Gregg's preference direction is toward the northeast, he prefers D to B. By comparing A with B and B with D, we conclude that Gregg prefers D to A. But indifference curve I_2 tells us that Gregg's indifferent between A and D. That Gregg prefers D to A contradicts that he's indifferent between D and A. Contradictions don't exist, so our original assumption that Gregg's indifference curves cross at some point A can't be true. Indifference curves don't cross.

Fourth, *indifference curves bow toward the origin*. Between points A and B in Figure 3.9d, Gregg's willing to give up no more than 32 ($= 85 - 53$) units of consumption to get 4 ($= 12 - 8$) extra hours of leisure. Giving up more than 32 units of consumption pushes him to a lower indifference curve; giving up less than 32 units puts him on a higher indifference curve. So over the range from A to B, the rate at which Gregg's willing to substitute leisure for consumption is 8 ($= 32 \div 4$) units per hour, which is (in absolute value) the slope of the line segment between points A and B. This means Gregg values his leisure time at 8 units of consumption per hour over this range.

We can also measure Gregg's value of leisure time for marginal changes. The slope of the line that is tangent to indifference curve I_1 at point C is –33 units of consumption per hour of leisure. So Gregg's willing to substitute out of consumption and into leisure time at the rate of 33 units of consumption per hour of leisure *for small changes in the neighborhood of* C. His **marginal rate of substitution** of leisure time for consumption is $MRS = 33$ at C. In somewhat simpler language, we say that Gregg's marginal value of leisure time is 33 units of consumption per hour at C.

Gregg's indifference curves bow toward the origin because his marginal value of leisure time falls as his pair of leisure and consumption moves down an indifference curve. If Gregg's preferences exhibit diminishing marginal rate of substitution, each of his indifference curves gets flatter as we move down along the curve. And this makes sense. If Gregg has lots of income but not much time outside of work (e.g., at point C in Figure 3.9d), he's willing to pay a lot (in terms of consumption) to get more leisure time; his marginal value of leisure time is high. Alternatively, if Gregg has plenty of leisure time but little income, he's not willing to give up much consumption to get a little more leisure; his marginal value of leisure time is low.

☑ PRACTICE   Choose some point in Figure 3.8b, and mark that point A. Draw an indifference curve through A that is consistent with Gregg's other indifference curves in the figure.

Preferences can differ across people, and having a higher value of time at home steepens the whole set of indifference curves. You have your own preferences, and your indifference curves might be steeper (or flatter) than Gregg's indifference curves. If you value your time at home more than Gregg does, then your willingness to pay for leisure time (in terms of consumption) is higher than Gregg's. At every point in Figure 3.8b, your indifference curve is steeper than Gregg's indifference curve. So having a higher value of time at home steepens the whole set of indifference curves. The flip side of this is that being more passionate than Gregg about consumption goods flattens your indifference curves relative to his.

Consumption–Leisure Choice

What does Gregg do? Of all the pairs of consumption and leisure that are available to him, which pair does he prefer over all others? He prefers the pair at the tangency of his budget line to one of his indifference curves, and that's his choice. Gregg takes 6 hours of leisure and works 10 hours each day, which is his point of tangency X in Figure 3.10. (The graph includes a second horizontal axis to track working hours h.) Since his wage w is \$10 per hour and the price of consumption p is \$1 per unit, his daily earnings of \$100 ($= \$10 \times 10$) fund his daily consumption of 100 units. And we have found one point on Gregg's labor supply curve: he wants to work 10 hours per day if his hourly wage is \$10 per hour.

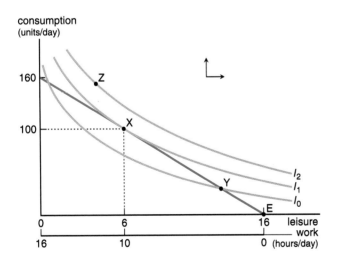

With $p = 1$, $w = 10$, and $y = 0$, Gregg's budget line is $c + 10l = 160$.

Of all the pairs of leisure and consumption in his budget set, which pair does Gregg choose? Or which pair (l, c) is on Gregg's highest indifference curve? The answer is X, a point of tangency between the budget line and an indifference curve.

At tangency point X, Gregg works 10 hours/day and enjoys 6 hours of leisure and 100 units of consumption/day.

FIGURE 3.10. Choosing How Much to Work

Why X? Gregg prefers points like Z, which is on a higher indifference curve, but he can't afford them. So we limit our attention to points on his budget line. Points like Y exhaust his income, but he can do better. That Gregg's indifference curve through point Y is flatter than his budget line indicates that he values his time less than the market does at point Y. So he can climb to a higher indifference curve by moving toward X, reducing leisure time and raising consumption along the budget line. Similarly, Gregg can do better by choosing X rather than any point between X and the budget line's vertical intercept. The indifference curve through any point between X and 160 on the vertical axis is steeper than the budget line, which means that Gregg values his time more than the market pays for his time. Again, he can climb to a higher indifference curve by pushing his choice toward X, increasing leisure time, working fewer hours, and cutting consumption along the budget line.

At Gregg's choice X, the slope of his indifference curve (i.e., his marginal rate of substitution) equals the slope of his budget line (i.e., his real wage). Consequently, Gregg chooses the length of his workday by equating the marginal value of his leisure time to his real wage w/p. At X, he values his time at the margin exactly the same as the market values his time.

 PRACTICE   Gregg chooses his leisure and consumption at X in Figure 3.10. His marginal value of leisure time at X is _____ units of _____ per _____.

The empirical content of our consumption–leisure choice model of labor supply derives from Gregg's response to changes in measurable factors that influence his choice. In particular, how does Gregg's quantity supplied of labor h vary with his nonlabor income y, his wage w, and other factors, such as the tax rate t? These factors don't influence Gregg's preferences, so we trace how each factor influences Gregg's quantity supplied of labor through its effect on his budget line.

Changing Nonlabor Income

An increase in nonlabor income expands opportunities, shifting out the budget line without changing its slope. Suppose Gregg receives a generous allowance of $40 per day. His nonlabor income increases from $0 to $40 per day, and his endowment point shifts up by 40 units of consumption per day. The slope of the budget line $-w/p$ doesn't depend on nonlabor income y, so his budget line with the allowance is parallel to his old budget line in Figure 3.11.

 PRACTICE   An increase in nonlabor income shifts the endowment point [up, down, not at all] and [steepens, flattens, doesn't change the slope of] the budget line.

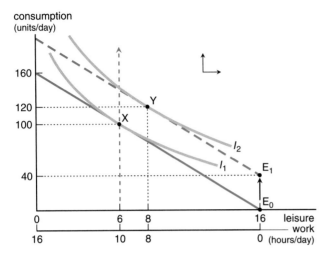

consumption
(units/day)

Gregg's nonlabor income y jumps from $0 to $40/day. His endowment shifts up 40 units from E_0 to E_1. Nonlabor income doesn't affect the slope of his budget line, which is −10, so Gregg's new budget line is parallel to his old budget line.

Since indifference curves get steeper moving up along any vertical ray, the tangency along the new budget line at Y lies northeast of the old tangency at X. Gregg spends $20 more each day, and he shortens his workday from 10 to 8 hours to enjoy more leisure.

FIGURE 3.11. Changing Nonlabor Income

Gregg responds to the increase in his nonlabor income by increasing his consumption c and leisure time l and decreasing his workday h. Figure 3.11 displays these **income effects**. The tangency at Y along Gregg's new budget line is northeast of X, the tangency along his old budget line. In particular, Gregg responds to his $40 increase in nonlabor income by lifting his daily consumption from $100 to $120, lengthening his time at home from 6 to 8 hours per day, and shortening his workday from 10 to 8 hours. Indeed, Gregg "spends" some of his extra income on leisure time, so higher nonlabor income reduces his quantity supplied of labor.

Leisure and consumption are **normal goods**—people enjoy more leisure and more consumption when their nonlabor incomes are higher. Figure 3.11 depicts this case. As a logical possibility, however, the choice of leisure time could fall as nonlabor income rises. But there's no reason to be distracted by this unusual case. We focus on the empirically relevant case with leisure as a normal good. The property of preferences that delivers leisure as a normal good is that indifference curves get steeper as we run up a vertical ray, such as the vertical ray through X in the figure.

The income effect can be so powerful that a man as passionate about work as Bill Gates transitioned from full-time to part-time work at Microsoft beginning in 2006 at age 50. Do you think the nonlabor income that flowed from his enormous wealth, a net worth of over $50 billion at the time, might have had something to do with his choice? Would he have transitioned to part-time work if his net worth had been $50,000? Similarly, people receiving and expecting to receive large inheritances work fewer hours, as do those who win big lottery games.

Leisure as a normal good also helps explain why people work shorter workdays and workweeks now than their ancestors did at the dawn of the twentieth century. People are richer now; they demand more leisure time. Much has changed since 1900 (e.g., wages have risen dramatically), so interpreting the shortening of the workday and workweek as purely an income effect would be a mistake. But the importance of the income effect can't be denied. If leisure weren't a normal good, we would all work *longer* days and *more* days each week than our ancestors did over a century ago. To see why, let's explore how the quantity demanded of leisure (i.e., home time) and the quantity supplied of labor (i.e., work time) vary with the wage.

Changing the Wage Rate

An increase in the wage expands opportunities by steepening the budget line without changing the endowment. If Gregg's hourly wage increases from $10 to $14, the slope of his budget line increases (in absolute value) from 10 to 14 units of consumption per hour. Gregg's endowment E doesn't depend on his wage, so his budget line pivots through E as Figure 3.12 illustrates. Working becomes more lucrative, leisure becomes more expensive, and his budget set expands. He can afford things that he couldn't afford with the lower wage.

Gregg responds to his raise by lengthening his workday. Figure 3.12a shows that case. His optimal pair of consumption and leisure moves to Z, a point northwest of X. Gregg takes advantage of his higher wage by extending his workday from 10 to 11 hours, and his time at home shrinks to 5 hours per day.

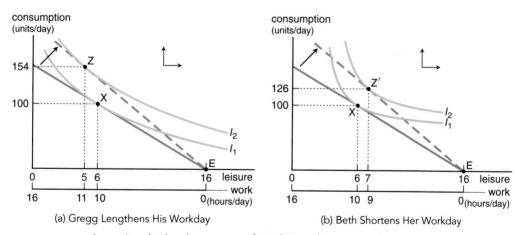

(a) Gregg Lengthens His Workday   (b) Beth Shortens Her Workday

Increasing the hourly wage rate from $10 to $14 rotates the budget line through the endowment point E in each panel.

(a) Gregg responds to his raise by lowering his leisure time and raising his work hours and consumption. That is, point Z lies northwest of point X. Gregg's workday lengthens to 11 hours, and his consumption grows from 100 to 154 units/day.

(b) Beth's preferences differ from Gregg's. She responds to the same raise by lowering her work hours and raising her leisure time and consumption. That is, for Beth, point Z' lies northeast of point X. Beth's workday shortens to 9 hours, and her consumption grows from 100 to 126 units/day.

FIGURE 3.12. Changing the Wage Rate

Gregg's daily pay grows from $100 to $154. (His daily consumption also jumps by 54 units.) If Gregg had retained his 10-hour workday, his pay would have grown by $40 (= 10 hours/day × $4/hour raise); adding an hour to his workday adds another $14 to his daily earnings.

Unlike Gregg, Beth responds to her raise from $10 to $14 per hour by shortening her workday to enjoy more time at home. Figure 3.12b shows that Beth chooses the same pair of leisure and consumption (point X) as Gregg when each person earns $10 per hour. In response to the $4 hourly raise, however, Beth's optimal choice moves to point Z′, which lies northeast of X. Beth takes advantage of the higher wage by shortening her workday from 10 to 9 hours to spend more time at home. If she didn't reduce her working time by an hour, Beth could increase her daily consumption by 40 units (= 10 hours × 4 units/hour). By taking more time at home, Beth raises her consumption by only 26 units.

How would *you* respond to an increase in your wage? Would you like to work longer hours like Gregg or shorter hours like Beth? Who's right? More precisely, who's rational? Gregg or Beth? They are both right and rational! Whether a person's hours of work respond positively or negatively to an increase in the wage is purely a matter of personal preference. The higher wage tilts the *terms of trade* in favor of consumption and against leisure, and Gregg takes advantage of work being more lucrative by lengthening his workday, substituting consumption for leisure time. The higher wage also expands the budget set, which means Gregg and Beth are richer. Beth spends some of her newfound riches on consumption and a lot on leisure time. Beth's choice of leisure time is very sensitive to her income, so she responds to the wage increase by choosing more time at home as an income effect.

To quantify these principles, we run a hypothetical experiment (Hicks 1946 [1939], pp. 36–37). First, while increasing Gregg's hourly wage from $10 to $14, we cut his nonlabor income by Δy, just enough to leave him no better off or worse off. Doing so isolates the effect of the wage increase changing the terms of trade between leisure and consumption. Then in a second step, we restore Gregg's nonlabor income by returning Δy to him. The end result is just the increase in his wage. But the intermediate step allows us to see how Gregg responds to a wage increase that leaves him no better off (i.e., the substitution effect) and how he responds to the restoration of his nonlabor income, which is an income effect. The payoff to the hypothetical is that we get a clear picture of each part and thus a better view of the total impact of the wage change.

In Figure 3.13, we decompose Gregg's wage increase into **substitution and income effects**. To isolate the substitution effect, we introduce a hypothetical budget line that is parallel to his new budget line (i.e., slope $= -14$) and is tangent to his original indifference curve I_1. The hypothetical budget line is tangent to the original indifference curve I_1 at Y, which lies northwest of X. So Gregg's response to a wage increase coupled with a reduction in his nonlabor income that leaves him on his original indifference curve is to substitute consumption for leisure, and he spends more time at work. This substitution effect raises Gregg's quantity supplied of labor. When we restore Gregg's nonlabor income by returning Δy, Gregg's choice jumps from Y to Z, increasing his leisure and consumption. The

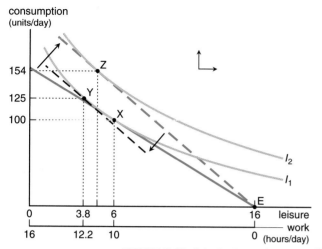

Increasing the hourly wage from $10 to $14 pivots the budget line through the endowment point E.

To decompose Gregg's total response (from X to Z) into substitution and income effects, we introduce a hypothetical budget line that has the slope of the new budget line but is tangent to the original indifference curve I_1. That's the dashed black line.

For Gregg, the substitution effect (X to Y) dominates the income effect (Y to Z), so Gregg's workday lengthens from 10 to 11 hours.

FIGURE 3.13. Substitution and Income Effects

shift from Y to Z involves a parallel shift in the budget line, so it's an income effect, and leisure and consumption both increase since they are normal goods. This income effect of Gregg's raise shortens his workday, lowering his quantity supplied of labor.

> ☑ **PRACTICE**   In Figure 3.13, the substitution effect of the increase in Gregg's hourly wage from $10 to $14 per hour increases his workday from _____ hours to _____ hours and his daily consumption from _____ units to approximately _____ units.

Key Principle.
A higher wage could lengthen or shorten the workweek because it also increases the value of leisure time.

Whether a worker's workday responds positively or negatively to a wage increase boils down to whether the substitution effect is bigger or smaller than the income effect for that worker. It's purely a matter of personal preference, which means it depends entirely on the shapes of the worker's indifference curves. If your indifference curves have little curvature (i.e., are close to linear), then your substitution effect of a wage increase is big, which pushes you toward a longer workday. If my indifference curves bend sharply, then my substitution effect of a raise is small, and I'm likely to shorten my workday. The strength of the income effect—working in the opposite direction—also reflects personal preference. If leisure time is a luxury, as it is for Beth, then the income effect is big, and a higher wage pushes toward a shorter workday. If leisure isn't very sensitive to income, a higher wage likely lengthens the workday.

Labor Supply Curve

Our graph of consumption–leisure choice contains all the information to construct a worker's labor supply curve. For instance, Figure 3.14 depicts Beth's choice for

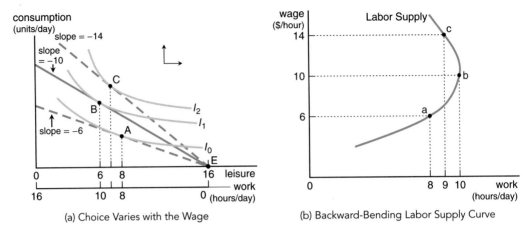

(a) Choice Varies with the Wage

(b) Backward-Bending Labor Supply Curve

(a) Increasing the hourly wage from $6 to $10 to $14 pivots the budget line through the endowment point E. As the wage rises from $6 to $10, Beth's choice moves from A to B, and her workday lengthens from 8 to 10 hours. As the wage climbs from $10 to $14, Beth's choice shifts from B to C, and her workday shrinks to 9 hours.

(b) We derive Beth's labor supply curve by plotting the three pairs of wage rates w and hours of work h from panel (a) and connecting the dots. Over a low range of wages, wage increases lengthen Beth's workday, and her labor supply curve slopes up. Over a higher range of wages, her work hours fall as the wage rises, and her labor supply curve bends backward.

The substitution effect dominates the income effect over the low range of wages; the income effect dominates the substitution effect over the high range of wages.

FIGURE 3.14. Deriving the Labor Supply Curve

each of three wages. For each tangency point (l^*, c^*), we collect the wage w that generates that choice and the implied workday $h^* = 16 - l^*$. The pair (h^*, w) is a point on Beth's labor supply curve. In Figure 3.14a, three wages—$6, $10, and $14 per hour—generate Beth's quantities supplied of labor—8, 10, and 9 hours per day, respectively. Figure 3.14b plots the three points (h^*, w) on Beth's labor supply curve: $(8, 6)$, $(10, 10)$, and $(9, 14)$.

Although a worker's labor supply curve can slope up everywhere, labor supply curves can bend backward. Beth's labor supply curve is an example of a **backward-bending labor supply curve**. Since the substitution effect of a pay raise increases hours worked (i.e., the quantity supplied of labor), the source of the bend backward in the labor supply curve must be the income effect of the raise. Indeed, the labor supply curve bends backward over the range of wages in which the income effect dominates the substitution effect.

Does the backward-bending labor supply curve strike you as bizarre? Beth's demand curve for consumption doesn't bend backward or slope up. (Nor do her demand curves for pizza, beer, music CDs, and so on.) Why does labor supply differ in such a spectacular way? Beth *buys* consumption goods, but she *sells* her time. And that makes all the difference. A higher price of pizza leaves Beth poorer, which leads her to eat less pizza, a normal good. But a higher wage enriches Beth, which leads her to take more leisure time, a normal good. And more leisure time means a shorter workday.

Why would a labor supply curve slope up for low values of the wage but bend backward for high wages? The income effect of a wage change Δw depends on the size of the parallel shift from the hypothetical budget line (tangent to the original indifference curve) to the new budget line. That shift is approximately $\Delta w \times h^*$, so it depends on Beth's workday h^*. If Beth works only two hours per day, then the pay raise Δw doesn't leave her much richer. If, however, Beth works a 12-hour workday, then the same raise Δw delivers six times the bang to her wallet. Thus the income effect is likely to dominate the substitution effect (and bend the labor supply curve backward) if Beth is working long hours.

 PRACTICE   How does increasing nonlabor income y affect Beth's backward-bending labor supply curve in Figure 3.14b?

3.3 Applications

We have three applications of our consumption–leisure model of labor supply. First, we establish the effects of a tax on earnings. Second, we show how a backward-bending labor supply might explain why the workweek has shrunk dramatically over the past century. Third, we apply the model to retirement to explore the determinants of retirement age.

Taxing Labor Income

The income tax also influences labor supply. Like changes in the wage rate, changes in the tax rate t generate substitution and income effects. Replace Gregg's wage w with his after-tax or take-home wage $(1 - t)w$, so introducing a tax or increasing the tax rate flattens Gregg's budget line, pivoting it through his endowment E. A 20 percent flat tax (i.e., $t = .20$), reduces Gregg's take-home wage from $10 to $8 per hour; indeed, a 20 percent flat tax is equivalent to a 20 percent wage cut. As such, the substitution effect of the tax pushes Gregg toward working shorter hours, while the income effect lengthens his workday.

If the government returns the proceeds of the tax to Gregg and other citizens in the form of government services, the income effect of the tax increase could vanish (Lewis 1957, pp. 202–203). Distribution of tax-financed government services shifts up Gregg's endowment point. If the government is amazingly efficient, the shift up in the endowment point can eliminate the income effect of the tax: combining the tax with efficient distribution of government services draws Gregg's choice down along his original indifference curve, reducing his workday and his consumption. That is, the income tax reduces the quantity supplied of labor if tax revenues are efficiently distributed as government services. It's purely a substitution effect.

Do high tax rates reduce hours of work? Figure 3.15 displays a scatter plot of tax rates and working hours across 29 developed countries in 2015. The tax rate measures the additional tax associated with a $1 increase in earnings for a single person without children who earns the average wage, and it includes employer contributions to social-security programs. Hours are measured per working-age adult. The scatter plot replaces dots with bubbles. The size of each bubble reflects the country's population, so large bubbles mark the data points for large countries.

The evidence across countries supports our prediction that high tax rates reduce hours of work. People in the lowest tax-rate countries (e.g., Mexico and Korea) work long hours. The workweek is shortest in high tax-rate countries like Belgium, France, and Germany. The slope of the regression line fit to these data is −0.27, so people in a country with a 50 percent marginal tax rate tend to work 2.7-hour-shorter workweeks than people in a country with a 40 percent marginal tax rate.

This inverse relationship pops right out of the data. But we should be cautious. One possibility is that governments can pay their bills with lower tax rates in countries where people work more; that's an example of causation running in reverse. (Refer to the discussion of causation in section 1.5.) And our analysis ignores plenty of other differences across countries. For instance, differences across countries in wages and nonlabor income might explain some of the variation in the workweek across countries. Government regulations and unions

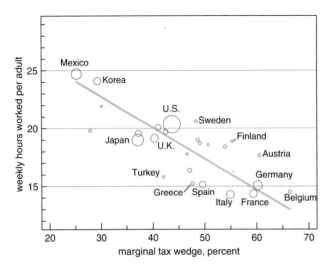

Notes: For each country, the center of the bubble marks the data point, and the size of the bubble reflects the country's population. The marginal tax wedge t is for a single person without children who earns the average wage; it includes employer contributions to social-security programs. The estimated regression line is

$h = 30.8 − 0.27t$ with $R^2 = .78$.
     (1.21)   (.03)

Source: Organisation for Economic Co-operation and Development (OECD), stats.oecd.org: Annual Labour Force Statistics, Hours Worked, and Taxing Wages databases, accessed March 17, 2018.

FIGURE 3.15. Hours of Work and Tax Rates Across 29 Developed Countries, 2015

are probably also important. So Figure 3.15 isn't the last word on the effect of taxes on working hours, but it does provide compelling first words.

Incredible Shrinking Workweek

Our ancestors in the early 1900s struggled to pay 5 cents for a loaf of bread. Farmers worked long hours, and production workers in manufacturing labored (on average) over 50 hours per week. Those production workers earned (on average) less than 20 cents per hour. (Some claim that, as students, our hard-working ancestors also "walked to school uphill, both ways, barefoot in the snow," but evidence to support this claim is rather thin.)

Fast forward to the current era. We measure the price of bread in dollars rather than nickels, and the typical consumption good is 20 times more expensive than it was early in the 1900s. Wages are also higher, a lot higher. The average hourly wage of production workers in manufacturing is now almost $21. For the typical production worker in manufacturing, an hour of work buys four times more consumption goods and services than it did in the early 1900s; that is, the real wage grew about 400 percent over the past century. Meanwhile, the workweek shrank about 20 hours. Our ancestors worked long and hard. Us? Not so much.

Figure 3.16 uses decadal averages to display the inverse relationship between the workweek and average hourly wages (in 2017 dollars). In the first half of the 1900s (for production workers in manufacturing), actual hours worked were quite sensitive to the rising real hourly wage. Since 1950 (for production and nonsupervisory workers in private nonfarm businesses), the workweek has been a little less sensitive to the real hourly wage.

Lewis (1957) and other mid-century labor economists detected a labor supply curve from the hours and hourly wage data from the first half of the century.

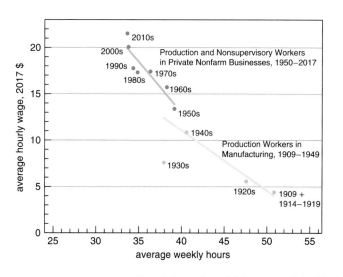

Notes: The Implicit Price Deflator for Gross Domestic Product (GDP) converts the average hourly wage to 2017 dollars.
Sources: Hours worked, 1909–1949: Jones, Ethel. 1963. "New Estimates of Hours of Work Per Week and Hourly Earnings, 1900–1957." *Review of Economics and Statistics* 45(4): 374–385. Average hourly earnings, 1909–1949: Bureau of Labor Statistics, *Employment and Earnings, United States, 1909–1971*, Bulletin No. 1312-8. 1950–2017: Bureau of Labor Statistics, Current Employment Statistics, Table B-2.

FIGURE 3.16. Decadal Averages of the Workweek and Real Hourly Earnings, 1909–2017

Faced with an inverse relationship between a price (i.e., the hourly wage) and a quantity (i.e., hours worked per week), demand is the first concept to pop into an economist's head, but Lewis argued that the inverse pattern isn't a downward-sloping demand for labor. On the demand side, as we learn in chapter 5, the hourly wage primarily influences the quantity demanded of *workers N* while other factors influence the employer's interest in the *workweek h*. So mid-century labor economists detected a labor supply curve that bends backward. The pattern of hours and hourly wage data in Figure 3.16 resembles the backward-bending section of a labor supply curve. Indeed, the income effect of dramatically increasing hourly wages over the past century appears to dominate the substitution effect, explaining the incredible shrinking workweek. But the workweek has been less responsive to the hourly wage since World War II, which suggests something more is going on.

Tempting as it is to see a backward-bending curve (or two) in Figure 3.16, our model of labor supply advises caution. A plot of pairs of weekly hours and hourly wages over the past century doesn't control for the many factors that shift labor supply curves, including nonlabor incomes y, income tax rates t, and demographic factors (e.g., family size) that influence the value of time at home. We find below that retirement benefits, welfare payments, unemployment benefits, and education also shift labor supplies, but Figure 3.16 ignores variation in these factors. And we've ignored the firm's interest in the workweek, which we study in chapter 5.

We should also improve the measurement of the key variables. By measuring hours paid rather than hours worked (beginning in the 1950s), we ignore the growth in pay for time not worked and understate the decline in the workweek. On the other hand, failing to account for the growing importance of employee benefits understates the growth in real hourly compensation.

Despite these caveats, we can be confident that the backward-bending curve provides an important (although incomplete) explanation of the incredible shrinking workweek.

Retirement

Our model of labor supply is also a model of retirement. We cast the model of labor supply in the context of Gregg's *daily* choice of leisure and consumption. Alternatively, we could analyze Gregg's allocation of time over the week to study how his workweek varies with his hourly wage rate. Or we could study how Gregg's choice of weeks to work over the year depends on his weekly wage. And we can apply the model of consumption–leisure choice over an even longer time period, the rest of a person's life. How does a worker split his or her remaining years into working years and retirement years, which is leisure time? In this context, our model of labor supply predicts how retirement age varies with annual values of nonlabor income, the wage, and retirement benefits.

To apply the model, we split a person's remaining life (rest of life ROL) into years of work and retirement years. For instance, Olivia at age 60 decides how to split the remaining 20 years of her life between work years and retirement years, recognizing that her consumption is lower if she retires earlier. Retirement years are an example of leisure time, which means we can replace leisure with retirement on the horizontal axis in Figure 3.17. Olivia's preferences are standard: she prefers more consumption and more years in retirement, so her preference direction is to the northeast; her indifference curves slope down and bow toward the origin.

What are Olivia's opportunities? Olivia's endowment E reflects the 20 years of retirement that she could enjoy if she retires immediately and the $80,000 in her savings account. Her annual wage is $40,000, so delaying retirement one year enables her to increase her spending on consumption by $40,000 over the rest of her life. Thus Olivia's budget line in Figure 3.17 emerges from her endowment E with slope $-40,000$ units per year. (The price of consumption is $1 per unit.) If Olivia never retires, she has $880,000 ($= $80,000 + (20 \times $40,000)$) to spend on consumption until she dies at age 80. So her budget line intersects the vertical axis at 880,000.

> ☑ **PRACTICE**   Mark the point in Figure 3.17 that corresponds to Olivia retiring immediately (i.e., at age 60).

Olivia chooses her retirement age by equating the marginal value of her time in retirement to her real wage. Point X in Figure 3.17, where her budget line is tangent to her indifference curve I_2, illustrates Olivia's retirement choice. She works 8 more years and retires at age 68; that leaves her 12 years to enjoy retirement. The $320,000 ($= 8 \times $40,000$) over the 8 years before retirement supplements the

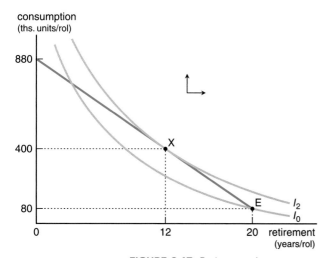

consumption
(ths. units/rol)

880

400

80

0   12   20   retirement
                               (years/rol)

Olivia prefers a longer retirement with more consumption, so her indifference curves slope down.

Olivia at age 60 expects to live to age 80. She has $80,000 in savings, and her annual wage is $40,000. Her budget line runs from her endowment E (retire now) to 880,000 on the vertical axis (never retire); the slope of her budget line is her real wage, 40,000 units/year.

Olivia's optimal choice is X. She works 8 more years, earning $320,000, and enjoys 12 years of retirement. She spends $400,000 on consumption over her remaining 20 years. That's $20,000/year.

FIGURE 3.17. Retirement Age

$80,000 she has in savings, which finances $400,000 of spending on consumption over 20 years. That's $20,000 per year.

The effect of the wage on retirement age is ambiguous. Figure 3.18a illustrates Olivia's response to her annual wage falling from $40,000 to $30,000. The lower wage means work is less lucrative to Olivia, which pushes her toward retiring earlier as a substitution effect. But the lower wage also leaves Olivia poorer, which reduces her demand for retirement (i.e., leisure time) as an income effect. Olivia responds to the cut in her annual wage by retiring two years earlier (at age 66), which extends her retirement from 12 years to 14 years. Olivia's response to her wage cut reveals that her labor supply curve slopes up.

> ☑ **PRACTICE**   Decompose Olivia's response to her wage cut into substitution and income effects in Figure 3.18. Show that the substitution effect shortens Olivia's working life while the income effect delays her retirement.

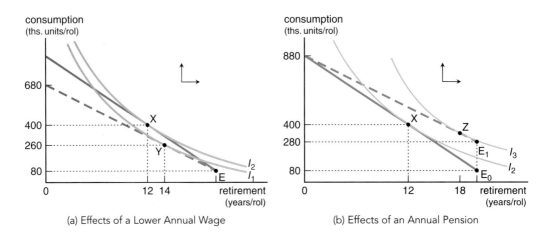

FIGURE 3.18. Wages, Pension Benefits, and the Age of Retirement

(a) Varying Olivia's wage rotates her budget line through the endowment point E, which generates substitution and income effects. Her choice moves from X to Y in response to a lower annual wage. As drawn, the substitution effect dominates: Olivia stops working sooner. She retires at age 66 rather than age 68. Over this range of wages, Olivia's labor supply curve slopes up.

(b) The $10,000 annual pension benefit is irrelevant if Olivia doesn't retire, so her budget line's vertical intercept doesn't depend on the pension. Varying Olivia's pension benefit rotates her budget line through its vertical intercept in panel (b). Her choice moves from X to Z in response to the pension benefit. Substitution and income effects both encourage Olivia to retire earlier. Her retirement age falls from 68 to 62.

Pension benefits encourage workers to retire earlier. Suppose Olivia's employer introduces a pension plan that pays Olivia and each of her coworkers $10,000 per year in retirement. If Olivia retires immediately, the pension benefit is worth $200,000 ($= 20 \times \$10,000$), which shifts her endowment point up by 200,000 units of consumption. Alternatively, if she never retires, she never collects the pension, so the pension doesn't affect her budget line's vertical intercept. Therefore, the pension benefit flattens Olivia's budget line and pivots it through the vertical intercept. (See Figure 3.18b.) Indeed, retiring a year early involves foregoing only $30,000 ($= \$40,000 - \$10,000$), so the slope of the budget line falls (in absolute value) to 30,000 units per year. Olivia responds to the pension benefit by retiring six years earlier (i.e., at age 62). (As drawn, her consumption over the rest of her life falls.) Since pension benefits reduce the real cost of a year in retirement and expand Olivia's opportunities, substitution and income effects of retirement benefits both push Olivia to retire earlier.

3.4   Whether to Work

In our analysis of labor supply to this point, workers work. But many people don't work, and most of those folks don't want to work. How do we model the choice whether to work? We start by deriving the **reservation wage**, the wage that leaves a person indifferent between working and not working. After exploring how a person's reservation wage varies with nonlabor income, we apply the analysis to commuting and other costs of work and to government programs that pay a cash grant to people who don't work.

Reservation Wage

Gregg's quantity supplied of labor varies with his wage, and he doesn't work at all if his wage is below some threshold, which we call his reservation wage. Gregg's reservation wage R is the wage that leaves him indifferent between working and not working. His reservation wage depends on his indifference curves, which reflect his preferences.

For Gregg to work, his budget line must be steeper than his indifference curve at his endowment. Figure 3.19 illustrates Gregg's indifference curve through his endowment E, which includes a $40 daily allowance. The thin blue line in the figure is tangent to that indifference curve I_0 at his endowment E. Thus the slope of the tangent line measures Gregg's marginal rate of substitution of leisure for consumption if he's not working. That's how much Gregg requires in consumption to give up his last hour of leisure. It's his reservation wage in real terms. Reservation wage R is (in absolute value) the slope of this tangent line if $p = 1$. (More generally, the slope of the tangent line is $-R/p$.)

For any $w > R$, the budget line emerging from E is steeper than the indifference curve I_0. If Gregg's wage is greater than his reservation wage, he can reach a higher indifference curve than I_0, so he participates in the labor market. For any $w < R$,

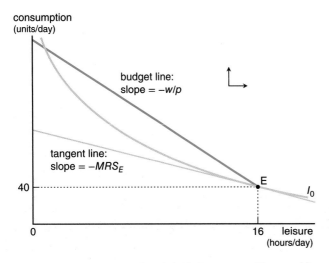

The slope of the thin blue line, the tangent to Gregg's indifference curve through his endowment point E, reveals his reservation wage R.

Gregg's budget line is steeper than the tangent line (i.e., $w > R$), so he works. If $w < R$, his budget line would be flatter than the tangent line, and he wouldn't participate in the labor market.

Suppose Beth values home time more than Gregg does. Her indifference curves are steeper, her reservation wage is higher, and it takes a higher wage to entice her to work.

FIGURE 3.19. Reservation Wage and Participation

the budget line is flatter than the indifference curve through E; Gregg can't reach an indifference curve higher than I_0, so he doesn't work.

 PRACTICE   Sketch a budget line in Figure 3.19 that keeps Gregg from working.

Gregg is more likely to want to work if his wage is higher. That is, a higher wage is more likely to satisfy $w > R$. The same result applies to all potential workers, so raising the wage draws workers into the labor market. Indeed, increasing the wage increases the participation rate.

The reservation wage for work is an increasing function of nonlabor income. For instance, if Gregg's daily allowance doubles from $40 to $80, his endowment shifts up from E_0 to E_1 in Figure 3.20. His reservation wage increases from R_0 to R_1 because the tangent line to I_1 at E_1 is steeper than the tangent line to I_0 at E_0. (We assume leisure is a normal good.) Thus the participation rate (and the employment rate) falls as nonlabor income rises. Winners of big lottery games, those who inherit fortunes, and those like Bill Gates who amass fortunes of financial assets are likely to work less (as we learned in section 3.2), and they are likely to withdraw from the labor market. They retire early.

Key Principle.
A higher wage increases the reward to working, which draws people into the labor market.

Application: Commuting and Other Costs of Work

Gregg and other workers might have **money costs of work** m, including bus or train fares, gasoline and parking fees for drivers, and laundry costs of uniforms and dry cleaning expenses of business attire. Gregg bears these costs if he works,

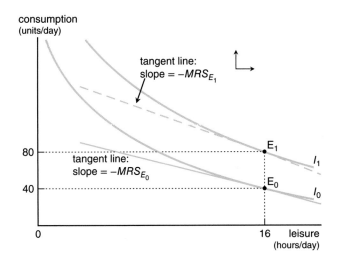

Increasing nonlabor income y shifts Gregg's endowment up from E_0 to E_1. Since leisure is a normal good, his indifference curve at E_1 is steeper than his indifference curve at E_0. Therefore, Gregg's reservation wage R increases with his nonlabor income.

Increasing nonlabor income increases the reservation wage and lowers the chance that $w > R$. So increasing nonlabor income lowers the participation rate.

FIGURE 3.20. Reservation Wage, Participation, and Nonlabor Income

but he avoids them if he doesn't work. Gregg can enjoy E in Figure 3.21 without working, but his budget line emerges from E′, a point m/p units of consumption below E.

To find Gregg's reservation wage with commuting costs, draw a line from E′ tangent to I_0, the indifference curve through E: the slope of this tangent line reveals the lowest wage that turns Gregg into a worker. Any wage higher than this reservation wage generates a budget line that's steeper than the tangent line, allowing Gregg to reach a higher indifference curve with a combination of leisure

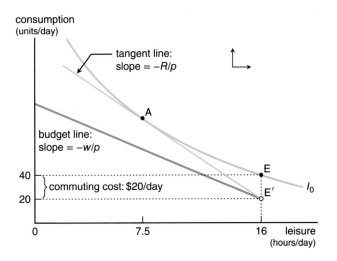

Gregg's endowment is point E. If he works, he loses $20/day in commuting costs, so his budget line emerges from point E′ rather than E.

The slope of the line from E′ tangent to I_0 reveals Gregg's reservation wage R. Commuting costs raise the reservation wage R and lower the participation rate.

As drawn, $w < R$, so Gregg doesn't choose to participate in the labor market, and he avoids the commuting costs m.

FIGURE 3.21. Reservation Wage, Participation, and Commuting Costs

and consumption that he prefers to his endowment E. If his budget line is flatter than the tangent line, then his wage is lower than his reservation wage, and the best Gregg can do is not work.

Commuting and other costs of work raise the reservation wage, lower the participation rate, and render short workdays uncommon. Gregg's reservation wage based on this new tangent line is higher than his marginal rate of substitution at E, his reservation wage without the money costs of work. By raising Gregg's reservation wage, commuting and other costs of work lower the chance that Gregg's wage exceeds his reservation wage; the odds that Gregg works fall, lowering the participation rate.

Commuting costs also endanger the short workday: Gregg might need to work several hours just to cover the costs of his daily commute. Without monetary costs of work, Gregg works a very short workday if his wage is only a little higher than his reservation wage. With money costs of work, Gregg jumps into the labor market with a whopping 8.5-hour workday at A in Figure 3.21.

Since costs of work can be avoided (by not working), paying commuting costs isn't the same as having less nonlabor income. If Gregg works, then paying *m* to commute or losing *m* in nonlabor income amount to the same thing: Gregg's budget line is lower by *m* units. But paying to commute and losing nonlabor income have opposite effects on Gregg's choice to work. Commuting costs raise the reservation wage and lower the participation rate. Cutting nonlabor income, however, lowers the reservation wage and raises the participation rate. That commuting and other costs of work can be avoided by not working drives the difference.

 PRACTICE   Commuting to work also takes time. Suppose Gregg's daily commute takes 30 minutes each way, so Gregg loses one hour per day *if he works*. Ignore his money cost of work, and mark the point in Figure 3.21 from which Gregg's budget line emerges. To illustrate Gregg's reservation wage with a *time cost of work*, draw a line from this point that's tangent to I_0. How does the time cost of commuting impact the reservation wage and participation rate?

Application: Cash Grants and Income Guarantees

Government antipoverty programs generate many complicated effects on labor supply. Here we focus on a simple program that pays a **cash grant** to people who don't work.

Like a money cost of work, a cash grant raises the reservation wage and lowers the participation rate. Suppose Beth has no nonlabor income (i.e., $y = 0$), but the government pays her $400 per week if she doesn't work. Beth's weekly endowment, point G in Figure 3.22, is $400/p$ units of consumption and 112 (nonsleeping) hours. Yet Beth's budget line emerges from her original endowment

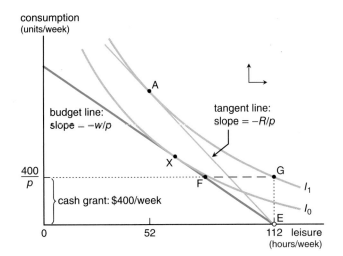

A take-it-or-leave-it cash grant of $400/week adds point G to Beth's budget set. She forfeits the $400 if she works, so her budget line emerges from E, her endowment without the cash grant.

The slope of the line from E tangent to I_1 reveals Beth's reservation wage R with the $400 cash grant. The cash grant drives up Beth's reservation wage, and she stops working. Cash grants lower the participation rate.

FIGURE 3.22. Reservation Wage, Participation, and Cash Grants

point E (without the cash grant) since she forfeits the $400 grant by working. So we derive her reservation wage by drawing a line from E tangent to indifference curve I_1. And that tangent line is clearly much steeper than the hidden indifference curve through E. That is, paying people not to work raises the reservation wage, lowers the participation rate, and reduces the supply of labor.

The Social Security Administration's Disability Insurance program (SSDI) makes monthly payments to "workers" with disabilities that are expected to prevent them from working for at least one year. Since only those with work-preventing conditions qualify for the program, SSDI appears to be a bad application of the model of cash grants, which emphasizes the choice whether to work. Appearances can be deceiving.

The disability rate—the number of disabled workers in the SSDI program divided by civilian employment—grew from about 2.4 percent in the late 1980s to 6.1 percent by late 2014. To get a better sense of the magnitude of the change, turn the disability rate upside down: in the late 1980s, there were 41 workers for every disabled person collecting benefits through SSDI. By the end of 2014, only 16 workers supported each disabled worker collecting SSDI benefits. The ranks of the disabled had grown so fast that the ratio of workers to disabled former workers had fallen by almost one worker per year over 25 years. Will we run out of workers to support the disabled by 2030? Recent history suggests not: the ratio of workers to disabled former workers rose from 16.4 in 2014 to 17.7 in 2017.

Over the past few decades, advances in medical care have been stunning, and the workforce has shifted from dangerous jobs in agriculture, mining, and manufacturing to safer jobs in services. Consequently, serious disabilities should have become rare like the 50-hour workweek and vinyl records. Why are so many more people disabled and not working?

To answer this question, let's apply the model of cash grants. First, SSDI's standards for work-preventing disabilities have slipped. Lowering the standards raises the number of people who qualify for the program. Qualifying for SSDI pushes the endowment point up, raises the reservation wage, and lowers the employment rate of the newly qualified pool of disabled workers. Second, disability benefits have grown more generous, which raises the reservation wage of those who qualify for the program. More disabled people who are capable of work find collecting the monthly SSDI check more attractive than working.

Recipients of disability payments aren't allowed to work, but other government antipoverty programs allow recipients to work. A welfare program that guarantees a weekly income of $400 is an example. In this case, the budget line in Figure 3.22 has two pieces: the dashed flat segment from G to F, and the regular budget line where the workweek generates more than $400 in earnings. Between G and F, the real wage is effectively zero; Beth collects a paycheck every week, which reduces her welfare payment dollar for dollar, and her consumption is unaffected.

A guaranteed weekly income of $400 delivers the same behavior as a cash grant of $400 per week. No one—except someone who wants to work for nothing—chooses to work along the line between G and F. So the reservation wage in the guaranteed-income program is the same as the reservation wage with a cash grant. And the guaranteed income matches the cash grant in discouraging work.

3.5   Family Labor Supply and Home Production

Labor supply choices aren't always made by rugged individualists. Many people choose whether to work and how much to work in the context of the family. For instance, a man's wage influences his spouse's labor supply (and vice versa), and the number and ages of kids at home impact the workweek of each parent. Modeling the internal working of the family is quite challenging, but we can illuminate the issues for family labor supply with some simple extensions of our model.

Family Labor Supply

Beth is married to Gregg. If they have children, especially young children, then time at home is particularly important. Recall that the slope of an indifference curve tells us how much consumption a worker is willing to forego for a marginal increase in time at home. Having children increases the amount of consumption that Beth and Gregg are willing to give up for a bit more time at home with the kids. That is, having children, especially young children, steepens each indifference curve. In response to the arrival of a new baby, Gregg's choice slides down his budget line toward his endowment point. He spends more time at home and less time at work, and he consumes less.

PRACTICE   Illustrate the effect of a first child on Gregg's indifference curves in Figure 3.10. Carefully indicate how Gregg's choice of consumption, leisure, and hours of work responds to the new arrival.

Marriage creates opportunities to specialize, which also influence indifference curves and labor supply. Thoroughly modern Gregg might specialize in caring for the home and family while Beth specializes in market work. Having Gregg home to attend to all the details of married life (e.g., shopping, washing clothes, paying the bills) lowers the value of Beth's time at home. Marriage flattens her indifference curves, and her choice of leisure and consumption moves up her budget line. She lengthens her workday. With Beth working long hours, there's more for Gregg to do at home, which steepens his indifference curves, and his workday shrinks.

Couples' labor supply curves are interrelated. Beth's labor supply depends on Gregg's wage, and vice versa. Suppose Gregg's wage increases from $10 to $14 per hour. If Gregg's raise simply translated into higher nonlabor income for Beth, then she would respond to Gregg's raise by shortening her workday as an income effect. But there's surely more to a family than a wife absorbing some of her husband's earnings.

Perhaps Gregg and Beth have *family preferences* over family consumption, Gregg's leisure time, and Beth's leisure time. If Gregg's hourly wage rises from $10 to $14, the family substitutes out of Gregg's leisure into family consumption. Gregg's raise also makes Beth's leisure relatively less expensive, so the family probably also substitutes into Beth's leisure. The substitution effects of the increase in Gregg's wage lengthen his workday and shorten Beth's workday. The family is also richer, and the income effect shortens each spouse's workday. Gregg's workday can rise or fall, which echoes our earlier finding that his labor supply curve might slope backward. Our new prediction is that Gregg's raise lowers Beth's labor supply.

Home Production

What's Gregg doing at home? He's involved in home production, using time at home to produce things of value. Time at home is spent shopping, cooking, cleaning, washing clothes, decorating rooms, paying bills, changing light bulbs, programming remote controls, checking homework, shuttling kids from one activity to another, and so on. Let's enrich our model of labor supply to distinguish between time in these household activities and genuine leisure time. How do people split their nonworking time between home production and genuine leisure?

To simplify our extension to home production, let's analyze Gregg's allocation of time before he married Beth. Figure 3.23 illustrates bachelor Gregg's split of his day into working time, home-production time, and leisure time (Gronau 1977). The figure adds a **home production function** to our model of consumption–leisure choice. Preparing a meal, decorating a room, and programming a remote control create consumption services, which we measure as consumption c on the vertical

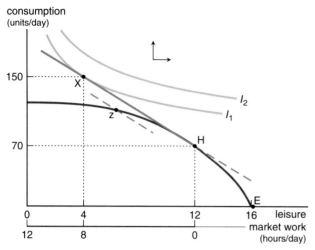

Gregg turns time on chores into consumption along his home production function (in gray). Gregg's optimal home production point H is where the slope of his production function (in absolute value) equals his real wage, which delivers the highest budget line. Gregg's choice of leisure and consumption is at X, the tangency of one of his indifference curves to his budget line.

Gregg works 4 hours on chores and 8 hours on his job, which leaves 4 hours for leisure. He consumes 150 units, 70 from home production and 80 from his earnings.

FIGURE 3.23. Allocating Time Between Market Work, Home Work, and Leisure

axis. The home production function is the relationship between time in these household activities and the output of consumption. In the figure, the home production function collects all the combinations of leisure and consumption that are feasible *without market work*. By shifting time from leisure to housework, Gregg moves up along his home production function from the endowment at point E and increases his consumption. Gregg accomplishes a lot in his first hour doing chores, but his production at home is subject to diminishing returns. As a result, his home production function in the figure bows out from the origin.

We analyze Gregg's optimal choice in two steps. In the first step, Gregg chooses how much time to devote to housework, and this choice determines his budget line for step two. He picks the point along his home production function that delivers the highest budget line. In Figure 3.23, that's point H, where the slope of his home production function (in absolute value) equals his wage w (with $p = 1$). Gregg's time doing housework shaves 4 hours from his day, leaving 12 hours for work on his job and leisure time. Point H then serves as an endowment point: H indicates Gregg's leisure and consumption if he doesn't work, given that he spends 4 hours per day on housework. His budget line emerges from H with slope $-w$. If Gregg chose any other point on his home production function (e.g., z), the resulting budget line would be inside the budget line through H. And that's why H is Gregg's best choice for home production.

In the second step, Gregg chooses the combination of leisure time and consumption that he most prefers among all the pairs (l, c) along the budget line. That is, he chooses point X, where one of his indifference curves is tangent to his budget line. So the points H and X in Figure 3.23 fully characterize Gregg's choice. Gregg works on a job for 8 ($= 12 - 4$) hours per day; he evenly splits the other 8 nonsleeping hours between housework and leisure time.

With home production, Gregg responds to a higher wage in a familiar way: his response combines substitution and income effects. But an important extra element follows from home production. As his time becomes more valuable in the market, Gregg substitutes out of housework into market work. His production point H slides down the production function (toward E) to a steeper point of tangency. Even if the higher wage leaves leisure time unchanged, Gregg's quantity supplied of labor to the market increases as he spends less time on housework.

The type of work that's done at home also depends on the wage. Home production combines time and market goods to produce things of value at home (Becker 1965). For instance, Gregg produces a meal with ingredients from the supermarket and time in the kitchen cooking. If Gregg gets a raise, he shifts from time-intensive to goods-intensive production at home. Take-out food replaces home-cooked meals. He buys a snowblower to speed up snow removal, and he hires Leisure Lawn to cut the grass.

The extension to home production helps explain the dramatic increase in labor force participation and the workweek of women over the second half of the twentieth century. First, time-saving innovations like the washing machine, the dishwasher, and the microwave oven shifted work around the house from time-intensive to goods-intensive production, and women responded by increasing the supply of their labor to the market. Second, the rising wages of women led them to substitute market work, as well as market goods, for time in home production. The fall in time in home production increased women's employment and hours of work. Since men weren't deeply involved in home production, their response to their own rising wages was entirely conventional: the income effect of men's rising wage dominated the substitution effect, so men's workweek fell. Furthermore, women leaving home for market work increased the value of men's time at home, which reinforced the decline in men's workweek.

3.6   Market Labor Supply

We have derived the labor supply curve of a person and specified the factors (i.e., nonlabor income y, tax rate t, pension benefits b, money costs of work m, cash grants from the government g, and spouse's wage) that shift a person's labor supply curve. Now it's time to aggregate the individual labor supplies to derive market labor supply.

The **market labor supply curve** sums the individual labor supply curves across workers. For instance, at $w = 10$, Gregg and Beth each supply 10 hours of labor per day. In their two-worker labor market, the quantity supplied of labor is 20 hours per day if the wage is $10 per hour. At $w = 14$, Gregg's quantity supplied of labor is 11 hours per day, and Beth's quantity supplied of labor is 9 hours per day. The quantity supplied of labor in their little market remains at 20 (= 11 + 9) hours per day. Summing the quantities supplied of labor across workers at each wage amounts to adding the individual supply curves horizontally on a graph. Those backward-bending individual labor supply curves can aggregate to a backward-bending market labor supply curve.

But there's more to it. As the wage increases, workers can increase or decrease hours along their labor supply curves, but the higher wage also draws people into the labor market. People who weren't participating in the labor market (i.e., people whose quantities supplied of labor equal zero) jump into the labor market. With money and time costs of work and cash grants, zero-hours people jump into employment with sizable hours. For instance, Al doesn't work at $w = 10$, but his quantity supplied of labor jumps to 5 hours per week at $w = 14$. With Al in the mix, the market quantity supplied of labor climbs from 20 hours per week at $10 to 25 hours per week at $14. The market labor supply curve slopes up, although Beth's labor supply curve bends backward.

Labor supply curves in particular markets typically slope up. The labor supply curves in chapter 2 slope up because we were working with particular markets—for instance, the market for nurses or the market for labor in Chicago—rather than the whole market for labor. Increasing the wage in any particular market draws workers from other markets, as well as from home. For instance, increasing the nurses' wage can increase or decrease the quantity supplied of labor of existing nurses. But the higher wage of nurses also draws people from out of the labor force into nursing, and it draws people from other occupations into nursing. In the long run, the time over which occupational choice is relevant, philosophers can become web designers, and costume designers can become architects. So labor supply curves in particular markets can be quite elastic in the long run.

 PRACTICE   Markets can be defined narrowly or broadly. The market for carpenters is narrower than the market for skilled craftsmen, and the market for labor in Nashua, New Hampshire, is narrower than the market for labor in New England. Are labor supply curves more or less elastic in narrowly defined labor markets? Why?

Summary

This chapter established how workers trading off consumption and leisure time determines working hours (e.g., the workday or workweek). For findings, we have:

☐ Driven by women entering the labor market in large numbers, labor force participation and employment rates trended up in the second half of the twentieth century. Over the first half of the twentieth century, the workweek of manufacturing production workers shortened dramatically. Although hours paid remain approximately 40 hours per week for production workers in manufacturing firms, the emergence and growth of pay for time not worked (e.g., holidays and vacations) contributed to the decline in hours worked over the past 60 years.

- [ ] Modeling labor supply combines opportunities with preferences to determine a person's choice of leisure and consumption. At the tangency of the budget line to an indifference curve, quantity supplied of labor equates the marginal value of the worker's home time (i.e., his marginal rate of substitution) to his real wage rate w/p.

- [ ] Increasing nonlabor income increases consumption and leisure time but decreases hours worked, our measure of the quantity supplied of labor.

- [ ] Workers can respond positively or negatively to an increase in the wage; it's a matter of personal preference. A person's labor supply curve slopes up (bends backward) if the substitution effect dominates (is dominated by) the income effect of the wage change.

- [ ] Introducing (or increasing) a tax on labor income would be equivalent to decreasing the wage if the proceeds of the tax weren't returned to workers in the form of government services. If government services are efficient, then the tax lowers the quantity supplied of labor as a substitution effect.

- [ ] The consumption–leisure choice model of labor supply applies directly to retirement because retirement years are a form of leisure time. More generous pension benefits encourage workers to retire younger, which reduces the supply of labor.

- [ ] The choice to participate in the labor market involves comparing the wage w to the reservation wage R. Increasing nonlabor income raises the reservation wage and lowers the participation rate and labor supply.

- [ ] Cash grants from the government also raise the reservation wage, lower the participation rate, and reduce labor supply.

- [ ] Workers respond to a higher wage by cutting time in home production, which leaves more time for market work and leisure time. A worker's labor supply tends to fall as the wage of his or her spouse rises.

- [ ] Although individual labor supply curves can bend backward, labor supply curves in specific markets typically slope up because a higher wage in one labor market draws workers from other labor markets as well as people from home.

There's plenty more to learn about labor supply and the workweek. In chapter 6, we see how schooling influences the workweek, and an extension to labor supply over a worker's career appears in chapter 7. In chapter 5, we explore the employer's interest in the workweek. Next we turn to the demand side of the labor market and employers' choices in pursuit of profit.

Key Concepts

- labor force participation rate, p. 82
- employment rate, p. 83
- budget line, p. 87
- budget set, p. 87
- nonlabor income, p. 87
- endowment, p. 88
- real wage, p. 88
- full income, p. 89
- indifference curves, p. 90
- preference direction, p. 91

- marginal rate of substitution, p. 93
- income effect, p. 96
- normal good, p. 96
- substitution and income effects, p. 98
- backward-bending labor supply, p. 100
- reservation wage, p. 107
- money cost of work, p. 108
- cash grant, p. 110
- home production function, p. 113
- market labor supply, p. 115

Short-Answer Questions

3.1 Figure 3.2 displays sharply different patterns in the participation rates of women and men. Without referring to any economic model, speculate about factors that might explain the different trends.

3.2 List at least seven factors that influence a worker's opportunities in the context of consumption–leisure choice. Explain how each factor affects the budget line or endowment point.

3.3 What features of our model of labor supply (a) allow for an ambiguous effect of the wage on the workweek but (b) deliver the definitive result that a higher wage rate increases labor force participation?

3.4 A lower wage flattens the budget line, and a higher tax rate does, too. But the two differ. Explain why a lower wage might lengthen the workweek but a higher tax rate likely shortens the workweek.

3.5 Decompose the effects of an increase in pension benefits on consumption, retirement years, and years of work into substitution and income effects. Does the substitution effect of the increase in pension benefits increase or decrease the age of retirement? Does the income effect increase or decrease the retirement age?

3.6 Does Beth's reservation wage depend on her opportunities, her preferences, or both? What effect does her wage have on her reservation wage? Does

Beth want to work if her wage is greater than her reservation wage, or vice versa?

3.7 Suppose a $200 weekly welfare payment has a weekly work requirement of 10 hours. Any work beyond 10 hours reduces the welfare payment dollar for dollar. Sheldon's real wage is 10 units of consumption, and he has 100 nonsleeping hours per week. Illustrate Sheldon's opportunities by supplementing his budget line to reflect welfare payments. Over what range of working hours is his consumption unaffected by his earnings? Does the work requirement increase or decrease Sheldon's reservation wage?

3.8 How is time in home production related to the wage rate? Explain why home production makes it more likely that a worker's labor supply curve slopes up.

3.9 Explain why the labor supply curve to a specific market probably slopes up even if the labor supply curves of workers in that market bend backward.

Problems

3.1 Ron chooses how many weeks to work each year. His time endowment T is 50 weeks per year, which conveniently lies on the grid in the figure below. His wage rate w is $400 per week, the price of consumption p is $10 per unit, and he has no nonlabor income (i.e., $y = 0$).

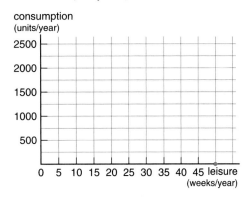

(a) If Ron doesn't work at all, how many units can he consume in a year? Label this point E.

(b) If Ron works all 50 weeks, how much can he consume? Label this point F.

(c) What is Ron's real wage? That is, if he works another week, how many more units of consumption does he enjoy?

(d) Draw Ron's budget line, and shade in the pairs (l, c) that Ron can afford.

There's also a proportional or flat tax on earnings (i.e., labor income); the tax rate is t, so Ron's take-home (or after-tax) wage is $(1 - t)w$.

(e) What is the effect of a 25 percent tax on earnings on Ron's real wage?

(f) What happens to Ron's budget line as the tax increases from zero to 25 percent? Illustrate the change in Ron's budget set.

3.2 The figure below displays several of Emma's indifference curves. Although there are 168 hours in every week, Emma sleeps and bathes exactly 68 hours weekly, so she has 100 hours to divide between work and play. Emma receives $50 per week in interest on her savings, which is her only income from nonwork sources. The price of the consumption good is $1 per unit, and her wage is $10 per hour.

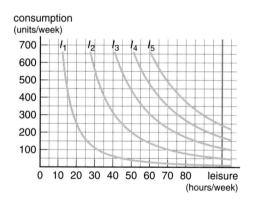

(a) In the range of 30 to 35 hours of leisure, what is Emma's marginal rate of substitution of leisure for consumption along indifference curve I_2?

(b) Mark Emma's endowment point E on the figure. What is the slope of the budget line in absolute value? Draw Emma's budget line.

(c) Emma chooses the combination of leisure and consumption that she values most. Mark Emma's optimal choice with an X. How many units of the consumption good does she consume?

(d) At Emma's optimal choice, how many hours of leisure does she enjoy each week? How many hours does she work?

(e) How much does Emma earn each week? That is, what is her wage income in dollars per week?

3.3 The indifference curves in the figure below display Hank's preferences over leisure l and consumption c. Hank has $50 per day in nonlabor income, and he's endowed with 16 hours every day. The price of consumption p is $5 per unit. You need to draw two or three budget lines in the figure to determine the effect of Hank's hourly wage increasing from $10 to $15.

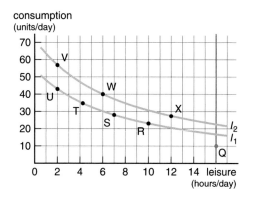

(a) If Hank's hourly wage is $10, which point is his optimal pair (l^*, c^*)? How much does he consume, how much leisure time does he enjoy, and how many hours does he work per day?

(b) If Hank's hourly wage is $15, which point does he choose? What are his daily values of consumption, leisure, and working hours?

(c) How does Hank's quantity supplied of labor vary with his wage for these two wages?

(d) The substitution effect of the increase in Hank's hourly wage from $10 to $15 is the movement from point _____ to point _____.

(e) The income effect of the increase in Hank's hourly wage from $10 to $15 is the movement from point _____ to point _____.

3.4 At age 50, Sondra finds herself in the unfortunate position of having neither retirement savings nor a pension benefit from her employer. For simplicity, let's assume that Sondra knows that she'll die at age 80. Her salary is $30,000 per year, and the price of consumption is $1 per unit.

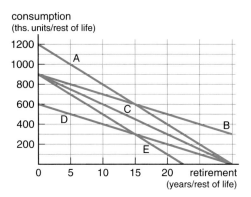

(a) Which line in the figure is the budget line governing the opportunities Sondra faces over the rest of her life?

(b) Draw an indifference curve so that Sondra chooses to retire in 15 years (i.e., at age 65).

(c) Sondra's employer introduces a pension plan. The plan pays Sondra $10,000 per year during retirement. Her salary remains at $30,000 per year while she works. Which line in the figure is Sondra's new budget line?

(d) Draw a second indifference curve, consistent with the first, to illustrate Sondra's retirement choice with the pension plan. Does she retire sooner or later?

3.5 Lois and Clark have the same preferences over leisure and consumption, two normal goods. They also have the same daily nonlabor income, $20, and hourly wage rate, $10. But they differ in two ways. Lois lives next to her office, so it takes her no time to commute to work. Clark, however, loses an hour every day commuting if he works at all. If Clark works, his employer provides a clean uniform for him every day. Lois, however, must have a clean business suit every day she works; if Lois works, her daily dry-cleaning cost is $5. Assume the price of the consumption good is $1.

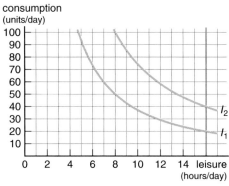

(a) Mark the common endowment point with an E in the figure.

(b) Use an open point to mark Lois's (l,c) if she pays for daily dry cleaning but puts in no hours at work; mark this point with L. Also, use C to mark the open point associated with Clark commuting to and from work without putting in any time at work.

(c) Draw Lois's budget line through L and Clark's budget line through C. Who has the bigger budget set?

(d) Lois and Clark both work. Is one person better off than the other? If so, who?

(e) Who works a longer workday?

(f) What effect does an increase in the cost of dry cleaning have on Lois's reservation wage? With the higher cost of dry cleaning, is she more likely or less likely to work?

3.6 The indifference curves in the figure below illustrate Alice's preferences over weekly leisure l and weekly consumption c. Alice has 110 hours each week to allocate between work and leisure activities. If Alice works, she has no nonlabor income, but she earns $10 per hour. (The price of consumption is $1 per unit.) If she doesn't work, she receives government aid in the form of a $300 weekly cash grant.

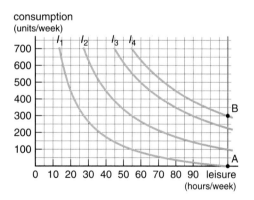

(a) Indicate the point in the figure that's Alice's endowment point with the $300 cash grant.

(b) Which indifference curve do we use to determine Alice's reservation wage?

(c) Draw a line from point A that's tangent to the indifference curve from your answer to the previous question. How is Alice's reservation wage related to this tangent line?

(d) Draw Alice's budget line in the figure. Illustrate all the pairs of leisure and consumption that are in Alice's budget set.

(e) Does Alice work? Use the budget line and tangent line to explain why she works or doesn't work.

3.7 Reuben splits the 16 nonsleeping hours of his day among market work, home work, and leisure time. He earns $10 per hour on his job, and the price of consumption is $1 per unit, so each hour of work in the market increases his consumption by 10 units per day. His home production function, the gray curve in the figure below, plots the relationship between hours of work at home and consumption. Reuben has no nonlabor income.

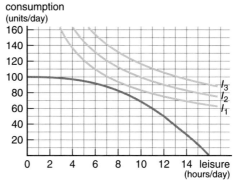

(a) Find Reuben's home production point H by drawing a budget line with slope -10 tangent to his home production function. [Hint: A line between 100 on the vertical axis and 10 on the horizontal axis has slope -10 and is "on the grid."]

(b) How many hours per day does Reuben devote to work at home?

(c) His work at home produces how many units of consumption per day?

(d) Find the tangency of the budget line through H with one of Reuben's indifference curves, and mark the point of tangency along the indifference curve with an X.

(e) How many hours does Reuben work on his job? How many hours of leisure does he enjoy?

(f) How much does Reuben earn per day, and what's his daily consumption?

References

Ashenfelter, Orley, Kirk Doran, and Bruce Schaller. 2010. "A Shred of Credible Evidence on the Long-Run Elasticity of Labour Supply." *Economica* 77(308): 637–650.

Becker, Gary S. 1965. "A Theory of the Allocation of Time." *Economic Journal* 75(299): 493–517.

Gronau, Reuben. 1977. "Leisure, Home Production, and Work—The Theory of the Allocation of Time Revisited." *Journal of Political Economy* 85(6): 1099–1123.

Hicks, J.R. 1946 (1939). *Value and Capital: An Inquiry into Some Fundamental Principles of Economic Theory*. London: Oxford University Press.

Lewis, H. Gregg. 1957. "Hours of Work and Hours of Leisure." In *Proceedings of the Ninth Annual Meeting*. Madison, WI: Industrial Relations Research Association, pp. 196–206.

4

Labor Demand

We are bombarded with images from around the world of back-breaking labor. In undeveloped regions, people work with only the simplest tools. A farmer plows the soil with a blade tied to an ox. A craftsman forms a table with a saw and chisel. A cabbie pedals tourists around in an oversized tricycle. In the language of economics, production in poor countries is labor-intensive.

A poor country like Ethiopia doesn't have access to the advanced technologies of developed countries like the United States, but the labor intensity of production in Ethiopia and other poor countries is more fundamental. Even if Ethiopia had the same technology as the United States, its production would be labor-intensive because wages in Ethiopia are so low. Differences in wages across countries help explain differences in labor intensities across countries.

This example illustrates an important principle that applies to every business, from a poor farmer in Ethiopia to technology giant Apple. An efficient mix of inputs depends on the prices of those inputs. Where the wage is low relative to the price of equipment (and other forms of capital), firms produce their goods and services with labor-intensive mixes of labor and capital. That's the Ethiopian farmer.

Our analysis of labor demand in chapter 2 specified factors that shift the labor demand curve and showed how the height of the labor demand curve measures the marginal value of labor. It was by no means superficial. But here we dig deeper to derive labor demand from the fundamentals of the production technology and a competitive firm's pursuit of profit.

Our analysis distinguishes between the short run and long run. Employment of labor can vary over short periods (e.g., day to day or week to week), but some inputs take quite a while to vary. We start by studying labor demand in the short run with equipment and other physical capital fixed. We also analyze how labor can substitute for other inputs (and vice versa) in the long run and explore how the time it takes to substitute between inputs impacts the elasticity of demand for labor.

4.1   Short-Run Labor Demand

Leisure Lawn is a competitive firm in the lawn-care business. Its workers use lawn mowers to cut the grass, weed whackers to trim the edges, and leaf blowers to remove the clippings. As a competitor, Leisure Lawn charges the market price for weekly lawn care, which is $30 per lawn. Leisure Lawn also operates in a competitive market for labor, so it pays its workers the going weekly wage of $300 per worker. To avoid the intricacies of measuring the cost of owned capital, let's assume that Leisure Lawn rents its mowers and other equipment in a competitive market, and the weekly rental price of capital is $200 per unit.

History matters. What Leisure Lawn can do this week depends on what it has done historically because changing capital—by investing or divesting—takes time. So we distinguish between choices that Leisure Lawn can implement quickly (i.e., in the short run) and those that take more time to implement. In particular, let's assume that Leisure Lawn can vary its employment of lawn-care workers in the short run; that is, labor is a **variable input** from week to week. Leisure Lawn's stock of mowers and other equipment, however, is fixed in the short run; capital is a **fixed input** week to week and perhaps within a season. In the long run, Leisure Lawn can vary its capital, too.

Leisure Lawn chooses how many workers to employ, and that choice depends on the value of the workers' contribution to production. So let's take a look at Leisure Lawn's production technology.

Production Function and the Total-Product Curve

The **production function** describes the technology that translates inputs into the output of a good or service. It links output q (e.g., the number of lawns cut per week) to the inputs of labor L (e.g., the number of lawn-care workers employed per week) and capital K (e.g., the number of lawn mowers used per week):

(4.1)
$$q = F(L, K)$$

where $F()$ is the production function. For instance, economists frequently work with a Cobb–Douglas production function: $F(L, K) = cL^a K^b$, where a and b are constants between zero and one and c is a positive number. (All the figures in this chapter derive from another production function, but let's leave the equation that describes that production function hidden in the background.)

TABLE 4.1. PRODUCTION RELATIONSHIPS

LABOR L (workers/week)	OUTPUT q (lawns/week)	AVERAGE PRODUCT OF LABOR AP_L (lawns/worker)	VALUE OF AVERAGE PRODUCT OF LABOR VAP_L ($/worker)	MARGINAL PRODUCT OF LABOR MP_L^* (lawns/worker)	MARGINAL PRODUCT OF LABOR MP_L (lawns/worker)	VALUE OF MARGINAL PRODUCT OF LABOR VMP_L ($/worker)
0	0				0.0	0
				3		
1	3	3.0	90		4.3	130
				6		
2	9	4.5	135		7.7	230
				8		
3	17	5.7	170		12.0	360
				12		
4	29	7.3	218		18.3	550
				18		
5	47	9.4	282		16.7	500
				16		
6	63	10.5	315		15.0	450
				—		
7	77	—	—		13.3	—
				12		
8	89	11.1	334		11.7	350
				11		
9	100	11.1	333		10.0	300
				9		
10	109	10.9	327		8.3	250
				8		
11	117	10.6	319		6.7	200
				6		
12	123	10.3	308		5.0	150

Notes: Capital is fixed at $K = 5$. Product price is $p = 30$. MP_L^* in column 5 compares output q across rows. MP_L in column 6 uses the slopes of lines tangent to the total-product curve. Entries in columns 3–6 are rounded.

How does output vary with employment of workers? The first two columns of Table 4.1 show how weekly output at Leisure Lawn varies with its weekly employment of labor for a fixed value of capital (at $K = 5$). Labor at Leisure Lawn is essential, as it is at most firms. If no one works, not one lawn gets cut. This principle is reflected in the first row of Table 4.1: $q = 0$ if $L = 0$. A second principle is that labor is productive, so employing more workers increases output. Because labor is productive, the number of lawns cut increases with the number of lawn-care workers it employs across the rows in Table 4.1. The pairs of employment L and output q in the table generate points (L, q) on the **total-product curve** in Figure 4.1. (Varying part-time employment traces out the curve between each pair of points.)

Average and Marginal Products of Labor

Businesses care a lot about worker productivity, and one measure of productivity is output per worker. We call this measure the **average product of labor**, which divides output by labor input: $AP_L \equiv q/L$. Since output depends on the input of labor, the average product of labor is a function of labor: $AP_L \equiv F(L; K)/L$. (The semicolon preceding K indicates that capital is held fixed at K in the expression.) Leisure Lawn's average product of labor in the third column of Table 4.1 is

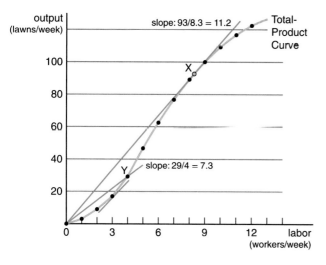

FIGURE 4.1. Total-Product Curve

Capital K is constant along Leisure Lawn's total-product curve $q = F(L; K)$.

The average product of labor q/L is 7.3 lawns/worker at $L = 4$, which is the slope of the ray to point Y: $(29 - 0)/(4 - 0) = 7.3$.

The marginal product of labor $\Delta q / \Delta L$ is the slope of the tangent to the total-product curve at each L. Labor's marginal product is 12 lawns/worker at $L = 3$ and falls to 5 lawns/worker at $L = 12$.

Average and marginal products of labor are equal at X, the point where a ray is tangent to the total-product curve.

output in the second column divided by labor input in the first column. Figure 4.2 illustrates the relationship between this measure of productivity and employment at Leisure Lawn. The average-product-of-labor curve is an inverted U that peaks with 8.3 workers employed each week cutting 11.2 lawns per worker.

An alternative measure of labor productivity computes the impact on production of small changes in the employment of labor. This **marginal product of labor** MP_L is the ratio of the change in output Δq to the change in labor ΔL, holding capital fixed: $MP_L \equiv \Delta q / \Delta L$. Table 4.1's fifth column displays marginal

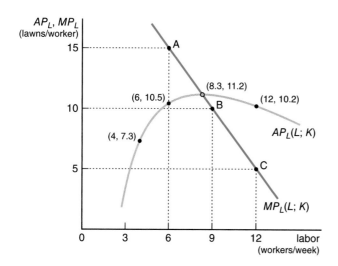

FIGURE 4.2. Average- and Marginal-Product Curves

Leisure Lawn's average- and marginal-products-of-labor curves are derived from its total-product curve in Figure 4.1.

Diminishing marginal productivity of labor applies to employment beyond $L = 4$. The marginal-product-of-labor curve MP_L slopes down for $L > 4$ and intersects its average-product-of-labor curve AP_L at the peak of the AP_L curve.

For $L < 8.3$, labor's marginal product exceeds its average product. At $L = 8.3$, the two curves intersect. For $L > 8.3$, the average product of labor is greater than it's marginal product.

products of labor for one-worker changes in labor (i.e., $\Delta L = 1$). For example, employing a sixth worker raises production at Leisure Lawn by 16 lawns per week, from 47 to 63 lawns per week. So the marginal product of labor is 16 lawns per worker between $L = 5$ and $L = 6$. Labor's marginal product starts low, rises to a maximum as employment at Leisure Lawn increases from 4 to 5 workers, and declines from there.

 PRACTICE Some entries in Table 4.1 are missing. Compute the average product of labor at $L = 7$ and the marginal product of labor from $L = 6$ to $L = 7$, and enter your results in the table.

For small changes in labor, the marginal product of labor at some L is the slope of the total-product curve at that L. For instance, the slope of the line that's tangent to the total-product curve at $L = 6$ in Figure 4.1 is 15 lawns per worker. (This isn't obvious; it's calculated in the background using the formula for the production function.) So the marginal product of labor in the neighborhood of $L = 6$ is 15 lawns per worker. The sixth column of Table 4.1 lists marginal products of labor calculated for these truly marginal changes in labor. Labor's marginal product increases with employment up to $L = 4$. The principle of **diminishing marginal productivity** applies beyond $L = 4$, so the marginal product of labor decreases with employment beyond the fourth worker. Figure 4.2 illustrates labor's marginal-product curve. Although the MP_L curve also has an inverted-U shape, only the downward-sloping part appears in the figure.

How are the average- and marginal-product-of-labor curves related? Let's think about the relationship between averages and marginals outside our production context before applying what we learn to production. The average score on the 10 quizzes I graded this morning is 85. Oops, I just found another student's quiz in my backpack. The score on that quiz is 96. Since the score on this marginal quiz (i.e., the eleventh) exceeds the average score of 85 among the first 10 quizzes, bringing the eleventh quiz into the average raises the average (from 85 to 86). If the score on the misplaced quiz had been below 85, then bringing it—the marginal quiz—into the average would have reduced the average. So the average rises (falls) if the marginal is greater (less) than the average.

And that's what we see in Figure 4.2. Over low levels of employment at Leisure Lawn, the marginal product of labor exceeds the average product of labor, and the average-product curve slopes up. The average-product-of-labor curve slopes down over higher-employment levels where the marginal-product curve lies below the average-product curve. And finally, labor's marginal-product curve crosses its average curve at the peak of the average curve. At the intersection, which corresponds to point X in Figure 4.1, Leisure Lawn employs 8.3 workers who cut 93 lawns each week. Output per worker is 11.2 ($= 93 \div 8.3$) lawns per worker, which is also the marginal product of labor with 8.3 workers employed.

PRACTICE Leisure Lawn adds some equipment for its workers to use. Suppose this increase in capital increases the marginal product of labor. What happens to the total-product curve in Figure 4.1 and the average- and marginal-product curves in Figure 4.2?

. . . .

ADVANCED We can derive the relationship between the average- and marginal-product-of-labor curves from the total-product curve in Figure 4.1. The figure includes a ray from the origin that is tangent to the total-product curve. The tangency is point X with 8.3 workers cutting 93 lawns per week. The slope of the ray ($= 93 \div 8.3 = 11.2$) reveals the average product of labor at the tangency X. (The rise is q and the run is L, so the slope q/L is the AP_L at $L = 8.3$.) A ray to any other point on the total-product curve (e.g., point Y) is flatter than the tangent ray, so the average product of labor peaks at X.

Since the ray is tangent at X, the slope of the total-product curve (i.e., the marginal product of labor) at X is also 11.2 lawns per worker. Therefore, the average product of labor equals the marginal product of labor at the tangency point X, which is where the average product of labor peaks.

For points shy of X, the total-product curve is steeper than the ray to the curve. For points beyond X, the marginal product of labor is less than the slope of the ray. Therefore, the marginal-product-of-labor curve is above (below) the average-product-of-labor curve for $L < 8.3$ ($L > 8.3$).

. . . .

Profit

For Leisure Lawn and other firms, sales revenue, productivity, investment returns, and so forth influence the bottom line, but the bottom line is profit. Profit π subtracts cost C from revenue R.

Since Leisure Lawn operates in a competitive lawn-care market, its weekly revenue is simply the $30 price per lawn times the number of lawns it cuts per week; more generally, revenue R is proportional to output q: $R \equiv pq$, where p is the price of the product. Columns 1 and 3 of Table 4.2 list the relationship between Leisure Lawn's revenue and its employment of labor. Raising employment from 9 to 10 workers per week raises production by 9 lawns per week and revenue by $270 ($= \$30 \times 9$) per week since the price of lawn care is $30 per lawn.

It costs money to run a business, and Leisure Lawn's costs vary with the number of workers it employs. Table 4.2 lists the relationship between cost and employment in columns 1 and 4. Since Leisure Lawn is a competitive firm in the labor market, its weekly cost of labor is simply $300 per worker. Capital is fixed at 5 units, and the weekly cost of capital is $200 per unit, so Leisure Lawn's fixed cost is $1,000 ($= \$200 \times 5$) per week. (See the cost entry in the table's first row.) Since each worker adds $300 to Leisure Lawn's weekly costs, cost grows $300 from row to row.

TABLE 4.2. REVENUE, COST, AND PROFIT

LABOR L (workers/week)	OUTPUT q (lawns/week)	REVENUE R ($/week)	COST C ($/week)	PROFIT π ($/week)
0	0	0	1,000	−1,000
1	3	90	1,300	−1,210
2	9	270	1,600	−1,330
3	17	510	1,900	−1,390
4	29	870	2,200	−1,330
5	47	1,410	2,500	−1,090
6	63	1,890	2,800	−910
7	77	2,310	3,100	−790
8	89	2,670	3,400	−730
9	100	3,000	3,700	−700
10	109	3,270	4,000	−730
11	117	3,510	4,300	−790
12	123	3,690	4,600	−910

Notes: Capital is fixed at $K = 5$. The price of lawn care is $30 per lawn, the wage is $300 per worker, and the price of capital is $200 per unit. Fixed cost is $1,000 (= $200 × 5) per week.

Leisure Lawn's profit varies with its employment of lawn-care workers. See columns 1 and 5 of Table 4.2. All the values of profit are negative, which implies that Leisure Lawn can't turn a profit if the price is $30 per lawn, the weekly wage is $300 per worker, and the rental price of capital is $200 per unit. Nevertheless, some levels of employment are more profitable (i.e., losses are smaller) than others.

Profit-Maximizing Choice of Employment

Leisure Lawn chooses labor to maximize profit with capital fixed in the short run. A principle that unifies economics is that maximizing choices compares benefits and costs *at the margin*. In this case, the *margin* refers to small changes in labor. Does a little more labor increase or decrease profit? The answer depends on how many workers the firm employs. For instance, adding a seventh worker might increase profit, but adding a twelfth worker might decrease profit. To pinpoint Leisure Lawn's employment choice, we investigate the benefits and costs of marginal changes in employment.

How does a marginal increase in labor affect Leisure Lawn's revenue? In chapter 2, we called the answer to this question the *marginal value of labor*. Marginal value is a powerful and general concept in economics. Indeed, we could study the marginal value of steam turbines in industry or ponder your marginal value of breakfast burritos. In the context of employment, however, we can be more specific.

Increasing employment by one worker increases Leisure Lawn's output by MP_L lawns per worker. At $L = 6$ in Table 4.1, Leisure Lawn's marginal product of labor MP_L is 15 lawns per worker. A marginal increase in labor from $L = 6$ raises production by 15 lawns per worker, and each of those extra cut lawns pays Leisure Lawn $30. Consequently, increasing labor raises Leisure Lawn's weekly revenue $450 $(= \$30 \times 15)$ per worker in the neighborhood of $L = 6$. Indeed, the change in revenue from a marginal increase in labor is the price of the product times labor's marginal product, which we call the **value of marginal product of labor**.

(4.2)
$$VMP_L \equiv p \times MP_L(L; K)$$

Since the product price is measured in dollars per lawn and the marginal product of labor is measured in lawns per worker, we measure labor's value of marginal product VMP_L in dollars per worker.

Table 4.1 lists the value of labor's marginal product and the analogous value of labor's average product $(VAP_L \equiv p \times q/L)$ at Leisure Lawn, and Figure 4.3 plots Leisure Lawn's VMP_L and VAP_L curves. With a low price such as $p = 2$, we could plot the VMP_L and VAP_L curves with the MP_L and AP_L curves in Figure 4.2. With $p = 2$, each point on the VMP_L curve is twice as high as the corresponding point on the MP_L (and similarly for the VAP_L and AP_L curves). More generally, we plot the VMP_L and VAP_L curves on a separate graph by changing the scale of the vertical axis. The vertical-axis units in Figure 4.3 are 30 times larger than the units in Figure 4.2 (and in dollars rather than lawns). Otherwise, the two graphs are identical.

 PRACTICE Suppose Leisure Lawn employs 7 workers per week. What are its values of the average product and marginal product of labor? Enter your answers in the fourth and seventh columns of Table 4.1, and mark these points on the VAP_L and VMP_L curves in Figure 4.3.

How does employing one more worker influence the cost of labor? The concept that answers this question is **marginal labor cost**. Since Leisure Lawn competes for lawn-care workers, the answer is simple: labor cost rises by the wage w. (In chapter 2, we derived marginal labor cost for a monopsonist; the derivation was more complex, and the answer was different.) One more worker means one more payment of the wage every week. So Leisure Lawn's marginal labor cost is a constant, which Figure 4.3 displays with the flat line at $300 per worker.

In the short run, a competitor maximizes profit by choosing employment to equate labor's value of marginal product with the wage. To see why, let's run through a series of marginal changes and trace their effects on profit. If Leisure Lawn employs 6 workers, we see in Figure 4.3 that $VMP_L > w$. In particular, a marginal increase in employment from $L = 6$ drives weekly revenue up by $450 (i.e., VMP_L at $L = 6$) and weekly cost up by $300 (i.e., w). Since $VMP_L - w = 150$ at $L = 6$, the marginal increase in labor raises Leisure Lawn's weekly profit by $150 per worker. Clearly, $L = 6$ doesn't maximize Leisure Lawn's

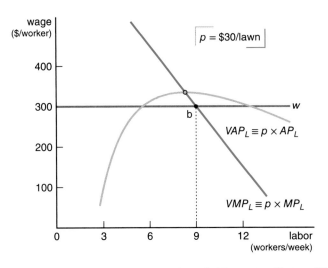

Leisure Lawn's product price is $30/lawn, so its VAP_L and VMP_L multiply its AP_L and MP_L curves by $30. This multiplication changes only the scale of the vertical axis.

As a competitive profit-maximizing firm, Leisure Lawn chooses employment to equate VMP_L and w at point b.

If the weekly wage is $300/worker, then Leisure Lawn maximizes its profit by employing 9 workers/week. At $L = 9$, VMP_L equals $300/worker.

FIGURE 4.3. Profit-Maximizing Choice of Employment

profit. And there's nothing special about $L = 6$. Any level of employment where the value-of-marginal-product curve is above the wage line (i.e., any $L < 9$ in Figure 4.3) leads to the same conclusion: profit grows by increasing employment.

Next let's try $L = 12$. A marginal increase in labor from $L = 12$ drives weekly revenue up by $150 and weekly cost up by $300. Since $VMP_L - w = -150$ at $L = 12$, a marginal increase in labor from $L = 12$ lowers profit by $150 per worker. A marginal *decrease* in labor from $L = 12$, therefore, increases profit by $150 per worker. Employing 12 workers doesn't maximize Leisure Lawn's profit, and there's nothing special about $L = 12$. Any level of employment where the value-of-marginal-product curve is below the wage line (i.e., any $L > 9$ in Figure 4.3) leads to the same conclusion: profit grows by decreasing employment.

 PRACTICE

Does $L = 8$ maximize Leisure Lawn's profit? In Figure 4.3, is the VMP_L curve at $L = 8$ above or below the wage line w? Use the positions of VMP_L and w at $L = 8$ to determine whether increasing employment a small amount raises or lowers Leisure Lawn's profit. Use Table 4.1 to quantify how a marginal increase in labor from $L = 8$ changes profit.

Having established that (1) any level of employment below 9 workers fails to maximize profit and (2) any level of employment above 9 workers also fails to maximize profit, we are left with a single logical possibility: employing 9 workers maximizes profit. Generally, we find a competitor's quantity demanded of labor in the short run at the intersection of the downward-sloping value-of-marginal-product-of-labor curve with the flat wage line. Leisure Lawn employs lawn-care workers until the value of the marginal product of labor is driven down to the wage. That is, employment adjusts to align labor's value of marginal product with the wage.

With Leisure Lawn's capital fixed at $K = 5$ in the short run, Leisure Lawn employs 9 lawn-care workers and cuts 100 lawns each week, which generates $3,000 (= 30×100) in revenue. Leisure Lawn's weekly cost of capital—its fixed cost—is $1,000 (= 200×5), and its weekly cost of labor is $2,700 (= 300×9). Profit is −$700. That is, the bottom line is that the best Leisure Lawn can do—faced with these prices for its product and its inputs—is to lose $700 per week. Ouch!

Short-Run Labor Demand Curve

We are ready to derive a competitor's short-run demand for labor. Let's change the wage and check how Leisure Lawn adjusts its employment of lawn-care workers.

The weekly wage of lawn-care workers falls from $300 to $200 per worker, so the wage line in Figure 4.4 shifts down from $w = 300$ to $w = 200$. As a profit-maximizing competitor, Leisure Lawn chooses how many workers to employ by equating labor's value of marginal product to the new $200 wage. That is, Leisure Lawn expands its workforce along its VMP_L curve from 9 workers to 11 workers.

For each wage, we read Leisure Lawn's quantity demanded of labor off the VMP_L curve. Therefore, the value of marginal product of labor is the competitive firm's **short-run labor demand curve**. The source of the downward-sloping demand for labor in the short run is diminishing marginal productivity of labor.

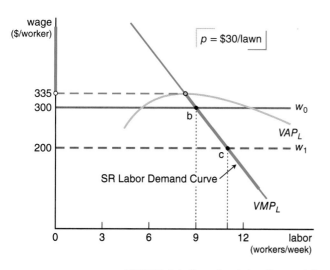

For a weekly wage less than $335/worker, Leisure Lawn's short-run (SR) labor demand curve and its VMP_L curve are the same relationship. Leisure Lawn's employment varies with w along the VMP_L curve.

For $w > 335$, Leisure Lawn shuts down (i.e., sets $L = 0$) because revenue wouldn't cover variable cost wL. That is, its quantity demanded of labor is zero for any wage above the shutdown wage.

FIGURE 4.4. Short-Run Labor Demand Curve

PRACTICE   Suppose the weekly wage is $250 per worker. Sketch the appropriate wage line in Figure 4.4. What quantity of labor does Leisure Lawn demand at the $250 wage?

Although we frequently refer to labor's value-of-marginal-product curve as the short-run labor demand curve of a competitive firm, the statement is a bit loose for two reasons. First, the VMP_L curve involves a vertical interpretation: its units are dollars per worker for each level of employment. The labor demand curve involves a horizontal interpretation of *the same relationship*: its units are workers per week for each value of the wage.

Second, if the wage is high enough, a firm like Leisure Lawn suspends business to avoid deeper losses. Leisure Lawn bears its cost of capital (i.e., its fixed cost) whether it produces or suspends production. So Leisure Lawn stops cutting lawns if its revenue fails to cover its labor costs: $R^* < wL^*$. (R^* and L^* denote the profit-maximizing values of revenue and labor if Leisure Lawn is open for business.) By dividing both sides of the inequality by L^*, we find that Leisure Lawn's quantity demanded of labor is zero for any wage greater than the value of labor's average product: $VAP_L < w$. Therefore, the short-run labor demand curve includes points along the vertical axis where the wage is greater than the **shutdown wage**, which is $335 per worker in this case.

Factors that Shift Labor Demand in the Short Run

What factors shift the short-run demand for labor? A payoff from deriving labor demand from the fundamentals of production is that profit maximization discloses the factors that shift labor demand. For instance, the rental price of capital r has no effect on short-run labor demand because r influences neither the VMP_L curve nor the shutdown wage. Since capital is fixed in the short run, its price is irrelevant for the firm's choice. But product price p, capital K, and the production function $F()$ do influence the VMP_L curve, the shutdown wage, and the demand for labor in the short run.

Key Principle. Innovations that raise workers' productivity increase employment and wages even though firms don't need as many workers after the innovations.

Higher product price, capital investment, and innovations that increase the productivity of workers increase the demand for labor. First, increasing the price of lawn care from $30 to $40 per lawn shifts up the VMP_L curve, increasing Leisure Lawn's quantity demanded of lawn-care workers at every wage. Second, if having more equipment to work with raises the marginal product of labor, then increasing capital (e.g., from 5 units to 6 units) increases labor's value of marginal product, shifting up the VMP_L curve and increasing the quantity demanded of labor at every wage. Alternatively, if increasing capital lowers the marginal product of labor, then the VMP_L curve shifts down, and short-run labor demand falls. Third, the process works the same way for innovations in the production technology: innovations that raise (lower) the marginal product of labor shift the VMP_L curve up (down) and increase (decrease) the demand for labor in the short run.

Our analysis of profit maximization clarifies a key principle from chapters 1 and 2. An innovation increases the demand for labor if it enhances labor productivity. (Recall how this principle illuminates historical innovations like the cotton gin and the assembly line.) Popular thought focuses on the innovation's effect on the product of labor: the innovation increases production, so fewer workers are needed. What's relevant for a profit maximizer, however, is the innovation's effect on the value of marginal product of labor. A profit-maximizing firm doesn't maintain production. It seizes the opportunity offered by a more productive workforce to increase employment and output.

 **PRACTICE**

The value of the marginal product of labor is the effect of a marginal increase in labor on the revenue of a firm in a competitive product market. For an employer without competitors in the product market, the **marginal revenue product of labor** tells us how revenue varies with marginal changes in labor: $MRP_L \equiv MR \times MP_L$. Carefully explain why, for a product market monopolist, marginal revenue MR replaces product price p in the condition for profit maximization (i.e., Equation 4.2). Removing or reducing competition in the product market has what effect on the demand for labor?

Payroll Tax and Short-Run Labor Demand

We concluded in chapter 2 that employer responsibility for a per-worker tax on labor decreases the demand for labor. The labor demand curve shifts down by the size of the tax. Let's see why. Since the government taxes the employer, marginal labor cost with the tax is $w + t$. To equate benefits and costs at the margin, Leisure Lawn's choice of employment solves $VMP_L = w + t$, or $VMP_L - t = w$. For each value of the wage w, Leisure Lawn chooses employment at the intersection of $VMP_L - t$ and the wage line. That is, the labor demand curve lies t dollars per worker below labor's value-of-marginal-product curve.

A payroll tax also reduces the demand for labor. Suppose t is the tax *rate* on an employer's payroll wL. Leisure Lawn's cost of labor with the payroll tax is $(1 + t)wL$, so its marginal labor cost is $(1 + t)w$. Leisure Lawn maximizes profit in the short run by choosing employment to equate VMP_L and $(1 + t)w$, or equivalently $VMP_L/(1 + t) = w$. If $t = .25$, then $1/(1 + t) = .8$, and the payroll tax scales down Leisure Lawn's short-run demand for labor from its VMP_L curve by 20 percent. So a payroll tax on employers also reduces the short-run demand for labor.

Like a tax on labor imposed on firms, government-mandated benefits, regulatory burden, and litigation costs also reduce the demand for labor. Regulations raise the gross cost of labor and consequently reduce labor demand. For instance, a government-mandated benefit shifts down the labor demand curve by the cost per worker, so it's like a per-worker tax levied on employers. If, however, a regulation generates a cost that's proportional to the payroll wL, then it scales down labor demand like a constant payroll tax rate. The details differ, but a single principle applies: regulations that raise businesses' costs of employing workers reduce the demand for labor.

4.2   Long-Run Labor Demand

Employers like Leisure Lawn have another option in the long run. Capital is fixed in the short run, but Leisure Lawn can vary its mowers and other equipment over time. With enough time, it can pick any amount for its capital. That is, capital is a variable input in the long run.

That Leisure Lawn can vary its capital in the long run introduces an entirely new issue. What's the best mix of labor and capital? Profit maximization in the long run requires an efficient mix of labor and capital. To find the efficient mix of inputs, we solve the cost-minimization problem using isoquant curves and isocost lines.

Production Function and Isoquant Curves

With capital as a variable input, we illustrate the production technology with isoquant curves. An **isoquant curve** collects all the pairs of labor and capital that produce a particular output q, such as 100 lawns per week. The equation $100 = F(L, K)$ implicitly defines Leisure Lawn's $q = 100$ isoquant curve. Replace 100 with q to define the isoquant curve for each level of output q.

Figure 4.5, a graph with labor and capital on the axes, displays three of Leisure Lawn's isoquant curves. Leisure Lawn can cut 100 lawns per week with 9 workers

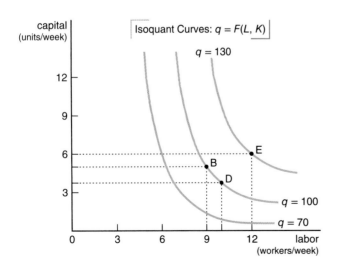

FIGURE 4.5. Isoquant Curves

Pairs of labor and capital that lie on an isoquant curve (e.g., isoquant $q = 100$) produce the same number of cut lawns. The pairs of L and K at points B = (9, 5) and D = (10, 3.75) cut 100 lawns/week. Labor–capital pairs on higher isoquant curves (e.g., E on $q = 130$) produce more output.

Isoquant curves slope down and don't cross. Diminishing marginal productivities of labor and capital imply that isoquant curves bow toward the origin.

using 5 units of capital (point B in the figure) or with 10 workers using 3.75 units of capital (point D). So B and D are two points on isoquant $q = 100$. At E, Leisure Lawn employs 12 workers using 6 units of capital. Since labor and capital are both productive, the added workers and capital (compared to either B or D) raise production to 130 lawns per week. Every other mix of labor and capital on isoquant $q = 130$ also cuts 130 lawns.

The properties of isoquant curves echo the properties of indifference curves.

- *Isoquant curves slope down.* Since labor and capital are both productive, employing more labor increases output unless capital falls. So more labor must be paired with less capital to preserve output along an isoquant curve.

- *An isoquant curve cuts through every mix of labor and capital.* If 9 workers use 5 units of capital to cut 100 lawns per week, then the labor–capital mix at B in Figure 4.5 is on isoquant $q = 100$.

- *Isoquant curves don't cross.* Nine workers use 5 units of capital to cut 100 lawns per week—no more, no less—so point B can't be on isoquant $q = 100$ *and* also be on some other isoquant curve.

- *Isoquant curves bow toward the origin.* That is, as we move from capital-intensive mixes of labor and capital (i.e., northwest points) to labor-intensive mixes (i.e., southeast points) along an isoquant curve, the curve flattens. This property is related to the diminishing marginal productivity of labor and capital.

To establish the relationship between marginal products and the curvature of isoquant curves, let's explore substitution of capital for labor along an isoquant. Between B and D in Figure 4.5, the rate of substitution of capital for labor is 1.25 $(= (5 - 3.75)/(10 - 9))$ units of capital per worker. For marginal changes in labor and capital around some point such as B, the rate of substitution of capital for labor along an isoquant curve is (in absolute value) the slope of the isoquant curve at B. We call this slope the **marginal rate of technical substitution** *MRTS* (or the marginal rate of substitution in production MRS_P).

As labor increases, the output-preserving reduction in capital depends on the marginal products of labor and capital. At point B in the figure, with nine workers, the marginal product of labor is 10 lawns per worker. (Refer to Table 4.1.) Employing another worker, therefore, expands Leisure Lawn's output by 10 lawns per week. Let's couple this increase in labor with some change in capital to keep Leisure Lawn cutting 100 lawns per week. The change in capital must reduce weekly lawns cut by 10 to preserve output at $q = 100$. Since the marginal product of capital is 6.7 lawns per unit of capital at B and capital falls from 5 units to 3.5 units per week, Leisure Lawn cuts 10 fewer lawns: $6.7 \times (3.5 - 5) = -10$. The change in capital along isoquant $q = 100$ is -1.5 $(= -10 \div 6.7)$ units of capital per worker, which is (in absolute value) the ratio of the two marginal products at B.

In general, the marginal rate of technical substitution is

$$(4.3) \qquad MRTS \equiv \frac{MP_L}{MP_K}$$

And this makes sense. The isoquant curve is steeper if the marginal product of labor is high because the fall in capital must be big to keep output fixed as employment grows. If the marginal product of labor is low, capital doesn't have to fall much to hold output fixed, so the isoquant curve is relatively flat.

 PRACTICE Suppose Leisure Lawn employs 4 workers using 3 units of capital to cut 16 lawns each week. The marginal products of labor and capital are 16 lawns per worker and 8 lawns per unit of capital. Employing a fifth worker raises production by how many lawns per week? How much must capital fall to preserve output at 16? What is the marginal rate of technical substitution at (4,3) in Figure 4.5? Is the isoquant curve at (4,3) steeper or flatter than the isoquant curve at B?

ADVANCED Let's derive the expression for the marginal rate of technical substitution. The definition of marginal product tells us that $MP_L \times \Delta L$ and $MP_K \times \Delta K$ give the changes in output from marginal changes in labor ΔL and capital ΔK. Simultaneous marginal changes in labor and capital cause output to change by $MP_L \Delta L + MP_K \Delta K = \Delta q$.

If these marginal changes in inputs move along an isoquant curve, then Δq equals zero. That is,

$$(4.4) \qquad MP_L \Delta L + MP_K \Delta K = 0$$

We find the slope of the isoquant curve by solving this expression for $\Delta K / \Delta L = -MP_L / MP_K$. Hence the marginal rate of technical substitution is the ratio of the marginal products.

Isoquant curves that bow toward the origin exhibit diminishing marginal rate of technical substitution. That is, each isoquant curve flattens as we move down along the curve from more capital-intensive to more labor-intensive mixes of labor and capital. Diminishing marginal productivities of both labor and capital drive the diminishing marginal rate of technical substitution. In Figure 4.5, isoquant curve $q = 100$ is flatter at D than at B *because* the marginal product of labor is lower and the marginal product of capital is higher at D than at B. Compared to B, D has more labor, which lowers the MP_L, and less capital, which raises the MP_K. Lowering the numerator and raising the denominator in Equation 4.3 decreases *MRTS*.

Cost Function and Isocost Lines

How much does each mix of labor and capital cost? We address this question graphically using isocost lines. Cost is the sum of labor cost wL and capital cost rK. (Recall that r is the rental price of capital.)

(4.5) $$C = wL + rK$$

With $w = 300$ and $r = 200$, mixes of labor and capital that cost Leisure Lawn $3,700 per week satisfy $3700 = 300L + 200K$. Figure 4.6 plots this isocost line. Nine workers using 5 units of capital cost Leisure Lawn $3,700 (= ($300 × 9) + ($200 × 5)) per week. The weekly cost of employing 12.3 workers with no capital is also $3,700. And any mix of labor and capital on the line through these points also costs $3,700 per week.

Replacing cost C with various numbers generates a family of isocost lines, one for each value of C. To see why, let's treat cost C as a constant (like the input prices w and r) rather than as a variable (like the inputs L and K). Then $K = C/r - (w/r)L$ defines an **isocost line**—combinations of L and K that cost the same—for each value of cost C. The position of each line is set by its cost C, but all the isocost lines share a common slope $-w/r$, which we call the wage–rental ratio. Changing C moves us to a different isocost line, such as from isocost $3,700 to isocost $3,000 in Figure 4.6. Varying the wage w, however, changes the whole family of isocost lines: every isocost line is flatter if w is lower.

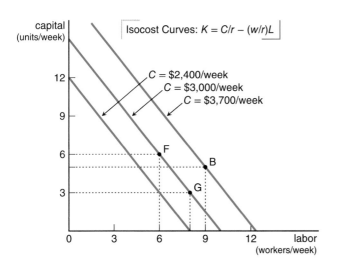

The wage rate is $300/worker, and the rental price of capital is $200/unit, so $K = C/200 - 1.5L$ is the equation of the isocost line with cost C. Isocost lines are parallel, and these isocost lines share a slope of –1.5.

Nine workers with 5 units of capital (i.e., point B) cost Leisure Lawn $3,700/week. Points F and G are two mixes of labor and capital that cost Leisure Lawn $3,000/week. On what isocost line is the point with $L = 4$ and $K = 3$?

FIGURE 4.6. Isocost Lines

Cost-Minimizing Mix of Labor and Capital

To maximize profit, a firm must choose the right quantity to supply, and it must produce that output efficiently. Every principles of microeconomics course carefully covers a competitor's profit-maximizing choice of output, and we revisit the key principle (i.e., $MC = p$) below. But a firm must also operate efficiently to maximize profit. That is, it must find and implement the cost-minimizing mix of labor and capital for any level of output.

What's the least-cost way for Leisure Lawn to cut 100 lawns per week? That is, what's the efficient mix of labor and capital? **Cost minimization** involves finding Leisure Lawn's lowest isocost line that reaches its output of 100 lawns. Leisure Lawn minimizes its cost of cutting 100 lawns by choosing its mix of labor and capital at the tangency of an isocost line to isoquant curve $q = 100$, point B in Figure 4.7. Each week, 9 workers (i.e., $L^* = 9$) use 5 units of capital (i.e., $K^* = 5$) to cut 100 lawns at a cost of $3,700. Any other mix of labor and capital on $q = 100$ (e.g., D′) is on a higher isocost line and costs more. Any less-costly mix of labor and capital (e.g., F) falls short of the 100-lawn target for production.

An efficient mix of inputs equalizes the "production bang" for the "input-price buck" across inputs. Point B in Figure 4.7 is an efficient mix of inputs because

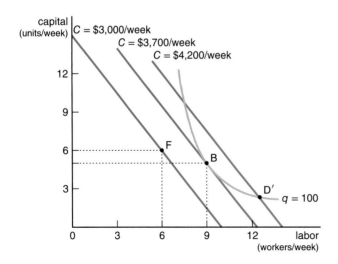

Employing 9 workers and 5 machines (i.e., the mix of labor and capital at point B) minimizes Leisure Lawn's cost of cutting 100 lawns each week. It's weekly cost is $3,700. Any other $K–L$ mix on isoquant 100 (e.g., D′) costs more: it lies on a higher isocost line. Lower cost $K–L$ mixes (e.g., F) don't cut 100 lawns/week.

At the efficient mix of labor and capital B, the slope of the isoquant curve equals the slope of the isocost line, which means that the marginal rate of technical substitution $MRTS$ equals the wage–rental ratio w/r.

FIGURE 4.7. Cost-Minimizing Mix of Labor and Capital

the isocost line is tangent to the isoquant curve at B. Thus the slope of the isocost $(-w/r)$ equals the slope of the isoquant curve $(-MP_L/MP_K)$. This property implies that marginal products per dollar are equated across labor and capital.

$$(4.6) \qquad \frac{MP_L}{w} = \frac{MP_K}{r}$$

At B, Leisure Lawn employs 9 workers using 5 units of capital. The marginal product of labor and capital are 10 lawns per worker and 6.7 lawns per unit of capital. Since the weekly input prices are $300 per worker and $200 per unit of capital, the ratios of marginal product to input price are 10/300 for labor and 6.7/200 for capital. These ratios are equal. Alternatively, if $MP_L/w > MP_K/r$, then Leisure Lawn could drive down its cost of cutting 100 lawns by substituting out of low "bang-for-the-buck" capital and into high "bang-for-the-buck" labor.

The efficient mix of labor and capital depends on the ratio of the wage to the rental price of capital. If the weekly wage falls from $300 to $200 per worker, the family of isocost lines gets flatter; in particular, the slope of each isocost line falls (in absolute value) from 1.5 to 1.0. In response to the lower wage, Leisure Lawn substitutes out of capital into labor, so its production becomes more labor-intensive. The tangency of one of these new, flatter isocost lines to the $q = 100$ isoquant curve is southeast of B on isoquant curve $q = 100$.

The magnitude of this substitution of capital for labor depends on the curvature of the isoquant. An isoquant curve that is close to linear affords enormous substitution possibilities, and Leisure Lawn's turn to labor-intensive production could be dramatic. Alternatively, if the isoquant curve is very curved, Leisure Lawn's move to a more labor-intensive mix of labor and capital could be negligible.

We measure the curvature of an isoquant curve, as well as substitution of labor for capital along an isoquant curve, by the **elasticity of substitution** of labor for capital, which can depend on the quantities of labor and capital.

$$(4.7) \qquad \sigma = \frac{\Delta(K/L)}{\Delta(w/r)} \times \frac{w/r}{K/L} \geq 0$$

where σ is the Greek letter sigma. Isoquant curves with less curvature (i.e., closer to lines) have higher values of σ and more substitution of capital for labor along the isoquant. The elasticity of substitution σ is smaller for isoquant curves with more curvature (i.e., closer to right angles).

Application: Cross-Country Differences in Capital Intensity

Have you every wondered why production in poor countries is so labor-intensive? To be sure, production technologies differ across countries, but differences in the relative prices of labor and capital cause cross-country differences in the mixes of labor and capital. Production in poor countries is labor-intensive because labor is so inexpensive in these countries.

A classic paper on production by Arrow, Chenery, Minhas, and Solow (1961) set the gold standard for working with substitution along an isoquant curve. They introduced a production function that summarizes substitutability of labor and capital along an isoquant curve with a single constant, the elasticity of substitution. And that constant allows us to connect cross-country differences in capital intensity to cross-country differences in wage–rental ratios.

Production in Japan was very labor-intensive in the 1950s. In fact, the capital–labor ratio K/L in the typical U.S. manufacturing industry was 10 times the capital–labor ratio in Japanese manufacturing (Arrow et al. 1961, Table 5). The U.S. capital–labor ratio was about 50 times higher in agriculture, 9 times higher in the production of nonferrous metals, and 3.4 times higher in the production of electricity. But the wage–rental ratios w/r were also higher in the United States: for 12 manufacturing industries, the average wage–rental ratio in the United States was 11 times the average wage–rental ratio in Japan. Wage–rental ratios in the United States were 27 times higher in agriculture, 7 times higher in nonferrous metals production, and 6 times higher in electrical production in Japan. Perhaps production in Japan was so labor-intensive because Japanese wages were so low relative to the price of capital.

Differences between capital intensities in the United States and Japan were stunning in the 1950s, but we can illustrate the source of the differences less dramatically in Figure 4.7. Suppose the United States and Japan have the same production technologies, so they share a common set of isoquant curves. Let's think of point B in the figure as the mix of capital and labor in the United States. Japan, with a lower wage–rental ratio, operates efficiently with a labor-intensive mix of capital and labor at point D′.

Two factors determine how far Japan's capital–labor mix is from the U.S. capital–labor mix. The first factor is the gap between the wage–rental ratios in the two countries. If the wage–rental ratio is much lower in Japan, then Japan's efficient mix of capital and labor is a labor-intensive point along the isoquant. (Plot D″ southeast of D′.) The second factor is the shape of the isoquant curve as measured by the elasticity of substitution. For a given gap in wage–rental ratios, an isoquant with less curvature generates more substitution out of capital into labor in Japan. So we use the elasticity of substitution to connect the cross-country gap in the wage–rental ratio to the cross-country difference in capital intensity.

> **Key Principle.**
> Production in undeveloped parts of the world is labor-intensive because wages in those places are so low relative to the cost of equipment and other forms of capital.

Do cross-country differences in input prices accurately predict the capital-intensities in Japanese industries at the time? Incredibly, the answer is yes. Arrow et al. (1961, Table 5) report capital–labor ratios and wage–rental ratios for 12 manufacturing industries in the United States and Japan. They also estimate an elasticity of substitution for each industry using data on labor productivities and wages across 19 countries (Arrow et al. 1961, Table 2). Combining the estimate of σ with the cross-country gap in the wage–rental ratio and the U.S. capital–labor ratio enables us to predict capital intensity in Japan industry by industry. For the average across the 12 manufacturing industries, we predict production in Japan to have been one-eighth as capital-intensive as

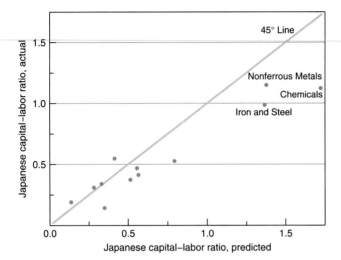

Notes: Data are from 1953 and 1954. To predict capital–labor ratios in Japan, we assume that Japan and the United States share the same constant-elasticity-of-substitution production function in each industry. The predicted capital–labor ratio in a Japanese industry scales the U.S. capital–labor ratio for that industry by a term that depends on the Japanese wage–rental ratio relative to the U.S. wage rontal ratio.

$$\widehat{\frac{K_J}{L_J}} = \left(\frac{w_J/r_J}{w_{US}/r_{US}} \right)^{\sigma} \times \frac{K_{US}}{L_{US}}$$

Source: Arrow et al. (1961, Table 5).

FIGURE 4.8. Actual and Predicted Capital–Labor Ratios in 12 Japanese Manufacturing Industries

U.S. production. That's quite close to the actual ratio, which was one-tenth. So differences in wage–rental ratios explain almost all the lower capital intensity in Japan in the 1950s.

Our cost-minimization model hits the capital-intensity target for the average across industries, and it also accurately predicts how capital intensity of Japanese production varies across the 12 manufacturing industries. Figure 4.8 plots the relationship between actual and predicted capital–labor ratios in Japan for the 12 industries. For all but the three most capital-intensive industries, the predicted capital–labor ratio (based on σ and the U.S.–Japan gap in w/r) accurately captures the actual capital–labor ratio in Japan; that is, the U.S.–Japan gap in the wage–rental ratio fully explains why production was so labor-intensive in Japan at the time. Furthermore, Figure 4.8 reveals the strong positive relationship across industries. Japanese production was more capital-intensive in industries where the wage–rental ratio was closer to the U.S. wage–rental ratio. The figure also reveals that the three most capital-intensive Japanese manufacturing industries weren't as capital-intensive as we would predict from their wage–rental ratios. Perhaps Japanese production technologies did differ from U.S. production technologies in these industries.

Overall, dramatic differences in wage–rental ratios explain the equally dramatic differences in capital intensities between the United States and Japan in the 1950s. Japanese production at the time was labor-intensive because labor was so inexpensive relative to capital in Japan. Equivalently, had wages been so low (relative to the price of capital) in the United States, production in U.S. industries would have been just as labor-intensive as production in the Japanese industries!

Profit-Maximizing Choice of Labor and Capital

To maximize profit, a firm must produce its good or service efficiently, minimizing its cost of whatever quantity it produces, *and* produce the most profitable quantity. One of the striking principles of economics is that a competitive firm maximizes profit by choosing its output to equate marginal cost MC to the price of the product p. We apply the $MC = p$ principle here. The intersection of Leisure Lawn's upward-sloping marginal cost curve and the flat price line $p = 30$ in Figure 4.9 determines its quantity supplied of lawn care, 100 lawns per week. Not only is B in Figure 4.7 the least-costly way to cut 100 lawns, but 100 lawns is the quantity that maximizes Leisure Lawn's profit because $MC = p$ at $q = 100$ with $p = 30, w = 300$, and $r = 200$. So B is Leisure Lawn's long-run choice given the three prices.

How does Leisure Lawn respond to a change in the wage? The weekly wage of lawn-care workers falls from $300 to $200 per worker, and Leisure Lawn substitutes labor for capital and expands production in its routine pursuit of profit. We establish this result in two steps. First, we hold output fixed at $q = 100$ to isolate the substitution effect of the wage cut. Second, we show how the lower wage decreases marginal cost and increases Leisure Lawn's supply of lawn care, shifting employment of labor and capital to a higher isoquant curve. Figure 4.10 illustrates these **substitution and scale effects** of a wage cut.

The lower wage flattens all the isocost lines, and the cost-minimizing mix of labor and capital slides down along isoquant curve $q = 100$ to a more labor-intensive mix. Since the slope of each isocost line is $-w/r$, cutting the wage from $300 to $200 lowers the slope (in absolute value) from 1.5 to 1.0 units of capital per worker. The cost-minimizing mix of labor and capital with the flatter isocost lines is point D, the tangency of a new isocost line to isoquant curve $q = 100$. Employment rises from 9 to 10 workers per week; use of capital falls from 5 to 3.75 units per week. The substitution effect of this wage cut (from B to D) tilts Leisure Lawn's production toward a more labor-intensive mix of inputs.

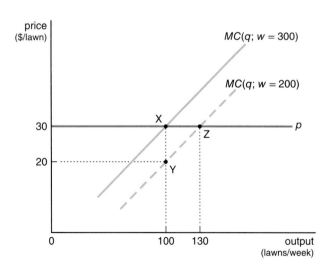

The intersection of the upward-sloping marginal cost curve MC with the price line p determines Leisure Lawn's quantity supplied. With $w = 300$ and $r = 200$, $MC = p$ at $q = 100$. That's point X.

The fall in the weekly wage from $300 to $200/worker shifts MC down (e.g., marginal cost at $q = 100$ falls from $30 to $20/lawn). Price p intersects the new MC further out along the price line, and Leisure Lawn expands its output from 100 to 130 lawns/week. That's point Z.

The lower wage pushes Leisure Lawn up to isoquant $q = 130$ in Figure 4.10.

FIGURE 4.9. Effect of Cutting the Wage on Production

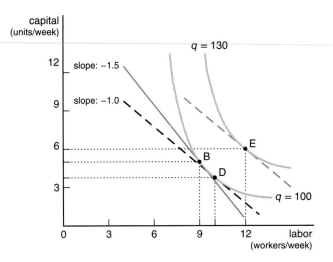

Leisure Lawn operates at B if w is $300/worker and r is $200/unit. If w falls to $200/worker, all isocost lines get flatter; the slope of the isocost lines falls (in absolute value) from 1.5 to 1.

The substitution effect from B to D holds output fixed. To find D, draw the new, flatter isocost line tangent to isoquant curve $q = 100$. Leisure Lawn substitutes out of K into L along $q = 100$.

Leisure Lawn also expands (based on $MC = p$) from 100 to 130 lawns/week, and the move from D to E is the scale effect. The scale effect reinforces the substitution effect in increasing L.

FIGURE 4.10. Substitution and Scale Effects of a Wage Cut

As a profit maximizer, Leisure Lawn responds to the lower wage by increasing its supply of lawn care. The lower wage decreases the marginal cost of lawn care. (How much cost rises to expand production by one unit depends on the prices of the variable inputs.) Lowering the wage shifts the marginal cost curve down. Leisure Lawn's quantity supplied of lawn care slides out along the product price line ($p = 30$) from $q^* = 100$ to $q^* = 130$, as Figure 4.9 illustrates.

Reflecting substitution and scale effects, Leisure Lawn's full response to the lower wage is to employ 12 workers using 6 units of capital, point E in Figure 4.10. As B to D marks the substitution effect of the wage decrease, the jump from D on isoquant curve $q = 100$ to E on isoquant curve $q = 130$ marks the scale effect. To cut 30 more lawns per week efficiently, Leisure Lawn raises employment from 10 to 12 workers per week and adds capital from 3.75 to 6 units per week. And Leisure Lawn turns a profit: weekly revenue rises from $3,000 to $3,900, weekly cost sinks from $3,700 to $3,600, and weekly profit climbs from $700 in the red to $300 in the black.

 PRACTICE   The government places a payroll tax on employers. The tax is proportional to the employer's payroll, so Leisure Lawn's cost of labor with tax rate t is $(1 + t)wL$. How does the tax affect Leisure Lawn's isocost lines? What are the substitution and scale effects (if any) of the payroll tax?

Long-Run Labor Demand Curve

Figure 4.10 contains all the information we require to construct Leisure Lawn's long-run labor demand curve. Its long-run response to the lower wage is to increase its quantity demanded of labor from 9 (at B) to 12 (at E) workers per week. (As

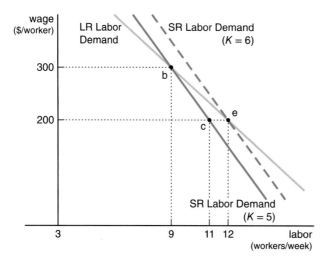

Leisure Lawn's long-run labor demand curve slopes down and is more elastic than its short-run (SR) labor demand curve. Allowing capital to vary delivers a larger employment response to the lower wage.

Leisure Lawn's long-run (LR) labor demand curve connects points from short-run labor demand curves. The initial short-run labor demand curve has $K = 5$. Employment in the short run grows from 9 to 11 workers. In the long run, capital increases to $K = 6$, which increases Leisure Lawn's short-run labor demand to the dashed line, and employment grows to 12 workers.

FIGURE 4.11. Long-Run Labor Demand Curve

drawn, capital rises from 5 to 6 units per week.) The pairs $(9, 300)$ and $(12, 200)$ are two points on Leisure Lawn's long-run demand curve in Figure 4.11.

The **long-run labor demand curve** collects points from many less-elastic short-run labor demand curves. In the short run (with capital fixed at $K = 5$), Leisure Lawn expands employment from 9 to 11 workers as the weekly wage falls from $300 to $200 per worker. In the long run, Leisure Lawn increases capital to 6 units per week. The extra capital raises the marginal product of labor, so the short-run labor demand curve with $K = 6$ lies to the right of the short-run labor demand curve with $K = 5$. With that sixth unit of capital in place, Leisure Lawn has a new, higher short-run demand for labor, the dashed line in Figure 4.11.

Labor demand in the long run is more elastic than labor demand in the short run. In the short run, Leisure Lawn adds two workers without changing capital. Leisure Lawn eventually adds another worker and a unit of capital. This more-elastic response in the long run doesn't require labor and capital to be complements. Indeed, even if labor and capital are substitutes in production, the dashed short-run labor demand curve with $w = 200$ lies to the right of the original short-run labor demand curve. In the case of complements, the additional capital raises the marginal product of labor; in the case of substitutes, capital falls in the long run, and *less* capital raises the marginal product of labor.

 PRACTICE   Leisure Lawn has fully responded to the $200 weekly wage. If the wage returns to $w = 300$, what happens to employment of lawn-care workers at Leisure Lawn in the short run? How does Leisure Lawn react in the long run?

Factors that Shift Labor Demand in the Long Run

Long-run labor demand depends on the wage, the price of the product, the price of capital, and the production technology. The long-run labor demand curve shifts with changes in the prices of the product and of capital and with innovations in the technology.

An increase in the price of the product shifts up the price line in Figure 4.9, increasing the scale of production. Leisure Lawn moves to a higher isoquant curve, which increases labor and capital as a **scale effect**. The higher product price, therefore, increases the demand for labor in the long run as well as the short run.

Although short-run labor demand depends on the firm's capital, the long-run labor demand curve shifts with the price of capital (rather than the amount of capital). Like a lower wage, a higher price of capital flattens all isocost lines, and Leisure Lawn substitutes labor for capital along an isoquant curve. The substitution effect of the higher price of capital increases the long-run demand for labor. A higher price of capital also shifts up the marginal cost curve in Figure 4.9, and Leisure Lawn downsizes as a scale effect, which reduces its long-run demand for labor and capital. Overall, the effect of capital's higher price on labor demand is ambiguous; it depends on whether the substitution effect increasing labor demand dominates the scale effect decreasing labor demand. If the higher price of capital increases (decreases) the demand for labor, labor and capital are substitutes (complements). That labor and capital can be substitutes or complements is no surprise, but our analysis illuminates how substitution and scale effects of the change in r determine whether the inputs are substitutes or complements.

Our analysis easily handles more than two inputs. Classical economists added land as a third input. Gasoline and space to store the mowers and other equipment are additional inputs at Leisure Lawn. Flour, yeast, mozzarella cheese, pepperoni, pizza ovens, plates, tables, chairs, electricity, and credit-card readers are all inputs at pizzerias. But for our analysis, the most important extension is to two types of workers: unskilled and skilled labor. Unskilled labor and skilled labor tend to be substitutes. In many contexts, unskilled labor is a substitute for and skilled labor a complement with capital. So a lower price of capital tends to reduce the demand for unskilled labor and raise the demand for skilled labor. And a lower wage of unskilled labor reduces the demands for skilled labor and capital.

Technological advances also shift the long-run labor demand curve. Suppose an innovation increases the number of lawns that Leisure Lawn cuts with any mix of labor and capital by 10 percent. The number on each isoquant curve rises by 10 percent, but the isoquant curves look the same. The marginal products of labor and capital also rise by 10 percent, and the marginal cost of lawn care falls at each pair (L, K). If Leisure Lawn continues to employ 9 workers and 5 units of capital, it cuts $110 (= 100 \times 1.1)$ lawns per week, and its marginal cost of lawn care falls from \$30 to \$27.27 $(= \$30 \div 1.1)$ per lawn. Expanding production from 100 to 110 lawns per week isn't enough to maximize profit because $MC < p$ at $q = 110$. So Leisure Lawn increases its demand for labor and capital as a scale effect.

Alternatively, if the innovation raises the marginal product of capital more than the marginal product of labor (i.e., if it's biased toward capital), then the isoquant curves turn flatter, and Leisure Lawn substitutes out of labor into capital. The substitution out of labor could be strong enough to swamp the scale effect and ultimately reduce the long-run demand for labor. Adoption of the printing press is a dramatic historical example of a capital-biased (or labor-saving) innovation. The substitution out of monastic scribes into printing presses dwarfed the scale effect associated with the increased production of books, and the demand for monastic scribes nearly vanished. (See chapter 2.)

Application: Short-Run vs. Long-Run Effects of the Minimum Wage

As we learned in chapter 2, a binding minimum wage lowers employment in a competitive labor market. How quickly is employment of teenagers and other minimum-wage workers predicted to fall? Businesses need time to adjust employment. The lesson from our analysis of long-run labor demand is that the longer employers have to vary inputs that are fixed in the near term, the bigger the escape from minimum-wage workers. The effects of the minimum wage can pile up over time.

With enough time to flee the expense of the minimum wage, businesses find creative ways to get by without unskilled labor. In the short run, cutting employment of unskilled minimum-wage workers translates into less output and lower revenue. The disemployment effect of raising the wage could be tiny in its first few weeks and small for months or even a year in some industries. In the long run, however, an employer can change its mix of inputs, replacing unskilled minimum-wage workers with capital. Raising the minimum wage even spurs innovations to replace artificially expensive unskilled workers.

Employers' flight from the expense of the minimum wage also includes substitution of skilled workers for unskilled minimum-wage workers. Suppose the two inputs are unskilled labor and skilled labor. The minimum wage increases the price of unskilled labor. In the long run, employers substitute skilled labor for unskilled labor, decreasing the quantity demanded of unskilled labor.

4.3   Market Labor Demand

We have derived labor demand for an individual employer and specified the factors that shift labor demand. Now it's time to aggregate the individual labor demands to derive market labor demand.

The **market labor demand curve** sums the individual labor demand curves across employers. For instance, if the wage is $300 per worker, the quantity demanded of labor is 9 workers per week at Leisure Lawn and nine other lawn-care firms. The quantity demanded of labor in this little labor market is 90 ($= 10 \times 9$) workers per week at $w = 300$. At $w = 200$, quantity demanded of labor at each of these employers grows to 11 workers per week (in the short run), and the market's quantity demanded of labor rises to 110 ($= 10 \times 11$) workers per week. These two pairs—(90, 300) and (110, 200)—are two points (x and y) on a market

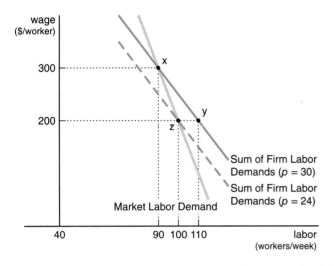

The weekly wage falls from $300 to $200/worker. Each of 10 firms employs 2 more workers. Market employment rises from 90 to 110.

Supply of lawn care increases, which drives the product price down from $30 to $24/lawn and reduces VMP_L at each firm. Each firm's quantity demanded of labor falls by 1 worker. The market's quantity demanded of labor falls to 100.

Due to this product-price effect, market labor demand through points x and z is less elastic than the sum of the firm demands.

FIGURE 4.12. Market Labor Demand and the Product–Price Effect

labor demand curve in Figure 4.12. Summing the quantities demanded of labor across employers at each wage amounts to adding the individual demand curves horizontally in the figure.

Application: Demand for Palestinian Labor in Israel

We can estimate the elasticity of demand for labor directly by measuring the change in employment associated with an exogenous change in the wage. That is, the change in the wage must be unrelated to the factors that shift the demand curve. A minimum-wage hike is an example, but minimum wages don't bind on many workers.

We can also estimate the elasticity of demand for labor by finding some exogenous shift in the supply of labor. The resulting movement along the labor demand curve estimates how the supply-driven change in employment impacts the wage. If the wage doesn't change much, the labor demand curve must be elastic.

The shifting supply of Palestinian men working in Israel provides an excellent application of this method. Curfews that restrict the mobility of Palestinians in Israeli-occupied territories reduce the supply of labor to Israel (Angrist 1996). (As a second application, we study the impact on wages of an exogenous influx of Cuban immigrants to Miami in chapter 7.) On a typical day, tens of thousands of Palestinians in the Israeli-occupied territories cross the border to work in Israel. Access to the Israeli labor market is restricted, and the number of Palestinians who are able to cross into Israel to work (legally or illegally) fluctuates with tensions, conflicts, and wars in the region. So the supply of Palestinian workers to Israel sometimes plummets for reasons unrelated to the demand for labor in Israel. By checking how the wage of Palestinian workers in Israel responds to restrictions on mobility that withdraw Palestinian workers, we can estimate the elasticity of demand for Palestinian labor in Israel.

Angrist (1996) studied the wages of about 40,000 Palestinian men in two Israeli-occupied territories, the West Bank and the Gaza Strip, between 1987 and 1991. For Palestinian men working in the occupied territories, wages varied inversely with the total number of days they worked in Israel (a measure of employment) from month to month. This finding suggests a downward-sloping demand for Palestinian labor in Israel. But nothing in the inverse relationship isolates movements along a labor demand curve. The labor demand curve might be shifting around, too.

The method of instrumental variables can help. (See section 1.5.) Angrist isolated variation in Israeli employment of Palestinian men that's linked to curfews, which limit Palestinians' mobility. This method purges the employment variable of variation that's due to factors that shift the demand for labor, and the result is an estimate of the elasticity of demand for Palestinian labor in Israel.

Angrist found that the number of Palestinian men working in Israel is sensitive to the number of curfew days per month in the territory (Angrist 1996, Figure 6). In addition, wages of Palestinians working in Israel are sensitive to curfew-driven variation in the number of Palestinians working in Israel. So the short-run demand for Palestinian labor isn't perfectly elastic. In particular, the estimate from Gaza indicates that withdrawing 10 percent of the Palestinians from the Israeli labor market increases the wages of Palestinian men in Israel by 13 percent (Angrist 1996, Table 4, column 4). The estimate also implies that the elasticity of demand for Palestinian labor in Israel is $-.76$ ($\approx .10 \div (-.13)$). Evidence from the West Bank points to a less-responsive wage and a more-elastic demand for labor. A 10 percent withdrawal of Palestinian workers raises the wage of Palestinian men in Israel by 9 percent (Angrist 1996, Table 4, column 9), so this estimate of the elasticity of demand for Palestinian labor in Israel is -1.1 ($= .10 \div (-.09)$).

Generating these estimates took creativity and a lot of hard work collecting and analyzing the data. Using the estimates is easy. A 10 percent fall in the wage of Palestinian men working in Israel lifts Israeli employers' quantity demanded of Palestinian labor by 7.6 percent in Gaza and 11 percent in the West Bank. Since the elasticity estimates derive from month-to-month changes, these are short-run responses.

Equilibrium Price Effects and Marshall's Rules

There's more to deriving labor demand in the market than adding firm demand curves horizontally. The wage falls, and Leisure Lawn increases its quantity demanded of labor and its supply of lawn care without any meaningful effect on the price of lawn care. If all lawn-care firms increase their product supplies, however, the market supply of lawn care grows (i.e., shifts right). If the price of lawn care remains at $30 per lawn, a surplus emerges in the lawn-care market. The price of lawn care must fall to clear the lawn-care market. Therefore, the market labor demand curve should allow the price of lawn care to move to its new equilibrium value.

Allowing the product price to vary to clear the product market lowers the elasticity of demand for labor. Figure 4.12 depicts this case. Each firm responds to the lower wage by increasing its supply of lawn care, and the price of lawn care falls from $30 to $24 per lawn. The lower price of lawn care scales down the value-of-marginal-product-of-labor curve at each firm, shrinking each firm's demand for labor. In particular, the lower product price reduces the quantity demanded of labor at $w = 200$ by 1 worker per week at each firm. At the market level, the quantity demanded of labor falls by 10 workers to 100 workers per week. Overall, dropping the weekly wage to $200 per worker lifts employment at the market level from 90 to 100 workers per week: half the effect of the lower wage on employment is lost.

As the figure displays, the market labor demand curve—recognizing the change in the equilibrium price of lawn care—is less elastic than the sum of the labor demand curves across the lawn-care firms.

 PRACTICE   In Figure 4.12, why does the sum of the labor demand curves across employers shift down as each lawn-care firm responds to the lower wage?

Market labor demand is also less elastic if the price of capital varies to clear the market for capital (e.g., mowers and other equipment). Although Leisure Lawn's demand for capital might have no meaningful effect on the price of capital, the lower wage changes the demand for capital at all firms, and the combined response can influence the price that clears the capital market. Suppose labor and capital are complements, so the lower wage raises the demand for capital at every lawn-care firm. If the supply of capital slopes up, the price of capital rises to clear the capital market. The higher price of capital lowers the demand for labor because the two inputs are complements. Each lawn-care firm trims its long-run quantity demanded of labor, and the market labor demand curve is less elastic than the sum of the labor demand curves across employers.

If labor and capital are substitutes, is this result turned on its head? No. If labor and capital are substitute inputs, the lower wage decreases the demand for capital, which reduces the price of capital. The lower price of capital reduces the demand for labor because labor and capital are substitutes. So again, allowing the price of capital to vary to clear the capital market gets each employer to trim its long-run quantity demanded of labor. And again, in this case with labor and capital as substitutes, the market demand for labor is less elastic than the horizontal summation of labor demand curves across employers.

Tucked deep within the pages of a classic treatise on economics are the first statements of how market clearing in the product and capital markets impacts the elasticity of demand for labor. Alfred Marshall identified these **product-price** and **input-price effects** and two other factors that influence the elasticity of demand for labor (Marshall 1920 [1890], pp. 316–320). In the context of labor and capital, **Marshall's rules** hold that the demand for labor at the market level is more elastic if

(1) labor and capital are more substitutable (i.e., the elasticity of substitution of labor for capital is bigger),

(2) the demand for the product is more elastic (i.e., the product-price effect is smaller),

(3) the supply of capital is more elastic (i.e., the input-price effect is smaller),

(4) labor's share of cost is bigger.

The first three of Marshall's rules have admirably survived 125 years of advances in economics and provided powerful guidance in practice. The fourth of these rules hasn't fared as well. For reasons too subtle for us to pursue, the effect of labor's share of cost on the elasticity of demand for labor depends on the difference between the elasticity of demand for the product and the elasticity of substitution (Hicks 1932, pp. 241–247). A bigger share of cost increases the elasticity of demand for labor if the elasticity of demand for the product exceeds the elasticity of substitution.

Summary

In this chapter, we identified—for profit-maximizing competitive firms—factors that influence employment in the short run when capital is fixed and in the long run when capital can vary. Some of the key findings are:

☐ The total-product curve plots output as an increasing function of labor holding capital fixed.

☐ Two measures of labor productivity are the average and marginal products of labor. With diminishing marginal productivity of labor (past some point), labor's average- and marginal-product curves are inverted-U shapes. The marginal-product-of-labor curve intersects the average-product-of-labor curve where the average curve peaks.

☐ To maximize profit, a competitive firm chooses employment in the short run to equalize the value of marginal product of labor and the wage. If, however, the wage is above the peak of the value-of-the-average-product-of-labor curve, the firm employs no one in the short run.

☐ A competitive firm's short-run demand for labor curve coincides with its value-of-marginal-product-of-labor curve for wages below the peak of the value of its average-product-of-labor curve.

☐ Product price, capital, technology, and employer taxes on labor shift the short-run demand for labor.

☐ Capital is a variable input in the long run. The efficient mix of labor and capital minimizes cost for a particular output. The efficient mix is the point where an isocost line is tangent to a particular isoquant curve. At the tangency, the marginal rate of technical substitution equals the ratio of input prices, so cost minimization equalizes the production bang per input-price buck across inputs.

☐ Across countries, differences in the ratios of input prices powerfully predict differences in capital intensity. Less capital-intensive production in less-developed countries is the efficient response to labor being relatively inexpensive in those countries.

☐ In the long run, a competitor maximizes profit by choosing an efficient mix of capital and labor and by choosing output such that marginal cost equals the price of the product. The long-run response to a lower wage combines the substitution effect toward a more labor-intensive mix along an isoquant curve with the scale effect to a higher isoquant curve.

☐ Long-run labor demand curves are more elastic than short-run labor demand curves.

☐ The labor demand curve at the market level is less elastic than the sum of labor demand curves across firms due to product-price and input-price effects.

Our analysis of labor demand has focused on firms choosing how many workers to employ. We have ignored the employer's interest in the workday or workweek. An employer's interest in the hours worked by each worker is one of the applications of the model of job attributes in the next chapter.

Key Concepts

- fixed and variable inputs, p. 127
- production function, p. 127
- total-product curve, p. 128
- average product of labor, p. 128
- marginal product of labor, p. 129
- diminishing marginal productivity, p. 130
- value of marginal product of labor, p. 133
- marginal labor cost, p. 133
- short-run labor demand curve, p. 135

- shutdown wage, p. 136
- marginal revenue product of labor, p. 137
- isoquant curves, p. 138
- marginal rate of technical substitution, p. 139
- isocost lines, p. 141
- cost minimization, p. 142
- elasticity of substitution, p. 143
- substitution and scale effects, p. 146

- long-run labor demand curve, p. 148
- scale effect, p. 149
- market labor demand curve, p. 150

- product-price and input-price effects, p. 153
- Marshall's rules, p. 153

Short-Answer Questions

4.1 Use the data in Table 4.2 to plot the relationships between revenue R, cost C, and profit π (on the vertical axis) and labor L (on the horizontal axis) at Leisure Lawn. At what level of employment does the "profit hill" peak?

4.2 At my local Wendy's franchise, the hourly wage is $9 per worker. The franchise employs 15 workers per hour, and the marginal product of labor is 3 burgers per hour. The price of a single with cheese, which we pretend is the only thing Wendy's sells, is $3.50. Is the franchise maximizing profit? If not, would it increase profit by employing more workers or fewer workers?

4.3 What effect does a higher wage have on isoquant curves, isocost lines, the marginal cost curve, and the firm supply curve?

4.4 If Ethiopia and the United States have a common technology, then Ethiopia's production is more labor-intensive because the wage–rental ratio w/r is lower in Ethiopia. Alternatively, suppose the marginal products of labor and capital are 10 times higher in the United States at every mix of inputs. How does the difference in technologies impact the capital–labor ratio K/L in the two countries?

4.5 The current mix of farm workers and farm equipment at Ruffles Potatoes in Minburn, Iowa, maximizes its profit in the long run. The hourly wage of farm workers is $11 per worker, and the hourly rental price of farm equipment is $55 per unit. What is the marginal rate of technical substitution? What is the slope of the isoquant curve at the current mix of inputs at Ruffles Potatoes?

4.6 Explain why the price of capital r doesn't influence short-run labor demand but does influence long-run labor demand.

4.7 Explain why the market labor demand curve isn't simply the horizontal summation of the firms' labor demand curves.

4.8 Suppose unskilled labor and skilled labor are substitutes in production, and ignore capital. How does an increase in the wage of skilled workers affect the demand for unskilled workers? To answer the next question, assume that immigration law prevents unskilled workers from poor countries from migrating to the United States. How does an increase in the wage of skilled workers affect the wage of unskilled workers in the United States? Does closing the borders to immigration increase or decrease the elasticity of demand for skilled labor in the United States? Which of Marshall's rules applies here?

4.9 Did Marshall overlook a rule? Use the principles from our analysis of long-run labor demand (of a competitive firm) to add a rule related to product supply. Carefully phrase the rule in terms of elasticities.

Problems

4.1 The daily production and cost data of a small manufacturer of smartphone cases are:

INPUT (hours/day)	OUTPUT (cases/day)	MARGINAL PRODUCT (cases/hour)	VALUE OF MARGINAL PRODUCT ($/hour)
0	0		
10	10		
20	40		
30	90		
40	130		
50	160		
60	180		
70	190		
80	190		

The price of a case is $10.

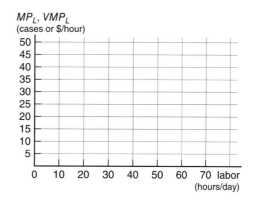

(a) In the range from 30 to 40 hours of labor per day, what are the marginal product ($\Delta q / \Delta L$) and value of marginal product of labor?

(b) Compute the marginal products and values of marginal product of labor from row to row.

(c) Plot the marginal-product- and value-of-marginal-product-of-labor curves on the graph. Use midpoints for labor, so plot the marginal product of labor over the range from 30 to 40 at $L = 35$.

4.2 Files+ is a small manufacturer of file folders, which sell for 30 cents per folder. In the short run, its daily production of file folders q is the following function of its daily employment of workers L:

$$q = 10L^2 - .05L^3$$

This implies that its average product of labor is

$$AP_L \equiv q/L = 10L - .05L^2$$

and its marginal product of labor is

$$MP_L \equiv \Delta q/\Delta L = 20L - .15L^2$$

(If you have had a course in calculus, you might remember how to derive this marginal product function from the production function.) Use a spreadsheet program, such as Excel or Numbers, to calculate AP_L, MP_L, and VMP_L for various values of L. Enter values of L in the sheet's first column, and enter the formulas for AP_L, MP_L, and VMP_L in the second, third, and fourth columns. Sketch the resulting combinations of (L, AP_L), (L, MP_L), and (L, VMP_L) in the figure below.

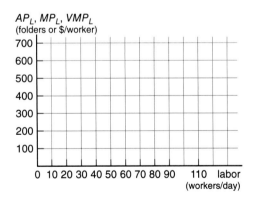

(a) At what level of employment L does the average product of labor AP_L peak?

(b) What are the values of AP_L and MP_L at the peak of the AP_L curve?

(c) Suppose the daily wage rate is $100 per worker. To maximize profit, Files+ employs approximately _____ workers per day, and the VMP_L is $_____ per worker.

4.3 The Muffin Maker bakes and sells muffins, corn muffins, blueberry muffins, banana-nut muffins, and so on. The size of the bakery is fixed, so the Muffin Maker expands or contracts its muffin production by varying its employment of workers. The Muffin Maker's hourly marginal-product-of-labor curve is Curve B in the figure below:

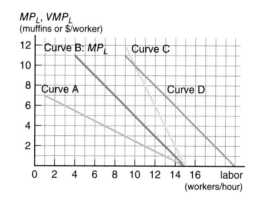

Muffins sell for $2.00 each, workers cost $6 per hour, and the bakery maximizes profit.

(a) Which curve represents the Muffin Maker's value of marginal product of labor?

(b) Depict the $6 wage by adding a line to the figure. The Muffin Maker's quantity demanded of labor is _____ workers per hour.

(c) The wage increases from $6 per worker to $8 per worker. What happens to employment at the Muffin Maker?

(d) In the original scenario with a wage of $6 per worker, how many workers does the Muffin Maker employ if the price of a muffin falls a whopping $1.50 from $2.00 to 50 cents? [Hint: How does the price cut affect the VMP_L curve?]

(e) The Muffin Maker is profitable, and it plans to invest in more ovens and increase the size of its kitchen by taking over the one-hour photo shop next door. Is the larger kitchen likely to increase or decrease the productivity of bakery workers? What effect will the expansion have on the Muffin Maker's marginal-product-of-labor curve?

4.4 UPS delivers packages using labor and trucks. The customers of UPS pay p dollars for delivery of a standard package. UPS pays each of its L workers an hourly wage w, and it pays r dollars per hour to use each of its K trucks. Suppose the price of capital falls.

(a) What happens to the efficient mix of labor and capital at UPS? That is, as a substitution effect, does UPS's delivery of packages become more or less labor-intensive? Does the substitution effect of the lower r increase or decrease UPS's demand for labor?

(b) What happens to UPS's marginal cost curve and profit-maximizing output as r falls? Does UPS move to a higher or lower isoquant curve?

(c) As a result of the decrease in r, does the scale effect lead UPS to increase or decrease its employment of labor?

(d) For a fall in the price of capital (i.e., a truck at UPS), do substitution and scale effects push employment in the same direction or in opposite directions?

4.5 In a typical week at TaxCrafters, L workers use K units of physical capital to prepare q individual tax returns. The figure below displays three of TaxCrafters's isoquant curves.

The weekly wage is $300 per tax preparer, and the weekly price of capital is $1,200 per unit.

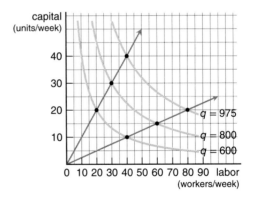

(a) What is the slope of each isocost line? Draw the isocost line through the point with 20 tax preparers using 5 units of capital.

(b) What is TaxCrafters's efficient mix of labor and capital to prepare 800 tax returns per week? That is, what combination of labor and capital minimizes its costs along isoquant curve $q = 800$? Mark this point with an X in the figure.

(c) The weekly wage jumps to \$1,200 per tax preparer. What happens to the slope of each isocost line? Illustrate what happens to the isocost line from part (a).

(d) How does TaxCrafters's efficient mix of labor and capital to prepare 800 tax returns per week respond to the wage increase? Mark the new efficient mix with a Y in the figure. The substitution effect of the increase in the weekly wage [decreases, increases] TaxCrafters's employment from _____ to _____ tax preparers per week and [decreases, increases] its use of capital from _____ to _____ units per week.

(e) Does the increase in the wage raise or lower the marginal cost of preparing tax returns? Does TaxCrafters increase or decrease the number of tax returns it prepares? Choose a point on isoquant curve $q = 600$ or $q = 975$ to illustrate the scale effect of the wage increase, and mark this point with a Z. The scale effect of the increase in the weekly wage [decreases, increases] TaxCrafters's employment from _____ to _____ tax preparers per week and [decreases, increases] its use of capital from _____ to _____ units per week.

(f) The total effect of the wage increase is to [cut, lift] employment from _____ to _____ tax preparers per week and to [lower, raise] TaxCrafters's use of capital from _____ to _____ units per week. Labor and capital in this case are [complements, substitutes] in production.

4.6 The figure below illustrates market demands for labor to make pizzas. The solid line is the market labor demand curve if the pizza price is \$10 per pie. The dashed line is the market labor demand curve if the pizza price is \$9.17 per pie.

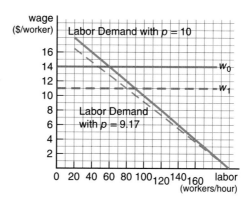

(a) The price of pizza is $10 per pie, and the hourly wage falls from $14 per worker to $11 per worker. The quantity demanded of labor increases by how many workers per hour?

(b) The lower wage of pizza workers increases the supply of pizzas. The demand for pizza slopes down, and the price of pizza sinks from $10 to $9.17 per pie to clear the pizza market. With this lower price of pizza, what is the quantity demanded of labor if the hourly wage is $11 per worker?

(c) Mark with a point the wage and quantity demanded of labor with $w = 14$ and $p = 10$. Mark with another point the wage and quantity demanded of labor with $w = 11$ and $p = 9.17$. Draw a line through the two points to illustrate the market labor demand curve that recognizes the equilibrium change in the price of pizza.

(d) Does the product-price effect increase or decrease the elasticity of demand for labor at the market level?

References

Angrist, Joshua D. 1996. "Short-Run Demand for Palestinian Labor." *Journal of Labor Economics* 14(3): 425–453.

Arrow, Kenneth J., Hollis B. Chenery, Bagicha S. Minhas, and Robert M. Solow. 1961. "Capital–Labor Substitution and Economic Efficiency." *Review of Economics and Statistics* 43(3): 225–250.

Hicks, J.R. 1932. *The Theory of Wages*. London: Macmillan.

Marshall, Alfred. 1920 (1890). *Principles of Economics: An Introductory Volume*, 8th ed. London: Macmillan.

Job Attributes

5

Why would anyone choose to work as a mortician, embalming, grooming, and otherwise preparing corpses for viewing and burial? Clearly there's more to a job than a paycheck, and working with corpses is an aspect of a job that repulses most of us. If morticians earned the same pay as workers on a typical job, then no one would work as a mortician. Perhaps morticians earn a bit more for their efforts, and that wage premium lures some of us into such repugnant work.

Interest in the connection among the wage and other aspects of a job isn't new. Adam Smith wondered about this connection when he dipped his pen into a bottle of ink to write these words: "The most detestable of all employments, that of public executioner, is, in proportion to the quantity of work done, better paid than any common trade whatever" (Smith 1998 [1776], p. 118). Smith's reasoning is one of many enduring contributions in the book that launched economics as a scholarly discipline: "The whole of the advantages and disadvantages of the different employments of labour ... must, in the same neighborhood, be either perfectly equal or continually tending to equality" (p. 117). He explained how wages vary with the "the ease or hardship, the cleanliness or dirtiness, the honourableness or dishonourableness of the employment" (p. 118). Employers must pay a wage premium to workers on jobs with attributes that people don't like.

A list of bad attributes of jobs in the modern era includes dirt, risk of injury, noise, long hours, odd hours (i.e., the "graveyard shift"), risk of job loss, and working with blood, guts, and corpses. Good features of jobs include a flexible work schedule, opportunity for career advancement, and a generous benefits package (e.g., health and pension benefits and vacation time). For many people, working with kids or in nature is a good feature of a job. Others prefer the kid-free and climate-controlled environment of corporate offices. Tastes differ.

The job's location is another important attribute. The great weather in southern California is surely a desirable attribute of working there. And the brutally cold winters of Alaska deter many of us from working there. Would you be surprised to learn that weekly wages in Alaska are among the highest in the country? According to Current Population Survey data (see section 1.4), the median weekly wage in 2017 was $839 in Alaska and $745 in the United States as a whole, so the typical worker in Alaska earns a 13 percent wage premium. Workers in Alaska aren't more educated than workers elsewhere in the United States, and the workweek in Alaska is just a little longer. It's the climate, of course. To attract workers to jobs in Alaska, employers pay premium wages. But the wage premium for work in Alaska has declined steadily from 61 percent in 1979 to 13 percent in 2017. The population in Alaska grew over this period at twice the clip of the United States as a whole. Perhaps Alaska's cold climate doesn't bother people as much as it once did.

Wages and the other aspects of jobs are linked in an implicit market for job attributes. A wage premium is simply the amount the employer pays to encourage workers to accept dirty, risky, or onerous work. The amount the worker implicitly pays the employer for job benefits and other desirable aspects of the job appears as a wage discount. The prices of these bad and good attributes of the job, which we call compensating wage differentials, clear the labor market.

This chapter contains two models and a series of applications. In the first model, supply and demand for labor determine the equilibrium wage premium on dirty jobs. In this model, each worker chooses between working on a clean job or a dirty job. In the second model, we treat dirt as a continuous variable, and we specify preferences of workers and firms over jobs. Workers and firms match together in the competitive equilibrium on the basis of workers' aversions to dirt and firms' costs of cleanup. We also apply the model to job risks and government regulation of job safety, the market value of human life, the lengths of the workday and workweek, and employee benefits.

5.1 Market for Work on Dirty Jobs

Trash collecting is a dirty job, but it pays a lot. To understand what determines the premium for dirty work, such as trash collecting, we begin with a simple model of the market for work on dirty jobs. Every job is either clean or dirty. Let's abstract from the firm's choice of how many workers to employ by assuming each firm employs one worker. The issue is whether that one worker enjoys a pristine work environment or suffers through the workday in a filthy mess. We also assume that the competitive wage for work on clean jobs w_c is \$10 per hour. Our task is to determine w_d, the wage on dirty jobs.

Supply of Labor to Dirty Jobs

Workers choose whether to work on clean or dirty jobs, and their choices determine the supply of labor to dirty jobs. Each worker has a **reservation wage for dirty work**. For instance, Alan accepts work on a dirty job only if the wage on the dirty job w_d is at least \$12 per hour. That is, Alan's reservation wage is \$12 per hour. Table 5.1 lists the reservation wages of Alan and three other workers, and the dashed horizontal lines in Figure 5.1 display their reservation wages.

We derive the supply curve in the market for dirty work by varying the wage on dirty jobs. If dirty jobs pay an hourly wage of \$14 (i.e., $w_d = 14$), then Alan and Barb choose dirty work; that is, the quantity supplied of labor to dirty jobs is two workers per hour. Since \$14 per hour is less than the reservation wages of

TABLE 5.1. RESERVATION WAGES FOR DIRTY WORK

WORKER	RESERVATION WAGE R ($/worker)	EMPLOYER	RESERVATION WAGE R ($/worker)
Alan	12	Wanda	22
Barb	13	Xena	19
Cassie	15	Yogi	15
Dan	18	Zach	13

Notes: A worker chooses a dirty job if the wage on the dirty job w_d is greater than or equal to his or her reservation wage R. An employer offers a dirty job if the wage on the dirty job w_d is less than or equal to his or her reservation wage R.

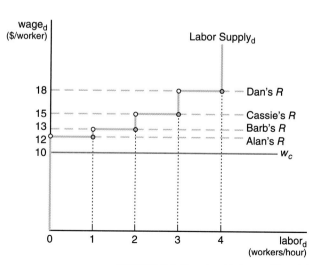

Each worker could earn \$10/hour on a clean job. Dashed horizontal lines depict workers' reservation wages for dirty work.

No one takes a dirty job if $w_d < 12$. If $12 \le w_d < 13$, only Alan takes a dirty job. If $13 \le w_d < 15$, Alan and Barb take dirty jobs. If $15 \le w_d < 18$, Cassie joins Alan and Barb on dirty jobs. And for any $w_d \ge 18$, all four workers take dirty jobs.

Labor supply to dirty jobs is an upward-sloping step function with a "tread" at each of the four reservation wages.

FIGURE 5.1. Supply of Labor to Dirty Jobs

Cassie and Dan, they prefer to work for $10 per hour on clean jobs. If, however, dirty jobs pay an hourly wage of $16, then Cassie (but not Dan) also chooses dirty work, and the quantity supplied of labor to dirty jobs is three workers per hour. The supply curve resembles a staircase with a "tread" at each worker's reservation wage. It's an upward-sloping **step function**.

 PRACTICE   Who wants to work on a dirty job if the hourly wage on dirty jobs is $12.50 per worker? What is the quantity supplied of labor to dirty jobs if $w_d = 12.50$? Mark this point in Figure 5.1.

Demand for Labor on Dirty Jobs

Firms also have a choice. Each firm decides whether to offer a dirty job at wage w_d or to bear the cost of cleaning up the workplace to offer a clean job. Cleaning up the workplace is costly in many ways; it includes the cost of pulling workers away from being productive.

Cleanup costs differ across firms. For instance, cleanup is so expensive at Wanda's firm that she is willing to pay up to $22 per hour to employ a worker on a dirty job. If the wage for dirty work is greater than $22 per hour, Wanda bears her high cost of cleanup and offers a clean job paying $10 per hour. Cleanup isn't so costly at Zach's firm; his reservation wage for offering work on a dirty job is $13 per hour. Table 5.1 lists the reservation wages for Wanda, Zach, and two other firms, and the dashed horizontal lines in Figure 5.2 illustrate their reservation wages.

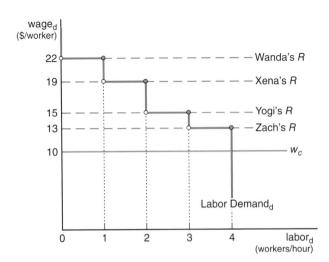

Each firm could pay someone $10/hour to work on a clean job. The dashed horizontal lines depict reservation wages for employing workers on dirty jobs.

No job is dirty if $w_d > 22$. If $19 \leq w_d < 22$, only Wanda offers a dirty job. If $15 \leq w_d < 19$, Wanda and Xena offer dirty jobs. If $13 \leq w_d < 15$, Yogi joins Wanda and Xena offering dirty jobs. And for any $w_d < 13$, all firms offer dirty jobs.

Labor demand on dirty jobs is a downward-sloping step function with a "tread" at each employer's reservation wage.

FIGURE 5.2. Demand for Labor on Dirty Jobs

We derive the demand curve in the market for dirty work by varying the wage on dirty jobs. If the wage on a dirty job is $20 per hour, then only Wanda offers a dirty job. Xena, Yogi, and Zach clean up their work environments and pay their workers $10 per hour to work on clean jobs. If the dirty wage is $18 per hour, Xena switches from offering a clean job to offering a dirty job, and the quantity demanded of labor on dirty jobs rises from one to two workers per hour. So the demand curve in the market for dirty work is a downward-sloping step function with a "tread" at each firm's reservation wage.

Equilibrium Wage Premium on Dirty Jobs

It's time for Alan and the other workers to meet Wanda and the other firms, and it's time for us to illustrate the labor supply and labor demand curves together in Figure 5.3. As always, we seek a wage that clears the labor market, so there's neither a surplus (or excess supply) nor a shortage (or excess demand) of workers to dirty jobs. That is, at the market-clearing wage, the number of workers who want to work on dirty jobs equals the number of dirty jobs that firms offer.

A surplus in the market for dirty work arises if the hourly wage on dirty jobs is $16. At $w_d = 16$, the quantity supplied of labor to dirty jobs is 3 (i.e., Alan, Barb, and Cassie), and the quantity demanded of labor is 2 (i.e., Wanda and Xena). Alternatively, if $w_d = 14$, then a shortage characterizes the market for dirty work: Wanda, Xena, and Yogi offer dirty jobs, but those dirty jobs interest only Alan and Barb. The only wage that clears the market for dirty work is $15 per worker. If $w_d = 15$, Alan, Barb, and maybe Cassie work on dirty jobs at Wanda's, Xena's, and maybe Yogi's firms. (This equilibrium pins down the wage at $15 per hour, but Cassie and Yogi don't care whether that third job is clean or dirty. Whether a third job is clean or dirty simply doesn't matter.)

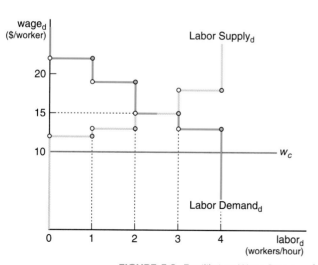

A surplus of workers to dirty jobs surfaces if $w_d > 15$, and any $w_d < 15$ causes a shortage of workers to dirty jobs. Thus the equilibrium wage on dirty jobs is $15/hour.

Wanda's, Xena's, and maybe Yogi's firms offer dirty jobs, and Alan, Barb, and maybe Cassie take those jobs. The equilibrium quantity of labor on dirty jobs is either two or three workers.

Gains from trade in dirty jobs are $16/hour, the area between the labor demand and labor supply curves up to 2 or 3 workers/hour.

FIGURE 5.3. Equilibrium Wage Premium for Work on Dirty Jobs

We now see how a **wage premium**—$5 (= \$15 − \$10)$ per worker in this case—emerges in equilibrium. Workers don't like dirt, so a wage premium is required to attract some of them to work on dirty jobs. It's expensive to clean up the work environment, so firms are willing to pay a wage premium to avoid the cost of cleanup.

Both sides of the market gain from having a market for dirty jobs. Each worker on a dirty job gains the difference between the actual wage and his or her reservation wage, and each firm offering dirty work gains the difference between its reservation wage and the actual wage. In our case, Alan gains $3, Barb $2, Wanda's firm $7, and Xena's firm $4 every hour. (Cassie and Yogi's firm, as the marginal worker and firm, don't gain anything.) Hence total surplus in this little market for dirty jobs is $16 (= \$3 + \$2 + \$7 + \$4)$ per hour.

These results generalize to a "thicker" market, a market with many workers and firms. Adding a worker to the market splits one of the vertical "risers" into two risers, so adding workers fills in the vertical gaps between the workers' reservation wages in Figure 5.1. Similarly, adding firms fills in the vertical gaps between the firms' reservation wages. Figure 5.4 measures employment on dirty jobs as a proportion of overall employment, and the labor supply and labor demand curves with many workers and firms return to their familiar smooth forms. As the

Key Principle.
Workers gain by having access to dirty, dangerous, and otherwise deplorable jobs.

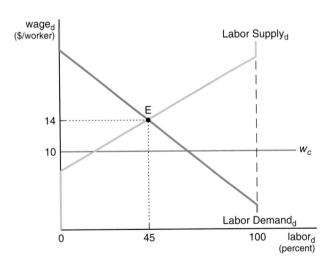

Having lots of workers and lots of jobs smooths out the labor supply and labor demand curves.

If nonlabor income increases, labor supply falls, and the equilibrium slides up along the labor demand curve. Fewer people work on dirty jobs, but the wage premium for dirty work rises.

What happens to the equilibrium if an innovation lowers the cost of cleaning up jobs? Demand for labor on dirty jobs falls, and the equilibrium slides down along the labor supply curve. Firms employ fewer people on dirty jobs, and the wage on those jobs falls.

FIGURE 5.4. Equilibrium Wage Premium in a "Thick" Market for Dirty Jobs

figure illustrates, the hourly wage premium for dirty work is $4 per worker, and 45 percent of the jobs are dirty.

What factors lead to higher or lower wages on dirty jobs? First, suppose nonlabor income jumps up for every worker. A clean work environment is surely a normal good, so each worker's reservation wage rises as an income effect. The supply of labor to dirty jobs falls, the equilibrium wage on dirty jobs rises, and employment on dirty jobs falls.

Second, if the technology for cleaning the work environment improves, then the premiums that firms are willing to pay workers on dirty jobs falls. Lowering firms' reservation wages reduces the demand for workers on dirty jobs, which results in a lower equilibrium wage on dirty jobs and more clean jobs.

Third, suppose the hourly wage on clean jobs jumps from $10 to $12. If we ignore that a clean work environment is a normal good, we shift the reservation wage of each worker and each firm up by $2. The equilibrium hourly wage on dirty jobs rises by $2, and employment on dirty jobs doesn't change. With the income effect, the labor supply curve shifts up by more than $2, the equilibrium wage on dirty jobs also rises by more than $2, and some workers switch from dirty jobs to clean jobs.

5.2   Model of Compensating Wage Differentials

Our model of the market for dirty jobs captures the key features of job attributes, including the determinants of the wage premium for work on a dirty job. But it ignores the spectrum of jobs that lie between clean and dirty jobs. Jobs range from the sterile environment of silicon-chip production to beyond the foul environment of septic-tank repair.

The relationship between wages and a job attribute such as dirt is the **compensating wage differential**. Here we explore the factors that determine compensating wage differentials for the dirtiness of jobs.

In the model of compensating wage differentials, a job is a pair of wages w and dirt d, and each firm chooses what job to offer while each worker chooses what job to take (Rosen 1974, 1986). So the market for jobs matches workers and firms on the basis of dirt-related preferences and technologies. Let's see how this process works.

Wage–Dirt Curve

The wage–dirt curve summarizes opportunities for both workers and firms. The axes in Figure 5.5 are wages w and dirt d, so any point on the graph is a job. Collecting all the jobs that are available in the labor market produces the **wage–dirt curve** $w(d)$. The wage–dirt curve slopes up because dirty jobs pay more, a principle that emerged from our analysis of the market for dirty jobs in section 5.1. We assume for simplicity that the wage–dirt curve is a line.

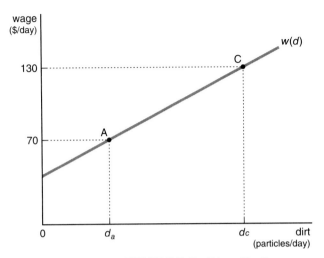

The wage–dirt curve w(d) collects all the jobs that are available in the labor market. That is, Sherwin's opportunities are all the points (i.e., jobs) on the wage–dirt curve, as well as all the points below the curve.

The curve slopes up because we assume (for the moment) that dirty jobs pay more. The compensating wage differential associated with the additional dirt on job C is $60/day.

FIGURE 5.5. The Wage–Dirt Curve

A worker like Sherwin chooses the job he likes best by comparing all the available jobs—that is, all the jobs along the wage–dirt curve. Similarly, a firm like Coalwood designs a job to offer by finding the job on the wage–dirt curve that maximizes its profit. Let's examine Sherwin's choice first.

Worker's Job Choice

Sherwin's preferences over jobs (d, w) derive from his more fundamental preferences over consumption (a *good*) and the dirtiness of his workspace (a *bad*). For simplicity, let's ignore nonlabor income. Then Sherwin cares about the wage on a job because it directly determines his consumption. And he dislikes dirty jobs just because he doesn't like dirt.

The indifference curves in Figure 5.6 illustrate Sherwin's preferences over jobs. Dirt is a bad, so his preference direction is to the northwest—toward cleaner and higher-paying jobs—and his indifference curves slope up. Since jobs A′ and C′ lie along an indifference curve (I_2), Sherwin is indifferent between the $80 daily wage on a job with dirt d_a and the $150 daily wage on a job with dirt d_c. That is, the $70 wage differential fully compensates Sherwin for the extra dirt $d_c - d_a$. Sherwin's indifference curve I_2 also divides the set of jobs into better jobs (above and left of I_2) and worse jobs (below and right of I_2). For instance, although job C pays more than job A′, it doesn't fully compensate Sherwin for the dirtier workplace.

Sherwin's indifference curves bow to the southeast, a property that follows from the diminishing marginal rate of substitution. The slope of the indifference curve through any job (d, w) in Figure 5.6 reveals Sherwin's willingness to pay (in terms of lower pay and consumption) for a marginally cleaner workplace from the starting point of that job. Let's compare Sherwin's willingness to pay at two jobs along indifference curve I_2. In the neighborhood of relatively clean job A′,

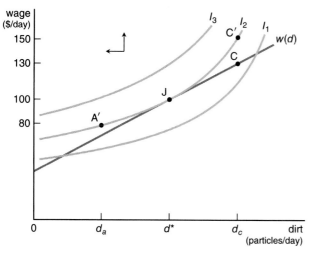

Each point on this graph is a job, a combination of wages and dirtiness of the work environment.

From job A′, Sherwin requires a wage premium of $70/day to take a job with d_c particles of dirt; that is, he is indifferent between jobs A′ and C′. Sherwin prefers job A′ to job C, although job C pays more. (Sketch the indifference curve that cuts through point C.)

Sherwin's optimal job is J, the point of tangency between the wage–dirt curve $w(d)$ and one of his indifference curves.

FIGURE 5.6. Sherwin's Preferences, Opportunities, and Job Choice

Sherwin isn't willing to forego a lot in wages for a slightly cleaner job. At job C′, however, he is willing to give up a lot in pay to introduce his filthy job to a bucket, a sponge, and a bottle of Mr. Clean. Thus the indifference curve is flatter at cleaner and lower-paying jobs and steeper at dirtier and higher-paying jobs.

 PRACTICE   Sharon's aversion to dirt is stronger than Sherwin's. She really hates dirty work. Sketch one or two of Sharon's indifference curves in Figure 5.6. Are Sharon's indifference curves steeper or flatter than Sherwin's?

Sherwin chooses the job at the tangency of the wage–dirt curve $w(d)$ to one of his indifference curves. Available jobs are on the wage–dirt curve. Which of the jobs on the wage–dirt curve is on the highest indifference curve? Job J, which is the point where $w(d)$ is tangent to Sherwin's indifference curve I_2. At this job, what Sherwin requires in compensation for a little dirtier workplace is exactly what the market pays for a little dirtier workplace. Cleaner jobs pay too little for Sherwin, and higher-paying jobs are just too dirty for him. Job J is just right.

Firm's Job Choice

Coalwood is a profit-maximizing firm, and **iso-profit curves** illustrate its preferences over jobs. Coalwood prefers to pay lower wages, and it also prefers a dirtier environment for its workers because cleaning the workplace is costly. Thus Coalwood's preference direction in Figure 5.7 is to the southeast, toward dirtier and lower-paying jobs.

Collecting all the jobs that generate a particular value for profit yields one of Coalwood's many iso-profit curves. As Figure 5.7 shows, Coalwood's iso-profit

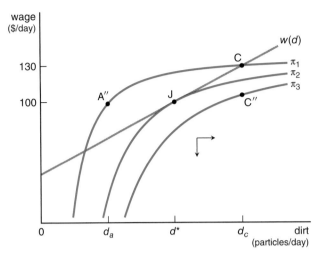

A", C, and C" are three of many jobs that Coalwood could offer to workers. Compared to job C, job A" saves Coalwood $30/day for each worker, but higher costs of cleanup exactly offset that cost saving. That is, jobs A" and C lie along an iso-profit curve. Coalwood prefers job C" to jobs A" and C because C" generates higher profit.

Coalwood's optimal job is J, the point of tangency between the wage–dirt curve w(d) and one of its iso-profit curves.

FIGURE 5.7. Coalwood's Iso-Profit Curves, Opportunities, and Job Choice

curves slope up. Jobs A" and C are on the same iso-profit curve, so the lower wage on job A" fully compensates Coalwood for the higher cleanup costs on that job: profit at A" equals profit at C. Iso-profit curve π_1 through job A" also divides the space into jobs that are more profitable than A" (below and right of π_1) and jobs that are less profitable than A" (above and left of π_1). C" is an example of a job that is more profitable than job A".

Coalwood's iso-profit curves bow to the northwest as a consequence of increasing marginal cost of cleanup. If air in the mine is a cloud of coal dust, then removing a small amount of the dust that reaches the lungs of Sherwin and his fellow miners doesn't take much: a ventilator draws dust-filled air from the mine and replaces it with dust-free fresh air, and each miner carries a rag to wipe his face. The cost of the marginal cleanup is low. However, if Coalwood has implemented nearly every means to rid the air in its mine of coal dust, then any further improvement in air quality comes at great expense. Perhaps the mine must (1) stop using the powerful and efficient equipment that cuts through rock, (2) equip each miner with a protective mask that impairs vision and communication, or even (3) surround each miner in a protective bubble—the "bubble miner" technology. The cost of this marginal cleanup is high. While Coalwood requires only a small cut in pay to remove a little dirt from job C, it requires a sharp cut in pay to push the workplace a little cleaner than job A". As a result, the iso-profit curve through these jobs is steeper at job A" than at job C. That is, Coalwood's iso-profit curves bow to the northwest.

 PRACTICE   The iso-profit curves in Figure 5.7 are for Coalwood's mining division. Cleanup is much less expensive at the Big Store, its retail store. Sketch one or two iso-profit curves for the Big Store. Are the Big Store's iso-profit curves steeper or flatter than the mine's?

Coalwood offers the job where the wage–dirt curve $w(d)$ is tangent to one of its iso-profit curves, which is job J in Figure 5.7. J is the job with highest profit among all the available jobs (i.e., points along $w(d)$). It could attract workers to a lower-paying job, but its cleanup costs would be too high. Coalwood could also economize on cleanup costs by offering a very dirty workplace, but the wage it must pay to attract workers would be too high. Job J is just right.

Equilibrium Compensating Wage Differential

The equilibrium matches workers to firms with a compensating wage differential for the dirtiness of the work environment. Coalwood offers job J, and Sherwin takes job J. For other jobs to exist, workers must differ from Sherwin in aversions to dirt, or firms must differ from Coalwood in cleanup technologies (e.g., coal mining vs. banking).

Figure 5.8 displays the matching of workers to firms. A worker seeking job A takes a job with a firm offering job A. For each worker choosing job B, one firm offers job B. So workers and firms match along the equilibrium wage–dirt curve. The wage–dirt curve is itself determined in the equilibrium. If $w(d)$ were flatter, meaning a smaller compensating wage differential for dirty work, then too many workers would choose clean jobs and too many firms would offer dirty jobs. Alternatively, if $w(d)$ were steeper, meaning a bigger compensating wage differential for dirty work, a surplus of workers would look for dirty jobs, and too many firms would offer clean jobs to avoid the high wages on dirty jobs. Therefore, the wage–dirt curve is determined in equilibrium to clear the job market for every amount of dirt d.

Two special cases should help us grasp how the wage–dirt curve is determined in equilibrium. First, consider the case of identical firms. All firms share the same "endowed" work environment and the same technology for cleaning up the

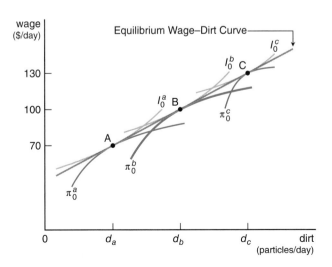

Different workers have different indifference curves, and different firms have different iso-profit curves. In the labor market equilibrium, workers and firms match on the basis of aversion to dirt and the cost of cleaning up the workplace. Each match is a job at a point of tangency between an indifference curve and an iso-profit curve.

The equilibrium wage–dirt curve collects all these tangency points and balances the two sides of the market at each amount of dirt d. A steeper (flatter) wage–dirt curve generates a shortage (surplus) of workers on clean jobs and a surplus (shortage) of workers on dirty jobs.

FIGURE 5.8. Equilibrium Compensating Wage Differential

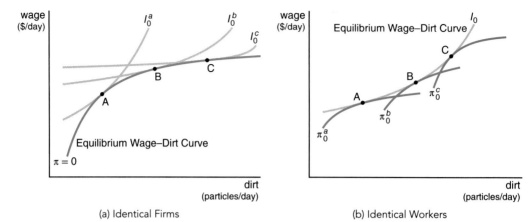

(a) Identical Firms   (b) Identical Workers

(a) If workers differ in their aversions to dirt but Coalwood and other firms are identical, then the equilibrium relationship between wages and dirt is the common zero-profit curve. Competition among firms drives the wage up to a point on the zero-profit curve for each value of dirt, and Sherwin chooses a job among all those on the zero-profit curve. The three types of workers depicted here choose jobs A, B, and C. In this special case of identical firms, the zero-profit curve doubles as the equilibrium wage–dirt curve.

(b) Suppose all workers share Sherwin's aversion to dirt but the cost of cleaning up the work environment differs across firms. Coalwood and other firms must offer jobs along a single indifference curve, so workers are indifferent among the jobs in the market. The three types of firms depicted here offer jobs A, B, and C. In this special case of identical workers, the equilibrium wage–dirt curve coincides with an indifference curve.

FIGURE 5.9. Equilibrium Compensating Wage Differential: Two Special Cases

workplace. This assumption implies that there is a single set of iso-profit curves, and panel (a) of Figure 5.9 graphs this case. Workers differ in their aversions to dirt, and they spread out along a single iso-profit curve, the zero-profit curve. The equilibrium wage–dirt curve is the zero-profit curve, so no job is more profitable or less profitable than any other job.

Second, if all workers share Sherwin's aversion to dirt, there is only one set of indifference curves over jobs. In panel (b) of Figure 5.9, firms differ in their cleanup costs, so the equilibrium involves matching the diverse firms to the identical workers. If workers preferred a particular job, then every worker would choose that job. To eliminate the implied surplus of workers to one job, the equilibrium leaves workers indifferent among the available jobs. The jobs Sherwin and the other workers take lie along a single indifference curve, which doubles as the equilibrium wage–dirt curve.

✓ **PRACTICE**   Suppose all firms have a common cleanup technology and all workers have the same aversion to dirt. Illustrate this case. How many jobs are there in the equilibrium?

Our results on the equilibrium determination of compensating wage differentials confirm our findings from the introductory model of a market for dirty jobs. A market for dirty work matches workers and firms on the basis of the workers' aversions to dirt and the firms' costs of removing the dirt, and the size of the wage premium or compensating wage differential for dirty work depends on these two factors.

Application: Occupational Safety Regulation

Risk of injury or even death on the job is another bad feature of work. To analyze compensating wage differentials for job risks, we simply replace dirt d with the risk of injury on the job r. (Risk is measured in nonfatal or fatal injuries per period.) In the market for job risks, risky jobs pay a premium, the most-risk-averse workers match with firms with the lowest costs of keeping the workplace safe, and the least-risk-averse workers (e.g., Sherwin) work at firms with the highest costs of reducing risks. Wages compensate workers for risks, so those who are lured to risky jobs by the compensating wage differential would be worse off if risky jobs didn't exist.

Enter OSHA, the Occupational Safety and Health Administration, the arm of the U.S. Department of Labor charged since 1970 with regulating workplace safety to reduce fatalities and other injuries on the job. OSHA sets standards for safety and health in the workplace. Risks beyond the safety standards are unlawful, so we can model OSHA regulation as a cap on job risks. Figure 5.10 includes a vertical reference line at the cap $\hat{r}$.

Since Sherwin works on a job (at J) with risks that exceed the OSHA standard, Coalwood adopts safety measures to reduce Sherwin's job risks. As a result, Sherwin enjoys a safer work environment and is better off overall, right? Wrong. Sherwin enjoys a substantial wage premium on his job because of the risks.

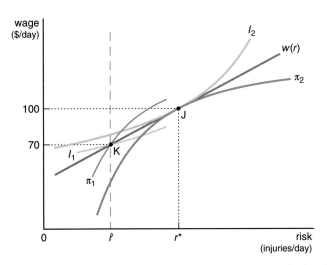

Without OSHA regulation of job safety, Sherwin and Coalwood match at job J, and Coalwood compensates Sherwin for the risks.

If OSHA enforces a binding cap on job risks at $\hat{r}$, job J is illegal. The job is redesigned from J to safer and lower-paying K.

The lower wage on job K pushes Sherwin to a lower indifference curve (I_1). The cost of reducing risk pushes Coalwood to a lower iso-profit curve (π_1). Sherwin and Coalwood are both hurt by the safety regulation.

FIGURE 5.10. OSHA Regulation of Job Safety

With Sherwin's exposure to risk capped at $\hat{r}$, Coalwood can pay Sherwin as little as \$70 per day, \$30 per day less than his wage without OSHA's safety standard. Most people (including policymakers) ignore that OSHA's safety regulation cuts Sherwin's wage, so they conclude that Sherwin gains at Coalwood's expense. But both Sherwin and Coalwood bear the pain of safety regulation. As Figure 5.10 shows, Sherwin's job slides down along the wage–risk curve from job J to job K to comply with the regulation. At K, Sherwin is on a lower indifference curve, and Coalwood is on a lower iso-profit curve. Sherwin and Coalwood lose; no one gains.

The prediction that safety regulation lowers wages is inescapable if employers pay a compensating wage differential for job risk. The compensating wage differential arises because workers understand the risks. No one has complete information of job risks, but workers have a good idea about the risks of work in various occupations. Everyone knows that working as a bank teller or librarian is much safer than working as a truck driver or logger. As we'll see in chapter 7, in the American colonial period, young emigrants from England commanded a compensating differential to work as servants on sugar plantations in the British West Indies compared to the less brutal work on farms in the mid-Atlantic colonies. The world was a lot bigger then, but information about the working conditions on sugar plantations flowed back to England. And workers in the Information Age surely have more information about jobs than the young emigrants from England had in the colonial period.

What if workers aren't informed about job risks? Does lack of information justify OSHA's regulatory activities? Let's assume that workers are utterly uninformed of job risks. So all jobs pay the same wage, a wage that reflects the average risk across safe and dangerous jobs. Some workers are lucky enough to find themselves on safe jobs, while other workers suffer the misfortune of workplace risks that jeopardize lives and limbs. In this scenario, a cap on risks helps those who would otherwise stumble onto risky jobs. The cap on risks, however, also hurts the fortunate workers on safe jobs: since risky jobs vanish, the equilibrium wage on all jobs falls.

A more direct policy would be to provide information about job risks. If workers like Sherwin are armed with the information about job risks, then firms like Coalwood with risky work environments must pay a wage premium. An advantage of this policy over capping risks is that well-informed workers can benefit from the high wage on risky jobs.

But what if workers' beliefs are biased? Perhaps workers systematically underestimate job risks. Sherwin takes the high-risk job (J) at Coalwood because he believes his risk is much lower than it is. If every worker errs in the same direction, then the resulting compensating wage differential is too small, and workers eventually regret taking those risky jobs. A cap on job risks can protect workers from their biased beliefs and bad job choices. Indeed, if workers have their heads in the sand, refusing to believe the evidence of job risks that the government could provide as an alternative policy, then OSHA regulation can help some workers. Other workers, however, would choose risky work even if they had correct assessments of the risks, and capping job risks hurts those workers.

Building the Brooklyn Bridge.   Erecting the Brooklyn Bridge across the East River was a tremendous engineering feat primarily because the foundations of its Brooklyn and New York towers sit deep in the bed below the river. Workers inside a massive open-bottomed box—a caisson—dug deep into the bed below the East River as other workers laid the foundation for the tower on top of the caisson. Pumps at the surface forced air into the caisson below to keep the river from flooding the interior space (David McCullough, *The Great Bridge*, 1972).

Work in the caisson was exhausting and oppressive. The air was hot, humid, smoky, and dense. According to McCullough, the work was "far more exhausting than anything any of [the workers] had ever done before" (p. 210). And it was dangerous. Twenty-seven people died in the construction of the bridge, and countless others suffered serious injuries. In a four-month period in 1872, caisson disease, which we now call decompression sickness or "the bends," struck over one hundred laborers in the New York caisson. As the caisson sunk deeper into the river bed, air pressure in the caisson rose to keep the river at bay, and workers toiled in more oppressive and dangerous conditions.

The daily wage started at $2, which was high for a laborer. (The daily wage for common laborers on the Erie Canal was $1.50 in 1872 (*Historical Statistics of the United States: Colonial Times to 1970, Part 1*, U.S. Department of Commerce, 1975, p. 64).) When the depth of the Brooklyn caisson reached 28 feet (and air pressure within the caisson rose to 12 pounds per square inch above normal air pressure at sea level), the daily wage rose to $2.25. The bridge company also trimmed 30 minutes from the usual eight hours (in two four-hour shifts) in the caisson. It cut another 30 minutes from the workday when the depth of the New York caisson reached 50 feet.

Workers in the caissons received a wage premium to compensate them for the onerous working conditions, and the wage premium increased as the conditions deteriorated. Shortening the length of the workday also compensated for the deteriorating conditions.

Although the river hid the mysterious workspace from sight, people in the neighborhoods on both sides of the East River were well informed of the oppressive working conditions. How each man handled or reacted to the conditions, however, wasn't known. Many gave it a go for a week; few stuck around. Most new hires decided the wage wasn't worth the effort and risks, so the quit rate was high. But other workers fought to keep their jobs. The company doctor carefully documented each reported case of decompression sickness, but he also understood that affected workers were hiding their symptoms from him for fear of being reassigned to safer and lower-paying work. These informed workers clearly preferred work in the caissons to safer work elsewhere.

Application: Value of Life

"You can't put a price on human life." Or can you? Economists and policymakers have been valuing human life in dollar terms since the mid-1970s (Thaler and Rosen 1976). The key insight is that the amount a person will pay to avoid risks to life and limb says something about how much that person values his life. We all do things that put our lives at risk. Riding in a car and swimming at the beach raise the odds of death, but they also typically deliver benefits. In trading off the costs and benefits of a risky activity, each person's personal **value of life** weaves its way into the cost side of the analysis. Let's see how the value of life influences the compensating wage differential for job risks.

The risk of death on the job varies dramatically across jobs. In the United States, the Department of Labor tracks every work-related fatality. In 2016, for instance, 5,190 workers died from job-related injuries. Not many of those deaths (5) were of people who work on management jobs in advertising, public relations, and sales. Job-related deaths were more common among firefighters (35), those in the military (62, excluding those on foreign soil), aircraft pilots and flight engineers (75), and police officers (109). But deaths on these risky jobs pale in comparison with deaths of construction workers (736) and truck drivers (918).

To identify job *risks*, however, we need to scale job fatalities by employment in each job or occupation. With this adjustment, driving a truck is less than twice as risky as police work. But being a pilot is almost four times as risky as being a cop. And the jobs with the greatest risk of a job-related fatality emerge: logging and fishing, which are, respectively, 9.3 and 5.9 times as risky as police work.

The compensating wage differential for the risk of job-related deaths reveals the market value of human life. To illustrate this incredible claim, suppose we have wage and risk data on two jobs. Security guards earn on average $27,000 per year for risky work that entails death at a rate of 10 per 100,000 workers per year. Loggers earn $33,400 per year for much riskier work: loggers' job-related deaths are 90 per 100,000 workers per year. Figure 5.11 illustrates the two jobs. The wage premium for nine times as much risk of death is $6,400, so the slope of the wage–risk curve $w(r)$ is $80 (= $6400 \div (90 - 10))$ per one-hundred-thousandth of a death.

This information isn't expressed in a very meaningful way. Let's make it easier to grasp by multiplying the numerator and denominator by 100: the slope of the wage–risk curve expressed this way is $8,000 per one-thousandth of a death. That means a typical worker reduces his risk of death by .001 by moving to a

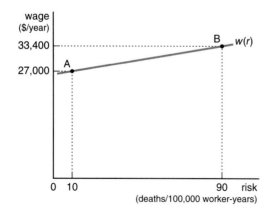

Measure	Value
Δw	$6,400/worker/year
Δr	80 deaths/100,000 workers/year
$\frac{\Delta w}{\Delta r}$	$80/death/100,000
	or $8,000/death/1,000
	or $8,000,000/death

The slope of the wage–risk curve is $80 per one-hundred-thousandth of a death, or $8,000 per one-thousandth of a death. That means each worker foregoes $8,000 to reduce the risk of death by .001. A thousand workers pay in total $8,000,000 to save one life, so the market value of that life is $8,000,000.

FIGURE 5.11. Market Value of Human Life

job that pays $8,000 less. So a thousand workers each pay $8,000 (or $8,000,000 in total) to reduce the risk of death on the job by .001 for each worker, which eliminates one death in total. That is, *workers pay $8,000,000 to save one life.* By simply expressing the slope of the wage–risk curve in terms of dollars per death, we uncover the market price—based on workers' aversion to death and firms' costs to make the workplace safer—of human life.

 PRACTICE   Suppose the annual wage premium for logging is $8,000 per worker. What's the slope of the wage–risk curve $\Delta w/\Delta r$? What's the implied value of a human life?

Estimation of the wage–risk curve $w(r)$ is tricky business (for reasons that we examine in section 5.4), so estimating the value of human life from compensating wage differentials for job risks is challenging. But with good estimates of the wage–risk curve in hand, as we assume in Figure 5.11, the steps to reveal the implied value of life are simple and few. All we have to do is express the slope of the wage–risk curve in the right units: dollars per death.

Ten million dollars is a good estimate of the value of life in the United States. Indeed, Viscusi and Aldy (2003) analyzed nearly 50 studies of the wage–risk curve. The typical compensating wage differential for risk of job fatality in U.S. samples translates into a value of life of almost $10 million when adjusted to 2017 dollars by the Consumer Price Index. Viscusi and Aldy's analysis also reveals that the value of life is lower for workers on the riskiest jobs. In particular, the wage–risk curve isn't linear: the compensating wage differential associated with a marginal increase in risk is smaller on the riskiest jobs. Income also matters. Workers in higher-income samples require a bigger compensating wage differential to accept a higher risk of death on the job. The implied value of life rises with income. In particular, workers in the developed world value their lives more, so it takes bigger compensating wage differentials to lure them onto risky jobs. Hence job safety appears to be a normal good.

Ten million dollars is an estimate of the *market value* of life. As such, it's analogous to expenditures on a good, and it certainly excludes consumer surplus. The slope of the wage–risk curve indicates how the wage changes for small changes in the risk of job-related death. We apply that "price" to many small (e.g., .001) changes in job risk to derive the total expenditure (in terms of foregone wages) to save one life. Personal values, such as how much you value your life, influence that market value, but you may value your life more or less than the market value of life.

5.3 Workday and Job Choice

What's the wage premium for working a long workday or a long workweek? We found in chapter 1 that occupations with long workweeks tend to pay high wages. For instance, doctors and lawyers typically work more than 45 hours per week. The length of the workweek is an attribute of the job, and here we apply our model of job attributes to illuminate the compensating wage differential for working long hours.

Employer's Interest in the Length of the Workday

The model of labor supply in chapter 3 is the starting point for determining the workday (or workweek), but the length of the workday is determined in equilibrium. The equilibrium also reflects the firm's interest in hours worked by an employee (Lewis 1969). Our analysis of labor demand in chapter 4 ignored the firm's interest in the length of the workday. But Leisure Lawn clearly isn't indifferent between having Gregg work 16 hours or having Gregg and seven coworkers each work 2 hours. Consequently, Leisure Lawn doesn't let Gregg choose hours h as in chapter 3. Indeed, there are few stronger empirical patterns in economics than that firms increase labor in the long run by expanding employment N with little or no change in working hours h. For instance, Leisure Lawn increases its labor (Nh) from 80 to 400 worker-hours per day in the long run by employing five times as many workers without changing the workday at all.

We remedy this omission by introducing several features that characterize the firm's preferences over hours and wages. The advantage of a short workday is that workers such as Gregg are fresh and productive early in the day and the day ends before they tire and lose focus. This is the **fatigue effect**: workers tire as the workday lengthens, which implies diminishing marginal productivity of working hours. Thus Leisure Lawn is willing to pay Gregg more for his second hour of work in the day than for his tenth.

Some disadvantage of a short workday must counterbalance the fatigue effect. Otherwise, a firm like Leisure Lawn would have a slew of workers each working only an hour or even a minute each day. There are many disadvantages of a short workday. First, getting the workday started typically takes a while, so there's a **start-up cost** for each worker. At Disney's Magic Kingdom, cast member Beth parks in an employee parking lot, rides a bus to the wardrobe department, changes into a costume in a locker room, and travels through a complex of tunnels to begin entertaining the guests on an attraction like the Jungle Cruise. The process repeats itself in reverse at the end of the workday. So Beth generates little or no value for Disney by working one hour per day.

Second, some costs of labor vary with employment N alone, so the cost of labor includes **per-worker costs**. Every worker gets a uniform (or an office). Payroll processing costs depend on the number of checks cut. Regulatory compliance often involves documentation for each worker (e.g., taxes, immigration status, no conflicts of interest). Providing some employee benefits (e.g., health insurance) involves a cost per worker that's unrelated to earnings. Worker training also involves a cost per worker. If Coalwood briefs each worker 30 minutes on its new safety procedures, then having one miner work a 10-hour day rather than having 10 miners each work a one-hour day cuts this training cost by 90 percent. Project coordination among members of a team also carries a cost per worker.

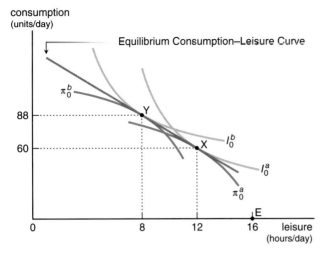

We extend the standard model of labor supply to include firms' interests in the length of the workday. The positions and shapes of the iso-profit curves reflect these interests.

Low per-worker cost leads Xena's firm to offer job X, which pays $60 for a 4-hour day, and workers who don't like to work much find that job attractive. Yogi's firm offers an 8-hour workday with job Y, and workers who don't mind working that much take that job and earn $88 for the day's work.

FIGURE 5.12. Choice of (l, c) with Firms that Care about the Length of the Workday

To avoid having "too many cooks in the kitchen," a firm adopts a long workday or workweek. Each worker handles a bigger chunk of the project, which economizes on the costs of coordinating activities among the team members.

Let's enrich our model of labor supply in chapter 3 to include the firm's interest in the workday. Start-up and other per-worker costs combine with the fatigue effect to form the iso-profit curves in Figure 5.12. The slope of an iso-profit curve (in absolute value) tells us the marginal product of working hours, so the fatigue effect implies that each iso-profit curve bows out from the origin. The relevant iso-profit curve starts below the endowment point; because of start-up and other per-worker costs, Gregg has to work a while each morning without pay to cover these costs.

The fatigue effect and start-up and other per-worker costs vary across firms, and iso-profit curves reflect these differences. In Figure 5.12, Xena's firm specializes in a short workday by offering job X. Start-up and other per-worker costs are low and the fatigue effect is strong at Xena's firm, so Xena employs people for only 4 hours per day. Workers who are averse to long workdays work for Xena; they earn $60 per day (or $15 per hour). Yogi's firm offers jobs with an 8-hour workday because its start-up and other per-worker costs are high and fatigue effects at Yogi's firm are weak. Workers who don't mind a long workday (or have a strong desire for consumption) work for Yogi, and they earn $88 per day (or $11 per hour).

Connecting these jobs (and many more like them) gives us the equilibrium consumption–leisure curve in Figure 5.12. The equilibrium consumption–leisure curve collects all the jobs available in the labor market, so it's like a budget line. Although Gregg can't choose his working hours on any job, he can pick his workday by selecting a job. The wage governing Gregg's choice (i.e., the slope of the consumption–leisure curve) isn't, however, the familiar hourly wage rate. If Gregg works for Xena on job X, his daily pay translates into a $15 hourly wage; if he works for Yogi on job Y, his hourly wage is $11. But the slope of the consumption–leisure curve is $7 per hour, and that's what's important for Gregg's labor supply choice.

 PRACTICE   In Figure 5.12, if Gregg works a 6-hour workday, how much does he earn for the day? Mark the point on the consumption–leisure curve. How much does he earn per hour?

Compensating Wage Differentials for Long Workdays

Transferring the information from the consumption–leisure graph in Figure 5.12 to a graph with daily wages (or earnings) w and working hours h in Figure 5.13 delivers a model of job choice with hours as the attribute of the job. Replace daily consumption c with the *daily* (not hourly) wage w on the vertical axis. Switching from leisure l to hours h involves flipping the content of the graph horizontally. The result is a familiar graph of compensating wage differentials for a job attribute—hours of work in this case—in Figure 5.13. A job with an 8-hour workday pays $28 (= $88 − $60) more per day than a job with a 4-hour workday.

We now have the foundation to interpret the empirical relationship between wages and workweeks across occupations. Workers' interests through labor supply and firms' interests based on fatigue effects and per-worker costs determine the equilibrium workweek. In our introduction to the Current Population Survey in

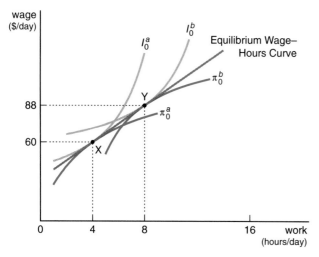

The consumption–leisure curve in Figure 5.12 implies an equilibrium relationship between the daily wage and the length of the workday. Flipping the curve horizontally replaces leisure l with work hours h on the horizontal axis.

Workers and firms match along the equilibrium wage–hours curve $w(h)$, and jobs with a long workday pay a compensating wage differential.

Job X pays $15/hour, and Y pays $11/hour, but extending the workday pays only $7/hour, the slope of the equilibrium wage–hours curve.

FIGURE 5.13. Equilibrium Compensating Wage Differential for the Length of the Workday

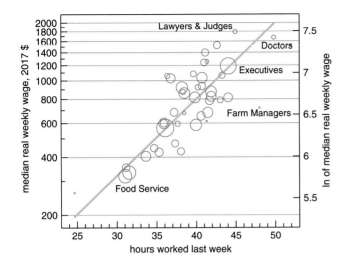

Notes: The left axis measures the wage on a logarithmic scale. The right axis measures the natural logarithm of the wage on the usual arithmetic scale. For each occupation, the center of the bubble marks the data point, and the size of the bubble reflects the occupation's employment.

Source: Current Population Survey, outgoing rotation group files, monthly 1979–2017.

FIGURE 5.14. Weekly Wage and the Workweek Across Occupations, 1979–2017

chapter 1, we plotted pairs of median weekly wages and the average workweek across 43 occupations. (See Table 1.2 and Figure 1.1.) The points are jobs that match workers to firms, and those points reveal the underlying wage–hours curve $w(h)$.

Fitting a line to the 43 "points" in Figure 5.14 identifies the wage–hours curve across occupations. Some occupations are much bigger in terms of employment than others, and the regression analysis should weight these occupations more heavily. Therefore, Figure 5.14 replaces the points from Figure 1.1 with bubbles: the size of the bubble reflects the number of people working in that occupation. The line that best fits the occupation data on weekly wages and hours appears in Figure 5.14, and the estimated regression line is

(5.1)
$$\ln w = 3.01 + .092h$$
$${}_{(.251)}{}_{(.007)}$$

with $R^2 = .730$. Lengthening the workweek by an hour increases weekly wages by 9 percent in this estimate of the wage–hours curve. (Increasing h by one hour per week increases $\ln w$ by .092, which is approximately the same as increasing the weekly wage w by 9.2 percent; see section 1.6's review of logarithms.) Hence workers in occupations with a 40-hour workweek tend to earn 92 percent more than those in occupations with a 30-hour workweek.

The length of the workweek alone captures much of the variation in weekly wages across occupations. Yet there's plenty of room for other factors (including those we study in subsequent chapters) to deepen our understanding of cross-occupation differences in weekly wages. Indeed, schooling, work experience, sex and race, and unionization help explain occupational wages, and these factors dampen the importance of the workweek. But our main finding survives: high-wage occupations tend to be occupations that have long workweeks.

Employee Benefits

Not all job attributes are bad. Jobs can be dirty, noisy, and dangerous, but they can also offer good prospects for career advancement, flexible work schedules, job security, paid holidays and vacations, and generous health and pension benefits. Here we tweak the model of compensating wage differentials to accommodate job amenities, the good features of jobs. The wage premium in this context emerges for jobs that don't provide many amenities.

Composition of Pay

Employee benefits are a big chunk of employee compensation. For the average civilian worker in the United States at the end of 2017, benefits—including paid leave, health and disability insurance, retirement plans, and legally required benefits (e.g., Medicare, Social Security, workers' compensation, and unemployment insurance)—cost employers $11.38 per hour. Wages and salaries average $24.49 per hour, so benefits add 46 percent to hourly pay. And total compensation of $35.87 per hour is split roughly 70–30 between wages (i.e., cash compensation) and benefits. What determines this split, the **composition of pay**?

Dirt, noise, and risk of injury or even death are byproducts of work activity. They occur naturally, and they're expensive to remove. Job benefits, however, aren't a natural byproduct of work. And in a simple economic environment, there is no reason to invite benefits to the compensation table. If workers prize health insurance, they simply buy as much as they want in the insurance market. Those who want more insurance buy more. Health insurance and other benefits are like shoes—none of the employer's business. So a reasonable starting point for the composition of pay is 100 percent wages, no benefits.

Benefits work their way into compensation if employers acquire some consumption goods or services at a discount. Suppose the price of a benefit b is $1,000 per unit for Disney and other employers. Beth and other workers would have to pay a higher price for the benefits. In competition with other employers, Disney offers the benefit to its workers at its cost, $1,000 per unit. Beth's annual value of marginal product is $50,000, so Disney pays her $50,000 without benefits, $0 with 50 units of b, or any combination of the two. Thus the wage–benefits curve $w(b)$ in Figure 5.15 depicts Beth's opportunities.

Beth's preferences over consumption goods and benefits interact with her opportunities along the wage–benefits curve $w(b)$ to determine her choice of a wage–benefits package. The downward-sloping indifference curves in Figure 5.15 illustrate her preferences. Beth chooses point C, the wage–benefits package where one of her indifference curves is tangent to the wage–benefits curve. Beth receives 15 units of the benefit, which costs Disney $15,000, and her wage income for the

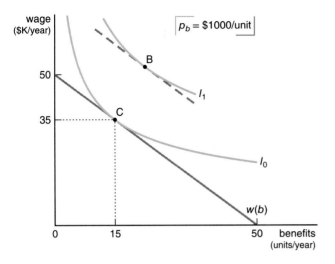

Indifference curves I_0 and I_1 represent Beth's preferences over wages w and benefits b.

Beth's $50,000 annual compensation is divided between wages and benefits, which cost $1,000 per unit. Each unit of b lowers w by $1,000 along the wage–benefits curve $w(b)$.

Beth chooses compensation package C. Her annual pay is $35,000, and the value of her benefits package is $15,000.

Gregg's earning potential is greater than Beth's; his wage–benefits curve (the dashed line) is higher, and he chooses compensation package B with a higher wage and more benefits.

FIGURE 5.15. Employee Benefits

year is $35,000. The composition of her pay is 70 percent wage and 30 percent benefits.

Disney and other employers might not allow each worker to design his or her own compensation package. Each competitive employer then offers a compensation package on the wage–benefits curve, and Beth controls her mix of wage and benefits by her job choice. She works for a firm that offers a 70–30 split of wage and benefits, point C in Figure 5.15. If she wants a different mix of wage and benefits along $w(b)$, she takes a job at a different firm.

Taxing Wages But Not Benefits

In the United States, the federal government taxes wages and salaries as individual income. It doesn't tax some employee benefits (e.g., health, disability, and life insurance). Pension contributions aren't taxed, but the government taxes income drawn from pensions during retirement. Thus pushing income into a pension plan delays taxation, which is valuable. Pay for time not worked (i.e., holidays, vacations, sick days) is taxed at the regular rates without any tax advantage.

Taxing wages but not benefits tilts Beth's compensation away from wages toward benefits. Beth switches to a more benefits-intensive compensation package to avoid taxes. To see why, consider point B in Figure 5.16 where the slope of Beth's indifference curve is −$1,000 per unit of benefits. At B, Beth is willing to forego $1,000 (meaning 1,000 units of consumption) to increase her benefits by one unit. Now we introduce a tax at rate t on Beth's wage income. Beth cares about her consumption, which she buys with her after-tax (or take-home) wage $(1 - t)w$. If the tax rate is 33.3 percent, Beth's after-tax wage is $.667w$.

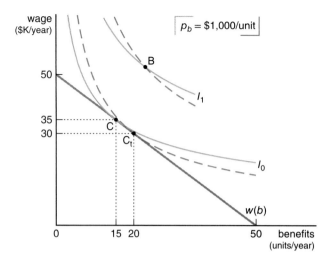

Indifference curves I_0 and I_1 represent Beth's preferences with no income tax. The steeper (dashed) indifference curves represent her preferences with a proportional income tax rate $t > 0$. The income tax steepens the indifference curve through each point on the graph (e.g., point B). The tax scales up the slope of the indifference curve at each point by $1/(1-t)$.

With steeper indifference curves, Beth's choice of a compensation package slides down $w(b)$ from C to more benefits-intensive C_t. She avoids part of the tax burden by replacing taxable wages with nontaxable benefits.

FIGURE 5.16. Taxing Wages But Not Taxing Benefits

If Beth foregoes $1,500 to get one more unit of b, her after-tax wage falls by only $1,000, which implies her consumption falls by 1,000 units. At point B, Beth is willing to forego $1,000 (meaning 1,000 units of consumption) to increase b by one unit without the tax, so she is willing to forego $1,500 (meaning 1,000 units of consumption) to increase b by one unit with the 33.3 percent tax. This calculation implies that the slope of Beth's indifference curve through point B increases (in absolute value) by the factor $3/2$. Indeed, at every point in Figure 5.16, the slope of Beth's indifference curve is scaled up by $3/2$. More generally, the scale factor is $\frac{1}{1-t}$, which equals $1/.667$ in this example.

> ✓ **PRACTICE**   Let $t = .20$. How does the tax affect the indifference curves in Figure 5.16?

Since Beth's family of indifference curves steepens and the wage–benefits curve remains fixed, Beth's optimal compensation package slides down along the wage–benefits curve from C to C_t in Figure 5.16. The composition of her pay tilts away from wages toward benefits.

But Cushy Jobs Pay More

Workers like Beth choose points along the wage–benefits curve, which implies an inverse (or negative) relationship between wages and benefits. Jobs with more benefits—like a corner-office view of the Brooklyn Bridge—should pay less! But the corner office with a view always goes with a high-paying job, and high-paying jobs tend to have more generous benefits packages, too. Is the model of compensating wage differentials just wrong?

Differences in productivity across workers—some workers are more productive than others—drive most of the variation in benefits across workers, and productivity differences don't trace out the downward-sloping wage–benefits curve $w(b)$. Suppose Gregg is more productive than Beth: his $w(b)$ curve is higher than (and parallel to) Beth's in Figure 5.15, and he chooses a compensation package with a higher wage and more benefits because benefits are a normal good. Comparing Gregg's and Beth's compensation packages reveals a direct relationship between wages and benefits, but that's simply the income effect associated with Gregg's higher productivity. Similarly, in the prime of her career, Beth earns more and receives more benefits, which again reflects the fact that benefits are a normal good.

To identify the wage–benefits curve empirically, we must compare compensation packages across equally productive workers. That is, we must control for earnings potential. In the chapters that follow, we study how attributes of the worker (e.g., schooling, work experience, race, and sex) influence productivity and wages. Lessons from that analysis help researchers control for differences in earnings potential across workers in estimating the wage–benefits curve. Such controls reduce the bias toward finding a positive relationship between wages and benefits due to the income effect. But we never fully control for earnings potential, so we never eliminate the bias toward finding that cushy jobs pay more. And thus we know that any compensating wage differentials that exist in the labor market will be difficult to find.

Summary

We opened this chapter with the observation that there's more to a job than its wage and that these other features—job attributes—are likely to influence wages. Our key findings are:

☐ Supply of and demand for workers on dirty jobs determine the wage premium for work on dirty jobs if dirt is a discrete variable. Workers require a wage premium to work on dirty jobs, and firms are willing to pay the wage premium to avoid the costs of cleaning the work environment.

☐ If jobs range from squeaky clean to deathly filthy, then compensating wage differentials emerge, and a wage–dirt curve matches workers to firms on the basis of (1) workers' preferences over jobs and (2) firms' cleanup technologies.

☐ Workers and firms both gain from the existence of an implicit market in dirt. Dirty work is simply a mutually advantageous trade between each firm that offers dirty jobs and each worker who takes one of those jobs.

☐ That workers gain from having access to dirty jobs challenges the justification for government regulation of safety and health in the workplace. The case for limiting job risks assumes that workers aren't compensated for job risks or their beliefs are biased. Our analysis points to workers, as well as firms, being hurt by the regulation.

☐ We calculate the market value of human life from the compensating wage differential for risk, which the slope of the wage–risk curve measures.

☐ Specifying firms' interests in the workday or workweek enriches our treatment of labor supply. A worker chooses his or her hours by choosing a job, and workers and firms of different types match along the wage–hours curve. The equilibrium includes a compensating wage differential for long hours.

☐ The relationship between the workweek and weekly wages across occupations, which is quite strong, is an empirical wage–hours curve.

☐ The compensation package tilts away from wages toward benefits in response to an income tax that exempts employee benefits from taxes.

This completes our analysis of job attributes, but the modeling methods and themes from this chapter carry over to our analysis of the attributes of workers, such as schooling, to which we turn in the next chapter.

Key Concepts

- reservation wage for dirty work, p. 165
- step function, p. 166
- wage premium, p. 168
- compensating wage differential, p. 169
- wage–dirt curve, p. 169
- iso-profit curves, p. 171

- value of life, p. 178
- fatigue effect, p. 180
- start-up and per-worker costs, p. 180
- employee benefits, p. 184
- composition of pay, p. 184

Short-Answer Questions

5.1 In Figure 5.3, shade the area that represents the gains from trade in the market for dirty jobs. Calculate the gains from trade.

5.2 Let's re-apply Figure 5.3 to illustrate the market for *risky* jobs. An innovation reduces the cost of making a job safe. What happens to reservation wages on each side of the market? Does the innovation increase or decrease the demand for labor on risky jobs? Does the innovation raise or lower the wage premium associated with risky work?

5.3 Sports franchises like the Los Angeles Lakers employ many non-athletes to work in the background managing team travel, drafting contracts, laundering uniforms, and so on. Many people are passionate about their sports teams. What effect does love of sports have on the supply of workers to sports franchises? Do you think sports franchises pay wage premiums or wage discounts to their non-athlete employees?

5.4 Sharon's aversion to risk is much stronger than Sherwin's. How is her choice of jobs related to Sherwin's? This difference in preferences generates two jobs along what curve?

5.5 Workers match with firms at various jobs along a wage–risk curve $w(r)$. Few firms offer low-risk jobs, but many workers want those jobs. Lots of firms offer high-risk jobs, but few workers want risky jobs. What happens in equilibrium to the wage–risk curve?

5.6 Workers surely aren't fully informed about job risks. Suppose they know that one in ten jobs involves serious exposure to a toxic chemical, but they don't know which jobs carry this risk. Are workers on risky jobs paid more in the competitive equilibrium? Are workers on risky jobs better or worse off than workers on safe jobs? Next, OSHA bans the chemical. What happens to the wage(s)? Are the workers who were on risky jobs better off? Does OSHA's ban help or hurt workers who had been lucky enough to be on safe jobs before the ban?

5.7 Suppose the wage–risk curve increases at a decreasing rate. How does the market value of life vary along the curve? Is the value of life higher for people on relatively safe jobs or for people on riskier jobs?

5.8 Workers don't like the risk of death or injury on the job, and they also don't like the risk of being laid off. Sketch a worker's job choice in a market that pays a compensating wage differential for the risk of layoff.

5.9 A common complaint about economists' modeling of labor supply is that workers can't choose their hours of work; employers set the workday or workweek. How does our model of compensating wage differentials address that complaint?

5.10 Wages are taxed; employee benefits are not. Why does the tax steepen the whole family of indifference curves? Be sure to refer to the marginal rate of substitution between consumption and benefits.

Problems

5.1 Jobs are either noisy or serenely quiet. Quiet jobs pay $10 per hour. Most workers don't like the noise, so they won't work on noisy jobs for $10 per hour. In particular, for the five workers in this labor market, Anna requires $17 per hour, Bart $14 per hour, Carmen $10 per hour, Davin $15 per hour, and Ellen $11 per hour to work on a noisy job.

It's costly for most firms to reduce noise on a job. For the five firms in this labor market, Al's Auto Body won't pay a wage more than $20 per hour on a noisy job; Bonnie's Bikini Boutique, $10 per hour; Carl's Custom Cabinets, $12 per hour; Debbie's Digital Demos, $14 per hour; and Elton's Entertainment, $16 per hour.

Each worker works on only one job, and each firm employs only one worker.

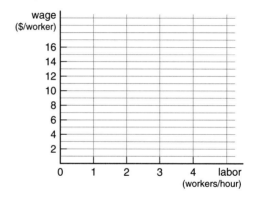

(a) Lightly sketch each worker's reservation wage in the graph.

(b) If the wage on the noisy job is $13 per hour, who wants to work on a noisy job? What is the quantity supplied of labor to noisy jobs if $w_n = 13$? Carefully sketch the supply of labor to noisy jobs.

(c) Lightly sketch each firm's reservation wage in the graph.

(d) If the wage on the noisy job is $13 per hour, which firms offer noisy jobs? What is the quantity demanded of labor on noisy jobs if $w_n = 13$? Carefully sketch the demand for labor on noisy jobs.

(e) What is the equilibrium wage for noisy work? How many people work on noisy jobs in the equilibrium?

(f) Noise is implicitly traded in this labor market. If government regulations require all jobs to be quiet, who suffers?

5.2 Jobs vary by the risk of injury, and the relationship between the hourly wage w and the risk of injury r is the wage–risk curve $w(r)$, which the figure below illustrates. The figure also depicts an indifference curve for each worker, Molly (M) and Nora (N).

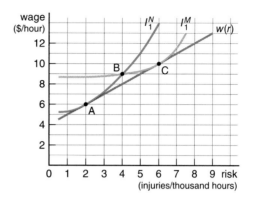

(a) Compared to job A, what's the wage premium for the riskier work on job C?

(b) How much more does Nora require in wages to accept a job with the risk of job C rather than take job A? That is, what wage differential $w_C - w_A$ leaves Nora indifferent between the risks on jobs A and C?

(c) Who is more averse to the risk of injury on the job: Molly, Nora, or neither?

(d) Consider the job choices of Molly and Nora. Molly works on job _____, and Nora works on job _____.

5.3 The figure below illustrates two jobs, A and B, on a hypothetical wage–risk curve.

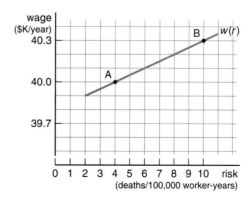

(a) What is the wage premium on job B compared to job A? That is, what is $\Delta w = w_B - w_A$? Carefully specify the units of the wage premium.

(b) What is the risk differential $\Delta r = r_B - r_A$? Carefully specify the units of the risk differential.

(c) What is the slope of the wage–risk curve? Carefully specify the units of the slope $\Delta w / \Delta r$.

(d) Simplify your answer to part (c) to solve for the implied value of human life.

5.4 The indifference curves in the figure below illustrate Dan's preferences over compensation packages, pairs of annual wages w and benefits b. The value of the marginal product of Dan's labor is $60,000 per year. Employee benefits come in standardized units, and the market price of each unit is $1,000. For example, if Dan's employer's annual cost of his health insurance is $4,000, then Dan's health insurance provides him with 4 units of the benefit b.

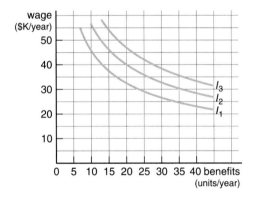

(a) Draw the wage–benefits curve, and determine Dan's optimal mix of wage and benefits. What is Dan's wage, and how many units of benefits does he receive?

(b) At Dan's optimal choice, what is his marginal rate of substitution between benefits and wages?

(c) The graph is drawn with a tax rate of zero. Suppose the government puts a 20 percent tax on wages but leaves employee benefits untaxed. In the neighborhood of Dan's optimal choice without the tax, what is his marginal rate of substitution with the tax? That is, at what rate is Dan willing to give up annual wages to get a bit more in benefits if the tax rate on wages is 20 percent?

(d) The 20 percent tax rate on wages scales up the slope (in absolute value) of Dan's indifference curve through each pair (b, w) by the factor _____.

(e) Illustrate how Dan's optimal composition of pay responds to the tax.

References

Lewis, H. Gregg. 1969. "Employer Interests in Employee Hours of Work." Unpublished manuscript, University of Chicago.

Rosen, Sherwin. 1974. "Hedonic Prices and Implicit Markets: Product Differentiation in Pure Competition." *Journal of Political Economy* 82(1): 34–55.

Rosen, Sherwin. 1986. "The Theory of Equalizing Differences." In *Handbook of Labor Economics*, vol. 1, edited by Orley Ashenfelter and Richard Layard. New York: North-Holland, pp. 641–692.

Smith, Adam. 1998 (1776). *An Inquiry into the Nature and Causes of the Wealth of Nations*. Washington, DC: Regnery Publishing.

Thaler, Richard and Sherwin Rosen. 1976. "The Value of Saving a Life: Evidence from the Labor Market." In *Household Production and Consumption, Studies in Income and Wealth*, vol. 40, edited by Nestor Terleckyj. New York: National Bureau of Economic Research, pp. 265–298.

Viscusi, W. Kip and Joseph Aldy. 2003. "The Value of a Statistical Life: A Critical Review of Market Estimates Throughout the World." *Journal of Risk and Uncertainty* 27(1): 5–76.

6 Schooling

oes the American Bar Association (ABA), as gatekeeper to the legal profession, restrict entry to elevate the pay of attorneys? According to data from the Current Population Survey in 2017, practicing attorneys with law degrees earn about $2,300 per week. By comparison, the average weekly pay of college graduates (without any graduate education) is about $1,300. The $1,000 weekly premium to practicing law might be due to ABA licensing, but perhaps less nefarious factors contribute to lawyers' wage premium. For instance, lawyers work long hours, 4.7 hours per week longer than the typical college graduate, and that explains about $250 of the $1,000 weekly premium. But what explains the remaining $750?

The most important factor explaining the wage premium to practicing law is schooling. Lawyers are well educated. Practicing law requires a law degree, which involves three expensive years of full-time study in law school. Law school is expensive in two ways. First, tuition and fees vary widely across law schools but average about $40,000 per year; that's approximately $800 per week of law school. An even greater cost of attending law school is foregone wages: law school is a full-time job, so a law student foregoes the pay of a typical college graduate, which is $1,300 per week. Therefore, practicing law involves weekly costs of $2,100 (= $800 + $1300) over the three years of law school to reap the weekly wage premium of $750 over a 35-year career. If the ABA elevates lawyers' pay, then this investment is unusually lucrative.

Does this investment strike you as a financial bonanza? In this chapter, we analyze schooling as an investment: the costs are up front in the form of out-of-pocket expenses like tuition and foregone wages, and payoffs come later in the form of higher pay over the career. Whether an investment like schooling is sensible depends on the interest rate.

Consider a law student who secures an unusual loan to finance the costs of law school: the loan requires weekly payments over the lawyer's entire 35-year career, with the final payment made at the aging lawyer's retirement party. If the loan's annual interest rate is 10.4 percent, then weekly payments on the loan are $750, and the wage premium to practicing law simply pays back the cost of law school with interest. The lawyer consumes not a dime more than a college graduate. If the interest rate is higher than 10.4 percent, then the $750 weekly wage premium to practicing law isn't enough to pay back the loan over a 35-year career, and law school is a bad investment.

Law schools are selective. They admit the best college students; average students need not apply. The typical lawyer was above average as a college student, and he or she would have earned more than $1,300 per week with only a college degree. So $750 exaggerates the weekly wage premium to practicing law, and a law-school education might be a bad investment even for interest rates much lower than 10.4 percent. Maybe the ABA isn't all that effective in elevating lawyers' pay.

Here we develop two models of schooling as an investment. In the first model, schooling is an investment in **human capital**: what you learn in school raises your productivity on the job after you leave school. In the second model, schooling is a means for higher-ability people to distinguish themselves from lower-ability people without improving their job skills at all. We also explore the effect of schooling on labor supply. Before we turn to the models of schooling, let's track how schooling choice (i.e., highest grade completed) has evolved over more than a century.

Some Historical Context.   The emergence of an educated workforce was one of the great social and economic transformations of twentieth-century America. In 1950, the typical working-age person had completed nine grades; by the end of the twentieth century, average schooling in the working-age population had reached one year of college. These numbers mix the schooling choices of young adults, senior citizens, and everyone in between. To get a better sense of the timing of schooling choices over the past century, let's examine completed schooling for each **birth cohort**, a group of people who were born in the same year.

Completed schooling of 25-year-olds grew rapidly from 7 grades in 1900 to 13 grades in 1970 and has grown slowly since then. Figure 6.1 displays highest grade completed (at age 35) by sex with time marked by the year the cohort turned 25. (Most but not all people complete their schooling by age 25; to accommodate the stragglers, the series in Figure 6.1 measure the highest grade those 25 year olds eventually complete.) On the basis of data in the 1940 Census of Population, the figure shows that the 25-year-olds in 1930 completed 9 grades on average. Twenty-five year olds in 1950 (based on data from the 1960 Census)

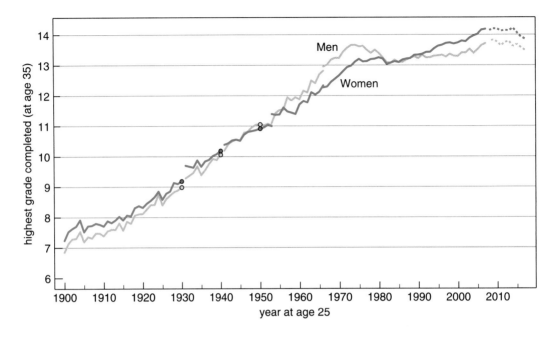

FIGURE 6.1. Eventual Completed Schooling of 25 Year Olds

Notes: (a) Each series measures the mean value of highest grade completed at age 35 and displays this with the year the respondents turn 25. For instance, in the 1940 Census of Population, 35-year-old men completed 9 grades on average, so 25-year-old men in 1930 eventually completed 9 grades on average. (b) In 1940, 1950, and 1960, we get three data points for women and another three data points for men from census data. In addition, we use the census data to estimate schooling earlier in the century and between the census years. (c) Since some 25- to 34-year-olds in 2017 hadn't completed their schooling, we project completed schooling for these younger cohorts on the basis of how average highest grade completed grows with age in earlier (complete) cohorts. Sources: Census of Population, Public Use Microdata Series (PUMS), 1-percent files, 1940, 1950, 1960. Current Population Survey, Annual Social and Economic Supplements (March), 1963–1976. Current Population Survey, basic monthly files, January 1976–December 2015. The data are available from IPUMS-USA and IPUMS-CPS (www.ipums.org) at the University of Minnesota.

completed 11 grades, a two-grade increase in two decades. And 25-year-olds in 1970 completed 13 grades. Schooling has continued to grow in successive cohorts, but the rate of growth has slowed since then.

Schooling choices of both men and women rose from 7 grades for the 25-year-olds in 1900 to over 13 grades for the 25-year-olds in 2015. That comparison hides small differences in the schooling choices of men and women that might surprise you. For the first four decades of the twentieth century, young women stayed in school slightly longer than young men. The pattern switched shortly after World War II. Men born between 1930 and 1955, who turned 25 between 1955 and 1980, stayed in school longer than women in those cohorts. Over the past 15 years, however, women have again been staying in school longer than men. For instance, based on data from the 2015 Current Population Survey, 25-year-old women in 2005 completed half a grade more than their male peers.

Schooling as an Investment in Human Capital

Jacob is a student. One of the biggest decisions in Jacob's life is when to quit school. Will he head straight to work after finishing high school, or will he attend college for four years and perhaps graduate school beyond that? That the answers to these questions depend on college tuition surely doesn't surprise you. The following analysis of schooling also points to the interest rate, life expectancy, taxes on labor income, and innate ability as key determinants of when to quit school.

We model schooling as an investment in human capital (Mincer 1958). As an investment, schooling involves costs up front that return payoffs down the road. Jacob's costs are in two forms. First, he or his parents might have to pay c dollars of tuition per grade (or year of college). Second, Jacob doesn't work while in school, so he foregoes the wage that someone with his education earns. By attending grade s, Jacob thus bears tuition cost c and foregoes the wage he could earn with that education for the promise of higher wages when he leaves school.

In this model, schooling generates higher wages over Jacob's career because schooling is productive. What Jacob learns in school raises his productivity throughout his career. That is, schooling increases his human capital.

Like all investors, Jacob evaluates his options for schooling investments by comparing costs and returns at different points in time. Since $1 today and $1 thirty years from today aren't valued equally, Jacob applies principles about the *time value of money*. In particular, Jacob compares **present values** of his different career options: he *discounts* dollar amounts in the future to the present.

If Jacob deposits $100 in the bank today and his deposit earns 10 percent annual interest, then he will have $110 in the bank in a year. That $110 bank balance earns 10 percent interest in the second year, so his balance after two years compounds up to $121. Simple enough. But earning 10 percent interest also means that $110 a year from now is worth $100 today. Indeed, the present value of $110 a year from now is $100 ($= \$110/(1 + .10)$), and the present value of $121 two years from now is also $100 ($= \$121/(1 + .10)^2$).

More generally, Jacob and other investors discount by the interest rate a stream of costs ($y_t < 0$) and payouts ($y_t > 0$) over years t from 0 to N. The present value is

(6.1)
$$PV = y_0 + \frac{y_1}{(1+i)} + \frac{y_2}{(1+i)^2} + \frac{y_3}{(1+i)^3} + \cdots + \frac{y_N}{(1+i)^N}$$

where i is the annual interest rate. In Jacob's case, y_t's in his early years are negative, corresponding to tuition payments while he is in school. Each subsequent y_t is Jacob's annual wage in year t of his career, and he retires $N + 1$ years from now.

☑ **PRACTICE**

Suppose workers with associate's degrees from two-year community colleges earn $38,400 per year, and the interest rate is 10 percent. Use a calculator to compute the factor $(1 + i)^t$ that discounts the $38,400 earned in year 37 (i.e., $t = 37$) back to the first year in college (i.e., $t = 0$). What is the present value of the $38,400 earned in year 37?

Wage Profiles and the Wage–Schooling Curve

The first two columns of Table 6.1 list Jacob's career options. Associated with each completed grade (or year of schooling) is the annual wage that he would earn throughout his career until he retires at age 65. (Wages that grow over a worker's career are the topic of chapter 7.) For instance, if he finishes high school but doesn't attend college (i.e., $s = 12$), he works on jobs that pay $32,000 per year. In Jacob's case, completing a grade of school adds $3,200 to his annual wage.

Wage profiles, one for each completed grade of school, summarize these career opportunities. The wage profiles in Figure 6.2 illustrate two of Jacob's many options. If Jacob takes his high school diploma and heads straight to work, he earns $32,000 per year for his whole career until he retires at age 65. Alternatively, Jacob attends another four years of college, pays $10,000 per grade in tuition, and starts working at age 23. With a college diploma, he earns $44,800 per year until he retires at age 65. By attending college, Jacob bears $10,000 per year in tuition and foregoes $32,000 per year in wages to raise his annual wage $12,800 over his 42-year career. The costs are hefty ($168,000 over the four years of college), but the returns are staggering ($537,600 over Jacob's 42-year career). Yet college could be a bad investment.

 PRACTICE   Suppose tuition at a community college is $5,000 per year, and workers with associate's degrees from two-year community colleges earn $38,400 per year until retiring at age 65. Sketch this wage profile in Figure 6.2.

TABLE 6.1.   SCHOOLING, WAGES, AND THE MARGINAL RATE OF RETURN TO SCHOOLING

SCHOOLING s (grade)	WAGE w ($/year)	WAGE CHANGE Δw ($/year/grade)	MARGINAL RATE OF RETURN $\Delta w/w$ (percent/grade)
10	25,600	3,200	12.5
11	28,800	3,200	11.1
12	32,000	3,200	10.0
13	35,200	3,200	9.1
14	38,400	3,200	8.3
15	41,600	3,200	7.7
16	44,800	3,200	7.1
17	48,000	3,200	6.7
18	51,200	3,200	____

Note: The marginal rate of return to schooling is Δw in column 3 divided by w in column 2.

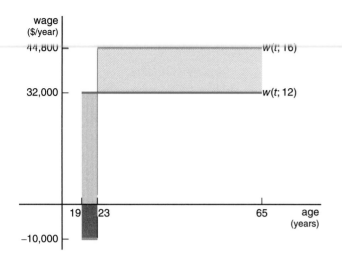

As an investment, college involves costs up front and payoffs down the road.

If Jacob quits school after grade 12, he earns $32,000/year from age 19 until he retires at age 65. His wage profile with a high school diploma is w(t; 12).

If Jacob graduates from college, he foregoes $32,000/year in wages and pays $10,000/year in tuition for four years. After graduating from college, Jacob earns $44,800/year until he retires. His wage profile with a college education is w(t; 16).

FIGURE 6.2. Wage Profiles and Schooling

The interest rate determines whether college is a good investment. Comparing the present values of Jacob's high school and college wage profiles reveals whether college is a good investment for Jacob. Let's assume Jacob can borrow money and lend (or save) money at the same interest rate, 7 percent. At age 18 (in his last year of high school), the present value of Jacob's high school wage profile is $451,518; the present value of his college wage profile is $446,506. Therefore, the 40 percent wage premium associated with a college education isn't enough to pay off four years of annual loans of $42,000 (= $10,000 + $32,000). (Alternatively, the 40 percent wage premium isn't enough to replenish Jacob's savings or investment accounts that were drawn down to pay for college.) If the interest rate is 7 percent, then college doesn't quite pay off. And the case for a college education is even weaker if the interest rate is 10 percent: the gap between the two present values widens. If, however, the interest rate is 5 percent, then college is a great investment for Jacob.

A single **wage–schooling curve** $w(s)$ collects all the information in the various wage profiles—one wage profile for each completed grade of school. Since each wage profile is flat, two numbers—schooling s and the wage w—fully describe the wage profile. (Let's ignore tuition for the moment.) Schooling s tells us when Jacob's pay jumps from nothing to w. Each pair (s, w) is a point on the wage–schooling curve $w(s)$; 12 and $32,000, 16 and $44,800, and 18 and $51,200 are three points on Jacob's wage–schooling curve in Figure 6.3a.

Since Jacob's wage–schooling curve is a line, the growth rate of Jacob's wage falls as schooling and the wage increase. By extending his education from high school to college, Jacob increases his wage $12,800, or $3,200 per year of college. To express this wage premium as a growth rate, we divide these values by the midpoint wage, which is $38,400, to find that college increases Jacob's wage 33 percent (or 8.3 percent per year).

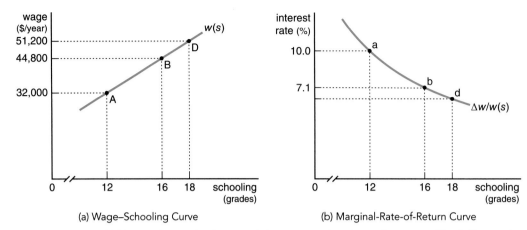

(a) Wage–Schooling Curve   (b) Marginal-Rate-of-Return Curve

(a) Two numbers, schooling s and the wage w, describe each wage profile. Collecting the pairs (s, w) across wage profiles gives Jacob's wage–schooling curve w(s), which shows how his annual wage varies with his schooling.

(b) Jacob's four years of college increase his wage $3,200/year, or about 8.2%/year of college. We compute the marginal rate of return $\Delta w/w(s)$ at each grade. The resulting marginal-rate-of-return slopes down.

FIGURE 6.3. Wage–Schooling Curve and the Marginal Rate of Return to Schooling

We can also express the growth rate of Jacob's wage for each year of school by dividing the wage change by the wage: $\Delta w/w(s)$. The slope of Jacob's wage–schooling curve is constant at $3,200 per grade; see column 3 of Table 6.1. (We're concerned with one-grade changes in schooling (i.e., $\Delta s = 1$), so we denote the wage–schooling curve's slope $\Delta w/\Delta s$ by Δw.) Since $w(12) = \$32,000$ and $w(16) = \$44,800$, Jacob's wage grows 10.0 percent ($= 3200 \div 32,000$) at $s = 12$ and 7.1 percent ($= 3200 \div 44,800$) at $s = 16$. These two points lie on the growth rate curve $\Delta w/w$ in Figure 6.3b.

 PRACTICE   What is the growth rate of Jacob's wage at point D in Figure 6.3a? Enter your answer in Table 6.1, and mark this value on the vertical axis for point d in Figure 6.3b.

We refer to the growth rate of wages with schooling as the **marginal rate of return to schooling**. By attending another year of school, Jacob foregoes the wage $w(s)$, which is the cost of his marginal schooling investment. (We continue to assume that tuition is zero.) The investment pays off Δw per year in higher wages. So the growth rate $\Delta w/w(s)$ is the marginal rate of return to schooling at s. The first and last columns of Table 6.1 list the relationship between wage growth $\Delta w/w(s)$ and schooling s, and the downward-sloping marginal-rate-of-return curve in Figure 6.3b illustrates the relationship.

Wealth and Iso-Wealth Curves

Jacob can compute the present value associated with each point on his wage–schooling curve, but a less direct approach allows us to derive his demand for schooling and to interpret the empirical relationship between wages and schooling. To keep things simple, assume that Jacob lives and works forever and that he doesn't have to pay for school ($c = 0$). In his last year of school, the present value of wages over his career is then

$$(6.2) \qquad PV_s = \frac{1}{1+i} \left\{ w + \frac{w}{1+i} + \frac{w}{(1+i)^2} + \frac{w}{(1+i)^3} + \cdots \right\}$$

The expression in braces is the present value of career wages evaluated in the first year on the job. It's an example of an infinite geometric series, and infinite geometric series simplify spectacularly. In fact, the expression in braces simplifies to $(1 + i)w/i$. (See the Advanced material below.) So the present value of career wages when evaluated in the last year of school s is simply the ratio of the wage to the interest rate.

$$(6.3) \qquad PV_s = \frac{w}{i}$$

No need for a financial calculator; ignore your spreadsheet program. We calculate the present value (the year before Jacob begins work) of career wages by simply dividing the wage w by the interest rate i.

 PRACTICE   With only a high school education, Jacob earns $32,000 per year. If the annual interest rate is 10 percent, what is the present value of career wages when Jacob is a senior in high school? (Assume Jacob lives and works forever.)

ADVANCED Establishing that the infinite geometric series in Equation 6.2 simplifies to Equation 6.3 is easy enough. Divide both sides of Equation 6.2 by $1 + i$ to yield

$$(6.4) \qquad \frac{PV_s}{1+i} = \frac{1}{1+i} \left\{ \frac{w}{1+i} + \frac{w}{(1+i)^2} + \frac{w}{(1+i)^3} + \frac{w}{(1+i)^4} + \cdots \right\}$$

Although there's an infinite number of terms on the right side of Equation 6.2 and another infinite number of terms on the right side of Equation 6.4, each term after w in Equation 6.2 matches up with an identical term in Equation 6.4. Subtracting one equation from the other leaves

$$(6.5) \qquad PV_s - \frac{PV_s}{1+i} = \frac{w}{1+i}$$

Solve this equation for PV_s (with $i > 0$) to find $PV_s = w/i$, which is Equation 6.3.

· ·

Since we don't know when Jacob finishes school, let's express the present value of Jacob's career wages before he starts school. Little Jacob's value of career wages the year before his parents walk him to his first day of school is

(6.6)
$$PV_0 = \frac{w}{i} \times \frac{1}{(1+i)^s}$$

which we call **wealth** W. Wealth commonly refers to the value of financial assets. Jacob's asset is his stream of wages over his career, so Jacob's wealth is the value of his career wages. In particular, wealth discounts the present value of Jacob's career wages back to before he starts school. Equation 6.6 shows how Jacob's wealth W varies with his wage w and schooling s, given an interest rate i. So Jacob (or his parents) can use Equation 6.6 to compare various pairs of wage w and schooling s.

 PRACTICE   With only a high school education, Jacob earns \$32,000 per year. If the annual interest rate is 10 percent, what's the present value of career wages in the year before little Jacob begins first grade? (Assume Jacob lives and works forever.)

Let's solve Equation 6.6 for the wage to illustrate the family of iso-wealth curves. An **iso-wealth curve** collects all the pairs of the wage w and schooling s that generate some value of wealth W (given an interest rate i). Solving Equation 6.6 for Jacob's wage gives an iso-wealth curve for some wealth W.

(6.7)
$$w = iW(1+i)^s$$

Wealth W and the interest rate i are constants in this equation; schooling s and the wage w are the variables.

Figure 6.4 displays the family of iso-wealth curves, one curve for each value of wealth. Along an iso-wealth curve, Jacob's wage grows at a constant rate, the interest rate i. (Such constant rate of growth is called *geometric* or *exponential growth*.) Equation 6.7 implies that the wage increase associated with another year of school is $\Delta w \equiv w(s+1) - w(s) = iw(s)$. (To derive this expression, use Equation 6.7 to express $w(s+1)$ as $iW(1+i)^{s+1}$ and $w(s)$ as $iW(1+i)^s$.) Therefore, the rate of growth of the wage along an iso-wealth curve $\Delta w/w(s)$ is the interest rate i.

Wealth-Maximizing Schooling Choice and the Demand for Schooling

Jacob chooses schooling to maximize his wealth. Since he can borrow or lend (or save) at the interest rate, his schooling choice separates entirely from his preferences for consumption over his lifetime.

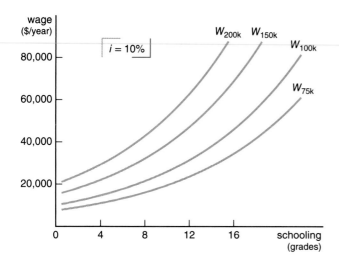

Iso-wealth curves illustrate Jacob's preferences over schooling and wages. Each iso-wealth curve collects pairs of schooling s and wage w that generate the same wealth W. This figure uses Equation 6.7 to display iso-wealth curves for four values of wealth.

Jacob's wage grows at a constant rate, the 10% interest rate, along each iso-wealth curve. Lowering the interest rate flattens each iso-wealth curve.

FIGURE 6.4. Iso-Wealth Curves

Whether Jacob is impatient (e.g., wanting to consume now at the expense of his future consumption) or quite patient (e.g., content with delaying his consumption until later in life) isn't relevant for his schooling choice. It might seem obvious that an impatient student quits school early because he doesn't care enough about the future consequences, but that's not correct. An impatient student goes to graduate school (if that maximizes his wealth) and lives lavishly while in school, borrowing against his future earnings or drawing down his (or his parents') savings and investment accounts.

The principle then is that access to a well-operating financial market enables Jacob to separate his schooling choice from his life-cycle consumption choice. He chooses schooling to maximize wealth, and he chooses how to allocate consumption over his lifetime, given his wealth, based on his patience or impatience, as well as the interest rate. Jacob's schooling choice is our only concern.

Of all pairs (s, w) on the wage–schooling curve, which one generates the highest wealth for Jacob? The wealth-maximizing choice of schooling is the point where an iso-wealth curve is tangent to the wage–schooling curve, which is point A in Figure 6.5. Jacob leaves school with a high school education and earns \$32,000 per year throughout his career. In his last year of school, the present value of his career wages PV_{12} is \$320,000 ($= \$32,000 \div .1$). To compute Jacob's wealth before he starts first grade, discount this present value back 12 years by dividing by 3.138 ($= 1.1^{12}$). Jacob's wealth is approximately \$102,000.

The wealth-maximizing choice of schooling s^* equates the benefits and costs of school at the margin; equivalently, the marginal rate of return to schooling equals the interest rate at s^*. The slope of the wage–schooling curve equals the slope of the iso-wealth curve at point A, Jacob's wealth-maximizing choice. Let the constant Δw denote the slope of the wage–schooling curve $w(s)$. The analysis following Equation 6.7 implies that the slope of the iso-wealth curve at s^* is $w(s^*)i$. The two curves have the same slope at A, so $\Delta w = w(s^*)i$ at Jacob's schooling choice s^*.

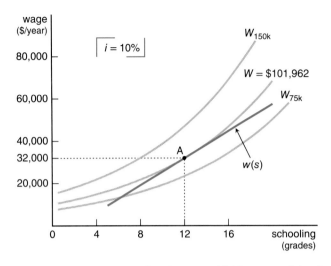

Jacob's wealth-maximizing choice of schooling is 12 grades, where iso-wealth curve $W \approx \$102{,}000$ is tangent to the wage–schooling curve $w(s)$ at A. He earns $32,000/year.

At point A, the slope of Jacob's iso-wealth curve iw equals the slope of his wage–schooling curve Δw. This equal-slopes condition implies that the marginal cost of school w equals the marginal benefit of school $\Delta w/i$ at Jacob's optimal schooling choice, A.

FIGURE 6.5. Wealth-Maximizing Schooling Choice

☑ **PRACTICE**   Mark the point (16, 44,800) with a B in Figure 6.5. Check Table 6.1 to confirm that B is a point on the wage–schooling curve. The annual interest rate is 10 percent. What is the slope of the iso-wealth curve through B? Is it steeper or flatter than the wage–schooling curve?

We can express this equal-slopes condition in two informative ways. First, divide each side by i to establish that Jacob's schooling choice equates the marginal benefit and the marginal cost of school: $\Delta w/i = w(s^*)$. The marginal benefit of school is $\Delta w/i$, the present value of the wage gain forever; the marginal cost of school is the foregone wage $w(s)$. Second, divide both sides of the equal-slopes condition by the wage $w(s^*)$ to reveal that the wealth-maximizing schooling choice equates the marginal rate of return to schooling to the interest rate: $\Delta w/w(s^*) = i$.

We can also illustrate the wealth-maximizing schooling choice by graphing the marginal-rate-of-return curve. Figure 6.6 depicts Jacob's marginal-rate-of-return curve and a horizontal line at the interest rate $i = 10$ percent. (The marginal-rate-of-return curve is drawn as a line to keep things simple.) Jacob chooses to finish school with a high school diploma (i.e., $s^* = 12$) at the intersection of the interest rate line and the marginal-rate-of-return curve. If Jacob drops out before finishing high school, then his marginal rate of return to schooling exceeds the interest rate: another year in school pays a higher return than the interest rate in the financial market. Since it's a good investment, Jacob stays in school. For any grade beyond $s = 12$, the interest rate exceeds the marginal rate of return to schooling: financial investments pay a higher return than schooling, so staying in school is a bad investment. Dropping out of school before the return to schooling falls below the interest rate raises Jacob's wealth. Consequently, Jacob

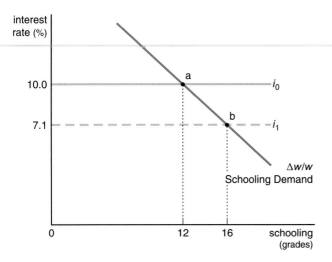

At tangency point A in Figure 6.5, the slope of Jacob's iso-wealth curve *iw* equals the slope of the wage–schooling curve Δw. So Jacob's optimal schooling choice s^* solves $\Delta w / w(s) = i$, where the marginal rate of return $\Delta w / w$ is a downward-sloping curve.

The quantity demanded of schooling varies along $\Delta w / w$ as the interest rate i varies, so the downward-sloping marginal-rate-of-return curve is Jacob's schooling demand curve.

FIGURE 6.6. Demand for Schooling

continues in school until he drives the marginal rate of return to his schooling investment down to the interest rate.

The quantity demanded of schooling is a decreasing function of the interest rate. You probably expect the demand for schooling to capture the relationship between schooling choice (i.e., the quantity demanded of schooling) and tuition, the price of attending school. In the context of investment, such as schooling as an investment in human capital, the interest rate plays the role of the price. Jacob completes 12 years of school if the interest rate is 10 percent. If the interest rate is about 7 percent, he equates the marginal rate of return to schooling to this lower interest rate by earning a college diploma. These two points—(12, .10) and (16, .071)—are two points on Jacob's schooling demand curve in Figure 6.6. Indeed, the marginal-rate-of-return curve is Jacob's demand for schooling.

Schooling is an investment, so maximizing the rate of return to the schooling investment sounds like an attractive goal. It's not! **Rate-of-return maximization** reduces Jacob's wealth. Jacob's marginal rate of return to schooling in third grade is 100 percent. Should he quit school after grade three to secure this stellar rate of return? If he did, he would earn a measly $3,200 per year throughout his career, and his wealth would be less than one-fourth its value with a high school diploma. So quitting school when the marginal rate of return is maximized would be a mistake. Indeed, the proper interpretation of the stellar marginal rate of return to a third-grade education is that continuing in school to fourth, fifth, and sixth grade and beyond is a wise move.

Equilibrium Wage–Schooling Curve

The rate of return to schooling investments is determined in equilibrium. Since the wage–schooling curve associates a wage with each grade completed, it implicitly embodies the rate of return to schooling. So now we explore how the wage–schooling curve is determined in equilibrium.

A steeper wage–schooling curve encourages Jacob and other students to stay in school longer. The quantities supplied of more-educated workers rise, and the quantities supplied of less-educated workers fall. On the other side of the market, quantities demanded of labor shift from more-educated workers to less-educated workers. Alternatively, a flatter wage–schooling curve lowers the return to schooling, which encourages Jacob and other students to drop out earlier. And employers' quantities demanded of labor shift from less-educated to more-educated workers. As an application of compensating wage differentials—here the attribute is the worker's schooling—the wage–schooling curve is determined in equilibrium to eliminate surpluses or shortages at every completed grade of schooling.

What happens if all workers are identical? In this special case, workers share a family of iso-wealth curves and a common wage–schooling curve. Every person graduates from high school just like Jacob, and the world is flooded with workers with only high school diplomas. No one trains to be a doctor, dentist, architect, engineer, or corporate executive, and that can't be an equilibrium. There's also a shortage of less-skilled workers, such as farm laborers and household cleaners. If everyone is identical, then the wage–schooling curve must adjust to leave everyone indifferent among the schooling options. That is, every pair (s, w) must lie on a single iso-wealth curve. More-educated workers earn more, but they are no wealthier. As Figure 6.7 shows, the wage–schooling curve $w(s)$ must coincide with (i.e., lie on top of) an iso-wealth curve in the equilibrium with identical people.

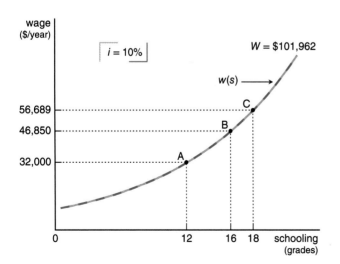

If everyone is identical, then the equilibrium wage–schooling curve leaves everyone indifferent among wage–schooling pairs, such as points A, B, and C. That is, pairs (s, w) must lie on a single iso-wealth curve. The equilibrium wage–schooling curve with identical people coincides with (i.e., lies on top of) an iso-wealth curve.

In this special case, the wage w grows with schooling s along the wage–schooling curve $w(s)$ at a constant rate, and that rate is the interest rate i.

FIGURE 6.7. Equilibrium Wage–Schooling Curve with Identical People

6.2 Estimating the Rate of Return to Schooling

Labor economists frequently estimate the rate of return to schooling by fitting a regression line to data on schooling and the logarithm of wages (e.g., Mincer 1974). Let's see why we can interpret the slope of the **log-wage equation** as the rate of return to schooling.

With identical people, the wage–schooling curve is an iso-wealth curve that easily fits wage and schooling data. Expressing the formula for an iso-wealth curve (i.e., Equation 6.7) in logarithms links the logarithm of the wage $\ln w$ to schooling s along the wage–schooling curve.

(6.8a) $$\ln w = \ln(iW) + \ln(1+i)s$$

(6.8b) $$\approx \ln(iW) + is$$

since $\ln w = s \ln x$ if $w = x^s$, and $\ln(1+i)$ is approximately i if i isn't too large. (See section 1.6.) Since i and W are constants, we can fit the line $\ln w = a + bs$ to data on $(s, \ln w)$ to estimate the constants a and b. The slope coefficient b tells us how an extra year of school increases $\ln w$, which is approximately the growth rate of wages $\Delta w / w$. Therefore, we often refer to b as the rate of return to schooling. In the equilibrium with identical people, the rate of return to schooling equals the interest rate, and an estimate of the slope coefficient b should be in the ballpark of the interest rate that governs schooling choice, perhaps 5–7 percent.

Rate of Return to Schooling Across Occupations

Figure 6.8 plots pairs of schooling and wages (s, w) for the 43 occupations in our CPS data on occupation averages since 1979. The scatter plot clearly reveals the positive correlation of schooling and wages across occupations: occupations with more-educated workers tend to pay higher wages. The estimated regression line is

(6.9) $$\ln w = 4.08 + .185s$$
$$\quad\quad\quad (.440)\quad (.031)$$

with $R^2 = .512$. Our estimate of the slope b is .185: staying in school another grade increases $\ln w$ by .185 and the wage w by 18.5 percent. That is, the estimated rate of return to schooling across occupations is 18.5 percent. We can be confident that the true value lies between 12.3 percent and 24.7 percent $(= .185 \pm (2 \times .031))$.

Adding the length of the workweek h to the regression tempers the effect of schooling on the wage.

(6.10) $$\ln w = 2.09 + .074h + .121s$$
$$\quad\quad\quad (.221)\quad (.006)\quad (.013)$$

with $R^2 = .920$. The estimated rate of return to schooling falls from 18.5 percent to 12.1 percent. This slope coefficient is precisely estimated: we can be confident that the true effect of schooling on $\ln w$ is between 9.5 percent and

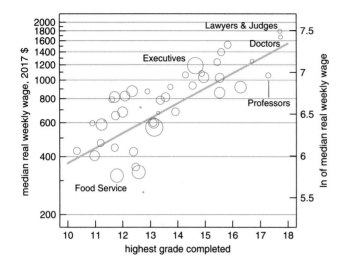

Notes: The left axis measures the wage on a logarithmic scale. The right axis measures the natural logarithm of the wage on the usual arithmetic scale. For each occupation, the center of the bubble marks the data point, and the size of the bubble reflects the occupation's employment.
Source: Current Population Survey, outgoing rotation group files, monthly 1979–2017.

FIGURE 6.8. Wages and Schooling Across Occupations, 1979–2017

14.7 percent ($= .121 \pm (2 \times .013)$). Omitting the workweek from the regression mistakenly attributes to schooling what we should attribute to the workweek because long-workweek occupations tend to have educated workers.

These estimates of the rate of return to schooling seem high: they are much higher than the 5–7 percent interest rate that we might expect. Perhaps we can do better by relaxing one or more of the many assumptions we invoked in deriving our model of schooling choice and casting it in the regression context. We assumed everyone has the same interest rate, pays no tuition, lives forever, pays no taxes, and has the same ability. Let's see how relaxing each of these assumptions affects our interpretation of the log-wage regression and whether relaxing these assumptions explains why the estimated slope coefficient b is greater than the interest rate.

Differences in the Interest Rate

People aren't identical. One way they differ is in their access to financial markets. Jacob borrows at a 10 percent interest rate to finance his schooling. Edward draws down his investment balances, which earn about a 7 percent return, to finance his education. As a result, Edward's schooling choice moves down along the schooling demand curve in Figure 6.6, and he graduates from college. Also, Edward's iso-wealth curves are flatter than Jacob's. Figure 6.9 illustrates how Edward's flatter iso-wealth curves push his schooling choice up along the wage–schooling curve $w(s)$. His tangency moves up the wage–schooling curve from Jacob's tangency (point A) to point B. He earns \$44,800 per year.

With differences in interest rates across people, observed pairs of schooling and wages trace out the wage–schooling curve, but differences in interest rates don't explain why the estimated rate of return to schooling is so high. The line through A and B is flatter than Jacob's iso-wealth curve but steeper than Edward's.

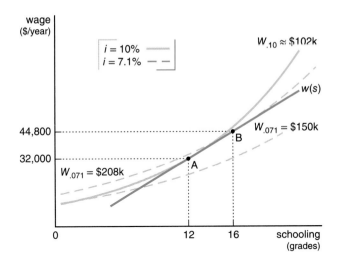

Jacob's and Edward's interest rates are 10 percent and 7.1 percent, respectively. Lowering the interest rate flattens the iso-wealth curves, so Edward's dashed iso-wealth curves are flatter than Jacob's solid iso-wealth curves.

Jacob starts working after high school and earns $32,000 annually. Edward, with the lower interest rate, graduates from college and earns $44,800/year.

The observations, points A and B, lie on the wage–schooling curve. Differences in i help estimate the true rate of return to schooling along $w(s)$.

FIGURE 6.9. Equilibrium Wage–Schooling Curve with Differences in Interest Rates

The implied estimate of the rate of return to schooling is some average of the two interest rates, 10 percent and 7.1 percent. With differences in interest rates, the slope of the regression line fit to $(s, \ln w)$ data identifies an average interest rate. Hence it doesn't explain why the estimated rate of return to schooling is so high.

Tuition, Death, and Taxes

Our analysis of the wealth-maximizing choice of schooling has ignored tuition, and now it's time to explore how tuition affects our interpretation of the schooling coefficient in the log-wage regression.

Tuition cost c lowers the rate of return from the rate of wage growth $\Delta w/w$ to $\Delta w/(w + c)$. Edward pays tuition cost c and foregoes the wage w to attend another grade of school. The cost of this investment is $w + c$, which returns the wage gain Δw. Thus Edward's marginal rate of return to schooling with tuition is $\Delta w/(w + c)$, which is lower than the growth rate of his wage $\Delta w/w$. For instance, in Figure 6.10, tuition of $13,700 per grade lowers Edward's marginal rate of return to schooling from 7.1 percent ($= 3200 \div 44{,}800$) to 5.5 percent ($= 3200 \div (44{,}800 + 13{,}700)$) at grade 16. Therefore, the marginal-rate-of-return curve in Figure 6.10 lies below the wage-growth curve.

Edward leaves school when his marginal rate of return equals the interest rate, so the negative effect of tuition on his marginal rate of return encourages him to leave school earlier. In Figure 6.10, Edward responds to tuition by quitting school after high school; he foregoes college. Indeed, at every interest rate, Edward's quantity demanded of schooling is lower than without tuition: tuition reduces the demand for schooling.

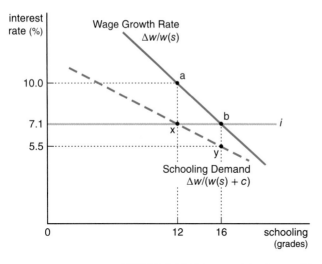

Edward's marginal rate of return to schooling is $\Delta w/(w(s) + c)$, so tuition c lowers the return to schooling. If $c = \$13,700/\text{grade}$, then tuition scales down his marginal return to schooling from 7.1% to 5.5% at grade 16.

If $i = .071$ and $c = \$13,700$, Edward gets only a high school education. Edward's quantity demanded of schooling falls at each interest rate, and his demand for schooling falls from the solid line to the dashed line.

Death (or retirement) and taxes also reduce the rate of return to and the demand for schooling.

FIGURE 6.10. Tuition and the Demand for Schooling

When Edward leaves school, his wage grows with schooling at a rate that exceeds the interest rate. In Figure 6.10, his wage grows 10 percent per grade when he leaves school with a high school diploma. But the interest rate is 7.1 percent. So the effect of schooling on log wages b exceeds the interest rate i if students pay tuition; that is, the regression coefficient is greater than the interest rate.

 PRACTICE Which of the four points in Figure 6.10 corresponds to Edward's schooling choice if his tuition is $13,700 per grade and the interest rate is 7.1 percent? At this schooling choice, Edward's wage grows with schooling at _____ percent per grade. Is his rate of wage growth greater than or less than the interest rate?

Our analysis of schooling choice assumes that Jacob, Edward, and others live and work forever. Jacob surely won't live forever, and recognizing that he will retire and eventually die helps explain the high apparent rate of return to schooling. Shortening Jacob's career reduces the payoff to his schooling investment and reduces his demand for schooling. Retirement drives a wedge between the rate at which Jacob's wage grows with schooling and his marginal rate of return to schooling. His schooling demand curve, which reflects the marginal rate of return to his schooling, lies below his wage growth curve $\Delta w/w$. So retirement and death echo the implication of tuition: Jacob leaves school before his wage growth sinks as low as the interest rate. That is, retirement and death cause the regression coefficient b to exceed the interest rate i.

Unemployment also reduces the demand for schooling and drives a wedge between wage growth and the interest rate. If Jacob's probability of being unemployed in any month of his long career is 10 percent, then he will have fewer months of work to earn a return on his schooling investment. Indeed, the 10 percent unemployment risk cuts his marginal rate of return to schooling by 10 percent, which reduces his demand for schooling. And again, Jacob leaves school before his wage growth sinks as low as the interest rate.

A tax on wage income lowers the payoff to schooling investment but also lowers the cost of schooling. In fact, a tax on wages doesn't affect the demand for schooling at all if Jacob pays no tuition and lives forever. With a flat tax rate t, the payoff to another year of school falls from Δw to $(1-t)\Delta w$. The lower payoff weakens Jacob's incentive to invest in human capital through schooling. But the flat tax also lowers the cost of going to school from w to $(1-t)w$, which strengthens Jacob's incentive to get educated. The marginal rate of return to schooling (without tuition or death) becomes $(1-t)\Delta w/((1-t)w(s)) \equiv \Delta w/w(s)$. The two tax terms cancel out, and the tax doesn't affect Jacob's demand for schooling.

A tax on wage income reduces the demand for labor if students pay tuition. While the tax lowers the foregone income from attending school (from $w(s)$ to $(1-t)w(s)$), it doesn't lower the tuition cost c. Indeed, the tax amplifies the effect of tuition in reducing the demand for schooling. (The gap between the wage growth curve and the demand for schooling curve in Figure 6.10 is bigger with the tax.) Thus taxes drive an additional wedge between the regression coefficient b and the interest rate i.

These extensions to tuition, death, unemployment, and taxes all point to (1) wage growth $\Delta w/w(s)$ exceeding the marginal rate of return to schooling, and (2) the demand for schooling lying below the wage-growth curve. In each case, the schooling coefficient b exceeds the interest rate i. So these factors go a long way toward explaining why our estimate of the "rate of return to schooling" in Equation 6.10 is so high.

Differences in Ability

A worker's wage profile depends on his or her ability a, as well as his or her schooling s. There are many elements of innate ability, but let's focus on smarts. Jacob is no slouch in the classroom or on the job, but Alice is just smarter. If she and Jacob get the same schooling, she earns a higher wage because her higher ability translates into better job performance. In addition, Alice gets more out of each year of school. Therefore, as Figure 6.11 illustrates, the wage–schooling curve of Alice and other high-ability people $w(s; a_1)$ is higher and steeper than the wage–schooling curve of Jacob and other low-ability people $w(s; a_0)$.

High-ability people demand more schooling. Alice and Jacob share a common set of iso-wealth curves, and the rate of growth along each iso-wealth curve is the interest rate i. As Figure 6.11 illustrates, Alice responds to her higher and steeper wage–schooling curve by getting a college education and earning \$64,000 annually. As before, Jacob completes high school and works for \$32,000 per year. The higher growth rate of wages along Alice's wage–schooling curve translates into a higher marginal-rate-of-return curve in Figure 6.12. That is, Alice and other high-ability workers have a higher demand for schooling.

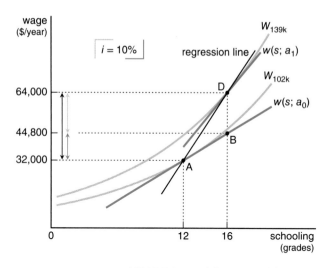

Alice is smarter than Jacob; her wage–schooling curve is higher and steeper than his.

Alice gets a college diploma and earns $64,000/year, twice what Jacob earns with his high school diploma. But Jacob would earn only $44,800/year (or 40% more) if he completed college. Here most of the college premium reflects Alice's higher ability.

The ability bias is that the thin black line, which runs through the two data points A and D, is steeper than either wage–schooling curve.

FIGURE 6.11. Ability Bias and the Rate of Return to Schooling

The difference in pay between high school and college graduates exaggerates the return to a college education. Comparing Alice's $64,000 wage to the $32,000 wage that Jacob earns with his high school diploma suggests that a college education doubles the wage. It doesn't. Much of the $32,000 gap in pay is due to Alice's higher ability rather than her college education. If Jacob graduated from college, he would earn $44,800 rather than the $64,000 that Alice earns. The $19,200 (= $64,000 − $44,800) difference reflects Alice's higher ability. Therefore, the college wage premium overstates the return to schooling if higher-ability people stay in school longer.

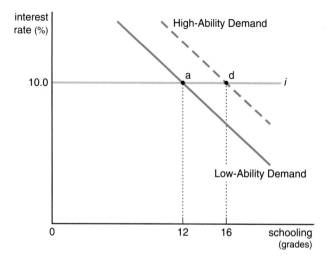

High-ability workers like Alice get more out of school; their marginal rate of return to schooling is higher, and they complete more grades.

By going to school the extra four years, Alice drives her marginal rate of return to schooling down to equality with Jacob's marginal rate of return to schooling.

FIGURE 6.12. Schooling Demand and Ability

PRACTICE   Use Alice's wage–schooling curve in Figure 6.11 to approximate her pay if she doesn't go to college. Use the curve to split the $32,000 wage premium that Alice receives into Alice's true return to a college education and Alice's ability advantage at $s = 12$.

The exaggerated return to schooling also appears in a regression line fit to data on wages and schooling. Fitting a line to the data generated by the choices of Jacob and Alice, points A and D, gives the thin black line in Figure 6.11. This line is steeper than either Jacob's or Alice's wage–schooling curve, so the estimated slope coefficient b exaggerates the rate of return to schooling. We call this overstatement the **ability bias** in estimating the rate of return to schooling.

Avoiding Ability Bias

There are many creative ways to avoid ability bias in practice. Early research added proxies for ability, such as scores on standardized tests and measures of family background, to the wage regression. Later researchers took an instrumental variables (IV) approach to purge the schooling variable of variation that could be driven by ability a. (See chapter 1's review of causation and instrumental variables estimation in section 1.5.) The IV estimator replaces schooling s with a variable closely tied to schooling but unrelated to ability. For instance, we can use college tuition, distance from home to the nearest college, and compulsory school attendance laws to predict schooling for each worker, and a regression line can be fit to log wages and the predicted schooling variable (i.e., the *instrumental variable*). IV estimates of the rate of return to schooling are typically high and sometimes higher than the simpler estimates that ignore ability bias. Yet another approach exploits differences in wages and schooling across workers of identical ability, which brings us to twins studies.

Avoiding ability bias would be easy if we could (1) clone high school graduates and send their clones to college or (2) clone college graduates and send their clones to work after high school. In your case, the original you—most likely the one reading these words—graduates from college with strong training in labor economics. By comparing your wage with your high-school-educated clone's wage, we calculate a return to college that's free of ability bias because you and your clone are genetically identical and equally able.

Ashenfelter and Krueger (1994) apply this method to a sample of hundreds of identical twins, which they collected at the Twins Days Festival in Twinsburg, Ohio, in the summer of 1991. For starters, they fit a line to their data, a pair of hourly wage and years of schooling for each working twin in their sample. The estimated regression line is

(6.11)
$$\ln w = 1.16 + .086s$$
$${\scriptstyle(.227)}\quad{\scriptstyle(.016)}$$

with $R^2 = .091$. Completing an additional grade raises the log wage .086 across the 298 workers in this sample, so the estimated "rate of return" to schooling is 8.6 percent per grade. This estimate does nothing to avoid ability bias, so we should expect the true effect of schooling on wages to be less than 8.6 percent.

Ashenfelter and Krueger then exploit the fact that the sample is composed of identical twins. Within roughly half the pairs of twins, the two twins share the same years of schooling, and this half of the sample isn't much use in avoiding ability bias. In the other half of the sample, one twin has more schooling than his or her genetically identical brother or sister. How much more does the more-educated identical twin earn?

Ashenfelter and Krueger use advanced econometric techniques to generate unbiased estimates of the effect of schooling on log wages, but we can extract the essence of their estimates with a few simple calculations from their data. For the half sample with different years of schooling within twin pairs, the average values of (s, w) are 15.45 grades and $16.24 per hour for the more-educated twin and 13.21 grades and $11.93 per hour for the less-educated twin. Figure 6.13a plots these two points. (The graph also plots points for the averages in the "same schooling" and "different schooling" samples for reference.) Since genetic makeup in the "More School" point is exactly the same as genetic makeup in the "Less School" point, differences between the two points aren't related to ability. The slope of the line through these two points is $\Delta w / \Delta s = \$1.92$ $(= (\$16.24 - \$11.93)/(15.45 - 13.21))$ per hour per grade or approximately 13.7 percent per grade; that is, a worker who completes one more grade than his

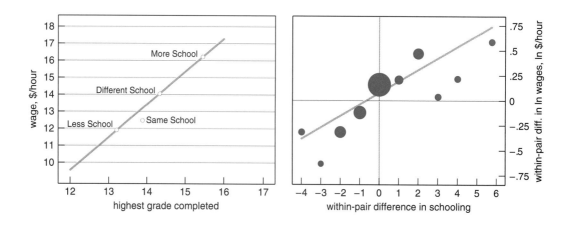

FIGURE 6.13. Average Hourly Wages and Schooling within Pairs of Identical Twins

Notes: In panel (a), the line connects the averages for the more-educated and less-educated twins in each not equally educated pair. In panel (b), a dot represents the average difference (across twins) in the log of the hourly wage for working twins with a specific within-pair difference in schooling. The size of the dot indicates the weight; that is, the largest dot, representing nearly half the sample, is for the equally educated twins $\Delta s = 0$.

Source: Calculations from the 1991 sample of 298 identical twins (Ashenfelter and Krueger 1994).

identical twin earns on average $1.92 more per hour or 13.7 percent more than his identical twin.

This pattern of wages and schooling for identical twins is confirmed in Figure 6.13b, which presents the data as differences *within each pair of identical twins*. Within each pair, we compute the difference in years of schooling and the difference in wages (in logs). For instance, Orley completed two more years of school and earns 33 percent more than his twin Morley, so the Orley–Morley pair contributes the data point (2, .33) to the sample. For each schooling difference (e.g., two grades), we plot the average within-pair difference in wages (in logs) in Figure 6.13b. For instance, one point on the graph indicates that the typical worker with two years of schooling more than his twin earns nearly 50 percent more than his twin. (The size of the dot reflects the number of twins used to compute the average.)

The scatter plot in Figure 6.13b clearly reveals that wages and schooling are positively related within pairs of twins. The regression line fit to these data points (and weighted by the number of observations represented by each point) is

(6.12)
$$\Delta \ln w = \underset{(.05)}{.08} + \underset{(.028)}{.115} \Delta s$$

with $R^2 = .678$. Hence our estimate of the rate of return to schooling within pairs of identical twins (and thus free of ability bias) is 11.5 percent. This estimate is a bit lower than our estimate in Figure 6.13a, but it matches our estimate across occupations in Equation 6.10. It's also in line with more advanced estimates in Ashenfelter and Krueger (1994).

Is our concern about ability bias unwarranted? These estimates suggest that removing ability bias *increases* the effect of schooling on wages, and that's a big surprise. But there's more to it. These estimates solve two problems simultaneously. They remove the upward bias from differences in ability, and they remove (or reduce) a downward bias from measurement error in the schooling variable. Survey participants, such as the identical twins in Twinsburg, don't always respond to survey questions accurately, so there are plenty of errors in schooling responses. Such errors bias the estimated effect of schooling on wages in Equation 6.11 toward zero. Averaging the data to produce the scatter plots in Figure 6.13 and the regression estimates in Equation 6.12 reduces the measurement-error bias, and Ashenfelter and Krueger's methods eliminate that bias. If ability bias (pushing up the estimate) is smaller than measurement-error bias (pushing down the estimate), then removing these biases increases the effect of schooling on wages. And that's what we've found.

6.3 Schooling as a Signal of Ability

In the model of schooling as an investment in human capital, higher-ability workers stay in school longer, and a rational employer can infer a worker's ability from his or her schooling. Could a rational employer infer ability from schooling even if schooling provides no useful skills? What if schooling is just jumping through a long series of intellectual hoops—memorizing state capitals in elementary school, identifying the characters and plot of *Macbeth* in a high school literature class, and grasping the analytic–synthetic dichotomy in a college philosophy course—to determine who's smart and who's not? Would schooling **signal ability**?

Signaling Model of Schooling

In the signaling model of schooling, low-ability and high-ability workers populate a single labor market (Spence 1973). The value of the marginal product of labor of Jacob and other low-ability workers is $40,000 per year *independent of schooling*; Alice and other high-ability workers have a value of marginal product of $60,000 per year no matter how much schooling they have. Employers don't observe ability. If employers can't figure out who's smart and who's not, then they treat all workers the same and pay each worker $50,000 per year, the average VMP_L.

Could Alice signal her ability by getting a college education? Can she separate herself from the pool of low- and high-ability workers to command the $60,000 annual wage that reflects the value of her contribution to production? Suppose Jacob and Alice choose between getting a high school education that pays $40,000 and earning $60,000 on a job that requires a college degree. As Figure 6.14 shows, the wage–schooling curve in this case is a step function with the wage jumping from $w = \$40,000$ to $w = \$60,000$ for schooling greater than or equal to 16 years. If Jacob chooses the high school career and Alice chooses the college career, then schooling reveals ability, Jacob is paid what he's worth, and Alice is paid what she's worth. But do Jacob and Alice sort this way?

If schooling is less valuable to low-ability people, then they skip college, and college can signal ability. What renders college less valuable to Jacob and other low-ability people? A higher interest rate would do it, but there's no reason to believe that low-ability people discount the financial returns to schooling at a higher interest rate.

Perhaps Jacob's cost of schooling is higher than Alice's even if he and Alice pay the same tuition. If Jacob struggles through school, then school frustrates him and his self-esteem suffers. These psychological costs of school are difficult to measure in dollars and cents, but they're real, and they're an important part of the cost of school. Consequently, the schooling cost for low-ability people like Jacob is higher than the schooling cost for high-ability people like Alice. Since the slope of the iso-wealth curve is $(w + c_a)i$ for a worker of ability a, Jacob's iso-wealth curves are steeper than Alice's iso-wealth curves. Figure 6.14a displays two of Jacob's iso-wealth curves; panel (b) displays two of Alice's iso-wealth curves. For simplicity (and to highlight the difference in slopes between Jacob and Alice), let's depict the iso-wealth curves (inaccurately) as lines.

While Jacob quits school after grade 12, Alice signals her ability to employers by graduating from college. In our context, there's no gain to attending college without completing a degree, and there's no advantage to going to graduate school. So the choice facing Jacob and Alice is between high school jobs paying $40,000 per year and college jobs paying $60,000 per year. This is the choice between the

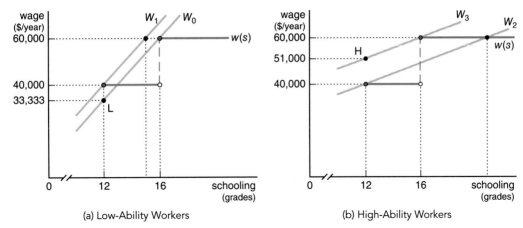

(a) Low-Ability Workers   (b) High-Ability Workers

High-ability and low-ability workers face a common wage–schooling curve, which here is a step function. College-educated workers earn $60,000/year; less-educated workers earn $40,000/year.

In panel (a), Jacob compares the high school job and the college job (i.e., the two gray dots). As a low-ability person, school frustrates him, and he discounts the college job more heavily than Alice in panel (b). To Jacob, the college job is worth no more or less than a high school job paying $33,333. He rejects college and heads straight to work. Alice doesn't mind college, and she values the college job the same as a high school job that pays $51,000. She goes to college.

Therefore, low-ability people take high school diplomas while high-ability people signal their ability by graduating from college.

FIGURE 6.14. Signaling Model of Schooling

two gray dots—points (12, 40,000) and (16, 60,000)—in Figure 6.14. For Jacob in panel (a), the high school job is on a higher iso-wealth curve. Indeed, he discounts the $60,000 college job down along his iso-wealth curve W_0 to $33,333, which he can compare directly to the $40,000 high school job. The high school job is more valuable, so Jacob and other low-ability workers begin working immediately after high school. For Alice in panel (b), the high school job is on a lower iso-wealth curve. She discounts the $60,000 college job down along her iso-wealth curve W_3 to $51,000, which is $11,000 more than the high school job pays. Alice and other high-ability workers graduate from college.

Employers notice that workers with college degrees are 50 percent more productive than high school graduates, and competition among the employers guarantees a 50 percent wage premium to college-educated workers.

 PRACTICE   Suppose Jacob discounts the college job more than Alice does, but his iso-wealth curves aren't as steep as the ones in Figure 6.14a. In this case, point L might be (12, 42,000). Would Jacob go to college? Would a college education signal ability?

. . . .

ADVANCED In our signaling model of schooling, a student must clear the hurdle of a college education to earn the $60,000 annual wage. Is this **schooling requirement** the only one that sorts workers by ability?

Varying the schooling requirement s' moves the upper gray dot in each panel left or right. Sliding the upper gray dot left until it meets Jacob's iso-wealth W_1 in panel (a) reveals the grade that leaves Jacob indifferent between high school and college jobs. Any higher schooling requirement (i.e., $s' > 15$) sends Jacob to work immediately after high school. Sliding the upper gray dot right until it meets Alice's iso-wealth W_2 in panel (b) reveals the grade that leaves Alice indifferent between high school and college jobs. Any higher schooling requirement (i.e., $s' > 21$) sends Alice to work right after high school. Therefore, any schooling requirement between 15 and 21 grades sorts workers by ability; schooling doesn't signal ability if the hurdle lies outside this range.

Competition among employers drives down the schooling requirement to the lowest value that delivers sorting by ability. That's 15 grades (or perhaps just a little more) in Figure 6.14. Any higher hurdle imposes costs without providing additional information or productive skills.

. . . .

Schooling must also be the least-cost way to signal ability. Might high-ability people like Alice have less-cost ways to distinguish themselves? First, standardized tests might be a more efficient means to identify ability. Many young people would take courses to improve their performance on the standardized test (to fool employers into thinking they're smarter than they are), but standardized tests would still be much cheaper than years of full-time school. Second, academic performance in elementary and middle school might predict ability quite well. As a byproduct of human-capital-generating schooling in elementary and middle schools, we develop a good sense of who the best students are. High school and college might do little to refine our assessments of who's smart and who's not. If that's true, then performance through middle school is a more efficient signal of ability than highest grade completed.

In a 1972 advertising campaign to encourage young blacks to enroll in college, the United Negro College Fund declared that "a mind is a terrible thing to waste." In the signaling model, sending a mind to school is a terrible waste. If Alice works rather than attending college, the value of what she produces over those four years totals $160,000 (= 4 × $40,000). The social cost of schooling as a signal includes these foregone earnings as well as the cost of providing the education (including subsidies from taxpayers). But schooling as a signal creates no value.

Schooling is simply an expensive means to end the subsidization of low-ability workers like Jacob by high-ability workers like Alice. If no one went to school, everyone would earn $50,000, which is the average VMP_L. Schooling increases Alice's annual pay from $50,000 to $60,000 but decreases Jacob's pay from $50,000 to $40,000. So in the signaling model, eliminating colleges and universities would raise our standard of living: the savings on educational expenses would be tremendous, and the value of production would rise as would-be college students begin their careers four years sooner. Furthermore, the windfall from eliminating education at all levels—from pre-K through graduate school—would be truly staggering if signaling (and only signaling) applied to all levels of education.

Signaling or Human Capital?

If schooling is so inefficient, why do we subsidize it? Schooling is either (1) productive in terms of career skills or (2) government folly on an epic scale. Clearly, distinguishing between human capital and signaling models of schooling is important. Can we distinguish the two models empirically?

Let's begin by isolating the proper context of the signaling model. Learning to read, to write, and to do arithmetic in elementary school is certainly productive. Likewise, training in medical, dental, veterinary, architectural, law, business, and other professional schools is productive. Even the strongest supporter of schooling as a signal won't go under the the knife for a medical procedure performed by a well-educated (i.e., quite able) person who hasn't attended medical school. So the signaling model is primarily about liberal-arts education. How does reading *To Kill a Mockingbird*, studying the culture of Bronze-Age Mesopotamia, or learning the chemical properties of trifluoroacetic acid contribute to a successful career? These are questions of the kind that many students ask, and signaling ability might be the answer.

Key Principle. Schooling is primarily an investment in cognitive skills, and those skills command a premium in the labor market. The wage premium associated with a college education might also reflect schooling's role in sorting people by innate ability.

While much of the liberal arts curriculum might be devoid of direct vocational or professional payoff, a liberal-arts education at its best teaches students how to think. Acquiring a liberal-arts education is like working out at the gym. Lifting the weights isn't the goal, but lifting weights strengthens your muscles. Likewise, a liberal-arts education isn't about *what to think*; it's about *how to think*. You exercise your mind to become a stronger thinker, which prepares you for a career in which you use your mind to solve problems never imagined in the classroom or lecture hall. Developing your reasoning skills prepares you for the vast and ever-changing unknown. So even a liberal-arts education generates human capital in the form of stronger thinkers.

Constructing a formal test to distinguish between human capital and signaling models of schooling is simple enough in principle. Just force everyone to attend another year of school: a high school dropout must finish high school; a high school graduate must attend one year of college; a college graduate goes to graduate school for a year. In the human capital model, worker productivity rises, and everyone's wage moves up the wage–schooling curve by one year. That is, the average wage increases. In the signaling model, no one is more productive, and the average wage doesn't change. This test would clearly distinguish the two models, but we can't implement it in a free society.

✓ PRACTICE   Compulsory school-attendance laws keep some kids in school longer. In groundbreaking research, Angrist and Krueger (1991) estimated that the rate of return to schooling associated with compulsory school attendance is about 10 percent per grade. Does this evidence favor the human capital model or the signaling model of schooling?

Evidence on the contribution of formal education to the level of development across countries favors schooling as an investment in human capital. The cross-country relationship between education and the standard of living is strong. As Figure 6.15 illustrates, gross domestic product (GDP) per capita is higher in more-educated countries like the United States. Lack of education explains why Mali and even India are quite poor. (Of course, other factors are at work, too. GDP per capita is much higher in oil-rich Qatar than in hyperinflation-ravaged Zimbabwe, although average years of schooling in the two countries are the same.) Are Americans signaling their high ability by getting more than 13 years of education to distinguish themselves from a worldwide pool of workers, including those from Mali and India? No. Wages and the standard of living are high in the United States in large part because American workers are so well educated, and the pattern is similar through time. Every country starts poor, and an educational surge characterizes the growth from poor country to rich country. These macroeconomic patterns linking education and the level of development favor the human capital model of schooling.

Evidence supporting schooling as human capital doesn't preclude schooling as a signal: the two aren't mutually exclusive alternatives. Indeed, the signaling

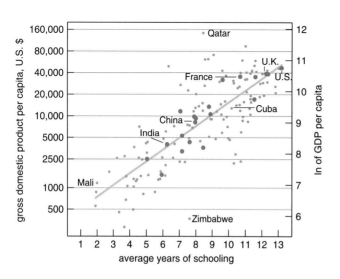

Note: The larger dots are data points for the twenty most-populated countries.
Sources: Schooling: Barro, Robert, and Jong-Wha Lee, 2013. "A New Data Set of Educational Attainment in the World, 1950–2010." *Journal of Development Economics* 104: 184–198. Gross domestic product per capita (cgdp): Heston, Alan, Robert Summers, and Bettina Aten. *Penn World Table, Version 7.1.* Center for International Comparisons of Production, Income and Prices at the University of Pennsylvania, 2012.

FIGURE 6.15. Development and Schooling Across 144 Countries in 2010

model can complement the human capital model. For instance, suppose a change in a compulsory school-attendance law extends schooling from age 15 to age 16. The schooling requirement in the signaling model must rise to preserve sorting by ability, so everyone stays in school longer. Lang and Kropp (1986) found that the effects of compulsory school-attendance laws extend beyond the directly affected high school dropouts to even well-educated workers. This evidence points to some role for signaling.

6.4 Application: Schooling and the Workweek

Why do more-educated people work longer workweeks? Our CPS data on occupation averages reveal that doctors, lawyers, and workers in other high-paying occupations work longer hours and are more educated than workers in lower-paying occupations. Indeed, the correlation of schooling (i.e., highest grade completed) and the workweek (i.e., hours worked last week) across occupations is .36. Through schooling, the workweek and the hourly wage are positively linked across occupations. That is, schooling might explain why the labor supply curve across occupations slopes up.

Schooling enters our model of labor supply in two ways: it raises the hourly wage, but schooling also lowers nonlabor income. Schooling is costly in terms of tuition (and other out-of-pocket expenses) and foregone income while in school. These costs from Gregg's school days reduce his nonlabor income after leaving school. If he borrowed to pay for college, payments on his student loans divert income from his current consumption. If he paid for college by drawing down his savings or investments, his current interest or investment income is lower. Either way, schooling lowers Gregg's nonlabor income.

Whether schooling is an investment in human capital or a signal of ability, the higher wage associated with more schooling increases the workweek as a pure substitution effect if people are identical. Figure 6.16 illustrates this case for two workers, Jacob and Gregg. Jacob has a high school diploma; his hourly wage is $10.94, and his nonlabor income is $250 per week. Jacob chooses to work 32 hours per week and collects $350 in weekly earnings. Gregg has a college education, and his hourly wage is $17.27. The cost of college lowers Gregg's nonlabor income to −$50, $300 below Jacob's nonlabor. Gregg chooses to work 55 hours per week, and he earns $950 per week.

Gregg earns almost triple what Jacob makes, and he consumes 50 percent more than Jacob, but he's no better off. Gregg's choice (X_{16}) and Jacob's choice (X_{12}) lie on a single indifference curve (I_1) in Figure 6.16. This is no accident: in the equilibrium with identical people, the wage and the cost of school must adjust to leave everyone indifferent as to how educated to become. And this principle applies to the current context with the workweek as a matter of choice. By increasing the wage and decreasing nonlabor income, education increases the workweek as a pure substitution effect (Lindsay 1971).

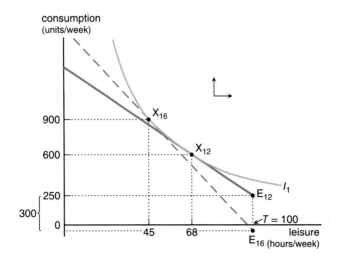

Gregg and Jacob have the same preferences. Jacob earns $10.94/hour with his high school education; Gregg earns $17.27/hour with his college degree. College was expensive, so Gregg has $300/week less than Jacob in nonlabor income. As a substitution effect, Gregg responds to his higher wage and lower nonlabor income by increasing his workweek.

Although Gregg's wage is 58% higher than Jacob's, and he consumes 50% more than Jacob, Gregg is no better off than Jacob: X_{12} and X_{16} lie on the same indifference curve.

FIGURE 6.16. Schooling and the Workweek

 PRACTICE

Beth, who has the same preferences as Gregg and Jacob, goes to graduate school for two years and earns an advanced degree. In Figure 6.16, draw a budget line for Beth that causes her workweek to respond to her higher education as purely a substitution effect. Illustrate the length of her workweek, her weekly consumption, and her weekly pay.

Schooling contributes to our understanding of variation in the workweek across occupations, and it also explains an important change in labor supply since 1900. Low-wage workers worked long hours a century ago. Now high-wage workers work long hours. A lot has changed in a century, and education is one of the most dramatic changes. Unlike high-wage workers at the dawn of the twentieth century, high-wage workers today get educated at great expense to command their high wages. The shift to buying higher wages through schooling dampens the income effect associated with higher wages and generates longer workweeks.

Summary

This chapter examined the link between schooling and wages. The key findings are:

☐ Schooling is an investment because it involves upfront costs, such as out-of-pocket expenses and foregone wage income, and payoffs down the road in the form of higher career wages.

☐ Discounting (to present values) the costs and returns to schooling investments at different points in time allows us to compare different career paths, one for each grade completed. If a worker has no tuition cost and lives and works forever, the present values of career wages are w/i in the last year of school and $(w/i)/(1+i)^s$ in the year before first grade.

☐ The tangency of an iso-wealth curve to the wage–schooling curve determines the wealth-maximizing time to finish school. At this choice, the marginal rate of return to schooling is driven down to the interest rate.

☐ The demand for schooling in the absence of tuition, death, and taxes is the marginal rate of return $\Delta w/w(s)$. The quantity demanded of schooling varies inversely with the interest rate.

☐ Tuition cost, a shorter career, and taxes (in the presence of tuition cost) lower the demand for schooling. At the chosen amount of schooling, the growth rate of wages along the wage–schooling curve exceeds the interest rate.

☐ If more innate ability increases the marginal rate of return to schooling, then higher-ability workers have a higher demand for schooling, which causes an ability bias: the college wage premium exaggerates the true return to schooling because part of the premium reflects the higher ability of college-educated workers.

☐ Even if schooling doesn't generate skills that employers value, educated workers earn more if schooling signals ability. For schooling to signal ability, low-ability workers must discount the college wage premium more than high-ability workers do.

☐ In the signaling model, schooling is a very costly way to redistribute wage income without increasing the value of what workers produce. It's highly inefficient.

☐ Educated workers work longer hours in an extension of the labor supply model to include schooling. In the equilibrium with identical workers, college-educated workers put in longer hours and consume more, but they aren't better off than workers with only high school diplomas.

In the next chapter, we extend the model of human-capital investment to explain why wages tend to grow over a worker's career and why that wage growth shrinks dramatically toward the end of the worker's career.

Key Concepts

- human capital, p. 195
- birth cohort, p. 195
- present value, p. 197
- wage profile, p. 198
- wage–schooling curve, p. 199
- marginal rate of return to schooling, p. 200

- wealth and iso-wealth curves, p. 202
- rate-of-return maximization, p. 205
- log-wage equation, p. 207
- ability bias, p. 213
- signaling ability, p. 216
- schooling requirement, p. 218

Short-Answer Questions

6.1 Our introductory analysis of law school as an investment used the average wage of college graduates (without any graduate education) to estimate foregone earnings. How would the cost of attending law school change if we used the average wage of *recent* college graduates? At some interest rate, a law-school career generates no more consumption than a college career. How would using the average wage of recent college graduates influence that critical interest rate?

6.2 Suppose tuition at a community college is $5,000 per year, workers with an associate's degree from a two-year community college earn $20,000 per year, and the annual interest rate is 10 percent. Use Equation 6.1 (with $N = 2$) to compute the present value (in the first year of community college) of two years in community college followed by one year of work.

6.3 How are the many wage profiles—one for each grade completed—related to the wage–schooling curve?

6.4 Jacob ponders a career that involves two years of graduate school and a $50,000 annual wage forever. If the annual interest rate is 10 percent, what is the present value of that career in Jacob's last year of school PV_{18}? What's the present value in the year before Jacob begins school PV_0?

6.5 Carefully explain why choosing when to leave school to maximize the rate of return to schooling is a terrible strategy.

6.6 We have assumed that people go to school early in their lives and work after leaving school. That's what most people do. Use our analysis of schooling demand to explain why going to school when young is better than working as a kid and going to school as a senior citizen.

6.7 If workers live and work forever and tuition is zero, what effect does an income tax have on the cost, benefit, and marginal rate of return to schooling? In this context, how does the tax shift the demand for schooling?

6.8 This one has the making of a science-fiction classic: Humans in an alternate reality (called Earth′) are much like you and me. But differences in ability on Earth′ only shift the wage–schooling curve; the slope of the wage–schooling curve doesn't depend on ability. Does ability increase or decrease the demand for schooling in this fictional world? Does the ability bias overstate or understate the actual effect of schooling on wages on Earth′?

6.9 Compare the signaling equilibrium displayed in the two panels of Figure 6.14 with the equilibrium in which Alice doesn't signal her ability. (We call the outcome without signaling the pooling equilibrium because Alice and Jacob are pooled together and treated the same by employers.) Who does better in the signaling equilibrium? Who does better in the pooling equilibrium? How is the social return to schooling related to Alice's private return to schooling in the signaling model?

6.10 The introduction to chapter 3 explains how hourly wages and weekly hours of work are positively related across occupations. Explain how schooling helps explain why the labor supply curve across occupations doesn't bend backward.

Problems

6.1 If Sally earns a college degree and goes to work, she earns $50,000 per year forever. The present value (in her last year of college) of $50,000 per year forever is $w/i = 50{,}000/.10 = 500{,}000$ if the interest rate is $i = .10$. Sally's wealth from a college career discounts w/i by $(1+i)^{16}$ to the present value before she started first grade: $W = 500{,}000/(1.1)^{16} = 500{,}000/4.595 = 108{,}815$.

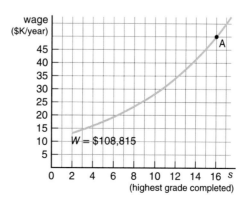

The formula for the iso-wealth curve that cuts through $(16, 50,000)$ is $w = .10 \times 108,815 \times 1.1^s$ for various values of s. The figure above displays this iso-wealth curve.

s (grade)	w ($/year)	Δw ($/year/grade)	Δw/w (%/grade)
12		—	—
13			
16	50,000	—	—
17			

(a) Sally contemplates quitting school after graduating from high school. What wage for a high school career generates the same wealth (i.e., $W = 108,815$) as she gets with a college education? Enter your answer in the table above, and mark this point in the figure.

(b) Use the figure to estimate the value of schooling on iso-wealth curve $W = 108,815$ that is associated with $w = 55,000$.

(c) Use the formula for iso-wealth curve $W = 108,815$ to calculate the wages associated with completing 13 and 17 years of schooling. Enter these wages in the table.

(d) Compute the wage change Δw associated with increasing schooling s from 12 to 13 years. Also compute wage-growth rate $\Delta w/w$ using the conventional method (rather than the midpoint formula). Repeat this calculation for an increase in s from 16 to 17 years.

(e) Use your calculations in the table to determine how the interest rate i affects iso-wealth curves.

6.2 Julio will live and work forever, he borrows and lends at a 4 percent annual interest rate, and he has no out-of-pocket expense of attending school. The table below lists Julio's weekly wage for each completed grade of school.

SCHOOLING (grade)	WAGE ($/week)	WAGE CHANGE ($/week/grade)	MARGINAL RATE OF RETURN (%/grade)
8	1,059		
9	1,175		
10	1,293		
11	1,409		
12	1,522		
13	1,628		
14	1,726		
15	1,812		
16	1,885		
17	1,941		
18	1,980		
19	2,000		
20	2,000		

(a) For each grade, use the conventional method to compute Julio's marginal rate of return to schooling $\Delta w/w$.

(b) Julio's marginal rate of return to schooling falls to 2 percent at grade _____.

(c) To maximize wealth, Julio quits school after completing which grade?

(d) If Julio chooses schooling s to maximize his marginal rate of return to schooling, he completes _____ grades.

(e) Lea and Julio have the same wage–schooling curve, but Lea faces an 8 percent annual interest rate. At what grade does wealth-maximizer Lea finish her education?

6.3 The table below lists the relationship between Maya's weekly wage and her schooling:

SCHOOLING (grade)	WAGE ($/week)	WAGE CHANGE ($/week/grade)	MARGINAL RATE OF RETURN (%/grade)
8	866		
9	944		
10	1,020		
11	1,091		
12	1,156		
13	1,214		
14	1,263		
15	1,301		
16	1,327		
17	1,340		
18	1,340		
19	1,327		
20	1,300		

(a) How does Maya's wage–schooling curve relate to Julio's wage–schooling curve in problem 6.2? Who earns a higher wage at each grade? Whose wage–schooling curve is steeper?

(b) Who is more able (and productive), Julio or Maya?

(c) Maya has no out-of-pocket expense of attending school. Compute Maya's marginal rate of return to schooling for each grade in the table.

(d) Who earns a higher rate of return to schooling, Julio or Maya?

(e) Like Julio, Maya will live and work forever, and she borrows and lends at a 4 percent annual interest rate. To maximize her wealth, Maya leaves school when she completes grade _____.

6.4 The figure below displays how the rate of wage growth $\Delta w / w$ varies with schooling s.

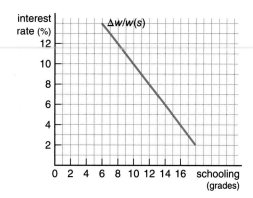

(a) Suppose Sadie lives and works forever, there's no tuition, and the annual interest rate is 9 percent. When does Sadie finish school? Graph her choice in the figure.

(b) The interest rate drops to 4 percent. Show how Sadie's schooling choice responds to the lower interest rate.

(c) The annual interest rate is again 9 percent, but now Sadie pays tuition, and tuition is higher for higher grades. In particular, tuition cost is one-third the wage associated with grade s; that is, $c = w(s)/3$. Express the marginal rate of return to schooling in terms of $\Delta w/w$.

(d) Plot the marginal-rate-of-return curve, which happens to be a line. Illustrate Sadie's schooling choice if the annual interest rate is 9 percent. How does tuition affect Sadie's school choice?

(e) Let s^* denote your answer to part (d). What's Sadie's marginal rate of return to schooling at s^*? And at what rate is Sadie's wage growing at her choice s^*?

6.5 We have a sample of 100 pairs of identical twins. In half these pairs, the two twins report equal grades completed. In the other 50 pairs of twins, one twin reports more schooling than the other. For this group of 100 people, years of schooling average 14 years, and the average hourly wage is $13. Among twins with different levels of education, the more-educated twins have on average 15 years of schooling and earn $14.30 per hour; the less-educated twins have 13 years of schooling and earn $11.70 per hour on average.

Plot these three points (s, w) in the figure below. Mark the point for the more-educated twins with an M, less-educated twins with an L, and different-educated twins with a D. Draw a curve or a line through the points.

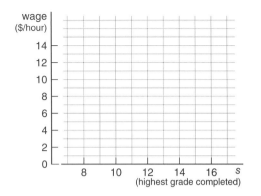

(a) Use points M and L to compute the slope of the wage–schooling curve $\Delta w / \Delta s$.

(b) Evaluate the marginal rate of return to schooling at the midpoint between points M and L. That is, on the basis of within-pair comparisons, what is the marginal rate of return to schooling at $s = 14$?

6.6 There are low-ability workers and high-ability workers. The annual values of marginal products are $40,000 for low-ability workers and $60,000 for high-ability workers. Competitive employers pay $60,000 annually to workers who have completed at least s' grades; others receive $40,000 annually. Everyone completes at least 12 grades. Employers don't directly observe ability, but they might rationally infer ability from schooling choices.

The figure below includes one iso-wealth curve for low-ability workers W_0^l and another iso-wealth curve for high-ability workers W_1^h. For each ability, other iso-wealth curves are parallel to the displayed curve.

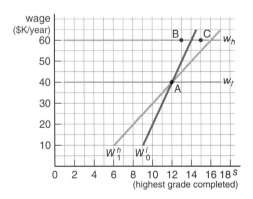

(a) Suppose $s' = 13$, so anyone who completes one year of college receives $60,000 annually. Draw the iso-wealth curves for low-ability and high-ability workers through point $B = (13, 60)$.

Who prefers meeting the schooling requirement for the higher pay: low-ability workers or high-ability workers?

(b) Suppose $s' = 15$. Draw the iso-wealth curves for low-ability and high-ability workers through point C. Who prefers meeting the schooling requirement for the higher pay: low-ability workers or high-ability workers?

(c) (Advanced) What is the lowest value of s' that induces (i) low-ability workers to pass on higher education and (ii) high-ability workers to continue their education beyond high school and complete s' grades? [Hint: Repeat the steps in parts (a) and (b) for other values of s'.]

References

Angrist, Joshua D. and Alan B. Krueger. 1991. "Does Compulsory School Attendance Affect Schooling and Earnings?" *Quarterly Journal of Economics* 106(4): 979–1014.

Ashenfelter, Orley and Alan B. Krueger. 1994. "Estimates of the Economic Return to Schooling from a New Sample of Twins." *American Economic Review* 84(5): 1157–1173.

Lang, Kevin and David Kropp. 1986. "Human Capital versus Sorting: The Effects of Compulsory Attendance Laws." *Quarterly Journal of Economics* 101(3): 609–624.

Lindsay, C.M. 1971. "Measuring Human Capital Returns." *Journal of Political Economy* 79(6): 1195–2015.

Mincer, Jacob. 1958. "Investment in Human Capital and Personal Income Distribution." *Journal of Political Economy* 66(4): 281–302.

Mincer, Jacob. 1974. *Schooling, Experience, and Earnings*. New York: Columbia University Press.

Spence, Michael. 1973. "Job Market Signaling." *Quarterly Journal of Economics* 87(3): 355–374.

7 Training, Turnover, and Migration

Ford Motor Company employed about 13,600 workers at a time in 1913. During March of that year, 7,300 workers left the company. Did production of the Model T plummet? No. While thousands of workers quit or were dismissed, Ford hired approximately the same number of workers. Through a rapidly revolving door, Ford replaced the 50,000 workers leaving the plant that year with 50,000 new hires entering the plant while only 13,600 workers inside the plant produced Model Ts. But in January 1914, Ford rolled out the revolutionary $5 workday for men with six months of service with the company, and its annual turnover rate promptly dropped from 370 percent in 1913 to 54 percent in 1914 and to 16 percent in 1915. Workers at Ford became permanent employees.

Ford was ahead of the curve. The annual turnover rate was over 100 percent in U.S. manufacturing in the 1910s. Early in the 1920s, the annual turnover rate dropped sharply. In fact, the annual turnover rate in manufacturing in the 1920s wasn't much higher than it is now for the U.S. labor market, about 40 percent. The years 1914 at Ford and 1920 more widely mark the dawn of workers' long-term attachment to their employers.

Turnover is about workers changing jobs; *migration* is about people changing locations. The two phenomena have much in common. Workers frequently quit to take higher-paying jobs. People frequently move to locations where higher-wage jobs are available. Job turnover and migration are activities of the young. Indeed, turnover and migration rates fall with age.

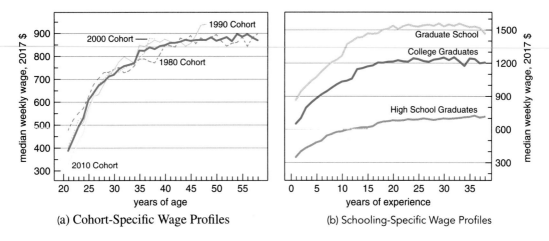

(a) Cohort-Specific Wage Profiles   (b) Schooling-Specific Wage Profiles

FIGURE 7.1. Wage Profiles in the Current Population Survey, 1979–2017

Notes: Panel (a) displays median wages by age for the 1980, 1990, 2000, and 2010 cohorts. The thick curve is the weighted average across the 39 wage profiles, one for each cohort, 1979–2017. In panel (b), wage profiles for each schooling group are averaged across 39 cohorts.
Source: Current Population Survey, outgoing rotation group files, monthly 1979–2017.

Job turnover and migration are connected to work experience, which is the main topic of this chapter. A worker acquires skills through work experience. Acquiring skills on the job is an investment in human capital, so this chapter extends the human capital model from learning in the classroom to learning on the job. The model explains why wages increase at a decreasing rate over workers' careers. Young workers have low wages, but they enjoy rapid wage growth. Experienced workers enjoy higher wages, but their wages grow slowly or even decline.

Figure 7.1 displays **wage profiles** for wage and salary workers in the Current Population Survey since 1979. Panel (a) plots the median wage by age for four **cohorts of workers**, groups of workers who were born in the same year. For instance, the wage profile of the 1980 cohort plots median real wages of workers who turned 21 in 1980 as they aged from 21 in 1980 to 58 in 2017. The median wage rises rapidly at low ages before slowing down and flattening out as these workers reach their mid-40s. (The wage bounces around a bit from age to age, which reflects economic conditions, as well as sampling error.) Wage profiles for the 1990 and 2000 cohorts display a similar pattern, but the 2010 cohort got off to an unusually bad start as we track those young workers from age 21 in 2010 to age 28 in 2017. The thick wage profile in panel (a) is the average across the 39 cohorts beginning with the cohort of workers who turned 21 in 1979 and ending with the 2017 cohort of 21-year-olds. This average wage profile demonstrates that wages increase at a decreasing rate over workers' careers.

Figure 7.1b illustrates how median wages vary with work experience for three schooling groups. Actual work experience isn't generally available in the CPS. Instead, we measure *potential* work experience as age minus 18 for workers with only a high school diploma, as age minus 22 for college graduates, and as age minus 24 for those with a graduate degree. For each schooling group, we average the wage profiles across the 39 cohorts from 1979 to 2017. Wages increase at a decreasing rate along each schooling group's wage profile. Furthermore, schooling raises and steepens the wage profile. More-educated workers earn more at each point in their careers, and the gap between the wages of more- and less-educated workers increases with experience.

Our primary task in this chapter is to explain why wages increase at a decreasing rate over workers' careers. The models that explain the empirical patterns of career wages intertwine with turnover, so our analysis also extends to job turnover and migration.

7.1   General Training

Learning doesn't stop at graduation. A typical worker acquires valuable skills over his working career, and those skills translate into fatter paychecks in the prime working years. To explain the empirical patterns of career wages, we model acquiring skills through on-the-job training (Becker 1962). The acquired skills are valued generally; that is, many employers value the skills.

On-the-Job Training as an Investment

Gary has just graduated from college. He's an ambitious kid, and he has plenty of prospects for his career. Some prospects are dead-end jobs. For instance, Gary might work as a lineman for a telephone company, climbing utility poles to solve problems with customers' phone service. If he climbs utility poles for his career, he will earn $600 per week until he retires in 40 years. Other jobs offer opportunities for growth or advancement: jobs that involve a lot of learning will enhance his job performance later in his career.

Among Gary's many prospects is a job at Rhythm Records, a major record label that develops recording artists and produces, manufactures, distributes, markets, and promotes their music. An entry-level position at Rhythm Records pays peanuts (i.e., $170 per week), but it offers great prospects for career advancement. If he takes the job at the record company, Gary will spend a lot of time early in his career learning the business. Eventually, with a large team of assistants, he will produce records or develop and manage artists. But only if he learns the business. Of course, the many competing record labels also value what he learns on the job. We call this type of learning **general training**.

Compared to the job as a lineman with the telephone company, the job at Rhythm Records includes an investment in Gary. Learning the business, which we call **on-the-job training**, is costly, but it pays a return by improving Gary's productivity later on. Training has direct costs (e.g., space for training sessions, wages of the staff who run the training sessions, training manuals, travel to conferences), as well as indirect costs in the form of foregone productivity. Training draws time away from making records, so Gary's current performance takes a hit if he devotes much time to learning new things. But spending less time producing now translates into better performance in the future, perhaps for the rest of Gary's long career.

Training declines over a worker's career. As his retirement approaches, Gary will have less time to reap the return to any new skills that he acquires. Therefore, the rate of return to his training investments falls as Gary ages. He rationally responds by getting a lot of on-the-job training when he is young and letting his training investments decline to zero as he nears retirement. Young Gary learns the business; old Gary puts his wisdom to work.

Productivity and Wage Profiles

Training declines with work experience, and past training boosts future productivity. These two features deliver a **productivity profile** that bows up: productivity increases at a decreasing rate over the worker's career.

Table 7.1 lists training costs and returns over Gary's 40-year career. Gary's productivity, the value of his marginal product, working as lineman is $600 per week, which Figure 7.2 plots as the flat line v_0. It takes some work to uncover Gary's value to Rhythm Records at each point in his career. We start by specifying his **potential productivity**, his value to Rhythm Records based on skills acquired through past training but assuming Gary doesn't train currently. It's a useful hypothetical.

A worker's potential productivity increases with work experience at a decreasing rate. Let's let x denote years of work experience (including the current year). Figure 7.2 displays Gary's potential-productivity profile $v_p(x)$ over his 40-year career. With the skills Gary acquired over his first four years on the job at Rhythm Records, Gary's productivity in his fifth year (i.e., $x = 5$) is $715 per week *if he devotes all his time to producing* (and doesn't train at all) in year 5. So $715 is his potential productivity at $x = 5$. The $115-per-week increase in his potential

TABLE 7.1. PRODUCTIVITY, TRAINING COSTS, AND WORK EXPERIENCE

EXPERIENCE x (years)	POTENTIAL PRODUCTIVITY v_p ($/week)	FOREGONE PRODUCTIVITY ($/week)	DIRECT TRAINING COST c ($/week)	NET PRODUCTIVITY v_n ($/week)
1	600	235	195	170
5	715	250	175	290
10	860	____	150	____
15	990	265	125	600
20	1,110	220	100	790
30	1,290	130	50	1,110
40	1,350	0	0	1,350

Note: Net productivity v_n is potential productivity v_p minus foregone productivity and the direct cost of training c.

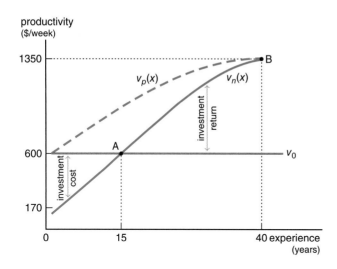

Gary's productivity without training is constant at v_0. Potential productivity with training $v_p(x)$ reflects his past training. His net productivity $v_n(x)$ subtracts training costs (including foregone productivity) from $v_p(x)$.

Gary's net productivity is lower than v_0 early in his career, and the difference $v_0 - v_n(x)$ is the opportunity cost of his training. The difference $v_n(x) - v_0$ turns positive later in his career when he earns a return on his training investment.

Gary's training shrinks to zero as he nears retirement, so net productivity $v_n(x)$ converges to potential productivity $v_p(x)$.

FIGURE 7.2. Productivity Profiles and Investment Costs and Returns

productivity since his first year on the job is the early return to his first four years of training. In Gary's tenth year on the job, his potential productivity is $860 per week, which reflects what he learned in his first nine years at Rhythm Records. Gary's productivity profile in Figure 7.2 increases at a decreasing rate because he trains less each year.

✅ **PRACTICE**

In Figure 7.2, Gary's potential-productivity profile $v_p(x)$ increases at a decreasing rate. For instance, his potential productivity rises $26 per week between years 5 and 10 and $24 per week between years 15 and 20. (See the first two columns of Table 7.1.) Why does Gary's potential productivity increase with his work experience? Why does the slope of $v_p(x)$ fall as Gary gets more experience?

Gary's actual productivity $v_n(x)$ reflects his current training, as well as past training, at each point in his career x. In his fifth year on the job at Rhythm Records, Gary spends 35 percent of his time learning, down from 39 percent in his first year. The value of the productivity he foregoes is $250 per week, so Gary's actual productivity in year 5 is $465 (= $715 − $250) per week. The direct cost of his training $c(x)$ in year 5 is $175 per week, down from $195 per week at the start of his career. So Gary's year-5 net productivity $v_n(5)$ is $290 (= $715 − $250 − $175), up from $170 per week in his first year on the job. In general, Gary's **net productivity** $v_n(x)$—his value to Rhythm Records—is his potential productivity $v_p(x)$ minus his foregone productivity and direct costs of training $c(x)$. His net-productivity profile $v_n(x)$ in Figure 7.2 increases with work experience x at a decreasing rate.

PRACTICE   In his tenth year working, Gary's potential productivity at the record label is $860 per week. He spends about 30 percent of his time training, and the direct cost of his training is $150 per week. What's Gary's foregone productivity with 10 years of experience? (Round to the nearest ten.) What are the actual and net values of his productivity at $x = 10$? Fill in these values in Table 7.1.

Net productivity increases with work experience for two reasons: (1) potential productivity rises, and (2) training costs fall. Gary's net productivity in year 15 of his career is $150 more than in year 10. Training in the intervening five years raises his potential productivity to $990 per week in year 15. In addition, he spends less time learning and more time producing in year 15 than in year 10: training costs fall from $410 $(= \$260 + \$150)$ to $390 $(= \$265 + \$125)$ per week over the five years. As training costs fall, the gap between potential and net productivity narrows, pulling net productivity closer to potential productivity. Gary's potential productivity rises from past training investments, and Gary's value to Rhythm Records grows even faster as his training costs shrink.

One way to measure training costs is to sum the direct cost c and foregone productivity at each point in Gary's career. Another way is to compare Gary's net productivity with training at Rhythm Records to his productivity as a lineman without training. Early in his career, Gary's net productivity is as much as $430 per week lower at Rhythm Records. By year 15, his net productivity with training catches up to the $600-per-week productivity as a lineman. Over the last 25 years of his career, Gary's training investment earns a positive return even while Gary continues to train. Figure 7.2 illustrates the net costs and net returns to Gary's training as the difference between the flat profile v_0 and his net-productivity profile $v_n(x)$ with Rhythm Records.

How does the wage vary over a worker's career? Competition among potential employers guarantees that Gary receives what he's worth over his career. That is, the present value of Gary's wage profile $w(x)$ equals the present value of his net-productivity profile $v_n(x)$ in a competitive labor market. Does competition for Gary's services guarantee that employers like Rhythm Records pay Gary what he's worth at each point in his career? No.

Rhythm Records could pay Gary a wage that equals his net productivity at each point in his career, which is competitive over his whole career, but there are plenty of alternative wage profiles. For instance, Rhythm Records could **front-load pay**, paying Gary more than he's worth early in his career and less than he's worth later on. A flat wage at $600 per week does just that. The wage profile $w_1(x)$ in Figure 7.3 is flatter than Gary's net-productivity profile, so $w_1(x)$ also front-loads pay. Paying Gary a huge signing bonus with no wage over his 40-year career is front-loading pay in the extreme, and it's competitive if the signing bonus equals the present value of the net value of his productivity $v_n(x)$.

The record company could also **back-load pay**, paying Gary less than he's worth early in his career in exchange for more pay later on. Wage profile $w_3(x)$ in Figure 7.3 fits this case. An extreme case of back-loading pay is also

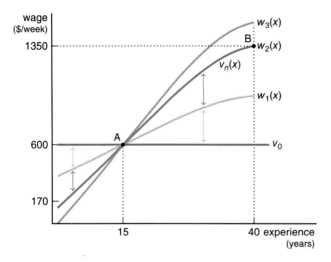

Wage profile $w_1(x)$ front-loads pay: Gary earns more than $v_n(x)$ until year 15; after that, the record company pays him less than he's worth. Along $w_1(x)$, Rhythm Records bears some of the costs and reaps some of the returns of Gary's training investment.

Wage profile $w_3(x)$ back-loads pay: Gary earns less than $v_n(x)$ until year 15; the record company overpays him after that.

Along wage profile $w_2(x)$, the record company pays Gary what he's worth week by week. In this case, Gary bears the costs of and earns the returns to his training investment.

FIGURE 7.3. Who Pays for General Training?

competitive: don't pay Gary a dime over his entire career and then award a fat check to him at his retirement party. If the present value of the amount on the check equals the present value of Gary's net productivity $v_n(x)$, then the single check at retirement is competitive.

Clearly, there are many options, so competition simply fails to pin down a unique wage profile. Perhaps other factors can pin down a unique wage profile that mimics the empirical wage profiles in Figure 7.1.

Who Pays for General Training?

The wage profile determines who pays for Gary's training. If Rhythm Records pays Gary what he's worth at each point in his career (i.e., along profile $w_2(x)$), then he pays for his training in the form of foregone earnings. He bears the investment cost early in his career by earning less than he could make on a job without training. He reaps the return on his training investment later in his career when he earns more than he could make on a job without training.

Alternatively, the record label could front-load or back-load Gary's pay. If Rhythm Records front-loads Gary's pay (e.g., his wage profile is $w_1(x)$), then it shares some of the investment cost and investment return with Gary. For the case that Figure 7.3 displays, Gary and the record label share Gary's training investment 50:50 along $w_1(x)$. Along wage profile $w_3(x)$, Rhythm Records back-loads Gary's pay. His wage is so low early in his career that he more than pays the cost of his training investment, and his wage later in his career is so high that he reaps more than the full return on his training investment.

The upshot is this: how the wage profile $w(x)$ compares to the net-productivity profile $v_n(x)$ and no-training productivity line v_0 reveals how Gary and Rhythm Records share the costs of and returns to his training.

PRACTICE Suppose Gary and Rhythm Records share the investment in his training 25:75, so the record label's share of the training investment is 75 percent. Sketch Gary's wage profile in Figure 7.3.

The wage profile must be competitive, but it must also be compatible with turnover incentives. With **employment at will**, a worker can quit at any time for any reason, and the employer can dismiss (i.e., lay off or fire) the worker at any time for any reason. Gary's incentives to quit and Rhythm Records' incentive to dismiss Gary pin down a unique wage profile.

If Rhythm Records front-loaded Gary's pay (e.g., wage profile $w_1(x)$ in Figure 7.3), then it would overpay Gary for the first 14 years of his career. After $x = 15$, Rhythm Records would pay Gary less than he's worth until he retires, so he'd quit when he reached 15 years of experience. The record label would be left with no chance to recoup the cost of its investment in Gary, so it wouldn't offer a wage profile that front-loads Gary's pay. Likewise, if the record label back-loaded Gary's pay (e.g., wage profile $w_3(x)$ in Figure 7.3), then it would dismiss Gary at $x = 15$ because Gary would be overpaid after that. Gary would be left with no chance to reap a return on his training investment, so he wouldn't take a job that back-loads his pay.

In fact, any competitive wage profile that underpays Gary at some point in his career must overpay him at some other point in his career. If the overpaying comes first, Gary quits when Rhythm Records tries to underpay him; if the underpaying comes first, the record label dismisses Gary when it's time to overpay him. Thus the only wage profile that's compatible with these turnover incentives (i.e., doesn't cause turnover) is the one that pays Gary what he is worth at each point in his career. That is, the competitive equilibrium wage profile is $w^*(x) \equiv v_n(x)$. Gary bears the full cost of his training by accepting lower wages early in his career and reaps the full return on his training investment later in his career. Rhythm Records has no stake in Gary's training.

Key Principle.
If workers can quit and employers are free to dismiss the workers, then employers must pay the workers what they're worth at every point in their careers.

Wages and Work Experience

This model of post-school investment in human capital predicts that wages increase at a decreasing rate as in Figure 7.1. It also explains some of the difference in median weekly wages across occupations. Although training investment can vary across occupations, occupations with more-experienced workers should have higher median weekly wages. Differences in work experience across occupations aren't dramatic, but public officials and administrators are older and more experienced than food-service workers and computer equipment operators. See Table 7.2. (We measure experience as *potential work experience*, $x = \text{age} - s - 6$, which is years since leaving school for a typical person.)

TABLE 7.2. EXPERIENCE AND WAGES ACROSS SEVERAL OCCUPATIONS

OCCUPATION	AVERAGE EXPERIENCE (years)	MEDIAN REAL WAGE (2017 $/week)
Food Service	13.9	318
Computer Equipment Operators	16.8	676
Mathematical & Computer Scientists	17.6	1,395
Lawyers & Judges	17.9	1,793
Health Diagnosing Occupations	18.4	1,671
Teachers, Excluding College & University	18.8	918
Teachers, College & University	20.1	1,056
Motor Vehicle Operators	23.5	681
Officials & Administrators, Public	24.9	1,239

Note: Experience is *potential work experience*: age minus highest grade completed minus 6.
Source: Current Population Survey, outgoing rotation group files, monthly 1979–2017.

In our CPS data of occupation averages since 1979, the regression of the median weekly wage (in logs) on work experience x suggests that occupations with more-experienced workers pay higher wages.

$$(7.1) \qquad \ln w = 5.19 + .069x$$
$$\underset{(.706)}{} \quad \underset{(.036)}{}$$

with $R^2 = .179$. Although the slope b isn't estimated precisely, let's get a sense of its magnitude. The point estimate is .069, so an additional year since leaving school increases $\ln w$ by .069 and the wage w by 6.9 percent. (We might say that the return to work experience across occupations is 6.9 percent per year.) Public officials and administrators average 11 years more experience than food-service workers. On the basis of regression Equation 7.1, we predict that the wage of public officials exceeds the wage of food-service workers by 76 percent ($= .069 \times (24.9 - 13.9)$). But that adjustment closes little of the gap in pay between the two occupations. Indeed, the regression's R^2 tells us that variation in average work experience across occupations captures only about 18 percent of the variation in median wages across occupations.

Let's estimate the effects of the workweek, schooling, and potential work experience on weekly wages in a single regression. The regression of the median weekly wage (in logs) on averages of the workweek h, schooling s, and potential work experience x across the 43 occupations is

$$(7.2) \qquad \ln w = 1.96 + .067h + .127s + .016x$$
$$\underset{(.191)}{} \quad \underset{(.007)}{} \quad \underset{(.014)}{} \quad \underset{(.007)}{}$$

with $R^2 = .929$. The effect of work experience on wages across occupations, 1.6 percent per year, is significantly different from zero (i.e., the confidence interval around .016 lies entirely above 0). Workers in an occupation with 10 years more experience tend to earn 16 percent higher wages.

The relationship between wages (in logs) and experience in Equation 7.2 is linear. But our model of general training predicts that wages increase with experience at a decreasing rate. We can capture the curvature by including another variable, the square of experience x^2. Unfortunately, detecting curvature in a sample of 43 occupation averages is too much to hope for, so let's use individual-worker data to estimate the regression with x and x^2.

On the sample of over 156,000 wage and salary workers in the 2017 CPS, the estimated regression equation is

(7.3)
$$\ln w = 3.53 + .030\,h + .103\,s + .039\,x - .0006x^2$$
$$\quad\;\;(.012)\quad(.0002)\quad\;(.0007)\quad\;(.0005)\quad\;(.0000)$$

with $R^2 = .460$. The estimates reveal that the typical worker with 10 years of experience earns 33 percent more than the typical worker with no work experience. To see why, let's define the experience expression $X \equiv .039x - .0006x^2$. Plug zero in for x to find that $X = 0$ at the start of the worker's career. But if $x = 10$, then $X = .33$ ($= (.039 \times 10) - (.0006 \times 10^2)$). So a worker with 10 years of experience earns 33 percent more than a worker with no work experience in these data. A similar calculation uncovers that workers with 20 years of experience earn only 21 percent more than workers with 10 years of experience. Indeed, the coefficient estimates in Equation 7.3 imply that wages increase with experience at a decreasing rate.

 PRACTICE Calculate the experience expression X for workers with 20 and 30 years of work experience. Subtract the value of X for $x = 20$ workers from the value of X for $x = 30$ workers to find that the typical worker with 30 years of experience earns _____ percent more than the typical worker with 20 years of experience.

Labor Supply over the Life Cycle

What are the consequences of career wages—that wages increase at a decreasing rate over workers' careers—for the workweek? Let's extend our model of labor supply to address predictable variation in wages over the life cycle.

Workers can allocate their working hours across weeks, seasons, and even years. For instance, lawns and shrubs don't grow in the cold of winter, so the value of marginal product of lawn-care workers at Leisure Lawn is quite low in January. If the wage of lawn-care workers reflects their value of marginal product month by month, then lawn-care workers push their hours of work from low-wage months like January to high-wage months like June. That is, their quantity supplied of labor responds positively to predictable changes in the wage from month to month.

Let's see how allocating labor supply across points in time applies to Gary's career. Gary allocates his labor supply over his career to take advantage of

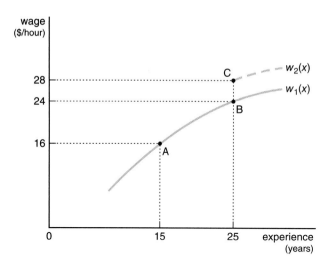

Along wage profile $w_1(x)$, Gary's hourly wage evolves from $16 at 15 years into his career to $24 at $x = 25$. This predictable (or expected) movement along his wage profile doesn't affect his wealth, so he responds by lengthening his workweek as a substitution effect.

If Gary is surprised by the good news that his wage profile is higher than expected beginning at $x = 25$, then an unexpected jump in his hourly wage from $24 to $28 at $x = 25$ increases his wealth. Gary's richer than expected, so his choice of hours to work reflects a wealth effect, as well as a substitution effect.

FIGURE 7.4. Wage Changes Along a Wage Profile vs. Shifts in the Wage Profile

differences in wages along his wage profile (Heckman 1974). He takes advantage of the high wages in the prime of his career by working more in those years and less in the low-wage years early in his career. He responds to predictable changes in his wage along his career wage profile by working more when work pays the most. (Gary might also choose to consume more in years when he's working long hours, but that's not our concern here.)

A predictable (or expected) difference in wages along a career wage profile doesn't modify wealth, so the implied **life-cycle labor supply curve** slopes up. Let's assume that Gary can borrow or lend at the interest rate i; borrowing and lending enables him to separate the question of when to work from the question of when to consume. To facilitate comparison with Gregg's labor supply choice in chapter 3, let's express Gary's wage profile in terms of an hourly wage. Gary's wage evolves along wage profile $w_1(x)$ in Figure 7.4. As expected, he earns $16 per hour 15 years into his career (i.e., at $x = 15$) and $24 per hour at $x = 25$. Gary has fully expected the 50 percent wage increase over those 10 years; it's no surprise. Indeed, he has been spending against this high income at $x = 25$ all along. He's no richer or poorer in terms of wealth, so his hours response to this movement along his wage profile is akin to a substitution effect. He exploits the higher wage when he has 25 years of work experience by allocating more work effort then and less effort in year 15. Thus his career hours profile $h(x)$ follows the same pattern as his wage profile $w_1(x)$, increasing at a decreasing rate.

Everything doesn't always work out as planned, and Gary's career is one example. Gary might be surprised to learn that he'll make more than he had expected, or he might be stunned by the bad news that his career is stagnating. Such surprises shift his wage profile. Gary's hourly wage 25 years into his career jumps from the expected $24 along wage profile $w_1(x)$ to $28, and his wage follows a new profile $w_2(x)$ from there. How Gary responds to this surprise (i.e., unexpected) wage change is a direct application of the model of labor supply in chapter 3. (In the career context, however, we refer to the income effect as the wealth effect.) The shift up in Gary's wage profile increases his wealth, so he wants more leisure time and a shorter workweek. As usual, the substitution effect of a higher wage pushes toward a longer workweek. The combination of substitution and wealth effects leads to an ambiguous effect of a surprise wage increase on the quantity supplied of labor. For surprise wage changes, the labor supply curve can bend backward even in the life-cycle context.

Casting labor supply in the life-cycle context generates a new implication: for predictable variation in the hourly wage over the life cycle, hours of work and the hourly wage move together. And the evidence supports this implication: hours and wage profiles are well aligned over the life cycle. Figure 7.5a illustrates the weekly hours and hourly wage profiles in the Current Population Survey averaged over the 39 cohorts of workers since 1979. They follow the same general pattern—increasing early in the career and falling in the years before retirement—although the hours profile is curiously flat in the middle years.

Figure 7.5b displays the same data as a scatter plot. The scatter plot reveals how the hours–wage pair (h, w) at each point in the life cycle is a point on a life-cycle labor supply curve. The workweek climbs up a life-cycle labor supply curve early in workers' careers, peaks at about 40 hours for the prime years of their careers, and slides down a lower (i.e., shorter workweek) life-cycle labor supply curve as retirement nears.

For additional evidence that the quantity supplied of labor responds positively to predictable differences in wages over time, consider the labor supply of vendors in a baseball stadium over the course of a season. Vendors walk around the stadium selling popcorn, peanuts, and beer, and they earn commissions on their sales. How much they make per hour is predictable: it depends on attendance, which varies

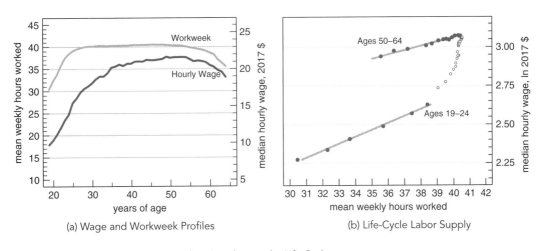

(a) Wage and Workweek Profiles   (b) Life-Cycle Labor Supply

FIGURE 7.5. Labor Supply over the Life Cycle

Note: Weekly hours and real hourly wage profiles are averaged across 39 birth cohorts.
Source: Current Population Survey, outgoing rotation group files, monthly 1979–2017.

by the day of the week, whether the game is played during the day or at night, the quality of the opponent, the weather, and so on. And each vendor decides whether to work a particular game. Oettinger (1999) found that the number of vendors who work a game is very sensitive to how much the vendors expect to earn for that game. In particular, the quantity supplied of labor is 6.5 percent higher for games in which the wage is predicted to be 10 percent higher. That's a very high elasticity of labor supply, and it reflects substituting labor supply over time.

7.2   Applications

Our finding that the worker pays for general training follows as a consequence of employment at will, that the worker can quit and the employer can dismiss the worker at any time for any reason. The importance of the principle emerges in the face of seemingly contradictory evidence—in cases where employers appear to pay for their workers' general training.

Military Training of Commercial Pilots

One way to become a commercial pilot in the United States is to graduate from college and head to a private aviation school for intense and expensive flight training. A six-month program can cost $50,000. Along this route, pilot trainees pay for their training as a typical student pays for his or her college education. This route is consistent with our model of general training: pilot trainees pay for their own training because the many airlines and commercial air-freight companies value skills in piloting aircrafts as general human capital.

Another way to become a commercial pilot is through the United States Air Force. The Air Force takes on the training of more than a thousand pilot trainees every year while it pays those trainees as second lieutenants. Pilot training in the Air Force is on-the-job training, and it's general training. The training is intense (i.e., 54 weeks of 16- to 18-hour days) and surely more costly to taxpayers than the $50,000 price tag at private flight schools. The Air Force front-loads pay with the expectation of underpaying the highly trained pilots over their military careers.

Can this strategy work? A typical employer that pays for its workers' general skills suffers the consequences when its trained workers quit. Quitting is less of a concern in the military. Indeed, the military has unusual means to deal with those who quit: a soldier or sailor who quits (i.e., goes absent without leave, or AWOL) is tracked down by the military police, tossed in a military prison (i.e., a stockade or brig), and tried in a military court. But trained military pilots quit when it's allowed, and that's a problem.

Military recruits typically commit to four years of active duty followed by two years in the active reserves and two years in the inactive reserves. A soldier or sailor can quit without repercussion when the term ends. So the military has four full-time years to capture a return on its training of young soldiers and sailors. That's not long enough for military pilots. The Air Force requires 10 years of active duty after a pilot receives his or her wings. To retain trained pilots beyond 10 years, the Air Force provides (1) supplementary pay to its pilots (i.e., aviator career incentive pay) that peaks at over $1,000 per month for pilots with 12 years of flight experience and (2) re-enlistment bonuses (i.e., aviator continuation pay) of $35,000 per year for the length of the commitment to active duty.

Raising pilots' pay stems the loss of pilots to commercial airlines, but it doesn't completely solve the problem. To compete with airlines and other commercial air carriers, the Air Force must pay the market wage for trained pilots. Aviator career incentive pay and aviator continuation pay raise the pay of Air Force pilots above the military pay schedule, but paying the market wage to trained pilots means that the Air Force is saddled with the training costs. It can't earn a return on the sizable training costs unless pilots are worth more in the military than in commercial flight. In that case, pilot training is military-specific training, and we explore specific training below.

MBAs

Many young executives in corporate America go to school part-time to earn MBAs, master's degrees in business administration. Their employers frequently pay for part or all of the tuition expense and accommodate the course time with reduced hours or flexible work schedules. But business-school education is the poster child for general training. Firms throughout the business world value the skills a young executive learns in business school. Does this practice violate our principle that workers must pay for their general training?

As a direct application of our model of general-training investments, the worker pays for his MBA. If Rhythm Records invests in Gary by paying for his business-school education, then it reluctantly watches Gary proudly market his new MBA-degree-certified skills to employers throughout the business world. Gary can put his MBA degree to work anywhere. His new business acumen warrants a higher wage, and Rhythm Records must pay that higher wage or he'll walk. But if Rhythm Records matches Gary's outside offers, it doesn't earn a return on its payment of Gary's tuition. If Gary can flee to a rival record label or any other employer, then Rhythm Records won't reimburse Gary for his MBA in the first place.

Who pays for MBA training is unrelated to who writes the tuition checks. In our model of general on-the-job training, employers like Rhythm Records pay the direct cost of training c, but workers like Gary pay for their general training by receiving lower wages while being trained. In the context of MBAs, Rhythm Records reimburses Gary's tuition cost $c(x)$, and accountants surely conclude that Gary's employer pays for his business-school education. But labor economists reserve judgment on who pays for the MBA until we identify what happens to Gary's wage.

If Gary's wage falls to reflect the net value of his productivity to Rhythm Records, then he pays for his MBA even if the record label reimburses his tuition expenses. In essence, he reimburses Rhythm Records for providing tuition assistance by receiving a commensurately lower wage. Therefore, that Rhythm

Records reimburses Gary for his tuition expenses (or writes checks directly to the business school) is irrelevant for determining who pays for Gary's MBA.

 **PRACTICE**   Twice a year, Rhythm Records writes a $10,000 check to the Anderson School of Management for Gary's MBA classes. The annual value of Gary's marginal product is $45,000, and taking classes doesn't hurt his job performance. If Gary's annual wage is $_____ , then Rhythm Records alone invests in Gary. Gary pays for his own MBA if his annual wage is $_____ .

No one in the HR (human resources or personnel) department at Rhythm Records has the faintest clue about our model of on-the-job training—including the principle that workers pay for their own general training. But even the dullest mind in HR realizes that the firm is paying more than it has to pay when a large pool of outstanding applicants for a few jobs overwhelms the recruiting process. If (1) Rhythm Records pays young executives the market wage on jobs that don't reimburse tuition costs for part-time MBA studies and (2) reimburses those tuition costs, then it is deluged with qualified applicants. It stops offering so much, and the young executives start paying for their MBAs by receiving the lower wage.

The principle that workers pay for their general training follows directly from the assumption that Gary can freely quit at any time. If, however, Gary can't quit, then Rhythm Records can pay for Gary's MBA by front-loading his pay. (We analyze an important historical example of no-quit clauses when we turn to indenture contracts in the context of migration in section 7.5.) Alternatively, Gary can quit at any time, but he must make a **severance payment** to Rhythm Records when he jumps ship. Rhythm Records reimburses Gary's business-school tuition costs, but his wage doesn't fall. If Gary leaves within the first year of receiving his MBA, he pays back 100 percent of the tuition costs. The severance payment slips to 50 (25) percent if he quits in the second (third) year post-MBA. He can leave free and clear in the fourth year. Rhythm Records takes on the investment, but Gary repays all or part of the investment cost if he leaves before his employer earns a return on its investment in Gary.

 PRACTICE   Gary and other young executives earn well above the minimum wage, but the minimum wage binds on many low-skill workers. Their wage can't fall in response to receiving on-the-job training. How does a binding minimum wage affect their on-the-job training?

So our principle that workers pay for their own general training doesn't apply if a worker like Gary can't quit or must pay to quit. Rhythm Records can pay for Gary's general training in this case. And this case has a lot to do with the player-development system and free agency in professional baseball.

Baseball's Reserve System

We concluded in chapter 2 that the **reserve clause** in baseball reduced competition for baseball players, but the reserve system also enabled baseball teams to develop their talent. Baseball clubs invest in young prospects who are frequently fresh from high school. The *farm system* in baseball builds from the premise that the major-league club can reap the return on its minor-league development costs by underpaying ballplayers who make it to "the Show." But learning to hit a curve ball or throw a slider is general training because all baseball teams value those skills. The reserve clause, which was essentially a no-quit clause, allowed major-league clubs to take on the general training of young baseball players. A system of delayed **free agency** replaced the reserve system in the late 1970s. A player becomes a free agent after six years of service in the major leagues, so his ball club has six years to earn a return on its investment in the player's development.

Without the reserve clause or delayed free agency, baseball would have an apprentice system. Rather than being paid about $1,000 per month in the farm system today, a young prospect would pay $15,000–$20,000 per month for training. That's more expensive than going to medical school, law school, business school, or even flight school. The upside is that the successful minor leaguer would be a free agent on day one in the major leagues; he wouldn't have to suffer through six years of receiving less than his value. The downside to immediate free agency is that apprenticing in the minor leagues would be a huge gamble. Many try, few succeed. That means many young prospects would have to pony up more than $100,000 per season for a long shot at becoming a big leaguer.

Such a risky investment isn't attractive to even the most confident ballplayer coming out of high school. Financial markets diversify risks, and major-league baseball clubs do, too. The club diversifies the risk by investing in a large portfolio of young prospects. (Each major-league team has at least six times as many minor-league prospects under contract as players on the major-league roster.) While the club doesn't know who will succeed and who will fail in the player-development process, it can be confident that two or three players per year will emerge as career major leaguers. (This pooling of risk is analogous to an insurance company knowing the proportion of houses that fire will destroy each year without knowing which houses will burn.) So risk-averse young players shift much of the risk of their training investment to the club, and the club earns a return on its training investment by underpaying players once they make it to the big leagues.

7.3   Specific Training

Much of what we learn on the job translates to other firms. A manager at General Electric learns about chemicals or steam turbines or light bulbs, and this knowledge is valuable to GE's competitors. Most important, a manager at GE learns to manage, and management skills are valued universally.

But some of what we learn on the job is **specific training** (Becker 1962). Commercial airlines highly value many of the skills of a fighter pilot in the

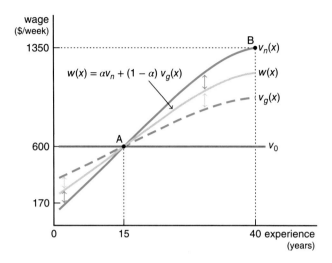

If workers like Gary pay for firm-specific training, then $w(x) = v_n(x)$. Their employers have insufficient incentives to retain them, so the dismissal rate is too high.

If Rhythm Records and other employers pay for their workers' specific training, then $w(x) = v_g(x)$. Workers' incentives to stay with their employers are too weak, so the quit rate is too high.

Sharing the costs of and the returns to specific training (i.e., $0 < \alpha < 1$) lowers the turnover rate, which is more efficient. But quit and layoff rates are still too high.

FIGURE 7.6. Who Pays for Firm-Specific Training?

Air Force, but they don't value skills in shooting down enemy aircraft. The "fighter" part of "fighter pilot" is a military-specific skill. Similarly, publishers' sales representatives learn the general skill of how to sell books, and they also acquire knowledge of the specific books their employer publishes. A sales rep who jumps to another publisher must learn the strengths and weaknesses of a new list of books. Even learning "to play as a team" is specific training in sports like basketball, football, soccer, and hockey.

Networking is also largely firm-specific. An experienced Gary continually reaches out by phone, email, and text to an extended team of specialists at Rhythm Records to get answers and to find solutions. He must do so to make records. If Gary switches to Melody Music, a rival record company, his knowledge of the business in terms of identifying talent, spotting a good tune, and getting the right sound carries over to Melody Music seamlessly. But he loses his networking knowledge. Solving problems takes longer because he doesn't know the strengths and weaknesses of his new team of specialists. He isn't quite sure whose expertise matches best to the current problem. Gary's networking skills recover as he gets experience at Melody Music, and his performance does, too.

With specific training, Gary's net productivity at Rhythm Records differs from his net productivity at rival firms like Melody Music. Figure 7.6 plots Gary's net-productivity profiles at Rhythm Records and other employers. His net-productivity profile at Rhythm Records $v_n(x)$ reflects Gary's general and specific training. The dashed profile $v_g(x)$ in Figure 7.6 is his net-productivity profile at other employers, which reflects only his general training. The difference between $v_n(x)$ and $v_g(x)$ captures the costs (early on) and returns (later on) to Gary's specific training at Rhythm Records. The difference between $v_g(x)$ and v_0 measures the costs (early on) and returns (later on) to Gary's general training.

To see why, let's take a close look at Gary's productivities five years into his career. In year 5 at Rhythm Records, Gary's potential productivity and net productivity are $715 and $290 per week. (See Table 7.1.) If Gary's training is split roughly equally between general and specific skills, then Gary's net productivity at Melody Music (based on his general training) is $500 per week, about halfway between $715 and $290. The difference between $500 and $290 is the $210-per-week cost of his specific training in year 5 at Rhythm Records.

 PRACTICE   The difference between $600 and $500 is the weekly [cost of, return on] Gary's [general, firm-specific] training in year 5.

What do other employers such as Melody Music offer Gary? Although these rivals cherish Gary's acquired knowledge of the business, some of his skills just won't transfer over if Gary jumps ship. So Gary is worth $v_g(x)$ to other firms, which is the amount outside competitors offer Gary to lure him away from Rhythm Records.

Who Pays for Specific Training?

How does Gary's wage at Rhythm Records vary over his career if he receives specific training? Let's apply the key principle from our analysis of general training: Gary pays for training by having his pay follow his net-productivity profile. What happens if Gary's wage profile $w(x)$ is his net-productivity profile $v_n(x)$, which reflects specific as well as general training? If everything evolves exactly as expected, Gary spends his entire career at Rhythm Records. Once he acquires some specific skills at Rhythm Records, his career at Rhythm Records can't be beat.

But a career isn't entirely predictable, and the randomness that interferes with the best-laid plans offers serious prospects for Gary to jump ship. Perhaps Gary's productivity at Melody Music soars, and Melody Music values him (without any specific capital) more than Rhythm Records values him with his specific capital. Or Gary's productivity at Rhythm Records falls so much that he becomes more productive at Melody Music. Although Gary accumulated specific capital at Rhythm Records, switching from Rhythm Records to Melody Music is efficient in these two cases.

Job separations can also be inefficient, and Gary and Rhythm Records share the costs and returns of Gary's specific training to reduce the inefficiency from excessive separations. If Gary undertakes the entire investment in his training, then Rhythm Records is indifferent between employing Gary and anyone else. With the slightest dip in the value of Gary's work—perhaps business is just a little slow or one of Gary's recording artists develops a drug problem that puts her in rehab—the record label cuts Gary loose. And Gary's left with skills that just aren't as valuable elsewhere. The smallest gain to Rhythm Records (by dismissing Gary) generates a huge loss to Gary. That's a problem for this wage profile, and Gary and Rhythm Records can design a better wage profile.

Having Gary pay for his training causes excessive dismissals (i.e., layoffs or firings), so let's have Rhythm Records undertake the costs and reap the returns to Gary's specific training. In this case, the wage profile follows the path of Gary's net productivity based on his general training, which is $v_g(x)$ in Figure 7.6. Rhythm Records pays Gary exactly what he's worth to rival firms like Melody Music at each point in his career. Therefore, Gary is indifferent between working at Rhythm Records and rivals like Melody Music throughout his career. Indifference isn't a good way to preserve an employment relationship. Indeed, a tiny bit of good fortune at Melody Music nudges Gary's productivity there up a nickel per week. Melody Music offers Gary up to a nickel more in weekly wages. It doesn't sound like much, but it's enough to get Gary to pack his desk, to collect the photos of his family from around his office, and to prepare for his new job at Melody Music. The problem with this wage profile is too many quits.

Next, let's try a wage profile along which Gary and Rhythm Records **share the costs of and returns to specific training**, while Gary shoulders his general training. If Gary's share of the specific investment is the Greek letter alpha α, which lies between 0 and 1, then his wage profile is $w(x) = \alpha v_n(x) + (1-\alpha)v_g(x)$. If $\alpha = .5$, then Gary's wage profile lies halfway between his net-productivity profile $v_n(x)$ and his net-productivity profile based on his general training $v_g(x)$. Figure 7.6 graphs this wage profile.

Sharing the costs of and returns to specific training reduces the problem of excessive quits and dismissals. Rhythm Records has a stake in Gary's specific training, so it's not inclined to dismiss Gary. Likewise, Gary has a stake in his specific investments, so it takes a particularly good outside offer to lure him away from Rhythm Records. By sharing the costs of and returns to specific training, Gary and Rhythm Records avoid the hypersensitivity of quits and dismissals to small doses of randomness.

This analysis of specific training also suggests an additional variable in the log-wage regression: **job tenure**, how long a worker has been with an employer. Since Gary's wage profile is steeper than $v_g(x)$, his net-productivity profile with only general training, job tenure reaps its own return. To see why, consider the wages of two workers with 15 years of work experience: Gary, who has spent all 15 years at Rhythm Records, and Walter, who has only three years of job tenure. Gary has acquired more firm-specific skills, is more productive, and earns a higher wage than Walter.

In data sets that include job tenure, the wage rises with job tenure in addition to rising with work experience. The basic monthly CPS doesn't collect information on workers' job tenures, but the BLS does collect job tenure data every other January in its Job Tenure and Occupational Mobility supplement to the CPS. Let's estimate the wage-tenure profile in the most recent Job Tenure supplement, which is from January 2016.

Wages rise with job tenure at a decreasing rate. We capture the curvature of the relationship between wages (in logs) and job tenure by including a squared term, the square of job tenure t^2, in the regression equation. On the sample of over 11,000 workers, the estimated regression equation is

(7.4) $$\ln w = 3.35 + .033\,h + .100s + .036x - .0006x^2 + .029t - .0006t^2$$
$$\quad\;\;(.034)\quad(.0004)\quad\;(.002)\quad\;(.001)\quad\;(.0000)\quad\;(.002)\quad\;(.0001)$$

with $R^2 = .530$. The estimated effects of the workweek h, schooling s, and work experience x are familiar, so let's focus on the relationship between the wage (in logs) and job tenure.

The regression estimates imply that—for workers with the same values for h, s, and x—workers with 10 years job tenure earn 23 percent more than new hires. To see this, let's work with the tenure expression $T = .029t - .0006t^2$. For new hires (i.e., workers with $t = 0$), T clearly equals zero. From this starting point, the effect of tenure on $\ln w$ is positive and rises with job tenure. For example, at $t = 10$, $T = .23\,(= (.029 \times 10) - (.0006 \times 10^2))$, so workers with 10 years job tenure earn 23 percent more than new hires with the same workweek, schooling, and experience. Furthermore, the negative coefficient on t^2 implies that the effect of job tenure on wages (in logs) falls with job tenure. In fact, $T = .34\,(= (.029 \times 20) - (.0006 \times 20^2))$ for workers with 20 years job tenure. So the second decade with an employer pushes up the wage about half as much (i.e., 11 percent ($= .34 - .23$)) as the first decade. Therefore, our regression estimates provide clear evidence that wages (in logs) increase with job tenure at a decreasing rate.

Specific Training and Turnover

In our model of general training, workers' incentives to quit and firms' incentives to dismiss workers combine to pin down the wage profile. But Gary is equally productive at all employers, so general training isn't a fertile environment to study job turnover. Our model of specific training, however, seriously addresses turnover throughout Gary's tenure at Rhythm Records.

Sharing the costs of and returns to training tends to preserve the employment relationship, and that's a good thing. As Gary accumulates specific skills, his value at Rhythm Records rises relative to his value at outside employers. Efficiency dictates that Gary should stay with Rhythm Records, and the sharing of specific training encourages just that. But Gary doesn't have the full stake in his investment in specific training, so he's too likely to quit. Likewise, Rhythm Records doesn't have the full stake in Gary's specific training, so the record company is too likely to dismiss Gary. Either way, one side captures the full benefit from separating but bears only a share of the cost of the lost specific investment.

If training is entirely general, then the amount of training Gary receives doesn't depend on how likely he is to change jobs. He just takes his acquired skills with him to his new job. But Gary's prospects for jumping ship are important if his training includes acquiring firm-specific skills. Specific skills have no value if Gary changes jobs, so specific training pays a low return if the turnover rate is high. Indeed, workers on jobs with high turnover rates should, on efficiency grounds, receive less specific training.

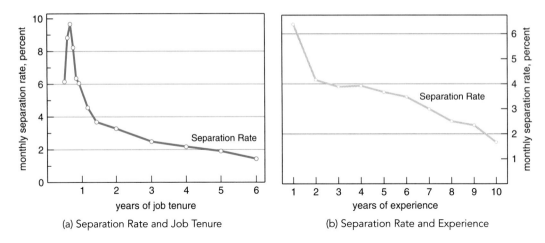

FIGURE 7.7. Separation Rates by Job Tenure and Experience

Notes: Years of experience starts at one for a worker in his or her first year as a long-term participant in the labor market. Similarly, years of job tenure starts at one for a worker on his or her first year on a job. In panel (a), the first six points are monthly, and the next two points are the third and fourth quarters of the first year on the job.

Sources: Unpublished calculations from Farber, Henry. 1994. "The Analysis of Interfirm Worker Mobility." *Journal of Labor Economics* 12(4): 554–593. The primary data source is the National Longitudinal Survey of Youth, interview years 1979–1988.

 PRACTICE   Where do you expect workers to receive more firm-specific training, on tech jobs in Silicon Valley or on jobs in a chemical plant in rural Ohio?

The model of specific training predicts that separations—the sum of quits and dismissals—become rare as job tenure lengthens. A worker who has been employed with a current employer for a long time has accumulated a lot of specific capital, so the odds don't favor an outside offer (based on general skills) exceeding his or her wage. That is, we predict the separation (or turnover) rate falls with job tenure. Figure 7.7a confirms that the separation rate falls with job tenure after the first two months on a new job. (Young workers in the first decade of their careers comprise the sample.) Roughly 75 percent of the jobs end within 36 months, and only 10 percent of the jobs last longer than 8 years. Panel (b) of Figure 7.7 demonstrates that the separation rate also falls with work experience.

7.4   Matching Models of Turnover

Gary is all tooled up with firm-specific human capital, so when he shows some interest in changing employers, he hears, "I'm afraid we wouldn't be a good fit for you," or "You're clearly a very talented person, but this job wouldn't be a good match for your skills."

Job seekers hear these polite rejections every day, and there's probably more to the rejections than accumulation of specific human capital. To see why, let's assume that Gary gets no training on the job; he doesn't accumulate general or specific human capital. But each employer has its own value of Gary's skills. The value of his match with Rhythm Records might be $675 per week, while his match value with Melody Music is $595 per week. Since Gary doesn't amass human capital on the job, these **match values** are fixed over his career.

If match values are known, then wage offers guide each worker to the employer that values his or her skills the most. While this principle is important, matching with known match values (and without accumulation of human capital) contributes nothing to our understanding of career wage profiles and turnover patterns. But the model becomes more interesting—and more powerful in explaining career patterns—by introducing learning *about the job*: the only thing Gary learns over his career is where his skills are valued most.

Here we sketch two models of matching workers to firms as an alternative to our training model. In the first model, a model of **job shopping**, the worker searches on the job for a better match, and the worker knows the match value before he or she accepts a new job. In the second model, the worker and the employer learn the value of their match by observing the worker's performance over time, refining their assessment every year. Let's see how these models explain the evolution of wages and turnover over workers' careers.

Searching on the Job

Workers move to better matches and higher-paying jobs as they age (Burdett 1978). Ken can work at many places, and a match value that doesn't vary over Ken's career characterizes each potential employer. Ken's match values vary across employers ranging from $100 to $1,100 per week, with any wage in that range as likely as any other.

Ken doesn't know where he's most valuable, so he searches. Searching generates one wage offer on a new job per year, and the wage offer reflects Ken's match value with that employer. If the wage offer exceeds his wage on his current job, he accepts the offer and starts work on the new job. Table 7.3 lists the wage offers and wages over the first 10 years of Ken's 30-year career. A computer simulation randomly generates the wage offers in the table. (The simulation distributes the match values uniformly between $100 and $1,100 per week.)

Upon graduation, Ken receives one job offer, and the job pays a mere $235 per week. That's much lower than Ken expected, but he accepts the $235 offer and continues searching for a better job. Since his first job doesn't pay well, it shouldn't surprise us that Ken receives a better offer for work in year 2; that job pays $743 per week. He accepts the offer and works on the new job in year 2. His wage offer in year 3 is awful (i.e., $188 per week), so he rejects it and continues working for his current employer at a weekly wage of $743. From there, Ken's wage profile continues as a series of flat lines in panel (a) of Figure 7.8, one for each job, with jumps from one line to the next marking a change of jobs.

PRACTICE   Ken's wage offer in year 5 is $784. (Refer to row 5 of Table 7.3.) What is his wage in year 5 if he doesn't change jobs? Does he take the job offer? Why does his wage in year 5 equal his wage offer in year 5 but his wage offer in year 4 is less than his wage in year 4?

Barbie, facing the same distribution of match values, travels along her own career path. Her first job is a good match, paying a weekly wage of $815. She turns down job offers over the next five years, but in year 7 she takes a new job that pays $907 per week. Figure 7.8a also displays her wage profile, again a series of flat lines.

With on-the-job search, workers always move to better matches, so wage profiles slope up. Ken moves to a higher-wage job in each of his five job changes, and Barbie's wage jumps in each of her two moves. Averaging these step-like wage profiles over thousands of workers generates a familiar wage profile, one that increases at a decreasing rate. (Along the average wage profile, the wage is the expected value of the wage at each point in a worker's career.) The "Average Wage" column of Table 7.3 lists this wage profile $w(x)$ for the first 10 years. Figure 7.8a illustrates the wage profile for all years. A typical worker like Ken expects to earn $600 per week in his first year. The expected wage grows to $767 in year 2, when half the workers find better matches.

TABLE 7.3. WAGE OFFERS, WAGES, AND SEPARATIONS IN A MODEL OF JOB SHOPPING

	——————— KEN ———————			—————— BARBIE ——————			———— ALL WORKERS ————	
Experience (years)	Wage Offer ($/week)	Wage ($/week)	New Job	Wage Offer ($/week)	Wage ($/week)	New Job	Average Wage ($/week)	Separation Rate (percent)
1	235	235	✓	815	815	✓	600	——
2	743	743	✓	542	815		767	50
3	188	743		144	815		850	33
4	514	743		497	815		900	25
5	784	784	✓	723	815		933	20
6	480	784		282	815		957	17
7	512	784		907	907	✓	975	14
8	666	784		136	907		989	13
9	174	784		442	907		1,000	11
10	971	971	✓	825	907		1,010	10

Note: A checkmark indicates that the worker accepts a new job, which happens if the wage offer for work on a new job exceeds the wage on the current job.
Source: Computer simulation with wage offers distributed uniformly between $100 and $1,100 per week.

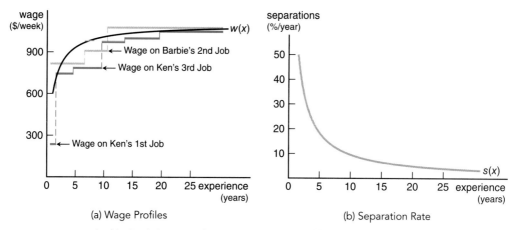

(a) Wage Profiles (b) Separation Rate

In this simulation, a worker receives one wage offer per year and changes jobs if and only if the wage offer exceeds his current wage. Thus a worker's wage profile in panel (a) is a series of flat lines, one flat line for each job. Over their 30-year careers, Ken has six jobs, and Barbie has three jobs.

Averaging over thousands of workers, the wage profile $w(x)$ in panel (a) rises from $600/week and converges toward $1,100/week after decades of job shopping. In panel (b), the separation rate $s(x)$ drops sharply from 50% in year 2 and converges to zero.

FIGURE 7.8. Wage Profiles and Separation Rates in a Model of Job Shopping

After 25 years of searching for better matches, the average wage has risen to $1,062 per week. It doesn't get much better than this. Few jobs have match values above $1,062—the upper limit is $1,100 per week—so the average wage grows slowly from year 25 to year 26. While the average wage increases with work experience as workers move to better jobs, the average wage increases at a decreasing rate.

The separation (or turnover) rate in this model of on-the-job search falls over workers' careers, so job changes are common early in the career. Ken works on six jobs over his career, but he starts his fifth job by the midpoint of his 30-year career. Barbie has three jobs, and she doesn't change jobs after her eleventh year of work. Ken and Barbie are two of thousands of workers. In this example, the average worker has about four jobs in a career, and each job lasts about 7.5 years. First jobs tend be short, and subsequent jobs last longer.

Figure 7.8b illustrates the separation rate, which is also listed in the last column of Table 7.3. Half the first jobs end after year 1, so the separation rate in year 2, which measures the change of employers from year 1 to year 2, is 50 percent. It declines from there and approaches zero well into a long career. The pattern that emerges from this simulation is that workers like Barbie and Ken eventually settle into career jobs by finding high-quality matches through search.

This simple example illustrates how moving to better matches—with fixed match values—over a career generates (1) a wage profile that increases (at a decreasing rate) without any increase in skills and (2) a decreasing separation rate without accumulation of firm-specific skills. The primary problem with the job-shopping model is, however, that it doesn't explain wage growth within jobs. To explain that pattern in a matching model, we turn to a model of **learning the match value**.

Learning the Value of the Match

The wage rises with job tenure if no one initially knows the value of the job match, but the employer and worker learn the match value by observing the worker's job performance (Jovanovic 1979). When media giant 20th Century Fox hires Barbie, Ken, and many other young professionals into entry-level management positions, no one knows who will sparkle and who will fizzle. The match will be good for some; for others, it just won't be a good fit. In contrast to Gary's experience at Rhythm Records, no worker at 20th Century Fox learns anything that makes him or her more productive in future years.

But there is learning. In the first year, everyone—including the HR folks at 20th Century Fox—observes that Barbie's doing super work, so everyone raises the assessment of the value of her match with 20th Century Fox a lot. Everyone also notices that Ken is struggling, so the assessment of his match value sinks. Wages adjust accordingly, and the worst-performing workers hit the road in search of better matches. The second year on the job brings new performance information; assessments of match values are updated in light of the new information, and a new crop of badly matched workers—not as bad and not as many as the first batch—leaves 20th Century Fox.

Cream rises to the top, and so do the wages of the best matched workers at 20th Century Fox. Year by year, more and more of the bottom performers exit in search of better matches. With each year, the group of retained workers is more select, so the average match value of the workers who remain increases with job tenure. Average performance increases with job tenure simply because retention of workers becomes increasingly selective. As a result, the average wage rises with job tenure, and the separation rate falls with job tenure. Voilà! These are precisely the patterns in the data.

 PRACTICE   Workers with 15 years of job tenure earn more than workers with 10 years of job tenure. Why? What happens over the five years to cause the average wage to rise?

Can this be the whole story? Was Jack Welch prepared to lead General Electric when he joined GE as a junior chemical engineer in 1960, or did he learn a lot about the business and managing workers in the 21 years before his promotion to CEO? With many bumps along the way, Steve Jobs led Apple Computer from his parents' garage to a worldwide empire. Could a hygiene-challenged, 21-year-old college dropout take the reins of Apple today and succeed? No chance. Jobs learned the business along the way. That's the human capital model of work experience. The model of learning match value, however, predicts that Welch or Jobs would have been wildly successful CEOs of their corporate empires from day one on their jobs. Perhaps it's best to think of learning match value as an insightful supplement to the human capital model.

Can we distinguish learning match values from human capital more formally? With rich data, the answer is yes. Suppose we have data on wages and job performance of individual workers over time. With such **panel data**—data that track individuals over time—we can plot the wage and productivity profiles of workers with, say, 20 years of job tenure. The learning model predicts that average wages in the group rose with tenure as everyone slowly learned that these workers are good matches. But the match value is fixed for each worker, so actual performance of workers celebrating 20 years with the employer should have been high all along; that is, their productivity profile should be high but flat. In the human capital model, performance, as well as wages, rise with job tenure. In a sample of workers with a specific tenure on the job, finding that the wage profile is lower and steeper than the productivity profile would be evidence of learning match values.

7.5   Migration

Over 1 million people per year legally migrate to the United States, and perhaps another 500,000 enter the United States illegally. Immigration is a politically charged issue in the United States, but there's a much wider principle at work here: people move across locations—across county lines, state borders, and regions of the United States, as well as across countries. Between 2016 and 2017, 10.8 percent of the working-age population changed residences. Most of these moves were local, but 4.1 percent crossed county lines, and 2.1 percent were moves to a different state or country. The 2.1 percent might seem small, but it compounds up over time. For instance, in 2016, 41 percent of U.S. residents weren't living in the state of their birth. Three of four residents of Nevada were born in other states or countries. And a lot of these moves are for work and wages.

Migration as an Investment in Human Capital

Migration is an investment in human capital. As an investment, the costs of migrating are borne early on; the benefits of the move, typically in the form of a higher wage, accrue down the line. A move to a location with better job prospects, for instance, is an investment in general human capital.

The choice to migrate, as an investment, depends on the **net present value** of the move, which in turn depends on the cost of migrating, the wage gain from the move, the interest rate, and length of the remaining career. Let c denote George's moving cost. The benefit of migrating takes the form of a higher wage Δw for

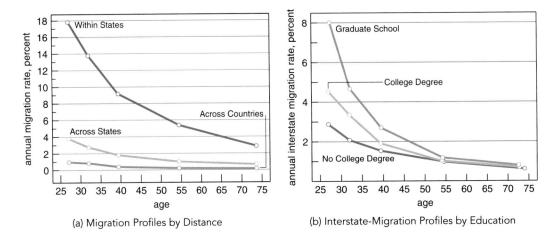

FIGURE 7.9. Migration Profiles by Distance and Education, 2016–2017

Note: In panel (a), each migration profile excludes narrower and wider crossings. For instance, "Across States" includes only migration that crossed state lines but didn't cross national borders. **Source:** Current Population Survey, Annual Social and Economic Supplement, March 2017.

the rest of George's working life, which is N years. Then the net present value of George's migration is

$$(7.5) \qquad NPV = -c + \frac{\Delta w}{1+i} + \frac{\Delta w}{(1+i)^2} + \frac{\Delta w}{(1+i)^3} + \cdots + \frac{\Delta w}{(1+i)^N}$$

where the annual interest rate i discounts the future wage gains Δw. If George lives and works forever, then the net present value of his migration simplifies to

$$(7.6) \qquad NPV = -c + \frac{\Delta w}{i}$$

(Chapter 6's analysis of the present values of wage profiles includes a parallel simplification; see Equations 6.2 and 6.4 for the steps to derive Equation 7.6 from Equation 7.5.)

George migrates if $NPV > 0$, so he's more likely to migrate the smaller the moving cost c, the greater the wage gain Δw, and the lower the interest rate i. Of course, George won't work forever, and the gains from migration shrink the closer he is to retirement (i.e., the smaller is N). So George is less likely to migrate the older he is. The graphs of annual migration rates for various age groups in Figure 7.9 confirm this prediction. For instance, the migration rate across states within the United States declines from 3.6 percent for 25- to 29-year-olds to 0.6 percent for people ages 65 and older.

The model also predicts that the migration rate falls with the length of the move. Long moves cost more, so longer distances decrease the net present value of migration NPV and lower the chance that George moves. Figure 7.9a illustrates how migration profiles depend on a proxy for distance. Moves that don't cross state lines are short; moves that cross state lines are longer, and migration to other countries tends to involve even longer distances. The figure demonstrates that the migration rate at every age falls as distance grows from Within States to Across States and ultimately to Across Countries.

How does schooling affect migration rates? Suppose wages are 20 percent higher in a thriving region of the United States. For a high-school-educated person making $32,000 per year, the wage gain to moving to a thriving labor market is $6,400 (= .20 × $32,000) per year. As a college-educated worker, George earns $44,800 per year in his current location; moving to the thriving region raises his wage almost $9,000 (≈ .20 × 44,800) per year. The effect of schooling on the cost of migration is likely to be less than proportionate, so the net present value of moving to a thriving labor market tends to be bigger for more-educated workers like George. Thus we predict that more-educated workers are more mobile, which the migration profiles in Figure 7.9b confirm. Workers with graduate degrees have the highest migration rates across states, and workers without college diplomas have the lowest migration rates.

Application: Indentured Servitude

In the modern world, migrating from one continent to another is a major investment with substantial moving costs. In the colonial period in America, the cost of migration was nearly insurmountable, approximately half a year's income and two to three months' passage on a ship. How could an unskilled youngster in Britain—the person with the most to gain from migrating to America—finance this investment in human capital?

Half to two-thirds of white immigrants to the British colonies in America came as indentured servants in the century and a half leading up to the American Revolution. An emigrant from Britain signed a contract that specified a period of work in exchange for passage to a colony, food, clothing, and lodging for the contract period and a monetary payment (i.e., freedom dues) at the conclusion of the contract. Colonial laws protected the servants, guaranteeing them access to adequate food, clothing, and lodging. Unlike slaves, indentured servants could even sue their masters.

Origins of the indenture system date to the Virginia Company in Jamestown, which financed the cost of passage with a work requirement that spanned several years. By 1620, the Virginia Company financed the costs of passage, about £5 per servant, and sold the contract to free planters when the servant arrived in Jamestown. Financing quickly shifted to European merchants involved in transatlantic trade through the major British ports, and the indenture system spread throughout the colonies. By the 1700s, indentured servants arrived from Scotland, Ireland, and Germany. But the indenture system became quantitatively insignificant by the end of the 1700s and played no part in the great transatlantic migration from Europe that began around 1820.

The **indenture contract** solved the problem of financing migration as a human-capital investment when more familiar forms of financing failed (Galenson 1981). Since migration is an investment in general human capital, we expect each

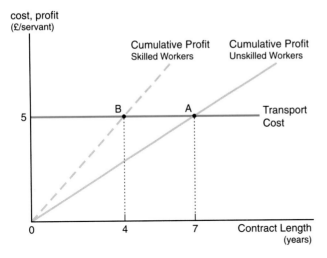

The period of indenture adjusts to equate the cumulative profit from the servant with the transport cost. Cumulative profit adds up the net value of the servant (productivity value minus maintenance costs) over the years the servant works.

A unskilled servant takes seven years to work off the cost of passage to America. The cumulative profit curve of a skilled servant is steeper, so the competitive period of indenture falls from seven to four years.

FIGURE 7.10. Compensating Differential in Length of the Indenture Contract

worker to bear the cost of moving and capture the return in the form of wage gains over his career. But the Brits with the most to gain from migrating to America were young and unskilled. (The landed aristocracy of Britain had less to gain.) These young people typically had no savings from which to finance passage to America.

A second possibility is for the worker to borrow the costs of passage from a bank. The world was a bigger place in the seventeenth and eighteenth centuries, and British banks weren't equipped to enforce loan payments 3,000 or so miles away. Defaulting would be too easy, so migrants couldn't borrow to pay their costs of passage.

A third possibility is to have the colonial farmer, desperate for labor, finance the cost of passage. This arrangement front-loads pay, so immigrants would quit on arrival in America. A colonial farmer attempting to recoup his investment by paying less than the market wage to the immigrants would find that his immigrants quit to work for other farmers who paid the market wage.

This reasoning suggests a fourth possibility: a no-quit clause in an employment contract. By precluding quits, the indenture contract allows the colonial farmer to front-load pay by paying passage and to earn a return on that investment over the length of the indenture contract.

The length of the indenture contract was determined in equilibrium in a competitive market for labor. In a typical labor market, a competitive wage emerges to clear the labor market. Since wages weren't an important part of the indenture system, a competitive process determined the length of the indenture. A short contract wouldn't be long enough for the colonial planter to recover the costs of passage, so there would be a surplus of servants. Long contracts would generate excess profit and a shortage of servants.

Figure 7.10 illustrates how competition drives the length of the indenture contract down to just cover the cost of passage. Cumulative profit adds the net

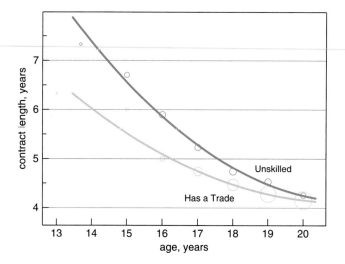

The 2,014 indenture contracts are split into (1) a skilled sample of 870 contracts that specified a profession, craft, or trade and (2) an unskilled sample of 1,144 contracts that didn't list any profession, craft, or trade or described the servant as unskilled, a poor lad, widow, and so on. The center of each bubble marks the average length of the contract for servants of the specified age; the size of the bubble reflects the number of servants of that age.

Source: London II Registers, Virtual Jamestown website: http://www.virtual jamestown.org. Microfilms of the original contracts are in the *Agreements to Serve in America* collection at Guildhall, London, England.

FIGURE 7.11. Age, Skill, and the Length of Indenture Contracts, London, 1718–1759

value of the servant (i.e., value of the marginal product net of costs of food, clothing, and shelter) from year to year. If the servant's net value is constant, then the cumulative profit curve is a ray from the origin. The intersection of this ray with a horizontal line at the cost of transportation determines the competitive contract length. As drawn, the period of indenture stretches to seven years for an unskilled servant, such as a 15-year-old without a profession or craft.

The indenture system solved the problem of financing passage to America, and servants signed (or marked) the contracts voluntarily. Furthermore, evidence in the form of compensating differentials indicates that servants captured the gain from migration in a competitive market for their services. In the context of indentures, we look for compensating differentials in the length of the indenture contract rather than in the wage. Compared to an unskilled servant, a skilled servant is more productive, so the farmer's net value of a skilled servant is higher. The dashed line in Figure 7.10 displays the cumulative profit curve for a 20-year-old carpenter. The equilibrium length of the indenture contract at point B is only four years. The carpenter works off the cost of passage three years faster than the unskilled servant.

Let's check if the evidence, in a collection of over 2,000 indenture contracts filed with the Lord Mayor of London between 1718 and 1759, supports these predictions. (This data set is one of two data sets in Galenson's (1981) analysis.) Servants ranged in age from 12 to 20 years. The indenture contracts specified the servant's profession, craft, or trade (e.g., farmer, carpenter, blacksmith, weaver, or bookkeeper) if he or she had one. A servant either signed or marked the contract, which reveals if he or she was literate.

Older workers and skilled workers negotiated shorter periods of indenture. Figure 7.11 displays the contract data averaged by age and skill. The length of the indenture contract falls with the servant's age for both skilled and unskilled workers. Since the whole age–length curve is higher for unskilled workers, contracts were longer for unskilled workers, as the analysis in Figure 7.11 predicts.

Let's estimate how age, skill, and literacy influenced the period of indenture of young workers. In the sample of over 2,000 indenture contracts, the estimated regression equation is

$$\text{(7.7)} \quad length = 30.03 - 2.439\,a + .058a^2 - .305trade - .161signed$$
$$\phantom{\text{(7.7)} \quad length = } \underset{(1.85)}{} \quad \underset{(.213)}{} \quad \underset{(.006)}{} \quad \underset{(.042)}{} \quad \underset{(.038)}{}$$

with $R^2 = .466$. (a is age in years, and *trade* and *signed* indicate whether the servant had a trade and whether he or she signed the contract.) The period of indenture decreased with age at a decreasing rate, so the regression estimates confirm the pattern in Figure 7.11. The regression estimates also confirm that skilled workers negotiated shorter contracts: having a trade shortened the period of indenture by about 31 percent of a year or nearly four months. In addition, literate servants also nabbed shorter contracts, almost two months (or 16 percent of a year) shorter.

So the evidence reveals that older workers, those with a trade, and literate workers signed shorter contracts, exactly as the model of a competitive market for servants predicts.

 PRACTICE   Islands in the West Indies are favorite Caribbean vacation destinations, but these islands were the home to sugar plantations, gang labor, and high mortality rates during the colonial period. An indenture contract specified passage to a particular colony. As a compensating differential, would indenture contracts be shorter or longer for servants heading to the West Indies?

Since the indenture system solved the problem of financing investments in general human capital in the form of migration, the decline of indentures should follow from falling costs of passage from and rising incomes in the source countries. That's exactly what happened. As the cost of transportation from Great Britain, Ireland, and Germany fell, and the Industrial Revolution ushered in an era of rising real wages, self-financing of migration became feasible, and the indenture system faded to insignificance. The indenture system revived in the second half of the nineteenth century as migrants from China and India were bound for the West Indies on indentures. Again, the indenture contract was the solution to the problem of financing migration as an investment in general human capital. The cost of passage from Asia to the West Indies was at least several years' income for the typical worker in India and China.

Selection on Skill

Who migrates isn't entirely random (Borjas 1987). Immigrants from Mexico are poor, not just poor compared to the typical American but poor compared to the typical Mexican. Immigrants from the United Kingdom and Sweden tend to be

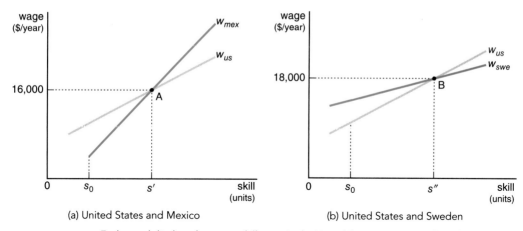

(a) United States and Mexico   (b) United States and Sweden

Each panel displays the wage–skill curve in the United States w_{us}. In panel (a), the wage–skill curve in Mexico is steeper than w_{us}. Mexican workers with skills *below* s' earn more by migrating to the United States. In panel (b), the wage–skill curve in Sweden is flatter than w_{us} because skills pay a lower premium in Sweden. Swedes with skills *above* s'' gain by migrating to the United States.

FIGURE 7.12. Selection on Skills: Low-Skill and High-Skill Immigrants

above-average workers both in the United States and in their countries of origin. What determines this selection on the skills of immigrants?

In our analysis of schooling choice in chapter 6, we found that higher-ability people stay in school longer because they get more out of school. So those who graduate from college are a group of higher-ability people. We also found that this sorting by ability has important repercussions for estimating the rate of return to schooling. Sorting by ability is an example of **self-selection**, sorting into a group by personal choice.

In the context of migration, immigrants to the United States are self-selected. Do more-skilled workers in some country do better there or in the United States? Do they self-select into the group of immigrants to the United States?

Figure 7.12 depicts two varieties of self-selection of immigrants. We analyze Mexican immigrants in panel (a). There's a range of skills for workers in Mexico, and the return to skill in Mexico is quite high. Low-skill Mexicans eke out a meager living. Skilled Mexicans can earn fabulous wealth. Indeed, Mexican telecom magnate Carlos Slim Helu has been the wealthiest person in the world. The return to skill in the United States isn't as high: low-skill workers in America do better, and high-skill workers in America can't match the fabulous wages of equally skilled workers in Mexico.

Do low-skill or high-skill Mexicans migrate to the United States? Mexicans with skills below s' in the figure would earn more in the United States (i.e., the U.S. wage–skill line is higher than the Mexican wage–skill line over this range of skills), so low-skill Mexicans want to migrate to the United States. High-skill Mexicans are happy to stay in Mexico to earn the higher return on their skills.

Thus the typical Mexican immigrant is drawn from the bottom of the distribution of skills in Mexico.

Immigrants from Sweden, however, are drawn from the top of the distribution of skills in Sweden. Figure 7.12b depicts this case. The wage–skill line in Sweden is flatter than the wage–skill line in the United States, and that pattern reflects the lower return to skill in Sweden. Consequently, low-skill workers in Sweden—all Swedes with skills below s''—do better staying in Sweden. High-skill Swedes would earn more in the United States, so they prefer to migrate to the United States. In this case, Swedish immigrants to the United States are drawn from the top of the Swedish distribution of skills.

 PRACTICE   A Mexican and a Swede have s_0 units of skill. Draw a line segment in Figure 7.12a to indicate what the Mexican gains in wages by migrating to the United States. In panel (b), draw a line segment to indicate what the Swede would lose in wages by migrating.

Effects of Immigration in the Short Run and Long Run

Probably the biggest issue in immigration policy is the effect of immigration on the employment and wages of native workers. Do immigrants take jobs away from Americans and drive down American wages, or are immigrants easily absorbed into the U.S. labor market with little or no effect on the employment and wages of native workers? Answers to these questions depend on how immigrants compare to natives in terms of skills. But the most dramatic case is the one with immigrants and natives as perfect substitutes. Let's see how immigration of perfect substitutes affects wages in the short run and long run.

In the short run, an influx of immigrants drives down wages. The increase in the supply of labor slides the equilibrium down the market's short-run labor demand curve. For employers to hire the immigrants (i.e., to employ the higher supply of labor), the wage must be lower. In the long run, however, capital adjusts, shifting the short-run labor demand curve. Let's see what happens.

The long-run response to immigration is to increase capital, restoring the capital–labor ratio and the wage to their pre-immigration values. Figure 7.13 illustrates this principle with isoquant curves and isocost lines, our tools of long-run labor demand from chapter 4. We start in a long-run equilibrium at point A with 10 million workers employed. An incredible shock drops 5 million immigrants into this market, increasing the supply of labor from 10 million to 15 million workers per year. The wage, the price of capital, and product prices adjust to fully employ the 50-percent-larger workforce at point B. Most important, the isocost line tangent to the isoquant curve at point B is flatter than the one tangent at point A: the wage falls in the short run to encourage firms to employ the extra workers. (Recall that the slope of an isocost line is, in absolute value, the ratio of the wage to the price of capital.) In other words, the influx of immigrants depresses the wage in the short run.

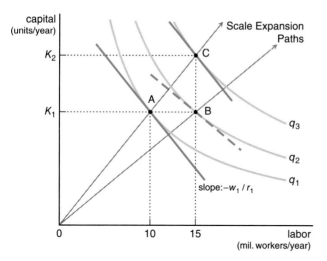

The wage w and capital price r adjust to employ the 10 million workers and K_1 units of capital at A. The slope of the isocost line tangent to isoquant q_1 at A is $-w_1/r_1$.

Immigration increases labor by 5 million workers. In the short run, w falls and r rises, so the isocost line at B is flatter than the isocost line at A.

In the long run, capital grows to match the 50% growth in labor, which restores the capital–labor ratio at C: w and r return to their initial values.

The labor market simply absorbs the immigrants in the long run without changing any price.

FIGURE 7.13. Wage Effects of Immigration in the Short Run and Long Run

In the long run, however, we accumulate capital. If production exhibits constant returns to scale, which is a reasonable approximation for the economy as a whole, then matching the 50-percent-larger workforce (from A to B in the figure) with 50 percent more capital (from B to C) expands production by 50 percent. Output per worker, therefore, returns to its pre-immigration value in the long run.

A special property of constant-returns production is that the slope of isoquant curves doesn't vary along a ray from the origin. The isoquant curves in Figure 7.13 come from a constant-returns-to-scale production function, so the slope of the isoquant curve at C equals the slope of the isoquant curve at A. That's important because the ratio of the wage to the price of capital in the long run at C must equal the initial ratio of the wage to the price of capital at A. Indeed, the wage w, the price of capital r, and the product price p all return to their pre-immigration values as the domestic labor market simply absorbs the immigrants.

Application: Mariel Boatlift

In the spring of 1980, Fidel Castro declared Cubans free to emigrate to the United States from the Cuban port of Mariel. Over the next six months, a private flotilla carried to Miami the 125,000 Cubans who took Castro up on his offer. Many of the boatlift immigrants ultimately settled elsewhere in the United States, but roughly half (about 60,000) settled permanently in Miami. Without warning, the Mariel boatlift increased the labor force of Miami by 7 percent and increased Miami's Cuban labor force by 20 percent.

Was the Mariel boatlift Castro's curse on Miami? What did the Mariel immigrants do after settling in Miami? Did they find jobs, or were they unemployed? How did their arrival affect the employment and wages of Miami's pre-boatlift workforce, including Cubans who immigrated to Miami in the years before the boatlift? Did Mariel immigrants take jobs from these people? Did the influx of Cubans drive down the wages of less-skilled workers in Miami, hurting those who had been employed in Miami before the boatlift?

Card (1990) used monthly data from the Current Population Survey to study the Miami labor market before and after the Mariel boatlift, and he compared the patterns of wages and unemployment in Miami with those in similar cities. His results are quite surprising. While the wages of non-Cuban workers in Miami fell in the early 1980s, wages fell roughly the same amount in comparable cities. (The United States suffered through a deep recession in 1981–1982.) Wages of Cuban workers in Miami dropped a whopping 9 percent from 1979 to 1983, but Hispanic workers in comparable cities suffered wage losses of 7 percent. And the remaining 2 percentage-point gap is likely explained by the fact that the average Cuban wage in Miami after the boatlift includes the wages of Mariel immigrants, who were younger, less skilled, less educated, and less proficient in English.

Unemployment patterns tell the same tale. While the unemployment rate in Miami rose in the early 1980s, comparisons with other cities provide no evidence that the Mariel boatlift caused unemployment of the native population in Miami. The unemployment rate of Cubans in Miami did rise more than the unemployment rate of Hispanics in comparable cities, but that difference was likely due to the high unemployment of the Mariel immigrants themselves (rather than earlier waves of Cuban immigrants losing their jobs).

Overall, Card's evidence paints a picture of a labor market that quickly (i.e., over a few years) absorbed the entrants to the labor market with little or even no effect on the native workforce. One way that Miami's labor market absorbed the Mariel immigrants was through a shift in the mix of products and services that Miami produced. Production shifted from goods and services that use lots of skilled workers toward goods and services that use unskilled labor intensively.

The Mariel boatlift shocked the supply of labor in Miami. Card's (1990) evidence that the effect of the influx of Cuban immigrants on the wages of native workers in Miami quickly diminished suggests that the demand for labor in Miami was quite elastic over a few years. The long run might not be so long.

Summary

In this chapter, we extended our analysis of human capital to on-the-job training and migration. The key findings are:

☐ On-the-job training involves foregone productivity as well as direct costs, and training investments reap returns in the form of higher productivity in the future. Training declines over the worker's career.

☐ Workers pay for their general training, which all employers value. Incentives to quit or to dismiss the worker prevent front-loading or back-loading pay over a worker's career. The worker's wage must equal his actual productivity minus the direct cost of training.

☐ Predictable variation in wages over a worker's career has no income effect on labor supply, so the life-cycle labor supply curve slopes up. Indeed, the wage and the workweek vary together over the life cycle.

☐ Employers can pay for the general training of their workers if workers can't quit or must compensate the employer for quitting. Limits on quitting help explain how employers are able to finance the training of military pilots, the MBAs of young executives, and the development of professional baseball prospects.

☐ Workers and their employers share the costs of and returns to firm-specific training investments to minimize losses from excessive turnover. Consequently, the wage rises and the separation rate falls with job tenure.

☐ A model of on-the-job search for better job matches predicts that the wage rises and the separation rate falls with work experience. The model of learning the value of the job match predicts that the average wage increases and the separation rate decreases with job tenure as low-quality matches are weeded out.

☐ Migration is an investment in general human capital. Higher wages in the new location are the return on the moving cost. The migration rate is higher for shorter moves, younger workers, and more-educated workers.

☐ Indentured servitude in colonial America solved the problem of financing migration as a human-capital investment. The indenture contract front-loaded pay by providing expensive passage from Britain to America. The contract required a no-quit clause to allow employers to earn back the cost of passage. Skilled servants worked off the cost of passage more quickly, and their periods of indenture were shorter.

☐ With differences in skills, above-average workers migrate to America if the return to skill is lower in the source country than in America. Below-average workers migrate to America if skills pay less in America than in the source country.

☐ Immigration drives down the wage in the short run. In the long run, capital grows to match the influx of immigrants, restoring the capital-to-labor ratio and the wage. That is, the labor market absorbs immigrants in the long run without hurting native workers.

Chapters 5 and 6 established the importance of job attributes (e.g., the workweek and job risks) and schooling as determinants of the weekly wage. Our analysis in this chapter adds work experience and job tenure to that list. In the next chapter, we turn to discrimination in the labor market. How much of the gap in wages between groups like men and women or whites and blacks isn't explained by job attributes, schooling, work experience, and job tenure? And how much reflects discrimination?

Key Concepts

- wage profile, p. 233
- cohorts of workers, p. 233
- general training, p. 234
- on-the-job training, p. 234
- productivity profile, p. 235
- potential productivity, p. 235
- net productivity, p. 236
- front-loading vs. back-loading pay, p. 237
- employment at will, p. 239
- life-cycle labor supply, p. 242
- severance pay, p. 246
- reserve clause and free agency, p. 247

- specific training, p. 247
- sharing training costs and returns, p. 250
- job tenure, p. 250
- match value, p. 253
- job shopping, p. 253
- learning the match value, p. 256
- panel data, p. 257
- migration as an investment, p. 257
- net present value, p. 257
- indenture contract, p. 259
- self-selection, p. 263

Short-Answer Questions

7.1 In what way is training on the job an investment in human capital?

7.2 Explain why the net-productivity profile converges to the potential-productivity profile in Figure 7.2.

7.3 Explain why the employment-at-will doctrine is important for determining who pays for training. Why can't the employer pay for training if employment is at will? What deviations from employment at will enable the employer to earn a return on its training investments?

7.4 Use the wage profile to carefully explain the difference between a surprise change in the wage and a predicted wage change. Why does only one of these carry an income (or wealth) effect on hours of work? How does the difference between surprise and predicted wage changes contribute to our understanding of why the hours profile follows the wage profile fairly closely over workers' careers?

7.5 Is the sharing of costs and returns of firm-specific training the perfect solution to the problem of excessive turnover? If workers and their employers share firm-specific investments in training, is turnover efficient?

7.6 Loan officers learn all about the banking industry. Production engineers pick up the ins and outs of oil and gas extraction. These workers and many others acquire industry-specific skills on the job. Do you think industry-specific training is more common in competitive or monopolistic industries? Explain how the extent of competition in an industry influences the amount of industry-specific training workers in that industry receive.

7.7 The value of a worker's match with an employer doesn't depend on work experience, but it does vary across employers. Explain how on-the-job search generates a wage profile that increases with experience at a decreasing rate. Also explain why the implied separation rate declines with experience.

7.8 Is migration more or less likely if the interest rate is higher?

7.9 How are immigrants absorbed in the long run? The short-run impact of an influx of immigrants includes a lower wage of native workers. In the long run, the wage of native workers returns to its pre-influx value. What happens in the meantime that restores the marginal product of labor?

7.10 Suppose the minimum wage binds on unskilled workers. Trace the short-run and long-run effects of a large influx of unskilled workers.

Problems

7.1 Donna works on a job that will involve lots of general training over her 40-year career. The figure below illustrates her net-productivity profile $v_n(x)$. Four wage profiles, each with the same present value as $v_n(x)$, also appear in the figure.

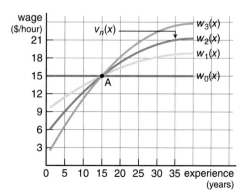

(a) Employment at will governs Donna's job. What does this term mean?

(b) To what does the term "net productivity" refer? Labor's value of marginal product with or without on-the-job training? With or without direct costs and lost productivity associated with training? Or with or without taxes?

(c) Why does Donna's net-productivity profile $v_n(x)$ slope up?

(d) Consider a flat wage profile that pays Donna $12 per hour throughout her career. If the interest rate is 0 percent, is this wage profile competitive?

(e) Suppose the employer pays Donna $w_0(x) = 15$ for her whole career. Does Donna or her employer pay for her training, or do they share the costs of and returns to her training with this flat wage profile?

(f) Which (if any) of the four wage profiles in the figure back-load(s) pay?

(g) Which (if any) of the four wage profiles encourage(s) Donna to quit in the 15th year of her career (i.e., at $x = 15$)?

(h) Which (if any) of the four wage profiles lead(s) Donna's employer to dismiss her in the 15th year of her career (i.e., at $x = 15$)?

(i) Which wage profile is the competitive-equilibrium wage profile?

7.2 Jessie has prospects of a 40-year career with her employer. She's learning a lot on the job, and much (but not all) of what she's learning would be valuable if she switched jobs to work for another firm.

The figure below illustrates two net-productivity profiles: $v_n(x)$ is Jessie's net-productivity profile with her current employer; $v_g(x)$ is a profile that reflects Jessie's net productivity based only on her general training and general-training costs.

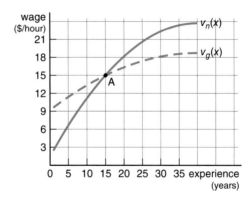

(a) Jessie's wage offers from other firms follow which profile?

(b) Suppose Jessie's wage profile coincides with her net-productivity profile $v_n(x)$. What are the likely consequences for Jessie's quits and dismissals?

(c) Suppose Jessie's wage profile coincides with the productivity profile $v_g(x)$. What are the likely consequences for Jessie's incentives to quit and her employer's incentives to dismiss her?

(d) Sketch a wage profile that reduces the inefficiencies from excessive turnover.

7.3 Boyan has worked at Nike for 10 years. Many of the workers who started with Boyan at Nike left when they learned that Nike wasn't a good match for them.

When Boyan had four years of tenure at Nike, the value of marginal product of workers with four years of tenure averaged $15.25 per hour. A little data work uncovers that that group's value of marginal product averaged $15.25 in years 1, 2, and 3, too. The value of marginal product of the group that remained at Nike through year 6 averaged $17.50 per hour in years 1 through 6. The figure below illustrates these (and several other) averaged value-of-marginal-product profiles.

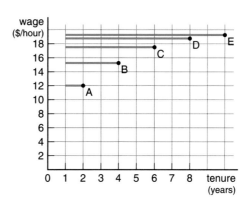

(a) Why is the VMP_L profile higher, on average, for workers with six years of job tenure than for workers with four years of tenure?

(b) Nike pays Boyan and his coworkers what they're worth, on average, at each point in their careers. Sketch the relationship between the wage w and job tenure t in the figure.

(c) Does the wage–tenure curve $w(t)$ increase at a decreasing, constant, or increasing rate?

7.4 Suppose Norma will live and work forever, and the interest rate i is 10 percent. What does it take to get Norma to migrate?

(a) Set *NPV* to zero in Equation 7.6 to solve for the wage gain Δw that leaves Norma indifferent between moving and not moving.

(b) Assume that the moving cost c (in dollars) increases linearly with distance d (in miles). In particular, let $c = 1000 + d$, and use this equation to express Norma's reservation wage gain as a function of distance d.

(c) For a move of 400 miles, Norma requires a wage gain of \$_____ per year.

(d) Norma has a job offer from an employer 1,000 miles away. The wage offer is \$250 per year more than she makes on her current job. Does she move to the new job?

7.5 Consider the market for indentured servants in the colonial period. For an unskilled servant working in a British colony in America, the annual value of marginal product was £8 (i.e., 8 British pounds). The value of marginal product of a skilled servant was £10 per year. An indenture contract required its owner (e.g., a colonial merchant or planter) to provide food, clothing, and shelter for his servant; the cost of this care c was £7 per year. Use the table below to track how the profit from an indenture contract accumulated over the length of the contract.

	UNSKILLED SERVANT		SKILLED SERVANT	
Year	$VMP - c$ (£/year)	Cumulative Profit (£)	$VMP - c$ (£/year)	Cumulative Profit (£)
1				
2				
3				
4				
5				
6				
7				
8				

(a) The owner of indenture contracts earns how much annually, net of the costs of care, per unskilled servant?

(b) How much more does an owner net annually on the indenture contracts of skilled workers?

The cost of passage from a British port to the colonies was £6 per servant, and the market for servants was competitive. Assume the interest rate was zero to simplify the analysis.

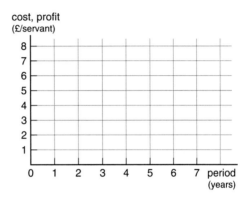

Use your entries in the table to illustrate cumulative profits and transport cost in the figure above.

(c) What is the equilibrium period of indenture of an unskilled servant?

(d) How much shorter or longer is a skilled servant's period of indenture?

(e) (Advanced) What are the prices of indenture contracts on the docks in America? How is the price of an unskilled servant's contract related to the price of a skilled servant's contract?

7.6 The figure below displays wage–skill curves for Mexico and the United States.

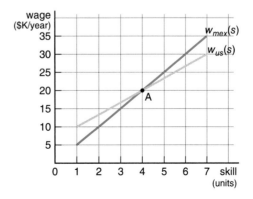

(a) If the least-skilled Mexican immigrates to the United States, how much does he or she gain in annual wages?

(b) Mexicans with skills ranging from _____ to _____ units want to emmigrate to the United States.

(c) Suppose the U.S. tax rate on labor income rises, which depresses the return to skill in the United States. Sketch the new U.S. wage–skill curve in the figure.

(d) How does the U.S. tax hike affect the quality of immigrants from Mexico?

(e) How does the U.S. tax hike impact the quality of immigrants from Sweden, a country with a wage–skill curve that's flatter than $w_{us}(s)$?

References

Becker, Gary S. 1962. "Investment in Human Capital: A Theoretical Analysis." *Journal of Political Economy* 70(5): 9–49.

Borjas, George J. 1987. "Self-Selection and the Earnings of Immigrants." *American Economic Review* 77(4): 531–553.

Burdett, Kenneth. 1978. "A Theory of Employee Job Search and Quit Rates." *American Economic Review* 68(1): 212–220.

Card, David. 1990. "The Impact of the Mariel Boatlift on the Miami Labor Market." *Industrial and Labor Relations Review* 43(2): 245–257.

Galenson, David W. 1981. "The Market Evaluation of Human Capital: The Case of Indentured Servitude." *Journal of Political Economy* 89(3): 446–467.

Heckman, James. 1974. "Life Cycle Consumption and Labor Supply: An Explanation of the Relationship Between Income and Consumption Over the Life Cycle." *American Economic Review* 64(1): 188–194.

Jovanovic, Boyan. 1979. "Job Matching and the Theory of Turnover." *Journal of Political Economy* 87(5): 972–990.

Oettinger, Gerald S. 1999. "An Empirical Analysis of the Daily Labor Supply of Stadium Vendors." *Journal of Political Economy* 107(2): 360–392.

Discrimination

8

Does racism influence the gap in wages between blacks and whites? Data on attitudes toward race are hard to come by. But since the early 1970s, researchers at the National Opinion Research Center have been collecting data on attitudes toward race by asking people questions like "Would you object if a family member brought a black friend home for dinner?" and "Would you resign from a social club that would not let blacks join?" Racism as measured by responses to questions like these varies across states, and so does the wage gap between blacks and whites. Is the black–white wage gap bigger in states where people are more racist?

Charles and Guryan (2008) found that the black–white wage gap in a state has next to nothing to do with the state's average value of racism. Put differently, lots of racist responses to these survey questions do not generate racial wage discrimination. Charles and Guryan did find, however, that the extent of racism among the least racist people explains a good portion of the variation in black wages relative to white wages across states. The difference is subtle but important. Turning Ku Klux Klanners into moderate racists would *not* raise black wages, but turning mild racists into non-racists would increase black wages. As mysterious as this seems, it's exactly what Becker (1971 [1957]) predicted when he developed the economic model of discrimination half a century ago.

Women are also victims of discrimination in the labor market. The gap between the wages of women and men immediately pops to mind, but discrimination also manifests itself in access to jobs. For instance, when retired Supreme Court Justice Sandra Day O'Connor graduated third in her class from Stanford

Law School in 1952, 40 law firms refused to interview her because she's a woman. Law firms at the time didn't employ women as attorneys, so she ultimately took a job working without pay for the county attorney in San Mateo, California. (It turned into a paying job after four months.) Justice O'Connor's troubling tale is one vivid example of the difficulty women have had breaking into traditionally male occupations.

Marriage bars also limited women's access to jobs. Marriage bars—the practice of refusing to hire married women and of firing women when they marry—denied married women access to many jobs before World War II (Goldin 1990). In 1942, 87 percent of the U.S. school districts refused to hire married women, and 70 percent of the school districts fired women when they married. Even the federal government implemented a marriage bar in 1932. In the face of downsizing in the executive branch, regulations required officials to fire workers whose spouses were federal employees. Although husbands could have been let go, government officials almost always fired the wives.

Discrimination in the labor market isn't just about sex and race. Discrimination can be by age, religion, sexual preference, height, weight, or even beauty. Does being attractive pay? Hamermesh and Biddle (1994) estimate that being below average in looks carries a 9 percent penalty in wages; workers with above-average looks capture a 5 percent wage premium for their attractiveness. The workers in Hamermesh and Biddle's study weren't fashion models, a job where looks count. Do employers, coworkers, or perhaps customers discriminate against the unattractive and in favor of the handsome and beautiful?

To understand discrimination, we must measure its consequences, especially for wages. And we need to know how each form of discrimination affects choices and ultimately the equilibrium in the market for labor. So our tasks are to measure the effects of discrimination and to model the consequences of discrimination.

8.1 Measuring Wage Gaps

Delegates to political conventions wear funny hats, wave big signs, and make lots of noise. In one of the political conventions in the summer of 1976, delegates also wore buttons that read "59 cents." I watched that political convention as a teenager and wondered what the "59 cents" was all about. Now I know. The National Organization of Women (NOW) distributed the buttons to support the movement for the Equal Rights Amendment to the U.S. Constitution; "59 cents" referred to women at the time earning on average 59 cents on the dollar that men earned. This **wage ratio** is our first measure of discrimination.

Wage Gaps by Sex, Race, and Ethnicity

Women in the United States are currently paid about 26 percent less than men. Table 8.1 collects average weekly wages in the 2017 Current Population Survey by sex, race, and ethnicity. In these data, the average wage of women is $847

TABLE 8.1. WAGE RATIOS AND WAGE GAPS BY SEX, RACE, AND ETHNICITY, 2017						
	BY SEX		**BY RACE AND ETHNICITY**			
	Women	**Men**	**Blacks**	**Asians**	**Hispanics**	**Whites**[a]
Mean Wage ($/week)	847	1,147	781	1,225	763	1,029 [1,092]
Wage Ratio[b] (%)	73.8		76.0	119.1	69.9	
Wage Gap (%)	26.2		24.0	−19.1	30.1	

Notes: [a]Whites are comprised of Hispanics and non-Hispanic whites. Non-Hispanic whites in brackets.
[b]Computed relative to men by sex, to whites by race, and to non-Hispanic whites by ethnicity.
Source: Current Population Survey, outgoing rotation group files, monthly 2017.

per week. The weekly wage of men is $1,147. The female–male wage ratio is, therefore, .738 (= 847 ÷ 1147) or 73.8 percent. (An updated version of the NOW button would read "74 cents.") How far is this wage ratio from wage equality? The answer to this question is the **wage gap**, which is 1 minus the wage ratio. The female–male wage gap is 1 − .738 = .263 or 26.2 percent in the most recent data.

Table 8.1 lists mean weekly wages by race and ethnicity in the recent CPS data. For black, Asian, white, Hispanic, and non-Hispanic white workers, weekly wages average $781, $1,225, $1,029, $763, and $1,092, respectively. Therefore, the black–white wage ratio is .760 (= 781 ÷ 1029), the Asian–white wage ratio is 1.191 (= 1225 ÷ 1029), and the Hispanic–white wage ratio is .699 (= 763 ÷ 1092). How far are these ratios from racial and ethnic wage equality? The black–white wage gap is 24.0 percent. The Asian–white wage gap is −19.1 percent; that is, the weekly wage of the average Asian worker is 19.1 percent *higher* than the weekly wage of the average white worker. The average Hispanic wage is 30.1 percent lower than the average wage of non-Hispanic white workers. So black workers in the United States currently earn 24 percent less than white workers; Asians receive 19 percent more than whites, and wages of Hispanics are on average 30 percent less than the wages of non-Hispanic whites.

 PRACTICE   The average wage of American Indians is $795 per week in these data. Compute the American Indian–white wage ratio. What is the American Indian–white wage gap?

Women's wages have been growing relative to men's wages since 1980. Figure 8.1 plots the U.S. Census Bureau's reports of wage ratios—based on median annual earnings of full-time, year-round workers—by sex, race, and ethnicity. ("Full-time" means usual hours worked of at least 35 hours per week; "year-round" means at least 50 weeks worked in the year; these data come from the Annual Social and Economic Supplement to the March CPS, which includes questions about annual earnings and usual hours worked "last year.") The female–male wage ratio fell in the late 1950s but remained steady at about "59 cents" in the 1960s and 1970s. Women's wages began growing relative to

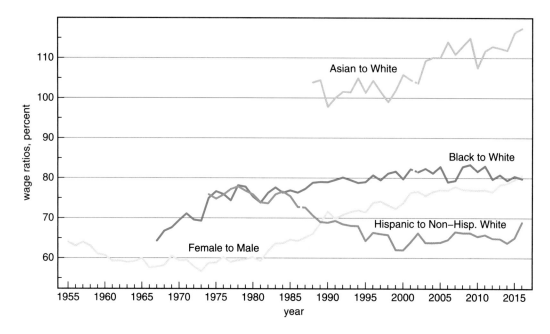

FIGURE 8.1. Wage Ratios by Sex, Race, and Ethnicity, 1955–2016

Notes: Median annual earnings of full-time, year-round workers by sex, race, and ethnic group.
Sources: For 1960–2016: U.S. Census Bureau, Historical Income Tables P-38 (1960–1973) and P-43 (1974–2016); for 1955–1959: Rytina, Nancy. 1983. "Comparing Annual and Weekly Earnings from the Current Population Survey," *Monthly Labor Review* 106(4): 32–35. Original data are from the Current Population Survey, Annual Social and Economic Supplements, 1956–2017.

men's wages around 1980. The ratio of women's to men's wages grew rapidly from 60 percent in 1980 to 72 percent in 1990. Since 1990, the female–male wage ratio in these data has risen slowly to 80 percent recently.

The black–white wage ratio has also risen. These data begin in 1967 when the median annual wage of black workers was 64 percent of the median annual wage of white workers. The black–white wage ratio grew quickly for a decade to about 75 percent and continued to grow until the late 1990s. Since 2000, the black–white wage gap has fluctuated between 17 and 21 percent in these data.

An Asian wage premium has emerged since the late 1990s, and wages of Hispanics have fallen relative to the wages of non-Hispanic whites since the late 1970s. Until the mid-1990s, annual wages of Asian workers were on par with the annual wages of white workers. Since 1998, the Asian–white wage ratio has grown from 99 percent to 117 percent. For Hispanics, the wage ratio fell from about 75 percent in the 1970s to 62 percent at the turn of the century. The Hispanic–non-Hispanic-white wage gap has fluctuated around 35 percent since 2000.

The wage gap is a flawed measure of discrimination. The wage gap mixes discrimination with other sources of differences in wages across groups. Consider the Asian–white wage gap in Table 8.1. Asian workers earn about 19 percent more than white workers. Is discrimination against white workers rampant in the U.S. labor market? Perhaps Asians pull the strings of corporate America, employing other Asians at wages that reflect the value of their marginal product while discriminating against whites and other racial groups. Or does nepotism favor Asian workers? Do employers pay Asian workers more than they are worth because they enjoy having Asians around? If these conjectures strike you as utterly unsatisfactory, you are ready to learn how measurable differences between groups (unrelated to discrimination) influence wage ratios and gaps.

The Asian–white wage comparison isn't the only peculiar one. Wage gaps for many ethnic groups go the "wrong way." Darity, Guilkey, and Winfrey (1995) calculated wage ratios for dozens of ethnic groups using annual earnings data from the 1980 and 1990 U.S. Census of Population. For instance, Austrian, Japanese, and Lithuanian men and women in the United States earned much more than the average U.S. worker, and the wage gaps for Russian workers were simply stunning. In 1990, the sun was setting on the Soviet Union, and the dissolution of the Soviet Union in December 1991 marked the end of the Cold War. But in the United States in 1990, the average wage of Russian men was 49 percent more than the wage of the average man in the United States. Russian women working in the United States earned on average 60 percent more than the average woman in the United States. The Russian wage premium must reflect something other than discrimination *in favor* of Russians in America.

Standardized Comparison

Asian workers earn more than white workers because they have more education. The average Asian worker has an extra year of schooling. Since schooling increases wages, the extra education should push Asian wages higher than white wages in the absence of discrimination. But how much higher?

Here we carefully parse differences in pay across groups into a part that is due to measurable differences in the characteristics of workers and their jobs and a part that is left unexplained. The unexplained or residual part is a better estimate of the effect of discrimination on wages.

The method of **standardized comparison** adjusts the wage gap for differences in average values of skill variables (and other characteristics of workers or their jobs) on the basis of estimated prices of the skill variables (Oaxaca 1973; Blinder 1973). (Economists also call this method the *Oaxaca decomposition*.) For instance, if the rate of return to schooling is 10–12 percent per grade, then Asians' extra year of schooling translates into a 10–12 percent higher wage for Asian workers. Put differently, if Asian workers had the same schooling as white workers (i.e., 14 years rather than 15 years), they would be paid 10–12 percent less than they receive. This standardizing of the racial wage comparison nearly eliminates any evidence of discrimination in favor of Asians or against whites.

Equal Slopes.   Figure 8.2 standardizes the wage comparison for a generic skill variable x. In this example, the average man is Mitch, who earns $800 per week and has 25 units of the skill variable. Mitch is point M in the figure. The line through point M is the wage–skill curve of men, which shows how the weekly wage w

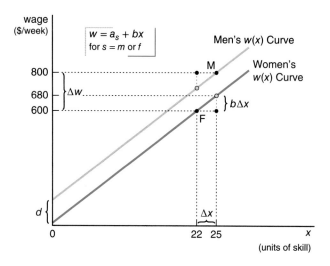

With weekly wage $600 and 22 units of skill x, Fran at F is the average woman. Average man Mitch at M earns $800/week with his 25 units of x. The weekly wage gap is $200 (or 25%).

Men's and women's wage–skill curves are parallel with slope $b = \$26.67$/unit of x. Fran would earn $680/week if she had $x = 25$ like Mitch, so the skill gap $\Delta x = 3$ explains $80 of the $200 wage gap. The residual wage gap is $120 (or 15%).

Mitch would earn $720/week if he had Fran's 22 units of skill.

FIGURE 8.2. Standardized Comparison with Equal Slopes

varies with skill x among men. Fran, as the average woman, earns $600 per week and has 22 units of skill, and F marks this point in the figure. Women's wage–skill curve is the line through F. In this case, men's and women's wage–skill curves are parallel with slope b. The weekly wage gap is $200, the female–male wage ratio is .75 ($= 600 \div 800$), and the female–male wage gap is 25 percent.

We use the wage–skill curves of men and women to adjust the wage gap for measurable differences in skills. Fran and Mitch have 22 and 25 units, respectively, of the skill variable x, so the **skill gap** is $\Delta x = 25 - 22 = 3$. The common slope of the wage–skill curves is $b = 26.67$, so the **skill price** is $26.67 per unit of skill. Therefore, employers value the 3-unit skill gap at $80 ($= \$26.67 \times 3$) per week. Indeed, if women like Fran had 3 more units of skill (to match the 25 units of men like Mitch), they would earn $680 rather than $600 per week. In the figure, this adjustment amounts to sliding F up along the wage–skill curve of women until it rests under M with $x = 25$. The skill gap then explains $80 of the $200 weekly wage gap, and the **residual (or adjusted) wage gap** shrinks to $120 per week. In percentage terms, the wage gap shrinks from 25 percent to 15 percent when we standardize the wage comparison by sex.

✓ **PRACTICE**   Fran and Mitch continue to be the average woman and average man at points F and M in Figure 8.2. But suppose the slope of each wage–skill curve is $20 per unit of x. The skill gap $\Delta x = 3$ explains how much of the $200 wage gap? What is the residual wage gap (in dollars)?

The method of standardized comparison also works in reverse. Rather than asking how much Fran would earn if she had as much skill as Mitch (the average man), we could ask how much Mitch would earn if he had the skill of Fran (the average woman). The calculation involves sliding Mitch's point M in the figure down the men's wage–skill curve until it lies directly above Fran's point F with $x = 22$. Mitch's wage falls by \$80 ($= \$26.67 \times 3$) per week from \$800 to \$720 per week. That is, the weekly wage gap again shrinks from \$200 to \$120. With parallel wage–skill curves, it doesn't matter whether we use men's or women's average skill as the standard for comparison.

. . . .

ADVANCED It does matter if we measure the wage gap in percentages. Adjusting men's wage down along men's wage–skill curve yields a residual wage gap of \$120 or 16.7 ($= 120 \div 720$) percent rather than the 15 percent residual wage gap working in the other direction. To avoid this discrepancy, we could use a midpoint formula, which we reviewed in the context of elasticities in chapter 1. (See section 1.6, "For Your Toolbox.") Wage ratios and adjusted wage ratios would be expressed with the midpoint of the wage (i.e., \$700 per week in this case) in the denominator.

This issue doesn't distract labor economists because we routinely work with log wages, and the issue vanishes with log wages. In Figure 8.2, we replace the wage w on the vertical axis with the natural logarithm of the wage $\ln w$. Suppose the log wage–skill curves are parallel lines with slope .033 per unit of skill x. The 3-unit skill gap absorbs .10 ($= .033 \times 3$) of the log wage gap. That's approximately 10 percent. And it doesn't matter whether we adjust the log wage of women up along women's log wage–skill curve or adjust the log wage of men down along men's log wage–skill curve. That is, the log approximation solves the problem.

. . . .

Using Regression Estimates. In practice, we estimate the prices of (or rates of return to) skill variables and other characteristics of workers and their jobs with a wage regression and use these prices to adjust the wage gaps. We regress the weekly wages (in logs) on the workweek h, schooling s, potential work experience x, and its square. (We include the squared term x^2 to capture that wages increase at a decreasing rate over workers' careers.) The regression also includes variables that indicate whether the worker is female ($F = 1$) or male ($F = 0$) or a member of a labor union ($U = 1$) or not ($U = 0$).

On the sample of over 156,000 wage and salary workers in the 2017 CPS, the estimated regression equation is

$$\text{(8.1)} \quad \ln w = 4.24 + \underset{(.051)}{} .026\,h + \underset{(.0002)}{} .066\,s + \underset{(.0008)}{} .033\,x - \underset{(.0004)}{} .0005x^2 - \underset{(.0000)}{} .173F + \underset{(.004)}{} .146U \underset{(.005)}{}$$

with $R^2 = .557$. The coefficient associated with the sex variable F indicates that the log wages of women are .173 lower than the log wages of men after controlling for the workweek, schooling, potential work experience, and union membership. (The regression also controls for state of residence and occupation, although Equation 8.1 doesn't report those estimated effects.) So women earn 17.3 percent less than

TABLE 8.2. COMPONENTS OF THE WAGE GAP BY SEX, 2017			
		BY SEX	
	Slope	Difference in Characteristics[a]	Contribution to Wage Gap[b]
Workweek (hours/worker)	.026	4.37	11.2
Schooling (grades)	.066	−0.42	−2.8
Experience (years)	—[c]	0.15	0.7
Union Member	.146	0.02	0.2
State[d]	✓	✓	0.1
Occupation[d]	✓	✓	3.5
Characteristics			12.9
Residual			17.3
Unadjusted[e]			30.2

Notes: [a]Men's average value minus women's average value. [b]Slope × difference in characteristics × 100. [c]This slope isn't a constant. [d]A ✓ marks that the regression includes variables indicating state of residence or occupation, although estimates of these effects aren't displayed. [e]100 × (mean log wage of women minus mean log wage of men).
Source: Current Population Survey, outgoing rotation group files, monthly 2017.

comparable men, which implies that standardizing the comparison shrinks the female–male wage gap from 30.2 percent to 17.3 percent.

How much does each measured characteristic contribute to the unadjusted female–male wage gap? Table 8.2 combines the gaps between men and women in average values of the regression variables (i.e., workweek h, schooling s, etc.) with the slopes from the regression line (i.e., Equation 8.1) to quantify each characteristic's contribution to the unadjusted wage gap. For instance, men on average work roughly 4.4-hour-longer workweeks than women. For men and women, an extra hour of work each week increases the weekly wage by 2.6 percent, which is the coefficient on the workweek h in Equation 8.1. Therefore, the predicted effect of women's 4.4-hour-shorter workweek is 11.2 ($\approx 2.6 \times 4.4$) percent lower pay. That is, the shorter workweek of women explains 11.2 percentage points of the 30.2 percent unadjusted wage gap.

> **Key Principle.**
> Measurable differences in skills and related worker characteristics partly explain gaps in wages based on sex and race.

The schooling gap works in the opposite direction. Working women are a bit more educated than working men. The schooling gap of −.42 years contributes −2.8 (= $6.6 \times (-.42)$) percentage points to the female–male wage gap.

Experience and union membership differ little across the sexes; women also live in the same places as men, so state of residence accounts for none of the female–male wage gap. But women tend to work in lower-wage occupations. This occupation gap explains 3.5 percentage points of the female–male wage gap. In total, differences between women and men in their skills and other characteristics explain nearly half of the wage gap between the sexes. What remains, the residual wage gap of 17.3 percent, is a measure of wage discrimination.

PRACTICE   Why does schooling contribute −2.8 percentage points to the female–male wage gap in these data? Why is this number less than zero?

We can also standardize the racial wage comparison. The estimated regression equation with indicators of race is

(8.2) $\ln w = 4.44 + .027\,h + .066\,s + .033\,x - .0005x^2 - .116B + .020A + .153U$
${}_{(.024)}\ \ {}_{(.0002)}\ \ \ {}_{(.0008)}\ \ \ {}_{(.0004)}\ \ \ {}_{(.0000)}\ \ \ {}_{(.005)}\ \ {}_{(.007)}\ \ {}_{(.005)}$

with $R^2 = .551$. The variables B and A indicate whether the worker is black ($B = 1$ and $A = 0$) or Asian ($B = 0$ and $A = 1$). (The regression also includes variables that indicate American Indian and Other/Mixed races, state of residence, and occupation, but the effects of these variables aren't reported in Equation 8.2.) The coefficients on the race variables indicate that, controlling for the workweek, schooling, and so forth, black workers receive 11.6 percent less than comparable white workers, and Asian workers earn 2 percent higher wages than comparable white workers. Therefore, standardizing the racial comparisons shrinks the black–white wage gap substantially and nearly eliminates the Asian wage premium.

Table 8.3 displays the components of the wage gaps by race. We find the wage adjustment (i.e., $b\Delta x$) for each characteristic by multiplying the characteristic's racial gap Δx by its estimated price in Equation 8.2. Small differences between black and white workers in average values of the workweek and schooling contribute 1.2 and 1.6 percentage points, respectively, to the black–white wage gap. But blacks tend to work in lower-wage occupations, and that factor contributes

TABLE 8.3. COMPONENTS OF THE WAGE GAPS BY RACE, 2017

		BLACK–WHITE		ASIAN–WHITE	
	Slope	Difference in Characteristics[a]	Contribution to Wage Gap[b]	Difference in Characteristics[a]	Contribution to Wage Gap[b]
Workweek	.027	0.43	1.2	0.55	1.5
Schooling	.066	0.24	1.6	−1.04	−6.9
Experience	—[c]	1.36	0.6	2.07	1.0
Union Member	.153	−0.02	−0.3	0.01	0.2
State[d]	✓	✓	−0.6	✓	−3.9
Occupation[d]	✓	✓	7.5	✓	−4.5
Characteristics			10.5		−14.0
Residual			11.6		−2.0
Unadjusted[e]			22.1		−16.0

Notes: [a]Men's average value minus women's average value. [b]Slope × difference in characteristics × 100. [c]This slope isn't a constant. [d]A ✓ marks that the regression includes variables indicating state of residence or occupation, although estimates of these effects aren't displayed. [e]100 × (mean log wage of women minus mean log wage of men).
Source: Current Population Survey, outgoing rotation group files, monthly 2017.

7.5 percentage points to the black–white wage gap. Overall, differences between blacks and whites in average values of worker and job characteristics explain almost half the 22.1 percent wage gap.

Adjustments for differences in characteristics push in the opposite direction for the Asian–white wage gap. In Table 8.3, the Asian–white wage gap is −16.0 percent, so Asian workers earn 16 percent *more* than white workers. Asian workers complete one grade of school more than white workers, which accounts for 6.9 percentage points of the 16 percent Asian wage premium. Asian workers tend to live in high-wage states and work in high-wage occupations, and those factors contribute 3.9 and 4.5 percentage points, respectively, to the 16 percent Asian wage premium. In total, these characteristics of workers and jobs explain almost all of the Asian–white wage gap.

The analysis in Tables 8.2 and 8.3 illustrates how standardizing wage comparisons operates in practice and reveals some of the key characteristics that differ on average between women and men and across races. But these data aren't sufficient to address some important differences in characteristics. First, replacing potential work experience (i.e., age minus schooling minus 5) with actual work experience is important for both sex and race: working women have historically had more career interruptions, and higher unemployment rates of black workers add up over decades to less accumulated work experience. So trivial differences in potential experience can mask meaningful differences in actual experience that absorb some of the remaining gap in wages by sex and race. Second, differences in school quality have been important for black–white wage gaps historically since many blacks attended separate and unequal schools in the segregated South. In the modern era, the concern is with lower-quality, inner-city schools: fewer black students attend resource-wealthy suburban schools.

Application: Wage Discrimination Against Muslims in America.   Let's apply our methods to standardize the comparison of wages of American-born children of immigrants from Muslim countries since the attacks of September 11, 2001. Do these second-generation Muslim immigrants earn more or less than non-immigrant workers in the United States? How do the wages of second-generation Muslim immigrants compare to the wages of second-generation immigrants from Europe?

The issue is religious discrimination. The Current Population Survey doesn't collect data on religions, but we can indirectly estimate wage discrimination against Muslim Americans in the CPS. The CPS collects data on country of birth, including parents' countries of birth. This allows us to study the wages of workers whose parents immigrated from predominantly Muslim countries from Morocco in North Africa through the Middle East (excluding Israel) to Pakistan. We compare the wages of these children of immigrants from Muslim countries to the wages in two other groups of American workers: those whose parents (1) were also born in America or (2) immigrated from continental Europe. (We exclude Ireland and the United Kingdom from the list of source countries because English is the primary language in these countries.) We're left with a data set of nearly 2 million American-born wage and salary workers since 2002.

Children of immigrants from Muslim counties earn as much as the children of non-immigrants. The average weekly wage in each of these two groups is right around $800. A wage gap appears, however, if we compare the wages of the second-generation Muslim immigrants ($796) to the wages of second-generation immigrants from Europe ($971). The wage ratio is .82 (= 796/971), so the children of immigrants from Muslim countries earn 18 percent less than the children of immigrants from continental Europe. This is one estimate of discrimination, but let's check whether evidence of wage discrimination against Muslim Americans survives standardizing the wage comparison.

Standardizing the comparison dramatically shrinks the measure of wage discrimination against Muslim Americans. To see this, let a variable $2GI$ indicate whether a worker is a second-generation immigrant and a variable $2GM$ indicate whether a worker's parents immigrated from a Muslim country. In the sample of nearly 2 million wage and salary workers since 2002, the estimated regression equation is

$$(8.3) \quad \ln w = 2.954 + .035\,h + .108\,s + .038\,x - .0006x^2 - .186\,F$$
$$ \underset{(.006)}{}\ \underset{(.0000)}{}\ \underset{(.0002)}{}\ \underset{(.0001)}{}\ \underset{(.0000)}{}\ \underset{(.0008)}{}$$
$$- .121B - .008A + .113U + .040(2GI) - .036(2GM)$$
$$\underset{(.001)}{}\ \underset{(.006)}{}\ \underset{(.001)}{}\ \underset{(.005)}{}\ \underset{(.014)}{}$$

with $R^2 = .531$. The estimated effects of the workweek h, schooling s, work experience x, sex F, race B and A, and union membership U are familiar. (Estimates of the effects of state of residence and year in the sample are suppressed to save space.) Let's focus on the effects of being a second-generation immigrant. The coefficient on the second-generation-immigrant indicator $2GI$ reveals that second-generation immigrants from Europe enjoy a 4.0 percent wage premium over workers whose parents were born in America. The coefficient on $2GM$ tells us that the wages of second-generation immigrants from Muslim countries are 3.6 percent lower than the wages of second-generation immigrants from Europe. This coefficient is the residual wage gap. It's much smaller than the 18 percent unadjusted wage gap, but 3.6 percent is a statistically significant estimate of wage discrimination against Muslims in America.

Unequal Slopes.   Wage discrimination can vary with skill. Suppose the skill price (or rate of return to skill) is higher for men than for women: women's price of skill is $26.67 per unit as in Figure 8.2, but men's skill price is $33.33 per unit. As Figure 8.3 depicts, men's wage–skill line is steeper than women's wage–skill line, so men's wages diverge from women's wages as skill increases. Increasing Fran's skill from 22 to 25 units increases her wage, the wage of the average woman, from $600 to $680 per week using the female price of skill. As before, the $200 wage gap shrinks to $120 per week.

But working in the other direction delivers a smaller estimate of wage discrimination. The $33.33 male price of skill adjusts Mitch's wage down by $100 (= $33.33 × 3) to $700 per week. Using the male price of skill shrinks the residual wage gap to $100 per week, $20 per week less than the residual wage gap using

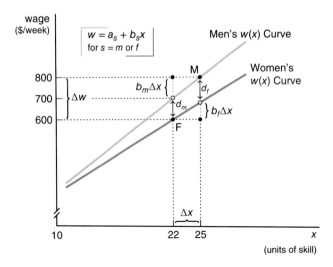

As in Figure 8.2, Fran's and Mitch's data points are F and M, and women's wage–skill curve has slope $b_f = 26.7$. Here, however, men's wage–skill curve is steeper with $b_m = 33.3$.

How much of the $200/week wage gap does the 3-unit skill gap explain? Along the line through F, Fran would earn $80 more/week if she had Mitch's skill. Along the line through M, Mitch would earn $100 less/week if he had Fran's skill. Using men's price of skill explains more of the wage gap.

The residual wage gap rises with skill x, indicating more discrimination against high-skill women.

FIGURE 8.3. Standardized Comparison with Unequal Slopes

the female price of skill. Using the higher (i.e., male) price of skill leaves a smaller residual gap—a smaller estimate of wage discrimination.

Left in the hands of unscrupulous researchers and policy analysts, the choice between the two measures of wage discrimination opens the door to political manipulation. Hoping to show large gaps in pay, supporters of affirmative-action programs might adjust up women's wages using the lower skill price. Those on the other side of the policy debate prefer to report less wage discrimination by using the higher skill price to adjust down men's wages.

Even the honest researcher finds two measures of wage discrimination to be a nuisance. The honest researcher standardizes the wage comparison both ways and hopes that the differences aren't big enough to cause distraction. But even this misses the point: with unequal slopes, the data are asking us to treat discrimination as a relationship rather than a number. If the wage–skill curves diverge (or even converge), measured discrimination is a function of skill. There might be more (or less) discrimination against high-skill women and blacks. That's important!

Accounting for Changes in Wage Gaps

Differences in worker characteristics and job attributes also explain changes in wage gaps over time. Figure 8.4 plots unadjusted (solid lines) wage gaps by sex, race, and ethnicity since 1979. Dashed lines depict residual wage gaps since 1983. (A key variable, union membership, wasn't available until 1983, so we analyze changes since 1983.) For instance, the unadjusted female–male wage gap has narrowed from 52 percent to 30 percent since 1983. The residual wage gap between women and men shrank less than half as much. The difference between these two wage-gap series—unadjusted and residual—identifies the combined effects of changing skill gaps and changing prices of those skills.

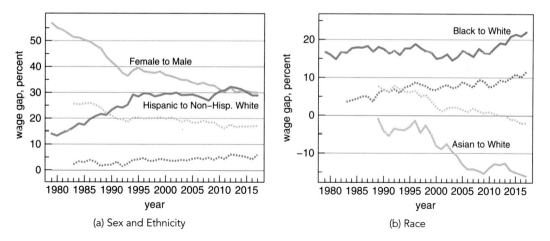

Notes: Solid lines are unadjusted wage gaps. Dashed lines are residual wage gaps, which begin in 1983.
Source: Current Population Survey, outgoing rotation group files, monthly 1979–2017.

FIGURE 8.4. Unadjusted and Residual Wage Gaps by Sex, Race, and Ethnicity, 1979–2017

Between 1983 and 2017, the female–male wage gap narrowed from 51.5 to 30.2 percent. What explains this decline? The first column of Table 8.4 decomposes the 20.6-percentage-point narrowing of the female–male wage gap into changing characteristics, changing skill prices, and the changing residual wage gap. (See Blau and Kahn (2017) for a detailed analysis of changes in the female–male wage gap since 1980.)

. . . .

ADVANCED Let's decompose the change in a wage gap into its three parts. Recall that Δ refers to the difference across groups, so Δw_{83} denotes the wage gap in 1983 and Δx_{17} denotes the skill gap in 2017.

The first component is the change between 1983 and 2017 in the skill gap, $\Delta x_{17} - \Delta x_{83}$, which we value using skill prices in 1983, b_{83}. The second component is the change in the price of skills $b_{17} - b_{83}$, which is weighted by Δx_{17}, the skill gap in 2017. The third is the change in the residual wage gap, which we denote by $d_{17} - d_{83}$. Thus the change in the wage gap between 1983 and 2017 is

$$(8.4) \quad \Delta w_{17} - \Delta w_{83} = b_{83}\left(\Delta x_{17} - \Delta x_{83}\right) + \Delta x_{17}\left(b_{17} - b_{83}\right) + \left(d_{17} - d_{83}\right)$$

We use this equation to explain changes between 1983 and 2017 in the wage gaps by sex, race, and ethnicity. Table 8.4 lists the results.

. . . .

One factor contributing to the narrowing wage gap is that women now look more like men in terms of the workweek. The gap between women and men

TABLE 8.4. ACCOUNTING FOR CHANGES IN WAGES GAPS, 1983 TO 2017

	FEMALE–MALE	BLACK–WHITE	ASIAN–WHITE[a]	HISPANIC–NON-HISPANIC
ΔCharacteristics[b]	−11.8	−2.8	−6.1	6.1
ΔPrices	−1.0	0.4	0.7	2.7
ΔResidual	−9.8	8.0	−9.8	3.8
ΔUnadjusted	−22.7	5.6	−15.1	12.5

Notes: [a]Asian–white changes are from 1989 to 2017. [b]Characteristics are the workweek, schooling, experience, and experience^2, along with indicators of union membership, state of residence, and occupation.
Source: Current Population Survey, outgoing rotation group files, monthly 1983, 1989, and 2017.

in the workweek shrank from −6.0 to −4.4 since 1983. In 1983, an extra hour of work increased wages 2.5 percent, so the shrinking hours gap contributed 4.0 (= 2.5 × (6.0 − 4.4)) percentage points to the narrowing of the wage gap. Overall, the shrinking characteristics gap explains 11.8 percentage points of the 22.7-percentage-point unadjusted decline. Changing prices accounted for 1.0 percentage point. For instance, the rate of return to schooling increased since 1983, and working women are now more educated than working men. Improving skills and other characteristics of women (relative to men) and changes in how these skills are valued combine to explain more than half the narrowing of the female–male wage gap since 1983. What's left over? Between 1983 and 2017, the residual wage gap fell 9.8 percent. The shrinking residual wage gap suggests that discrimination against working women has weakened.

Table 8.4 also displays similar accountings of the changes in wage gaps by race and ethnicity. The unadjusted black–white wage gap increased by 5.6 percentage points—from 16.5 percent in 1983 to 22.1 percent in 2017. The skill gap between blacks and whites shrank over the period: black workers now are more like white workers in terms of the workweek and schooling. This fact points to the black–white wage gap narrowing by 2.8 percentage points. The change in the prices associated with skills and other characteristics had essentially no effect on the black–white wage gap. But the black–white wage gap grew by 5.6 percentage points. Indeed, the residual black–white wage gap increased by about 8 percentage points from 3.7 percent in 1983 to 11.6 percent in 2017. To the extent the residual wage gap identifies the effect of racial discrimination on wages, this calculation exposes increasing discrimination against blacks since 1983.

The patterns are much different for Asian workers. The Asian–white wage gap "fell" from −0.9 (i.e., an Asian wage premium of 1 percent) to −16.0 (i.e., an Asian wage premium of 16 percent). What explains the 15-percentage-point increase in the Asian wage premium? The change in the skill gap explains 6.1 percentage points. For instance, Asians worked a significantly shorter workweek in 1989, but the hours gap between Asian and white workers vanished by 2017. And the Asian schooling advantage widened between 1989 and 2017. Although the increase in the rate of return to schooling contributes to the increase in the Asian wage premium, the overall effect of changing prices of worker characteristics *reduced* the Asian wage premium about 1 percentage point. Also contributing to the emergence of a significant Asian wage premium is a decline of 10 percentage points in the residual wage gap. Any evidence of wage discrimination against Asians in 1989 vanished by 2017.

 PRACTICE

The wage gap between Hispanic and non-Hispanic white workers widened from 16.6 percent in 1983 to 29.1 percent in 2017. Use the last column of Table 8.4 to identify the sources of the widening wage gap. The Hispanic–white gap in the workweek grew by 0.4 hours, which is reflected in what number in the table? The rate of return to schooling increased between 1983 and 2017, and Hispanics are less educated than non-Hispanic whites. Which number in the table captures the combination of these two facts? Changing characteristics and prices explain how much of the widening wage gap? How much is left unexplained?

Wage Gaps by Sex Across Countries

Wage gaps are a worldwide phenomenon. Table 8.5 lists unadjusted wage gaps by sex for full-time workers in many developed countries. The female–male wage gap in the United States is typical of wage gaps in these and other developed countries.

The wage gap in the United States shrank as women entered the labor market, and the same is true in other countries. In the United States between 1970 and 2015,

TABLE 8.5. WAGE GAPS BY SEX ACROSS COUNTRIES, 1995–2015

COUNTRY	1995	2000	2005	2010	2015
Australia	14	17	16	14	13
Canada	26	24	21	19	19
France	10	10	11	14	10
Germany	23	21	24	21	17
Ireland	24	20	18	11	14
Japan	37	34	31	29	26
Korea	43	40	39	39	37
New Zealand	15	7	9	7	6
Sweden	19	15	15	14	13
United Kingdom	27	25	21	18	17
United States	25	23	19	19	19
OECD Countries[a]	23	21	18	16	16

Notes: Wage gaps are calculated for full-time workers using the ratio of the median wage of women to the median wage of men and expressed as percents. [a]Average over 20 countries in the Organisation for Economic Co-operation and Development (OECD).
Source: *OECD Employment Outlook*, Statistical Annex Table H in 2007, Table I in 2012, and Table P in 2017.

the participation of women in the labor market rose 17 percentage points, and the female–male wage gap shrank 20 percentage points. The pattern is similar for the average of 20 developed countries: between 1995 and 2015, the participation rate of women rose 5 percentage points, while the female–male wage gap shrank 7 percentage points. Changes in the wage gap appear to be linked roughly point for point (in absolute value) with changes in the participation rate of women.

What could explain the inverse relationship between the participation rate of women and the female–male wage gap? First, less discrimination against women would narrow the wage gap, and the increase in women's wages would draw more women into the labor market. Second, as more women participate in the labor market, the typical woman would look more like the typical man in terms of skills and other characteristics, and the shrinking skills gap would translate into a shrinking wage gap. Either way, we predict that countries with the biggest increases in the participation rate of women have the biggest decreases in the wage gap.

Wages and the Sex and Race Compositions of Occupations

Let's apply the method of standardized comparison to the occupational averages in the Current Population Survey since 1979. Do the sex and race compositions of occupations help explain differences in wages across occupations?

Wages are lower in occupations with lots of women and blacks. In Figure 8.5, panel (a) displays the inverse relationship between median weekly wages and the female proportion of employment, and panel (b) shows how the black proportion of employment varies across occupations. These two scatter plots suggest that race

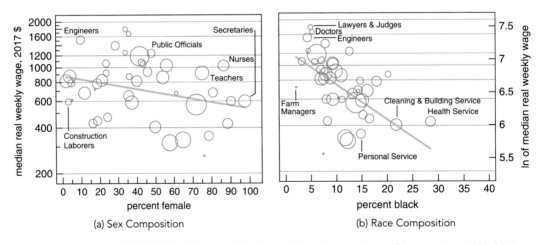

FIGURE 8.5. Wages and the Sex and Race Compositions of Occupations, 1979–2017

Notes: The left axis measures the wage on a logarithmic scale. The right axis measures the natural logarithm of the wage on the usual arithmetic scale. For each occupation, the center of the bubble marks the data point, and the size of the bubble reflects the occupation's employment. The slopes of the regression lines are −.496 (with a standard error of .241) in panel (a) and −5.299 (with a standard error of 1.152) in panel (b).

Source: Current Population Survey, outgoing rotation group files, monthly 1979–2017.

composition is more important than sex composition in explaining differences in wages across occupations.

In chapter 7, we analyzed the regression of the median weekly wage (in logs) on averages of the workweek h, schooling s, and potential work experience x across the 43 occupations. Let's add sex and race variables to the regression: f is the proportion (of total employment in the occupation) female, b is the proportion black, and a is the proportion Asian.

$$(8.5) \quad \ln w = 2.55 + .045h + .137s + .033x - .245f - 1.066b + 1.079a$$
$$\quad\quad\quad (.319) \quad (.010) \quad (.012) \quad (.009) \quad (.107) \quad (.376) \quad (.861)$$

with $R^2 = .951$.

We interpret the estimated coefficients on the sex and race variables as residual wage gaps. A fictional occupation with no women (i.e., $f = 0$) tends to pay 24.5 percent higher wages than a fictional occupation with all women (i.e., $f = 1$). This suggests that the 50 percent gap in female employment between mathematical and computer scientists ($f = .286$) and personal-service workers ($f = .785$) captures $12.2 (= 24.5 \times (.785 - .286))$ percentage points of the huge gap in pay between these two occupations.

The estimated effects of race on wages are crazy big, too big to make sense as wage discrimination. To see why, replace some white workers with black workers to increase the proportion black in an occupation from 5 percent to 15 percent. Since the estimated coefficient on proportion black in the regression is -1.066, the wage in the occupation falls by $10.7 (= 1.066 \times (15 - 5))$ percent. That's huge! To make the arithmetic work, either the black–white wage ratio is zero, or everyone—black, white, Asian, man, or woman—gets paid less in occupations with lots of black workers.

There's more going on here than just reducing the median wage in an occupation by replacing some higher-wage white workers with lower-wage black workers. Racial composition captures something about occupations, something that isn't measured elsewhere in the wage regression. Some occupations are collections of low-skill jobs that attract low-skill workers. If some skills aren't measured and those skills differ by race, then even the residual wage gap can exaggerate the true effect of race on wages. Let's see how.

8.2 Identifying the Effects of Discrimination

Adjusting the wage gap for measurable differences across groups improves the estimates of wage discrimination. But are the standardized comparisons good enough to identify wage discrimination? Could unmeasured differences across groups contribute to the residual wage gap?

Omitted Skill Variables

If unmeasured skills differ on average by sex, then the residual wage gap mixes wage discrimination with the **gap in unmeasured skill**. Suppose there are two skill variables x and y, and assume for simplicity that the two variables aren't correlated. The female–male wage gap Δw is

(8.6) $$\Delta w = b\Delta x + c\Delta y + d$$

where Δx and Δy are the two skill gaps (across sexes), b and c are the positive skill prices, and d is the wage effect of discrimination. If skill y were measured, then we would use it to adjust the wage gap just like x. (See Tables 8.2 and 8.3.) But since y is an unmeasured skill that differs by sex (i.e., $\Delta y \neq 0$), the adjustment for differences in measured skill $b\Delta x$ leaves the residual wage gap $\Delta w - b\Delta x$:

(8.7) $$\text{residual wage gap} = c\Delta y + d$$

Thus the residual wage gap reflects a gap between the sexes in unmeasured skills Δy, as well as the wage effect of discrimination d. If men tend to have more of skill y, then $\Delta y > 0$, and the residual wage gap overstates wage discrimination d.

 **PRACTICE**   In our analysis of Fran and Mitch in Figure 8.2, the wage gap is $200 per week, and $\Delta x = 3$ and $b = 26.67$. A second skill gap is $\Delta y = 2$, and the price of the second skill is $c = 25$. Compute the residual wage gap with and without skill y. If skill y isn't measured in the data, how is the estimate of wage discrimination affected? ·

Is there any reason to believe that unmeasured skill gaps work in the same direction as measured skill gaps? What's available in the data isn't determined by the needs of labor economists and other researchers. Easily measured data are collected; factors that are difficult to quantify are not. So ease of measurement largely determines the partition into measured and unmeasured skills. Whatever leads men (or whites) to have more x also likely leads men (or whites) to have more y since ease of measurement is what typically distinguishes x from y. Therefore, if standardizing the comparison shrinks the wage gap, then the resulting residual wage gap likely overstates wage discrimination.

One approach to address this bias is to search for richer data with better measures of skill. But there are other, more creative methods.

Control Group of Nondiscriminators

If some workplaces are free of discrimination, then differences in wages by sex and race in those workplaces are informative about gaps in unmeasured skills. Being free of discrimination means that the wage effect of discrimination is zero: $d = 0$. Standardizing the wage comparisons for workers in discrimination-free workplaces leaves a residual wage gap that equals $b\Delta y$, the effect of the gap in unmeasured skills on the wage gap. That is, the residual wage gap in discrimination-free workplaces estimates the bias from the gap in otherwise unmeasured skills. That's exactly what we need to identify discrimination.

In workplaces that are subject to discrimination, Equation 8.7 gives the residual wage gap. Since the residual wage gap is $c\Delta y$ in workplaces that are free of discrimination, differencing residual wage gaps between discriminating and discrimination-free workplaces identifies the wage effect of discrimination d: $(c\Delta y + d) - (c\Delta y) = d$.

This is a difference-in-difference estimator. Most workplaces are "treated" with a dose of discrimination d; workers in those workplaces are the treatment group. Some workplaces are free of discrimination; workers there are the control group. The difference-in-difference estimate of the wage effect of discrimination subtracts the residual wage gap in the control group from the residual wage gap in the treatment group.

The challenge, of course, is to find a group of nondiscriminators. In his study of wage discrimination at the U.S. Department of Health, Education, and Welfare (HEW), Borjas (1978) didn't intend to use a difference-in-difference estimator to deal with unmeasured skills. But he did think it was informative to compare residual wage gaps by sex and race at HEW with residual wage gaps for the labor market in general. HEW was the government department charged with enforcing federal anti-discrimination law, so (1) HEW shouldn't have discriminated against women and blacks in its own employment practices, and (2) HEW likely attracted workers who were less sexist or racist. Hence workers at HEW might be a reasonable control group.

Borjas found that the residual wage gaps at HEW were quite similar to the residual wage gaps elsewhere. If the folks at HEW weren't discriminating, that means (or suggests) that our usual estimates of wage discrimination are due to unmeasured skill gaps between men and women and blacks and whites.

Are you confident that HEW was free of discrimination in 1977? Borjas wasn't. He also entertained the equally interesting idea that employment practices at HEW were every bit as discriminatory as those in the rest of the labor market. Perhaps the doctor was as sick as the patient!

Test Scores and the Long Shadow of Discrimination in Childhood

Neal and Johnson (1996) take an entirely different approach to the same issue. They understand that the residual wage gap could reflect unmeasured differences in skills between the races, and they suspect that skill differences could originate during childhood. In particular, Neal and Johnson wonder how much of the sizable unadjusted wage gap between blacks and whites in their late 20s can be explained by differences in performance on a standardized academic test taken before leaving high school?

Neal and Johnson use the National Longitudinal Study of Youth (NLSY) to study the wages of several thousand black and white workers. The wage data are from 1990 and 1991, when the workers were 26 to 29 years old. The workers were ages 15–18 in 1980 when they took the Armed Forces Qualification Test (AFQT). (The military uses the test, but the NLSY sample isn't related to military

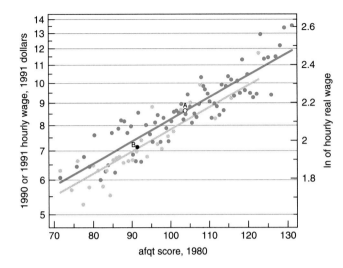

Notes: Each point is a race-specific average over 30 workers grouped by AFQT score. The data points for whites are blue; black data points are gray. The left axis measures the wage on a logarithmic scale; the right axis measures the natural logarithm of the wage on the usual linear scale. The mean values for whites and blacks are points A and B, respectively. The slope of the parallel regression lines is .0117 with a standard error of .0006.

Sources: Neal and Johnson (1996). Original data are from the National Longitudinal Surveys of Youth including the supplemental samples of blacks and Hispanics.

FIGURE 8.6. Wages, Test Scores, and Race

enlistment.) Performance on the AFQT is a measure of cognitive development and academic achievement. Studies in the military indicate the test isn't racially biased, although blacks don't score as high as whites on the test.

Teens who scored higher on the AFQT test in 1980 worked for higher wages in 1990 and 1991. That is, test scores of 15- to 18-year olds predict the wages of these workers a decade later. The scatter plot in Figure 8.6 displays the strong positive relationship between teen test scores and their wages a decade later in Neal and Johnson's data. (The AFQT scores have mean a mean of 100 and a standard deviation of 15.) This pattern suggests that we can use the AFQT score as a skill variable to standardize the wage comparison.

Let's use test scores to standardize the racial wage comparison. Points A and B in Figure 8.6 mark the means of AFQT scores and hourly wages for white and black workers, respectively. (These points are analogous to Mitch and Fran's points in Figure 8.2.) In these grouped data, the wage gap is 19.7 percent, and whites score 12.3 points higher on the AFQT test. The wage–score curve for whites lies above the wage–score curve for blacks, and the slope of the parallel lines is .0117 (with standard error .0006). The residual wage gap is .053 (= .197 − .0117 × 12.3). That is, the vertical distance between the parallel lines in the figure is 5.3 percent. So performance on a standardized test as a teen explains nearly three quarters of the black–white wage gap of workers in their late twenties.

In Neal and Johnson's sample of over 3,000 workers, the estimated regression equations with and without the test-score variable are

(8.8a)
$$\ln w = 1.445 - .030a - .191F - .217B - .073H$$
$$(.284)\quad(.010)\quad(.017)\quad(.020)\quad(.022)$$

(8.8b)
$$\ln w = 30.03 - .031a - .206F - .024B - .069H - .012AFQT$$
$$(1.85)\quad(.010)\quad(.016)\quad(.020)\quad(.022)\quad(.001)$$

with $R^2 = .079$ in Equation 8.8a and $R^2 = .195$ in 8.8b. Variables that indicate sex, race, and ethnicity (i.e., F, B, and H, respectively) reveal significantly lower wages of women (19.1 percent), blacks (21.7 percent), and Hispanics (7.3 percent) in the first regression equation.

How do test scores affect the black–white wage gap? The second regression equation shows that controlling for AFQT score virtually eliminates the black–white residual wage gap. The black–white wage gap falls from 21.7 percent without controlling for AFQT score to 2.4 percent with the extra variable. In fact, the effect of being black on wages isn't statistically significant in the second regression.

This evidence suggests that a racial skill gap that arises before young people enter the labor market causes the racial wage gap. What causes the racial skill gap of 15- to 18-year-olds? Neal and Johnson found racial differences in family-background variables (e.g., parental education) and school quality (e.g., student–teacher ratio) are important sources of the sizable racial gap in AFQT scores. In particular, family-background variables that reflect the cost or difficulty parents face in developing their children's skills explain roughly one-third of the racial gap in test scores.

By overstating the effect of current labor market discrimination on wages, we confuse the barriers that black children face in acquiring job skills with the obstacles that black adults face in the labor market (Neal and Johnson 1996, p. 871). The disadvantages young black workers now face in the labor market arise mostly from the obstacles to acquiring productive skills that they faced as children.

Discrimination in Hiring: Audit Studies and Blind Auditions

Another way to detect discrimination is by experiment. In an ideal experiment of discrimination in hiring, race would be assigned randomly to each job applicant, and racial differences in hiring rates would demonstrate discrimination. Race, of course, can't be assigned in an experiment. As an alternative, black and white participants can be paired and directed to apply for the same jobs. In these **audit studies**, each black job applicant must match his or her white partner in terms of qualifications. Black job applicants in audit studies receive fewer job offers than their white partners, which suggests discrimination against blacks.

Heckman (1998) summarized and evaluated several audit studies of hiring. In these studies, each audit pair applied to dozens of employers. In some pairs of job applicants, the white applicant was more successful; the black applicant was more successful in other pairs. The most common outcome was equal treatment: neither applicant was offered a job, or both applicants were offered jobs. Nevertheless, blacks tended to be offered jobs a bit less often.

There are several reasons to be suspicious of these audit studies. First, these are entry-level jobs for which the pretend job applicants (typically college students working on the audit study as a summer job) are overqualified. Second, nothing in the pairing of black and white job applicants guarantees that they are equally qualified. Third, in preparing pretend job applicants to apply for jobs, audit agencies sometimes instruct them on the importance of their work for detecting discrimination in America. The pretend applicant could innocently (or complicitly) influence job interviews to tilt the outcomes toward discrimination. Fourth, at best, audit studies detect the *average effect* of discrimination on hiring. As we see in section 8.3, economic models of discrimination point to the importance of discrimination *at the margin*.

A study of blind auditions for positions in symphony orchestras avoids these criticisms of audit studies. These aren't college students pretending to be interested in a job. These are professional musicians hoping to land permanent jobs in leading orchestras. Here the issue is discrimination by sex. We can't assign sex randomly, but orchestras have done the hard work for us. Almost every orchestra in the United States introduced blind auditions in the second half of the twentieth century. In a blind audition, the candidate performs behind a screen so the audition committee doesn't know the sex of the candidate.

In the not-too-distant past, renowned conductors asserted that female musicians couldn't match their male counterparts. If they were right, then women would tend to lose to men in blind auditions, and the introduction of blind auditions wouldn't tilt the sex composition of orchestras toward women. But over the same period that orchestras were turning to blind auditions, women were landing positions in these orchestras. While this correspondence suggests discrimination, other factors could be at work. For instance, perhaps the talent of female musicians increased relative to the talent of male musicians over this period.

Goldin and Rouse (2000) sorted through these possibilities by quantifying the effect of blind auditions on moving to the next round of auditions and ultimately to being hired. Without blind auditions, the probability a woman was ultimately selected to join an orchestra was 1.7 percent; for male musicians, the probability was 2.7 percent. That's a big difference. With blind auditions in every round, the success rate of women matched the success rate of men. Goldin and Rouse showed that introducing blind auditions explains about 25 percent of the increase in female participation in orchestras between 1970 and 1996. Twenty-five percent is a big effect, but it leaves plenty of room for other factors, including that the talent of female musicians has grown faster than the talent of male musicians.

Career Wage Ratios and Family Demands

Other than discrimination, what could explain the residual gap in wages between women and men? Are there unmeasured factors that differ by sex? One possibility is family demands. Perhaps children and housework distract even full-time working women from their jobs. Is there evidence to put this nagging issue to rest, or do the wages of working women take a hit when the work–family balance tilts toward the family, distracting them from their jobs? Let's see.

Is the gap between women's and men's wages bigger over the ages when many women raise children? By tracking birth cohorts of workers over their careers, we can plot how the female–male wage ratio varies with age (Goldin 2014). To do this, we analyze the wages of college graduates in the Current Population Survey by age and birth cohort since 1979. For instance, we can track the weekly wages of college graduates who were born in 1960. We pick these workers up in 1985 at age

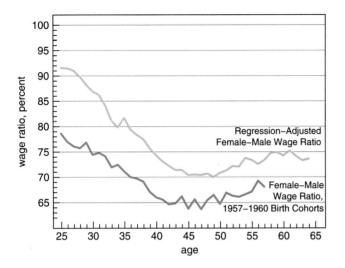

Notes: The dark-blue series tracks the female–male wage ratio of the four cohorts of workers born between 1957 and 1960 over their careers from age 25 to age 54. The light-blue series connects the estimated effects of age–female interactions, expressed as a wage ratio, in a ln-wage regression that includes age, cohort, year, race, and state effects, as well as the workweek and schooling. **Source:** Current Population Survey, outgoing rotation group files, monthly January 1979–December 2017.

FIGURE 8.7. Wage Ratio of College-Educated Women and Men by Age

25 and follow them for more than three decades until they turn 57 in 2017. In each year (i.e., at each age), we compute the cohort's female–male wage ratio. (We can do this for workers in each birth cohort, but we don't capture workers in earlier cohorts early in their careers or workers in later cohorts late in their careers.)

Figure 8.7 displays a U-shaped career pattern of female–male wage ratios. First, for the four cohorts born between 1957 and 1960, the ratio of the weekly wages of women to the weekly wages of men is 79 percent at age 25, and the ratio drops rapidly to 64 percent for workers in their mid-40s. The female–male wage ratio recovers a bit over the next decade for workers in these birth cohorts.

Second, a similar U-shaped career pattern emerges from regression estimates of residual wage gaps. Here we control for the workweek, schooling, race, occupation, state of residence, birth cohort, and year to estimate the residual wage gap (and ratio) separately for each age. As Figure 8.7 illustrates, the U-shaped career pattern survives standardizing the wage comparisons. Educated women earn only 8 percent less than comparable men at ages 25 and 26. The regression-adjusted wage ratio drops to 70 percent for workers in their late 40s and rebounds to nearly 75 percent for workers in their late 50s and early 60s.

Goldin (2014) argues that family demands explain this pattern for college-educated workers. First, full-time working women with children at home devote nine hours more per week than their full-time working husbands on household chores and childcare. (See American Time Use Survey, Table A-7A at bls.gov/tus.) Second, the U-shaped career pattern for the female–male wage ratio doesn't exist for less-educated workers. Perhaps there's something special about women on professional jobs. Third, Goldin shows that the pattern is there in high-wage, high-hours-premium occupations but not so much in other occupations. On some jobs (e.g., investment banking, corporate law), people work long hours and earn a big wage premium (per hour). The long workweek is fine for professional women early in their careers. When family demands draw time away from work, however, the hourly wage of women in those long-workweek/big-premium jobs takes a hit. Indeed, some jobs impose heavy penalties on anyone (man or woman) who wants to work fewer and more flexible hours.

But some high-wage jobs don't pay a premium for long hours. Pharmacy, which is one of the highest-paying occupations, is an example. There's little difference in the services provided by one pharmacist filling prescriptions for 12 hours or two pharmacists working 6-hour shifts, so pharmacy doesn't pay an hourly wage premium for long hours. And the lack of a wage penalty for short workweeks makes pharmacy a family-friendly occupation for professional women. In fact, balancing work and family shouldn't penalize the wages of mid-career women in pharmacy. And empirically, the women's mid-career wage penalty in pharmacy is rather small.

So the evidence points to family-induced, mid-career wage penalties for women on jobs that pay a premium for long (and inflexible) hours. On these jobs, the wages of anyone who works a short workweek or needs to arrange working hours around childcare suffer. That tends to be working women with families. This isn't to say that there's no discrimination against women in wages. But when we routinely standardize the wage comparisons by sex, we overlook the work–family balance that tends to be more important for working women with families. And the evidence suggests that these women endure a wage penalty that working men with families escape.

8.3   Modeling Discrimination

Discrimination against women and blacks in the United States and women and various ethnic groups around the world are historical facts, and in many cases discrimination persists. Let's model discrimination to answer some important questions. Does discrimination cause gaps in wages among people doing the same work? Does discrimination segregate workers, pushing those who suffer discrimination into low-wage jobs? Let's see.

There are five primary models of discrimination in the labor market (Becker 1971 [1957]; Arrow 1972). Three are models of **taste discrimination**. The source of the discrimination is the tastes or preferences of employers, coworkers, or customers. The fourth model, the monopsony model of discrimination, links wage gaps by sex, race, and ethnicity to differences across groups in the elasticity of supply of labor. The fifth is a model of statistical discrimination, which is now commonly known as profiling. In a labor market with statistical discrimination, an employer pays a worker on the basis of group identity rather than on that worker's skills.

Employer Discrimination

Profit-maximizing employers do *not* discriminate, and a sexist or racist employer does *not* maximize profit. Indeed, the discriminator foregoes profit to exercise

TABLE 8.6. DISCRIMINATION COEFFICIENTS AND RESERVATION WAGES TO EMPLOY WOMEN

EMPLOYER	DISCRIMINATION COEFFICIENT d	RESERVATION WAGE RATIO	RESERVATION WAGE R
Archie	.43	.70	14
Ben	.25	.80	16
Carl	.11	.90	18
Dan	.00	1.00	20
Ed	−.09	1.10	22

Notes: The reservation wage ratio is $1/(1+d)$. The hourly wage of men is $w_m = 20$, so the reservation wage to employ women is $R = 20/(1+d)$.

his sexist or racist preferences. Women and men are equally productive in this model of **employer discrimination**. In fact, they are essentially the same input, so production depends on $L_f + L_m$, the sum of female and male labor. But each sexist employer acts as if the price of employing women is more than the wage of women w_f. Indeed, the perceived cost of employing a woman is $(1+d)w_f$, where d is the employer's **discrimination coefficient** (Becker 1971 [1957]).

In this context, a firm's employment choice boils down to choosing whether to employ all women or all men. If men's wage is less than the perceived cost of women (i.e., $w_m < (1+d)w_f$), then women are too expensive, and the firm employs all men. But if the inequality is reversed, then men are too expensive, and the firm employs all women. So a higher wage of women lowers the chance that firms employ women. Furthermore, if the sexist employer perceives the costs of men and women to be equal, then $w_m = (1+d)w_f$. If the female–male wage ratio equals $\frac{1}{1+d}$, the sexist employer is indifferent between employing all women or all men. That is, the employer's reservation wage ratio is $\frac{1}{1+d}$.

Table 8.6 displays the discrimination coefficients of five employers. Archie, Ben, and Carl discriminate against women. Dan doesn't discriminate; he maximizes profit. Ed discriminates in favor of women. Archie strongly dislikes employing women, and he treats the cost of employing a woman as 43 percent higher than the wage he pays her (i.e., $d = .43$). He is indifferent between employing women and men only if the wage men receive is 43 percent higher than the wage women receive (i.e., $w_m = 1.43w_f$). So Archie's reservation wage ratio is $1/1.43 = .70$. Archie, therefore, employs only men if the wage ratio w_f/w_m is greater than 70 percent; he employs only women if $w_f/w_m < .70$. If men earn a $20 hourly wage, then Archie's reservation wage to employ women is $14 ($= .70 \times \$20$) per worker.

Ben and Carl aren't as sexist as Archie. Their discrimination coefficients (.25 and .11, respectively) translate into reservation wage ratios of .80 and .90, respectively. So the hourly reservation wages to employ women are $16 ($= .80 \times \$20$) at Ben's firm and $18 ($= .90 \times \$20$) at Carl's firm. Dan doesn't discriminate against women; with $d = 0$, Dan's reservation wage to employ women is the wage of men, $20 per worker. Ed, however, discriminates in favor of women; he wants to employ only women unless the female wage exceeds $22 ($= 1.10 \times \$20$).

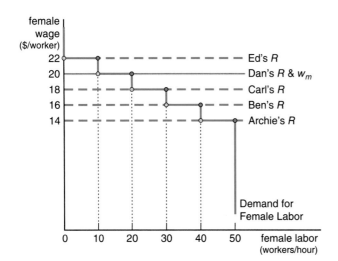

The hourly wage of men is $20/worker. A dashed horizontal line displays each employer's reservation wage to employ women.

If the hourly wage of women is $17, then Carl, Dan, and Ed employ only women. Each firm employs 10 workers/hour, so the quantity demanded of female labor is 30 workers/hour.

The demand for female labor is a downward-sloping step function with a 10-worker-wide flat segment at each employer's reservation wage.

FIGURE 8.8. Demand for Female Labor

From employer to employer, lower discrimination coefficients yield higher reservation wages to employ women.

What's the sex composition of each firm's workplace? All men? All women? Or a mixture of the two sexes? In this little five-firm labor market, the reservation wages generate a downward-sloping demand for female labor. To avoid unnecessary complication, let's abstract from the choice of how many workers to employ, which was the focus of chapter 4. Instead, assume that each firm employs 10 workers.

Figure 8.8 uses a horizontal dashed line to illustrate each employer's reservation wage to employ women. For any value of the wage of women w_f, we find the quantity demanded of female labor by checking whether each employer wants to employ women. For instance, if the hourly wage of women is $17 per worker, then Carl, Dan, and Ed want to employ only women, and the market's quantity demanded of female labor is 30 workers per hour. The pair $(30, 17)$ is one point on the demand curve for female labor.

We derive the rest of the curve, the downward-sloping step function in the figure, by trying other wages. The flat sections of the steps correspond to reservation wages. For instance, with $w_f = 18$, Carl is indifferent between employing women and men, and the quantity demanded of female labor can range from 20 to 30 workers.

 PRACTICE   If the hourly wage of women is $15, which firms employ women, and what is the quantity demanded of female labor? Mark this point in Figure 8.8.

Women earn less than men in this labor market's equilibrium. To focus on the wage effect of discrimination, let's fix the quantity supplied of women at the

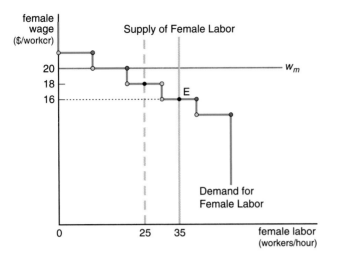

The supply of women is fixed at $L_f = 35$. The $16 hourly wage of women at the intersection of the labor demand and labor supply curves of women clears the labor market. Ed, Dan, and Carl employ only women; Archie employs only men. Ben employs 5 women and 5 men.

The wage gap, which is 20% $\left(= \frac{20-16}{20}\right)$, reflects the reservation wage to employ women of Ben, the marginal employer of women. If Ben's reservation wage jumps from $16 to $17, the equilibrium wage gap shrinks from 20% to 15%.

The equilibrium hourly wage of women rises to $18 if the supply of female labor falls to $L_f = 25$.

FIGURE 8.9. Equilibrium Wage Gap

number of women in the population L_f. Figure 8.9 displays the labor supply of women by a vertical line at $L_f = 35$. The figure also includes the demand for female labor from Figure 8.8. For any hourly wage of women greater than $16, the quantity demanded of women is less than 35 women per hour, so there's a surplus of women. Alternatively, if the hourly wage of women is less than $16, female workers are such a good deal that there's a shortage of them. Only $w_f = 16$, at the intersection of the labor demand and labor supply curves for women, clears the labor market.

Women are fully employed in this equilibrium. Since neither Ed nor Dan discriminates against women, they employ only women. Carl discriminates against women, but the $16 hourly wage of women is low enough to entice him to employ only women. Employment of women in these three firms totals 30. Ben, who is indifferent between employing women or men, employs the remaining 5 women. Archie, our poster boy for sexism, employs only men and fails to take advantage of the lower cost and higher profit from having an all-female workplace. The equilibrium wage ratio is .80 (= 16 ÷ 20), and the female–male wage gap is 20 percent. Women and men also tend to segregate into different firms in this equilibrium with employer discrimination.

The discrimination coefficient of the marginal employer of women and the relative supply of women determine the equilibrium wage gap. Decreasing the supply of women raises the equilibrium up along the female labor demand curve, and the wage gap narrows. Fewer women wanting to work means that the female wage need not be so low as to lure Ben, an employer with a strong distaste of employing women, into employing women.

This illustrates an important principle: discrimination *at the margin* is what matters. For instance, whether Archie's reservation wage to employ women is $14, $12, or even $8 doesn't matter for the equilibrium. If Archie's discrimination

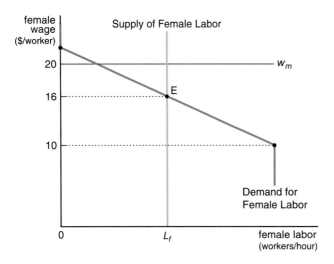

With lots of employers, gaps between the reservation wages fill in, and the labor demand curve smooths out. Reservation wages to employ women range from $10 at the most sexist employer to $22 at a firm that favors women.

The equilibrium hourly wage of women is $16, so the wage gap is 20%. The labor market segregates by sex, with each firm employing only men or only women.

Reducing discrimination lifts the demand for women and narrows the wage gap. Increasing the supply of women widens the wage gap.

FIGURE 8.10. Equilibrium Wage Gap in a "Thicker" Labor Market

coefficient is bigger, his reservation wage to employ women is smaller. But the intensity of Archie's sexist preferences doesn't affect the equilibrium wage gap as long as Archie doesn't employ women.

 PRACTICE An anti-discrimination campaign targets the most serious discriminators, such as members of the Ku Klux Klan (KKK), and the campaign moderately reduces discrimination coefficients of these racists but no one else. What effect does the campaign have on the black–white wage gap?

These results generalize to a "thicker" market with many workers and firms. Let's add a few firms. Adding a firm fills in a vertical gap between two of the reservation-wage lines in Figure 8.6, and one of the steps of the female labor demand curve turns into two shorter steps. With many employers, we measure labor demand and labor supply in percentages, and the female labor demand curve slopes down in its familiar smooth form. Figure 8.10 depicts this case. In this context, a widespread reduction in sexism increases the demand for female labor, which shifts the female labor demand curve to the right and raises the equilibrium wage of women. The female–male wage gap shrinks.

 PRACTICE Apply the graph in Figure 8.10 to the Great Migration of blacks from the low-wage South. How does an increase in the supply of blacks in the North affect the black–white wage gap in the North?

ADVANCED Our assumption that each firm employs 10 workers is a useful simplification, but let's explore the consequences of relaxing that assumption. Since the value of marginal product of labor is $20 per worker with 10 workers, employment at every all-male firm is indeed 10 workers. Allowing total employment to vary with the wage of women doesn't affect employment in all-male firms.

All-female firms, however, employ more than 10 women, and the least sexist all-female firms employ the most women. A sexist employer of all women chooses employment such that the value of marginal product of labor equals the perceived price of female labor $(1+d)w_f$, which is less than w_m in every all-female firm. Therefore, $L_f^* > 10$ in all-female firms, and employment of women is biggest in the least sexist firms (e.g., Dan's and Ed's firms).

The demand for labor in the market for women continues to have flat sections, but we replace the vertical segments with smoother downward-sloping sections as each employer of women responds to a drop in the wage of women by increasing its quantity demanded of female labor.

If all employers discriminate equally, they share a common discrimination coefficient d. In this special case, we illustrate the demand for the labor of women and men with the downward-sloping value-of-marginal-product-of-labor curve in Figure 8.11. The quantity supplied of labor is fixed at the total population $L_m + L_f$. At the intersection of the labor demand and labor supply curves, the value of marginal product of labor equals $20 per worker. In a competitive labor market,

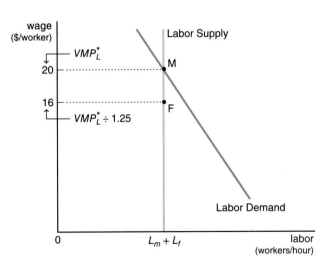

Labor demand is the downward-sloping VMP_L curve, which depends on labor $L = L_m + L_f$ rather than L_m and L_f separately. With a fixed supply of labor, the equilibrium hourly wage of men is the equilibrium VMP_L, which is $20/worker.

The common discrimination coefficient is $d = .25$. To leave firms indifferent between employing women and men, the wage of men must equal 1.25 $(= 1 + d)$ times the wage of women. So $w_f^* = \$20 \div 1.25 = \$16$. The female–male wage gap is 20%, and workplaces integrate.

FIGURE 8.11. Employers Discriminate Equally

men receive what they're worth; that is, $w_m^* = 20$. For discriminating employers to employ both women and men, they must be indifferent between the two sexes. That is, the relationship between the two wages must be $(1+d)w_f = w_m$. Since men receive a wage equal to labor's value of marginal product, the wage of women must be $w_f^* = VMP_L^*/(1+d)$. With $VMP_L^* = 20$ and $d = .25$, the equilibrium hourly wage of women is $16 (= \$20 \div 1.25)$ per worker. In this equilibrium, the female–male wage ratio is .80, and the female–male wage gap is 20 percent.

 PRACTICE   Suppose the common discrimination coefficient falls from $d = .25$ to $d = .111$. What happens in equilibrium to the wage of women and the female–male wage gap?

With employer discrimination, segregation is possible, but the case of employers that discriminate equally demonstrates that employer discrimination need not deliver segregation. Every employer is indifferent between employing women and men, so nothing points to segregating women from men. The main consequence of employer discrimination is the wage gap.

Employee Discrimination

Coworkers can also discriminate. Men can discriminate against their female coworkers; whites can discriminate against their black coworkers. To explore the consequences of **employee discrimination**, let's continue to assume that women and men are equally productive, perfect substitutes in production. And let's restore the traditional assumption that firms maximize profit; that is, employers don't discriminate against women.

Let's explore the consequences of men discriminating against the women they work with. In particular, suppose men require a wage premium to work with women. These sexist men care about the sex composition of the workplace as an attribute of the job. With more women in the workplace, their male coworkers require higher wages as a compensating wage differential for the undesirable (to them!) job attribute.

The equilibrium is immediate without any graphs or mathematics. It costs less for a firm to employ either all women or all men than to integrate the workplace because men in integrated firms require a wage premium. No profit-maximizing employer integrates its workplace. The labor market completely segregates into all-female firms and all-male firms. Competition among employers guarantees that women and men receive a wage that reflects the value of labor's marginal product. Firms that employ women and firms that employ men are separate but equal in every way. Women and men are equally productive, so output, revenue, cost, and profit are the same in all-female and all-male firms. Most important, employee discrimination doesn't deliver a wage gap. In our case, $w_f^* = w_m^* = 20$.

Segregation is the main implication of employee discrimination, but complete segregation is a bit strong to be important empirically. Can we tweak the model to get some integrated employers? The integrated firm operates at a cost disadvantage that must be counterbalanced by a revenue advantage. Suppose women and men are complements in production. Men don't like working with women, but women enhance the productivity of men in this extension of the model. In the equilibrium, integrated firms operate alongside all-female and all-male firms. Again, women and men in the segregated firms receive the same wage. Women in the integrated firm are also paid that wage. Men in the integrated firm, however, receive a wage premium to work alongside women. Despite the higher wage of men in integrated firms, men are indifferent between working there or in all-male firms.

The most important implication of this extension is that a female–male wage gap exists only in integrated firms. So employee discrimination doesn't deliver female–male (or black–white) wage gaps across occupations (or other job classifications); wage gaps exist only within jobs where women and men (or blacks and whites) work together. Nor does discrimination by coworkers segregate women or blacks into low-paying occupations and jobs.

Customer Discrimination

Customers can also discriminate. In this third model of taste discrimination, firms maximize profit, coworkers don't give a hoot about whom they work with, but customers care about who serves them. Let's cast this model of **customer discrimination** in the context of race: whites don't like being served by blacks.

Precision Tools, a manufacturer of construction tools and equipment, sells its products through retailers like Maycomb Building Supply. Precision employs a racially integrated team of sales representatives who work in the field schmoozing retailers like Maycomb to push its products, to improve the placement of its products in the store, and so on. An effective sales rep develops a good rapport with the wholesale buyer at each retailer.

But Robinson, the black sales rep for Maycomb, has an awful rapport with Ewell, the racist buyer at Maycomb. Ewell doesn't want to deal with a black man, so he tends to order products through the white sales reps at Precision's competitors. Precision's sales through Maycomb suffer, and it considers assigning a white sales rep to Maycomb and moving Robinson to another retailer. That's not easy because many of the wholesale buyers are racists like Ewell. Robinson is simply less valuable to Precision because the wholesale buyers of Precision's products discriminate against blacks.

Customer discrimination reduces the demand for and lowers the wage of black sales reps like Robinson. A black–white wage gap emerges among equally skilled sales reps. To avoid the lower pay, Robinson and other black workers gravitate toward jobs serving black customers (or to jobs without contact with racist customers). So customer discrimination generates some segregation.

PRACTICE   Many technological innovations have decreased contact between employees and customers. ATM and Internet transactions come to mind. Predict the effect of these innovations on wage gaps if the source of wage gaps is customer discrimination.

If sports fans are racists, then sports is another example of customer discrimination. The racist alumni of a college basketball powerhouse don't want a black point guard, and their charitable contributions to the university depend on the race of the team's primary ball handler. A more-talented black point guard can be worth less to the university than a less-talented white point guard. And many football fans don't want a black quarterback to lead their NFL team on the field. The team's owner, general manager, and coaching staff might all be racially neutral, judging their players on the basis of talent without regard to race. While that approach puts the best team on the field, it doesn't maximize the team's profit. The profit-maximizing team passes over a more-talented black quarterback in favor of a less-talented white quarterback to improve ticket sales, TV viewership, and sales of jerseys and ball caps. The team loses more games, but the fans prefer losing with a white quarterback to winning with a black quarterback. Go figure.

These examples show that customer discrimination can produce wage gaps and segregation. The empirical importance of customer discrimination hinges on black workers' inability to escape the discrimination by working on jobs without meaningful contact with racist customers. The model of customer discrimination doesn't predict wage gaps on jobs without customer contact.

Did Soccer Fans in England Discriminate Against Black Players?   English league soccer is a competitive business with lots of professional clubs. A club can win more matches and improve its ranking in league play by acquiring better players. Since the market for players is quite competitive, acquiring better players drives up the club's payroll. In fact, the relationship across clubs between performance and payroll is strong. But payroll expenses might also reflect the racial composition of the club's players. Can a club win more matches without inflating its payroll by having more black players? If so, there would be evidence of race discrimination against black players.

Using data from a period when black players were breaking into English league soccer (1978–1993), Szymanski (2000) analyzes how club performance depended on the club's payroll and the racial makeup of its players. He shows that, holding payroll fixed, having more black players on the roster improved the club's ranking in league play. So clubs sacrificed wins to keep black players off the field. Is this evidence of racial discrimination by soccer fans? Szymanski finds that the club's racial composition had no effect on its revenue or attendance, given its performance. His evidence, therefore, casts doubt on customer discrimination and favors employer discrimination against black players.

Monopsony Discrimination

Coalwood has nothing against women, but it finds that women just aren't as sensitive as men (in terms of labor supply) to the wage. If women's labor supply is less elastic than men's labor supply, then a profit-maximizing employer like Coalwood pays women less than men. **Monopsony discrimination** applies our model of labor market monopsony to wage gaps by sex, race, and ethnicity.

We learned in chapter 2 that Coalwood reduces employment to drive the wage down along the labor supply curve. Now Coalwood faces separate labor supply curves of equally productive men and women. In Figure 8.12, the labor supply of women is less elastic than the labor supply of men. The figure also displays the marginal-labor-cost curves of women and men. Recall that marginal labor cost exceeds the wage if labor supply slopes up, so each marginal-labor-cost curve lies above its labor supply curve. For simplicity, the value of the marginal product of labor is constant at $500 per worker.

Faced with the labor supply curves in Figure 8.12, Coalwood cuts its employment of women and men in half (compared to competitive employment) to maximize profit. To see why, we apply the usual principle of profit maximization twice, once for each sex. Coalwood chooses the number of workers of each sex to employ where the value of the marginal product of labor equals the sex-specific marginal labor cost. That's point A in the figure. To attract 300 women and 300 men to work at Coalwood, the firm pays women a weekly wage of $250 per worker at point F and men a weekly wage of $400 per worker at M. The female–male wage ratio is 62.5 percent ($= 250 \div 400$), and the wage gap is 37.5 percent.

This example illustrates the key principle of the monopsony model of discrimination: firms pay groups with less-elastic labor supplies less. The monopsony explanation for the female–male wage gap hinges on the assumption that women's

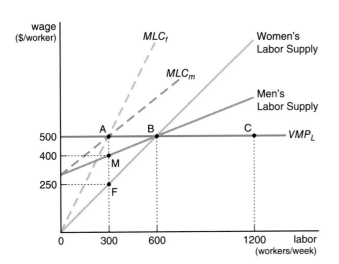

If Coalwood behaved competitively, it would employ 600 women and 600 men at a $500 wage.

Coalwood faces two upward-sloping labor supply curves, but the labor supply of women is less elastic. To maximize profit, Coalwood chooses employment of each sex at A, where the value of the marginal product of labor equals each sex's marginal labor cost. Points M and F reveal the lowest wages that attract 300 men and 300 women to work at Coalwood. The weekly wages of women and men are $250 and $400, respectively.

FIGURE 8.12. Monopsony Discrimination

labor supply is less elastic than men's labor supply. The validity of this essential assumption is by no means obvious. For instance, for most of the twentieth century, men were the breadwinners in American families. Many of these men felt locked to their jobs and were unwilling to take the risks associated with quitting to search for jobs with slightly higher wages. Working women, as second-income earners, were probably better positioned to quit to search for higher wages. That factor points to a more-elastic supply of female workers.

We might also wonder why minorities tend to be the groups with low elasticities of labor supply. For instance, if blacks have more-elastic labor supplies than whites, then the monopsony model predicts that blacks earn a wage premium over whites.

Historical examples of discrimination abound: Germans discriminated against Jews, Greeks against Albanians, Turks against Armenians, Russians against Koreans, and Kashmiris against Hindus. Was the source of German discrimination against Jews a less-elastic supply of Jewish labor? Monopsony discrimination probably partially explains wage gaps in some contexts, but the source of pervasive discrimination against minority groups historically and around the world today isn't that the victims of discrimination are always and everywhere less-elastic suppliers of labor.

Statistical Discrimination

"There is nothing more painful to me … than to walk down the street and hear footsteps and start thinking about robbery—then look around and see someone white and feel relieved," remarked civil-rights activist Jesse Jackson to an audience at Operation PUSH in Chicago in 1993. Jackson was racial profiling, harboring a belief that the footsteps of a black man are more dangerous than those of a white man; just as New Jersey state troopers harbor a belief that young black men driving expensive cars are more likely to be drug dealers; just as agents at airport security checkpoints harbor a belief that young Middle-Eastern men are more likely to be explosive-carrying terrorists; and just as employers harbor a belief that young women are more likely to interrupt their careers to have children. In each case, an assessment is made on the basis of group identity (i.e., race, ethnicity, or sex) without knowing whether the belief about the group, which might be correct, applies to the individual.

Profiling is an exercise in statistical inference. In many contexts, we don't have the information—it's too costly to obtain or we don't have the time to obtain it—to evaluate the individual accurately. We form quick judgments on limited information, and that process involves applying averages of the group to a member of the group. It's pervasive. A nice smile or a firm handshake counts for something. When you were in high school, your parents were surely less likely to let you ride home from a movie with your 16-year-old friend at the wheel than to let the unknown parent of your friend drive you home. No one from the construction trades lands a project at my house by wearing lots of gold chains and otherwise looking like a wiseguy from *The Sopranos*.

In the simplest model of **statistical discrimination**, wage gaps reflect productivity gaps (Phelps 1972). In the hiring process, an employer doesn't observe an applicant's skills. The employer just doesn't know how productive the worker is. A résumé, a school transcript, and the content of an interview reveal a lot, but much remains unknown. Perhaps sex or race provide additional information. For instance, if women are less likely to stay employed because they frequently interrupt their careers to have children, a rational employer uses sex to inform his prediction of each worker's value. So young women get paid less than young men, which illustrates how statistical discrimination translates a turnover gap into a wage gap. Does this wage gap measure discrimination? Most labor economists don't think so. The resulting wage gap simply reflects an underlying productivity (or turnover) gap.

Statistical discrimination isn't really about discrimination against the profiled group. It's about ill-treatment within groups. For instance, the young woman committed to a business career is pooled with all women and ill-treated in the comparison with men. Her wage, as well as her opportunities to advance through on-the-job training, suffer. That much is clear. But we shouldn't ignore that the women who will interrupt their careers to have children gain by statistical discrimination. If they were paid on the basis of their weak commitment to a career, then their wage would be lower than the wage they enjoy by hiding among career women. Statistical discrimination hurts some women, helps other women, but doesn't mistreat women overall.

How might a career-oriented young woman escape the ill-treatment she suffers by being profiled as a future homemaker? She signals her commitment to the labor market. One way to do this is by getting an MBA from an expensive business school. What a woman learns in business school contributes to her human capital, but an MBA also signals that she's in it for the long haul. Paying the high price of an MBA doesn't make sense if she expects to work for only a few years (or even a decade) before transitioning to the rigors of raising a family. Of course, medical, dental, and law schools offer the same opportunities to signal while acquiring valuable professional training as human capital.

An advanced degree is a strong signal, but weaker signals of skills or career commitment are also informative and shift some of the weight from sex and race in wage determination. The better the information about individual skills, the less important are group identifiers like sex and race. For instance, the influence of sex and race on wages should quickly fade with work experience. Once hired, a worker's actual performance reveals his or her productivity and replaces rough measures like sex and race in determining pay. Thus the importance of statistical discrimination is limited to the hiring process, newly hired workers, and contexts where the personal performance of workers is difficult to measure.

Can the beliefs at the foundation of statistical discrimination be self-confirming? Suppose employers mistakenly believe that blacks are less-able workers than whites. The statistical discriminator then tends to assign blacks to lower-level and lower-wage jobs. Young blacks, anticipating this treatment, don't acquire the skills to justify placement in higher-level jobs. Employers' beliefs that blacks are less productive reduce the incentives for blacks to acquire skills, which confirms their beliefs.

Not so fast. A rational statistical discriminator understands the process and is surprised to see such a small skill gap. Because blacks and whites are equally able, the skill gap that emerges is the gap in acquired skills only. It's smaller than the gap that the employer expects. It's simply inconsistent with the employer's belief that blacks are less able. The rational statistical discriminator learns from his mistake and updates his belief about the ability of blacks. Having correctly parsed black productivity into the ability component and the stereotype-induced lack of skill acquisition, the rational statistical discriminator subsequently uses a stereotype-free belief of black ability. Blacks in the next round of hiring train as much as whites and land the same jobs as whites. Indeed, rational employers quickly dispel their beliefs of black inferiority, and black workers quickly respond by acquiring more skills. If statistical discriminators update their beliefs rationally, then mistaken stereotypes do *not* survive.

Our analysis of statistical discrimination suggests that racial profiling and sexual stereotypes tend to reflect actual productivity-related differences because, to the extent initial beliefs are erroneous, employers can correct them quickly. Furthermore, statistical discrimination is primarily a practice that affects new hires and otherwise inexperienced workers.

But there's a second flavor of statistical discrimination. A profit-maximizing employer uses race to infer productivity, but a racist employer might use incidental information to infer race. For instance, employers pass over the résumés of Lakisha and Jamal in favor of the comparable (or, in field experiments, identical) résumés of Emily and Greg (Bertrand and Mullainathan 2004). This form of statistical discrimination is the racist employer's means to exercise his taste-based end of discriminating against blacks.

8.4   Can Discrimination Survive in the Long Run?

How do discriminators fare in the long run? Are sexist and racist preferences driven from an unregulated labor market? Let's explore these issues in the context of taste-based discrimination.

Paying a Price to Discriminate

In a world of racist corporate leaders, one CEO has a dream: what if he stops discriminating against black workers by adopting color-blind employment practices? That CEO is Gary, who has risen through the ranks of the recording industry to become the CEO of Rhythm Records. Like every other employer, Gary discriminates against blacks. Gary and other CEOs share a common discrimination coefficient $d = .25$, so they employ blacks at a 20 percent wage discount. One night Gary wakes with what he thinks is a brilliant idea. What seems brilliant at 3 AM frequently doesn't pass muster in the light of dawn, so Gary has to give this one more thought. He wonders, "What if I stop discriminating?"

Gary searches for the consequences of such a change in his preferences, a change from $d = .25$ to $d = 0$. He would run Rhythm Records to maximize profit. Equally productive black workers come at a 20 percent discount. Rather than employ any white workers, he would employ only blacks. Blacks are equally productive, so output and revenue wouldn't suffer. But his labor costs would fall by almost 20 percent; labor costs are by far his biggest cost, and his costs fall by 15 percent. Profit, as the accountants measure it, would quadruple from 5 percent to 20 percent of revenue. The share price of Rhythm Records' stock would quadruple on the announcement of the discrimination-free employment policies.

Gary would be richly rewarded, and he would be the darling of Wall Street. His headshot would grace the covers of *Forbes*, *Fortune*, *Business Week*, and the *Wall Street Journal*. Publishers would compete for the rights to his life story. Offers to be on the boards of directors of major corporations would pour in. Participation on boards of trustees of museums, orchestras, and other nonprofits would keep him in the cultural limelight well into retirement.

Some dream. Fame and fortune follow from simply maximizing profit rather than discriminating against blacks. If Gary continues to discriminate, fame and fortune remain just a dream, and he labors away in the shadows generally unknown. The fame and fortune that follow from not discriminating are Gary's **costs of discriminating**. So discriminating costs Gary (and other discriminators) a lot.

Gary kicks the racist habit, and a corporate star is born. He runs Rhythm Records to maximize profit, which involves replacing white workers with black workers in the long run. Gary's mission isn't to rid the world of the evils of racism. As a profit maximizer, he pays black workers the market wage for black labor. Some might call Gary a discriminator for paying blacks less than they're worth. Labor economists don't. Gary's discrimination coefficient is $d = 0$, so his preferences aren't racist. He simply pays the market prices for his inputs, including black labor.

 PRACTICE   Alan Greenspan, the Chairman of the Board of Governors of the Federal Reserve System from 1987 to 2006, argues that hiring women economists in the 1960s and 1970s at his economic consulting firm "just made great business sense." He writes in his memoir, *The Age of Turbulence*, "I valued men and women equally, and found that because other employers did not, good women economists were less expensive than men" (2007, p. 74). What was Greenspan's discrimination coefficient d? How did he profit from valuing men and women equally?

Gary isn't unique. The heads of Coalwood, Leisure Lawn, and thousands of other firms face the same choice—to discriminate or not to discriminate—and with the same consequences. Every CEO has a strong incentive not to discriminate.

The advantages of not discriminating encourage some, perhaps many, CEOs to kick the racist habit. Competition among these color-blind firms lifts the black–white wage ratio toward one, reducing or even eliminating wage discrimination.

As discrimination weakens and the wage ratio rises, the cost of discriminating falls. In a reasonably rich model, some discrimination can survive. But in the very long run, why would anyone discriminate at all? Discrimination is costly, so why would mommas let their babies grow up to be sexists and racists? Loving parents raise their kids not to discriminate because discrimination just gets in the way of their kids' success.

These principles aren't limited to Gary's case, the case of employer discrimination. Workers who discriminate against their coworkers pay a price in an integrated workplace. Sexist and racist workers have difficulty competing against nondiscriminating workers for jobs because the sexist and racists require a wage premium to work in the integrated firm.

Customers who discriminate also pay a price. Teams with racist fans lose more games, so the color-blind fan enjoys more wins. The wholesale buyer in a supply house gets more attention and even better deals by working with a black manufacturer's rep.

Or consider the case of a racist loan officer in a bank. The quality of the loans he approves (i.e., his performance) determines his raises and promotions. If he passes over higher-quality black applications to approve lower-quality white applications, the performance of the loans he writes suffers: too many of his borrowers default on their payments. His raises are smaller, and it takes him longer to get promoted. The racist loan officer pays a price to discriminate.

Key Principle.
Discrimination isn't free. Discriminators pay a price to exercise their sexist or racist preferences.

 PRACTICE   The manager of radio station KOOK's sales department discriminates against women. The women he employs earn the market wage for women, but his hiring and promotion decisions favor men over women. His pay depends on the revenue (or profit) that his sales team generates. How does he pay a price for his sexist policies?

Discrimination is costly, and the cost of discriminating provides pressure that can root out discrimination in free labor markets in the long run, perhaps the very long run. That's not true in regulated labor markets.

Institutionalized Discrimination

Archie likes whites, Christians, and attractive young people. He owns a McDonald's franchise. In the absence of laws against discrimination, Archie can discriminate until his heart's content. How so? The minimum wage. Archie's franchise has a queue of willing and able applicants, an excess supply of workers. He can't drop the wage without violating the minimum-wage law. But he can pick and choose favorites from the long queue of applicants. No blacks, no Jews, no Muslims, no atheists, no environmentalists, no Yankee fans. Is Archie foregoing profit by discriminating? No. The queue of workers eliminates his cost of discriminating. So the minimum wage encourages discrimination.

Everyone knows the manifestations of **racial segregation** in the South during the **Jim Crow era**, the 90 years ending in 1965: segregated schools, restrooms, hotels, restaurants, drinking fountains, bars, trains and streetcars and later buses, ticket windows, cemeteries, prisons, reading rooms in libraries, theaters, and so on. Such segregation was institutionalized by law; that is, the legal system required businesses and other organizations to segregate. If powerful white racists succeeded in exploiting blacks, why did they go to the trouble of codifying it as law? Perhaps governments institutionalized racism to accomplish what racism alone could not. Let's explore this possibility in the context of employment law under Jim Crow.

Some examples are simple and obvious. A law that requires employers to provide separate restroom facilities for black and white workers raises costs. Were employers so racist that they would bear these additional costs and forego profit? For some, yes. But why did those racists impose by law what they could do on their own? The law forced other employers to segregate restrooms, which kept the less-racist employers from having a competitive advantage. That is, by forcing segregated restrooms on all employers, the law allowed the most racist employers to survive.

Other examples of racist employment law under Jim Crow are more subtle. For instance, vagrancy laws supported wage discrimination against black workers in the Jim Crow era. Roback (1984) argues that white solidarity wasn't adequate to overcome the economic incentives for individual planters to offer higher wages to attract black workers. The purpose of vagrancy laws and other elements of Jim Crow was to accomplish what racism alone could not. An unemployed black worker, perhaps hiking to a town in search of work, was charged with vagrancy. Even blacks who traveled to visit relatives faced the risk of arrest. Although vagrancy was a misdemeanor, the courts sentenced black vagrants to work on chain gangs on public-works projects or leased them to farmers. (An editorial in an Atlanta newspaper in 1904 admonished the police to get busy rounding up the "vags" because the cotton was ripening.) The conditions of leased convict labor were at least as bad as under slavery, and mortality rates were high. (Farmers had no incentive to keep the black convicts healthy beyond the period of incarceration.) Consequently, quitting a job on one farm to look for work on another farm carried serious risks, even the risk of death. So vagrancy laws reduced black workers' mobility, which eased competition among planters for black labor. This element of monopsony reduced the wages of black workers.

Fast forward to the 1980s and the banking industry. Banks have been highly regulated historically. Interest-rate regulations (e.g., caps on the interest that banks could pay on deposits) and branch-banking restrictions were common until the 1980s. For instance, most states prohibited or strongly limited bank branching until the 1970s. These regulations limit competition among banks. Lack of competition boosts profit, and it also breeds discrimination. Free from competition, a discriminator that would be driven from a competitive market can survive. Deregulation of branch banking and the rise of interstate banking injected a dose of competition, which reduced banks' profitability. If bank employees had captured some of the excess profit (i.e., "rents") from regulation, then deregulation should have reduced wages.

Wages of bank employees did fall, and they fell more in states that had tighter restrictions on branching before deregulation (Black and Strahan 2001). Wages of men fell 12 percent, and wages of women fell 3 percent. Regulated banks had been doling out super-competitive wages to men and roughly competitive wages to women. Deregulation ushered in competition, which eliminated the super-competitive wages that male bank employees had enjoyed. Regulation had fostered discrimination against women, and deregulation reduced the female–male wage gap in banking.

8.5   U.S. Anti-Discrimination Policy

Since the 1960s, the federal government has prohibited employment discrimination by sex, race, religion, and national origin. Federal anti-discrimination programs have targeted sexist and racist employment practices by, in most cases, increasing the cost of discriminating. One act, however, raised the cost of employing women.

The Equal Pay Act of 1963 requires employers to pay women the same wages as men with similar skills, efforts, and responsibilities working under the same conditions. Raising the wages of women reduces the quantity demanded of female labor. (That implication doesn't depend on whether an employer discriminates.) So the Equal Pay Act would have reduced the employment of women. But Congress quickly remedied this deficiency with Title VII of the Civil Rights Act of 1964, which prohibits employers from discriminating (a) in hiring, dismissing, or promoting workers or (b) with respect to compensation and job conditions on the basis of sex, race, religion, or national origin.

Title VII proscribes equal employment opportunities for women and minorities. But federal programs against sex discrimination in the workplace don't appear to have had much effect. The dramatic rise in female labor force participation began decades before these acts, and the narrowing of the female–male wage gap didn't begin until about 1980. (See Figure 8.1.) So the timing is off. The narrowing of the female–male wage gap since 1980 probably has more to do with the increasing commitment of women to the labor market.

Title VII prohibits sex discrimination in the workplace, but the primary target of the Civil Rights Act was racism, especially the deeply institutionalized racism in the South. Indeed, Title VII was part of a comprehensive dismantling of Jim Crow in the South. The battle against racism in the workplace began in 1961 when President Kennedy ordered federal contractors to "take affirmative action to ensure that applicants are employed and that employees are treated during employment without regard to their race, creed, color, or national origin"

(Executive Order 10925). President Johnson's Executive Order 11246 (1965) requires each federal contractor to document its hiring and employment practices. For federal contractors with more than 50 employees, taking *affirmative action* includes forming goals and timetables to increase the employment opportunities of protected groups. While Title VII prohibits employers from using sex and race in hiring and employment, Executive Order 11246 requires federal contractors to use sex and race to increase the employment opportunities of women and minorities. Critics call this reverse discrimination.

Did the 1960s anti-discrimination programs narrow the black–white wage gap and improve the employment opportunities of black workers? The economic prospects of black workers had been improving well before the landmark civil rights policies of the 1960s. Blacks' gains in the amount and quality of schooling were continual, and the racial wage gap narrowed continually as a result. In addition, black emigration from the low-wage South increased the average wage of black workers and narrowed the black–white wage gap. Against this backdrop of continual racial progress, however, the period from 1965 to 1975 in the South stands out as a dramatic episode of black economic progress.

The employment and wage effects of the 1960s civil rights policies were striking in the South, where the resistance to anti-discrimination policy was strongest (Donohue and Heckman 1991). Employment of blacks increased sharply in Southern firms that were required to implement affirmative action programs. For instance, few blacks worked in South Carolina's textile mills, the state's largest manufacturing industry, between 1910 and 1964. Executive Order 11246 covered South Carolina's textile mills since they supplied textiles to the federal government, and textile manufacturers rapidly increased their employment of blacks beginning in 1965. Blacks' wage gains between 1965 and 1975, which were unusually high, were also concentrated in the South. And black economic progress between 1965 and 1975 extended beyond the benefits of increasing the quantity and quality of black education. Young blacks captured the benefits of more schooling and better schooling, but the black–white wage gap narrowed for young workers and old workers alike.

Summary

In this chapter, we learned how to measure wage discrimination and how to model discrimination. The principal findings are:

☐ Adjusting wage gaps (by sex or race) for differences in measurable characteristics (e.g., skill variables such as schooling and work experience) improves estimates of the wage effects of discrimination. Standardizing the wage comparisons shrinks the female–male and black–white wage gaps and eliminates the otherwise mysterious wage premium earned by Asians.

☐ Standardizing the wage comparisons also exposes otherwise hidden patterns over time. The black–white wage gap has changed little over the past three decades, but the residual wage gap has widened by 8 percentage points. Although the wage gap between Hispanics and non-Hispanic white workers has grown by 13 percentage points, the residual wage gap has barely increased at all.

☐ The residual wage gap reflects gaps in typically unmeasured characteristics, as well as discrimination. An academic achievement gap through high school captures much of the black–white wage gap. Family demands of college-educated women contribute to the female–male wage gap.

☐ Employer discrimination against group-B workers generates a wage gap that reflects how strongly the marginal employer of B workers discriminates. Weak discriminators take advantage of the wage gap and employ B workers. Strong discriminators employ only A workers. An increase in the relative supply of B workers or an increase in discrimination of the marginal employer widens the wage gap. If all employers discriminate equally, then A and B workers don't segregate into different firms.

☐ Discrimination against coworkers is a strong force toward segregation. With sufficient complementaries across groups, sexists work with women and racists work with blacks in an integrated firm, but the sexist and racist workers receive a wage premium. In segregated firms, however, women receive the same wage as men, and blacks' wages equal whites' wages.

☐ Equally talented A and B workers differ in value to the employer if customers discriminate against B workers. A profit-maximizing employer pays B workers less because the firm's customers value B workers less. Customer discrimination produces wage gaps only to the extent B workers can't escape to jobs without contact with the sexist or racist customers.

☐ Monopsony employers pay lower wages to groups with less-elastic labor supplies.

☐ Wage gaps reflect productivity gaps if employers are statistical discriminators. In the labor market, statistical discrimination applies primarily to the hiring process and new workers; it's predicted to wane with experience as employers replace low-quality information like sex and race with high-quality information on actual job performance.

☐ Discrimination is costly. Financial incentives for employers, coworkers, and customers not to discriminate are strong in free labor markets. Queues of willing and able workers in regulated markets encourage discrimination. Jim Crow laws in the South institutionalized racial discrimination. Without Jim Crow, discriminators would have paid a higher cost to discriminate, there would have been less discrimination, and discrimination likely would have diminished in influence over the decades.

We have established the importance of the workweek, schooling, work experience, job tenure, sex, and race for understanding weekly wages. In the next chapter, we add one last variable: union status, which shapes the bargaining relationship between an employer and its workers.

Key Concepts

- wage ratio, p. 276
- wage gap, p. 277
- standardized comparison, p. 279
- skill gap and skill price, p. 280
- residual (or adjusted) wage gap, p. 280
- gap in unmeasured skill, p. 291
- audit study of hiring, p. 295
- taste discrimination, p. 298
- employer discrimination, p. 299

- discrimination coefficient, p. 299
- employee discrimination, p. 304
- customer discrimination, p. 305
- monopsony discrimination, p. 307
- profiling, p. 308
- statistical discrimination, p. 309
- cost of discriminating, p. 311
- racial segregation in the Jim Crow era, p. 313

Short-Answer Questions

8.1 Standardizing comparisons adjusts wage gaps for differences in skills and other characteristics across groups. Why is this method appropriate?

8.2 There is one skill variable x, white workers (on average) have more of the skill than black workers, and the skill price is higher for white workers. How are the black and white wage–skill curves related? To standardize the comparison, should we use the black skill price to adjust black wages up or the white skill price to adjust white wages down? Which method leads to a bigger residual wage gap?

8.3 Differences in characteristics between women and men absorb nearly half of the female–male gap in weekly wages. Which variable is the most important factor explaining the female–male wage gap?

8.4 Summarize the Asian–white wage gap. What are the unadjusted and residual Asian–white wage gaps in the recent data? How has the residual Asian–white wage gap evolved since the late 1980s?

8.5 Differences across groups in unmeasured skills contaminate estimates of the effects of sex or race on wages and job offers. Discuss three approaches to solving the problem.

8.6 How does the female–male wage ratio vary with age? If women's family demands drive this pattern, do you think the pattern would be more or less pronounced in occupations that pay a large hourly wage premium for working long hours? Do you think the pattern would be more or less pronounced for workers without a college diploma?

8.7 Explain why a racist would employ all blacks in equilibrium.

8.8 Suppose employers are identical. If their discrimination coefficient is 33 percent, the equilibrium wage gap is 25 percent. If their discrimination coefficient is 25 percent, the equilibrium wage gap is 20 percent. And an 11 percent discrimination coefficient translates into a 10 percent wage gap in equilibrium. What explains this pattern?

8.9 The marginal discriminator is quite important. Extreme discriminators are not. Explain why the most extreme racists and non-racists have no effect on the black–white wage gap.

8.10 Two colleges offer the same education, but their grading systems differ greatly. Everyone at Feel Smart U. gets As and Bs. Grades at Old School U. extend from A down to F. Employers and graduate schools understand how grades at the schools differ. A students at FSU complain that they don't get the jobs and spots in graduate schools that A students at OSU get. Does it make sense for employers and graduate admissions committees to use school identity, as well as grades, as admission criteria? Are employers and graduate schools statistical discriminators?

8.11 Assume that anti-discrimination laws don't exist. For each model of discrimination, give one example (if appropriate) of how a discriminator bears a cost to discriminate. (Use your own examples, or draw examples from the chapter.) Do statistical discriminators bear such a cost?

Problems

8.1 The figure below displays the relationships between hourly wages w and a skill variable x for blacks and whites. The average values of the skill variable are $x = 8$ for blacks and $x = 12$ for whites.

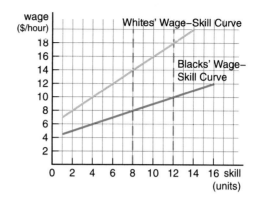

(a) What are the average hourly wages of blacks and whites?

(b) What are the black–white wage ratio and wage gap?

(c) Bernard, who is black, has the skill of the average white worker. What is his hourly wage? How does his wage compare to the wage of the average black worker and the wage of the average white worker?

(d) Woody, who is white, has the skill of the average black worker. What is his hourly wage? How does his wage compare to the average wage of blacks and the average wage of whites?

(e) Standardize the comparison to compute a measure of discrimination (in dollars per hour) for workers with 10 units of skill.

8.2 Between 1989 and 2011, the American Indian–white wage gap widened from $110 to $130 per week (in 2011 dollars). The table below displays the wage gaps Δw, as well as the skill gaps in the workweek h and schooling s, in 1989 and 2011.

	WAGE GAP	SKILL GAPS		CONTRIBUTION TO Δw	RESIDUAL WAGE GAP
Year	Δw	Δh	Δs	Δw	Δs
2011	130	0.8	1.00		
1989	110	1.1	0.75		
Change					

Assume the skill prices were $25 per hour for h and $60 per grade for s in each year (i.e., $\Delta b = 0$).

(a) In each year, the gaps between American Indians and whites in the workweek and schooling explain how much of the wage gap? List these contributions to the wage gap in the table.

(b) Compute the residual wage gap, in dollars per week, for each year.

(c) Subtract the wage gap in 1989 from the wage gap in 2011 to find the change in the wage gap. Repeat this subtraction for the two skill gaps, the contribution to the wage gap, and the residual wage gap. Enter your results in the bottom row of the table.

(d) Changes in the skill gaps explain how much, in dollars per week, of the $20 per week widening of the wage gap? How much is left as a change in the residual wage gap?

8.3 Men and women are equally productive, but some employers discriminate against women. The table below lists the discrimination coefficient of each of five employers.

EMPLOYER	d	RESERVATION WAGE RATIO	RESERVATION WAGE R
Al's Auto Body	0.000		
Billy's Bagels	0.053		
Chris's Cuts	0.111		
Danny's Decor	0.176		
Ed's Eyecare	0.250		

Each firm employs 100 workers. On the supply side, there are 250 women and 250 men in this labor market. At full employment, the value of marginal product of labor is $20 per worker. Competition among employers guarantees that men earn the value of the marginal product of labor.

Compute each employer's reservation wage ratio and reservation wage to employ women in the table, and illustrate the market for female labor in the figure below.

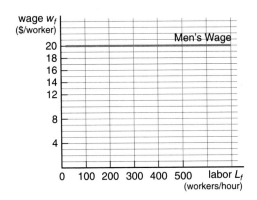

(a) If the hourly wage of women is $18.50 per worker, how many women and how many men does Chris's Cuts employ?

(b) If the hourly wage of women is $18.50 per worker, what is the quantity demanded of female labor?

(c) What is the equilibrium hourly wage of female workers in this market?

(d) In the equilibrium, how many women does each firm employ?

8.4 Blacks and whites are equally productive, and only the sum of black and white labor matters for production. All employers are racists, and their common discrimination coefficient is 1/3.

There are 20 blacks and 80 whites, and every person wants to work no matter what the wage is. The figure below illustrates the demand for labor.

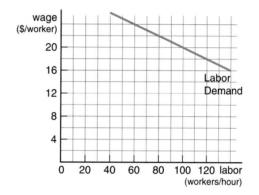

(a) What is the hourly value of the marginal product of labor in the competitive equilibrium?

(b) What is the equilibrium hourly wage of whites?

(c) Use the discrimination coefficient to solve for the equilibrium hourly wage of blacks.

(d) What are the equilibrium black–white wage ratio and wage gap?

8.5 Half the workers in a labor market are women, and the other half are men. All firms are identical: they have the same production functions, and they are operated by employers with a common discrimination coefficient $d = .50$. If workers of both sexes are fully employed, each firm employs 100 workers, and the hourly value of the marginal product of labor is $15 per worker.

(a) What is the equilibrium hourly wage of men?

(b) Use the discrimination coefficient to determine the equilibrium hourly wage of women.

(c) What is the equilibrium mix of women and men employed in the typical firm?

(d) If one firm stops discriminating, how does it change its mix of women and men to maximize profit?

(e) What happens to the nondiscriminator's hourly revenue, labor costs, and profit?

(f) Other nondiscriminators emerge. What are the effects of competition among profit-maximizing employers on the wages of women and men, the female–male wage ratio, and the female–male wage gap?

8.6 Suppose men require a higher wage to get them to work. Coalwood, a profit maximizer, faces upward-sloping labor supply curves, and the labor supply curve of men L_m^S is simply higher (vertically) than the labor supply curve of women L_f^S. A marginal-labor-cost curve pairs with each labor supply curve, and the value the marginal product of labor is $500 per week. The figure below displays these five curves.

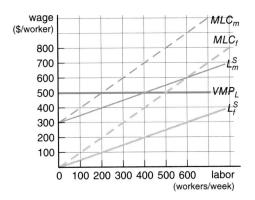

(a) Coalwood employs _____ women and _____ men each week.

(b) In the monopsony equilibrium, Coalwood pays each woman a weekly wage of _____ and each man a weekly wage of _____.

(c) The equilibrium female–male wage gap is _____ percent.

(d) Although women receive less than men in the monopsony model of discrimination with parallel labor supply curves, this specification delivers an unsatisfactory prediction. What prediction is inconsistent with the evidence?

8.7 The only information that ColdCall has about job applicants is their English proficiency. An applicant with strong English skills is worth $500 per week An applicant with weak English skills is worth only $400 per week on average. The labor market is competitive, so ColdCall pays wages that equal the expected value of marginal product of each worker.

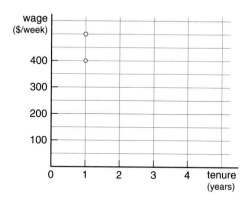

(a) What are the entry wages of strong and weak English speakers, w_s and w_w? Mark w_w in year 1 in the figure. What are the strong–weak wage ratio and wage gap based on these entry wages?

At the end of year 1, ColdCall learns the performance of each worker with weak English skills. One-third of these workers performed as expected; another one-third performed better than expected, and ColdCall adjusts up its expected value of marginal product of this group by $50 per week. Workers in a third group underperformed, and their expected value of marginal product sinks by $50 per week.

(b) In the same figure, mark the three wages that ColdCall pays to weak-English-skill workers in year 2. What is the average wage of workers with weak English skills in year 2? Mark this point with a small circle in the figure.

At the end of year 2, ColdCall gets enough information to determine each worker's productivity. Again, one-third of these workers performed as expected; one-third performed better than expected; and another one-third underperformed. Performing better (worse) than expected raises (lowers) ColdCall's final determination of value of marginal product by positive (negative) $50.

(c) In the figure, mark the five wages that ColdCall pays to workers with weak English skills in year 3 and all subsequent years. Also mark the average wage of these workers with a circle in the figure above.

(d) Sketch the wage profiles of workers who, in years 1 *and* 2, (i) overperformed or (ii) underperformed. Also sketch the profile of the average wage of weak-English-skill workers.

(e) How does the wage gap vary with job tenure? ColdCall doesn't statistically discriminate against workers who have completed two or more years of job tenure. Is the wage gap bigger in years when ColdCall statistically discriminates?

References

Arrow, Kenneth J. 1972. "Models of Job Discrimination." In *Racial Discrimination in Economic Life*, edited by Anthony H. Pascal. Lexington, MA: Lexington Books, pp. 83–102.

Becker, Gary S. 1971 (1957). *The Economics of Discrimination*. Chicago: University of Chicago Press.

Bertrand, Marianne and Sendhil Mullainathan. 2004. "Are Emily and Greg More Employable than Lakisha and Jamal? A Field Experiment on Labor Market Discrimination." *American Economic Review* 94(4): 991–1013.

Black, Sandra and Philip Strahan. 2001. "The Division of the Spoils: Rent-Sharing and Discrimination in a Regulated Industry." *American Economic Review* 91(4): 814–831.

Blau, Francine D. and Lawrence M. Kahn. 2017. "The Gender Wage Gap: Extent, Trends, and Explanations." *Journal of Economic Literature* 55(3): 789–865.

Blinder, Alan S. 1973. "Wage Discrimination: Reduced Form and Structural Estimates." *Journal of Human Resources* 8(4): 436–455.

Borjas, George J. 1978. "Discrimination in HEW: Is the Doctor Sick or Are the Patients Healthy?" *Journal of Law and Economics* 21(1): 97–110.

Charles, Kerwin Kofi and Jonathan Guryan. 2008. "Prejudice and Wages: An Empirical Assessment of Becker's *The Economics of Discrimination*." *Journal of Political Economy* 116(5): 773–809.

Darity, William, David Guilkey, and William Winfrey. 1995. "Ethnicity, Race, and Earnings." *Economics Letters* 47(3–4): 401–408.

Donohue, John J. III and James Heckman. 1991. "Continuous versus Episodic Change: The Impact of Civil Rights Policy on the Economic Status of Blacks." *Journal of Economic Literature* 4(29): 1603–1643.

Goldin, Claudia. 1990. *Understanding the Gender Gap: An Economic History of American Women*. New York: Oxford University Press.

Goldin, Claudia. 2014. "A Grand Gender Convergence: Its Last Chapter." *American Economic Review* 104(4): 1091–1119.

Goldin, Claudia and Cecilia Rouse. 2000. "Orchestrating Impartiality: The Impact of 'Blind' Auditions on Female Musicians." *American Economic Review* 90(4): 715–741.

Hamermesh, Daniel and Jeff Biddle. 1994. "Beauty and the Labor Market." *American Economic Review* 84(5): 1174–1194.

Heckman, James. 1998. "Detecting Discrimination." *Journal of Economic Perspectives* 12(2): 101–116.

Neal, Derek and William Johnson. 1996. "The Role of Premarket Factors in Black–White Wage Differences." *Journal of Political Economy* 104(5): 869–895.

Oaxaca, Ronald. 1973. "Male-Female Wage Differentials in Urban Labor Markets." *International Economic Review* 14(3): 693–709.

Phelps, Edmund. 1972. "The Statistical Theory of Racism and Sexism." *American Economic Review* 62(4): 659–661.

Roback, Jennifer. 1984. "Southern Labor Law in the Jim Crow Era: Exploitative or Competitive?" *University of Chicago Law Review* 51(4): 1161–1192.

Szymanski, Stefan. 2000. "A Market Test for Discrimination in the English Professional Soccer Leagues." *Journal of Political Economy* 108(3): 590–603.

9

Unions

I n August 2000, Firestone and Ford recalled 14.4 million tires that were suspected of being defective. Rubber tread was detaching from the steel belt in these tires, and tread failures had caused 271 fatalities and 800 more injuries. In many of the tread failures, the tires were on Ford Explorers. There were many hypotheses: design problems with the Explorer or the tires themselves, low air pressure, and problems in the manufacturing process (e.g., insufficient cooling time), plant conditions (e.g., moisture), and materials (e.g., outdated rubber).

The evidence, however, points to labor strife (Krueger and Mas 2004). Bridgestone–Firestone was in a contentious battle with the United Rubber Workers (URW) union representing the workers at its Decatur, Illinois, plant. The URW rejected Bridgestone–Firestone's demands for concessions. After working a few months without a contract, the workers voted to strike in July 1994. Management responded by hiring temporary replacement (nonunion) workers, who were paid 30 percent below the union rate, and the firm converted the replacement workers to permanent employees six months into the strike. By May 1995, the plant was running around the clock on two 12-hour shifts. The URW had depleted its strike fund (to pay its striking workers), and the union faced a serious risk of replacement workers voting to decertify it.

The URW called off the strike. Replacement workers kept their jobs, and Bridgestone–Firestone recalled URW workers only as they were needed. The dispute continued for 19 more months until Bridgestone–Firestone and the URW reached a settlement in December 1996. In the interim, recalled strikers worked alongside replacement workers; other union workers waited for work. And the union called for a worldwide boycott of Bridgestone–Firestone tires.

Were the defective tires produced by inexperienced replacement workers while union workers struck? No. Were the defective tires made by exhausted workers on the new 12-hour shifts? No. Most of the defective tires were produced during two periods: (1) the months between the time management demanded concessions and the time the union struck (i.e, the first half of 1994), and (2) the months after the strike when recalled union workers worked alongside replacement workers (Krueger and Mas 2004). Bridgestone–Firestone demanded deep concessions at the bargaining table, and union workers responded badly to the demands by producing defective tires.

This example illustrates some key features of union bargaining: concessions, strikes, boycotts, strike funds, replacement workers, decertification, and working without a collective bargaining agreement. In this chapter, we focus on the effects of unions on wages and employment. Strikes, boycotts, strike funds, and replacement workers influence the power that unions wield at the bargaining table. Bargaining power translates into a union wage premium that can influence the employment of union and nonunion workers.

9.1 Historical Context

Unions' bargaining power depends on legal institutions—the court rulings, legislative actions, and executive orders that underlie the rise and fall of union membership in the United States.

Union Membership

The previous century witnessed the rise and decline of unions in the United States, and the decline of unions in the private sector continues. Figure 9.1 depicts the evolution of union membership (as a percentage of overall employment) since 1900. **Collective bargaining agreements** cover the jobs of some nonunion workers, and a measure of unionism that includes these workers is the *union coverage rate*. Figure 9.1 also depicts the union coverage rate since it became available in 1979. The figure reveals the meteoric rise of unions in the 1930s and 1940s and the gradual decline of unions over the past four decades.

A union is essentially an agreement among workers to act in concert (i.e., to bargain collectively) rather than competitively, and such collusive agreements are difficult to implement. Unions struggle to overcome the same problems that confront colluding firms: (1) members' incentives to cheat on the agreement and (2) competition from outside the agreement. (The incentive of members to cheat on a cartel agreement is one of the more important principles in microeconomics.) In the union context, the incentives of individual workers diverge from the incentives of the union. For instance, while Richard favors a strike for higher wages, he prefers to work while his coworkers walk the picket lines. Similarly, nonunion

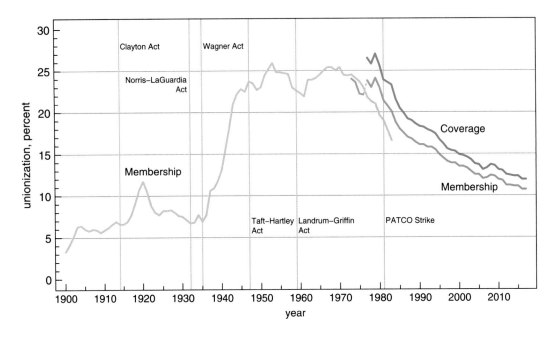

FIGURE 9.1. Union Membership and Coverage, 1900–2017

Notes: Current Population Survey's measure of unionism expanded in 1977 to include union-like associations. Data on unionism isn't available in the Current Population Survey in 1982.
Sources: 1900–1983: Hirsch, Barry and John Addison. 1986. *The Economic Analysis of Unions: New Approaches and Evidence.* Boston, MA: Allen and Unwin, Table 3.1. 1973–2017: Hirsch, Barry and David Macpherson. 2018. *Union Membership and Earnings Data Book: Compilations from the Current Population Survey.* Washington, DC: Bureau of National Affairs, Table 1.

workers in a firm can thrive while the union reduces its employment to drive up wages. And nonunion firms with lower labor costs drive unionized firms out of business. To succeed, unions must solve these problems. The history of unions in the United States identifies the institutions that helped U.S. workers implement their collusive agreements.

In the nineteenth century, courts working within the common law viewed unions as a violation of workers' freedom to contract with their employers and protected workers from being forced to unionize. Organizing efforts in the nineteenth century were largely unsuccessful, and few workers were members of unions at the time. The Sherman Antitrust Act of 1890 made unionizing even more difficult. While the target of the Sherman Antitrust Act might have been John D. Rockefeller's Standard Oil and other large firms, unions fell within the scope of the legislation. Workers banding together in any activity in restraint of trade among the states violated the act. The Sherman Act even prohibited a union from orchestrating a national boycott of hats made by a nonunion firm (Loewe v. Lawlor 1908). Thus the Sherman Act made the difficult job of unionizing more difficult, and union membership at the time reflected the challenging legal landscape. Only 5–6 percent of U.S. workers were union members in the early twentieth century.

For unionism to take hold, it would need to be set free from the grip of the Sherman Act, and the Clayton Antitrust Act (1914) did just that. The Clayton Act specified that unions were free to strike, peacefully picket, boycott, and do other activities without interference from the courts even if the union activity was in restraint of trade in interstate commerce. In the wake of the Clayton Act, union membership grew to nearly 12 percent in 1920, but union gains were short-lived. The Supreme Court ruled in 1917 that unions induce a breach of contract: unionizing breached the pledge not to unionize that many employers required as a condition of employment (i.e., a **nonunion pledge** or **yellow-dog contract**; Hitchman Coal Co. v. Mitchell 1917). From its peak of 11.7 percent in 1920, union membership fell to 7.7 percent in 1924 and returned to its pre–Clayton Act rate of about 7 percent by the early 1930s.

Rapid Rise of Unions.   At the dawn of the 1930s, workers were free to form and to join unions, to bargain collectively, to strike, to picket, and to boycott, but employers weren't obligated to bargain collectively with workers; they were free to ignore unions, to contract with workers to make nonunion status a condition of employment, and to dismiss union organizers or any worker who joined a union. (Two exceptions were that the federal government required the Post Office and all interstate railroads to bargain collectively with their workers.) Employers could also seek relief from the courts in the form of injunctions to stop trespassing, damage to property, violence, and threats of violence by union workers during strikes.

The political table tilted in favor of unions in the 1930s, and unionism flourished. In advance of the New Deal agenda of the Roosevelt administration, the Republican Congress and President Hoover enacted the first significant pro-union legislation, the Anti-Injunction Act of 1932, more commonly known as the Norris–LaGuardia Act. The Norris–LaGuardia Act declared as public policy that workers must be free to join unions for collective bargaining. Anything that conflicted with that policy couldn't be enforced by federal courts, so pledges not to unionize became unenforceable. The legislation also declared unions, their leaders, and their members immune from prosecution in federal courts for unlawful acts committed by anyone else in the union. Most important, the Norris–LaGuardia Act severely limited court injunctions in labor disputes. Federal courts couldn't issue injunctions to stop strikes and picketing even if the collective bargaining agreement included a no-strike clause. Indeed, the Norris–LaGuardia Act prevented federal courts from intervening to protect person and property of the employer, nonunion workers, and replacement workers. But this empowering of unions had no discernible effect on union membership in the following few years. (see Figure 9.1.)

. . . .

ADVANCED The premise of the Norris–LaGuardia Act was that "the individual unorganized worker is commonly helpless to exercise actual liberty of contract." The legislation even assumed that powerful employers forced powerless unions to accept no-strike clauses in collective bargaining agreements. But an employer can't set the wage at the lowest value that would keep these helpless workers on the job *and* impose a no-strike clause on the union. If the employer wants a no-strike clause from the union, it must raise the wage above the workers' reservation wage without a no-strike clause; that is, the union agrees not to strike in exchange for a higher wage. Removing court enforcement of no-strike clauses, therefore, lowers the union wage.

Removing court enforcement of nonunion pledges (i.e., yellow-dog contracts) doesn't help workers either. If the nonunion pledge is a bad attribute of the job, then employers that require the pledge must pay a wage premium. (As with no-strike clauses, the result doesn't require a competitive labor market.) Alternatively, if the nonunion pledge is a desirable feature of the job—many workers at the time vehemently opposed unions, strikes, threats of violence from union members, and so forth—then employers require nonunion pledges as a way to commit to remaining nonunion. Workers who don't like unions value the employer's commitment. Either way, eliminating nonunion pledges hurts the workers who sign the pledges.

But nonunion pledges were probably window dressing anyway. At that time, employers could fire anyone for any reason or for no reason at all. An employer could fire Al for becoming a union organizer or Richard for joining a union *with or without a nonunion pledge*. Removing court enforcement of nonunion pledges, therefore, didn't limit employers' ability to dismiss unionizers and probably had little effect on efforts to unionize.

· ·

The National Labor Relations Act of 1935, also known as the Wagner Act, declared that the labor policy of the United States is to "eliminate obstructions to the free flow of commerce" by "encourag[ing] the practice and procedure of collective bargaining." The act created the National Labor Relations Board (NLRB), a group of political appointees, to hear labor disputes, replacing the federal courts that had been handing down anti-union rulings for decades. The act prohibits resisting unions: an employer must bargain collectively with a union representing its workers, must not interfere with efforts to unionize or with union activities, and must not discriminate against or penalize its workers for their union activities. The Wagner Act also confers exclusive (or monopoly) bargaining rights to a single union representing a group of workers, so the law prohibits competition among unions to provide bargaining services. (Strikes not authorized by the union, so-called *wildcat strikes*, are therefore prohibited.) The NLRB certifies each union as the exclusive representative of a group of workers on the basis of a majority-rule election. To insulate union workers from competition from nonunion workers, collective bargaining agreements (including union pay scales) apply to all workers, including workers who aren't members of the union.

The Wagner Act tilted the legal landscape in favor of unions, and unionism took off like a rocket from a launch pad. Figure 9.1 shows that union membership exploded from 7 percent in 1935 to about 24 percent by 1947.

 **PRACTICE**   After the passage of the Wagner Act in 1935, workers were free to do which of the following: organize a union, organize a second union, join a union, bargain collectively, strike with union approval, strike without union approval, picket, boycott? Employers were able to do which of the following: bargain with unions, ignore unions, enforce nonunion pledges, pay nonunion workers less than union workers, dismiss union organizers and union members for their union activities?

The explosive growth of unionism in the United States ended in the late 1940s with an act that amended the Wagner Act and chipped away at the pro-union labor policy of the time. The Labor Management Relations Act of 1947 (commonly known as the Taft–Hartley Act) prohibits some union activities, such as political strikes and sympathy strikes, pickets, and boycotts in support of other unions. The act bans *closed shops* (in which only union workers could be hired) and requires a *union shop* (in which nonunion new hires must promptly join the union) to be approved by a majority of its members. Most important, Taft–Hartley allows states to ban union shops. In these *right-to-work states*, a worker can't be required to join the union or to pay dues to cover the costs of collective bargaining. (As of 2018, right to work is protected in 27 states, including all the states from Virginia to Texas.) Taft–Hartley also empowers the federal government to seek injunctions in federal courts to prevent or to stop strikes that imperil national health or safety and specifies the legal procedure for workers to remove (i.e., decertify) their union.

Twelve years later, the Labor Management Reporting and Disclosure Act of 1959 (also known as the Landrum–Griffin Act) backed up these limits. Landrum–Griffin requires complete disclosure of union finances and regularly scheduled elections to protect workers from the control of union bosses. The growth of unionism ended soon after Congress enacted Taft–Hartley, and for the next two decades membership in unions varied between 22 and 26 percent without any clear trend.

Slow Decline of Unions.   In an era with strong legal protections of unions (and without any landmark legislation or legal rulings), union membership declined from about 25 percent in 1970 to about 11 percent in recent years. Many believe that President Reagan's response to the Professional Air Traffic Controllers Organization's (PATCO) strike in 1981 marks the dawn of an anti-union era in government policy. As a public-sector union, PATCO was prohibited from striking, but it struck for higher pay, better working conditions, and a shorter workweek on August 3, 1981. Reagan ordered the air-traffic controllers back to their jobs and threatened to fire anyone who failed to return to work within 48 hours. Only one in eight air-traffic controllers reported to work. On August 5, Reagan fired the 11,345 workers who ignored his order, and the NLRB decertified PATCO from its authority to represent workers two months later.

Replacing the striking air-traffic controllers killed PATCO; does it also explain the more general decline of unions over recent decades? Probably not. First, the decline of unions began a decade before the 1981 PATCO strike. Second, the decline in union membership and coverage continued unabated through the sixteen years of the Clinton and Obama administrations. Third, public-sector unions should have felt the chilling effect of Reagan's response to PATCO most: Reagan fired and replaced government workers in a public-sector union, but public-sector unions have thrived since their emergence in the 1960s. We evaluate other explanations for the decline of private-sector unions in section 9.3.

Public-Sector Unions.   Although the federal government has forced private employers to recognize and to bargain in good faith with their workers' unions since the 1930s, Washington refused to deal with unions until President Kennedy signed Executive Order 10988 in 1962. Prior to Kennedy's executive order, federal workers could be members of unions, but federal departments and agencies couldn't recognize the unions as representatives of the employees. Executive Order 10988, however, granted limited collective bargaining rights to federal government workers. Unions could represent federal workers (but not workers at the FBI or CIA or any military personnel), but unions of federal workers couldn't bargain over wages or other elements of compensation, and strikes of federal workers were (and continue to be) illegal. Arbitration resolves labor disputes in the public sector.

Public-sector unionism grew rapidly in the 15 years following Kennedy's executive order, and unions have maintained their position in the public sector while unions in the private sector have declined. Figure 9.2 displays the growth of public-sector unionism since the 1950s and the decline of private-sector unionism since the 1970s. In the years preceding Executive Order 10988, 22–23 percent of government workers at all levels (i.e., federal, state, and local) were members of unions and similar associations. Public-sector unionism grew moderately through the 1960s and accelerated in the first half of the 1970s. Between 1969 and 1976, union membership of government workers increased from 27 percent to 40 percent. Over the past three decades, while unions in the private sector lost two-thirds of their membership, public-sector unions continued to thrive. Indeed, union members now hold 34 percent of government jobs at all levels.

Unionism Across Countries.   Union membership varies widely across countries, and unions have been in decline in most countries. In Belarus, Belgium, Iceland, and Sweden, at least half of the workers are union members, but unionization rates are below 5 percent in India, Thailand, Kuwait, Tanzania, Nicaragua, and many other countries. Unionization even varies significantly across developed countries. (See Table 9.1.) Coverage of collective bargaining agreements also differs across countries. The coverage rate is only slightly higher than the membership rate in the United States. In France, however, where 8 percent of the workers are union members, collective bargaining covers almost all private-sector jobs.

Union membership has been falling for decades in most countries. Table 9.1 reports that union membership averaged across 23 OECD countries fell from about 47 percent in 1980 to nearly 32 percent in 2015. Union membership in New Zealand fell from 69 percent in 1980 to 22 percent in 2000 (and continues to fall),

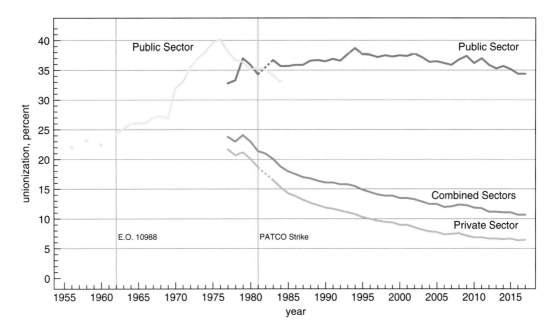

FIGURE 9.2. Private- and Public-Sector Unionism in the United States, 1956–2017

Notes: Union membership includes members of union-like associations, and values before 1962 are imputed from related series. Union data aren't available in the Current Population Survey in 1982. **Source:** 1956–1984: Freeman, Richard, Casey Ichniowski, and Jeffrey Zax. 1988. "Appendix A: Collective Organization of Labor in the Public Sector." In *When Public Sector Workers Unionize*, edited by Richard Freeman and Casey Ichniowski. Chicago: University of Chicago Press, Table 2. 1977–2017: Barry, Hirsch and David Macpherson. 2018. *Union Membership and Earnings Data Book: Compilations from the Current Population Survey.* Washington, DC: Bureau of National Affairs, Table 1.

and bargaining coverage has fallen from 67 percent in 1990 to 15–16 percent in recent years. In New Zealand, changes in government policy toward organized labor precipitated the decline, and other countries have also changed their labor policies. But the worldwide decline of unions suggests that country-specific explanations (e.g., Reagan's response to PATCO) can go only so far.

Union Wage Premium

Unions raise wages, and Figure 9.3 illustrates the **union wage premium** in the United States since 1973. From the mid-1970s through the mid-1990s, union workers earned on average 25–30 percent more than nonunion workers. Since the mid-1990s, the union wage premium has trended down from nearly 30 percent to under 20 percent recently. The residual union wage premium in Figure 9.3 standardizes the comparison for many characteristics of the worker and job, and the residual wage premium has trended down from 20 percent in 1984 to 14 or 15 percent in recent years.

TABLE 9.1. UNION MEMBERSHIP RATES ACROSS COUNTRIES, 1980–2015

COUNTRY	1980	1990	2000	2010	2015
Australia	49.6	45.4	28.2	21.8	18.3
Belgium	54.1	53.9	56.2	53.8	54.2
Canada	34.0	32.8	31.2	30.1	29.4
France	18.3	9.8	8.0	8.0	7.9
Germany	34.9	31.2	24.6	18.9	17.6
Israel[a]	84.0	71.0	37.7	30.3	22.8
Italy	49.6	38.7	34.4	35.5	35.7
Japan	30.8	25.2	21.5	18.3	17.4
New Zealand	69.1	49.6	22.4	21.4	17.9
Sweden	78.0	81.5	80.1	69.3	66.8
United Kingdom	52.2	39.6	29.7	26.8	24.5
United States	22.3	15.5	12.9	11.4	10.6
OECD Countries[b]	47.5	43.0	37.5	33.8	32.2

Notes: Data are from administrative sources except for Australia (beginning in 1997) and the United States, which draw membership rates from surveys of workers. [a]Israel's most recent data are from 2007 and 2012. [b]Average over 23 of the 24 OECD countries in 1980; Turkey is excluded due to missing data. **Source:** Organisation for Economic Co-operation and Development, stats.oecd.org: Trade Union Density data set, accessed March 14, 2018.

Unionization rates also help explain differences in wages across occupations in our sample from the Current Population Survey (CPS). Figure 9.4 plots combinations of median weekly wages (on a log scale) and unionization rates for the 43 occupations. A bubble represents each occupation, and the size of the bubble reflects the size of the occupation.

The figure includes a regression line fit to these "points." The regression line appears to be quite flat, and its slope isn't measured precisely, but the estimated slope is sizable. To see this, take two occupations along the regression line. The unionization rate of health technicians is 10 percent, and their median weekly wage is $660. The most unionized occupation is mail and message distributing. The unionization rate of mail carriers (and related workers) is 53 percent, and they earn about $840 per week. The 43-percentage-point difference in unionization rates accounts for $135 of the $180 difference in weekly wages. One hundred and thirty-five dollars per week is a lot of money.

Let's tentatively add unionization to the list of factors that explain how median wages vary across occupations. We fit a regression equation to the 43 occupation averages in the CPS (since 1983) to estimate the effect of union membership. The estimated regression equation is

$$(9.1) \quad \ln w = \underset{(.313)}{2.61} + \underset{(.009)}{.046h} + \underset{(.013)}{.127s} + \underset{(.008)}{.031x} - \underset{(.107)}{.169f} - \underset{(.434)}{1.393b} + \underset{(.880)}{1.705a} + \underset{(.203)}{.321u}$$

with $R^2 = .956$; h is hours worked last week, s is highest grade completed, x is years of potential work experience, f is the proportion female, b is the proportion black,

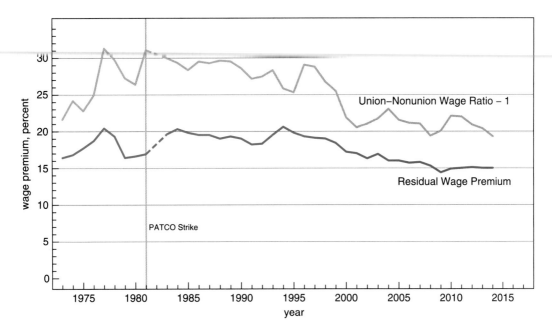

FIGURE 9.3. Union Wage Premium, 1973–2017

Note: Data on workers' union status aren't available in the Current Population Survey in 1982.
Source: Hirsch, Barry and David Macpherson. 2018. *Union Membership and Earnings Data Book: Compilations from the Current Population Survey.* Washington, DC: Bureau of National Affairs, Table 2.

a is the proportion Asian, and u is the union membership rate. The estimated effects of most regressors are familiar from earlier chapters. For instance, occupations with longer workweeks tend to pay 4.6 percent higher weekly wages per hour of work; occupations with more-educated workers pay 12.7 percent higher wages per grade.

Our estimate of the effect of unionization on occupational wages is new. The coefficient on the union variable implies that wages in a fictional fully unionized occupation (i.e., $u = 100$ percent) would be 32.1 percent (i.e., .321 log points) higher than wages in a fictional occupation without any union members (i.e., $u = 0$ percent). That is, our estimate of the union wage premium across occupations is 32.1 percent. In a more realistic comparison, we predict that construction workers earn 5 percent more than health technicians because the construction workers' unionization rate exceeds health technicians' unionization rate by 15 percentage points: $.05 \approx .321 \times (.25 - .10)$.

This cross-occupation estimate of the union wage premium is large but imprecisely estimated. To improve the precision, let's analyze the relationship between wages and union status *across workers* rather than across occupations. We can estimate a wage regression using data on the over 156,000 wage and salary workers who report weekly wages in the 2017 CPS. Let U indicate whether a worker is a union member; that is, $U = 1$ for union members, and $U = 0$ for

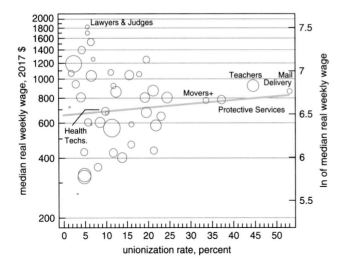

Notes: The left axis measures the wage on a logarithmic scale. The right axis measures the natural logarithm of the wage on the usual arithmetic scale. For each occupation, the center of the bubble marks the data point, and the size of the bubble reflects the occupation's employment. The regression line is $\ln w = 6.49 + 0.436u$.

Source: Current Population Survey, outgoing rotation group files, monthly 1983–2017.

FIGURE 9.4. Weekly Wage and Unionization Across Occupations, 1983–2017

other workers. (F, B, and A indicate sex and races.) The estimated regression equation is

$$(9.2) \quad \ln w = 4.66 + \underset{(.020)}{.026}\,h + \underset{(.0002)}{.066}\,s + \underset{(.0008)}{.033}\,x - \underset{(.0004)}{.0005}x^2 - \underset{(.0000)}{.172}F - \underset{(.004)}{.092}B$$
$$+ \underset{(.007)}{.058}A + \underset{(.005)}{.172}U$$

with $R^2 = .554$. (The regression equation also includes variables that indicate each worker's occupation.) The estimated slope coefficients are familiar, and the effect of union status U is measured precisely. Our cross-worker estimate of the union wage premium is .172 or 17 percent, roughly half the size of the cross-occupation estimate from Equation 9.1. This comparison holds occupation fixed, so 17 percent is our estimate of the wage premium *within* occupations in 2017.

9.2   Models of Unions

Unions increase wages. That's true empirically, and it's the main implication of every economic model of unions. Here we explore three models of unions. In the first model, underpaid workers organize to bargain collectively with a monopsony employer, such as Coalwood from chapter 2. In the second model, workers organize to act as a monopoly seller of labor to competitive employers, and these employers respond to the union wage by reducing employment. In the third model, workers bargain collectively with competitive firms, and the union and firms choose an efficient wage–employment pair in the collective bargaining agreement. Each model predicts that unions increase wages, but the three models differ regarding the effect of unions on employment.

Union Bargaining with a Monopsony Employer

Many people believe that powerful employers underpay workers and that unions help workers to get wages that better reflect their contribution to production. In chapter 2, we found that firms in competitive labor markets pay workers what they're worth and a monopsony employer pays its workers less than the value of their contribution to production. So unions can help exploited workers only in monopsony (and other noncompetitive) labor markets. Let's explore the consequences of the workers at Coalwood—or any other firm facing an upward-sloping labor supply curve—forming a union to **bargain with a monopsonist** for a higher wage. The result is stunning: the union can increase the wage *and* increase employment.

As we learned in chapter 2, Coalwood drives the wage down along the labor supply curve by reducing its employment of competitive workers. If those workers unionize, however, Coalwood can't drive the wage down along the supply curve because collective bargaining fixes the wage. Bargaining for a union wage changes the form of Coalwood's marginal-labor-cost curve: bargaining eliminates Coalwood's gain from reducing employment.

In Figure 9.5, the union bargains for a $13 hourly wage—still less than the $15 per hour competitive wage but more than the $12-per-hour monopsony wage. Over the range of employment from 0 to 830 workers per hour, Coalwood pays a $13-per-hour union wage, and increasing employment by one worker increases hourly labor cost by $13. That is, marginal labor cost MLC over this range is $13 per worker. To employ more than 830 workers per hour, Coalwood has to pay more than $13 per worker, which the union surely welcomes, and marginal labor cost exceeds the wage. (See Table 2.3 in chapter 2.) So the marginal-labor-cost

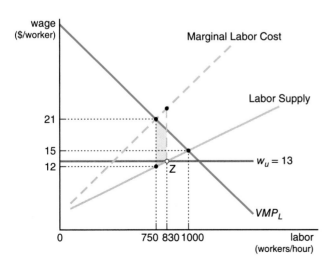

A competitor employs 1,000 workers/hour and pays an hourly wage of $15/worker. As a monopsonist, Coalwood reduces the wage to $12 by reducing employment to 750 workers/hour.

Workers unionize and bargain for a $13 hourly wage. As a result, MLC equals $13/worker between 0 and 830 workers (at Z), and Coalwood employs 830 workers/hour along the labor supply curve. Unless the union is quite strong (i.e., bargaining for an hourly wage greater than $21/worker), union bargaining increases employment.

FIGURE 9.5. Union Bargaining with a Monopsony Employer

curve with a union wage is the union wage w_u up to the labor supply curve and the original *MLC* curve at all higher levels of employment.

PRACTICE

If the union bargains for a $15 hourly wage per worker, Coalwood's marginal labor cost is $_____ per worker from _____ to _____ workers per hour. At higher levels of employment, marginal labor cost is the height of which curve in Figure 9.5: marginal labor cost, labor supply, or labor's value of marginal product?

Coalwood increases employment in response to the union increasing the wage from the monopsony wage to the collectively bargained union wage. Coalwood maximizes its profit by choosing employment to equate the workers' value of marginal product with marginal labor cost. Over the range of employment from 0 to 830 workers per hour, VMP_L is greater than *MLC*, which is the $13 union wage. Therefore, increasing employment increases profit over this range. For any level of employment above 830 workers, VMP_L is less than *MLC*, which is the dashed marginal-labor-cost curve in Figure 9.5 over this range. Therefore, decreasing employment increases profit over this range. That employment neither below 830 nor above 830 maximizes profit points us to our result: Coalwood maximizes profit by employing 830 workers per hour, the level of employment that equates the value of marginal product of labor with marginal labor cost.

Thus workers organizing to bargain collectively against a monopsonist increase their wage *and* increase employment. (If we replace the union wage w_u with minimum wage w_{min}, this model also delivers our result from chapter 2 that the minimum wage increases employment in a monopsony labor market.)

The workers in Coalwood form a union to increase their pay, and their union enhances efficiency. For starters, the monopsony equilibrium is inefficient: Coalwood employs too few workers. Since Coalwood responds to the union wage by increasing employment, the deadweight loss from underemployment shrinks. In Figure 9.5, the efficiency gain is the area of the shaded trapezoid between the VMP_L curve and the labor supply curve.

In the bargaining-with-a-monopsonist model of unions, wages and employment move together. A more powerful union bargains for a higher wage, $14 per worker, for instance, and employment rises. If the union is so powerful that it can bargain for wages above the competitive wage, then pushing the union wage up (from there) lowers union employment. But the overall impact of the union on employment is positive if the union wage doesn't exceed $21 in Figure 9.5 (or more generally, labor's value of marginal product in the monopsony equilibrium).

This model applies to unions of professional athletes, which raise player salaries and reduce the exploitation of players. As we learned in chapter 2, the reserve system and delayed free agency in baseball and other sports reduce competition for players and depress player salaries. Players unionize to bargain collectively with team owners, and collective bargaining agreements influence each player's contract negotiation. In particular, the rules governing salary caps, luxury taxes, and when players qualify for arbitration hearings and free agency influence each player's ability to capture the value of his contribution to the team.

Monopoly Union

The wage in a competitive labor market equals the value of labor's marginal product, but workers might still bargain collectively to raise their pay above the competitive wage. Workers at Leisure Lawn and other lawn-care firms form the Union of Lawn Care Workers (ULCW), a monopoly seller of labor to lawn-care firms. The ULCW bargains for a higher wage, and employment of lawn-care workers falls as a result. This is the **monopoly model of unions**.

The objective of a product-market monopolist is to maximize profit, and profit is also the objective of the ULCW. **Union profit** measures the workers' gain to organizing. As a seller of labor, the union's revenue is the **wage bill** $w_u L_u$. But there's also an **opportunity cost of union labor**: these unionized lawn-care workers could earn the nonunion wage w_n outside the union, so the opportunity cost of L_u union workers is $w_n L_u$. Therefore, union profit π_u is the union wage premium $w_u - w_n$ times the number of union workers.

(9.3)
$$\pi_u = w_u L_u - w_n L_u = (w_u - w_n)L_u$$

By organizing, workers' gain the product of the union wage premium and union employment.

The ULCW is a monopolist, a single seller of labor. As a monopolist, the ULCW faces a downward-sloping labor demand curve: it must accept a lower wage to place a larger workforce. The ULCW is in business to maximize its profit. (Many labor economists refer to this specification as the *rent-maximizing model of unions* (Dunlop 1944).) As a profit maximizer, the ULCW chooses the size of its workforce by comparing benefits and cost at the margin. Does a marginal increase in union employment increase or decrease union profit? To answer this question, we need to know how revenue and cost respond to the marginal increase in labor. The nonunion wage tells us how much the marginal increase in union employment increases cost. So the nonunion wage plays the role of marginal cost in the standard model of monopoly. Now we need to develop marginal revenue, how the wage bill paid to ULCW's workers varies with small changes in union employment.

Marginalizing the Labor Demand Curve. For the ULCW or any other union facing a downward-sloping labor demand curve, the **marginal wage bill** is less than the wage. ULCW's wage bill grows less than the wage paid to the extra worker. Employing another worker means that the union wage bill rises by the wage of that extra worker. But it also means that all the union workers receive a lower wage because increasing employment decreases the wage along the labor demand curve. This second effect drives a wedge between the wage and the marginal wage bill.

TABLE 9.2. LABOR DEMAND, THE WAGE BILL, AND THE MARGINAL WAGE BILL

UNION EMPLOYMENT L_u (worker-hours/day)	UNION WAGE w_u ($/worker-hour)	UNION WAGE BILL $w_u L_u$ ($/day)	MARGINAL WAGE BILL MWB^* ($/worker-hour)	MARGINAL WAGE BILL MWB ($/worker-hour)
50	25	1,250		15
			13	
60	23	1,380		11
			9	
70	21	1,470		7
			5	
80	19	1,520		3
			1	
90	17	1,530		−1
			−3	
100	15	1,500		−5

Notes: Comparing the wage bill $w_u L_u$ across rows gives MWB^* in column 4. MWB in the fifth column uses the formula $MWB = 3 - 2L/5$.

Table 9.2 lists values of ULCW's employment, wage, wage bill, and marginal wage bill MWB. The first two columns combine to give six points (L_u, w_u) on the demand curve for lawn-care workers in Figure 9.6. The union wage bill in the third column is the product of union employment and the union wage in the first two columns. In the fourth column, we compute the marginal wage bill by comparing the wage bill across rows. For instance, the wage bill grows by $50 (= $1520 − $1470) per day as employment grows from 70 to 80 worker-hours per day; the marginal wage bill over this range is $\Delta WB / \Delta L = \$50$ per day/10 worker-hours per day $= \$5$ per worker-hour.

The marginal wage bill in column 4 of Table 9.2 is less than the wage in column 2 at any level of employment. The pairs (L_u, MWB) give

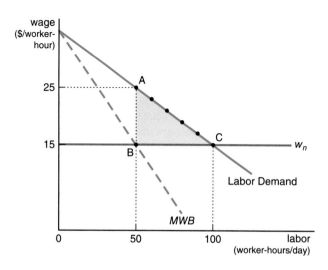

To maximize its profit $\pi_u = w_u L_u - w_n L_u$, the union sets its wage w_u such that employment L_u equalizes the marginal wage bill MWB with the marginal cost of union employment, the nonunion wage w_n. Employment at Leisure Lawn falls from 100 to 50 worker-hours/day, and the hourly wage increases from $15 to $25/worker.

The area of the triangle formed by points A, B, and C, $250/day, is the deadweight loss from underemployment at Leisure Lawn.

FIGURE 9.6. Monopoly Union: Marginalizing the Wage Bill

the marginal-wage-bill curve, which is the dashed line in Figure 9.6. The marginal-wage-bill curve in the figure lies below the labor demand curve because the marginal wage bill is less than the wage.

 PRACTICE

The ULCW also unionizes Cutting Edge Landscapes, where increasing employment from 100 to 120 worker-hours per day drives the wage down from $16 to $14 per worker-hour. What's the marginal wage bill over this range of employment?

ADVANCED The labor demand curve in Figure 9.6 is linear, and the equation of the line is $w = 35 - L/5$. Let's derive the marginal-wage-bill curve for a linear labor demand curve with intercept a and slope $-b$: $w = a - bL$.

The wage bill is $WB \equiv wL = aL - bL^2$. For those who learned and recall the power rule from a first course in calculus, $MWB = a - 2bL$ is the derivative of WB with respect to L.

The derivation for everyone else uses only algebra. Let's start with the marginal change in labor $\Delta L = L_1 - L_0$, where L_1 is one unit (i.e., worker-hour) to the right of L and L_0 is one unit to the left of L. Then $\Delta WB = \left(aL_1 - bL_1^2\right) - \left(aL_0 - bL_0^2\right) = a(L_1 - L_0) - b\left(L_1^2 - L_0^2\right)$. As the difference of two squares, $L_1^2 - L_0^2$ factors to $(L_1 + L_0)\Delta L$, so $\Delta WB = a\Delta L - b(L_0 + L_1)\Delta L = a\Delta L - 2bL\Delta L$. Finally, divide both sides by ΔL to find

(9.4)
$$MWB \equiv \frac{\Delta WB}{\Delta L} = a - 2bL$$

The marginal-wage-bill curve and the labor demand curve share the same intercept a, but the marginal-wage-bill curve is twice as steep. Thus MWB lies below the labor demand curve at every (positive) level of employment.

In the case of lawn-care workers at Leisure Lawn, $a = 35$ and $b = 1/5$, so $MWB = 35 - 2L/5$. This formula generates the values for marginal wage bill in the final column of Table 9.2 and in Figure 9.6.

As a monopolist, the ULCW reduces the employment of its workers to drive up the union wage. The wage–employment pair (L_u, w_u) that maximizes its profit π_u (i.e., the gain to its members) is point A in Figure 9.6: employment equates the marginal wage bill with the nonunion wage, and the union wage is the highest wage that gets Leisure Lawn to employ those 50 worker-hours per day. (Recall that a product-market monopolist sets its price along the demand curve at the quantity where marginal revenue equals marginal cost.) Unionizing lawn-care workers drives up the wage by limiting employment. In Figure 9.6, employment falls from 100 to 50 worker-hours per day, and the hourly wage jumps from $15 to $25 per worker.

PRACTICE Why doesn't employing 70 worker-hours per day maximize union profit? What are the marginal wage bill and the opportunity cost of union labor at $L_u = 70$? What happens to the union's profit if employment falls from 70 to 69?

The equilibrium with a monopoly union is inefficient. To increase the wage, the ULCW reduces employment below its efficient level, 100 worker-hours per day in Figure 9.6. The deadweight loss from underemployment is the area of the triangle defined by points A, B, and C: $(100 - 50)(\$25 - \$15)/2 = \$250$ per day, which is quite a lot for a firm that employs only 50 worker-hours of labor per day.

The union's success in driving up the wage without suffering massive cuts in employment hinges on the elasticity of demand for its labor. The ULCW is more successful if the demand for its labor is very inelastic. If the labor demand curve is quite steep, the union can lift its wage with minimal loss of union jobs. Alternatively, if the demand for lawn-care workers is very elastic—so the labor demand curve is quite flat—the only way to command a significant union wage premium is by suffering drastic cuts in union employment. We investigate the factors that influence the elasticity of demand for labor in section 9.3.

Even as a monopoly union, the ULCW probably doesn't hold all the cards. Leisure Lawn likely has some power at the bargaining table, too. Let's generalize the monopoly-union model to include bargaining power. The ULCW's goal in negotiations is the wage–employment pair at point A in Figure 9.6. Leisure Lawn's goal is the competitive equilibrium at point C in the figure. The collective bargaining agreement, then, lies somewhere between A and C and depends on the relative bargaining strengths on the two sides of the table. If the ULCW is stronger, the agreement is closer to the wage–employment pair at point A; union wage and employment are closer to point C if Leisure Lawn is stronger. (We identify factors that influence bargaining strength later in this chapter.) Therefore, the union wage and employment are inversely related in the bargaining extension of the monopoly-union model.

Preferences and Opportunities. We can also illustrate the monopoly-union equilibrium and its inefficiency by modeling the union's preferences and opportunities. This representation is particularly useful for comparing the monopoly-union equilibrium with the equilibrium for an efficient-contracting union, which we turn to next. Since the ULCW can choose any wage–employment pair along the demand curve for its labor, the demand curve for lawn-care workers is essentially the budget line facing the union. Associated with each point on the labor demand curve is a value for union profit π_u, which we illustrate with the ULCW's iso-profit curves.

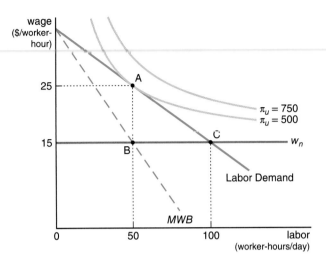

The union's opportunities are the wage–employment pairs along the labor demand curve. The union's preference direction is toward higher wages and employment, and the union's downward-sloping iso-profit curves illustrate its preferences. Each of the union's iso-profit curves asymptotes to the nonunion wage line.

A monopoly union maximizes its profit π_u by choosing a wage w_u and employment L_u where a union iso-profit curve is tangent to the labor demand curve. So the union bargains for $w_u = 25$ and $L_u = 50$ at point A.

FIGURE 9.7. Monopoly Union: Preferences, Opportunities, and Choice

Iso-profit curves illustrate the preferences of a profit-maximizing union. The union prefers a higher wage and higher employment, so the ULCW's preference direction is toward the northeast in Figure 9.7. The iso-profit curves slope down and bow toward the origin just like indifference curves with two goods (e.g., consumption and leisure in chapter 3). But here we can be precise. Since union profit is $\pi_u = (w_u - w_n)L_u$, the ULCW's iso-profit curve for $\pi_u = 500$ is $w_u = w_n + 500/L_u$. Each iso-profit curve in Figure 9.7 has the vertical axis as one asymptote and the nonunion wage as another asymptote.

 PRACTICE   In Figure 9.7, shade the set of wage–employment contracts that the ULCW prefers to point A, the monopoly union contract.

To maximize its profit, the ULCW selects a wage–employment pair where one of its iso-profit curves is tangent to the demand curve for its labor. That's point A in Figure 9.7, exactly the solution we had for the monopoly union using the marginal wage bill. Since these are simply two ways to illustrate the same equilibrium, it should be no surprise that (1) ULCW reduces employment to drive up the wage along the demand curve, and (2) the lower employment under the monopoly union is inefficient.

Efficient-Contracting Union

The inefficiency of the monopoly-union equilibrium suggests the following question: "Can the union and the firm bargain to an agreement that they both prefer

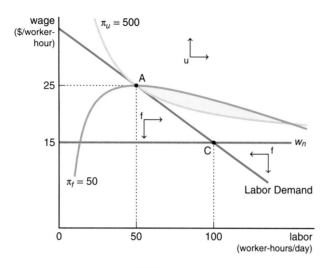

Each of Leisure Lawn's iso-profit curves is a hill that peaks at a point on its labor demand curve.

The intersection of Leisure Lawn's iso-profit curve $\pi_f = 50$ with the ULCW's iso-profit curve $\pi_u = 500$ at the monopoly union contract A defines the shaded set of points southeast of A. Any point in this set is a wage–employment pair that the ULCW and Leisure Lawn prefer to the monopoly union contract. Each side increases profit by moving from A to any point in the shaded set, so the monopoly union contract A can't be efficient.

FIGURE 9.8. Inefficiency of a Monopoly Union

to the monopoly union contract?" Put differently, is there some wage–employment pair that the ULCW and Leisure Lawn prefer to the monopoly union contract at point A in Figure 9.7? Answering these questions lays the foundation for the efficient-contracting model of unions (Leontief 1946). Our analysis builds from the iso-profit curves of firms.

The iso-profit curves of Leisure Lawn and other lawn-care firms are hills (or inverted U-shapes) that peak along the labor demand curve. Leisure Lawn prefers lower wages at any level of employment, so that preference direction is to the south. The labor demand curve guides us in determining Leisure Lawn's preference direction in terms of higher or lower employment. The labor demand curve tells us the quantity of labor that maximizes Leisure Lawn's profit (meaning its most preferred quantity of labor). Therefore, to the left of the labor demand curve, Leisure Lawn prefers higher employment; to the right of the labor demand curve, Leisure Lawn prefers lower employment. (Figure 9.8 displays Leisure Lawn's preference directions.) Consequently, Leisure Lawn's iso-profit curves slope up to the left of the labor demand curve and slope down to the right of the labor demand curve. Each iso-profit curve peaks at a point along the labor demand curve.

 PRACTICE   Figure 9.8 contains one of Leisure Lawn's iso-profit curves. Sketch one or two other iso-profit curves. Clearly indicate the peak of each iso-profit curve.

We see from the two iso-profit curves that cut through point A in Figure 9.8 that there are many wage–employment pairs that both the ULCW and Leisure Lawn prefer to the monopoly union contract. Wage–employment contracts that

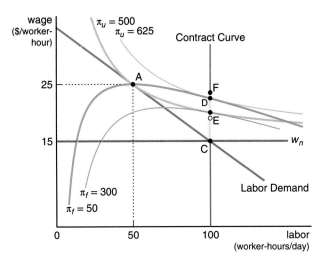

At an efficient bargain, a union iso-profit curve is tangent to a firm iso-profit curve. The vertical line at $l = 100$ is the contract curve, a collection of these efficient contracts.

Even the weakest union doesn't bargain for a wage below w_n, and Leisure Lawn doesn't accept a wage that generates significant losses. So we also trim the contract curve below w_n and above some threshold point F. Between F and C, relative bargaining strength determines the equilibrium, such as at point E. Employment is efficient and independent of the union wage.

FIGURE 9.9. Efficient-Contracting Union

the ULCW prefers to point A are all the points (L_u, w_u) above iso-profit curve $\pi_u = 500$ in Figure 9.8. Leisure Lawn prefers wage–employment contracts below its $\pi_f = 50$ iso-profit curve to the monopoly union contract, point A. These two sets of contracts overlap, and that's incredibly important. It implies that there are collective bargaining agreements that generate higher profit for the ULCW *and* higher profit for Leisure Lawn compared to the monopoly union contract. Switching from the monopoly union contract to one of these contracts improves matters on both sides of the bargaining table.

We have a formal name for this property: any wage–employment pair in the shaded region southeast of point A *Pareto-dominates* the monopoly union contract at point A. Or less formally, the monopoly union contract isn't efficient.

For a wage–employment pair to be efficient, no other wage–employment pair can generate more profit for the union *and* the firm, which means an efficient wage–employment pair can't be Pareto-dominated. Since the hallmark of inefficiency is the shaded region formed by the intersection of the union's and firm's iso-profit curves, efficiency requires that the iso-profit curves across the two sides of the bargaining table don't intersect: they must be tangent. Therefore, an **efficient union contract** is a wage–employment pair where an iso-profit curve of the union is tangent to an iso-profit curve of the firm.

The collection of these tangencies is called the **contract curve**, and points C, D, E, and F in Figure 9.9 are four points on the contract curve. With a profit-maximizing union, the contract curve is a vertical line at the competitive value for employment, so the efficient contracts are the wage–employment pairs along a vertical line at 100 worker-hours per day in Figure 9.9.

To find the equilibrium in the **efficient-contracting model of unions**, we eliminate efficient wage–employment pairs that (1) drive workers to nonunion jobs or (2) drive firms out of business. This involves trimming the contract curve from below and above. First, although wage–employment pairs below point C are efficient, the ULCW can credibly threaten to reject them because those efficient contracts involve wages below the nonunion wage w_n: the lawn-care workers prefer to work at the nonunion wage rather than work at a lower union wage.

Second, we also trim away efficient wage–employment pairs that drive Leisure Lawn out of business. In the short run, the ULCW might be able to drive the union wage so high that the wage bill and other variable costs soak up all of Leisure Lawn's revenue. Leisure Lawn would be unprofitable, and any higher wage causes Leisure Lawn to close shop and eat its losses. That's point F in the figure. (In the long run, the union can't drive the union wage any higher than Leisure Lawn's zero-profit curve at the competitive level of employment, $L = 100$ worker-hours per day in Figure 9.9.) The efficient-contracting equilibrium, therefore, lies on the line segment between points C and F in Figure 9.9.

 PRACTICE   Union contracts below C and above F in the figure are efficient. Why isn't the efficient-contracting equilibrium a point below C or above F?

Bargaining strength determines the equilibrium union contract between points C and F in Figure 9.9. If the ULCW is powerful at the bargaining table, the solution is closer to point F. Perhaps the ULCW's strike fund is flush with cash, so striking lawn-care workers can pay their bills during a long strike. The collective bargaining agreement is closer to point C if Leisure Lawn is a strong bargainer. Perhaps Leisure Lawn can replace the striking workers with capable nonunion workers during a strike. Without replacement workers, Leisure Lawn suffers deep losses during a strike because lawn care is a service rather than a product. For instance, if Leisure Lawn were a manufacturer of lawn equipment like Toro, it could build up an inventory of its product in advance of the contract negotiations. A manufacturer can bargain tough knowing that it can sell its product from inventory in the event of a strike.

The main implication of the efficient-contracting model is that unionization pushes employment off the labor demand curve: the vertical line of efficient wage–employment pairs lies to the right of the labor demand curve. Unions like the ULCW neither increase nor decrease employment. Furthermore, employment in the efficient-contracting model is independent of the union wage. Relative bargaining strengths can push the union wage up or down the trimmed contract curve, but union employment doesn't budge from the competitive level. Thus a key implication of the efficient-contracting model of unions is that union employment is independent of the union wage.

ADVANCED The conclusion that the contract curve is vertical hinges on our specification of the union's preferences over the union wage and union employment. To isolate the impact of bargaining over the wage *and* employment, we retained the natural assumption of the monopoly-union model that the ULCW maximizes its profit, and we depicted its preferences with union iso-profit curves.

In a more general specification, we replace the union iso-profit curves with union indifference curves that slope down and bow toward the origin. An efficient union contract is a point of tangency between one of the ULCW's indifference curves and one of Leisure Lawn's iso-profit curves. The contract curve that collects these points of tangency can slope up or down in this more general specification.

. . . .

9.3   Applications

We now turn to three applications of our union models. First, we compare and contrast the three models. Second, we investigate factors that render labor demand less elastic and monopoly unions more successful. Third, we explore the effects of unions on the wage and employment on nonunion jobs.

Comparing Union Models

What impact do unions have on employment and firm profit, and how does the union wage bargain affect employment and profit in union firms? Answering these questions allows us to sort through the three competing models of unions. In the model of bargaining with a monopsony employer, bargaining collectively increases employment, and a stronger union increases employment along the upward-sloping labor supply curve. In the monopoly-union model, unionization decreases employment as the equilibrium slides up the labor demand curve, and a stronger union decreases employment along the downward-sloping labor demand curve. The employment effect is zero in our specification of the efficient-contracting model, and a stronger union has no effect on union employment.

Although there's plenty of debate in labor economics about the effect of the union wage on union employment, I think it's fair to say that unions reduce employment. The main issue is whether the monopoly-union model paints a complete picture of unions' effect on employment or whether unions push employment beyond the labor demand curve.

Predictions.   Firms suffer substantial losses in market value from successful unionization drives, and the magnitude of the losses might allow us to distinguish among the union models. Do firms' losses from unionization exceed the gains to workers, or vice versa? The answer to that question depends on the union model.

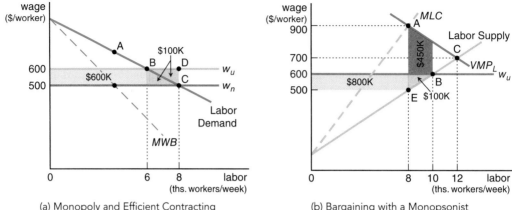

(a) Monopoly and Efficient Contracting   (b) Bargaining with a Monopsonist

(a) An efficient-contracting union bargains for a $600 wage at D. Unionizing transfers $800,000/week, the area of the rectangle defined by points C and D and the vertical axis, from employers to their workers. A monopoly union bargains for B, halfway between C and A. Workers gain $600,000/week, but the damage to employers totals $700,000/week because employers also lose the area of the triangle below the labor demand curve between B and C.

(b) The union bargains the wage up from the monopsony wage of $500 to $600/week, and the monopsonist increases employment. Workers gain $900,000 (= $800,000 + $100,000)/week, while the monopsonist loses $350,000 (= $800,000 − $450,000)/week. The profit the monopsonist generates from the additional 2,000 workers buffers its loss.

FIGURE 9.10. Comparing Models: Worker Gains and Employer Losses from Unionization

    Figure 9.10 illustrates the gains to workers and the losses to their employers from unionization. Prior to unionization, firms employ 8,000 workers and pay each worker a $500 weekly wage. The new union bargains for a $600 weekly wage.

    In the efficient-contracting model, employment remains at 8,000 workers per week. Figure 9.10a depicts this case. The efficient union contract D lies directly above the competitive equilibrium at C. The gain to those workers is $800,000 (= ($600 − $500) × 8000) per week, and the loss to their employers is also $800,000. The gain to workers is matched dollar for dollar by the loss to employers if the collective bargaining agreement is efficient.

    Figure 9.10a also depicts the effects of unionization in the monopoly-union model. The new union exercises all its power to get bargaining agreement B, which lies halfway between the competitive equilibrium C and the monopoly union's ideal contract A. In this contract, employers respond to the union wage premium by reducing employment from 8,000 to 6,000 workers per week. The net gain to workers is $600,000 (= ($600 − $500) × 6000)) per week, but the damage to employers is even bigger. Each of the 6,000 remaining workers receives $100 more per week. This $600,000 loss to firms matches the gain to workers. But firms also lose the profit they earned on the workers who lose their jobs. This amount is $100,000 (= ($600 − $500) × 2000 ÷ 2), which is the area of the right triangle below the labor demand curve between B and C. So unionization damages employers to the tune of $700,000 per week. In the monopoly-union model, therefore, workers' gains from unionization translate *more than* dollar for dollar into employer losses.

 PRACTICE

In the monopoly-union model, firms maximize profit by cutting employment in response to the union wage bargain. Firms lose less by cutting employment. In Figure 9.10a, how much bigger would firms' losses be if they didn't cut employment from 8,000 to 6,000 workers per week?

In the model of bargaining with a monopsony employer, workers' gains from unionization translate *less than* dollar for dollar into employer losses. That is, workers gain more than firms lose. Figure 9.10b demonstrates this principle. Our starting point is the monopsony equilibrium E in which 8,000 workers receive a weekly wage of $500 per worker. The new union bargains for a $600 wage, which is halfway between the monopsony wage and the competitive wage at C, and the monopsonist reacts to the union wage by increasing employment to 10,000 workers per week. The net gain to the delighted workers is $900,000 per week, which includes a $100,000-per-week net gain to the extra 2,000 workers. Unionization damages the monopsony employer, but the firm loses less than workers gain. In particular, the monopsonist takes a hit by paying every one of the original 8,000 workers an extra $100 per week. But the profit the monopsonist earns on the 2,000 extra workers, which is $450,000 per week, partially offsets that weekly loss of $800,000. So the net loss to the monopsony employer is $350,000 (= $800,000 − $450,000), much less than the gain to its workers.

So our three union models carry three different predictions for the effect of unionization on firms' losses relative to workers' gains. In the efficient-contracting model, workers' gains from unionization equal employers' losses. In the monopoly-union model, employers' losses exceed the gains to workers. But the workers' gains from unionization exceed the losses to their employer if the union bargains with a monopsonist.

Formal Evidence.   Using data on petitions to unionize and certification elections, Ruback and Zimmerman (1984) estimate that a successful unionization drive decreases the stock-market value of a firm by nearly 4 percent. Ruback and Zimmerman also express firms' losses in per-worker terms. Firms lose $139,250 per worker (in 2017 dollars) as a result of unionization. Do workers gain that much? To answer this question, let's express the $139,250 loss per worker in weekly terms for comparison with a worker's weekly wage gain. How much must weekly costs per worker rise to cut the present value of the firm's profit $139,250 per worker? The answer depends on the rate that the firm discounts future profits. The discount rate depends on the firm's risk of going belly-up in any year, as well as the interest rate, so an 8 percent annual discount rate probably isn't excessive.

The present value of $214 per week is $139,250 if the firm discounts future profits at 8 percent per year. That is, we estimate that unionization increases weekly costs by $214 per worker, which we compare to a typical worker's gain in weekly wages from unionization. In a standardized comparison, the union wage premium is 15 percent. (See Figure 9.3.) That's a weekly wage premium of $149 per worker. So our estimate of the increase in cost (i.e., $214 per worker per week) is almost 50 percent bigger than our estimate of the increase in the wage (i.e., $149 per worker per week). This evidence supports the monopoly-union model since the firm loses more than its workers gain.

The calculations, however, are sensitive to the discount rate that we use to compute the present value. Firms discount the future at much higher rates than a risk-free interest rate. An 8 percent discount rate might be reasonable. But a lower discount rate delivers a lower weekly loss per worker and weakens the evidence in favor of the monopoly-union model. Indeed, the gap between the loss per worker and the wage premium vanishes if the discount rate is as low as 5 percent.

Evidence from stock-market responses to bargaining agreements establishes that union gains at the bargaining table translate into large losses to their employers. The magnitude of those losses might also help us distinguish among the models. Since predictable outcomes of collective bargaining agreements are old news, they don't influence stock prices at the time of the agreement. Surprise outcomes are what move the firm's market value. To study the impact on a firm's market value of surprise wins and losses in thousands of bargaining agreements, Abowd (1989) split changes in union profit into predictable and surprise components. Abowd then calculated how a surprise win that is worth, for example, $10 million to the union over the course of the contract translates into a loss in the firm's market value.

Evidence from surprises at the bargaining table aren't consistent with the monopoly-union model. Abowd (1989, Table 4, column F) calculates that a surprise $10 million union win at the bargaining table translates into a $6.3 million loss to shareholders (i.e., less than dollar for dollar), which is consistent with unions bargaining with monopsonists. Abowd's estimate, however, isn't precise enough to reject the hypothesis that the true effect is dollar for dollar, so these results are also consistent with the efficient-contracting model.

The formal evidence is decidedly mixed. Ruback and Zimmerman's (1984) evidence from successful unionization drives supports the monopoly-union model. Abowd's (1989) evidence from bargaining surprises doesn't. Let's turn to less-formal methods to sort through the competing models of unionism.

Informal Evidence.   Union contracts rarely specify employment, a fact that casts doubt on the efficient-contracting model. But union work rules do push labor on employers. For instance, by limiting class size, unions push teachers on school districts. Is adding teachers efficient? There's more to limiting class size than pushing teachers on school districts. Class size is an attribute of the job: smaller classes mean less work for each teacher, but that's *not* part of the efficient-contracting model. Indeed, small class sizes are an extremely expensive employee benefit that has little if any positive effect on student performance. In an efficient contract, classes are bigger.

Limiting class size is an example of a union work rule that pushes labor on employers. Work rules that push labor on employers might be consistent with efficient contracting, but work rules frequently amount to **featherbedding**—pay for little or no work or for work that is discarded. (Featherbedding was banned in 1947 by the Taft–Hartley Act, but courts have interpreted featherbedding narrowly, and the practice continues.)

The inefficiency of featherbedding is obvious in the following notorious historical examples: painters' unions limit the size of paint brushes and the use of spray equipment and have even required painting pre-painted pipes with a dry brush. Electrical unions have required the wiring of factory-wired switchboards to be torn out and rewired by union workers. For decades after diesel locomotives replaced steam locomotives, each train was required to have a fireman to shovel nonexistent coal into a nonexistent boiler. And railroad unions limited the workday of a train crew to 108 miles, so crews were paid a full day for a few hours of work, and trains carried multiple nonworking crews. The union of typographical workers required resetting of advertising copy that came already typeset by the advertisers and has required digitally typeset news copy to be typeset manually and then discarded. Stagehands' unions set the minimum size of the crew and even require a stage crew for performances that have no scenery. Musicians' local unions require employment of standby musicians when an out-of-town orchestra or band performs. Skilled craftsmen are sometimes required to do unskilled work like operating an elevator.

Several of these examples follow from union attempts to stifle efficiency-enhancing innovation. As these examples highlight, the efficient-contracting model finds no support in the inefficiencies of featherbedding.

Recipe for a Successful Monopoly Union

Since unions prefer higher employment to lower employment and higher wages to lower wages, a monopoly union's success hinges on its ability to raise the demand for its labor and to lower the elasticity of demand for its labor. Job loss tempers the benefit to a monopoly union of raising the wage of its union members. Employment falls less where the demand for labor is less elastic (i.e., labor demand is steeper), and the monopoly union responds to a less-elastic demand for its labor by choosing a higher union wage. Overall, the monopoly union is more successful where the demand for its labor is less elastic. The monopoly-union model, therefore, predicts that workers unionize in contexts where demand for their labor is less elastic.

Parable of the UAW.   Let's start with a parable about workers in an industry with several firms and a product demand that isn't very elastic. This is a parable, but let's give the players names. The industry is the U.S. auto industry without unions and before competition from foreign carmakers was serious. Automakers in the United States would share the monopoly profit if they could reduce quantity supplied to the monopoly level and drive up the price of cars to the monopoly price by a collusive agreement. Collusion is illegal in the United States, and it tends to fail because each firm's incentive is to produce more than its share of monopoly output. To the benefit of U.S. car buyers, collusion among the big three automakers fails, and the auto industry remains competitive.

Next, workers unionize. If the autoworkers at Ford (and only Ford) unionize, driving up costs and lowering Ford's profit, they send business to nonunion General Motors and Chrysler, and union employment plummets. Alternatively, autoworkers form the United Auto Workers (UAW) to unionize the auto industry—General Motors, Ford, and Chrysler. The UAW raises the wage, which shifts up marginal cost at each automaker and reduces the supply of cars. The equilibrium slides up the demand curve for cars.

If the demand for cars isn't very elastic, much of the increases in wages and costs is passed on to car buyers in the form of higher car prices. In fact, there's one value of the union wage that increases marginal cost and decreases the supply of cars by enough that the equilibrium slides up the car-demand curve all the way to the monopoly equilibrium. By choosing this wage, the UAW implements the monopoly equilibrium in the market for cars and effectively cartelizes the industry. The monopoly profit from car sales, of course, flows directly from car buyers to the autoworkers, skipping past the owners of General Motors, Ford, and Chrysler.

 **PRACTICE** The Railway Labor Act of 1926 mandated collective bargaining for workers in all interstate railroads, even railroads where unions hadn't been successful. The Interstate Commerce Commission fixed rail rates on the basis of costs, so higher union wages were passed on to shippers in the form of higher rates to ship cargo. Carefully explain how this act enabled rail workers to share in the bounty of cartelizing the railroads.

Marshall's Rules. This parable illustrates an important principle: workers are more successful organizing a whole industry because the demand for labor is less elastic at the industry level, and less-elastic labor demand encourages bigger union wage gains with smaller job losses. Why is labor demand less elastic at the industry level? Product demand at a competitive firm is perfectly elastic at the market price of the product. Introducing the union wage drives up marginal cost, and the competitive firm reduces supply, sending plenty of its sales to other firms and its workers to nonunion jobs. (It would lose *all* its business if it raised its price.)

Product demand at the market or industry level slopes down—it's less elastic. Applying the union wage to all firms in the industry reduces supply, and product price rises up the less than perfectly elastic product-demand curve. Unionization of the whole industry causes product price to rise, which buffers some of the blow to employment. Less-elastic demand for the product at the industry level translates into less-elastic labor demand at the industry level. Therefore, workers organizing a whole industry can increase their wage without losing as many jobs (in percentage terms).

The difficulty of organizing farm workers in the United States illustrates how an elastic demand for labor can be linked to elastic supplies of other inputs. In response to unionization efforts and demands for higher wages in the 1950s and early 1960s, farmers substituted *braceros*, seasonal workers from Mexico. Having plenty of willing and able workers across the border made it easy to replace the unionizing farm workers. In the longer run, farmers could also substitute out of high-priced farm workers into capital equipment, such as tractors, tillers, and harvesters, which are elastically supplied. Substituting other inputs for labor without driving up the wages or prices of these other inputs isn't a recipe for union success. Indeed, workers' organizing efforts are more successful if employers' attempts to substitute other inputs for union labor drive up the prices (and wages) of these other inputs. Therefore, a less-elastic supply of other inputs helps workers raise their wage with fewer jobs lost. As such, it is an ingredient for a successful union.

Airline pilot unions in the United States are quite successful, and the source of their success is that the demand for pilots isn't elastic. Pilot unions can increase the pay of pilots with few jobs lost in the cockpit. Higher pilot pay pushes up the marginal cost of air travel (although the cost of pilots is a small part of the marginal cost of flights), so employment of pilots falls by the scale effect. The substitution effect, however, is small: airlines can't substitute flight attendants, baggage handlers, or jet fuel for pilots, although they can fly bigger planes (i.e., increase capital) with a smaller workforce of pilots. The technologically driven limit on substitutability generates a less-elastic demand for pilots. Therefore, airline pilot unions can raise pilots' pay with little loss of employment. More generally, limited substitutability among inputs is an ingredient for union success.

The preceding examples apply the monopoly-union model to Marshall's rules from chapter 4 (Marshall 1920 [1890], Book 5, chapter 12). In general, a union is more successful where the demand for its labor is less elastic, which is where (1) demand for the product or service is less elastic; (2) supplies of other inputs, such as physical capital and other types of labor, are less elastic; and (3) union labor is less substitutable with other inputs.

Key Principle.
Unions are more successful where demand for the product of their labor and the supply of other inputs are less elastic.

 PRACTICE   Work rules in many union contracts limit employers' ability to substitute physical capital and nonunion labor for union labor. Carefully explain how these rules affect the elasticity of demand for union labor.

Unions and Politics.   But institutions matter, and Marshall's rules also help us understand the political positions that unions take by identifying the laws and regulations that enrich unions. A public policy that increases the demand for union labor and decreases the elasticity of demand for union labor raises union profit, and unions actively support the policy with political contributions and votes. Which public policies push labor on employers and render the demand for union labor less elastic? Let's consider a few.

A monopoly union favors high tariffs and tight quotas on imported goods because protectionism raises the demand for labor in protected industries (at the expense of jobs in export industries) and lowers the elasticity of demand for the products of union labor. Protectionism shifts sales from imports to domestically produced products and jobs from the export sector to the protected industries, which benefits workers, including union workers, in protected industries. But trade restrictions, such as tariffs and quotas on imports, also reduce the elasticity of demand for the domestically produced goods. For instance, the demand for American cars is less elastic because "Detroit" can limit imports of Hondas, Mazdas, and Toyotas. Without restrictions on foreign imports, raising the wage of auto workers reduces the domestic supply of cars, driving car sales abroad and jobs to the nonunion sector. With imports restricted, the union wage reduces the domestic supply of cars, but the equilibrium slides up the domestic auto-demand curve. The price of cars rises, which buffers some of the blow to the jobs of autoworkers. Sales of fewer cars are lost to foreign competition, and fewer jobs shift from the unionized auto industry to other industries. Protectionism lowers the elasticity of demand for labor in a protected industry, and a monopoly union responds by demanding a higher wage. Unions have always enthusiastically supported trade restrictions because they deliver bigger union wage gains with fewer union jobs lost.

A monopoly union favors immigration restrictions because limiting the flow of immigrants raises the demand for skilled union workers and lowers the elasticity of supply of nonunion labor. Restricting immigration of typically less-skilled workers increases the demand for more-skilled resident workers, which benefits resident workers, including union workers. But immigration restrictions also lower the elasticity of supply of alternatives to union labor. Recall how the large pool of seasonal workers from Mexico (i.e., *braceros*) raised the elasticity of supply of alternatives to union farm labor. By lowering the elasticity of supply of alternatives to union farm workers, restricting immigration (including ending the *bracero* program in 1964) lowers the elasticity of demand for unionized farm labor, and a monopoly union responds by demanding a higher wage while losing fewer jobs. Indeed, farm workers didn't successfully unionize until the federal government prevented seasonal workers from Mexico from crossing the border to work on American farms. Through the lens of monopoly unions and Marshall's rules, unions' influential support of immigration restrictions is no surprise.

A monopoly union also supports minimum wages because high-skill union workers benefit by raising the wage of their lower-skill substitutes. The minimum wage shifts employment from low-skill workers to high-skill workers, which benefits union workers. But the minimum wage also lowers the elasticity of supply of low-skill alternatives to union workers, such as teenagers and high school dropouts. As ending the *bracero* program dried up the pool of replacement farm workers, the minimum wage shrinks the pool of low-skill substitutes for union labor. By lowering the supply of low-skill alternatives to union labor, the minimum wage lowers the elasticity of demand for unionized labor, and a monopoly union responds by demanding a higher wage while losing fewer jobs. That unions have long been enthusiastic and influential supporters of higher minimum wages should be no surprise.

Monopoly unions working on federal contracts also benefit from the Davis–Bacon Act of 1931, which requires the federal government to pay prevailing wages. Davis–Bacon prevents nonunion federal contractors from underbidding union contractors because the prevailing wage has always been interpreted to be the union wage. By preventing the federal government from substituting lower-wage nonunion workers for higher-wage union workers, Davis–Bacon insulates union workers from nonunion competition in public-works projects. This insulation lowers the elasticity of demand for union workers on federal projects, and a monopoly union responds by demanding a higher wage. Unions always vocally oppose suspensions and outright repeal of Davis–Bacon.

A monopoly union also favors occupational licensing to limit the supply of nonunion labor. Success of a monopoly hinges on its ability to prevent the entry that the monopoly price invites, and that goes for a monopoly union, too. Suppose the plumbers' union acts as a monopoly seller. It can raise the wage of plumbers only by reducing the employment of plumbers, but the union wage in plumbing lures other workers into the lucrative field of plumbing *as nonunion workers*. Success of the plumbers' union depends on its ability to limit entry of the nonunion workers, and licensing is one of the tools to limit entry. Occupational licensing requirements artificially hold down the number of nonunion workers to elevate the wage of union workers. So it's not surprising that unions strongly support occupational licensing.

A monopoly union advocates work-rule regulations that masquerade as safety regulations. We have already examined how featherbedding pushes union labor on employers. What's new here is that safety rules that specify the number of workers per piece of equipment (e.g., per train, per movie projector) also limit or even eliminate the employer's ability to substitute other inputs for union labor along an isoquant curve. Limiting substitutability reduces the elasticity of demand for union labor, which leads to a higher union wage with fewer jobs lost. So it shouldn't be surprising that unions are vocal supporters of safety regulations, even when the regulations' apparent purpose is to improve the safety of consumers rather than workers.

These predictions about union policy positions follow from applying the monopoly-union model to Marshall's rules, and they are right on target. To the extent these predictions follow from the effect of the law or regulation on the elasticity of demand for union labor, the evidence favors the monopoly-union model over the bargaining-with-a-monopsonist or the efficient-contracting model of unions.

Key Principle.
Unions support government policies that reduce the elasticities of demand for the product and supply of other inputs.

Decline of Unions.   What explains over four decades of declining union membership in the United States? Since unions have declined throughout the developed world (see Table 9.1), pinning blame on U.S. government policies provides at best an incomplete explanation. Structural shifts from unionized manufacturing jobs to nonunion service and information jobs also falls short (explaining perhaps one-fourth of the decline in the United States) because union membership has fallen even within narrowly defined industries and occupations.

What drivers of union success have changed throughout the developed world? The world is evolving toward globalization with a rapid pace of innovation. It's becoming more competitive and dynamic, and private-sector unions don't do well in a highly competitive world. Competition limits the success of unions. (Public-sector unions, absent the usual competitive pressures of the market, can continue to thrive.) So the leading candidate to explain the decline of private-sector unions in the United States and other developed countries is the rise of global competitiveness and dynamics.

Effects of Unions on Nonunion Wages

Unions directly control the wages of their workers, and they indirectly impact the wages of nonunion workers. When I was 16 years old working as a car hop at Steak 'n Shake, my father told me that the only reason I earned as much as $3 per hour (including tips) was that the local Ford and General Electric plants were paying $18 per hour to their inexperienced union workers. He was referring to what we call the **union threat effect**: nonunion firms pay their workers more to reduce the risk of their workers unionizing. It never dawned on my father that a second effect of the unions at Ford and General Electric pushed in the opposite direction, lowering my pay at Steak 'n Shake: people who can't find work in the high-wage union sector spill over into nonunion jobs, driving wages down there.

The union threat effect involves nonunion firms offering higher wages to reduce workers' incentives to unionize. Since unionizing is costly, Leisure Lawn doesn't have to pay its nonunion workers the union wage to keep them from unionizing, but paying a higher nonunion wage renders the ULCW union less attractive to the lawn-care workers. The threat of unionization typically causes firms like Leisure Lawn to pay a bit more, accepting the certain increase in labor costs of its nonunion workforce to lower the risk of a bigger increase in labor costs of a union workforce.

Workers displaced by the union wage in the union sector spill over to the nonunion sector, raising employment and lowering the wage there. Let's apply chapter 2's model of a minimum wage with an uncovered sector to the union context. The three-panel diagram in Figure 9.11 illustrates these **union spillover effects** from manufacturing to retail. Before manufacturing workers unionize, the wage and employment are determined in one labor market, panel (a) of Figure 9.11. The demand for labor, which is the sum of labor demands in manufacturing and retail, interacts with the supply of labor to determine the equilibrium wage ($15 per hour) and employment (100 million worker-hours per week), point E in panel (a). Tracing the $15 hourly wage to panels (b) and (c)

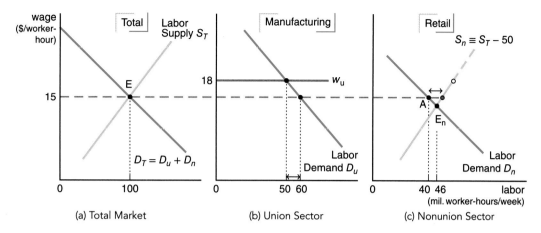

Point E is the no-union equilibrium, and the $15/hour equilibrium wage yields employment of 60 and 40 million worker-hours/week in the two sectors. Manufacturing workers unionize and bargain an $18/hour wage. Manufacturing employment falls, and 10 million worker-hours spill over to nonunion retail. For $w_n < 18$, quantity supplied of labor in retail is the total quantity supplied of labor from panel (a) minus the 50 million worker-hours in manufacturing. This new labor supply curve is 10 million worker-hours to the right of point A. Not all the displaced labor is employable in retail firms at $15/hour, so the nonunion wage falls.

Unionization increases the union wage, shrinks employment in the union sector, expands employment in the nonunion sector, lowers the nonunion wage, and reduces employment overall. The resulting allocation of labor across sectors is inefficient.

FIGURE 9.11. Union Spillover Effects

reveals equilibrium employment in the two sectors: 60 million worker-hours per week in manufacturing and 40 million worker-hours per week in retail.

Workers in manufacturing unionize, and their monopoly union sets the hourly wage at $18. Employment in manufacturing slides up the manufacturing labor demand curve in Figure 9.11b. Manufacturing employment fall from 60 to 50 million worker-hours per week, and the remaining 10 million worker-hours of labor spill over into retail.

To determine the effect of the spillover into retail, we need to derive the supply of labor to retail in the presence of the $18 union wage in manufacturing. (Without the union in manufacturing, neither sector has its own upward-sloping labor supply curve; there's the upward-sloping labor supply curve in the combined market S_T and perfectly elastic (i.e., flat) labor supply curves at the competitive wage in manufacturing and retail.) With the union wage in manufacturing, the supply of labor in retail is the supply of labor in the whole labor market minus employment in manufacturing (for $w_n < 18$). For instance, if the retail wage w_n remained at $15 per hour, then the quantity supplied of labor would remain at 100 million worker-hours per week. Of those worker-hours, 50 million would be in manufacturing, so the quantity supplied of labor in retail at $w_n = 15$ would be 50 million worker-hours per week. Thus one point on retail's labor supply curve is 10 million worker-hours per week to the right of point A. And the slope of the labor supply curve in retail is the slope of the total labor-supply curve (up to $w_n = 18$). Figure 9.11c plots retail's labor supply curve.

The new equilibrium in retail slides down retail's labor demand curve, increasing employment and decreasing the wage in retail. As drawn, the retail sector absorbs 6 million of the 10 million worker-hours of labor. The other 4 million worker-hours aren't employed. The hourly wage in retail falls to $14. Unionizing manufacturing jobs increases the manufacturing wage, shifts employment from manufacturing to retail, and reduces the wage in retail.

 PRACTICE   Suppose the labor supply curve S_T is less elastic (i.e., steeper in Figure 9.11a). How do the new equilibrium wage and employment in retail compare with the equilibrium in retail as Figure 9.11 illustrates? Does less-elastic labor supply produce a higher or lower wage in retail? Is employment in retail higher or lower?

Some workers displaced by the union wage might wait for jobs in manufacturing. Searching for a union job in manufacturing while unemployed might be as valuable (in present value terms) as being employed at the lower wage in retail. In this case, the union wage in manufacturing causes unemployment but doesn't lower the wage in retail as much as Figure 9.11 illustrates.

With a nonunion sector, a monopoly union causes an inefficient allocation of labor across the two sectors: manufacturing is too small, and retail is too big. In the monopoly-union equilibrium in Figure 9.11, labor's values of marginal product are $18 per worker-hour in manufacturing and $14 per worker-hour in retail. Shifting one hour of a worker's time from retail to manufacturing lifts the combined value of production by $4 (= $18 − $14). The same principle applies to every hour of labor where labor's value of marginal product in manufacturing exceeds its value of marginal product in retail. Again, efficiency requires that the value of marginal product of labor be equated across all markets.

How well does the union wage premium—the wage gap between union and nonunion workers—measure the effect of unions on the wages of union workers? Unless the threat and spillover effects of unions exactly offset, the union wage premium reflects the effect of unions on nonunion wages, as well as its effect on union wages. Part of the union–nonunion wage premium is due to unions increasing the wages of their workers; the other part of the union–nonunion wage gap is the effect of unions on nonunion wages. If the threat effect is particularly strong, the union wage premium understates the effect of unions on the wages of union workers. Alternatively, if the spillover effect is particularly strong, the union wage premium exaggerates the effect of unions on their workers' wages.

Summary

This chapter opened with a detailed history of unionism in the United States. We also explored how wages and employment are determined in three models of unions: the model of bargaining with a monopsony employer, the monopoly-union model, and the efficient-contracting model. Our key findings are:

☐ The rise of unions in the twentieth century followed passage of important pro-union legislation, especially the Wagner Act of 1935. Membership in private-sector unions has declined over the past four decades, and only 6–7 percent of jobs in the private sector are currently unionized. Union membership of government workers took off in the 1960s and 1970s, and public-sector unions continue to thrive: 34 percent of jobs in the public sector are currently unionized.

☐ Union workers earn 15–20 percent more than comparable nonunion workers, and this union wage premium has trended down toward 15 percent over the past three decades.

☐ Underpaid workers who unionize to bargain collectively against a monopsony employer increase the wage and increase employment. The source of this surprising result is that the monopsony employer's gain from reducing employment (i.e., driving down the wage) is lost when it faces a fixed union wage.

☐ In a monopoly union, workers organize to raise pay above the competitive wage, and employers respond by decreasing employment along the labor demand curve. Employment in the monopoly-union equilibrium equates the marginal wage bill with the nonunion wage.

☐ The monopoly union contract is inefficient because employment falls in response to the union wage. Indeed, other wage–employment pairs yield higher profits for both the union and the employer, improving matters on both sides of the bargaining table.

☐ An efficient-contracting union pushes labor on employers—beyond the labor demand curve and up to the competitive level for employment. Relative bargaining strength determines the union wage. Union employment is independent of the union wage.

☐ Evidence of union effects on stock prices doesn't allow us to confidently choose between the monopoly-union and efficient-contracting models. But (1) featherbedding's inefficiencies and (2) union support of government policies that reduce the elasticity of demand for its labor favor the monopoly-union model.

☐   Success of a monopoly union hinges on its ability to raise the wage of its workers without suffering significant job loss. That is, a monopoly union is more successful where the demand for its labor is less elastic. Unions support government policies—including immigration restrictions and minimum wages—that decrease the elasticity of demand for their labor.

☐   Unions influence nonunion wages in two ways. First, the threat of unionization can increase the wages of nonunion workers. Second, employment in the unionized sector shrinks as a result of monopoly unions, and the spillover of workers to the nonunion sector reduces the wages of nonunion workers.

This chapter completes our study of the primary factors that explain variation in average wages across occupations and among workers. In the next chapter, we turn our attention from *averages* of wages to the *dispersion* of wages. For instance, why is the distribution of wages skewed to the right?

Key Concepts

- collective bargaining agreement, p. 327
- nonunion pledge or yellow-dog contract, p. 329
- union wage premium, p. 333
- bargaining with a monopsonist, p. 337
- monopoly union, p. 339
- union profit, p. 339
- wage bill, p. 339
- opportunity cost of union labor, p. 339

- marginal wage bill, p. 339
- iso-profit curves, p. 343
- efficient union contract, p. 345
- contract curve, p. 345
- efficient-contracting model of unions, p. 345
- featherbedding, p. 351
- union threat effect, p. 356
- union spillover effects, p. 356

Short-Answer Questions

9.1 What makes it difficult for unions to succeed in the absence of any laws to help or to hinder unions? Identify several features from one or two laws or court rulings that helped unions overcome these difficulties.

9.2 Summarize how private- and public-sector unions have evolved differently since the 1960s.

9.3 A small hospital in rural Alaska is a monopsony employer of nurses. The nurses unionize. They have little power at the bargaining table, but they do bargain for a slightly higher wage. What happens to the number of nurses employed? What happens to labor costs and marginal labor costs?

9.4 We explored two flavors of the monopoly-union model. One flavor's equilibrium is point A in Figure 9.6. The equilibrium lies between points A and C in the other flavor. What's the key difference between the two?

9.5 Suppose E is a union contract between A and C in Figure 9.8, and it's the best the ULCW can get by bargaining as a monopoly union. Sketch the set of contracts that both the union and the employer prefer to contract E.

9.6 Why are pairs of union wages and union employment above point F in Figure 9.9 excluded from the set of equilibrium union contracts for an efficient-contracting union? Are they inefficient?

9.7 Why are Marshall's rules important for determining the success of monopoly unions?

9.8 Explain how protectionism—tariffs and quotas that restrict imports—influences the elasticity of demand for domestic labor.

Problems

9.1 A fabric mill in rural South Carolina is the only employer in town. The figure below depicts three curves: the mill's value of marginal product of labor VMP_L, labor supply, and marginal labor cost MLC. The MLC curve is drawn assuming that workers aren't unionized.

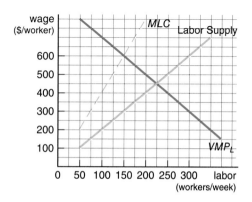

(a) If workers don't bargain collectively, the profit-maximizing mill employs _____ workers per week and pays a weekly wage of $_____ per worker. Mark this point with an A in the figure above.

(b) The mill workers unionize and successfully bargain for a $350 wage. How does this union wage affect the mill's marginal-labor-cost curve? Carefully illustrate the two parts of the new *MLC* curve.

(c) How many workers are employed in the equilibrium with $w_u = 350$? Illustrate the equilibrium with a B in the figure.

(d) A ruling by the NLRB limits the mill's ability to operate during a strike, which increases the union's bargaining strength. The union threatens to strike if the mill doesn't raise the weekly wage to $400. The mill concedes. Illustrate the new union equilibrium with a C. How does employment of union workers vary with the union wage in this model?

(e) Apply this model to predict the effect of a minimum wage in a monopsony labor market. Assume the minimum wage is less than the wage in the competitive equilibrium.

9.2 A union bargains collectively for workers in a hospital. The union's objective is to maximize its profit, which is the wage bill $w_u L_u$ minus the opportunity cost of the workers $w_n L_u$. The hourly wage on nonunion jobs w_n is $10 per worker.

The table below lists the hospital's labor demand schedule. The figure below plots its labor demand curve.

LABOR (workers/hour)	WAGE ($/worker)	WAGE BILL ($/hour)	MARGINAL WAGE BILL ($/worker)
0	30	0	
10			——
20	25		
30			——
40	20		
50			——
60	15		
70			——
80	10		
90			——
100	5		
110			——
120	0	0	

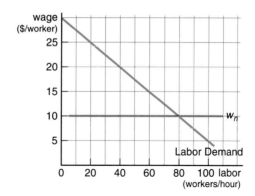

(a) Without the union, the hospital employs workers in a competitive labor market. How many workers does it employ per hour, and what is its hourly cost of labor?

(b) For each row in the table with a wage, compute the wage bill.

(c) Compute the marginal wage bill over the ranges of employment from 0 to 20, 20 to 40, 40 to 60, and so on. In the last column, enter each marginal wage bill on the appropriate line.

(d) Plot the combinations of labor (as the midpoint in the range) and the marginal wage bill in the figure for labor up to $L_u = 70$. Connect the dots to illustrate the marginal-wage-bill curve.

(e) The union behaves as a monopoly seller of labor. How many workers does the hospital employ in the monopoly-union equilibrium?

(f) In the monopoly–union equilibrium, what is the union wage? Plot the equilibrium in the figure.

(g) As a consequence of union wage bargaining in the hospital, how many workers spill over to the nonunion sector?

9.3 In the figure below, two sets of iso-profit curves illustrate the preferences on the two sides of the bargaining table.

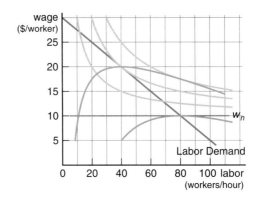

(a) The union's preference direction is toward the _____.

(b) Which curves are the union's iso-profit curves?

(c) Label the point that represents the monopoly union contract with an A. That is, which point in the figure maximizes the union's profit given the hospital's demand for labor?

(d) Which curves in the figure are the hospital's iso-profit curves?

(e) Use the two iso-profit curves through the monopoly union contract to define the set of wage–employment pairs that both the union and the hospital prefer to contract A. Shade in this set of contracts.

(f) Which points represent efficient bargains between the hospital and its workers? Illustrate the contract curve in the figure.

(g) If the hospital employs 80 workers per hour at an hourly wage of $20 per worker, its profit is zero. Mark this point in the figure. Illustrate the range of efficient wage–employment pairs that are profitable to the hospital and its union.

(h) Among these efficient contracts, what determines the unique efficient-contracting equilibrium?

References

Abowd, John. 1989. "The Effect of Wage Bargains on the Stock Market Value of the Firm." *American Economic Review* 79(4): 774–800.

Dunlop, John. 1944. *Wage Determination Under Trade Unions*. New York: Macmillan.

Krueger, Alan B. and Alexandre Mas. 2004. "Strikes, Scabs, and Tread Separations: Labor Strife and the Production of Defective Bridgestone/Firestone Tires." *Journal of Political Economy* 112(2): 253–289.

Leontief, Wassily. 1946. "The Pure Theory of the Guaranteed Annual Wage Contract." *Journal of Political Economy* 54(1): 76–79.

Marshall, Alfred. 1920 (1890). *Principles of Economics: An Introductory Volume*, 8th ed. London: Macmillan.

Ruback, Richard and Martin Zimmerman. 1984. "Unionization and Profitability: Evidence from the Capital Market." *Journal of Political Economy* 92(6): 1134–1157.

10 Wage Inequality

Computers have changed everything, even the distribution of wages. The price of computing has fallen rapidly over several decades, and businesses have responded. Computers are unrivaled at carrying out tedious calculations and storing information, so technology has replaced many low-level workers. For instance, computerized switches now route telephone calls, and telephone switchboard operators are found only in black-and-white movies. Computers also generate data, the information for decision makers. With more information, managers make more decisions and better decisions. Information arrives more quickly, so managers respond more quickly. Decentralized authority throughout the business organization replaces top-down rules. Business organizations become more flexible. All this information places a premium on workers' cognitive skills.

In terms of the tools of economics, the falling price of computing increased the quantity demanded of computing in business. Computers are *substitutes* for workers on many low-level jobs, so the demand for unskilled labor fell. Computing and skilled labor are *complements*; the fall in the price of computing raised the demand for skilled labor. The full response takes time: as firms adapt to the information age, they reorganize the workplace to take advantage of the flow of information. Workers throughout the business organization become decision makers. The reorganization craves cognition, further increasing the demand for skilled labor in the long run. The skilled get richer, and the less skilled get poorer. Wage inequality increases.

The computer revolution is only the latest manifestation of innovations that increase the demand for skills. Starting with the electrification of production, the twentieth century was a period of continual innovation that increased the demand for skilled workers, even skilled blue-collar workers, relative to the demand for unskilled laborers. For much of the nineteenth century, however, innovation involved shifting production from skilled artisans (e.g., weavers and gunmakers) to factories where complex tasks were simplified and standardized to be executed repetitively by workers with few skills. Innovations like interchangeable parts and the assembly line continued the shift away from skilled workers. So the computer revolution isn't unique in transforming the workplace and shaping the distribution of wages.

Why do different people receive different wages? That's a question about wage inequality. It's also a question we've been answering chapter by chapter. For instance, in our model of schooling choice, educated workers earn higher wages to compensate them for delaying their wages, as well as for tuition, while they attend school. Schooling and other variables from our models explain how much wage inequality? Do our models explain why wages at the top of the wage distribution are so high, why the "1 percent" make so much?

J.K. Rowling has amassed immense wealth by delivering boundless joy to hundreds of millions of readers of her *Harry Potter* books. Others become rich through theft, corruption, and political pull. Rowling grew rich by creating value; riches acquired through theft don't create value. Most of us don't object to riches that follow from honest value-creating effort; some of us even find value-creation heroic. No one admires the people who embezzle their way to riches. These are ethical issues, and they're missing from our exploration of the wage inequality in this chapter. You will have to satisfy your thirst for knowledge about the ethics and politics of inequality elsewhere.

The goal of this chapter is to understand wage inequality. Here we develop the tools to measure wage inequality and the principles to explain it. We also (1) apply the tools and principles to the evolution of wage inequality since 1940 and (2) look to the future to evaluate the prospects for automation-driven job loss.

10.1 Measuring Wage Inequality

One of the most important principles of labor economics is that the amount a worker is paid is far from arbitrary. As we have seen in the preceding nine chapters, differences across workers in the workweek, schooling, work experience, sex and race, and union membership explain much of the differences in weekly wages across workers in competitive labor markets. "How big are the differences in wages across workers?" Answering this question focuses on the distribution of wages across workers and offers a fresh perspective on essentially the same issue.

Let's begin by plotting the distribution of wages in the Current Population Survey and proceed by introducing a few statistics that measure wage dispersion and asymmetry.

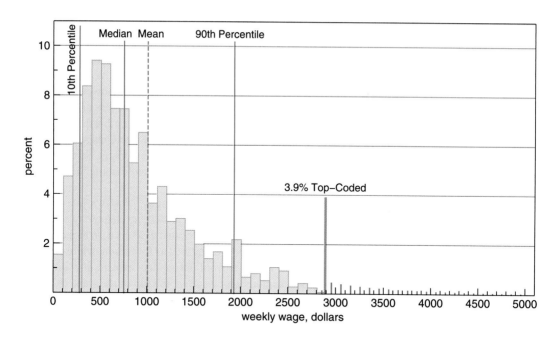

FIGURE 10.1. Distribution of Weekly Wages, 2017
Notes: The CPS top-codes weekly wages at $2,884, and 3.9 percent of the wage and salary workers earn at least $2,884 per week. Thin vertical lines display estimates of the histogram bars above $2,884.
Source: Current Population Survey, outgoing rotation group files, monthly 2017.

Dispersion

We illustrate the distribution of wages with a **histogram**, a bar chart that displays proportions (or percentages) over fixed-width intervals of wages. Figure 10.1 depicts the histogram of weekly wages from the outgoing rotation groups from over 156,000 wage and salary workers in the 2017 Current Population Survey. We partition the wage data into $100-wide bins; the height of each bin's bar measures the percentage of the 156,236 observations on weekly wages that lie within that bin. Figure 10.1 reveals that 6 percent of the workers earn between $200 and $300 per week; 2 percent of the workers earn between $1,500 and $1,600 per week. These percentages sum across all the bins to 100 percent.

 PRACTICE   Use the heights of the histogram bars in the figure to estimate the percentage of workers with wages between $1,000 and $1,200.

Unfortunately, the CPS top-codes weekly wages so that annual wage income can't exceed $150,000. Weekly wages of 3.9 percent of the wage and salary workers are top-coded at $2,884. (See the bar at $2,884 in the figure.) Top-coding hides the upper end of the wage distribution's right tail and confounds measurement

TABLE 10.1. SUMMARY MEASURES OF WEEKLY WAGES, 2017		
MEASURE	WAGE ($/worker)	ln WAGE (ln $/worker)
Median	750	6.58
Mean	999	6.60
Standard Deviation	—	0.80

Note: The mean and standard deviation of ln w are corrected for top-coding as described in the text.
Source: Current Population Survey, outgoing rotation group files, monthly 2017.

of wage dispersion. To address this problem, let's replace the top-code bar with reasonable estimates of the upper tail of the wage distribution. (Replacing the bar involves fitting the shape parameter of the Pareto distribution, but don't let that distract you.) Replacing the top-code bar at $2,884 with the estimated series of thin vertical lines in the figure suggests that the wage distribution's right tail extends out quite far.

The **mean** and **median** of wages are two measures of central location of the wage distribution. The mean (or average) wage simply sums wages across all workers and divides by the number of workers. Table 10.1 reports that the mean of the weekly wage in these data is $999. The median wage marks the middle of the wage observations, as ordered from lowest to highest. The median wage is $750 per week, so half the workers report weekly wages below $750, and the other half report wages above $750. The mean wage exceeds the median wage because the right tail extends farther than the left tail from the median.

Percentile Ratio.   Everyone isn't paid the same wage, and this dispersion of wages is certainly visible in Figure 10.1. But how disperse are wages? That is, how do we quantify **wage inequality**? One way is by comparing wages at various **percentiles of the wage distribution**, and Table 10.2 lists wages at several percentiles of the wage distribution. Ten percent of the workers earn wages at or

TABLE 10.2. WAGES AT PERCENTILES OF THE WEEKLY WAGE DISTRIBUTION, 2017			
PERCENTILE p	WAGE ($/worker)	CUMULATIVE WAGE ($)[a]	CUMULATIVE WAGE SHARE (%)[b]
10	273	1,886	1.9
25	460	7,571	7.5
50	750	22,625	22.3
75	1,250	47,013	46.3
90	1,923	70,482	69.5

Notes: [a]The cumulative wage at percentile p (e.g., 25) sums the wages from percentile 1 to percentile p. [b]Cumulative wage share divides the cumulative wage by the sum of all percentiles, which is $101,448.
Source: Current Population Survey, outgoing rotation group files, monthly 2017.

below $273 per week, so the weekly wage at the 10th percentile of the distribution is $273. Ten percent of the workers earn above $1,923 per week, so $1,923 is the wage at the 90th percentile. Vertical reference lines in Figure 10.1 mark the wages at these two percentiles, as well as the median wage (i.e., the wage at the 50th percentile). That the wage at the 90th percentile is well above the wage at the 10th percentile tells us that weekly wages are quite disperse. The difference between these two wages is $1,650 per week. Or, the worker at the 90th percentile earns 7 times as much as (or 600 percent more than) the worker at the 10th percentile. This is the **90–10 percentile ratio**, or 90–10 ratio for short. A bigger 90–10 ratio means there's more wage inequality.

 PRACTICE   The weekly wage at the 25th percentile is $460 per worker. What does this mean? The wages of _____ percent of workers are at or below $460. _____ percent of workers earn more than $460. [Advice: Do not proceed until you fully grasp the concept of wages at percentiles of the distribution.]

Standard Deviation.   A second measure of wage dispersion is the **standard deviation of the log of wages**. The standard deviation quantifies dispersion by computing the average distance of a random variable from its mean. It's the perfect measure of dispersion if the random variable is distributed normally (so the familiar bell curve describes its distribution). Values of a normally distributed variable are scattered symmetrically around its mean, a property that's clearly violated by the wage distribution in Figure 10.1. But the logarithm of wages is reasonably symmetric and close to normal.

Figure 10.2 displays a new histogram of wages with bins based on the logarithm of wages rather than wages. Each bin is .25 log-units wide, which means that the upper limit of each bin exceeds its lower limit by about 25 percent. Since few of us can easily interpret values of $\ln w$ like 5.521, 6.215, or 6.908, a second horizontal axis along the top of the graph displays the corresponding wages (e.g., 250, 500, and 1,000). This second horizontal axis measures the weekly wage on a logarithmic scale, which means the distance between 250 and 500 is the same as the distance between 500 and 1,000. (This figure uses properties of the normal distribution to fill out the right tail by replacing the bar of top-coded wage observations.)

Figure 10.2 overlays the **normal distribution** or bell curve that best fits the data on log wages. The bell curve doesn't really match the log-wage data, but it does provide a reasonably good fit. Therefore, the standard deviation of log wages should be a good, although imperfect, measure of wage dispersion. The top-code-corrected standard deviation is .8 log points. With a normal distribution, 68 percent of the data lie within one standard deviation of the mean, which is 6.6 for log wages. So 68 percent of the wage observations are predicted to lie on the interval between 5.8 and 7.4 on the figure's bottom axis and between $330 and $1,636 on the top axis. This range would be narrower if the standard deviation of log wages were lower.

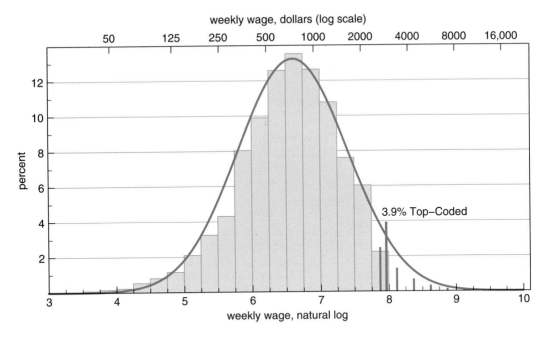

FIGURE 10.2. Distribution of the Logarithm of Weekly Wages, 2017
Notes: (a) The normal distribution with mean 6.6 and standard deviation .8 is projected over the histogram. (b) The bottom axis measures the natural logarithm of the wage on the usual arithmetic scale; the top axis measures the wage on a logarithmic scale. (c) The thin vertical lines display projections of the histogram bars above the $2,884 top-coded wage.
Source: Current Population Survey, outgoing rotation group files, monthly 2017.

Lorenz Curve and Gini Coefficient. The **Lorenz curve** recasts the histogram data in Figure 10.1 to focus on wage dispersion or inequality. To build the Lorenz curve, we answer questions like "How much in total does the bottom 90 percent of the wage distribution earn?" In the recent CPS, the weekly wage at the 90th percentile is $1,923, and workers at or below the 90th percentile earn 69.5 percent of all wages. So 69.5 percent is the **cumulative wage share** at the 90th percentile. Table 10.2 lists the cumulative wage shares at the 10th, 25th, 50th, 75th, and 90th percentiles of wages. By repeating this calculation for every percentile, we can plot pairs of cumulative wage shares (on the vertical axis) and percentiles of workers (from 1 to 100 on the horizontal axis). Figure 10.3a displays the resulting Lorenz curve.

 PRACTICE   Mark the 90th percentile's contribution to the Lorenz curve by plotting a point in Figure 10.3a. The point lies below the 45° line. Why can't a point on a Lorenz curve lie above the 45° line? [Hint: You must grasp the meaning of the wage at the "pth percentile of the distribution" to answer this question.]

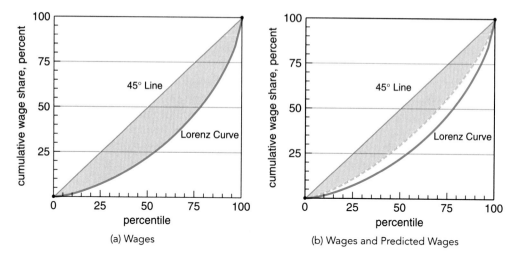

FIGURE 10.3. Lorenz Curves of Weekly Wages, 2017
Note: The dashed curve in panel (b) is the Lorenz curve for wages predicted from Equation 9.2.
Source: Current Population Survey, outgoing rotation group files, monthly 2017.

The Lorenz curve slopes up, emerges from the origin $(0,0)$, terminates at $(100,100)$, and bows down to the right. The most important feature of the Lorenz curve is the way it pictures wage dispersion: the shaded area between the Lorenz curve and the 45° line measures inequality.

To see why, let's imagine two extremes. First, if everyone earns the same wage, then workers up to the 10th percentile earn 10 percent of all wages, the bottom half of workers earn 50 percent of all wages, and workers up to the 90th percentile of wages account for 90 percent of all wages. The resulting Lorenz curve coincides with the 45° line, which eliminates the shaded region. Second, if all wages are bestowed on one worker and everyone else works without pay, then the Lorenz curve runs along the bottom and right edges of the graph; that is, the cumulative wage share is zero for every percentile shy of the 100th, and the curve jumps to 100 percent at the right edge of the graph. Between these extremes of no inequality and complete concentration of wages, a bigger shaded area means more wage inequality.

The dashed Lorenz curve in Figure 10.3b uses predicted rather than actual wages. (The solid curve is a copy of the Lorenz curve from panel (a).) A regression line fits the weekly wage data (in logs) to the key variables from our analysis over the preceding five chapters: the workweek, schooling, work experience, sex, race, and union membership. Equation 9.2 in chapter 9 reports the estimates. We find the predicted wage for each worker by plugging his or her values for the regressors (hours of work, schooling, etc.) into the right side of Equation 9.2 and solving the equation for w.

These predicted wages form the dashed Lorenz curve in Figure 10.3b. The shaded region clearly shrinks, which indicates there is less inequality in predicted wages than actual wages. But the startling feature is that there is *so much inequality in predicted wages*. Wages aren't arbitrary. Measurable differences across workers in the workweek, schooling, work experience, sex, race, and union membership generate a lot of inequality in weekly wages. Can we be more precise?

The Lorenz curve helps us visualize wage dispersion; the Gini coefficient translates the picture into a single number. The **Gini coefficient** measures the area of the shaded region between the Lorenz curve and the 45° line relative to the area below the 45° line. Since a Lorenz curve lies within the triangle below the 45° line, the Gini coefficient ranges from zero to one. If everyone earns the same wage, the Lorenz curve coincides with the 45° line, and the Gini coefficient is zero. If all wages are claimed by one worker, the Lorenz curve runs along the bottom and right edges of the graph, and the Gini coefficient is one. More generally, a higher value of the Gini coefficient indicates more wage dispersion or inequality.

To calculate the Gini coefficient, we measure the vertical distance between the 45° line and the Lorenz curve at each percentile from 1 to 100. The numerator of the Gini coefficient sums these gaps across percentiles. The Gini coefficient's denominator sums the vertical distances between the 45° line and the horizontal axis, which is the sum of the percentiles.

The Gini coefficient associated with the Lorenz curve in Figure 10.3a is .416; that is, the Gini coefficient of weekly wages in these data is 41.6 percent. The Gini coefficient derived from the dashed Lorenz curve in Figure 10.3b is .303; that is, 30.3 percent is the Gini coefficient of predicted weekly wages. In these data, differences across workers in a short list of worker-related variables explains almost three-quarters (i.e., $30.3 \div 41.6$) of the inequality in weekly wages as measured by Gini coefficients.

Earnings Inequality Around the World. Figure 10.4 displays the positive relationship between 90–10 ratios and Gini coefficients for annual earnings in 20 countries. That high 90–10 countries tend to be high Gini countries helps us classify countries: by either measure, Belgium, Italy, and Taiwan are low earnings-inequality countries, and earnings inequality is high in Mexico, South Africa, and India. In the middle are Germany, Japan, and the United States; 90–10 ratios in these countries are about 15, and their Gini coefficients are roughly 45 percent.

Figure 10.4 also illustrates the curious cases of Finland, Norway, and Sweden, three countries with surprisingly high 90–10 ratios. The Gini coefficients in these three countries suggest moderate earnings inequality, but their 90–10 ratios place them among the highest inequality countries in the figure. But aren't Finland, Norway, and Sweden pillars of equality? Yes, if we measure inequality of *total* income, which includes government transfers. Indeed, the 90–10 ratios and Gini coefficients for total income in Finland, Norway, and Sweden are among the lowest in the world. But switching from total income to earnings unmasks lots of inequality in these countries.

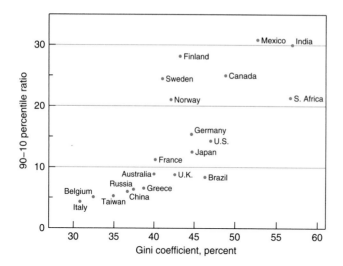

Income is annual labor income (LIS variable pil) of people ages 16+. Sample excludes negative and zero values of labor income; to handle outliers, extreme values in the left tail are set to 10 percent of the median and in the right tail to 10 times the median. Years: 2000 (Belgium), 2005 (Sweden), 2008 (Japan), 2010 (Australia, France), 2011 (India), 2012 (Mexico, South Africa), 2013 (Brazil, Canada, China, Finland, Greece, Norway, Russia, United Kingdom), 2014 (Italy), 2015 (Germany), 2016 (Taiwan, United States).

Source: Luxembourg Income Study. LIS Database accessed on April 2, 2018, at http://www.lisdatacenter.org.

FIGURE 10.4. Earnings Inequality Around the World

Asymmetry

Wages aren't distributed symmetrically. Let's return to the wage distribution in Figure 10.1 with an eye toward detecting and quantifying **asymmetry (or skewness)**. We begin by matching histogram bars on each side of the $750 median. Over 9 percent of the sample of wage and salary workers earn between $500 and $600 per week, so the height of the histogram bar for the bin between 500 and 600 is over 9 percent. But the histogram bar on the other side of the median, between 900 and 1,000, is 6.5 percent. Within several hundred dollars of the median, each histogram bar to the left of the median is taller than its matching bar to the right of the median. The pattern reverses farther from the median as a consequence of the long right tail of the wage distribution. That is, the *distribution of wages skews to the right*; its right tail extends much farther than its left tail.

One measure of asymmetry of wages compares the mean and the median. The difference between mean and median wages is $249 (= $999 − $750) per week in the recent CPS. By expressing this number in percentage terms, we can compare **mean–median differences** at different points in time and even across countries with different currencies. The mean wage in the CPS is one-third higher than the median wage.

A second measure of asymmetry compares percentiles of the wage distribution. How far from the median are the 10th and 90th percentiles? The answer involves a **comparison of the 90–50 and 50–10 percentile ratios**. If the wage distribution were symmetric, then the distance from the 10th percentile of wages to the median wage would equal the distance from the median wage to the 90th percentile of wages. The worker at the 10th percentile earns $477 (= $750 − $273) less than the median worker in these data. The worker at the 90th percentile earns

$1,173 (= $1923 − $750) more than the median worker. So the 90th percentile is 2.5 (= 1173 ÷ 477) times as far as the 10th percentile from the median.

Application: Wage Inequality Across Occupations

Let's apply these measures of wage dispersion and asymmetry to our data on occupation averages in the Current Population Survey, 1983–2017. Table 1.2 in chapter 1 lists the median wages in the 43 occupations. With only 43 observations, plotting the histogram of wages in these data isn't very informative. But percentiles of the wage distribution across occupations are informative. The median weekly wage is $778, which is associated with workers in other transportation and material moving occupations; the 10th and 90th percentiles of weekly wages are $329 (sales workers in retail trade and personal services) and $1,193 (executives, administrators, and managers in the private sector). Executives earn about three-and-a-half times as much as retail sales workers; that is, the 90–10 ratio across occupations is 3.6 (= 1193 ÷ 329). Wages across occupations aren't skewed to the right. Indeed, the 90th percentile of wages is closer than the 10th percentile to the median.

We can also use the occupation wage data to plot a Lorenz curve: each occupation contributes a line segment to the Lorenz curve in Figure 10.5. For instance, the line segment between points A and B is the contribution of clerical workers (other than secretaries, stenographers, and typists). Workers in this occupation comprise 9.4 percent of the wage and salary workers, and they earn 6.6 percent of total wages. Therefore, the slope of the line segment between A and B is .7 (= 6.6 ÷ 9.4). Executives, administrators, and managers in the private

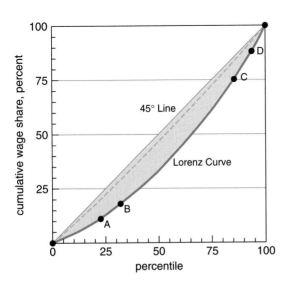

Point A marks shares of employment and total wages in occupations that pay less than clerical workers (other than secretaries, stenographers, and typists). Point B includes these clerical workers in the shares. Moving along the Lorenz curve from A to B adds 9.4 percentage points to the percentiles on the horizontal axis and 6.6 percentage points to the cumulative wage share on the vertical axis.

The dashed Lorenz curve uses residual wages. Little wage inequality remains across occupations after accounting for differences across occupations in average values of the workweek, schooling, etc.

Note: The dashed Lorenz curve uses each occupation's residual wage, the difference between its median wage and the median wage predicted from Equation 9.2.

Source: Current Population Survey, outgoing rotation group files, monthly 1983–2017.

FIGURE 10.5. Lorenz Curves of Median Weekly Wages in 43 Occupations, 1983–2017

sector contribute the line segment between points C and D in the figure. These executives make up 8.2 percent of wage and salary workers, and they earn 12.8 percent of total wages; the slope of the line segment between C and D is thus 1.6 ($= 12.8 \div 8.2$). The Lorenz curve in the figure combines the line segments from all 43 occupations.

Like the Lorenz curves in Figure 10.3, the Lorenz curve on occupation data runs below the 45° line from the origin $(0,0)$ to $(100,100)$ and increases at an increasing rate. But the Lorenz curve on median wages across occupations is much closer to the 45° line. The Lorenz curve in the earlier figure captures wage dispersion across all workers, combining wage differences within occupations and wage differences across occupations. The Lorenz curve on occupation wage data is much closer to the 45° line, which means that there is much less wage inequality across occupations and plenty of wage inequality within occupations. Comparison of the two Gini coefficients allows us to be more precise. The Gini coefficient based on median wages across occupations is 20.7 percent, down from 41.6 based on the individual wage data. So wage inequality is evenly split within and across occupations.

We can also parse occupation wages into two parts: one that contains wages predicted on the basis of our analysis in the preceding five chapters, and a residual that is left unexplained. To predict each occupation's wage, we use the wage regression reported as Equation 9.1 in chapter 9. Most predictions are on target. For instance, we predict that executives earn $1,187, and their median weekly wage is $1,186. And clerical workers (other than secretaries) earn just $27 per week more than predicted. On the other hand, lawyers receive $83 per week more than we predict, and college teachers earn $220 per week less than predicted.

Key Principle.
Wages reflect skills, and differences in worker skills explain almost all of the differences in pay across occupations.

We use the residual differences in wages across occupations to plot a Lorenz curve that reflects only residual (i.e., unexplained) wage inequality across occupations. That's the dashed curve nestled quite close to the 45° line in Figure 10.5. The variables from the preceding five chapters absorb so much of the wage differences across occupations that little cross-occupation inequality remains. Indeed, the Gini coefficient falls from 20.7 percent to 4.1 percent using residual wages. As measured by Gini coefficients, little of the inequality in median wages across occupations remains after accounting for differences across occupations in averages of several key characteristics of workers.

10.2   Economic Models of Wage Inequality

The distribution of wages isn't arbitrary. In corrupt societies, a worker thrives by seizing what others produce by theft, fraud, deceit, or political pull. In a free labor market, the wage depends on a worker's ability to produce valuable goods and services. Our purpose here is to sketch how the elements of wage inequality—dispersion and skewness—emerge in free labor markets. That is, let's move from measuring to explaining wage inequality.

Ability

Suppose ability is distributed normally. In particular, let's assume that ability follows a normal distribution with mean 100 and standard deviation 15. The familiar bell curve in Figure 10.6a illustrates the distribution of ability.

Workers in a competitive market receive wages that reflect the value of their marginal products. How is productivity related to ability? Higher-ability workers are clearly more productive, but here we can be more precise. The function that transforms ability into productivity is the wage–ability curve in Figure 10.6b. The wage w increases with ability a at an increasing rate. As drawn, the wage grows exponentially (i.e., at a constant rate of growth) with ability, so the wage–ability curve is the following exponential equation:

(10.1)
$$w = 660e^{.03a-3}$$

where the constant e is 2.71828…. Along this curve, the wage grows at a constant growth rate, 3 percent per unit of ability. Set a to 65 to find that a worker with 65 units of ability earns about $230 per week; a worker at the mean of the ability distribution, at point A in the figure, earns a weekly wage of $660. And a worker with 135 units of ability receives about $1,885 in weekly wages.

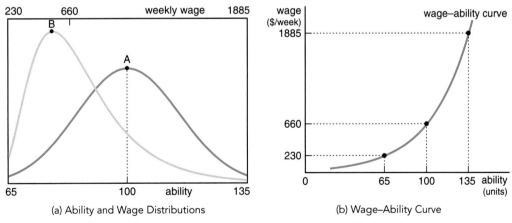

(a) Ability and Wage Distributions

(b) Wage–Ability Curve

Ability is distributed normally around the mean at 100; the bell curve that peaks at A in panel (a) plots this distribution. In panel (b), the weekly wage grows as an exponential function of ability. In panel (a), the curve that peaks at B is the implied distribution of wages. (The top axis measures wages.) This distribution of wages is log normal.

FIGURE 10.6. From a Normal Distribution of Ability to a Log–Normal Distribution of Wages

> **PRACTICE**   Judy has 119.22 units of ability, which puts her at the 90th percentile of the distribution of ability. Plug 119.22 into Equation 10.1 to calculate Judy's wage.

Small differences in ability magnify to large differences in wages for high-ability workers. For instance, increasing ability from 65 to 70 units raises the weekly wage by $63; increasing ability from 130 to 135 units raises the weekly wage by $263.

This magnification of ability differences generates a long right tail in the wage distribution. In Figure 10.6a, the wage distribution is plotted against the wage scale along the graph's top edge. (The range of wages measured on the top scale matches the range of abilities measured on the bottom scale.) The generated distribution of wages clearly isn't normal; these wages are distributed log-normally with a long right tail.

This example illustrates how an exponential transformation of abilities to wages generates wage inequality with a long right tail, a prominent feature of the actual wage distribution. And the result generalizes. Any wage–ability curve that **increases at an increasing rate** stretches the right tail of the wage distribution. If ability is distributed symmetrically and the wage increases with ability at an increasing rate, then the distribution of wages skews to the right.

Why would the wage increase with ability or skill at an increasing rate? Let's explore three economic models in which the wage–skill curve does just that: our schooling model from chapter 6, a model of job assignments in hierarchies, and a model of superstars.

Schooling

In our model of schooling with identical workers (in section 6.1), the equilibrium wage–schooling curve coincides with an iso-wealth curve. The growth rate of the wage $\Delta w/w$ along an iso-wealth curve is constant, and that rate is the interest rate i. (See the discussion following Equation 6.7.) This property means that the wage–schooling curve is an exponential function as in Figure 10.6b. If the distribution of schooling is symmetric, then wages skew to the right.

Voilà! In the blink of an eye, we have an equilibrium model that generates wage dispersion with a long right tail.

Schooling choice can generate plenty of dispersion and skewness of wages, but none of the identical workers in the model fares any better than any other worker. Wealth is equalized. Educated workers earn more as a compensating wage differential for delaying the time they start receiving wages. They are no wealthier than their less-educated coworkers.

Mincer (1958) developed our model of schooling choice to explain the distribution of wages, and he focused on the wage distribution's long right tail. Mincer's principle is that schooling choice skews the distribution of wages relative to the distribution of schooling. Unfortunately, the distribution of schooling is far from pretty. It's not normal; it's not symmetric; it's not even nice. High school dropouts aren't so common, so the distribution of schooling is thin up to a dramatic spike of high school graduates at $s = 12$; the distribution thins out again before spiking at $s = 16$ for those with college degrees. And there's a smaller spike for those with advanced degrees.

Messy as the distribution of schooling is, it delivers Mincer's principle: the transformation of schooling to wages produces substantial dispersion of wages with a long right tail. We establish this result by estimating the relationship between log wages and schooling in our sample of wage and salary workers in the 2017 CPS. On the basis of the estimated rate of return to schooling (i.e., 11.7 percent per grade), we compute a predicted weekly wage for every worker. All variation in these predicted wages across workers is due to differences in schooling across workers.

How are these predicted wages distributed? If Mincer's principle is important in practice, then the distribution of these predicted wages must skew to the right. It does. Spikes in the distribution of schooling transfer to spikes in the distribution of predicted wages, but the 90–10 percentile ratio is a substantial 2.0 ($= 1183 \div 586$). Most important, the 90th percentile of predicted wages ($1,183 per week) is nearly three times as far as the 10th percentile ($586) from the median ($741). Thus schooling choice skews the distribution of wages to the right in practice.

Differences in ability and schooling separately contribute a lot to our understanding of wage inequality, including that wages are skewed. The interaction of ability and schooling amplifies their separate effects. In chapter 6, we learned that ability increases the demand for schooling: able workers become educated workers. Able workers reap the wage benefits of both ability and education; low-ability workers make due with wages that reflect both low ability and little education. So the positive matching of ability and schooling increases wage inequality.

Job Assignment in Hierarchies

Most firms organize their **jobs into hierarchies** from low-level tasks like sorting mail to high-level tasks like developing the firm's strategic plan. Assigning workers to jobs within a hierarchy skews the distribution of wages relative to the distribution of skills. Let's explore this principle in the context of a start-up firm in the infant industry of private space transportation.

SpaceZ organizes its jobs into a three-level hierarchy. Production and similar low-level jobs comprise level 1, the bottom of the corporate hierarchy. Supervisors and low-level managers responsible for handling day-to-day operations occupy level 2. They keep everything running smoothly by ordering materials, filing regulatory forms, processing the payroll, and doing thousands of other things. The third level is upper management, which develops long-term plans, pricing and marketing strategies, and so forth. Decisions whether to build a private space port, where to build it, and whether to outsource parts production to Indonesia are made by the workers who populate level 3 of the hierarchy.

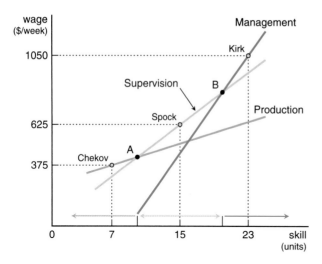

Each line depicts how the wage varies with skill within a level of SpaceZ's job hierarchy. Wage–skill lines get steeper from lower levels to higher levels of the hierarchy because skills are more valuable in jobs with more responsibilities and wider spans of control.

For workers like Chekov with up to 10 units of skill, the wage is highest on production jobs; Spock and other workers with skills between 10 and 20 units earn the highest wages by working on middle-level supervisory jobs. Kirk's wage is highest if he manages the enterprise.

FIGURE 10.7. Job Assignments in Hierarchies

Workers at SpaceZ are assigned to jobs on the basis of their skills, and the payoff to skill rises as we go up the hierarchy. Having more skill makes a worker a bit more productive sorting mail or entering data in a computer. That extra skill delivers a bigger bang on supervisory jobs. With a low-skill worker in a supervisory position, everything goes to hell, and production suffers. A supervisor with more skill coordinates the day-to-day activities seamlessly, which enhances performance of every level-1 worker on the supervisor's team. Skill delivers the biggest bang in management: better decisions influence the future of the enterprise, raising the value of every worker's labor. Figure 10.7 illustrates these relationships between skill and productivity by three upward-sloping lines, one for each level in the hierarchy.

The assignment of workers to jobs takes advantage of the higher return to skill on higher-level jobs. Suppose the "money" backing the SpaceZ venture assigns workers to jobs. Points A and B in Figure 10.7 mark the cutoff points for job assignments. The production line is highest for skills up to $x = 10$ at A; the supervisory line is above the production and management lines for skills between $x = 10$ and $x = 20$ (i.e., between points A and B); and the management line is highest for skills beyond $x = 20$. The investors assign workers with skills below 10 units, such as Chekov, to production and related jobs on level 1. Spock and other supervisors on level 2 are drawn from workers with skills in the range from 10 to 20. Investors assign workers like Kirk with more than 20 units of skill to upper-management jobs on level 3.

This assignment of workers to jobs also ensues without the top-down control of investors. If every worker's wage on each job equals his or her productivity, then wage-maximizing workers self-select into jobs that maximize their productivities. That is, as an invisible hand, a competitive wage structure efficiently sorts workers to jobs. Figure 10.7 displays the three wage–skill lines, one for each level in the job hierarchy. Chekov, who has 7 units of skill, earns the most in production; he takes a production job working for $375 per week. Spock is the median worker in terms of skills; he has 15 units of skill x. By working as a supervisor in level 2, he earns $625 per week. He would earn less as a production worker and a lot less as an upper-level manager. Kirk has 23 units of skill. His weekly wage on a level-3 job is $1,050. Kirk can earn more than Spock as a supervisor and a lot more than Chekov on a production job, but he can earn the most and produce the most value for SpaceZ by commanding the enterprise.

 PRACTICE   Picard has even more skill than Kirk, two more units in fact. Draw a dashed line to indicate Picard's skill in Figure 10.7, and mark the wages he can earn in production, supervision, and management.

Skills are distributed symmetrically around Spock at the median ($x = 15$), but the distribution of wages skews to the right. We can establish this result with only our three workers. Kirk and Chekov are equidistant from Spock in terms of skills: Kirk has 8 more units of skill; Chekov has 8 fewer units of skill. Chekov's wage is $250 below the median wage, which is Spock's $625 per week. The extra 8 units of skill raises Kirk's weekly wage $425 above Spock's median wage. That Kirk's wage is farther than Chekov's from the median wage means that the right tail of the wage distribution extends farther than the left tail. The wage distribution skews right relative to the distribution of skills.

This model of skill-based selection to jobs demonstrates how sorting in the labor market skews the distribution of wages. The key principle is *convexity* of the wage–skill curve: the wage increases with skill at an increasing rate. In Figure 10.7, the wage–skill curve $w(x)$ combines three linear pieces: the production wage–skill line up to $x = 10$, the supervisory wage–skill line for $10 < x < 20$, and the management wage–skill line for $x > 20$. Although linear in pieces, the wage–skill curve increases at an increasing rate overall.

We can also extend the model to include meaningful job assignments within each level. For instance, supervisors with more skill than Spock supervise larger teams or activities; they accept more responsibility and have a bigger span of control. Without the extra responsibility, a more-skilled supervisor produces more and earns a higher wage than Spock. That wage premium, however, magnifies as the responsibilities of the more-skilled supervisor expand. This extension applies the convexity of $w(x)$ to within levels of SpaceZ's hierarchy and further skews wages relative to skills.

This model also explains why employers organize workers into job hierarchies. A job hierarchy leverages the skills of the best workers to raise the performances of low-skill workers in lower-level jobs. By just doing his own thing on a low-level job, a high-skill worker like Kirk can produce more than a low-skill worker like Chekov. But Kirk's biggest impact in terms of producing value is in making decisions that increase the productivity of other workers. On a high-level job, Kirk leverages his plentiful skills to the advantage of others. (And his wage reflects this.) Dozens, hundreds, or even thousands of workers gain from just one of his good ideas.

 PRACTICE   Kirk does quite well. Do you think this model of job assignments explains much of the lavish compensation of chief executive officers (CEOs)? Or do you think that CEO compensation is less about the ability to create value and more about corruption and pull? (We investigate CEO compensation in the next chapter, but thinking about these questions in the context of wage inequality helps frame the issues.)

Superstars

Superstars make the big bucks, super-big bucks: LeBron James in basketball, Cristiano Ronaldo in soccer, Johnny Depp and Jennifer Lawrence in film, Jerry Seinfeld in his day on television, Beyoncé and Taylor Swift in music, and J.K. Rowling in fiction. Their earnings populate the far-reaches of the right tail of the wage (or income) distribution. No lawn cutter, coal miner, or cast member at Disney World's Splash Mountain, no matter how talented, is a superstar. Why does the cream of the crop in some activities rise to superstar status, while the best and brightest in other activities labor away without notice?

Superstar markets differ from typical markets in two ways (Rosen 1981). First, in terms of production technology, a single exemplary effort is sold over and over at little marginal cost in sports and many other forms of entertainment. Costs don't rise in proportion to the size of the audience or market. Second, in terms of the preferences of consumers, the satisfaction from a string of several mediocre performances doesn't match the pleasure from a single great performance. Let's see how these two features combine to generate superstars.

Technologies that allow **joint (or nonrivalrous) consumption** characterize superstar markets. With the typical technology, you can't eat your cake and let your neighbor eat it, too. If you eat your cake, then I (as your neighbor) have to get my own cake. That's the **cake technology**. But the technology in superstar markets is a **sunset technology**: you can enjoy a beautiful sunset, and I can enjoy that same sunset, too. If entertainment were like cake, LeBron James would play basketball in my driveway today, Jerry Seinfeld would make witty observations in my living room tonight, Taylor Swift would sing a few songs while riding along on my morning commute tomorrow, and J.K. Rowling would battle to keep me awake with a thrilling bedside story night after night.

Even the best performers and authors wouldn't make much money playing private gigs every day. They must sell each performance to a wide audience to command the big bucks. And they do it through large arenas, television, films, CDs and digital music files, and books. You and I can watch the same game, laugh at the same TV show, play air guitar to the same recording of a song, and drift off to sleep with the same book.

PRACTICE Let's add Mark Zuckerberg of Facebook to our list of superstars. How does the technology for developing and deploying software applications resemble the sunset technology? If Internet applications were produced by a cake technology, what would be a private gig for Zuckerberg?

Limited substitution between quantity and quality is also important in superstar markets. If two mildly funny comedians are just as good as one side-splittingly funny comedian, then the funniest comedian must compete with many not-so-funny rivals. Even with large arenas, television, films, and records, competition would limit the funniest comedian's stardom. But two mediocre performances are a poor substitute for one exceptional performance. Why settle for second best? We all can enjoy the funniest comedian, the most gut-wrenching drama, the greatest tunes, and the most thrilling read. We all pay to watch, to listen to, and to read the best, and that's how superstars are born.

The consequence of joint consumption and limited substitutability is a wage structure that magnifies differences in skill near the top. The market concentrates vast earnings on a few. LeBron James's annual salary is about $36 million, and toss in another $52 million per year in earnings from endorsements. Real Madrid pays Ronaldo $61 million per year, and his endorsements push his annual income to about $108 million. Jerry Seinfeld turned down $110 million for a tenth season of *Seinfeld* in the 1990s, and he continues to rake in tens of millions of dollars annually in syndication residuals. An A-list actor gets tens of millions of dollars in up-front payments to star in a film—Johnny Depp's fee for starring in *Pirates of the Caribbean: On Stranger Tides* was $35 million—and back-end payments based on box-office revenue can add tens of millions, too. From June 2017 through May 2018, Taylor Swift raked in about $80 million from record sales, live performances, and endorsements, which outpaced Beyoncé's $60 million over the same period. J.K. Rowling has made a billion or so dollars from her *Harry Potter* series.

But for every superstar, there are dozens or even thousands of entertainers struggling to make a living, waiting tables between auditions, and writing novels that no one will read. Being the best pays big bucks; being less than the best ... not so much.

Talent is one thing; the size of the market is another. If we hold a performer's personal market fixed, being a little better translates into a little more pay, which is like moving along one level's wage–skill line in Figure 10.7. But the size of the personal market grows with talent, and pay increases with talent at an increasing rate. That means differences in wages across workers magnify differences in their talents.

The size of the overall market is also quite important. The introductions of film, radio, television, cable television (especially for sports), and the Internet greatly expanded the markets for entertainers. One performance is sold to listeners, viewers, and fans throughout a city or around the world. And the evolution of recording technology is a nice example of market size in music.

Without records, great voices would be recognized by peers but enjoyed by few. And they wouldn't earn that much either. But Elizabeth Billington, an opera singer over two centuries ago, was an exception to this rule. In the 1801 season in London, Billington earned 10,000–15,000 pounds performing at Covent Garden (i.e., the Royal Opera House) and Drury Lane (i.e., the Theatre Royal). It could only happen in London, which was one of the two largest cities in the world and the world capital of trade and finance at the time. Billington put fannies in the seats of two large opera houses. (Competition between the two houses helped, too.) Writing in his *Principles of Economics*, Marshall (1920 [1890]) predicted that no singer would ever match Billington's earnings for the 1801 season. But Marshall qualified his prediction with this clause: "… so long as the number of persons who can be reached by a human voice is strictly limited" (p. 571). The invention of mass-produced recordings removed the limit on the reach of the human voice.

Early recording technology didn't turn music from a cake technology to a sunset technology. In the early days of acoustic recording, the band played once to create a single cylinder recording. One performance, one recording, no copies. Later pantograph technology mechanically connected the playing stylus moving along the recorded cylinder to a recording stylus on another cylinder to make a single copy. But every pantograph-generated recording deteriorated the sound quality of the original cylinder. Music couldn't be mass produced from master recordings until the mid-1890s when the gramophone's recorded discs (i.e., records) challenged recorded cylinders. It took more than a decade for disc recordings to rival cylinder recordings in sound quality. But by 1910, a single recording session could generate good-quality mass-produced records, and that year marks the dawn of the age of stars in music.

Elizabeth Billington was a star, and her earnings for the 1801 season were astonishing *for the time*. But her earnings reflected the technology at the time. Would her earnings astonish us today? We can adjust Billington's earnings for inflation and use the average exchange rate between pounds and dollars to express her earnings in 2017 dollars. The result is $1.2 million to $1.8 million. Nothing to sneeze at, but also nothing remarkable in the era of mass-produced records and digital streaming of music.

10.3   Application: Increasing Wage Inequality

Wage inequality has been growing since the late 1960s, and labor economists have been carefully documenting the patterns since the early 1990s (e.g., Juhn, Murphy, and Pierce 1993; Katz and Murphy 1992). Juhn, Murphy, and Pierce analyze the evolution of wage inequality in the CPS between 1963 and 1989. Little happened until the late 1960s. From 1968 to 1989, however, weekly wages of workers at the 10th percentile of the distribution fell about 25 percent in real terms. The wage at the 90th percentile rose about 25 percent in real terms over the same period. Thus the ratio of the 90th to 10th percentiles of wages increased about 50 percent over these 21 years. Wage inequality grew most rapidly between 1968 and 1973 and between 1979 and 1989.

Increasing wage inequality since the late 1960s reversed a period of wage compression earlier in the century. The wage distribution narrowed dramatically

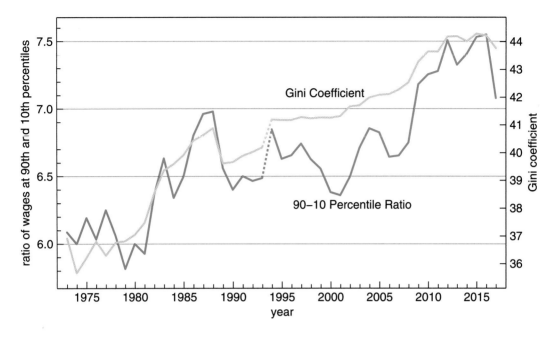

FIGURE 10.8. Increasing Wage Inequality, 1973–2017
Notes: Monthly values of the Consumer Price Index adjust weekly wages for inflation. Top-coded wage observations are multiplied by 1.5. The Bureau of Labor Statistics introduced a major redesign of the CPS in 1994.
Source: Current Population Survey, May Supplement files, 1973–1978; and outgoing rotation group files, monthly 1979–2017.

between 1940 and 1950 (Goldin and Margo 1992). The ratio of the 90th percentile to the 10th percentile of wages shrunk by about one-third between 1940 and 1950. The compression of the wage distribution was so dramatic in the 1940s that the 90–10 percentile ratio didn't return to its 1940 value until the mid-1980s. Wage inequality rebounded a little in the 1950s, but it took nearly two decades of rising inequality from the late 1960s to reverse the compression of the wage distribution in the 1940s.

Rising inequality continues. Figure 10.8 plots annual values of the 90–10 percentile ratio and the Gini coefficient for the weekly wages of wage and salary workers in the CPS. On the heels of the rapid rise of wage inequality in the 1980s, the 1990s witnessed little change in the dispersion of wages. But widening of the wage distribution surfaced again at the turn of the twenty-first century, and the rise of wage inequality has been nearly as rapid since 2000 as it was in the 1980s. One-third of the rise in the Gini coefficient and half of the rise in the 90–10 ratio since 1979 have occurred since 2000.

Increasing Return to Skills

What explains the pattern of falling and rising wage dispersion over the previous seven decades? The main principle from our economic models is that wage

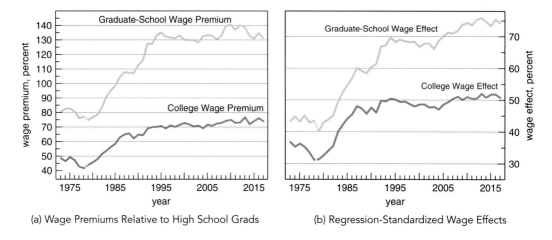

FIGURE 10.9. Wage Premiums to College and Graduate School, 1973–2017

Notes: Sample includes wage and salary workers with 12 or 16 or more grades completed. Monthly values of the Consumer Price Index adjust the weekly wage for inflation. Top-coded wage observations are multiplied by 1.5. In panel (a), the wage premium is the mean wage of the group (college or graduate school) relative to the mean wage of high school graduates (minus 100 percent). The wage effects in panel (b) are estimates from annual regressions of the weekly wage (in logs) on indicators of educational attainment (i.e., college or graduate school), as well as the workweek, potential experience and its square, and indicators of sex, race, and union membership.

Sources: Current Population Survey, May Supplement files, 1973–1978; and outgoing rotation group files, monthly 1979–2017.

inequality is a product of the return to skills (i.e., the skill price). So our point of departure for understanding periods of increasing wage dispersion, such as the last five decades, is an **increasing return to skill**. Juhn, Murphy, and Pierce (1993, Table 8) document strong evidence of an increasing price of skill: the rate of return to schooling rose sharply in the 1980s, and the premium to experience began growing in the late 1960s and continued growing through the 1980s.

Figure 10.9 displays dramatic increases in the wage premiums to college and graduate school since the 1970s. Panel (a) tracks the mean wage of these educated workers relative to the mean wage of high school graduates: this college wage premium has risen from a little over 40 percent in 1978 to nearly 75 in 2017; over the same period, the graduate-school wage premium has risen from 75 percent to over 130 percent. Panel (b) standardizes the wage comparisons using estimated effects of educational attainment from annual log-wage regressions that control for the workweek, potential work experience, sex, and race: by this measure, college graduates now earn about 50 percent more than comparable high school graduates, up from about 30 percent in the late 1970s; workers with graduate-school educations now earn nearly 75 percent more than comparable high school graduates, up from 40 percent in the late 1970s. Today's labor market is paying an unusually high price for well-educated workers.

Increasing wage inequality follows directly from an increasing return to skills. But what causes the increasing return to skills? What factors would increase the demand for skilled labor (relative to the demand for unskilled labor) or increase the supply of unskilled labor (relative to the supply of skilled labor)'?

Skill-Biased Innovations and the Baby Boomers

A **skill-biased innovation** is a change in the production technology that increases the demand for skilled workers relative to the demand for unskilled workers. With fixed quantities supplied of skilled and unskilled workers, the increase in the relative demand for skilled workers increases the skill premium and widens the distribution of wages, increasing wage inequality.

Figure 10.10 illustrates this result. The graphs contain familiar demand and supply curves, but they're relative demands for skilled labor and relative supplies of skilled workers. Each demand curve links the proportion of skilled workers demanded to the ratio of the wage of skilled workers w_s to the wage of unskilled workers w_u. If skilled workers become relatively less expensive, employers respond by increasing employment of skilled workers relative to unskilled workers; that's the downward-sloping relative demand for skilled workers, D_1 in panel (a).

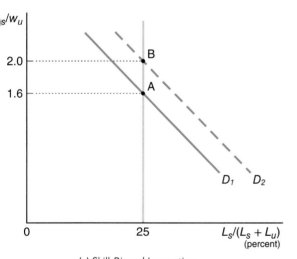

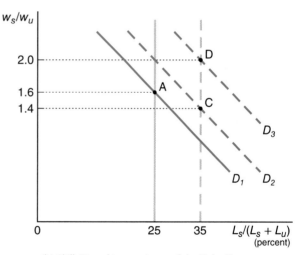

(a) Skill-Biased Innovation

(b) Skill-Biased Innovation and the Baby Boom

Each demand curve depicts the inverse relationship between the proportion of skilled labor that employers demand and the relative wage of skilled labor w_s/w_u. The proportion of skilled labor supplied is assumed to be independent of the relative wage.

Skilled-biased innovation raises the relative demand for skilled labor. The equilibrium shifts from A to B, lifting the relative wage w_s/w_u. If growth in the supply of skilled labor outpaces the growth in demand, the equilibrium shifts from A to C, and the relative wage w_s/w_u falls.

FIGURE 10.10. Increasing Demands for and Supplies of Skilled Workers

The relative supply of skilled workers reflects the mix of skills in the workforce in the short run and the incentives to acquire skills in the long run. For starters, let's assume that the relative supply of skilled workers is vertical (i.e., perfectly inelastic) in the short run at 25 percent in Figure 10.10a.

To employ the mix of skilled and unskilled workers in this labor market, the relative wage of skilled workers must be 1.6. Skill pays a 60 percent wage premium in the equilibrium at point A in Figure 10.10a.

A skill-biased innovation increases the demand for skilled workers (relative to unskilled workers), shifting the relative demand for skilled workers to the right. The relative wage of skilled workers w_s/w_u rises to clear the labor market. In panel (a), the wage premium rises from 60 percent at A to 100 percent at B.

Skill-biased innovation is a leading explanation for the widening of the wage distribution, but a declining rate of return to schooling in the 1970s is a bit of problem. What gives? The supply of skilled workers. In particular, the supply of college graduates grew exceptionally fast in the 1970s, shifting the relative supply of skilled workers to the right in the figure. Skill-biased innovations continued in the 1970s, sliding out the relative demand for skilled workers, but the relative supply of skilled workers shifted out a lot, driving down the rate of return to schooling. In panel (b), the increase in the relative supply of college graduates outpaces the increase in the relative demand for college graduates, so the equilibrium moves from A to C, and the wage premium falls. As the growth of college-educated baby boomers tailed off, the equilibrium moves from C to D over the 1980s, increasing the wage premium and wage inequality.

 **PRACTICE**   College education is one source of skills; work experience is another. As young baby boomers flooded the labor market in the 1970s and early 1980s, the supply of inexperienced workers increased. Sketch the effect on the relative supply of experienced (i.e., skilled) workers in Figure 10.10a. Use the model to predict the effect of the entry of young baby boomers on the wage premium. Does the entry of baby boomers in the 1970s and early 1980s (1) steepen or flatten the wage profile and (2) increase or decrease wage inequality?

Juhn, Murphy, and Pierce (1993) also document rising residual wage inequality since the late 1960s. That is, within schooling–experience pairs, wage inequality has been growing. So rising inequality reflects more than increasing returns to schooling and work experience. For instance, even among inexperienced high school graduates, the wage distribution widened starting in the late 1960s. This pattern is consistent with skill-biased innovations, but there are other possibilities.

International Trade and Immigration

Coupling skill-biased innovations with supply shifts of college-educated baby boomers goes a long way toward explaining the pattern of wage inequality since the 1960s. Increased international trade is a second source of increased relative demand for skilled workers. Globalization shifts domestic production to more skill-intensive products as the United States imports fewer skill-intensive goods from other countries.

With the growth of international trade, production in the United States and other developed countries shifts toward goods and services that take advantage of skilled labor; these countries import products of low-skill workers in less-developed countries. Thus domestic demand for labor shifts from unskilled labor toward skilled labor, and jobs of unskilled workers head to Honduras, Vietnam, and China. Growth of international trade, therefore, mimics skill-biased innovation in increasing the relative demand for skilled workers, lifting the wage premium, and increasing wage inequality.

Although imports from less-developed countries (LDCs) have been increasing as a share of GDP, the timing of the growth doesn't match the timing of the most rapid rise in inequality. Borjas, Freeman, and Katz (1997) studied the impact of international trade on the U.S. labor market. They demonstrated that the periods of fastest growth of imports from less-developed countries are the 1970s and 1990s; from 1979 to 1989, the value of imports from LDCs relative to GDP barely grew (Borjas, Freeman, and Katz 1997, Figure 2). So the period of rapidly rising wage inequality was *not* the period of rapidly rising imports from the less-developed world.

An influx of low-skill immigrants increases wage inequality. Adding more observations to the bottom end of the wage distribution raises inequality directly. But there's more to it. Immigration of low-skill workers reduces the relative supply of skilled workers, mimicking the effect of entry of young baby boomers in the 1970s and early 1980s. The wage of skilled workers rises relative to the wage of unskilled workers to clear the labor market, and wage inequality grows.

Institutions

Institutions matter, and two institutional features of the 1940s compressed the distribution of wages (Goldin and Margo 1992). In the wartime command economy of the first half of the decade, the National War Labor Board's (NWLB) authority to approve or to reject requests for wage increases compressed the wage distribution. The NWLB set ranges of acceptable wages by occupation and region, and the board routinely approved requests to increase wages that were below the range. The NWLB also routinely approved raises that eliminated occupational differences in wages within plants.

Wage compression continued after World War II, and a second institutional factor had a lot to do with it. The GI Bill offered subsidized college educations for returning war veterans. Veterans headed to college, which caused an unprecedented increase in the supply of college graduates over just a few years. While the GI Bill increased the supply of skilled labor, the relative demand for skilled workers didn't grow. The wage premium fell, and the Great Compression continued until the demand for college graduates began to grow in the 1950s.

Unions are the great wage compressors, an antidote to wage inequality. That is, unions compress the wages of workers covered by union contracts. Of course, the union wage premium is a source of inequality between union and nonunion workers. Compression of wages within unions tends to be the stronger effect, so the decline of private-sector unions since the early 1970s might contribute to rising wage inequality. The decline of unions seems to be a small but important piece of the rising-wage-inequality puzzle.

And then there's the minimum wage, which eroded in real terms in the 1980s. In the late 1970s, wages of low-wage workers bunched at the minimum wage. As inflation eroded the real minimum wage in the 1980s, real wages of these low-wage workers spread down the left tail of the wage distribution. Wage inequality increased in the bottom half of the wage distribution, which raised the 90–10 percentile ratio. But the eroding real value of the minimum wage fails to explain the tremendous widening in the top half of the wage distribution. Like the decline of unions, erosion of the minimum wage is at best one piece of the puzzle.

There's clearly a role for institutions, but common patterns across developed countries underscore the importance of skill-biased innovations in increasing wage inequality. Changes in institutions are specific to each country. For instance, the minimum wage erodes in real terms in the United States while some other countries hike their minimum wages. But technological innovations diffuse throughout the developed world. Is there evidence of skill-biased innovations and increasing wage inequality outside the United States? The increase in the employment of skilled workers (relative to unskilled workers) has been pervasive in developed countries despite the increase in the relative wage of skilled workers (Berman, Bound, and Machin 1998). And the pattern doesn't reflect a shift in demand from goods produced by unskilled workers to goods produced by skilled workers: within industries (and even within plants), production has shifted from unskilled workers to skilled workers.

In most developed countries, the shift toward skilled workers is associated with falling relative wages of unskilled workers. Institutions in some developed countries prevent wages from falling, so the skill-biased innovations leave less of a mark on wage inequality and more of a mark on unemployment of unskilled workers in these countries. (See the discussion of European unemployment in section 12.4.)

10.4   Technology and Jobs in the Long Run

Our equilibrium model of relative skills and relative wages in Figure 10.10 is a powerful tool to understand the wage premium to skill and wage inequality in the short run. In the long run, however, we should address the incentives to acquire skills. After all, people choose whether to get skills. A high wage premium (or return) to skill encourages workers to acquire skills. In the long run, skill-biased innovation increase skills rather than wage inequality.

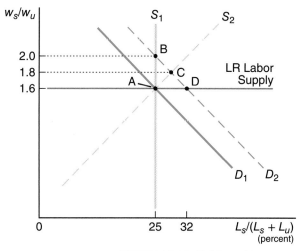

With a fixed mix of skills in the short run, skill-biased innovation increases wage inequality. The equilibrium jumps from A to B in the short run, and the relative wage of skilled workers rises from 1.6 to 2.0.

Increasing the return to skill encourages skill formation, so the relative supply of skilled workers slopes up in the intermediate run. As the quantity supplied of skilled labor (relative to unskilled labor) increases, the wage premium falls to 80 percent at C.

Skill formation continues until the relative wage of skilled workers returns to 1.6 in the long run. That is, the relative supply of skilled labor is perfectly elastic in the long run.

FIGURE 10.11. Skill-Biased Innovations in the Short Run and Long Run

Skill-Biased Innovations in the Short Run and Long Run

Figure 10.11 illustrates how the equilibrium evolves from the short run to the long run. In response to a skill-biased innovation that increases the demand for skilled workers relative to unskilled workers, the equilibrium jumps from point A to point B in the short run: the relative wage of skilled workers rises from 1.6 to 2.0, so the wage premium to skill rises from 60 percent to 100 percent, which increases wage inequality.

The 100 percent wage premium encourages skill formation. More kids go college; workers get more training on the job. These choices increase the relative supply of skilled workers. The equilibrium slides down the new relative demand for skilled labor D_2 from B to C in the intermediate run: firms employ more workers with skills, and the wage premium to skill falls from 100 percent to 80 percent. And wage inequality falls.

People acquire skills until the wage premium to skill falls back to its long-run value. In Figure 10.11, the long-run equilibrium is point D where the wage premium to skill returns to its long-run value of 60 percent. From the initial equilibrium at A to the new long-run equilibrium at D, growth in the supply of skilled workers matches growth in the demand for skilled workers. Since the wage premium to skill eventually returns to 60 percent, the skill-biased innovation doesn't affect wage inequality in the long run. The source of this stunning result is the perfectly elastic long-run relative supply of skilled workers. In the long run, workers just follow the jobs.

Encouraging Skill Formation

Increasing wage inequality signals the need (on efficiency grounds) for more skilled workers; that is, rising inequality is a skill-supply problem. Increasing the relative supply of skilled workers mitigates or even solves the inequality problem.

Redistributing income from high-skill to low-skill workers, however, dampens the incentive to acquire skills. But it's the incentive to acquire skills that increases the number of skilled workers and decreases wage inequality. That is, equity-driven income redistribution perpetuates the underlying problem of too few skilled workers.

Key Principle.
Increasing wage inequality encourages workers to acquire skills, which reduces inequality in the long run.

Even those who don't acquire extra skills gain from the skills that others acquire. Suppose skilled workers are college graduates, and the low-skill workers have only high school educations. A high return to skill (schooling in this case) encourages more students to go to college, increasing the relative supply of skilled workers and depressing the college wage premium. The extra college graduates gain, of course. But the high school graduates who they leave behind also gain because fewer workers are available to fill those low-skill jobs. The wage premium to skill shrinks to the advantage of the low-skill workers.

Many students enroll in college and later drop out. This suggests that many high school graduates want the wages that go with a college education but aren't prepared to succeed in college. Are public high schools failing to prepare these students for college and careers as high-skill workers? If so, addressing rising inequality might be more about education policy and less about tax and welfare policies.

Application: Automation and Job Loss

Do you have a case of automation anxiety? Are you afraid that robots and computers are destroying jobs? Innovation has definitely eliminated some jobs. One example is blacksmiths, a job that the automobile industry nearly eliminated. In the modern era, bookkeeping and payroll software applications are replacing bookkeepers and payroll clerks. But there's good reason to be skeptical of widespread technology-driven joblessness.

Two-hundred years ago, almost everyone worked on farms. Now farms employ only 1 in 50 workers. Mechanical harvesters and other innovations in farm technology combined with inelastic demand for agricultural products to drive down the price of farm goods so much that the innovations reduced the value of marginal product of farm workers. (Recall our discussion of farm innovations in section 2.1.) Have you noticed how the loss of all those farm jobs from the early 1800s has caused economy-collapsing mass unemployment? Actually, workers have fared quite well over the past two centuries.

We've fully responded to the shift from farm employment to manufacturing and service employment without a catastrophe. Of course, two centuries is a long time. More recently, ATMs replaced bank tellers for most in-branch transactions, but more people work as bank tellers now than in the pre-ATM era. And less than two decades ago, 190,000 people worked at Blockbuster and other video stores. At the end of 2017, Blockbuster has 10 stores (most in Alaska), and employment in all video stores has dropped to 10,800 workers. Are state unemployment offices overrun with claims for unemployment insurance benefits from former video store clerks looking for work that no longer exists? Nope. Jobs in video stores are long gone, but other jobs have popped up.

Robots and computers are great at routine and codifiable tasks. They aren't so good at tasks that require judgment, intuition, flexibility, creativity, and persuasion. Advances in technology shift demand from many low-skill jobs to high-skill jobs that complement the new technology. In the short-run, automation reduces employment of low-skill workers and increases the wage premium to skill; robots and computers increase wage inequality in the short run. But in the long run, people follow the jobs. They acquire the skills to do cognitively demanding work, jobs that complement computers and make use of the traits (e.g., intuition, creativity, etc.) that computers currently lack. The wage premium to skill vanishes as the relative supply of skilled workers catches up with the increases in the relative demand for skilled workers. And wage inequality returns to its long-run basis.

Technology might also polarize the job market, carving out the middle of the job distribution (Autor and Dorn 2013). With **job polarization**, innovations eliminate repetitive motion or routine jobs that require moderate skills (e.g., machine operator or bookkeeper). Janitors, hair stylists, home health-care aides, and other low-skill workers are safe on their difficult-to-automate jobs. Many professional, technical, and managerial jobs complement the advances in computing, so the demand for high-skill workers on these non-routine jobs increases. Thus jobs shift from the middle to the bottom and top of the skill distribution.

In the long run, workers follow the jobs to both ends of the distribution, hollowing out the center. But low-skill jobs aren't bad jobs in the long run because the wage on low-skill jobs must be high enough for those jobs to be attractive compared to high-skill jobs that require advanced schooling and lots of work experience. The inequality that remains in the long run simply reflects the wage premium that encourages enough workers to acquire skills.

Summary

In this chapter, we developed the tools to measure and the principles to explain the distribution of wages. Our main findings are:

- ☐ A histogram depicts the wage distribution by measuring the proportion of workers in various intervals of wages (e.g., between $600 and $700 per week). Most workers earn between $400 and $1,000 per week, but the right tail of the weekly wage distribution extends beyond several thousand dollars.

- ☐ The ratio of the wage at the 90th percentile to the wage at the 10th percentile of the distribution measures wage dispersion or inequality. A worker with wage w_p is at percentile p of the wage distribution if p percent of workers earn no more than w_p. The wage w_p is then the wage at the pth percentile. The standard deviation of log wages is a second measure of wage dispersion.

☐ The Lorenz curve illustrates wage dispersion by plotting the share of wages earned by workers at or below percentile p (i.e., the cumulative wage share) and p itself. The Gini coefficient measures wage dispersion by comparing gaps between the cumulative wage shares and percentiles along the Lorenz curve. Gini coefficients indicate that (1) India and South Africa are among the countries with the most wage inequality, and (2) wage inequality in Italy is quite low.

☐ Wages skew to the right. Comparing either (1) the mean to the median or (2) the 90–50 percentile ratio to the 50–10 percentile ratio quantifies the asymmetry or skewness of wages.

☐ Measurable differences in the workweek, schooling, potential work experience, and other factors across workers absorb at least three-quarters of wage inequality as measured by the Gini coefficient. Measurable differences across occupations in averages of our key variables explain almost all wage inequality across occupations.

☐ A wage–skill (or wage–ability) curve that increases at an increasing rate skews the distribution of wages to the right. In chapter 6's model of schooling with identical workers, the equilibrium wage–schooling curve increases at an increasing rate, and schooling choice contributes to the skewness of wages. Self-selection to jobs and superstar technologies also magnify small differences in skills or talents into large differences in pay.

☐ Wage inequality in the United States grew slowly in the 1970s, accelerated in the 1980s, and has continued to grow since then. The Great Compression of the 1940s was a period of falling wage inequality.

☐ Many factors contributed to rising wage inequality since the late 1960s. Skill-biased innovations increased the demand for skilled labor relative to unskilled labor, which increased the wage premium to skilled labor. While the premium to other dimensions of skill and wage inequality overall increased in the 1970s, an unusually rapid growth in the supply of college graduates reduced the college wage premium in that decade.

☐ Skill-biased innovation doesn't generate wage inequality in the long run—when the increase in the supply of skilled workers matches the increase in the demand for skilled workers.

In the next chapter, we investigate the form of pay, including strategies that link pay to performance. A tight link between pay and performance widens the distribution of wages, but we focus on how to structure compensation to attract, to retain, and to motivate workers.

Key Concepts

- histogram, p. 368
- mean and median, p. 369
- wage inequality, p. 369
- percentiles of the wage distribution, p. 369
- 90–10 percentile ratio, p. 370
- standard deviation of log wages, p. 370
- normal distribution, p. 370
- Lorenz curve, p. 371
- cumulative wage share, p. 371
- Gini coefficient, p. 373
- asymmetry or skewness, p. 374

- mean–median difference, p. 374
- comparison of 90–50 and 50–10 percentile ratios, p. 374
- increases at an increasing rate, p. 378
- hierarchy of jobs, p. 379
- superstar market, p. 382
- joint (or nonrivalrous) consumption, p. 382
- cake vs. sunset technologies, p. 382
- limited quantity-quality substitution, p. 383
- increasing wage inequality, p. 384
- increasing return to skill, p. 386
- skill-biased innovation, p. 387
- job polarization, p. 393

Short-Answer Questions

10.1 What is the wage at the 75th percentile of weekly wages in Table 10.2? Workers in the bottom 75 percent of the wage distribution earn what percent of all wages? Workers with wages between the 75th and 90th percentiles earn what percent of all wages?

10.2 In constructing the Lorenz curve, we order workers from lowest wage to highest wage. Explain why the ordering causes the Lorenz curve to increase at an increasing rate.

10.3 We studied three measures of wage dispersion and two measures of wage asymmetry in the chapter. What are they?

10.4 If the wage grows with ability at an increasing rate (as in Figure 10.6b), then the wage isn't very sensitive to ability among low-ability workers and is very sensitive to ability among high-ability workers. Explain how this differential effect tends to skew the distribution of wages to the right.

10.5 The Occupy Wall Street movement is deeply concerned with wage inequality, such as differences in wages between investment bankers and farmers. The movement doesn't appear to be concerned with differences in wages among investment bankers. Summarize our findings about wage inequality within and across occupations. Do you think the evidence is relevant to the debate?

10.6 How did we establish that, in Figure 10.7, (1) skills are distributed symmetrically and (2) wages skew to the right? How does the process of job assignment (i.e., self-selection) skew wages?

10.7 What are the two key features of superstar markets? Pick a superstar. What business is he or she in? Do the two key features fit the example of your superstar?

10.8 Wage inequality has been rising since the late 1960s, and skill-biased innovations have a lot to do with it. But something else was going on when the college wage premium fell in the 1970s. What was it? Work with the relative demand and relative supply of skilled workers to explain why the rate of return to schooling fell while the premium to other skills rose in the 1970s.

10.9 Skill-biased innovation is a leading candidate to explain increasing wage inequality over nearly 50 years. Name at least four other candidates, and explain how each hypothesis might contribute to increasing wage inequality.

Problems

10.1 Here are the weekly wages in a sample of 10 wage and salary workers: 150, 250, 300, 350, 400, 450, 550, 650, 800, and 1,000.

In small samples like this one, the gaps between the wages are a source of ambiguity in computing wages at percentiles of the distribution. Let's resolve the ambiguity by using midpoints. With an even number of observations, the median is halfway between the highest value in the bottom half of the sample and the lowest value in the top half of the sample. Also, 30 percent of the workers earn $300 or less, but 30 percent also earn $349.99 or less. To be consistent with the calculation of the median wage, the wage at the 30th percentile is halfway between $300 and $350.

(a) Compute the mean and median of wages in this sample.

(b) What are the wages at the 10th and 90th percentiles in this sample?

(c) What is the 90–10 percentile ratio? That is, the worker at the 90th percentile earns _____ times as much as the worker at the 10th percentile.

(d) How far from the median wage are the wages at the 10th and 90th percentiles? Do wages in this small sample skew to the right?

10.2 We sort weekly wages in a large sample of workers from lowest to highest, and the table below lists the wage at each *decile* of the wage distribution—the 10th percentile, 20th percentile, and so on.

PERCENTILE p	WAGE ($/worker)	CUMULATIVE WAGE ($)	CUMULATIVE WAGE SHARE (%)	GAP (%)
10	0	0	0	10
20	100	100		
30	200	300		
40	300			
50	400			
60	600			
70	700			
80	800			
90	900			
100	1,000			

Although 10 percent of the sample wages lie between the wages at adjacent deciles (e.g., between $200 at percentile 30 and $300 at percentile 40), ignore these wages for the purpose of calculating cumulative wages: just add the wages across the listed percentiles.

(a) What are the total wages of workers at or below the 40th percentile? Complete the column of cumulative wages in the table.

(b) What is the sum of all wages in this sample? That is, what is the cumulative wage at the 100th percentile?

(c) Divide the cumulative wages in the third column by the sum of all wages to compute the cumulative wage shares in the fourth column.

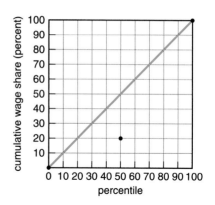

(d) Plot the 10 pairs of percentiles and cumulative wage shares in the figure above. Connect the points to illustrate the Lorenz curve in this sample.

(e) For each of the 10 percentiles, subtract the cumulative wage share from the percentile and enter the result in the last column of the table.

(f) Calculate the Gini coefficient by (i) summing the percentiles in the first column, (ii) summing the gaps in the last column, and (iii) dividing the sum of the gaps by the sum of the percentiles.

10.3 There are two types of jobs: blue-collar jobs and white-collar jobs. Workers with 10 years of education earn $400 per week on blue-collar jobs and $200 on white-collar jobs. Completing another year of school increases the wage on a blue-collar job by $50 per week and the wage on a white-collar job by $100 per week.

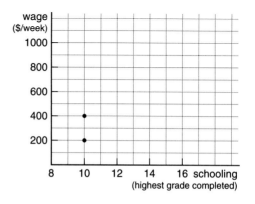

(a) Graph the wage–schooling line on blue-collar jobs in the figure above. Also graph the wage–schooling line on white-collar jobs.

(b) Where do the two lines intersect? Over what range of schooling do blue-collar jobs pay more? Over what range of schooling do white-collar jobs pay more?

Schooling is distributed uniformly between grades 10 and 18. That is, 11.1 percent of the workers leave school after completing each grade from 10 to 18.

(c) If everyone worked on blue-collar jobs, wages would be distributed uniformly between $_____ and $_____.

(d) If everyone worked on white-collar jobs, wages would be distributed uniformly between $_____ and $_____.

(e) Each worker takes the job that pays him or her the higher wage. How does the wage gap between the top worker and the median worker compare to the wage gap between the median worker and the bottom worker? What does your answer reveal about the distribution of wages in this problem?

10.4 The figure below illustrates the market for skilled labor relative to unskilled labor.

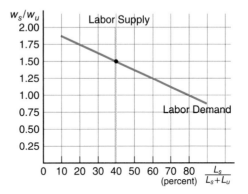

(a) The GI Bill draws war veterans to colleges, and the relative supply of skilled labor subsequently increases by 20 percentage points. What happens to the relative wage of skilled workers? Does the college wage premium rise or fall?

(b) Alternatively, a massive influx of unskilled workers enters the country, and the relative supply of skilled labor falls by 10 percentage points. What happens to the relative wage of skilled workers?

(c) Introduction of assembly-line production a century ago shifted the demand for labor away from skilled craftsmen toward unskilled workers. Suppose the innovation reduces the relative demand for skilled labor by 20 percentage points at each relative wage. What happens to the relative wage of skilled labor?

10.5 The figure below shows the market for skilled workers relative to unskilled workers in the short run.

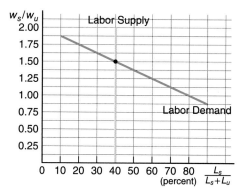

(a) An innovation increases the relative demand for skilled workers by 20 percentage points at each value of the relative wage. Graph the effect of the innovation in the figure, and mark the new equilibrium point.

(b) How does the innovation affect the wage premium in the short run?

(c) How does the innovation influence the incentives to acquire skills by investing in human capital?

(d) In the intermediate run, the relative supply of skilled workers increases 10 percentage points. Illustrate the intermediate-run equilibrium in the figure. Does the wage premium to skill rise or fall from the short run to the intermediate run? What happens to wage inequality in the intermediate run?

(e) In the long run, the wage premium returns to its original value. How much must the relative supply of skilled workers increase to reach the long-run response to the innovation? Illustrate the new long-run equilibrium.

(f) In the context of this problem, discuss how the race between the demand for and the supply of skilled workers influences wage inequality.

References

Autor, David H. and David Dorn. 2013. "The Growth of Low-Skill Service Jobs and the Polarization of the U.S. Labor Market." *American Economic Review* 103(5): 1553–1597.

Berman, Eli, John Bound, and Stephen Machin. 1998. "Implications of Skill-Biased Technological Change: International Evidence." *Quarterly Journal of Economics* 113(4): 1245–1279.

Borjas, George J., Richard B. Freeman, and Lawrence F. Katz. 1997. "How Much Do Immigration and Trade Affect Labor Market Outcomes?" *Brookings Papers on Economic Activity* 1997(1): 1–90.

Goldin, Claudia and Robert A. Margo. 1992. "The Great Compression: The Wage Structure in the United States at Mid-Century." *Quarterly Journal of Economics* 107(1): 1–34.

Juhn, Chinhui, Kevin M. Murphy, and Brooks Pierce. 1993. "Wage Inequality and the Rise in the Returns to Skill." *Journal of Political Economy* 101(3): 410–442.

Katz, Lawrence F. and Kevin M. Murphy. 1992. "Changes in Relative Wages, 1963–1987: Supply and Demand Factors." *Quarterly Journal of Economics* 107(1): 35–78.

Marshall, Alfred. 1920 (1890). *Principles of Economics: An Introductory Volume*, 8th ed. London: Macmillan.

Mincer, Jacob. 1958. "Investment in Human Capital and Personal Income Distribution." *Journal of Political Economy* 66(4): 281–302.

Rosen, Sherwin. 1981. "The Economics of Superstars." *American Economic Review* 71(5): 845–858.

11

Compensation Strategies

Workers at Safelite in the early 1990s probably thought they were doing a good job popping out damaged windshields and installing new ones. The typical installer earned $10 to $12 per hour replacing 2.7 windshields per day. It takes about an hour to replace a windshield, so Safelite President John Barlow wondered why his workers weren't installing more windshields each day. Could he motivate his workers to install more windshields?

Safelite began rolling out piece-rate performance pay in January 1994. Safelite paid each installer $20 per windshield with a guaranteed minimum pay of $11 per hour. (If weekly performance pay based on the $20 piece rate added up to less than $11 per hour, then Safelite paid the worker the guaranteed $11 per hour for the week.) If the typical worker continued to install only 2.7 windshields in an 8-hour day, the guaranteed $11 hourly wage would exceed hourly compensation based on the piece rate ($= 2.7 \times \$20 \div 8$). But many workers responded to the incentive system. The number of windshields installed per worker per day increased 44 percent (Lazear 2000). About half of the increase came from existing workers hustling to install more windows. The other half was from raising the quality of Safelite's installers. Slow installers left Safelite, and faster installers—lured by the wages they could earn with performance pay—came to Safelite. The average hourly wage increased 10 percent. But cost per windshield fell, and profit rose.

Safelite's experience with performance-based compensation in the 1990s illustrates the main issues in the design of compensation systems. First, performance incentives matter. Linking pay to performance motivates workers to work harder; that is, they increase their quantity supplied of effort. Second, performance incentives also affect worker quality. A compensation system that rewards performance attracts and retains talented workers. So compensation strategies affect worker performance, recruiting, and retention.

The strategy of paying for performance worked at Safelite. In this chapter, we identify the advantages and disadvantages of each form of compensation—profit sharing, piece rate, bonus pay for reaching a sales or production quota, prizes for high performers, paying super-competitive wages, and back-loading pay. And we apply the principles to the compensation of chief executive officers (CEOs) of corporations.

11.1 Introduction to Compensation

How does the wage vary with performance—performance of the firm, performance of the individual worker, or performance of a reference group of coworkers? A strong link between pay and performance motivates workers to work hard, to supply effort. It also attracts skilled workers. As we compare various forms of compensation, let's focus on how each form motivates and attracts workers.

Effort on the job is unknown to anyone but the worker, and some skills aren't known by anyone else either. If effort on the job were observable, then the employer could contract with each worker to supply a specified amount of effort, the contract would be enforceable in court, and motivating workers wouldn't be a problem. Let's assume effort, as well as some skills, are unobservable, so a compensation system must motivate the worker to provide effort and attract quality workers.

Production Environment

Julie and Katie are two service professionals. They might check in travelers at the airport, edit manuscripts for publication, report the news, treat infected root canals, or surgically repair damaged knees. Let's assume they prepare tax returns for individual taxpayers like you and me. The price to prepare a typical return is $125. The number of tax returns that Julie (or Katie) can prepare in a week depends on her effort. By working hard—keeping focused and avoiding idle chatter, personal telephone calls, Facebook updates, and online shopping while on the job—Julie prepares lots of tax returns in a week; if she doesn't work hard, she doesn't complete many returns. Julie's output also depends on a random element. If she's lucky, the tax returns are straightforward, and she prepares lots of easy returns. If several complicated returns appear on her desk, she doesn't prepare as many returns.

For a tax preparer like Julie, output q therefore depends on effort e and randomness u. To keep things simple, let's assume that the marginal product of effort is a constant. Giving five more units of effort for the week translates into one more completed tax return; that is, the marginal product of effort MP_e is 1/5 tax returns per unit of effort. Then Julie's production of tax returns is

(11.1) $q = e/5 + u$

where u is a random variable with mean zero. The random element is essential. Without it, effort could be deduced by observing output, and the problem of motivating performance would vanish.

The value of marginal product of Julie's effort VMP_e is the price of preparing a return (i.e., $p = 125$) times the marginal product of her effort (i.e., $MP_e = 1/5$). In this case, VMP_e is $25 (= \$125 \times 1/5$) per unit of effort. That is, one more unit of effort from Julie for the week raises weekly revenue by $25.

Efficient Effort

Effort is costly. The cost of effort isn't something that's paid with cash or a credit card; it's an implicit cost. People don't like to work hard because hard work is physically or mentally draining. Maybe it just gets in the way of happy thoughts. Workers don't like being tired, sore, mentally drained, or perhaps so wired that they can't relax at the end of the day. We reduce all these downsides of effort into a single function: the cost of effort is an increasing function $C(e)$.

The **marginal cost of effort** is also an increasing function of effort. Julie, Katie, and other tax preparers don't mind doing a little work. It relieves the boredom, provides a bit of mental exercise, and so forth. (On other jobs, it can provide physical exercise, too.) So the marginal cost of effort is low if effort is low. If Julie and her coworkers are working a grueling schedule, however, then putting in a little more effort can be exhausting or even depressing; that is, it can be quite costly. Thus the marginal-cost-of-effort curve slopes up, as Figure 11.1 illustrates.

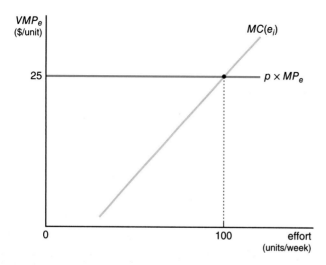

The marginal product of effort is 1/5, and the price of the product is $p = 125$, so the value of the marginal product of effort is $25 (= \$125 \div 5$)/unit of effort. $MC(e)$ is the marginal-cost-of-effort curve.

The efficient level of effort $\hat{e}$ equates the value of the marginal product of effort with the marginal cost of effort. The intersection of the horizontal VMP_e line with the upward-sloping $MC(e)$ curve at $\hat{e} = 100$ reveals that the efficient level of effort in this case is 100 units/week.

FIGURE 11.1. Efficient Level of Effort

Efficiency requires that the value of the marginal product of effort equals the marginal cost of effort; that is, the solution to $VMP_e = MC(e)$ is the **efficient effort** $\hat{e}$. For our tax preparers, the marginal value of effort is \$25 per unit of effort, which Figure 11.1 displays as a horizontal line. Any effort short of 100 units has $VMP_e > MC(e)$ in the figure, so a little more effort increases the value of what Julie produces more than it costs her in terms of the cost of her effort. Increasing effort creates value. For any effort beyond $e = 100$, $VMP_e < MC(e)$, so increasing effort increases the value of what Julie produces less than it increases the her cost of effort. Decreasing effort creates value. The efficient amount of effort is $\hat{e} = 100$ at the intersection of the marginal-value-of-effort and marginal-cost-of-effort curves.

 PRACTICE   How does the efficient amount of effort vary with the price of the product, the marginal product of effort, and factors that shift the marginal cost of effort?

Self-Employment

What forms of compensation achieve or approach the efficient effort $\hat{e}$? Let's start with self-employment. If Julie works for herself, her incentives to work hard are strong. In fact, self-employed workers have incentives to supply the efficient level of effort.

Julie prepares tax returns for individual taxpayers. She's self-employed. She works hard because she alone captures the benefit (in terms of revenue) of her effort. The benefits of giving it her all (e.g., really pushing herself, avoiding distractions, and so on) are entirely hers. Alternatively, if she takes a long weekend or cuts out early to watch her kid's soccer game, she suffers the lost income. So an additional unit of effort increases Julie's self-employment income by \$25, the value of the marginal product of her effort VMP_e. She also bears the full cost of her effort, so her marginal cost of effort is $MC(e)$. As a result, Julie supplies the efficient level of effort $\hat{e} = 100$.

The strong incentive to perform is the main reason why about 1-in-10 workers in the United States choose self-employment over working as employees. But why do 9-in-10 workers choose to be employees? To answer this question, we compare the advantages and disadvantages of several forms of compensation, including profit sharing.

Profit Sharing and Shirking

Julie partners with Katie in preparing tax returns. They share the accounting profit of their two-person partnership, which dilutes each partners incentive to work hard.

Julie knows her own effort, but she doesn't know Katie's effort. Katie knows exactly how hard she works, but she doesn't know whether Julie is working hard or just daydreaming. The number of tax returns that their partnership prepares is $q = (e_j + e_k)/5 + u$, where $u = u_j + u_k$ is a random variable. (Since we have more than one tax preparer, we use the subscripts j and k to identify who's who.)

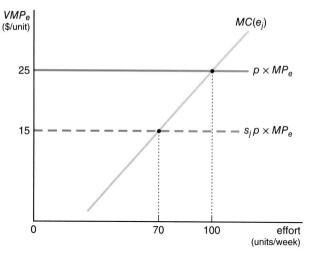

FIGURE 11.2. Effort in a Partnership

Julie's share of the partnership's accounting profit is $s_j = .6$. She bears the full marginal cost of her effort but receives only 60 percent of the value of the marginal product of her effort. Julie chooses her effort to equate $.6VMP_e$ with $MC(e)$. The 70 units of effort that she puts in is inefficiently low. Julie shirks.

Since partner shares sum to one, Katie's share is $s_k = .4$, and she supplies less effort than Julie. In a partnership with N partners, the average share is $1/N$, so profit-sharing incentives are quite weak in large partnerships.

The partnership's accounting profit is $\pi = pq - c = 125((e_j + e_k)/5 + u) - c$, where cost c does *not* include the cost of effort. Since the mean of u is zero, the expected value of profit is

(11.2) $$\mathrm{E}\pi = 25(e_j + e_k) - c$$

(The E operating on profit π tells us to compute the expected value or mean of π.) Every unit of effort generates, on average, \$25 in revenue and accounting profit for the partnership.

Profit sharing divides the accounting profit between the partners. Julie's share of the accounting profit is 60 percent; Katie's profit share is 40 percent. So Julie earns $.60\pi$ from the partnership, and Katie earns $.40\pi$.

Let's explore how Julie decides how hard to work—how much effort to supply. Julie cares about her compensation from the firm, but she also cares about her effort. In particular, assume that Julie's objective is to maximize the expected value of her partner earnings net of her implicit cost of effort. Her **expected net earnings** is $y_j = .6\mathrm{E}\pi - C(e_j)$, so

(11.3) $$y_j = .6(25(e_j + e_k) - c) - C(e_j)$$

Although Julie benefits from Katie's effort e_k, she couldn't care less about Katie's cost of effort $C(e_k)$.

Julie chooses her effort by equating the benefit and cost of her effort at the margin. Putting in an extra unit of effort increases the number of tax returns she completes by 1/5 on average. That increases partnership revenue and profit by \$25 since $p = 125$. Julie's profit share is 60 percent, so the extra unit of effort increases her weekly partner earnings by \$15 ($= .6 \times \$25$). The dashed horizontal line in Figure 11.2 depicts this marginal benefit of effort. Her marginal cost of effort is the upward-sloping line in the figure. The quantity of effort that Julie supplies is

$e_j^* = 70$ where her marginal cost of effort equals 15. Since Julie's effort is short of the efficient effort $\hat{e} = 100$, we say she **shirks**.

PRACTICE

Katie solves a very similar problem. If Katie exerts another unit of effort, how much do Katie's partner earnings rise? Sketch this marginal benefit in the figure. Her marginal-cost-of-effort curve is the same as Julie's. Indicate the solution to Katie's effort-supply problem in the figure. Does Katie shirk? Does she supply more or less effort than Julie?

Why do partners shirk? Because each partner bears the full cost of her effort but receives only a share of the product of that effort.

A higher share of profit raises the marginal reward for effort, which increases the quantity supplied of effort. If Julie's share of partnership profit rises from 60 percent to 70 percent, the marginal reward for her effort increases from $15 to $17.50. And Julie's quantity supplied of effort slides up the marginal-cost-of-effort curve from $e = 70$ to $e = 77.5$. Therefore, the marginal-cost-of-effort curve is the **effort supply curve** of partners. (The usual caveat applies: we measure marginal cost vertically in dollars per unit of effort; effort supply is measured horizontally in units of effort per week.)

Profit sharing is inefficient. Each partner shirks. Since the profit shares sum to 100 percent, motivating one partner to work harder (by increasing her share) necessarily dilutes the other partner's incentives to supply effort (as her share falls). This problem is particularly bad in large partnerships. With 10 partners, partner shares average 10 percent. So the typical partner's effort solves $.10 \times VMP_e = MC(e)$, and the incentives to supply effort are weak. If the number of partners N is 100 or 5,000, the typical partner's marginal benefit of effort sinks toward zero. Indeed, in large partnerships, incentives from profit sharing are negligible. We call this the $1/N$ problem.

There are thousands of partners in each of the Big Four accounting firms, and most of these partners work very hard. Each partner's share of profit is small, so why do they work so hard? Each firm divides its profit among the thousands of partners at the close of every fiscal year. But the key feature of profit distribution in these partnerships is that a partner's profit share depends on *personal* performance. The primary gain to a partner's hard work is that it increases the partner's share of partnership profit. The firm rewards high-performing partners with larger shares of partnership profit. Partner compensation ends up being a complicated way to compensate workers on the basis of personal performance while avoiding the double taxation associated with corporations.

11.2 Performance Pay

Profit sharing provides only weak incentives to supply effort, especially in large partnerships, so let's explore how performance pay can strengthen workers' incentives to supply effort. Performance pay links a worker's compensation to his or her job performance.

Julie and Katie continue to crank out 1040s and Schedule Cs, but now they work at TaxCrafters, where each tax preparer's wage depends on performance. Julie's pay depends on the number of tax returns she prepares in a week. Her pay might also depend on her performance relative to a group of her coworkers. Let's uncover the advantages and disadvantages of various forms of performance pay at TaxCrafters.

Personal Performance

Personal performance pay links a worker's wage to his or her personal performance. Julie's pay depends on the rate at which she prepares tax returns. TaxCrafters might pay her by the piece (i.e., per tax return), a commission, or a bonus. Or TaxCrafters might tie Julie's annual salary to her annual performance evaluation. To identify the key principles of personal performance incentives, we analyze how piece rates and bonuses motivate performance and attract and retain workers.

Piece Rate.   With a **piece rate**, the wage is a linear function of performance. Julie's wage is the sum of a guaranteed payment that she receives every week a and performance pay, which is the product of the piece rate b and Julie's output q. (Here we hide the subscripts.)

(11.4) $$w = a + bq$$

Julie's guarantee is $75 per week, and her piece rate is $50 per return, so her weekly wage is $w = 75 + 50q$. The line in Figure 11.3 illustrates the relationship between Julie's pay and performance.

 PRACTICE   Liz sells flat-screen TVs at Best Buy. Best Buy pays Liz $4 per hour plus a commission rate of 10 percent on her sales revenue pq. Express Liz's hourly wage (or earnings) in terms of the commission rate, the price of TVs p, and her sales of TVs q.

Julie's objective is to maximize her expected earnings net of the cost of her effort. Her wage is $w = 75 + 50q$; since q is random, her wage is random. The expected value of her wage is $Ew = 75 + 50(e/5) = 75 + 10e$, so the expected value of Julie's net earnings is

(11.5) $$y = 75 + 10e - C(e)$$

Exerting more effort lifts her weekly wage on average, but it also raises the cost of her effort.

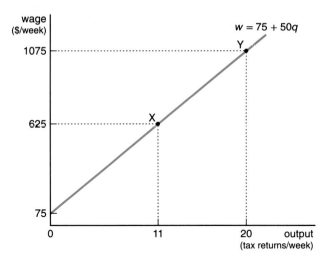

In a piece-rate compensation system, Julie's weekly wage w is a linear function of the number of tax returns she prepares q. The intercept $a = 75$ is her guaranteed weekly payment. The piece rate $b = 50$ determines the slope of the wage line. If Julie prepares 20 tax returns in a week, TaxCrafters pays her $1,075 (= \$75 + (\$50 \times 20))$ for the week.

The higher the piece rate, the steeper the wage line and the stronger the incentive to supply effort.

FIGURE 11.3. Piece-Rate Compensation

Julie chooses her effort to equate the marginal value and marginal cost of her effort. An extra unit of effort increases Julie's average output by one-fifth of a tax return. Since the piece rate is $50 per return, the extra effort increases her average weekly wage by $10 (= \$50 \times 1/5)$. The dashed horizontal line at $VMP_e = 10$ in Figure 11.4 illustrates Julie's marginal reward for effort. At low levels of effort, the marginal cost of effort is less than $VMP_e = 10$, and Julie does better by working harder. At high levels of effort, the marginal cost of effort exceeds $VMP_e = 10$, so exerting less effort improves matters for Julie. Julie's optimal effort e^* is 55 units per week at the intersection of the horizontal VMP_e line and the marginal-cost-of-effort curve $MC(e)$.

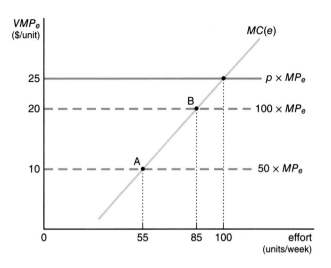

The piece rate is $b = 50$, so Julie's marginal reward for effort bMP_e is $10 (= \$50 \times 1/5)$/unit of effort. Julie's effort choice equates her marginal reward for effort to the marginal cost of her effort at point A. She supplies 55 units of effort/week.

Doubling the piece rate to $100 per tax return causes Julie to increase her effort from 55 to 85 units/week.

$MC(e)$ is the effort supply curve.

FIGURE 11.4. Effort with a Piece Rate

PRACTICE   With a piece rate of $50 per tax return, each tax preparer at TaxCrafters supplies 55 units of effort. How many returns does a tax preparer like Julie complete in a typical week? What is the average weekly wage of a tax preparer at TaxCrafters?

The $50-per-return piece rate doesn't generate more effort than profit sharing in Julie and Katie's partnership. In fact, Julie, Katie, and the other tax preparers at TaxCrafters put in only as much effort as Katie did in the partnership. So shifting to personal performance incentives doesn't encourage much effort if the piece rate is as low as $50 per tax return. We need a higher piece rate to get Julie, Katie, and the other tax preparers at TaxCrafters to really perform.

Increasing the piece rate increases effort. If the piece rate doubles from $50 to $100 per tax return, then (1) Julie's marginal reward for effort doubles from $10 to $20 per unit, and (2) her effort rises from 55 to 85 units per week. Julie's quantity supplied of effort slides up the marginal-cost-of-effort curve from A to B in Figure 11.4. The marginal-cost-of-effort curve is, therefore, Julie's effort supply curve.

Setting the piece rate equal to the product price delivers efficient work effort. For any piece rate less than the price of the product or service, workers like Julie shirk. But if TaxCrafters pays a piece rate of $125 per return (i.e., $b = p$), then Julie's marginal reward for effort pMP_e equals $25 per unit of effort, and she supplies 100 units of effort. Such high-powered incentives motivate Julie and the other tax preparers to supply the efficient level of effort.

But what does it mean for tax preparers to be paid a piece rate that equals the price of tax-preparation services? Since performance pay absorbs all TaxCrafters's revenue, the guaranteed weekly pay a falls to zero. Julie is essentially self-employed. That makes sense. A self-employed worker receives all the benefit and bears all the cost of her effort, so she chooses the efficient effort $\hat{e} = 100$. But this result implies that piece rates always produce shirking in any meaningful employment relationship.

PRACTICE   A taxi driver pays a daily fee to rent the cab and keeps all the revenue from fares. What are the driver's guarantee a and commission rate b?

Advantages and Disadvantages.   What are the advantages and disadvantages of high-powered piece-rate compensation? Let's start with the advantages. A high piece rate motivates workers to give a lot of effort. It also attracts and retains the most-talented workers. In Figure 11.5, talented workers—those who can prepare more than 15 returns per week—do better by working for employers with high-powered incentives. Less-talented workers sort into jobs with low-powered

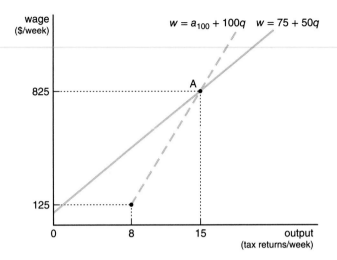

$$w = a_{100} + 100q \qquad w = 75 + 50q$$

Performance incentives are strong along the dashed wage line with the $100 per return piece rate. That piece rate applies only to output exceeding 8 tax returns/week.

The intersection of the two lines at point A determines the output that leaves workers indifferent between the two piece rates. Talented workers, those who expect to produce more than 15 returns/week, earn more with the higher piece rate. Less-talented tax preparers, those who expect to complete fewer than 15 returns/week, earn more with the lower piece rate.

FIGURE 11.5. Talented Workers Prefer High-Powered Incentives

incentives. So a tight link between pay and performance attracts and retains talented workers.

High-powered piece-rate compensation also has disadvantages. The first is risk. The higher the piece rate, the riskier is Julie's weekly wage. Some weeks, she breezes through 15 tax returns with her 55 units of effort. Other weeks, she prepares only 9 returns with the same effort. Julie might not mind bearing that risk. She probably can smooth her consumption spending across weeks, building up her savings in good weeks and drawing it down in bad weeks. But she might be averse to risk. In that case, wage risk is a bad attribute of the job, and TaxCrafters must pay Julie more on average to compensate her for the extra risk associated with high-powered incentives. More-talented and less-risk-averse workers find high-powered incentives most attractive. Less-talented and more-risk-averse workers sort into low-*b* jobs.

Key Principle.
How workers are paid (e.g., performance incentives) is important for motivating, recruiting, and retaining workers.

A second disadvantage of piece rates is the cost of measuring performance. Counting the number of tax returns that Julie prepares is easy enough; similarly, it is easy to count the number of flat-screen TVs that Liz sells at Best Buy. But in many contexts, precisely measuring the worker's contribution to production is challenging. For instance, for nurses, authors, professors, web designers, illustrators, and boxers, we get a sense of performance (e.g., whether the person is having a good week or year, or who's doing better), but measuring performance precisely borders on impossible. That's why piece rates and commissions are most common in production and sales, where output is easily measured.

A third disadvantage of piece rates is that quality suffers. Where performance can be measured, we tend to simply count output or sales because the quality element of performance is usually much more difficult to measure. TaxCrafters easily measures how many tax returns Julie prepares in a week. The quality of her work is more difficult to assess. She might overlook deductions or forget to fill out a supplementary schedule. Imagine compensating nurses by the number of patients they care for, authors by the number of words they write, professors by the number of research papers they publish, web designers by the number of webpages they post, illustrators by the number of drawings they sketch, and boxers by the number of punches they throw. In every case, quality would suffer. For instance, authors would write lengthy books that no one would read. So high-powered personal incentives linked to quantity generally encourage quantity at the expense of quality.

 PRACTICE   For each of the previous example jobs, clearly identify the quality dimension and spell out how quality suffers if the worker's pay is tightly linked to quantity.

Key Principle.
Designing compensation to solve one problem tends to create other problems.

A fourth disadvantage of high-powered piece rates and commissions is that they don't encourage teamwork. Julie might increase TaxCrafters's output, revenue, and profit more by helping Katie (i.e., shifting some effort from Julie's own production to Katie's production); that is, teamwork is productive. With piece-rate compensation, however, the only way for Julie to increase her wage is by preparing more tax returns herself. If she helps Katie, Julie prepares fewer returns herself, and her pay suffers. The lack of teamwork can be a serious problem. Julie and Katie might battle for credit for good ideas and against blame for bad mistakes. Indeed, Julie might "throw Katie under the bus" to avoid wage-reducing blame for a failure.

Our analysis points to the importance of performance measurement. A good measure of a worker's performance is tightly linked to the firm's profit. Unfortunately, easily available measures of performance are frequently only weakly tied to profit. Where measuring the performance that really matters to the firm—performance that includes product quality (including treating customers and clients well), and teamwork, and so on—is fairly easy, piece rates and commissions can thrive.

Bonus Pay.   A second form of personal performance pay is **bonus pay** for meeting a standard for performance, such as a production or **sales quota**. Suppose Julie's weekly wage is a fixed amount w_0 if her performance falls short of q' tax returns per week. If she prepares q' or more returns per week, her weekly wage jumps to $w_1 > w_0$; that is, she gets a bonus of $\Delta w = w_1 - w_0$ if her performance reaches the quota q'. The quantity of effort that Julie supplies depends on the bonus Δw.

A big bonus has several advantages. First, Julie works hard because a big bonus provides strong incentives. Second, a big bonus also attracts talented workers (and those who are less averse to risk). Third, bonus pay economizes on the cost of measuring performance. TaxCrafters needs to know only whether Julie's performance meets the quota, so only marginal cases require precise measurement. Consequently, bonus pay can bring in quality dimensions of performance since only marginal cases require precise (and costly) measurement of quality.

Bonus pay also has its disadvantages, and several of these echo the disadvantages of piece rates. Large bonuses generate wage risk, which risk-averse workers dislike. And to the extent the quota is measured in terms of quantity, bonus pay neglects quality.

An additional problem with bonus pay is its lack of **marginal incentives**. In the following scene from *The Office* ("Turf War," 2012), two salesmen explain how, faced with a windfall of new clients, they respond to the lack of marginal incentives that stems from a cap on sales commissions:

> **Jim**: "The salesmen have a commission cap, but we've figured out a way around it."
> **Dwight**: "Lloyd Gross is a fictional salesman we invented to—how do I put this?—steal from the company, embezzle, to commit fraud."
> **Jim**: "Okay, it sounds sketchy, but it helps us get more money."

Bonus pay suffers from the same problem. Once Julie reaches the quota for the week, her incentives to work vanish. She coasts. Similarly, the most-talented tax preparers coast all week because they know they will reach the quota with minimal effort. And the bonus provides the least-talented tax preparers with only weak incentives because the quota is typically beyond their reach.

 PRACTICE Workers in a corporate hierarchy advance from level to level on the basis of performance. The firm promotes a worker if his or her performance reaches a standard q', and the promotion comes with a salary increase $\triangle w$. What are the advantages and disadvantages of promotion-based incentives?

Relative Performance

Sometimes everyone is hit with bad luck. Network access is slow all day. An air-conditioner compressor fails in the dog days of summer, and everyone sweats though a week of stifling heat. A snowstorm delays delivery of parts, and production grinds to a halt. The wind is blowing out, so even a weak-hitting shortstop looks like a homerun hitter. These are examples of what economists call **common shocks**, random factors that hit everyone equally. With a common shock z, Julie's production of tax returns is $q_j = e_j/5 + u_j + z$. (Replace the j subscripts with k subscripts to express Katie's production of tax returns.)

Why should workers bear the risk of these shocks that hit everyone? Risk-averse workers don't like wage risk from any source, but common shocks can be avoided without dampening incentives to work hard. **Relative performance pay** sweeps away the effect of the common shock on wages.

Piece Rate.   A relative-performance piece rate links Julie's wage to her performance relative to Katie's performance.

(11.6) $$w_j = a + b(q_j - q_k)$$

Likewise, Katie's wage w_k is linked to $q_k - q_j$, her performance relative to Julie's performance.

Neither Julie's nor Katie's wage depends on the common shock. Relative performance is $q_j - q_k = (e_j - e_k)/5 + (u_j - u_k) + (z - z)$, so the common shock z differences out. Consequently, Julie's weekly wage doesn't depend on z.

(11.7) $$w_j = a + b(e_j - e_k)/5 + b(u_j - u_k)$$

(Recall that the marginal product of effort is 1/5.) So everyone's performance sinks when the network grinds to halt, but that doesn't affect the wages of Julie, Katie, or anyone else who prepares returns at TaxCrafters.

The principal advantage of relative performance pay is that it eliminates the risk from common shocks. That's not important to workers who aren't bothered by risk, but risk-averse workers value this buffer. Relative performance pay does introduce a new risk: Julie bears some of the risk of Katie's performance, and Katie bears some of the risk of Julie's performance. If Katie's a little lucky this week—the tax returns assigned to her are simple—she prepares more returns, which lowers Julie's relative performance and pay.

But expanding the reference group addresses this problem. Rather than measuring Julie's performance relative to Katie's performance, let's measure Julie's performance relative to the average performance in a reference group. That reference group includes Katie and plenty of other tax preparers at TaxCrafters. Averaging performance in the reference group of coworkers eliminates the common shock without exposing Julie to much randomness in the performances of Katie and the other tax preparers. This result is an application of the *law of large numbers*, an important principle in statistics. There's less risk in an average, especially in large groups.

Although expanding the reference group avoids one disadvantage of relative performance pay, another disadvantage can't be avoided. Relative performance pay encourages **sabotage**. Julie can raise her wage by working harder to improve her own performance. She can also raise her wage by hindering Katie's performance. Julie badmouths Katie in front of clients. She edits Katie's electronic calendar, and Katie arrives 30 minutes late to important meetings. She deletes a critical file on Katie's computer. And, of course, she throws Katie under the bus whenever there's a critical error. It frequently takes less effort to bring down a coworker's performance than to raise one's own. There's no avoiding it: relative performance pay encourages sabotage.

In small groups, these back-stabbing workers might collude to reduce effort. Since wages depend only on relative performance, tax preparers can maintain their wages and reduce their costs of effort if they all reduce effort together. The lower level of effort isn't, however, compatible with incentives facing each tax preparer. Katie, for instance, wants to supply 85 units of effort if the relative performance piece rate is $b = 100$ even if all her coworkers agree to supply 50 units of effort. So the collusion has to be enforced, and enforcement's likely to be difficult in any but the smallest groups.

 PRACTICE   Explain how grading on a curve is a form of relative performance "pay." Does grading on a curve foster teamwork among students? How strong are the incentives to collude to reduce study time in small classes and large classes?

Contest.   A **contest** (or **tournament**) is a form of relative performance pay. The prize in a contest resembles bonus pay. But rather than receiving a bonus for reaching quota q', Julie wins a prize for out-performing Katie (Lazear and Rosen 1981).

A contest's prize motivates hard work and also eliminates the wage risk from common shocks. Since TaxCrafters awards the prize on the basis of relative performance, compensation in a contest is immune to common shocks. The prize to the winner of a boxing match doesn't vary with the quality of the fight. The prize to the winner of the Masters golf tournament doesn't depend on the winner's score, only that it's the lowest score. If it's windy and the course is dry, the scores are high (i.e., bad), but the conditions don't affect the prize structure. The winner still pockets the same amount. Contests also economize on the cost of measuring performance: it's frequently easier to determine who performed better without measuring precisely how much better.

But contests also have several disadvantages. First, every worker has an incentive to sabotage his opponent. Second, opponents have an incentive to collude, like taking a dive in a boxing match. Third, in a contest with a single prize, the lack of marginal incentives echoes the disadvantage of bonus pay: the less talented give up; the most talented coast. For instance, if one salesperson has a big sales lead by the end of October, he coasts through November and December and still captures the prize that goes to the annual sales leader.

Contests pop up in some surprising places. The race to become a firm's next chief executive officer (CEO) resembles a contest, and the lavish compensation at the top of the corporate hierarchy is the prize that goes to the winner. (See section 11.4 on the compensation of chief executive offers.) And contests appear throughout management. For instance, during Jack Welch's two-decade reign as CEO of General Electric, supervisors at GE classified business professionals into three groups. They singled out the top 20 percent for special attention, development, and fast tracking. The middle 70 percent were distinguished from the problem workers in the bottom 10 percent; workers in the bottom tier were also flagged for special attention, which often involved being fired.

The annual battle at GE to be in the top 20 percent and the struggle to escape the cellar were two parts of a contest. GE's performance evaluation relied on relative performance, and the percentages were fixed. If every one of GE's professionals had a "career year" in 1999, then still only the top 20 percent would have been singled out for their achievements. Ranking was a hallmark of GE's performance-driven culture, but the system was dropped (after Welch stepped down) in favor of a system without strict percentages. GE still strives to identify top performers and to address problems with underperformers, but the company no longer grades on a pure curve.

Application: Self-Employment and Entrepreneurship

Self-employment has a big advantage over work as an employee: a self-employed worker has strong incentives to supply effort. In addition, self-employment attracts the most talented workers (in a line of work) because the self-employed worker captures the full return to his or her talent. So self-employment carries an advantage over working for others in terms of motivating performance and attracting quality workers. Consequently, we predict that self-employed workers earn more than comparable employees doing similar work.

What's the downside of self-employment? Risk! Self-employment removes the buffer between the worker's paycheck and fluctuations in sales revenue. Self-employment isn't for workers who are strongly averse to risk. Indeed, risk-averse workers are willing to accept lower earnings on average in exchange for less earnings risk. So they work as employees in other firms.

Entrepreneurs are different. If Julie prepares tax returns with the help of an assistant, she's self-employed. If she starts, owns, and operates a tax-preparation business with dozens of employees in several offices, she's an entrepreneur. As an entrepreneur, she deals with payroll, hiring, business loans, insurance, advertising, and regulatory compliance. She must be knowledgable in accounting, finance, marketing, and management. Self-employed Julie needs to know taxes. Entrepreneur Julie needs skills in all aspects of business.

Workers with specialized knowledge can thrive as employees, but entrepreneurs require broad knowledge. And the evidence supports this implication. Studying the careers of graduates from Stanford University's Graduate School of Business, Lazear (2005) found that students who took a broad range of business courses, rather than specializing in one area like marketing, were more likely to subsequently start their own businesses. And Stanford MBAs who worked in several areas of business were more likely to subsequently become entrepreneurs. So entrepreneurs are generalists—jacks of all trades.

11.3   Efficiency Wage and the Threat of Dismissal

A theme is emerging: no system of compensation is perfect. Each has its advantages and disadvantages. And that theme also applies to the two forms of compensation we explore in this section. One option is to pay a wage premium if the higher wage gets workers to work harder. For instance, in undeveloped regions of the world, workers suffer from malnutrition, which undercuts their productivity. Paying these workers higher wages raises their food intake, which strengthens them and increases their productivity. Maybe the high wage pays for itself. None of the tax preparers at TaxCrafters is starving, but higher wages might elicit effort from Julie and the other tax preparers to cut the odds of losing their lucrative jobs. (Or the higher wage attracts higher-ability workers.) A second option is to fire workers who shirk. In some circumstances, the threat of dismissal motivates workers to behave.

Here we sketch (1) a model of an **efficiency wage** in which TaxCrafters pays a super-competitive wage to increase the effort of its tax preparers and (2) a model that combines the threat of dismissal with back-loading pay to keep workers honest.

Efficiency Wage

TaxCrafters pays a weekly wage that's independent of performance. If effort increases with the wage, then TaxCrafters chooses a wage that trades off the higher cost with the higher productivity of a higher wage. To attract and retain workers like Julie, the weekly wage TaxCrafters pays to its tax preparers can't be less than the competitive wage, which is $750 per worker.

If a higher wage stimulates effort, paying a higher wage increases output and revenue. Labor input L is the product of the number of tax preparers N and the effort of each tax preparer e: $L = eN$. TaxCrafters can't pay Julie, Katie, and its other tax preparers per unit of effort, so the weekly wage w is per worker. Thus TaxCrafters's profit is

(11.8) $$\pi = pF(e(w)N) - wN$$

where p is the price to have a tax return prepared, the production function $F()$ translates labor input eN into prepared tax returns, and $e(w)$ is the supply of effort as a function of the wage w. Effort supply $e(w)$ slopes up, so a higher wage increases effort, labor input, the number of prepared tax returns, and revenue.

TaxCrafters has two choices: (1) how many tax preparers to employ N and (2) how much to pay each tax preparer w. It maximizes profit along both margins. In particular, it chooses employment N such that the value of the marginal product of workers equals the wage; that is, $pMP_L \times e = w$. The presence of e in this equation distinguishes it from Leisure Lawn's profit-maximizing condition in chapter 4 on labor demand. Here's why. The value of the marginal product of *labor* L is the product price p times the marginal product of labor MP_L. The value of the marginal product of *employment* N includes the extra term e because one extra worker increases labor input by e units; that is, $VMP_N = VMP_L \times e$.

TaxCrafters also chooses the wage to maximize its profit. The efficiency wage (i.e., profit-maximizing wage) equates the marginal effect of the wage on revenue with the marginal effect of the wage on cost. A $1 higher weekly wage per worker

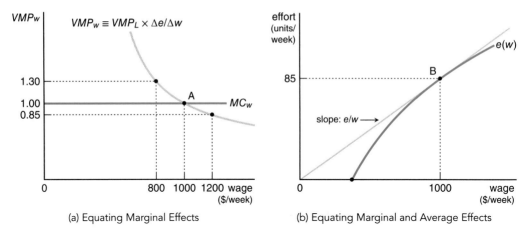

(a) Equating Marginal Effects   (b) Equating Marginal and Average Effects

(a) The value of the marginal product of the wage VMP_w is a downward-sloping function of the wage. TaxCrafters maximizes profit by choosing the wage at point A, the intersection of the VMP_w curve and the horizontal line at 1.00. The efficiency wage is $1,000/week.

(b) The efficiency wage equates the marginal $\Delta e/\Delta w$ and average e/w effects of the wage on effort supply. Hence point B also depicts the efficiency wage. A ray from the origin is tangent to the effort supply curve at point B.

FIGURE 11.6. Efficiency Wage

increases weekly cost by N or $1 per worker. The impact of a higher wage on revenue depends on the slope of the effort supply curve $e(w)$. A $1 higher weekly wage per worker lifts effort by Δe, which raises labor input by $N\Delta e$, which increases revenue by $pMP_L N\Delta e$ or $pMP_L \Delta e$ per worker. To maximize profit, TaxCrafters equates the marginal revenue of the wage to the marginal cost of the wage.

(11.9)
$$pMP_L \frac{\Delta e}{\Delta w} = 1$$

where $\Delta e/\Delta w$ is the slope of the effort supply curve.

 PRACTICE   The slope of the effort supply curve depends on the wage, but the value of the marginal product of labor in Equation 11.9 also depends on the wage. Does a higher wage increase or decrease labor input L and pMP_L? How so?

Graphing the Solution. Figure 11.6 displays the solution to this problem in panel (a) for the effort supply curve $e(w)$ in panel (b). The downward-sloping curve in panel (a) is the value of the marginal product of the wage. The higher the wage, the smaller the revenue gain from a marginal increase in the wage. The marginal cost of the wage is the flat line at 1. The intersection of these two curves at point A identifies the efficiency wage: paying tax preparers like Julie a $1,000 weekly wage, which is one-third more than the $750 competitive wage, maximizes TaxCrafters's profit. Panel (b) reveals that the 33 percent wage premium delivers 85 units of effort from each tax preparer. Since the marginal product of effort is 1/5 tax returns per unit of effort, each employee at TaxCrafters prepares 17 ($= 85 \times 1/5$) tax returns per week.

This result is stunning. Without performance pay of any kind, Julie, Katie, and the other tax preparers at TaxCrafters work quite hard. Indeed, the efficiency wage has many advantages. Workers face no wage risk. Quality doesn't suffer because TaxCrafters doesn't pay tax preparers for quantity. And the efficiency wage encourages teamwork. Julie is indifferent between allocating effort to prepare her own tax returns and helping Katie with hers.

But these advantages come at a steep price, the 33 percent wage premium. Let's compare TaxCrafters's wage cost with the efficiency wage to its wage cost with a piece rate that also delivers 85 units of effort and 17 tax returns per week. Recall that a piece rate of $100 per tax return (for $q > 9$) encourages tax preparers to supply 85 units of effort and to prepare, on average, 17 returns per week. The average weekly wage with this piece rate is $900 per worker. In this example, the efficiency wage is a more expensive method for TaxCrafters to generate the same performance from its tax preparers.

The success or failure of the efficiency wage hinges entirely on the response of effort to the wage. If the quantity supplied of effort isn't very responsive to the wage, then even a high efficiency wage does little to solve the shirking problem. Alternatively, if the quantity supplied of effort is very responsive to the wage, then a small wage premium can generate hard work, and the efficiency wage can dominate piece-rate compensation.

A special property of the efficiency wage is that the elasticity of effort with respect to the wage equals one (Solow 1979). TaxCrafters chooses the number of workers to employ preparing taxes N to satisfy $VMP_N \equiv pMP_L \times e = w$. So we replace pMP_L with w/e in Equation 11.9 to give

$$(11.10) \qquad \frac{w}{e} \cdot \frac{\Delta e}{\Delta w} = 1$$

Therefore, maximizing profit implies that the elasticity of effort with respect to the wage equals one. This in turn implies that the marginal effect of the wage $\Delta e/\Delta w$ equals its average effect e/w. And that suggests a second way to illustrate the efficiency wage. In Figure 11.6b, sketching a ray from the origin that is tangent to the effort supply curve identifies the efficiency wage. At tangency point B, the slope of the ray, which is e/w, equals the slope of the effort supply curve, which is $\Delta e/\Delta w$. That is, the elasticity of effort with respect to the wage equals one at point B.

Effort and the efficiency wage are unrelated to the price of the product. Increasing the price to have a tax return prepared increases the demand for tax preparers but has no effect on the efficiency wage of tax preparers. The efficiency wage is rigid with respect to changes in the product price, so employment fluctuates up or down without changing the wage.

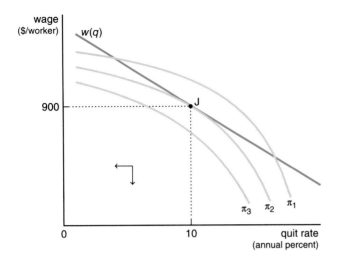

The wage–quits curve $w(q)$ slopes down because fewer tax preparers quit if their wage is higher. TaxCrafters's profit is higher if its wage and quit rate are lower, so its iso-profit curves slope down. Increasing marginal cost of hiring and training bows each iso-profit curve out from the origin.

To maximize profit, TaxCrafters offers job J where its wage–quits curve is tangent to iso-profit curve π_2.

FIGURE 11.7. Paying a Wage Premium to Reduce Quits

An important application of the efficiency-wage model blends our analysis of turnover from chapter 7 with our model of job attributes from chapter 5. TaxCrafters is quite concerned with the quit rate of its tax preparers. If the quit rate is high, its hiring rate must be high to maintain employment. Training all those newly hired tax preparers in TaxCrafters's proprietary system for preparing taxes is expensive. Paying a higher wage reduces the quit rate, which economizes on training costs.

Application: Paying a Wage Premium to Reduce Quits.   Paying an efficiency wage premium can increase effort and profit. Paying a wage premium also reduces quits, and a lower quit rate cuts hiring and training costs. In fact, TaxCrafters chooses its quit rate by trading off wage costs with the costs of hiring and training tax preparers.

If TaxCrafters pays a higher wage, fewer tax preparers quit each year. Figure 11.7 displays this downward-sloping, wage–quits curve $w(q)$. The figure also illustrates three of TaxCrafters iso-profit curves. Each iso-profit curve slopes down and bows out from the origin, a property that follows from increasing marginal cost of hiring and training. Since TaxCrafters prefers lower wages and lower quit rates, profit along an iso-profit curve closer to the origin (e.g., π_3) is higher than profit along an iso-profit curve that's farther from the origin (e.g., π_1).

To maximize profit, TaxCrafters offers job J where its wage–quits curve is tangent to one of its iso-profit curves. In the figure, TaxCrafters pays each tax preparer $900 per week, and 10 percent of its workers quit annually.

PRACTICE Rhythm Records is in the same labor market as TaxCrafters, and the two firms face the same wage–quits curve. But hiring and training costs are higher at Rhythm Records. Sketch one or two of the record label's iso-profit curves in Figure 11.7. Does Rhythm Records pay a higher or lower wage than TaxCrafters?

Threat of Dismissal

Profit sharing, personal performance pay, relative performance pay, and the efficiency wage use carrots to encourage effort. Now comes the stick. Firms can fire workers for misbehaving, for shirking or stealing from the firm. For instance, if Best Buy catches Liz "transferring" a bit of the inventory of flat-screen TVs to her SUV, Best Buy doesn't just dock her pay; it fires her. So we now turn to the threat of dismissal as a motivator (Becker and Stigler 1974). For the threat of dismissal to motivate performance and keep workers like Liz honest, workers must lose something by being dismissed. If Best Buy fires TV-thief Liz on Tuesday and another electronics retailer hires her at the same wage on Wednesday, then she loses nothing. The threat of dismal wouldn't be effective.

Let's clarify this principle in the case of Julie, who has put her accounting skills to a different use. She's now involved in managing TaxCrafters's finances at its corporate headquarters, where she earns annual salary w. The value of her marginal product on this job v is $45,000 per year, and that's how much she can make at other firms. If Julie's honest, she receives an annual wage $w(t)$ in year t of her tenure at TaxCrafters. But Julie has a chance to embezzle $10,000 each year. The chance that she's caught is 10 percent. If TaxCrafters catches Julie embezzling, it dismisses her and recovers Julie's ill-gotten gain with the help of the legal system. (To highlight the role of the threat of dismissal, let's assume that TaxCrafters doesn't press criminal charges against Julie.) Julie immediately finds work at another firm paying $45,000.

Keeping Julie honest is most difficult just before she retires, 30 years into her career at TaxCrafters. What wage in the last year of Julie's career would keep her honest? Julie isn't averse to risk, so the risk associated with the gamble of embezzling funds doesn't bother her. What matters is how the expected value of embezzling compares to the honest wage $w(30)$.

If TaxCrafters catches Julie embezzling, which happens with probability .1, the firm dismisses her, and she works elsewhere earning $45,000 per year. If Julie successfully embezzles $10,000 from TaxCrafters in the year before she retires (i.e., $t = 30$), she gets her wage $w(30)$ plus her ill-gotten gain of $10,000; that happens with probability .9. So Julie's expected value of embezzling is $.1(45,000) + .9(w(30) + 10,000)$. The lowest wage that keeps Julie honest is the wage that leaves her indifferent between embezzling and not embezzling. It's the wage that solves

(11.11) $$w(30) = .1(45{,}000) + .9(w(30) + 10{,}000)$$

Solve this equation to find $w(30) = 45{,}000 + 90{,}000 = 135{,}000$. To keep Julie honest in her last year on the job, TaxCrafters must pay her $135,000, which is a $90,000 wage premium. Ouch.

 PRACTICE   The wage on the left side of Equation 11.11 is a sure thing; the right side is the expected value of the embezzling gamble. Simplify the right side to express the expected value of embezzling in terms of Julie's wage 30 years into her career.

Keeping Julie honest one year earlier doesn't take much of a wage premium. Here's why. If Julie loses her job in year $t = 29$, she foregoes the $90,000 wage premium in her last year on the job. That alone is a strong incentive to behave in the second-to-last year of her career. To leave Julie indifferent between behaving and embezzling at $t = 29$, TaxCrafters must pay her a $5,000 wage premium. That is, $w(29) = 50{,}000$. And this wage applies to every year of her career with TaxCrafters up to $t = 30$.

. . . .

ADVANCED Let's derive Julie's wage at $t = 29$. The present value of behaving honestly on the job is $w(29) + w(30)/(1 + i)$, where i is the annual interest rate. Let v denote Julie's productivity value, so the present value of detected embezzling is $v + v/(1 + i)$, which happens with probability .1. With probability .9, Julie receives the present value of successful embezzling, which is $10{,}000 + w(29) + w(30)/(1 + i)$. The wage $w(29)$ that leaves Julie indifferent between behaving on the job and embezzling solves

(11.12) $$w(29) + \frac{w(30)}{1 + i} = .1\left(v + \frac{v}{1 + i}\right) + .9\left(10{,}000 + w(29) + \frac{w(30)}{1 + i}\right)$$

Replace $w(30)$ with $135,000$ and v with $45,000$ to solve for

(11.13) $$w(29) = 45{,}000 + \left(\frac{i}{1 + i} \times 90{,}000\right)$$

If the interest rate is 5.88 percent, then $w(29) = 50{,}000$.
     We could repeat this calculation for $w(28)$ and $w(27)$ and so on. Conveniently, the solution is the same for every year except the last year. In general, the formulas are

(11.14) $$w(t) = v + \frac{1 - \pi}{\pi} \cdot \frac{ib}{1 + i}$$

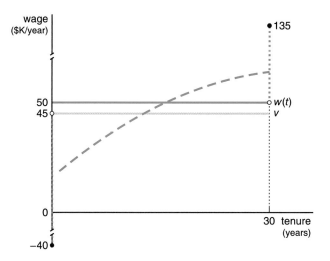

TaxCrafters fires Julie if she is caught embezzling funds. To keep Julie honest, it pays a $5,000 annual wage premium plus an $85,000 pension at retirement, and Julie pays an $85,000 fee for the job.

Interest on the fee funds the wage premium, and TaxCrafters returns the fee to Julie as a pension at retirement. Since she forfeits her pension if she is caught embezzling, Julie is posting an $85,000 bond. This wage profile back-loads pay.

The dashed wage profile also back-loads pay: Julie accumulates the bond early in her career and draws it down late in her career.

FIGURE 11.8. Bonding and the Threat of Dismissal

for all $t = 1, \ldots, T-1$, and $w(T) = v + ((1-\pi)/\pi)b$,
where v is Julie's productivity value, π is the probability
of detection, b is the value of the ill-gotten gain, and i is the interest rate.

. . . .

The solution is a wage profile that pays Julie an annual wage premium of $5,000 and an additional premium of $85,000 at the end of her career, and this wage profile keeps Julie honest throughout her career. The dark blue line (and the point marked 135) in Figure 11.8 illustrates Julie's wage profile.

This is Julie's dream job, but not because she takes pride in being honest. It just pays a lot—so much that she'd buy the job if she had to. How much would Julie pay for the job managing finances at TaxCrafters's corporate headquarters? $85,000 because the job at TaxCrafters is worth $85,000 more in present-value terms than a standard job paying a $45,000 annual wage. The annual interest rate is 5.88 percent. At that rate, the annual interest on an $85,000 deposit is $5,000. If Julie pays $85,000 for her job, the annual interest on that fee funds her $5,000 annual wage premium throughout her career. And TaxCrafters returns the $85,000 fee to her as a pension at retirement. That is, if she pays $85,000 for the financial manager job at TaxCrafters, the present value of compensation on that job equals the present value of a $45,000 wage on a standard job. It's competitive.

The fee Julie pays for her job is a **performance bond**. If TaxCrafters doesn't catch Julie embezzling funds, then it returns the $85,000 bond to her in the form of a pension at the end of her career. TaxCrafters fires Julie if it catches her embezzling funds. Since she won't be around to collect the $85,000 pension at retirement, she forfeits the bond.

The competitive bonding contract back-loads pay, which increases the cost to the worker of behaving badly. The principle of back-loading pay to encourage honesty (and to reduce shirking) also applies without the unrealistic assumption that Julie buys her job. Consider the dashed wage profile in Figure 11.8. Along this upward-sloping wage profile, Julie doesn't post a bond to secure her job at TaxCrafters. She builds up a bond early in her career by being underpaid. She is overpaid later in her career, and she might also receive a pension in retirement. Back-loading pay—having the wage profile be steeper than the productivity profile—puts some teeth in the bite of the threat of dismissal.

Jobs that back-load pay attract workers who expect to stay a long time. Honest workers are happy with delayed rewards; dishonest workers prefer jobs with smaller penalties for bad behavior. In addition, workers who frequently change jobs avoid jobs that back-load pay. So back-loading pay attracts honest and low-turnover-rate workers.

Back-loading pay discourages the worker's bad behavior; unfortunately, it also encourages the employer to misbehave. TaxCrafters overpays Julie late in her career, so it has an incentive to falsely accuse Julie of embezzling. It dismisses Julie, and she forfeits her $85,000 pension, as well as her $5,000 annual wage premium over the rest of her career. The incentive to falsely accuse Julie is particularly strong as she approaches retirement.

This model of back-loading wages plays an important role in age-discrimination cases related to reductions in force (RIFs). In response to a fall in business, such as in a recession, firms look to cut costs, and they frequently eliminate jobs and the workers doing those jobs. A recession presents an opportunity to cut loose underperforming or overpaid workers, and plenty of those workers might be old. But federal employment law bans age discrimination. By dismissing too many old workers, the employer runs the risk of being served with a class-action suit for age discrimination.

Our model illuminates the issues. Since pay is back-loaded, older workers are likely to be targets of RIFs. And evidence that these dismissed workers underperform relative to their wages misses the point. Dismissed workers might justifiably accuse the employer of reneging on an implicit agreement to overpay them toward the end of their careers and in retirement.

Application: Mandatory Retirement

Mandatory retirement was common for managerial workers in corporate America decades ago. Managers could retire early, but they typically worked until age 65 and collected retirement benefits thereafter. Beginning in 1979, amendments to the Age Discrimination in Employment Act banned mandatory retirement in the federal government and prohibited mandatory retirement for most workers in the private sector before age 70. So the age of mandatory retirement in the private sector jumped from 65 to 70. The 1986 amendments prohibited mandatory retirement altogether, although there are exceptions: military personnel, FBI agents, park rangers, air-traffic controllers, and airline pilots can be forced to retire.

Banning mandatory retirement has had a striking effect on some jobs. For instance, tenured faculty at colleges and universities historically had job security

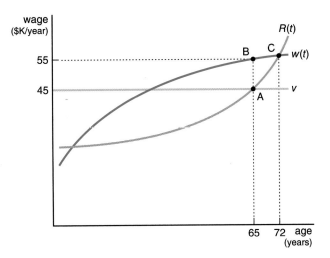

Julie's reservation-wage profile R(t) reflects the marginal value of her time if she doesn't work. The efficient time to retire is when R(t) equals Julie's value of marginal product v, which is when she turns 65.

Back-loading pay distorts Julie's incentive to retire. Julie retires when her reservation–wage profile R(t) crosses her wage profile w(t), which is at age 72.

Mandatory retirement at age 65 increases efficiency by preventing Julie from delaying her retirement.

FIGURE 11.9. Mandatory Retirement

until retirement at age 65. A professor would retire at age 65 or work thereafter on a series of annual contracts. Now that mandatory retirement is banned, a tenured professor has a truly lifetime job.

To evaluate the impact of banning mandatory retirement, we must understand why mandatory retirement existed in the first place. Why was mandatory retirement an element of firms' employment policies? Or, why did workers in a competitive labor market agree to be bound by mandatory retirement? Our model of back-loading pay has the answer (Lazear 1979).

Back-loading pay solves one problem, the malfeasance of workers, but creates another. Back-loading pay distorts Julie's labor supply choices. Let's look at her retirement choice. Julie's reservation wage for work $R(t)$, which reflects the marginal value of her time not working, rises with age t. The efficient time to retire is when that reservation wage reaches the value of her marginal product on the job. In Figure 11.9, Julie's efficient age to retire is 65. (See point A.) If Julie's wage profile coincides with her productivity profile, then she retires at age 65.

Back-loading Julie's pay, however, distorts Julie's retirement choice. Her wage exceeds the value of her marginal product late in her career, so she delays retirement until her reservation wage $R(t)$ reaches her wage $w(t)$. That's age 72 at point C in the figure. Over the last seven years of her career, the value of Julie's contribution to production is less than the value she places on her time outside of work. That's inefficient.

Mandatory retirement at age 65 eliminates this distortion. So mandatory retirement is efficient if firms back-load pay.

☑ **PRACTICE**   Why is 65 the efficient age for Julie to retire? Why does she want to keep working past age 65?

Julie enjoys a productive and honest career at TaxCrafters, and she expects to retire in a few years at age 65 as TaxCrafters's employment policy requires. The government bans mandatory retirement, and Julie decides to delay her retirement. The unexpected prospect of employing Julie at a loss for seven extra years burdens TaxCrafters. When business slows, TaxCrafters seizes the opportunity to cut Julie loose. In this case, TaxCrafters is *not* reneging on an implicit agreement to overpay Julie in her later years. TaxCrafters is simply responding to Julie reneging on the implicit agreement to retire at age 65. Since the law prohibits TaxCrafters from ushering Julie to the door on her 65th birthday, the firm disguises mandatory retirement as an age-based reduction in force. And it's efficient.

TaxCrafters has another tool at its disposal, and this one is legal. TaxCrafters's pension plan rewards years of service, so Julie increases her annual pension benefit by delaying her retirement. But delaying retirement also shortens the period Julie will have to collect her pension. Death looms! Impending death and rewarding years of service combine to give Julie a profile for the present value of pension benefits that peaks at some age $\hat{a}$. TaxCrafters designs its pension plan so that $\hat{a}$, the age at which the present value of pension benefits peaks, is young enough (and the profile falls rapidly enough with age beyond $\hat{a}$) to encourage Julie and other workers to retire at age 65.

11.4 Compensation of Chief Executive Officers

Leslie Moonves, the former chief executive officer (CEO) of CBS, raked in over $68 million in total compensation in 2017. That placed him seventh on the list of America's highest-paid chief executives. A quick look at Table 11.1 reveals that the main source of compensation of the top CEOs isn't salary or even cash compensation (i.e., salary plus bonus). Awards of company stock and stock options are the biggest slice of the compensation pie. For instance, grants of CBS stock worth almost $44 million accounted for 64 percent of Moonves's total compensation. The value of Stephen Kaufer's stock awards and options to buy TripAdvisor stock comprised 98 percent of his compensation.

Moonves, Kaufer, and the other CEOs don't have bosses. Do they set their own pay? The CEO reports to the corporation's board of directors, which represents the stockholders. The board's compensation committee, usually in consultation with a private compensation-consulting firm, sets the CEO's pay. Yet there's still room for influence.

Can this unique feature at the top of the corporate hierarchy explain the incredible sums paid to top executives? The level of executive compensation is one issue. A second issue is the sensitivity of executive compensation to the performance of the firm: are CEOs rewarded for decisions that increase the value of the firm, or are they paid like bureaucrats? Let's explore these two issues.

TABLE 11.1. HIGHEST-PAID CHIEF EXECUTIVE OFFICERS, 2017

RANK	NAME (COMPANY)	SALARY	BONUS	OTHER COMPENSATION	STOCK & OPTION AWARDS	TOTAL COMPENSATION
1	Hunter Harrison (CSX)	1.9	3.5	29.3	115.9	150.5
2	Hock Tan (Broadcom)	1.1	3.7	0.1	98.3	103.2
3	Frank Bisignano (First Data Corp.)	1.3	0.6	0.5	99.9	102.2
4	Alex Molinaroli (Johnson Controls)	1.5	0.0	64.8	11.9	78.2
5	Michael Rapino (Live Nation)	2.4	7.8	0.1	60.4	70.6
6	Mario Gabelli (Gamco Investors)	0.0	0.0	69.4	0.0	69.4
7	Leslie Moonves (CBS)	3.5	20.0	1.2	43.7	68.4
8	Nicholas Howley (Transdigm)	0.0	0.0	51.2	9.8	61.0
9	Douglas Lebda (LendingTree)	0.6	1.0	0.6	57.4	59.6
10	Douglas Ingram (Sarepta Therapeutics)	0.3	0.4	0.0	56.1	56.9
11	Thomas Dooley (Viacom)	0.4	0.0	53.2	0.0	53.6
12	Ronal Clarke (FleetCor Technologies)	1.0	1.1	0.0	50.5	52.6
13	Stephen Kaufer (TripAdvisor)	0.7	0.4	0.0	46.9	47.9
14	Gregory Maffei (Liberty Interactive)	1.1	2.5	0.2	44.1	47.8
15	Brian Duperreault (AIG)	1.0	14.1	0.3	27.3	42.8

Notes: Compensation figures are in millions of dollars. Bonus includes annual non-equity incentive payments. Stock and stock-option awards are valued when granted. Total compensation includes long-term non-equity incentive payments but excludes changes in the value of pension benefits.
Source: AFL-CIO's CEO Pay Database, https://aflcio.org/paywatch/highest-paid-ceos, accessed July 13, 2018.

Level of CEO Pay

Chief executives of large corporations are superstars. The key feature of a superstar market is that small differences in talent at the top translate into huge differences in pay. Why would small differences in skill among the most talented executives translate into huge differences in their pay? Because small differences in executive skill translate into billion-dollar differences in the corporate bottom line. A superb decision sparks an innovation that creates a new market and generates an annual flow of billions of dollars in profit. A dim-witted decision tarnishes the firm's reputation, its products lose out to the competition, the firm's profits turn to losses, and its corporate life hangs in the balance.

How do the decisions of a CEO translate into billions of dollars gained or lost? The CEO chooses among competing projects, and a talented and motivated CEO funds profitable projects and shuts down unprofitable projects (e.g., product lines, plants, or divisions). The CEO defines a business strategy, makes financing choices (e.g., debt, equity, dividends, and share repurchases), decides whether to acquire other firms (or to be taken over by another firm), and evaluates whether

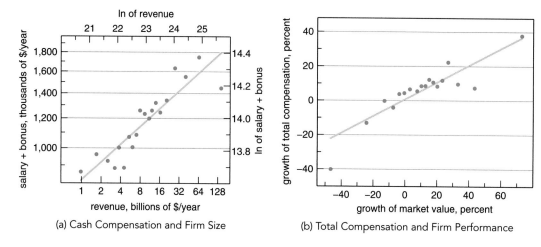

FIGURE 11.10. Compensation of Chief Executive Officers
Notes: The analysis excludes CEOs with annual cash compensation below $10,000. For 2017 in panel (a), the slope of the regression line (in logs) is .151 (.024), and R^2 = .692. The slope of the regression line in panel (b) is .277 (.089), and R^2 = .375. We compute the growth rates in panel (b) using changes from 2016 to 2017.
Source: Compustat's ExecuComp database, 2016 and 2017.

to enter one market or exit another market. The CEO influences the development of new products by setting the R&D budget and shapes human resource policies (e.g., piece rates at Safelite). Should the CEO close an aging (and unprofitable) plant or update it for the twenty-first century at great expense? If the firm enjoys a nice cash flow from its historical investments, should it put that cash to work expanding some of its not-so-profitable current endeavors, acquire firms in new lines of business, or return the cash to stockholders by buying back stock? Does the CEO continue to subsidize one division at the expense of another, distorting production choices in each division, cutting corporate profit, and eroding the value of the firm? Or does the CEO make the tough call to let the less-profitable division sink or swim on its own? Billions of dollars are at stake. Superb decisions create the superstar CEO.

Cash Compensation and Firm Size.   As the superstars model predicts, executive compensation rises rapidly with firm size. A CEO in a bigger firm has a deeper and broader impact, so better decisions have bigger payoffs in bigger firms. One wise choice is leveraged across a dozen divisions, each with tens of thousands of workers, selling to millions of customers. A firm in a small market doesn't leverage a similarly brilliant idea as far. The large firm values the extra skill the most, and competition among large firms aligns the compensation of CEOs in large firms with the value they create.

The evidence supports this implication. Figure 11.10a depicts the positive relationship between CEO cash compensation and firm revenue among the firms in the Standard & Poor's 500, a list of the largest publicly traded firms. Each dot in the scatter plot represents 25 firms grouped by revenue, from highest to lowest. For instance, in the 25 largest firms in 2017, cash compensation of CEOs (in logs) averaged 14.15 or almost $1.4 million, and revenue in those firms (in logs) averaged 25.72 or $148 billion; the point (148, 1.4) is one of the 20 points in the scatter plot.

The graph also depicts the regression line fit to these data, and the slope of the regression line is .151 (.024). To get a sense of the magnitude of this effect, let's compare three firms of vastly different sizes. Sales revenue at E*Trade, the online brokerage firm, was $2.45 billion in 2017. On the basis of the regression line in Figure 11.10a, we predict the cash compensation of E*Trade's CEO Karl Roessner to be $970,000 per year. Sales revenue at McDonald's is 10 times as high as at E*Trade; the predicted cash compensation of McDonald's CEO Steve Easterbrook is $1.4 million, 41 percent more than Roessner's cash compensation. Apple's sales revenue is 10 times as high as McDonald's and 100 times as high as E*Trade's, and we predict the cash compensation of Apple's CEO Time Cook to be $1.9 million. That's 41 percent more than Easterbrook's and 99 percent more than Roessner's cash compensation. Managing one of the largest firms translates into a sizable—but not extraordinary—premium in cash compensation.

Top executives aren't as valuable in firms where they have less scope to apply their skills creatively. CEOs of companies in tightly regulated markets have less scope for managerial creativity, so the superstars model predicts that CEOs in tightly regulated firms earn less. Indeed, a strong empirical pattern across industries is that executive compensation in tightly regulated industries (e.g., electrical utilities) is much lower than in less-regulated industries.

 PRACTICE   Suppose the wage–skill curve (or line) of CEOs in unregulated markets is steeper than CEOs' wage–skill curve in regulated markets. Draw the two wage–skill curves, and indicate the range of skills that generate higher CEO wages in regulated markets. Are CEOs in regulated markets drawn from the top or the bottom of the skill distribution? [Hint: See Figure 7.12.]

Lucrative compensation of the typical CEO might also be the prize in a contest to become the next CEO. If the firm's senior vice presidents compete in a contest to become CEO, then the compensation of the CEO is the prize that goes to the winner, like the winner of the U.S. Open in tennis or golf. CEO prize money motivates senior vice presidents, as well as workers hoping to become senior vice presidents, to work crazy hard.

Stock Options and Total Compensation.   Cash compensation is one thing, but the lion's share of CEO compensation comes from **employee stock options**. To get a handle on stock options, suppose TaxCrafters granted Kevin, its fictional CEO, 100,000 stock options on July 1, 2012, when shares of TaxCrafters stock traded at $25 per share. Each stock option grants Kevin (and only Kevin) the right to buy one share of TaxCrafters stock at an exercise price P^e of $25. Using the option to buy a share of stock is called *exercising the option*. Kevin's options won't fully vest for four years (i.e., he can't exercise any of them in the meantime), and they expire after 10 years. He also forfeits the options if he quits. Anytime between the vesting date and the expiration date, Kevin can exercise his options at the $25 exercise price.

The payoff from these stock options depends on the price of TaxCrafters stock in the future. Kevin's stock options become quite valuable if the price of TaxCrafters stock rises dramatically. For instance, if the price of the stock doubled from $25 in 2012 to $50 in 2016, Kevin could exercise each option for a $25 gain. Those 100,000 options turned into $2.5 million in stock gains. But his stock options become worthless if the stock price permanently falls below the exercise price. So Kevin's stock options constitute a risky gamble on the stock price.

How much were Kevin's stock options worth when TaxCrafters granted them on July 1, 2012? Exercising one stock option at some time t costs TaxCrafters the difference between the stock price P_t and the exercise price P^e. The present value (when they were issued) of Kevin's 100,000 stock options is $100,000 \times (P_t - P^e)$ discounted back to July 1, 2012. If we know when and at what price Kevin exercises his options, computing this present value is easy enough. But the stock price bounces around randomly, so valuing Kevin's stock options involves computing expected values, as well as discounting those expected values back to July 1, 2012. You don't want to do that, and I don't want to do that; frankly no one on TaxCrafters's compensation committee wants to do that either!

Thankfully, two financial economists have done the heavy lifting for us. Black and Scholes (1973) derived a relatively simple formula for valuing publicly traded stock options, the **Black–Scholes options pricing formula**. An important element of the formula is that a stock option with a longer term until expiration or a more volatile stock price is more valuable at its grant date: lengthening the term or raising the volatility increases the odds of cashing in the option for a big gain.

Annual lists of the highest-paid executives in the *Wall Street Journal*, the *New York Times*, and other periodicals now use the value of stock options when they are granted to calculate total compensation. But for decades, *Forbes* and other business periodicals included the gains from exercising stock options in calculating total compensation.

For instance, *Forbes* wouldn't include the value of Kevin's 100,000 stock options when they were granted in 2012. Rather, *Forbes* would include the $2.5 million that Kevin pocketed when he exercised those options in 2016 in Kevin's 2016 total compensation. Kevin's stock gain in 2016 really reflected his compensation from 2012 as well as the growth in the market value of TaxCrafters over the four years. Furthermore, stock gains in any one year can reflect grants of stock options over several years. TaxCrafters granted stock options to Kevin in 2009, 2010, and 2011, as well as 2012, and he exercised all those options in 2016. So *Forbes* would report amounts that he earned over those four years, as well as his salary and bonus in 2016, as 2016 compensation.

Reported compensation of the highest-paid executives can be truly staggering. Does this mistreatment of stock options contribute to that? If total compensation includes the gains from exercising previously granted stock options, then the executives at the top of the compensation list are the big winners in the stock-price gamble. Executives in firms with falling stock prices tumble down the rankings.

Larry Ellison's compensation in 2008 provides a revealing example. Oracle paid Ellison $1 million in salary, no bonus, and about $12 million in other compensation. He also received stock options valued at about $72 million. So his total compensation for the year was a hefty $85 million. But Ellison also exercised stock options that Oracle granted to him years before. His gains from exercising the stock options totaled $544 million! So *Forbes* reported that Ellison raked in a whopping $557 million for the year. All these numbers are huge, but using realized gains from exercising stock options (rather than the value of newly granted options) grossly exaggerated Ellison's compensation in 2008.

Sensitivity of CEO Pay to Firm Performance

Do corporations motivate their CEOs to do a good job? Does the form of compensation encourage CEOs to work hard and to make decisions that maximize the wealth of the firms' shareholders?

The incentives from cash compensation are primarily through the bonus, which depends on accounting measures of firm performance and sometimes achievement of specific goals for the CEO. The typical bonus formula includes (1) a threshold for performance y_l, (2) a minimum bonus a, (3) a slope b, and (4) a cap on the bonus B_h. Kevin's annual salary S is $1 million, and Figure 11.11 depicts his cash compensation $w = S + B$. If firm performance reaches the threshold y_l, Kevin receives the $500,000 minimum bonus, and his cash compensation jumps from his $1 million salary to $1.5 million. From there, Kevin's compensation grows at rate b per dollar of net income y until his bonus reaches the cap of $2 million at y_h. So Kevin's annual cash compensation tops out at $3 million. In general, the

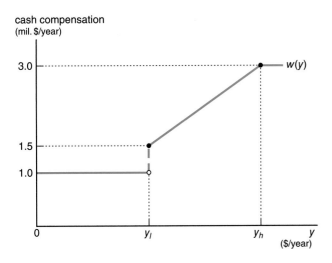

TaxCrafters CEO Kevin has a base salary of $1 million. He pockets a $500,000 minimum bonus if TaxCrafters's performance reaches y_l. In the incentive zone between y_l and y_h, his bonus increases with performance. Kevin's bonus is capped at $2 million, so his cash compensation can't exceed $3 million/year.

The typical CEO bonus plan includes a minimum performance standard y_l to receive the minimum bonus, a link between the size of the bonus and the performance measure, and a cap on the size of the bonus.

FIGURE 11.11. Cash Compensation with a Performance-Based Bonus

bonus follows $B = a + b(y - y_l)$ for a performance measure y (e.g., corporate net income) between y_l and y_h, and performance incentives are more powerful if the slope b or the threshold y_l is higher.

Cash Compensation.   How sensitive is CEO cash compensation to the performance of the firm? Jensen and Murphy (1990) estimate the effect of changes in the firm's value (i.e., shareholder wealth), a measure of firm performance, on changes in CEO cash compensation. Suppose a little more effort from the CEO increases the firm's value by $1,000. How much of this $1,000 does the CEO capture in higher cash compensation? On a sample of 1,668 CEOs spanning the years 1974–1986, Jensen and Murphy (1990, Table 1) estimate that increasing the firms' value by $1,000 increases the CEO's cash compensation by a statistically significant and economically trivial 1.35 *cents*. Peanuts! Broadening the measure of compensation (but continuing to exclude stock options) lifts the effect from 1.35 to 3.29 cents. These numbers are way too small to generate meaningful incentives to perform.

The relationship between CEO cash compensation and firm performance is weak, but cash compensation does bounce around a lot for each CEO, and this variation might reflect *personal* performance incentives. The market value of the firm's stock and accounting measures of firm performance (e.g., sales revenue or profit) surely depend on factors other than the CEO: the 400,000 other workers in the firm, or interest rates, or oil prices, or government regulations, or whether there's a war, and on and on. If the CEO's cash compensation bounces around from year to year in ways that measures of firm performance don't capture, then the board of directors is probably distinguishing the CEO's personal performance from the performance of the firm. For instance, Kevin could be doing a great job sailing a sinking ship.

Total Compensation and Market Value.   Stock options also provide incentives, potentially strong incentives. Stock options richly reward the CEO for actions that increase the price of the firm's stock. But they are also very risky, so risky that CEOs require substantial premiums in option-based compensation relative to cash compensation. For instance, our CEO Kevin is indifferent between $800,000 in cash compensation and $1,000,000 worth of stock options. If the stock price sinks once and for all, Kevin's options become worthless. Kevin loses the $800,000 he could have had if he had taken the cash compensation instead of the stock options. If the stock price takes off, he might exercise those stock options for $20 million. He's buying an $800,000 lottery ticket for the chance to win $20 million but with one important difference. Kevin's actions on the job—setting corporate strategies and all—affect his chances of winning the $20 million. If he does a better job, the firm does better, the price of its stock rises, and Kevin reaps the gain by exercising his stock options. That's a strong motivator.

Figure 11.10b illustrates the positive relationship between total compensation of the CEO (including the Black–Scholes value of newly granted stock options) and the market value of the firm. (Each data point is an average of 25 firms in the Standard & Poor's 500, ordered from highest to lowest growth in the stock's market value during the fiscal year.) The slope of the regression line fit to these data indicates that increasing the growth rate of market value by 10 percentage points increases the growth rate of the CEO's total compensation (including newly granted stock options) by 2.8 percentage points.

For instance, by keeping on task and doing a splendid job, Kevin raises the market value of TaxCrafters by 25 percent this year. How much is he rewarded for his hard work? As a typical CEO, Kevin's total compensation is 7 (= .28 × 25) percent higher than if he coasted and the market value of TaxCrafters stagnated. Since Kevin represents the average CEO (who earns $10.7 million), his hard work bumps his total compensation up $750,000 (≈ .07 × $10,700,000). Not bad.

But Kevin's extra $750,000 is pocket change compared to the several billion dollars that his extra effort generates for TaxCrafters's shareholders. Indeed, the implied sensitivity of total compensation to stock-market performance in this case is about 7 cents per thousand dollars. That's much bigger than Jensen and Murphy's estimate based on cash compensation but economically tiny nonetheless.

CEO stock holdings also provide incentives. Bill Gates hasn't been the CEO of Microsoft for a long time, but in 1999 (the year before he stepped down from being CEO) he owned almost 800 million shares of Microsoft stock. Those shares were worth about $37 billion. If Bill had a good idea that increased Microsoft's stock price by 5 percent, and he had a few of those, his financial wealth climbed $2 billion. And a long series of bad decisions could wipe out his wealth. Those are some strong financial incentives to get it right.

Grants of stock to CEOs are restricted: a CEO like Kevin must hold the stock rather than sell it. Restricting stock ownership makes sense. Stock provides Kevin with incentives going forward only if he holds the shares. Grants of stock options are also restricted: Kevin can't sell his options either.

The primary distinction between stock and stock options stems from Kevin's exposure to downside risk. With stock, Kevin bears downside as well as upside risk from fluctuations in the stock price. With stock options, his risk is largely upside: if the stock price falls once and for all, the options become worthless, but that's the limit of Kevin's loss. This difference between stock and stock options carries over to the incentives to take risks. CEO stock holding encourages a risk-averse CEO like Kevin to be too cautious. But stock options strongly reward good outcomes and insure Kevin against bad outcomes. As a result, stock options encourage Kevin to take risks, and overcoming the CEO's risk aversion is generally a good thing for shareholders.

Application: Personal Use of the Corporate Jet

There's more to doing a good job than putting in a lot of effort. For instance, excessive perquisites (i.e., perks) at the top of the corporate hierarchy might fleece the stockholders. Surely some perks, chauffeurs and business use of the corporate jet for instance, are time savers that increase the corporation's profit. They're productive benefits. But what about the most extravagant perk: access to the corporate jet for *personal* use? Perhaps the CEO is taking advantage of his cozy relationship with the board of directors at the stockholders' expense.

Not so fast. Access to the corporate jet for personal use is an attribute of the job. On the basis of our model of job attributes from chapter 5, we should expect the CEO's wage to adjust as a compensating wage differential. Apple's experience with Steve Jobs is a good example. Jobs had been working in the late 1990s as interim CEO of Apple. The board of directors was negotiating with Jobs to remove "interim" from his job title when Jobs expressed interest in having a jet for personal use such as for quick family trips to Hawaii. Apple gave Jobs a $43.5 million Gulfstream V jet (and another $40.5 million to cover the associated tax liability), and Jobs announced his permanent return to Apple as CEO in January 2000. Where's the compensating wage differential? Jobs worked every year for a $1 salary without any bonus or any grants of stock or stock options. He was the lowest paid worker at Apple! (Apple did reimburse Jobs for business use of his jet.)

Another example follows from CEOs being members of prestigious and exclusive golf clubs long distances from their corporate headquarters. Kevin puts TaxCrafters's corporate jet to good personal use shuttling him to his golf club, Augusta National Golf Club in Augusta, Georgia. Is Kevin paid less as a consequence?

Fleecing stockholders, compensating wage differential, or a productive benefit? One way to bring evidence to bear on this question comes from checking the response of the stock price to legally required disclosures of the corporate-jet perk. If personal use of the corporate jet signals excess at the top of the corporate hierarchy, then the stock price falls when the firm discloses the new perk. If personal use of the corporate jet simply shifts costs from compensation to the jet, then disclosing the new perk has no effect on the stock price. If, however, personal use of the corporate jet is a time saver that actually improves the CEO's job performance, then announcing that the CEO can use the corporate jet for personal use pushes up the stock price.

What's the evidence? Yermack (2006) found an otherwise unexplained drop in the stock price of 1.65 percent (with a standard error of 0.65 percent) when a corporation discloses its first corporate-jet perk in a filing to the Securities and Exchange Commission. That's huge, much bigger than the cost of providing the jet. So investors appear to treat personal use of the corporate jet as evidence of a board of directors that's ineffective in reigning in corporate excess and uninterested in protecting the stockholders' interests.

Summary

In this chapter, we explored compensation strategies to motivate workers and to attract and retain talented workers. Our key results are:

☐ The efficient level of effort equates the value of the marginal product of effort to the worker's marginal cost of effort.

☐ The incentives to perform from profit sharing are weak, especially in large partnerships. The typical partner bears the full cost of his or her effort but receives only a $1/N$ share of the product of that effort.

☐ Personal performance pay, such as piece rates and bonuses, encourage hard work and attract and retain talented workers. But personal performance incentives also subject workers to the risk associated with wage variability and promote quantity over quality.

☐ Bonus pay economizes on the cost of measuring performance, and the standard or quota for personal performance might broaden to include dimensions of quality. But bonus pay lacks marginal incentives: strong performers coast while weak performers give up.

☐ Relative performance pay shifts the risk of common shocks to the employer, but it also invites sabotage of coworkers.

☐ Paying an efficiency-wage premium can elicit effort from workers without (1) subjecting them to wage risk, (2) neglecting product quality, or (3) inviting sabotage of coworkers. But an efficiency wage can be expensive. In one application, employers pay a wage premium to reduce the quit rate to economize on the costs of training replacement workers.

☐ Back-loading pay puts teeth in the bite of the threat to fire badly behaved workers. Back-loading pay can elicit honesty and effort from workers, but it can also distort labor supply choices. The distortion probably explains why mandatory retirement was popular before federal law banned it.

☐ CEOs are superstars in the sense that small differences in CEO skill generate huge differences in the firm's profit. The spectacular sums paid to each year's highest-paid CEOs are partly the result of stock options being accumulated over many years and exercised all at once. The weak sensitivity of CEO salary and bonus to firm performance is a cause for concern, but strong performance of the firm can have a big impact on broader measures of compensation.

The final topic in our exploration of labor economics is unemployment, one of the most important topics in the field. In the next chapter, we investigate how factors that influence strategies for job search influence the unemployment rate.

Key Concepts

- personal performance pay, p. 408
- piece rate and commission, p. 408
- bonus pay and sales quota, p. 412
- marginal incentives, p. 413
- common shock, p. 413
- relative performance pay, p. 414

- sabotage, p. 414
- contest (or tournament), p. 415
- efficiency wage, p. 417
- performance bond, p. 423
- employee stock option, p. 429
- Black–Scholes options pricing formula, p. 430

Short-Answer Questions

11.1 Safelite guaranteed an $11 hourly wage when it rolled out performance pay, so it paid installers $20 per windshield or $11 per hour, whichever was greater. How many windshields must a worker install in an 8-hour day for performance pay to equal the $11 hourly wage? Workers installed 2.7 windshields per day before performance pay. Did it take a little or a lot of extra effort to reach the "incentive zone"?

11.2 Explain why randomness and limited information are at the heart of compensation strategies. For instance, how would our analysis differ if everyone directly observes effort?

11.3 Explain why bonus pay and contests have an advantage over personal and relative performance piece rates in terms of measurement costs.

11.4 Why does the risk from common shocks play an important role in the comparison of personal performance pay and relative performance pay? Furthermore, what is the advantage of using a large reference group (rather than one or two coworkers) with relative performance pay?

11.5 Have you ever observed coasting on the job as a consequence of the form of compensation? Did the typical worker put in a lot of effort while the best workers (or worst workers) coasted? Did workers cycle through periods of hard work and coasting? Was there a lack of marginal incentives for some workers (but not others) or at some times (but not others)?

11.6 Yahoo requires each supervisor to rank the members of his or her staff from best to worst. Bonuses and raises must conform to the ranking. How does this system resemble a contest? Discuss the advantages and disadvantages of this system of performance evaluation and compensation.

11.7 Carefully explain the advantages of an efficiency wage in terms of effort, risk, measurement costs, product quality, and teamwork.

11.8 TaxCrafters's job design involves trading off the wage and the quit rate. If TaxCrafters's training costs fall (perhaps it ditches its proprietary software in favor of a widely used program like TurboTax), what happens to its iso-profit curves and its optimal job choice? Does it raise or lower its wage?

11.9 If Liz works hard this year, she produces more this year, and she becomes more productive for the rest of her career. Her hard work creates some general human capital. Do you think Liz might work hard when she's young out of concern for her career? Will career concerns provide strong incentives to supply effort when Liz is age 60 or 65?

11.10 Order the following forms of compensation from weakest to strongest in terms of the incentives for workers to cooperate: profit sharing, personal piece rate, relative-performance piece rate, efficiency wage.

11.11 Beth from chapter 3 has an upward-sloping life-cycle labor supply curve. To keep Beth honest on the job, her employer pays her along a profile that resembles the dashed curve in Figure 11.8: her hourly wage is lower than the value of her marginal product early in her career and vice versa later in her career. How does back-loading Beth's pay distort her labor supply? Does she want to work too much (or too little) early or late in her career?

11.12 In your own words, explain what an employee stock option is. Also, how does receiving stock options (rather than cash) now encourage Kevin, the CEO of TaxCrafters, to perform later?

Problems

11.1 The marginal product of effort of Mac, a typical worker in a fast-food burger joint, is one-fourth burgers per hour; that is, $MP_e = .25$. The price of a burger is $2. The figure below graphs Mac's marginal cost of effort.

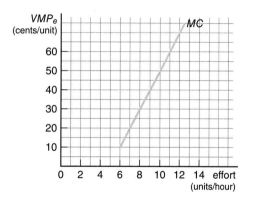

(a) If Mac increases his effort by one unit per hour, the change in the burger joint's revenue is $_____ per hour. That is, what is VMP_e, the value of Mac's marginal product of effort? Plot the VMP_e curve in the figure.

(b) Mac's efficient effort $\hat{e}$ is the solution to what equation? Illustrate the solution in the figure. Mac's efficient effort is $\hat{e} =$ _____ units of effort per hour.

(c) If the price of a burger rises from $2.00 to $2.80, what happens to Mac's efficient level of effort?

(d) If the marginal-cost-of-effort curve shifts down, what happens to $\hat{e}$?

(e) Suppose the market for fast-food workers like Mac is competitive. If Mac's quantity supplied of effort is efficient, how much does he earn per hour?

11.2 Some ophthalmologists specialize in LASIK vision-correction surgery. Performing LASIK takes effort, as well as skill. For a skilled ophthalmologist, correcting the vision in one eye takes 10 units of effort on average. So the number of vision-corrected eyes (i.e., output q) is a random function of effort e: $q = e/10 + u$, where u is a mean-zero random variable.

Effort is costly to the doctor. Each doctor's weekly cost of effort function is $C = 1000 - 20e + e^2/10$. The marginal cost of effort is $MC = -20 + e/5$, which the figure below depicts.

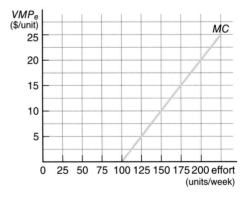

The price of LASIK is $500 per eye, but there are $300 in non-effort costs per eye. So the net price of the doctor's service is $200 per eye. [Hint: Use the net price to answer the questions.]

(a) On the basis of the information in the scenario and the figure, what is the efficient amount of a doctor's effort?

(b) Two doctors form a partnership, and they split the accounting profit 50:50. On average, what does a partner gain by increasing effort by one unit? Plot this marginal benefit in the figure.

(c) Each doctor chooses effort to maximize his expected partner earnings minus his personal cost of effort. How much effort does each partner supply?

(d) The partnership grows to a practice with eight doctors, and they share the accounting profit equally. How much effort does each partner supply?

11.3 The eight doctors in problem 11.2 sell the practice to an outside investor who receives the practice's profit as the owner. The eight doctors become employees of the LASIK firm, and each doctor receives a guaranteed weekly amount a plus performance pay of $150 per eye.

(a) How much effort does each doctor supply?

(b) On average, how much does each doctor receive per week in performance pay? That is, how much does the firm pay each doctor on top of guaranteed pay?

11.4 Randy and the other used-car salesmen at Pick-a-Plum Car Sales receive commissions. In particular, Randy's annual wage is $w = 25{,}000 + .05R$, where R is sales revenue from the cars Randy sells. Cars at Pick-a-Plum sell for $10,000 each. Putting in a bit more effort increases the odds of selling a car by 1-in-20; that is, the marginal product of Randy's effort is 1/20 cars per year.

(a) What's Randy's guaranteed pay? What is his commission rate?

(b) Randy's commission is equivalent to a piece rate of $_____ per car.

(c) How much does a marginal increase in effort increase Randy's annual wage?

(d) Use the figure below to determine the quantity of effort that Randy supplies: $e^* = $ _____ units per year.

(e) How many cars does Randy sell in a typical year? His sales generate how much revenue? How much does he receive (on average) in commissions? What is the expected value of Randy's annual wage?

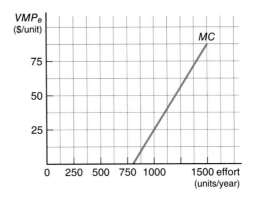

11.5 Terri's production of custom-made windows is the sum of her effort e and a random term u. Each one of the five values of u from -2 to $+2$ is equally likely. Terri earns a bonus of $50 if her daily production reaches 11 windows; that is, $\Delta w = 50$ if and only if $e + u \geq 11$.

    (a) Suppose Terri supplies 10 units of effort per day. Which of the five values of the random variable u enable Terri to earn the $50 bonus?

    (b) If $e = 10$, what is the probability that Terri earns the bonus?

    (c) If $e = 11$, what is the probability that Terri earns the bonus?

    (d) For the marginal increase in effort from $e = 10$ to $e = 11$, Terri's expected gain in wages is $MB_e = \$$_____ per day.

11.6 One theme of our analysis of employment strategies is that each form of compensation has advantages and disadvantages. Each of the five concepts listed in the table below connects to a particular form of compensation. Explain each concept, and match it to a form of compensation. More than one concept can apply to each form of compensation.

CONCEPT	FORM
1/N problem	bonus pay
worker collusion	relative performance pay
false accusation of wrongdoing	profit sharing
worker sabotage	back-loading pay
lack of marginal incentives	

11.7 Workers at Sparkling Pools clean swimming pools, which takes some effort. Sparkling Pools pays its workers an efficiency wage because it has found that workers clean more pools per week if the wage is higher. The relationship between the quantity supplied of effort e and the wage w is $e = \sqrt{w} - 12.5$. The figure below graphs the effect of a marginal increase in the weekly wage on weekly revenue at Sparkling Pools.

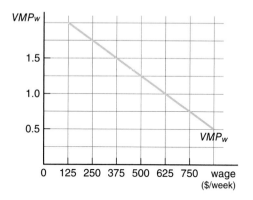

(a) What value of the wage maximizes Sparkling Pools's profit? That is, what is the efficiency wage w^*?

(b) What is the quantity supplied of effort of the workers at Sparkling Pools? That is, $e^* =$ _____ units per week.

(c) The marginal product of effort is two pools per unit of effort, so each worker at Sparkling Pools cleans _____ pools per week.

(d) The price of pool cleaning is $50 per pool, so each worker generates $_____ in weekly revenue.

11.8 *Old Republic*, a fictional monthly magazine, back-loads the pay of its journalists to avoid fabrications: falsifying events, concocting quotations, inventing sources, and so on. Each journalist receives a monthly wage w over his or her whole career; at retirement, the journalist receives a one-time pension benefit P. The value of a journalist's marginal product is $5,000 per month. The value to the journalist of a typical fabrication is $10,000, and the probability that *Old Republic* detects a fabricated article is 5 percent. The magazine dismisses a journalist whom it catches fabricating a story, and the journalist forfeits any claim to the retirement benefit.

(a) What is the smallest amount of pay in the last month (including the pension benefit) that keeps a journalist honest?

(b) How does this pay in the last month on the job compare to the journalist's value of marginal product?

(c) If the monthly interest rate is .0264 percent, then the ratio $i/(1+i)$ equals .00263. Use this number to compute each journalist's wage premium in every month except the last. (See Equation 11.14.)

(d) To keep its journalists honest, *Old Republic* pays each journalist $\_\_\_\_\_$ every month plus a pension benefit of $\_\_\_\_\_$ at retirement.

References

Becker, Gary and George Stigler. 1974. "Law Enforcement, Malfeasance, and Compensation of Enforcers." *Journal of Legal Studies* 3(1): 1–18.

Black, Fischer and Myron Scholes. 1973. "The Pricing of Options and Corporate Liabilities." *Journal of Political Economy* 81(3): 637–654.

Jensen, Michael C. and Kevin J. Murphy. 1990. "Performance Pay and Top-Management Incentives." *Journal of Political Economy* 98(2): 225–264.

Lazear, Edward P. 1979. "Why Is There Mandatory Retirement?" *Journal of Political Economy* 87(6): 1261–1284.

Lazear, Edward P. 2000. "Performance Pay and Productivity." *American Economic Review* 90(5): 1346–1361.

Lazear, Edward P. 2005. "Entrepreneurship." *Journal of Labor Economics* 23(4): 649–680.

Lazear, Edward P. and Sherwin Rosen. 1981. "Rank-Order Tournaments as Optimum Labor Contracts." *Journal of Political Economy* 89(5): 841–864.

Solow, Robert M. 1979. "Another Possible Source of Wage Stickiness." *Journal of Macroeconomics* 1(1): 79–82.

Yermack, David. 2006. "Flights of Fancy: Corporate Jets, CEO Perquisites, and Inferior Shareholder Returns." *Journal of Financial Economics* 80(1): 211–242.

Unemployment

12

Poison-tipped arrows fly in one direction. Guns fire in the other direction. That's the extent of the rare interaction between the Arrow People (or *Flecheiros*) of the Brazilian Amazon and the rest of the world. The Arrow People are an uncontacted tribe, so we know little about them. We don't even know what language they speak. But from distant observations, we know that they gather, garden, hunt, and fish. They work to survive. I'll bet a nickel that none of the Arrow People—or the members of any other uncontacted tribe—is unemployed.

A person is unemployed if he or she isn't working but wants to work. What would it mean to be unemployed in a tribe of Amazon Indians? If an Amazon Indian isn't working, it's not from lack of opportunities to work. There's no shortage of work to do in the rainforest, but there's no shortage of work to do in the developed world either. So what gives rise to unemployment in the developed world? In the simple society of the Arrow People, a person doesn't need to search for work. In complex modern societies, a worker searches for a good job. While searching for work, the person is unemployed.

So unemployment is a consequence of job search. Some good workers lose their jobs through no fault of their own. Business slows, workers are cut loose, and many of them become unemployed. They begin the process of searching for job prospects (through friends, professional contacts, classified ads, and websites), applying for jobs, interviewing, and eventually evaluating a job offer or two. How long do the unemployed search? Most people exit the ranks of the unemployed in

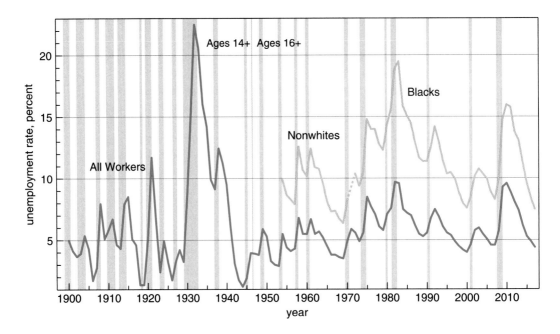

FIGURE 12.1. Unemployment Rates, 1900–2017
Notes: Shaded periods are recessions. Unemployment rates for whites, which are hidden, would lie just below the series for All Workers.
Sources: For all workers, see Figure 3.1. For nonwhites from 1954 to 1970, see *Historical Statistics of the United States, Colonial Times to 1970*, Series D14 and D18, p. 128. For blacks beginning in 1972, see Bureau of Labor Statistics, Current Population Survey, series LNU01000006 (Civilian Labor Force—Black or African American) and LNU03000006 (Unemployment Level–Black or African American).

just a month or two; others suffer through spells of unemployment that stretch past a year.

There are ebbs and flows in every business, and workers continually come and go. The labor market is quite dynamic. While a worker searches for the right job, an employer searches for the right person to fill a job vacancy. Information is difficult to come by, and unemployment—people looking for work while out of work—surfaces as a persistent feature rather than just an unwelcome visitor in economic downturns. The omnipresence of unemployment is apparent in Figure 12.1, which presents unemployment rates in the United States since 1900. The unemployment rate fluctuates from year to year, but on average, 5 percent of the labor force searches for work at any time.

Unemployment is valuable. It's a valuable activity for the people who are unemployed, and the unemployed are a valuable resource. With limited information, search while unemployed directs workers to the jobs where they're most productive. Unemployment is also valuable as an inventory of workers. In our dynamic world with imperfect information, idle resources are valuable, and they are all around us. Restaurant tables are empty at most times on most days, but wait times to get tables on a Saturday night can be long. The inventory of tables

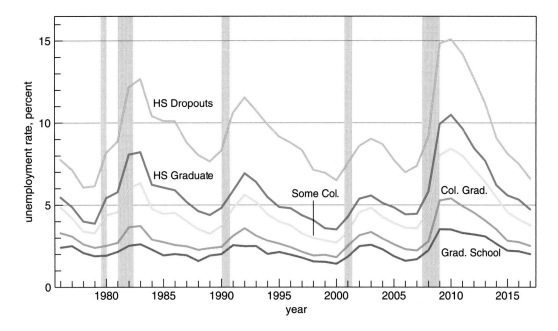

FIGURE 12.2. Unemployment Rates by Education, 1979–2017
Notes: The series are constructed using highest grade completed for the years 1979–1991 and more detailed education responses for 1992–2017. Sample includes people ages 25 and older. Shaded periods are recessions.
Source: Current Population Survey, outgoing rotation group files, monthly 1979–2017.

buffers fluctuations in demand at restaurants. The new cars that pack the lots at auto dealerships sit idle waiting for the new-car buyer searching for the perfect combination of color, accessories, and price. Empty tables at restaurants, cars on dealers' lots, and other idle resources help match buyers and sellers. Workers are idle resources while unemployed, and unemployment facilitates the matching of workers' skills to the tasks to be performed on jobs.

More-educated workers have lower unemployment rates, as Figure 12.2 illustrates, and that's efficient. Efficiency dictates that more valuable resources have less idle time (smaller buffers or inventories). In a ballpark, the empty seats are an idle resource that buffers fluctuations in demand for seats from game to game. But the best seats always sell first, so the least valuable seats (e.g., in the nose-bleed sections) have high "unemployment" rates. The most skilled workers are like the best seats at the ballpark, too valuable to be unemployed long. So the unemployment rate is lower for more-educated workers.

All this idleness isn't disturbing unless you limit your economic reasoning to a model in which markets clear instantly with perfect information. In this chapter, we shake things up (by adding some randomness) and dumb things down (by limiting the information that workers and employers have). The result is a model of job search and frictional unemployment. The model identifies factors that influence the unemployment rate, the length of time people stay unemployed, and the wages they earn on their new jobs. It also illuminates the effects of unemployment insurance.

12.1   Disequilibrium Unemployment

Our first model treats unemployment as an excess supply of workers. Figure 12.3 illustrates an hourly market for labor straight from chapter 2. The market clears at an hourly wage of $6 per worker with 5 million workers employed per hour. Any wage greater than $6 produces a surplus or excess supply of labor. At any super-competitive wage, the quantity demanded of labor is lower than, and the quantity supplied of labor is higher than, 5 million workers. Many people who want to work are left without jobs. They are unemployed.

A super-competitive wage causes **disequilibrium unemployment**, but what causes the wage to exceed its market-clearing value? Labor markets surely don't clear instant by instant, but why would an hourly wage greater than $6 per worker be any more common than a wage less than $6? That is, why aren't periods of vast shortages of labor and widespread job vacancies as common as periods of unemployment?

Minimum Wage and Efficiency Wage

A binding minimum wage causes unemployment. If the minimum wage is $7.25 per hour, then the excess supply of workers is $L_S - L_D$. The excess supply of workers in Figure 12.3 is 1.5 ($= 6.0 - 4.5$) million workers per hour. These people want to work at the $7.25 wage, so they are unemployed. Therefore, we predict high unemployment rates of those for whom the minimum wage binds: unskilled and inexperienced workers such as high school dropouts and teens.

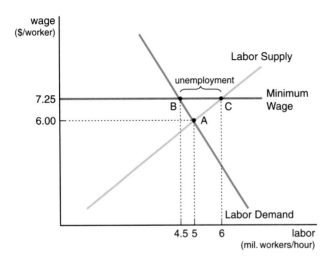

For any wage above the $6 equilibrium wage, there is an excess supply (or surplus) of labor and unemployment.

Why is a higher-than-equilibrium wage with unemployment any more likely than a lower-than-equilibrium wage with job vacancies? And what prevents the wage from clearing the labor market, eliminating unemployment or vacancies? The minimum wage is one possibility; an efficiency wage is another.

FIGURE 12.3. Unemployment as a Surplus of Labor

PRACTICE   How much of the unemployment in Figure 12.3 is due to the disemployment effect of the $7.25 wage? (The disemployment effect of the minimum wage is a key concept in chapter 2.) What accounts for the rest of the unemployment?

There's something to this. The unemployment rate of teens was 14.0 percent in 2017 when the overall unemployment rate was 4.4 percent. The unemployment rate of young black men also illustrates the principle. In 2017, the unemployment rate of black men ages 16–19 was 30.0 percent, and their unemployment rate has been at least 30 percent in every year except one over the past four decades. Other factors might also be in play, but the fact that the wage of young black men can't by law fall below the minimum wage undermines the equilibrating process that would encourage firms to employ more young black men.

An efficiency wage also causes unemployment. As we discovered in chapter 11, in some circumstances, it's profitable for an employer to pay an efficiency wage premium. It might be to motivate performance, to attract better workers, to reduce costly quits, or even to improve morale. If the profit-maximizing wage exceeds the market-clearing wage, the resulting excess supply of workers causes unemployment. In one variety of the efficiency-wage model, the resulting reserve army of unemployed workers also motivates performance. People work hard to avoid being dumped into unemployment because finding a job takes a long time with an efficiency-wage-induced excess supply of workers.

With multiple labor markets of the sort we studied in chapter 2, workers can be unemployed as they move from one labor market to another. One aspect of these flows across markets reveals important dynamics: employment adjusts along a path to a new long-run equilibrium. What happens to steel workers when the domestic steel industry declines? The demand for labor among steel firms falls, so employment and the wage in the steel industry fall. Displaced steel workers are unemployed while they look for work in the steel industry and elsewhere. In time, displaced steel workers find work in other industries and even other occupations. The supply of labor to steel decreases, and labor supply to other labor markets increases. In the long run, the wage in the steel industry returns to its long-run value, but employment of steel workers falls to a permanently lower level *without any unemployment*. Along the path to the new long-run equilibrium, there's **structural unemployment**, the unemployment associated with the changing structure of the economy.

12.2 Steady-State Unemployment

Minimum wages, efficiency wages, and the dynamics of structural unemployment contribute to our understanding of unemployment, but there must be more to unemployment than disequilibrium. Unemployment is widespread and persistent. It's not a temporary phenomenon, and vacancies are widespread and persistent, too. In the disequilibrium model, a wage that's too high causes unemployment; a wage that's too low causes vacancies. But unemployment and job vacancies coexist. We need a model of workers looking for work while firms search for workers to fill vacant positions. We need a model of **frictional unemployment**.

Flows Between Labor-Market States

The labor market is dynamic. People enter the labor market to get their first jobs. Some people return to the labor market after having a child or when the kids head to school. Others drop out of the labor market to get more education. Disabilities force others to exit the labor market; workers who recover from disabilities return to work. Old workers retire; some bored retirees return to work part-time. Firms put some workers on temporary layoffs while other firms recall workers from temporary layoffs. And some people, after months of searching for work, find a job and are thrilled to head to work every morning and collect a pay check at the end of every week. From week to week and month to month, there's definitely a lot of coming and going in the labor market.

Most adults in the United States are employed, but a relatively small group of people is unemployed. A third group of adults isn't in the labor force at all. These are the people who attend school, manage a home and raise a family full-time, enjoy retirement, and so on. So everyone is in one of these three **labor-market states**: employed (**E**), unemployed (**U**), and not in the labor force (**N**).

For the years 1990–2006 in the United States, Figure 12.4 lists and portrays the number of people in each labor-market state. (The size of each circle reflects the number of people in the state.) Employment averaged 130.5 million workers, unemployment averaged 7.5 million workers, and 69.3 million adults weren't in the labor force (NILF) on average. That is, in a typical month, 63.0 percent of the working-age population was employed, 3.6 percent was unemployed, and 33.4 percent was not in the labor force.

From month to month, people flow from one labor-market state to another. A graduating student who finds a job moves from not in the labor force (**N**) to employed (**E**); a worker recalled from a temporary layoff moves from **U** to **E**; a discouraged person who drops out of the labor market after unsuccessfully searching for work for nearly a year moves from **U** to **N**.

Figure 12.4 also displays the monthly **labor-market flows**, which measure workers' moves across the labor-market states. In a typical month, 3.4 million working-age people flow from **N** to **E**; that is, 4.9 percent of the people who aren't in the labor force (**N**) in one month are employed (**E**) in the next month. Another 1.8 million workers flow from **E** to **U**; that is, 1.4 percent of employed workers in one month are unemployed in the next month. And 2.0 million unemployed workers (27.3 percent of the unemployed) find jobs in a typical month. The figure also lists the other three flows (i.e., **E** → **N**, **U** → **N**, and **N** → **U**).

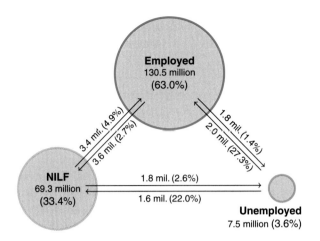

In each month, a worker is either employed, unemployed, or not in the labor force (NILF), which are the three labor-market states. Transitions from state to state between months are flows. For instance, 2.0 million workers flow from unemployment to employment from month to month. This flow is 27.3% of the unemployed workers.

This diagram illustrates a steady state because the number of people In each labor-market state doesn't change between months. That is, the combined flows into each state equal the combined flows out from each state.

FIGURE 12.4. Average Stocks in and Flows Between Labor-Market States, 1990–2006

 PRACTICE Use Figure 12.4 to find how many people exit unemployment in a typical month. Those who exit unemployment in a month are what proportion of the unemployed?

These flows between labor-market states bounce around a lot from month to month and even year to year. But the averages over the years 1990–2006 describe a steady state. In a **steady state**, flows into a state equal the flows out of the state, so the size of the state (e.g., the number of people unemployed) doesn't change. Consider unemployment. In a typical month, 3.6 million workers become unemployed, 1.8 million from employment ($E \rightarrow U$) and another 1.8 million who hadn't been in the labor force ($N \rightarrow U$). But 3.6 million workers also escape unemployment: 2.0 million by finding jobs ($U \rightarrow E$) and 1.6 million by exiting the labor market to N. Inflows to unemployment equal outflows from unemployment, so the number of people unemployed doesn't change.

An analogy might help. The number of people unemployed in a month is like the volume of water in a lake. As people flow into unemployment from employment and outside the labor market, water flows into the lake from the sky (as rain) and from streams. As the unemployed escape unemployment by finding jobs or exiting the labor market, water evaporates from the lake and flows out of the lake to form a river. For the lake's water level not to change, the volume of water entering the lake through rainfall and streams must equal the volume of water exiting the lake by evaporating into the air or flowing into the river. If the level of water in the lake neither rises nor falls, the lake is in a steady state. But the particular molecules of water in the lake are constantly changing: some molecules enter the lake while others leave the lake. How long a typical molecule of water remains in the lake depends on the exit rate—the volume of water that leaves the lake per hour relative to the volume of water in the lake.

PRACTICE   Apply the lake analogy to the average time people spend unemployed. In terms of stocks and flows of the sort that Figure 12.4 illustrates, what determines the length of time that a typical unemployed person spends unemployed?

In the steady state, what fraction of participants in the labor market is unemployed? The answer to this question is the **steady-state unemployment rate**. To be in a steady state, the flow of workers into unemployment must equal the flow of workers out from unemployment. For the moment, let's work with only two states, **E** and **U**, so assume that **N** doesn't exist. E and U are the numbers of people employed and unemployed in the steady state. Let s denote the **job separation rate** from employment to unemployment, and let h denote the **hiring rate** from unemployment. The separation rate measures how often workers become unemployed (i.e., the **incidence of unemployment**), and the hiring rate determines how long people stay unemployed (i.e., the **duration of unemployment**).

In the steady state, the flow into unemployment sE equals the flow from unemployment hU; that is, $sE = hU$. This simple expression and an expression for the unemployment rate are all we need to derive the steady-state unemployment rate. In general, the unemployment rate u is the ratio of unemployment to the sum of employment and unemployment; that is, $u = U/(E + U)$. By expressing the steady-state condition $sE = hU$ in terms of $U/(E + U)$, we solve for the steady-state unemployment rate. Add sU to both sides of the steady-state condition to find that $s(E + U) = (h + s)U$. Dividing both sides by the parenthetical expressions delivers the steady-state unemployment rate.

(12.1)
$$u^* = \frac{s}{h + s}$$

So the steady-state unemployment rate u^* is an increasing function of the separation rate s and a decreasing function of the hiring rate h. Recognizing the importance of flows of workers across states identifies the two key determinants of unemployment: the separation rate from employment (or the rate of job loss) s and the rate of job finding h.

 PRACTICE   In Figure 12.4, the monthly separation rate to unemployment is 1.4 percent, and the monthly hiring rate from unemployment is 27.3 percent. Plug these values into Equation 12.1 to solve for the steady-state unemployment rate over the years 1990–2006. (This calculation assumes there are only two labor-market states.)

Let's extend the model of steady-state unemployment to three states. With three labor-market states, the indirect flows from employment (**E**) through NILF

(**N**) to unemployment (**U**) and the reverse flows from unemployment through NILF to employment influence the steady-state unemployment rate. Tracking all the flows is tedious algebra, but the bottom line is easily understood. The steady-state unemployment rate with three states is

(12.2)
$$u^* = \frac{s + \alpha}{(h + \alpha) + (s + \beta)}$$

That is, we replace the separation rate to unemployment s with $s + \alpha$, where α reflects the indirect path from employment to unemployment ($\mathbf{E} \to \mathbf{N} \to \mathbf{U}$). We also replace the hiring rate h with $h + \beta$, where β captures the indirect path from unemployment to employment ($\mathbf{U} \to \mathbf{N} \to \mathbf{E}$). In this specification, the equilibrium unemployment rate continues to be an increasing function of the separation rate to unemployment s and a decreasing function of the hiring rate h. The most important extra effects through α and β are (1) a higher entrance rate from NILF to unemployment raises the steady-state unemployment rate and (2) a higher exit rate from unemployment to NILF lowers the steady-state unemployment rate.

What was the steady-state unemployment rate over the years 1990–2006? To answer this question, plug the relevant values from Figure 12.4 into Equation 12.2. The monthly separation and hiring rates are $s = 1.4$ percent and $h = 27.3$ percent. The extra terms are $\alpha = 0.9$ percent and $\beta = 14.4$ percent. (α and β depend on the numbers in Figure 12.4, but the calculations are omitted.) So the adjusted rates are $s + \alpha = 2.3$ percent and $h + \beta = 41.7$ percent. The implied steady-state unemployment rate is 5.2 percent over this period.

Distribution of Lengths of Spells of Unemployment

J.J. loses his job. He licks his wounds, and his friends and family express their sorrow and offer encouragement as he joins the ranks of the unemployed. How long will it take J.J. to find work? It depends on many factors, including how intensively he searches and how finicky he is in searching for and evaluating job offers, but let's start with a simple observation: it's random. J.J. could get lucky and find a job quickly, or he might have awful luck, taking a year or more to find an acceptable job. So the length of a spell of unemployment is a random variable, and random variables are characterized by their distributions. What's the distribution of lengths of unemployment spells?

Our steady-state model has the key ingredient: the rate at which J.J. and other unemployed workers escape unemployment. Between 1990 and 2006, the hiring rate from unemployment in a typical month was 27 percent. An additional 22 percent of the unemployed exited unemployment by leaving the labor market. So roughly half the unemployed in one month weren't unemployed the next month.

There's good reason to believe a 50 percent monthly escape rate from unemployment is excessive. People make mistakes (or even lie) in survey interviews, and we sometimes misclassify their responses. Janet in December reports being unemployed; in January, she suggests that she's not in the labor force; in February, she declares that she's unemployed; and she's employed when

TABLE 12.1. DISTRIBUTION OF LENGTHS OF UNEMPLOYMENT SPELLS

MONTHS	MONTHS UNEMPLOYED (m)	BEGINNING UNEMPLOYMENT (%)	LEAVING UNEMPLOYMENT (%)
January	1	100.0	40.0
February	2	60.0	24.0
March	3	36.0	14.4
April	4	21.6	8.6
May	5	13.0	5.2
June	6	7.8	3.1
July	7	4.7	1.9
August	8	2.8	1.1
September	9	1.7	0.7
October	10	1.0	0.4
November	11	0.6	0.2
December	12	0.4	0.1
January	13	0.2	0.1

Notes: The formulas for Beginning Unemployed and Leaving Unemployment are $(1-x)^{m-1}$ and $(1-x)^{m-1} \times x$, respectively, where x is the exit rate from unemployment. The calculations assume that x is 40 percent per month.

we interview her in March. Janet might have left the labor market for a month in January. Alternatively, the distinction between unemployed and not in the labor force isn't that sharp, and the interviewer misclassifies her in January. In Janet's case, misclassification turns one unemployment spell of three months into two spells of one month each. That is, misclassification tends to exaggerate short spells of unemployment. Farber and Valletta (2015) study these short spells of reported unemployment and conclude that a lot of the short spells are erroneous. A better measure of the exit rate from unemployment is 40 percent. So let's work with that.

Constant and Common Exit Rate.   If the monthly escape rate from unemployment is 40 percent—a constant that's independent of how long the person has been unemployed—then 40 percent of the unemployed leave unemployment in the first month. The other 60 percent are unemployed in the second month, and 40 percent of those 60 percent (i.e., 24 percent) find jobs in the second month. The process continues month after month, and the last column of Table 12.1 lists the resulting distribution of lengths of unemployment spells.

Let's see where the numbers come from. If J.J. and 999 other workers become unemployed in January, then 400 (40 percent) of them find jobs (or leave the labor market) in January, and 600 (60 percent) continue looking for work in February. Forty percent of those second-month job searchers find jobs (or leave the market) in February; that's 240 workers or 24 percent of the original pool of unemployed.

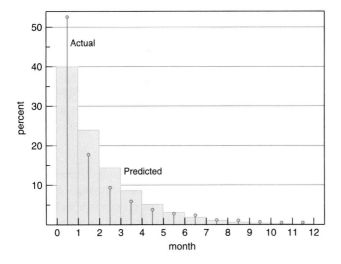

The height of each bar gives the predicted proportion of unemployment spells ending in each month assuming the exit rate from unemployment is constant at 40%. The predicted distribution of spell lengths is geometric since the proportions decline at a constant rate, 40%/month.

The gray dots with thin drop lines measure the actual proportion of unemployment spells that end in each month, 52.6% in the first month, 17.8% in the second month, and so on.

The model with a constant exit rate underpredicts very short spells and overpredicts spells that end in months 2–5.

FIGURE 12.5. Distributions of Lengths of Unemployment Spells

Then 360 workers (36 percent) carry over to search in March. And on and on. By October, only 10 workers (1 percent) still look for work, and only 2 workers (0.2 percent) remain unemployed after 12 months. The bar graph in Figure 12.5 illustrates this distribution of lengths of unemployment spells—as predicted by the 40 percent escape rate from unemployment.

 PRACTICE   Through July, 97.2 percent of the unemployed have escaped unemployment, and the other 2.8 percent are still unemployed in August. Explain how to calculate that 1.1 percent of Januarys crop of freshly unemployed workers find jobs in August. Also explain how to calculate that 1.7 percent of the unemployment spells continue into September.

How long can J.J. and other freshly unemployed people expect to be unemployed? Six hundred workers start February unemployed, and 360 start March unemployed. So half the 1,000 workers who began searching for work in January find work or drop out of the labor market by sometime in February. In fact, the median spell of unemployment ends at about Presidents' Day, 1.35 months after it began. The average spell of unemployment, however, is longer. For a distribution that falls off geometrically (i.e., at a constant rate), the expected value is the inverse of the exit rate. In our case, the mean length of unemployment spells is 2.5 (= 1 ÷ .4) months. So J.J. can expect to find a job by the middle of March.

This example captures a puzzling property of unemployment: most spells of unemployment are short, but the lion's share of unemployment is due to long spells. In this example, 64 (= 40 + 24) percent of the unemployment spells end in the first two months. Those spells are quite short. Although few people remain unemployed longer than three or four months, each of those people is counted as unemployed several or even many times. For instance, only 1 percent of the spells end in the tenth month, but we count each of those searchers as unemployed 10 times, once for each month. In Table 12.1, searchers who are fortunate enough to exit unemployment in the first two months (64 percent of the spells) account for only about one-third of unemployment. Workers with longer spells of unemployment (36 percent of the spells) account for roughly two-thirds of unemployment. Puzzling but true.

Exit Rates that Vary.   All our results follow from a single assumption: the exit rate from unemployment is constant at 40 percent. Although 40 percent fits the flows across labor-market states, it misses the distribution of lengths of unemployment spells. Figure 12.5 overlays the actual distribution of spell lengths over the years 2000–2005 (Farber and Valletta 2015, Table 3) with gray dots and thin drop lines. More than half (52.6 percent) of the unemployed workers find jobs in their first month of job search, but the exit rate from unemployment drops rapidly. In the second month, the exit rate falls to 37.6 percent, so only 17.8 (= 37.6 × (1 − .526)) percent of the spells of unemployment end in the second month, which is well below the 24 percent predicted by a constant exit rate of 40 percent. Figure 12.5 reveals the systematic pattern of the errors. The constant exit-rate simulation understates very short spells of unemployment and exaggerates exits from unemployment in months 2–5.

Where did we go wrong? To be consistent with the steady-state flows in Figure 12.4 (corrected for reporting errors), the unemployed must escape unemployment at a 40 percent rate. But to be consistent with the distribution of lengths of unemployment spells, the exit rate from unemployment must vary with time unemployed. There are two ways to resolve this conflict: let the exit rate depend on the duration of the unemployment spell, or let the overall exit rate from unemployment mix values from groups with different exit rates.

Perhaps the exit rate from unemployment is quite high in the first month, and it declines rapidly from there. J.J. might line up a new job before he leaves his old job; he's just waiting to start the new job. Or it might be relatively easy for a newly unemployed worker to find a job, but being unemployed a long time carries a stigma. If J.J. has been unemployed for nine months, each employer wonders why another employer didn't hire him months ago. Is there something wrong with him? Such suspicions reduce J.J.'s chance of exiting unemployment.

Stigma seems like it would kick in much later, not as early as the second or third month. After all, readers of this chapter aren't the only ones to grasp that finding a job is a random process; employers know that, too. And there's another element pushing in the opposite direction: J.J. might run out of money. He might be picky in his first month or two of job search, but he'll search more aggressively and be less picky as he depletes his savings and runs up balances on his credit cards. J.J.'s cash-flow problem points to his exit rate from unemployment increasing as his time unemployed grows. But that pattern isn't consistent with the declining exit rates in the data.

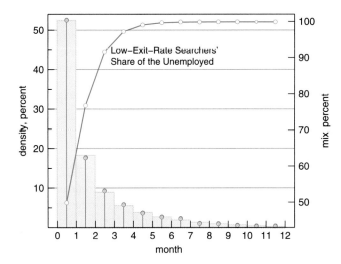

Half the newly unemployed escape from unemployment at a rate of 78%. The other half have a 27% exit rate. The first group finds jobs fast, so the mix of unemployed workers rapidly shifts to low-exit-rate workers. The connected dots track the share of unemployed workers who have low exit rates from 50% in month 1 to nearly 100% in month 4.

The overall escape rate from unemployment is very high in the first month but declines rapidly as high-exit-rate searchers escape unemployment. The resulting distribution of lengths of unemployment spells is the bar graph, which fits the actual distribution of spell lengths remarkably well.

FIGURE 12.6. Mixing Low- and High-Exit-Rate Searchers

There's also a logical problem with the stigma explanation: if J.J. and his fellow workers in the ranks of the unemployed are identical, then it doesn't make sense for any employer to treat the long-time unemployed with stigma. For stigma to make sense, we need meaningful differences among workers.

Some workers escape from unemployment faster than others. Some are better searchers. They have lots of business contacts, or they are just good at marketing themselves. Other equally productive workers are more modest about their skills and aren't tied into a network of people who feed them job prospects.

Let's assume there are two types of unemployed workers. J.J. and 499 other newly unemployed workers have an escape rate from unemployment of 27 percent per month. Steve and 499 other unemployed workers exit unemployment at rate 78 percent per month. We don't know who's who, so we track the exit rate from unemployment for the combined group of 1,000 people who start looking for work in January. In January ($m = 1$), 135 ($= .27 \times 500$) low-h searchers and 390 ($= .78 \times 500$) high-h searchers find jobs. So 525 ($= 135 + 390$) people or 52.5 percent find jobs in the first month. That rate fits the actual month-1 escape rate from unemployment in Figure 12.5 quite well.

Those who didn't find a job in January continue to look for work in February. That's 365 ($= 500 − 135$) low-h workers like J.J. and only 110 ($= 500 − 390$) high-h workers like Steve, so the composition of the unemployed shifts from 50–50 in January to 81–39 low-h in February. Ninety-nine of the 365 low-h searchers find work in February, with 266 left to continue searching in March; 86 of 110 high-h searchers find work in February, and 24 continue to be unemployed in March. Overall, 185 ($= 99 + 86$) or 18.5 percent of the spells end in February ($m = 2$).

Figure 12.6 displays the bar chart of completed lengths of unemployment spells by continuing these calculations for March, April, and so on. Predictions from this model, which mixes low- and high-escape-rate groups, fit the actual distribution incredibly well. Month by month, the proportion of unemployment spells that are predicted to end matches the proportion of spells that do end. What delivers the result? Early exits from unemployment are mostly high-h searchers like Steve. As the length of unemployment spells increases, the mix of unemployed workers shifts toward low-h workers like J.J. So the overall exit rate sinks from 52.5 percent in January and approaches 27 percent for seriously long spells.

12.3 Job Search

The exit rate from unemployment is one of two broad determinants of the steady-state unemployment rate. But what determines the exit rate from unemployment? Here we model job search with a **reservation wage**: J.J. accepts a job only if the wage offer w is at least as high as his reservation wage R. As we'll see, J.J.'s reservation wage depends on how intensively he searches, how long jobs last, the interest rate, and the net cost of job search, which is related to unemployment insurance benefits.

J.J. searches for a job. He casts a wide net, job offers sometimes come and sometimes not, and he accepts or rejects job offers along the way. He **searches sequentially**. And J.J. searches because he doesn't know which firm would pay him the highest wage. His skills are valued differently across employers. One firm would pay him no more than $550 per week; another firm would pay him close to $1,000 per week; and plenty of firms would offer him wages between those extremes.

Although J.J. doesn't know what he's worth at any firm, he does know the distribution of wage offers. He knows what to expect on average and even his chances of landing a job that pays more that $1,000 per week—the proportion of employers that value him more than $1,000 per week. That is, he knows his distribution of wage offers. Let's assume that J.J.'s wage offers are distributed normally, so they follow the bell curve in Figure 12.7. J.J.'s mean wage is $800 per week, and 90 percent of his wage offers are in the range between $635 and $965 per week.

Reservation Wage

As an unemployed job searcher, J.J. could hold out for a job that pays at least $1,200 per week or even one that pays more than $2,000 per week. If he does, he'll be unemployed for a very long time. This example illustrates the fundamental trade-off that every unemployed worker faces. Holding out for a great job has its reward in the form of a high expected wage, but setting your sights high invites a long spell of costly unemployment.

J.J.'s optimal search strategy involves a reservation wage (McCall 1970). He accepts a job if it offers a wage greater than or equal to his reservation wage: $w \geq R$. In Figure 12.7, the height of the wage distribution $f(w)$ at some wage w tells us the probability of receiving a job offer at that wage. The area under the wage

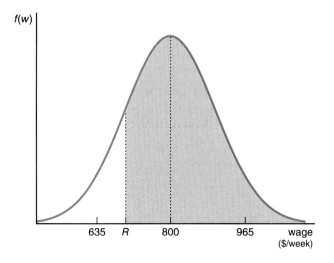

J.J.'s wage offers are normally distributed; the distribution follows the familiar bell curve with the peak at his mean wage, $800/week.

J.J.'s reservation wage R in the context of search sets the minimal acceptable wage offer. J.J. accepts any wage greater than or equal to R.

The probability that J.J. accepts a wage offer is the shaded area below the curve relative to the entire area below the curve. Raising his reservation wage lowers the probability that he'll receive an acceptable job offer.

FIGURE 12.7. Distribution of Wage Offers

distribution above R—the shaded area in the figure—is the probability that an offer is acceptable to J.J. By raising his reservation wage R, he shrinks his chance of receiving an acceptable offer and lengthens his time unemployed. But the job he eventually accepts will, on average, pay a higher wage.

 PRACTICE

Raise J.J.'s reservation wage in Figure 12.7 from R to $800 per week. Illustrate what happens to the probability that J.J. accepts a job offer. At what rate does J.J. accept job offers if his reservation wage is $800 per week?

How does J.J. trade off the advantage of a higher reservation wage (i.e., a higher wage on average as long as he holds the job) with the disadvantage of a higher reservation wage (i.e., a longer spell of unemployment)? He chooses his reservation wage by comparing the benefits and costs of small changes in the reservation wage. Since a higher reservation wage increases his time searching, let's call these the **marginal benefit of search** and **marginal cost of search**.

By increasing his reservation wage a bit, J.J. remains unemployed longer, and he bears the cost of search c and foregoes a wage over the extended period of search. The marginal increase in his reservation wage also raises the wage he'll receive on an acceptable job. The benefit of a higher reservation wage depends on the distribution of wages: how much a little higher reservation wage raises the average value of the wage over the range above R. And the expected wage gain needs to be expressed as a present value. The gain is more valuable the longer the job and the lower the interest rate. The present value also depends on how rapidly job offers arrive. For any reservation wage, the gain from a little higher reservation wage is bigger if J.J. starts the job sooner, and that happens if job offers come in quickly.

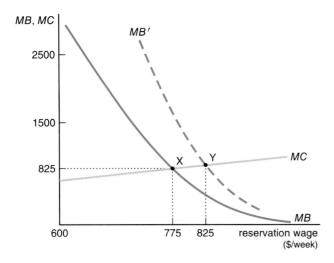

J.J.'s marginal cost of search—of a marginally higher reservation wage R—is $MC = c + R$, a line with slope one. His marginal benefit of search is a downward-sloping curve that depends on the arrival rate of job offers, how long jobs last, and the interest rate, as well as the distribution of wage offers. J.J.'s optimal reservation wage R^* equates the costs and benefits of search at the margin: $R^* = 775$.

More frequent job offers, longer jobs, and a lower interest rate shift the MB curve up, which increases J.J.'s reservation wage from $775 to $825 per week.

FIGURE 12.8. Optimal Reservation Wage

J.J.'s job search boils down to this. A marginal increase in his reservation wage from R means that J.J. rejects a job offer with a wage equal to R. He spends another week searching for work, which costs him c in out-of-pocket expenses, and he foregoes the wage he could have earned $w = R$. So his marginal cost of search is $MC = c + R$, which is the upward-sloping line in Figure 12.8 (with $c = 50$).

By rejecting a job offer with $w = R$, J.J.'s gain from searching this week depends on the probability he receives a wage offer this week a, the probability the offer is acceptable to him $\Pr(w \geq R)$, the expected wage gain (relative to R), how long he'll hold the job, and the interest rate i. The marginal benefit of search is a decreasing function of the reservation wage, as Figure 12.8 shows. (The marginal benefit curve is drawn using the wage distribution in Figure 12.7, a weekly arrival rate of job offers $a = .10$, a weekly interest rate $i = .0015$, and a weekly job separation rate $s = .005$. This job separation rate implies that jobs last on average 3.3 years.) With a low R, J.J. has big gains to nudging up R primarily because he's likely to get an acceptable offer quickly. But with a high R, a little higher R carries little benefit because he's unlikely to get a much better offer anytime soon.

The intersection of his marginal cost and marginal benefit curves at $775 per week in Figure 12.8 identifies J.J.'s optimal reservation wage R^*. Sixty percent of the wage distribution lies above $R^* = 775$, so the probability a job offer is acceptable to J.J. is 60 percent. Since there's a 1-in-10 chance that J.J. receives an offer in any week, the probability that he receives an acceptable offer this week is 6 percent. That implies that he should expect to be unemployed for nearly 17 $(= 1 \div .06)$ weeks. The average acceptable wage turns out to be $865 per week. So his optimal reservation wage extends his unemployment spell to almost 17 weeks but raises the wage he expects to get from $800 to $865 per week.

PRACTICE

In Figure 12.7, half the distribution of J.J.'s wage offers lie above $800 per week. Suppose J.J. mistakenly chooses $800 per week for his reservation wage. What's the probability that a job offer is acceptable to him? There's a 1-in-10 chance that he receives an offer this week, so the probability that he receives an acceptable offer this week is _____ percent. How long should J.J. expect to be unemployed?

ADVANCED The optimal reservation wage R^* is the value of R that solves

$$(12.3) \qquad c + R = \frac{a \Pr(w \geq R)}{s + i} \left(E[w \text{ for } w \geq R] - R \right)$$

where c is the out-of-pocket cost of search, a is the arrival rate of job offers, s is the job separation rate, and i is the interest rate. The left side of the equation is the marginal cost of search.

The marginal benefit of search (on the right side of the equation) combines three expressions. The first expression is the probability of receiving an acceptable job offer this week. That's the product of the arrival rate a and the probability that a job offer is acceptable $\Pr[w \geq R]$, which is a decreasing function of R. The second expression is the expected wage gain, which is the difference between the average acceptable wage $E[w \text{ for } w \geq R]$ and the reservation wage R. The third expression converts the marginal benefit to a present value by dividing by the sum of the job separation rate s and the interest rate i.

Career Jobs, Low Interest Rates, and Being Well-Connected

Would you search longer for a day job, a summer job, or a career job? The answer is obvious because the gain to job search is bigger for jobs that last longer. Jobs that last longer have lower separation rates. Lowering the separation rate raises the marginal benefit of search and shifts up the marginal benefit curve in Figure 12.8. J.J.'s choice slides up the marginal cost curve in response to the lower separation rate, so he adopts a higher reservation wage. Becoming more selective reduces the odds that he'll accept a job offer in any week. He remains unemployed longer, so we predict a higher unemployment rate for searchers on career jobs. When he finds a job, it will tend to pay more since his search is more selective. Likewise, a lower interest rate i increases the marginal benefit of search, raises the reservation wage, lengthens spells of unemployment, lifts the unemployment rate, and raises the average accepted wage.

The arrival rate of job offers a also influences the reservation wage, the length of spells of unemployment, the unemployment rate, and the average accepted wage. Unlike J.J., Steve is well-connected professionally. He has a great network of professionals who feed him serious job prospects. Consequently, Steve receives job offers twice as rapidly as J.J. If Steve shared J.J.'s $775 reservation wage, he would remain unemployed half as long as J.J., eight weeks or so. But Steve has good reason to be more selective in his search. As Figure 12.8 shows, the higher rate of job offers shifts up the marginal benefit curve. Steve's optimal reservation wage is $825, $50 higher than J.J.'s, and the probability he finds a job offer acceptable is 40 percent (compared to J.J.'s 60 percent). The probability that Steve receives an acceptable job offer in any week is 8 percent ($= .2 \times .4$), so he can expect to be unemployed 12.5 ($= 1 \div .08$) weeks. His average accepted wage is almost $900 per week, about $35 more than J.J.'s. So being well-connected—or being in a thicker market—shortens spells of unemployment, lowers the unemployment rate, and raises the average accepted wage.

 PRACTICE   Increase the out-of-pocket costs of search c. What happens to the two solid curves in Figure 12.8? Trace out the effects of a higher c on the reservation wage, the odds of receiving an acceptable job offer, the length of spells of unemployment, the unemployment rate, and the average accepted wage.

Key Principle.
Unemployment isn't primarily a surplus (or excess supply) of labor. Unemployment is a natural consequence of a two-sided search process: a worker searches for a high-wage job, and a firm looks for the best workers to fill its vacant positions.

What happens in equilibrium if every worker is identical to J.J.? Every worker solves J.J.'s search problem, so all workers share J.J.'s $775 reservation wage. Employers understand this (or quickly figure it out), so every employer offers a weekly wage of $775, the lowest wage that workers accept. Therefore, the purpose of job search—to find a high-wage job—vanishes if workers are identical.

This paradox shouldn't disturb us. It simply points us to an important foundation of search: differences across workers and firms. Each employer has its own value of a worker's skills. (See the discussion of matching models in section 7.4.) J.J.'s search for a high wage is simply a search for a good match. While workers like J.J. search for high-wage jobs, employers search for high-value workers. In the two-sided search process, workers are unemployed and firms have job vacancies. So unemployment and job vacancies coexist.

12.4   Applications

How does unemployment insurance (UI) affect unemployment? Our first application extends the model of job search to answer this question. In our second application, UI is one of several factors that contribute to our understanding of the

European unemployment problem—decades of persistently high unemployment rates.

Unemployment Insurance

Unemployment insurance, a joint program of the federal and state governments that originated in the Social Security Act of 1935, covers U.S. workers. Employers pay unemployment insurance premiums through a payroll tax, and workers who become unemployed through no fault of their own receive weekly unemployment compensation (i.e., UI benefits) while they search for work. To be eligible for unemployment compensation, a worker must meet employment and earnings requirements in the base period (typically a year) before becoming unemployed. Eligible workers can receive compensation for up to 26 weeks in most states, although the benefit period automatically extends to 39 weeks in recessions when (and in states where) the unemployment rate is high. In the 2007–2009 recession, the Bush administration extended the benefit period to 59 weeks, and the Obama administration extended it to 99 weeks.

Unemployment compensation replaces roughly half of pre-tax weekly wages. The **UI replacement ratio** varies somewhat across states, and it varies a lot with the worker's pre-unemployment wage. Mississippi replaces exactly half the average weekly wage (in the highest earnings quarter in the year before unemployment). Michigan and Pennsylvania replace 2–3 percent more. But every state caps unemployment compensation, so low-wage workers enjoy higher replacement ratios. Caps on unemployment compensation also vary a lot across states; for instance, the caps in Mississippi, Michigan, and Pennsylvania are, respectively, $235, $362, and $575 per week. So the replacement ratio for high-wage workers is quite low in Mississippi and much higher in Pennsylvania. Indeed, the replacement ratio for a worker who earns $1,000 per week (or $52,000 per year) is 23.5 percent in Mississippi, 36.2 percent in Michigan, and 52.2 percent in Pennsylvania.

UI and the Duration of Unemployment. Unemployment compensation enters our model of job search as the opposite of an out-of-pocket expense. Unemployment compensation reduces or even reverses the out-of-pocket cost of search. So the effects of unemployment compensation b on the reservation wage and unemployment variables are exactly the opposite of the effects of out-of-pocket costs c. In particular, unemployment compensation shifts down the marginal-cost-of-search curve in Figure 12.9. J.J. responds to his $400 weekly unemployment compensation by increasing his reservation wage from $775 to $820. He becomes more selective in evaluating job offers, and his odds of receiving an acceptable job offer in a week fall from 6 percent to 4.2 percent. The time that J.J. can expect to be unemployed lengthens from 17 ($= 1 \div .06$) to 24 ($= 1 \div .042$) weeks. So unemployment compensation increases the unemployment rate. This result should be intuitive: unemployment compensation pays people to be unemployed, so people collecting unemployment compensation stay unemployed longer. But the average accepted wage also rises because longer

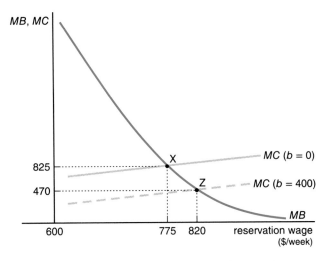

J.J.'s weekly unemployment compensation b is $400, which shifts down his marginal-cost-of-search curve by $400. J.J.'s optimal reservation wage increases from $775 to $820/week. The higher reservation wage lowers the chance he'll accept a job offer from 60% to 42%/week, so the weekly probability that he'll exit unemployment falls from 6% to 4.2%. J.J.'s spell of unemployment stretches from 17 to 24 weeks.

Unemployment compensation increases the unemployment rate, but it also increases the expected value of accepted wages. In J.J.'s case, his accepted wage rises on average from $865 to $893/week.

FIGURE 12.9. Unemployment Compensation and the Optimal Reservation Wage

searches tend to improve the quality of job matches. In J.J.'s case, the expected value of an acceptable wage rises from $865 to $893.

PRACTICE   Larry in Mississippi and Bruce in Pennsylvania had each been working for $1,000 per week before losing their jobs. Assume that the replacement ratio in each state is 50 percent, but recall that weekly unemployment compensation is capped at $235 in Mississippi and $575 in Pennsylvania. Which worker has the (1) higher reservation wage, (2) longer spell of unemployment, and (3) higher wage on the new job? The differential cap on unemployment compensation across these two states causes the unemployment rate of high-wage workers to be higher in which state?

Unemployment insurance also weakens the incentive to search while unemployed. Our search model predicts that workers with generous unemployment compensation spend less time searching, and data on time use confirm this implication (Krueger and Mueller 2010). Searching less intensively generates fewer job offers and longer spells of unemployment.

The effect of unemployment compensation on search can also be detected from changes in behavior as benefits expire. Meyer (1990) used administrative records from the UI systems in 12 states to analyze how exit rates from unemployment change as the time when UI benefits lapse nears. Figure 12.10 illustrates how the exit rate from unemployment varies week by week running up to the week when benefits lapse or expire. Weekly exit rates fluctuate around 5 percent until the final weeks before benefits lapse. Exit rates from unemployment

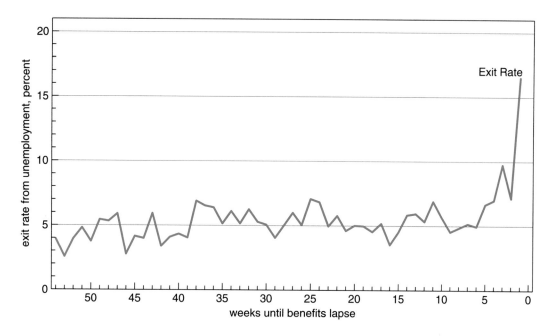

FIGURE 12.10. Exit Rate from Unemployment in the Weeks Before Benefits Lapse
Source: Meyer (1990, Table IV).

rise rapidly in the final five weeks before benefits lapse, spiking at 16.5 percent in the last week of eligibility. Unfortunately, the administrative data don't follow workers after their benefits lapse, so we don't know from these data whether the exit rate remains high after benefits expire (as our model predicts) or falls back toward 5 percent.

Nothing in Figure 12.10 ensures that the composition of the pool of unemployed workers remains the same from week to week. Meyer skillfully addresses this concern in estimating exit rates from unemployment week by week for a typical worker by controlling for schooling, age, state of residence, the wage prior to unemployment, unemployment compensation, and weeks until benefits lapse (Meyer 1990, Tables V and VII, specification 5). He finds that a 10 percent increase in unemployment compensation b (e.g., from \$300 to \$330 per week) lowers the exit rate from unemployment 8.8 percent. If the baseline exit rate is 5 percent per week, the 10 percent increase in b lowers the exit rate to a little more than 4.5 percentage points and lengthens the average spell of unemployment by nearly two weeks. In addition, between six and two weeks prior to benefits lapsing, the exit rate rises 109 percent; in the last week of eligibility, the exit rate jumps another 95 percent. In total, the exit rate more than quadruples in the six weeks immediately preceding the lapsing of unemployment benefits.

Unemployment compensation dulls the incentive to search, but perhaps workers are too quick to take jobs without UI. In our model of sequential search, workers pay their bills while unemployed by drawing down bank balances, borrowing against their retirement accounts, or running up credit-card balances.

But what if J.J. has no funds to pay the bills while he searches? No surprise. He lowers his reservation wage and finds a job faster. Unemployment insurance, in this case, finances J.J.'s search, and he efficiently lengthens his time unemployed.

There's evidence to support this interpretation. Chetty (2008) finds that the dulling effect of unemployment compensation on incentives to work is much smaller for searchers with liquid assets (or with a second income earner in the family). Furthermore, severance payments from previous employers lead to longer spells of unemployment only for job searchers with little or no wealth. So cash on hand matters, and unemployment insurance puts cash in the hands of job searchers.

But there's also an alternative policy. A simple and more direct way to confront the problem of financing job search is through a loan that could be paid back from the earnings on the new job. If the financial market doesn't offer these loans, then the government could offer a loan program.

UI and the Incidence of Unemployment.   Unemployment insurance also influences the flow of workers into unemployment—the incidence of unemployment—by encouraging layoffs, especially temporary layoffs (Feldstein 1976). With fluctuations in product demand and hiring and training costs, having an inventory of workers makes sense. In periods of high demand, everyone works. When demand slackens, the firm puts some workers on temporary layoff, and it recalls those workers when demand recovers. The workers on temporary layoff are unemployed, although we don't expect them to search intensively for new jobs. And workers on temporary layoffs have historically been a big part of unemployment.

Let's explore the impact of unemployment insurance on temporary layoffs in two steps. First, suppose that the UI system is financed by a payroll tax rate t that's unrelated to each employer's history of layoffs and dismissals. An employer can place workers on temporary layoff without having to pay a dime of their unemployment compensation. So employers use temporary layoffs excessively. In particular, an efficient contract between a firm and its workers exploits unemployment insurance by increasing temporary layoffs. Some workers are sent home even when the value of the marginal product of their labor is greater than the marginal value of their time at home (i.e., when $v_H < VMP_L < v_H + b$, where v_H is the marginal value of time at home). So rational employment policy exploits the UI system by increasing temporary layoffs, and the unemployment rate is too high year in and year out.

Second, unemployment insurance premiums are **experience-rated**. Firms with a history of laying off lots of workers pay a higher UI payroll tax. But the experience rating is far from perfect. UI tax systems have minimum and maximum tax rates. The minimum tax rate means that employers that draw the least from the UI system overpay. The maximum tax rate implies that employers that lay off lots of workers and generate lots of unemployment claims are a drain on UI finances. Most importantly, an employer that pays the maximum tax rate can increase its use of temporary layoffs without any impact on its UI tax rate. Such a firm adopts an employment policy with a high temporary layoff rate. Again, unemployment insurance encourages temporary layoffs, increasing the unemployment rate, but the effect is primarily among employers at the highest tax rate. Topel (1983) estimated that subsidies in unemployment insurance from imperfect experience rating account for one-fourth of all layoffs.

Some industries are more prone to seasonal and cyclical fluctuations, and imperfect experience rating subsidizes these industries. The auto industry relies on temporary layoffs while it retools its production lines for two weeks every summer. Seasonal workers in construction and agriculture are regularly placed on temporary layoffs and collect unemployment compensation while waiting to be recalled. So UI is an industrial policy that, by subsidizing seasonal and cyclical industries over more stable industries, distorts the mix of employment across industries. As a result, the unemployment rate is higher year in and year out.

 PRACTICE   Do you expect seasonal jobs to be more common where experience rating of unemployment insurance premiums fully reflects experience or where UI premiums aren't experience-rated?

One policy implication is striking. By simply aligning employers' UI tax rates with their UI experience, we can reduce the unemployment rate without cutting unemployment compensation.

European Unemployment

Why have unemployment rates in most European countries been so high for decades? The European unemployment problem is widespread (i.e., it includes France, Germany, Ireland, Italy, Spain, and the UK) and persistent: high unemployment in Europe isn't a temporary situation that fades away as the European economies recover from each recession. In sharp contrast, the unemployment rate in the United States has been relatively low for decades, and the U.S. experience with high unemployment has been (until recently) limited to short periods of recession.

What explains the difference in the unemployment situation across the two sides of the Atlantic? Any explanation for the European unemployment problem must also address an important fact: Europe was the low-unemployment side of the Atlantic not so long ago, so the rise of European unemployment is a relatively recent phenomenon. Figure 12.11 portrays the U.S. unemployment rate and the average unemployment rate in 15 European Union (EU) countries since 1960. European unemployment rates rose for three decades beginning in the mid-1960s, and the European–U.S. unemployment gap reversed in favor of the United States by the mid-1980s.

The generous social-entitlement programs and high tax rates that characterize European welfare states emerged in the 1960s and 1970s. The typical European welfare state features a high minimum wage, extensive collective bargaining, generous unemployment compensation, ample job-security provisions, and high

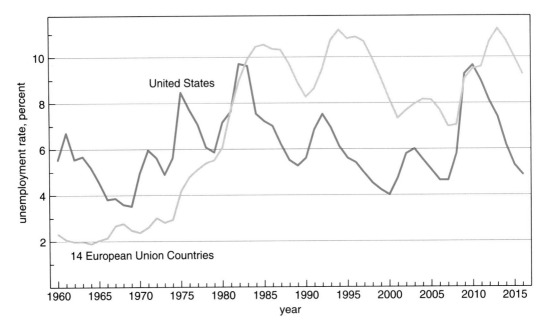

FIGURE 12.11. U.S. and European Unemployment Rates, 1960–2016
Notes: The European unemployment rate is the weighted average of the unemployment rates in the following 15 European Union (EU-15) countries: Austria, Belgium, Denmark, Finland, France, Germany, Greece, Ireland, Italy, Luxembourg, Netherlands, Portugal, Spain, Sweden, and the UK. The weighting variable is population ages 15–64.
Source: Organisation for Economic Co-operation and Development (OECD), stats.oecd.org: Annual Labour Force Statistics Summary Tables, accessed March 14, 2018.

taxes. Perhaps changes in these labor-market institutions in Europe beginning in the 1960s caused the European unemployment problem.

 PRACTICE On the basis of what you have learned in this and preceding chapters, what do you think the consequences are of each feature of the European welfare state on employment and unemployment rates?

Minimum wages cause disequilibrium unemployment, and minimum wages are much higher in Europe than in the United States. Data from the OECD indicate that the minimum wage relative to the average wage of full-time workers averaged almost 40 percent among nine EU countries in 2007 (before the global recession). In the United States, the minimum wage in 2007 was only 24 percent of the average wage of full-time workers. The minimum-wage ratio has doubled (from 25 percent to 50 percent) in France since the late 1960s, but the French experience isn't typical. The minimum-wage ratio has declined in many European countries, although several European countries have introduced minimum wages since the 1960s.

Collective bargaining is much more common in Europe, and the resulting union wage premium can contribute to the European unemployment problem. Collective bargaining raises the wage above the market-clearing wage. If employment falls in jobs covered by union contracts, displaced workers spill over to the nonunion sector. But coverage of collective bargaining agreements extends to over 90 percent of jobs in many of the major EU countries. Since the uncovered sectors are quite small, many people end up without work. The lure of high wages in the covered sector, however, causes an excess supply of labor and disequilibrium unemployment. Unions in Europe also contribute to unemployment through minimum wages. Some European countries don't have legal minimum wages, but their collective bargaining agreements set wage floors on most jobs.

Unemployment compensation is more generous and lasts longer in Europe than in the United States. For instance, Germany set its UI replacement ratio at 90 percent in 1975 (before scaling it back some in the 1980s and 1990s). The unemployed in France and Germany receive unemployment compensation for two years (or three years for older workers in France), much longer than the typical 26 weeks in the United States. In the Netherlands, an unemployed worker can collect unemployment compensation for over three years. Is unemployment in Europe distinctively long-term? Data from 2007 (before the global recession) reveal that unemployment spells longer than one year accounted for 34 percent of the average unemployment in the 15 EU countries; only 10 percent of the unemployed in the United States were people with spells lasting longer than one year. Incredibly, the long-term unemployment rate in every one of the 15 EU countries exceeded the long-term unemployment rate in the United States.

Strong job-security provisions are common in Europe. Dismissing workers, eliminating shifts, and closing plants are difficult and costly in Europe. Workers who are laid off must be given ample notice, and employers must make generous severance payments to the displaced workers. These regulations must lower the unemployment rate, right? Wrong. Employment protection lowers the incidence of unemployment by reducing layoffs of protected workers. But job security also raises the cost of employing workers, which reduces the employment rate. Coupled with minimum wages, collective bargaining, and other factors that elevate wages above their market-clearing levels, the lower employment rate presents itself as a higher unemployment rate. In addition, employment protection doesn't apply to workers on temporary jobs, which just encourages employment of temporary workers. Strong employment protections in some European countries have created a permanent underclass of people working on temporary contracts. And these temporary workers experience lots of unemployment as they move from job to job.

Taxes finance unemployment compensation, social insurance benefits, old-age pensions, and other social spending, and taxes in the new Europe are high. The relevant taxes include personal income taxes on labor income, payroll taxes paid by workers and their employers, and even value-added and sales taxes. The marginal tax rate (not including value-added and sales taxes) averages about one-half for the typical production worker in the 15 EU countries, which is significantly greater than the one-third marginal tax rate in the United States. In addition, value-added taxes in these European countries are much higher than sales taxes in the United States. As you learned in chapter 2, a tax on labor reduces employment, so high taxes in Europe should reduce the employment rate there. Combining high tax rates with minimum wages and union wage premiums generates an excess supply of labor and unemployment.

Why did it take so long for a serious European unemployment problem to emerge? The European unemployment rate rose rapidly from the mid-1970s to the early 1980s. Should Europe's unemployment problem have materialized a decade or so earlier? Ljungqvist and Sargent (1998) argue that the rise of the European welfare state was a time bomb waiting for the first serious recession to explode into a persistent European unemployment problem. The essence of their argument is that the unemployed, especially the long-term unemployed, are scarred by their period of inactivity. In a free labor market, a recession pushes up the unemployment rate, the economy recovers fairly quickly, and unemployment returns to its long-run rate. In the European welfare state, institutional rigidities cause recessions to last longer, and the unemployed suffer through longer spells of unemployment. The long-term unemployed lose skills, and their job opportunities deteriorate. This **scarring effect of unemployment** casts a long shadow: it raises unemployment in the long run, well after the recession ends. And each recession scars more long-term unemployed workers, and post-recession unemployment ratchets up to a higher long-run rate.

If this analysis of Europe's unemployment problem is right, then the blame for high unemployment rates in Europe rests squarely with unemployment insurance and other policies that distort the labor market. But Figure 12.11 also suggests that unemployment rates on the two sides of the Atlantic converged in 2009: for a few years, the United States looked very European in terms of unemployment. That convergence in unemployment rates might have been a temporary consequence of the deeper U.S. recession. But there might have been more to it.

U.S. policies became very European during the 2007–2009 recession. The federal government hiked the minimum wage in the summers of 2007, 2008, and 2009. Unemployment insurance became more generous, and unemployment benefit periods reached 99 weeks. The alarming upward trend in disability enrollments continued. Monthly food-stamp benefits per person rose 28 percent in real terms from 2007 to 2011 (before retreating since 2014), and participation in the food-stamp program grew from 11.3 percent of the working-age population in 2007 to 19.4 percent in 2013, four years into the recovery. These factors might explain the "jobless recovery" and the rise of long-term unemployment in the United States. Spells lasting a year or more comprised about 10 percent of unemployment before the recession, but this long-term unemployment rose to about 30 percent of unemployment between 2010 and 2012.

The recent data on unemployment rates in Europe and the United States, however, suggest a return to form. The higher rate of unemployment in Europe reappeared in 2012 and 2013, and the U.S. unemployment rate dropped from its peak at 9.6 percent in 2010 to 4.4 percent in 2017.

The U.S. employment rate tells a more somber tale of recovery. From 2006 to 2011, the employment rate in the United States fell a whopping 4.7 percentage points (from 63.1 percent to 58.4 percent), and it hasn't recovered.

The employment rate in 2017 remains 3 percentage points below its rate before the recession. In addition, long spells of unemployment remain unusually common: in 2017, 15.1 percent of unemployed people had been unemployed a year or more.

12.5 Unemployment in the Macroeconomy

Unemployment is always and everywhere, but unemployment also varies with fluctuations in the macroeconomy. To be specific, the unemployment rate rises in recessions. That's **cyclical unemployment**.

Inflation and Unemployment

A remarkable and influential pattern materialized in the 1960s. Figure 12.12a displays how the unemployment rate fell as the inflation rate rose year after year. By the end of the 1960s, the inflation rate had reached 5 percent, which was unusually high for the time, and the unemployment rate had dipped below 4 percent. The relationship between the inflation rate and the unemployment rate is the **Phillips curve**, which is named after economist A.W. Phillips, who studied the relationship in the late 1950s.

This strong empirical pattern ushered in an era of macroeconomic policy that emphasized the trade-off between inflation and unemployment along the Phillips curve. Most economists and policy makers at the time viewed a little higher inflation rate as a small price to pay to lower the unemployment rate and to boost employment and output.

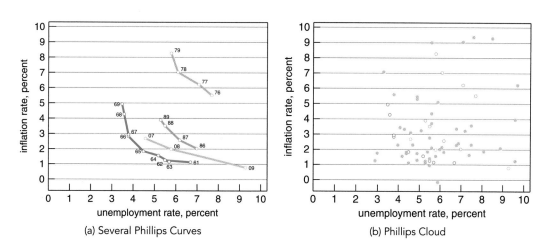

FIGURE 12.12. Phillips Curves and Phillips Cloud, 1948–2017
Sources: Unemployment rate: Bureau of Labor Statistics, Current Population Survey, Table A-1. Inflation rate: computed using the annual GDP deflator from the Bureau of Economic Analysis, National Income and Product Accounts, Table 1.1.9, line 1.

Figure 12.12a graphs Phillips curves for short periods in the 1970s, 1980s, and 2000s, as well as the 1960s. The Phillips curve for the second half of the 1970s reflects *stagflation*, a combination of high inflation and high unemployment in a stagnating economy. What caused the 1970s stagflation? Or more formally, why did the Phillips curve from the 1960s shift to the higher inflation *and* higher unemployment Phillips curve in the second half of the 1970s?

Such shifts in the Phillips curve must be quite common because there's no apparent relationship between inflation and unemployment in general. Figure 12.12b plots all annual combinations of inflation and unemployment in the United States since World War II. The Phillips curve is a Phillips cloud.

Why does a short-run relationship between inflation and unemployment, such as in the 1960s, vanish in the long run? To answer this question, we must do a little macroeconomic modeling. The goal is to illustrate cyclical unemployment in a simple model that distinguishes between the short run and long run. After uncovering the key principle in one specific model, I explain how the same or similar results follow from alternative macroeconomic approaches.

Phillips Curves in a Model of Aggregate Fluctuations

The model's key ingredients are (1) aggregate demand that comes from equilibrium in the market for money, (2) aggregate supply that's unrelated to monetary policy and inflation in the long run, (3) short-run aggregate supply in which real growth increases with inflation, and (4) a relationship between the growth rate of the real economy and the unemployment rate. We combine these ingredients to deliver a short-run Phillips curve that slopes down and an unemployment rate that's independent of the inflation rate in the long run.

Real economic growth depends on factors like savings, investment, innovations, and population growth. It doesn't depend on the inflation rate. Let's assume the growth rate of real output g_Q is 3 percent annually. Figure 12.13a is a graph with real growth and inflation rates on the axes. Since the real growth rate is independent of the inflation rate π, the **aggregate supply curve** is the vertical line at $g_Q = 3$ percent. If the real economy grows at a faster clip, the vertical aggregate supply curve shifts to the right to perhaps 4 percent. Easy enough.

To derive aggregate demand, we begin with the demand for money. People hold money to handle their buying and selling, so desired money holding (i.e., the quantity demanded of money) is proportional to spending: $M_D = \alpha PQ$, where P is the price level, Q is aggregate real output (a weighted average of the quantities of all goods), and α is a constant that depends on access to ATMs, credit cards, etc. (i.e., the transactions technology). If prices are higher (i.e., higher P) or we're all more productive (i.e., higher Q), we all want to carry more money.

The government or its monetary authority controls the supply of money M. For markets to clear, the quantity demanded of money M_D must equal the quantity supplied of money M. If $M = \alpha PQ$, people willingly hold the money that's in

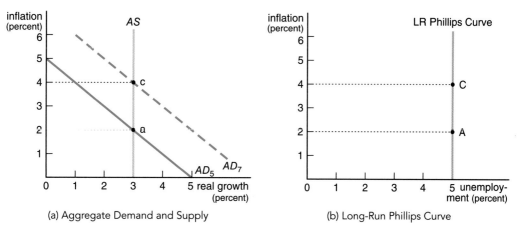

(a) Aggregate Demand and Supply (b) Long-Run Phillips Curve

The long-run (LR) aggregate supply curve AS is vertical at 3% real growth in panel (a). If money grows 5% per year, the aggregate demand curve is AD_5. The aggregate equilibrium at point a is 2% inflation and 3% real growth. In panel (b), the equilibrium is point A: $\pi = .02$ and $u = .05$, the natural rate of unemployment.

Monetary expansion shifts aggregate demand up to AD_7. The long-run equilibrium rises from a to c along AS: the equilibrium inflation rate rises to 4% without changing real growth or unemployment. So the long-run Phillips curve is vertical through points A and C in panel (b).

FIGURE 12.13. Inflation, Real Growth, and Unemployment in the Long Run

circulation. Since the real economy (for the moment) determines output Q, the price level P adjusts to clear the market. The market clears if the price level satisfies

(12.4) $$P^* = \frac{M}{\alpha Q}$$

We can also express this equilibrium condition in terms of growth rates. With the transaction technology fixed, the inflation rate π (approximately) equals the growth rate of money g_M minus the real growth rate g_Q; that is, the inflation rate that gets people to hold the money that's being introduced to the economy is the difference between monetary and real growth rates.

(12.5) $$\pi = g_M - g_Q$$

Figure 12.13a graphs this simple relationship as the **aggregate demand curve**. If the supply of money grows at an annual rate of 5 percent, then the aggregate demand curve is the line that runs from 5 percent inflation on the vertical axis to 5 percent real growth on the horizontal axis: $\pi = 5 - g_Q$.

Aggregate Equilibrium.   The intersection of the aggregate demand and aggregate supply curves in Figure 12.13a determines the equilibrium rate of inflation. Since real output grows at 3 percent per year, the inflation rate must be 2 percent to get people to hold the 5 percent increase in the supply of money. So the equilibrium is point a in Figure 12.13a.

PRACTICE   If the annual inflation rate were 3 percent, people would want to increase their money holdings [more, less] than the 5 percent annual increase in the supply of money. If the annual inflation rate were 1 percent, people would want to increase their money holdings [more, less] than 5 percent per year.

What about unemployment? Behind the scenes, people flow between employment, unemployment, and not in the labor force. Business is good at Leisure Lawn, and the company hires a couple more workers to cut lawns. Album sales are sinking at Rhythm Records, so Gary puts the brakes on a few new projects and decides not to replace one sound engineer who quit and the marketing guy who retired. TaxCrafters simultaneously hires and fires workers. Steve finds a job; J.J.'s still looking.

The unemployment rate that emerges from all this activity is the **natural rate of unemployment** (Friedman 1968). In our context, the unemployment rate consistent with no changes in the aggregate demand or aggregate supply curves is the natural rate. If the natural rate of unemployment u^* is 5 percent, then the long-run equilibrium includes a 2 percent inflation rate and a 5 percent unemployment rate, point A in Figure 12.13b.

Changes in Monetary Policy.   If the government increases the growth rate of the money supply, then aggregate demand increases, and the inflation rate rises. In particular, if monetary growth increases from 5 percent to 7 percent annually, the aggregate demand curve shifts up by 2 percentage points; the aggregate equilibrium slides up the aggregate supply curve from a to c, and the equilibrium inflation rate rises from 2 percent to 4 percent. So the 2 percent increase in the growth rate of money translates into a 2 percent higher inflation rate. The change in monetary policy doesn't affect real economic growth, and the unemployment rate holds steady at the natural rate. (Product prices, values of marginal products of labor, and wage offers all rise by 4 percent; unemployed job searchers like J.J. and Steve respond by increasing their reservation wages by 4 percent, so the exit rate from unemployment doesn't change.) Since the new combination of inflation and unemployment rates is point C in Figure 12.13b, the long-run relationship between inflation and unemployment is the vertical long-run Phillips curve through points A and C.

Things are different in the short run if the increase in the rate of monetary growth takes everyone by surprise. Firms like Leisure Lawn, Coalwood, Rhythm Records, SpaceZ, and TaxCrafters increase prices by only 2 percent. Similarly, people want to expand their money holdings only 2 percent, which means more new money drops into the economy than people want to hold. They spend the

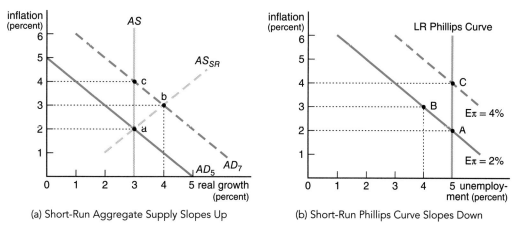

(a) Short-Run Aggregate Supply Slopes Up   (b) Short-Run Phillips Curve Slopes Down

If the change in monetary policy isn't anticipated, the aggregate equilibrium slides up the short-run aggregate supply curve AS_{SR} to b, and real growth rises to 4%. In panel (b), unemployment slips to 4% (at B) as a cyclical reduction in unemployment along a short-run Phillips curve. As expectations of inflation $E\pi$ increase from 2% to 4%, the short-run Phillips curve shifts up, and the unemployment rate returns to 5% at C. In panel (a), real growth returns to 3% as the aggregate equilibrium climbs from b to c.

FIGURE 12.14. Inflation, Real Growth, and Unemployment in the Short and Long Runs

extra bucks. Strong sales surprise the typical firm, and it expands production along its upward-sloping supply curve. Product prices creep up (and the inflation rate ends up at 3 percent), which increases the demand for labor. Wages rise a bit, which increases the quantity supplied of labor. Job searchers like J.J. and Steve are also fooled: they don't raise their reservation wages enough, so the exit rate from unemployment rises, and the unemployment rate falls to 4 percent. That's a cyclical reduction in unemployment.

So surprise monetary growth increases inflation a bit but less than predicted by the increase in g_M. In Figure 12.14, the real growth rate g_Q rises from 3 to 4 percent, and the unemployment rate falls from 5 to 4 percent. The short-run equilibrium combination of inflation and real growth is point b in panel (a); the short-run equilibrium combination of inflation and unemployment is point B in panel (b). The line that runs through points a and b in panel (a) is the **short-run aggregate supply curve**; it slopes up because buyers, sellers, and workers were all "nominally confused." The line that cuts through points A and B in panel (b) is the short-run Phillips curve; it slopes down because more people work and fewer people search when the economy booms. The source of the dip in the unemployment rate, however, is nominal wage confusion: workers mistake a higher nominal wage for a higher real wage.

From Short-Run Surprise to Long-Run Understanding. People correct their mistakes. Surprise inflation generates short-term growth with a lower unemployment rate, but with time everyone realizes they've been confused by the monetary shock. The quantity demanded of money grows to reflect the actual growth rate of money. The real responses of output, employment, and unemployment vanish. The inflation rate rises to 4 percent, the real growth rate retreats to 3 percent, and the unemployment rate returns to the natural rate. That is, the economy moves from the short-run equilibrium at b to the long-run equilibrium at c in Figure 12.14a. The labor market in panel (b) moves from B to C: unemployment returns to its natural rate, but the inflation rate rises to 4 percent.

 PRACTICE   This process also works in reverse. Sketch the short-run and long-run responses to lower-than-expected monetary growth in the two panels of Figure 12.14. To start things off, which curve shifts in which direction? Let b' and B' mark the short-run equilibrium in the two panels. What happens to inflation, real growth, and unemployment in the short run? Mark the long-term equilibrium with c' and C', and explain how inflation, real growth, and unemployment respond to lower-than-expected monetary growth in the long run.

The principal message from this model is that inflation doesn't reduce the unemployment rate; *surprise inflation* reduces unemployment. The unemployment rate at time t is the natural rate of unemployment u^* unless higher- or lower-than-expected inflation surprises people. So we've derived the **expectations-augmented Phillips curve**.

(12.6) $$u_t = u^* - \beta(\pi_t - \mathrm{E}\pi_t)$$

where $\mathrm{E}\pi_t$ is the expected rate of inflation at time t and β is positive. A fully anticipated increase in the inflation rate doesn't influence the unemployment rate. Surprise inflation, however, sinks the unemployment rate below its natural rate u^*.

So expected inflation $\mathrm{E}\pi_t$ is the factor that shifts the short-run Phillips curve up and down. For instance, inflation rose in the 1960s and early 1970s. By the mid-1970s, people expected significantly higher inflation, so the short-run Phillips curve was higher in the late 1970s than in the 1960s. And this shift explains why the 1976–1979 Phillips curve in Figure 12.12a lies above the 1960s Phillips curve.

This model generates cyclical unemployment from monetary misperceptions. The key feature generating differences between short-run and long-run responses is the upward-sloping, short-run aggregate supply curve. Other macroeconomic models shift the emphasis from money to other factors that shift aggregate demand. Wartime defense spending (increasing aggregate demand) and fear of financial collapse (decreasing aggregate demand) are two examples. But the primary response to fluctuations in aggregate demand is through inflation unless prices and wages are inflexible. An important class of models uses downward wage and price rigidities to generate a short-run aggregate supply curve that slopes up below the initial aggregate equilibrium at point a. In this case, fiscal contractions and fear of financial collapse decrease real growth and increase unemployment cyclically.

Yet another class of models approaches aggregate fluctuations from the supply side. Real shocks to the economy (e.g., new discoveries, natural disasters, oil price shocks, and government regulations) shift the vertical aggregate supply curve left (negative shocks) or right (positive shocks). A positive real shock increases real growth and decreases the inflation rate along the aggregate demand curve. Positive real shocks typically increase the marginal product of labor and wages. Employment rises and unemployment falls. But inflation and unemployment rates vary together in this model without any downward-sloping Phillips curve.

Job Vacancies and Unemployment

For more than half a century, the Phillips curve has been center stage in the study of macroeconomic fluctuations. Now a second curve features prominently in macrolabor studies. The **Beveridge curve** is the relationship between the unemployment rate and the job-vacancy rate, which measures job openings relative to employment. Since unemployment is more than just an excess supply of labor, unemployment and job vacancies happen simultaneously: workers search for good jobs while firms search for the right workers to fill their jobs.

Unemployment and job vacancies coexist, but the unemployment rate tends to be higher when there aren't many job openings—that is, when the vacancy rate is low. That's the Beveridge curve. Figure 12.15 displays the empirical relationship between the unemployment rate and the vacancy rate in monthly data since December 2000. The data from 2000 to 2007 display a stable inverse relationship. The thin blue line is an estimate of the Beveridge curve over these years.

What underlies such a strong empirical relationship? The Beveridge curve captures the idea that it's easier to find a job if firms have lots of job openings. But what determines the position along the Beveridge curve in any month? To close the model, we turn to firms' incentives to create jobs, which follows from their prospects for profit. If the unemployment rate is high, offering a job is more profitable (in present value terms) for several reasons. First, firms find workers quicker. Second, the wage might be lower. And third, if the high unemployment rate persists, workers stay on their jobs longer. So the job-creation curve in the right panel of Figure 12.15 slopes up because the incentive to create jobs increases with the unemployment rate.

Each pair of equilibrium rates of job vacancies and unemployment is a point on the Beveridge curve that's consistent with firms' incentives to create jobs. For instance, 01/08 is the point where the job-creation curve intersects the Beveridge curve in Figure 12.15b. At 01/08, the mix of job vacancies and unemployment (based on search and matching) is consistent with firms' incentives to create jobs.

The pace of business slows, and the economy sinks into a recession. At any unemployment rate, the profitability of employing a worker falls. That is, the job-creation curve pivots down in a recession, and the equilibrium slides down the Beveridge curve from 01/08 to 11/08. Job vacancies fall, and unemployment rises.

That's what happened early in the Great Recession. The macroeconomy declined from its peak in December 2007. In Figure 12.15a, the series of connected

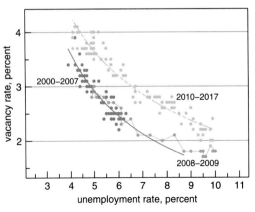

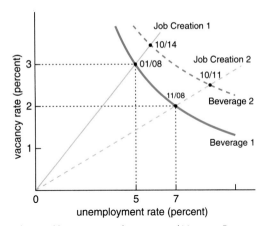

(a) Beveridge Curves in the United States, 2000–2017   (b) Equilibrium Unemployment and Vacancy Rates

FIGURE 12.15. Job Vacancies and Unemployment

Notes: (a) With u denoting the unemployment rate and v the vacancy rate, the estimated regression equation for 2000–2007 is $\ln v = 2.595 - .947 \ln u$ with $R^2 = .844$. For 2010–2017,
 $_{(.073)}$ $_{(.045)}$
the estimates are $\ln v = 2.536 - .763 \ln u$ with $R^2 = .926$. (b) Dates of the form mm/yy label
 $_{(.044)}$ $_{(.023)}$
the four points; e.g., "01/08" is January 2008.

Sources: For the unemployment rate, Bureau of Labor Statistics, Current Population Survey, series LNS14000000; for the vacancy rate, Bureau of Labor Statistics, Job Openings and Labor Turnover Survey, series JTS00000000JOR. December 2000–December 2017.

dots displays how unemployment fell as vacancies rose over the next two years. For the first year (2008), the relationship followed the standard pattern, but the Beveridge curve began to shift out early in 2009. Since early 2010, the unemployment rate has fallen as the vacancy rate has risen along a higher Beveridge curve.

What causes the Beveridge curve to shift? If finding the right worker to fill a job takes a long time, and finding the right job also takes a worker a long time, then search isn't very efficient. In this case, the Beveridge curve lies far from the origin, so reducing search efficiency shifts the Beveridge curve up and out. (See Figure 12.15b.) This happens if (1) unemployment benefits are generous, (2) jobs aren't in the same places as the unemployed workers (and moving costs are high), and (3) vacant jobs require skills that most unemployed workers don't have. Factors (2) and (3) are examples of *mismatch*: vacancies and qualified job searchers aren't finding each other because the unemployed don't match the open jobs in terms of location or skills.

 PRACTICE   In October 2009, the unemployment rate reached 10 percent, and the vacancy rate was 1.8 percent. Plot this point in panel (b) of Figure 12.15. Draw a Beveridge curve and a job creation curve such that this point is the equilibrium.

Was job creation in October 2009 more or less profitable than job creation 11 months earlier? Was search more efficient in October 2009 or late in 2008?

The Beveridge curve that fits our experience since the Great Recession suggests that search has become less efficient. The unemployment rate is currently (in June 2018) down to 4 percent, but the vacancy rate is unusually high for such a low unemployment rate. So firms aren't filling lots of jobs that they want to fill.

One important piece of the puzzle is long-term unemployment. If we exclude the long-term unemployed in measuring the unemployment rate, the Beveridge curve since 2000 has been stable: unemployment (excluding the long-term unemployed) rose as vacancies fell early in the Great Recession, and the pattern reversed along a stable Beveridge curve during the recovery and continuing through 2017. So the less-efficient matching of workers to jobs since 2008 is really about people who have been unemployed a long time. The long-term unemployed are finding it more difficult to find jobs.

Summary

In this chapter, we studied unemployment that reflects an excess supply of labor and unemployment that's part of the equilibrium in a dynamic labor market with imperfect information. We also distinguished among frictional, structural, and cyclical unemployment. Our key findings are:

☐ Binding minimum wages and efficiency wages cause disequilibrium unemployment as an excess supply of labor.

☐ Workers flow between the labor-market states—employment, unemployment, and not in the labor force—from month to month. In a steady state, flows into each state equal flows out from the state.

☐ The steady-state unemployment rate increases with the job separation rate and decreases with the exit rate from unemployment, which depends on the hiring rate.

☐ Lengths of spells of unemployment depend on the exit rate from unemployment. Most unemployment spells are short, but a lot of unemployment in any month is attributable to people who have been unemployed longer than a few months.

☐ The distribution of lengths of unemployment spells isn't consistent with a single constant exit rate from unemployment. Spells that end in months 2–5 aren't common enough to be consistent with the high exit rate in the first month. Mixing of high- and low-exit-rate job searchers can explain the pattern.

☐ A worker searches for a job sequentially by choosing a reservation wage that equates costs and benefits of search at the margin. The disadvantage of a higher reservation wage is that the spell of unemployment lasts longer. The advantage is a higher wage for the length of the new job.

☐ Unemployment compensation raises the reservation wage, lowers the exit rate from unemployment, lengthens spells of unemployment, and increases the unemployment rate; UI also increases the average accepted wage. Imperfect experience rating of UI premiums (paid by employers as payroll taxes) subsidizes temporary layoffs, distorting the mix of employment toward the most seasonal and cyclical industries.

☐ The rise of the European welfare state—with high minimum wages, extensive collective bargaining, generous unemployment compensation, strong job-security provisions, and high taxes—likely caused the European unemployment problem, including the preponderance of long-term unemployment in Europe.

☐ The relationship between inflation and unemployment rates isn't stable. A fully anticipated increase in the inflation rate $\Delta \pi$ shifts up the short-run Phillips curve by $\Delta \pi$, so the long-run Phillips curve is vertical.

☐ Inflation surprises, as well as a variety of other factors, produce an upward-sloping short-run aggregate supply curve, a downward-sloping short-run Phillips curve, and cyclical unemployment.

☐ Since the Great Recession, the unemployment rate has fallen and the vacancy rate has risen along a higher Beveridge curve, which suggests that search has become less efficient.

This concludes our exploration of labor economics. I'm sure you've learned a lot and developed an appreciation of the content and methods of labor economics. And I sincerely hope that the key principles of labor economics stick with you for a long time.

Key Concepts

- disequilibrium unemployment, p. 446
- structural unemployment, p. 447
- frictional unemployment, p. 448
- labor-market states, p. 448

- labor-market flows, p. 448
- steady state, p. 449
- steady-state unemployment rate, p. 450
- job separation and hiring rates, p. 450
- incidence and duration of unemployment, p. 450
- reservation wage in search, p. 456
- sequential search, p. 456
- marginal benefit and marginal cost of search, p. 457
- UI replacement ratio, p. 461

- UI experience rating, p. 464
- scarring effect of unemployment, p. 468
- cyclical unemployment, p. 469
- Phillips curve, p. 469
- aggregate supply curve, p. 470
- aggregate demand curve, p. 471
- natural rate of unemployment, p. 472
- short-run aggregate supply, p. 473
- expectations-augmented Phillips curve, p. 474
- Beveridge curve, p. 475

Short-Answer Questions

12.1 Explain how we use randomness and limited information to understand unemployment.

12.2 One application of structural unemployment is to a mismatch of skills: employers search for workers with one set of skills, and workers have another set of skills. Explain how this mismatch leads to unemployment in the short run but not in the long run.

12.3 What is the meaning of "steady state" in the context of the labor market? Does it mean that no one changes "states"?

12.4 In Table 12.1, what percentage of the unemployed in one month aren't unemployed in the next month?

12.5 What does a plot of the distribution of lengths of unemployment spells measure? Why is the first bar the tallest, and why does each successive bar get shorter? Is this pattern consistent with a constant exit rate from unemployment?

12.6 Explain how mixing high- and low-exit-rate people improves the fit of the distribution of lengths of spells of unemployment.

12.7 You graduate from college and begin searching for a career job. Why is holding out for the highest wage offer (and best match) anywhere a bad strategy for search?

12.8 List at least three factors that increase the marginal benefit of search. Explain how one of these factors influences the reservation wage, the average length of time unemployed, and the averaged accepted wage.

12.9 How does unemployment compensation enter the model of job search? How does unemployment compensation affect the reservation wage, time unemployed, and post-unemployment wages? Do you expect the unemployment rate to be higher or lower in states with high replacement ratios?

12.10 It's more difficult to dismiss workers in most European countries than in the United States. Explain why more job security in Europe leads to lower employment and higher unemployment rates.

12.11 Figure 12.12a plots several short-run Phillips curves. On the basis of our model of the macroeconomy, what shifts the Phillips curves?

12.12 Labor economists frequently classify unemployment as frictional, structural, or cyclical. We analyzed several models of unemployment in this chapter. Which model(s) generate frictional unemployment, structural unemployment, or cyclical unemployment?

Problems

12.1 The figure below displays a market for teenage labor with a minimum wage of $6 per hour.

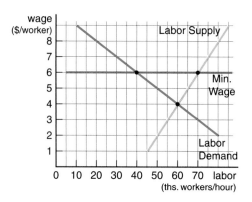

(a)   How many workers are unemployed at the $6 minimum wage?

(b)   The government places an hourly tax of $1 per worker on employers. Show the effect of the tax on the demand for labor.

(c) With both the minimum wage and the labor tax, how many workers do firms employ? What is the incremental effect of the tax on employment?

(d) With both the minimum wage and the labor tax, how many workers are unemployed? What is the incremental effect of the tax on unemployment?

12.2 Suppose everyone in a population of 140 million people is either employed or unemployed. (No one is out of the labor force.) The monthly exit rate from unemployment h is 38 percent, and the monthly separation rate from employment s is 2 percent.

(a) Use the two rates, h and s, to compute the steady-state unemployment rate u^*.

(b) In the steady state, _____ people are employed, and _____ people are unemployed.

(c) In the steady state, how many people exit unemployment to enter employment in a month?

12.3 Suppose the monthly exit rate from unemployment doesn't depend on the length of time a person has been unemployed; it's constant at $h = .333$.

(a) What fraction of spells of unemployment end within the first two months?

(b) What is the mean length of spells of unemployment?

12.4 The figure below displays Steve's marginal benefits and marginal costs of search. The three marginal benefit curves are drawn for low, middle, and high job separation rates. For simplicity, we assume that the marginal benefit curves are linear.

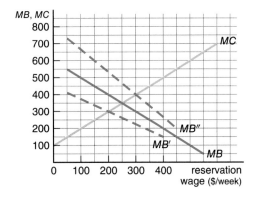

(a) For the middle job separation rate and with out-of-pocket costs of search of $100 per week, what is Steve's optimal reservation wage R^*?

(b) Steve's out-of-pocket costs of search rise from $100 to $200 per week. Illustrate the effect of this change in the figure. Steve's new reservation wage is $_____ per week.

(c) In the original case with $c = 100$, the job separation rate falls from the middle rate to the lower rate. When Steve finds a job, will it tend to last shorter or longer? Is his new marginal benefit curve the lower or higher dashed curve? How does Steve's reservation wage respond to the lower job separation rate?

12.5 Julie and Katie had each been earning $800 per week before losing their jobs at TaxCrafters. Julie and Katie live in states with 50 percent replacement ratios, but Katie's state caps unemployment compensation at $300 per week. The figure below graphs their marginal benefit and marginal cost of search assuming no unemployment compensation. For simplicity, the marginal benefit curve is linear.

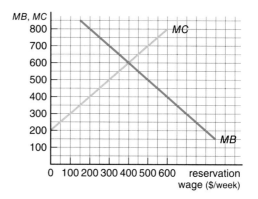

(a) Unemployment compensation b shifts the _____ curve [up or down] by b.

(b) Adjust the curve(s) in the figure to reflect Julie's unemployment compensation. Julie's optimal reservation wage is $_____ per week.

(c) Draw a curve that reflects Katie's unemployment compensation. What is Katie's optimal reservation wage?

(d) Who is likely to remain unemployed longer, Julie or Katie?

12.6 Below, the left figure graphs the long-run aggregate supply curve AS. The right figure displays a short-run Phillips curve.

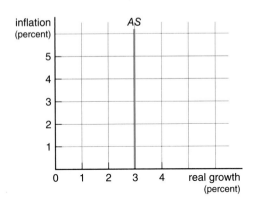

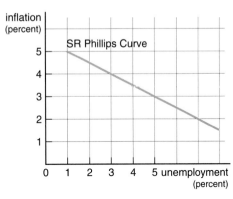

(a) The supply of money grows 6 percent annually. Draw the aggregate demand curve AD_6. What is the equilibrium rate of inflation?

(b) The natural rate of unemployment is 5 percent. Mark the equilibrium in the right panel with an A.

(c) Monetary growth slows to 4 percent, and it's a complete surprise. Assume the slope of the short-run aggregate supply curve is 1. What happens to the real growth rate, the inflation rate, and the unemployment rate in the short run? Mark the short-run equilibrium with a b in the left panel and a B in the right panel.

(d) People adjust their expectations to reflect the lower rate of monetary growth. What happens to the real growth rate, the inflation rate, and the unemployment rate in the long run? Mark the new long-run equilibrium points with a c in the left panel and a C in the right panel.

(e) Draw the long-run Phillips curve. Also draw the short-run Phillips curve that's associated with the new inflation rate.

12.7 The Beveridge curve in the figure below displays the relationship between unemployment and job vacancy rates. Firms create jobs or vacancies, and the relationship between vacancies and unemployment is the job-creation curve $v = .25u$.

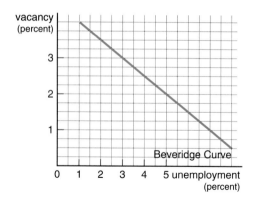

(a) Plot the job-creation curve, and indicate the equilibrium values of u and v with point A.

(b) Business picks up, and the new job-creation curve is $v = .5u$. Plot the new job-creation curve, and mark the new equilibrium point B. The new unemployment rate is _____, and the new vacancy rate is _____.

(c) Return to the original job-creation curve. An improvement in the search process shortens the time it takes for workers to find jobs and for firms to fill their job vacancies. Shift the appropriate curve to find the new equilibrium. The innovation in search [increases, decreases] the unemployment rate and [increases, decreases] the vacancy rate.

References

Chetty, Raj. 2008. "Moral Hazard versus Liquidity and Optimal Unemployment Insurance." *Journal of Political Economy* 116(2): 173–234.

Farber, Henry S. and Robert G. Valletta. 2015. "Do Extended Unemployment Benefits Lengthen Unemployment Spells? Evidence from Recent Cycles in the U.S. Labor Market." *Journal of Human Resources* 50(4): 873–909.

Feldstein, Martin. 1976. "Temporary Layoffs in the Theory of Unemployment." *Journal of Political Economy* 84(5): 937–958.

Friedman, Milton. 1968. "The Role of Monetary Policy." *American Economic Review* 58(1): 1–17.

Krueger, Alan B. and Andreas Mueller. 2010. "Job Search and Unemployment Insurance: New Evidence from Time Use Data." *Journal of Public Economics* 94(3–4): 298–307.

Ljungqvist, Lars and Thomas J. Sargent. 1998. "The European Unemployment Dilemma." *Journal of Political Economy* 106(3): 514–550.

McCall, J.J. 1970. "Economics of Information and Job Search." *Quarterly Journal of Economics* 84(1): 113–126.

Meyer, Bruce D. 1990. "Unemployment Insurance and Unemployment Spells." *Econometrica* 58(4): 757–782.

Topel, Robert H. 1983. "On Layoffs and Unemployment Insurance." *American Economic Review* 73(4): 541–559.

Answers to the Practice Questions

Chapter 1: Introduction to Labor Economics

PAGE 4—Busboys work 20 hours (= 4 hours per busboy × 5 busboys) serving 40 meals per night. That's two meals per busboy-hour, so a busboy earns $2 per hour in tips if customers tip $1 per meal. The payroll wage falls $2 per hour to $4 per hour to clear the busboy market. Busboy costs fall by $40 per night, so revenue must fall by $40 per night to clear the market for restaurant meals. The price of a meal falls from $25 to $24 to preserve profit at $0.

PAGE 11—At bls.gov, find the current unemployment and employment rates in "Employment Situation Summary Table A. Household data, seasonally adjusted." CPS Annual Table 1 reports that the employment rate rose from 58.5 percent to 60.1 percent and the unemployment rate dropped from 9.6 percent to 4.4 percent from 2010 to 2017.

PAGE 14—Farm managers work long hours (48 hours per week), but their median wage is only $720 per week. The height of the regression line in Figure 1.1 is about $1,680 at $h = 48$, so we predict that farm managers earn about $1,680 per week.

PAGE 16—The point estimate is .121, and its standard error is .013. So the confidence interval runs from $2 \times .013 = .026$ below .121 to $2 \times .013 = .026$ above .121. That is, the confidence interval is $.121 \pm .026$. Therefore, we can be confident that the true effect of schooling on wages is between 9.5 percent and 14.7 percent. The confidence interval includes 10 percent, but 15 percent is above the upper limit.

Chapter 2: Labor Markets

PAGE 33—The height of the labor demand curve at $L = 4$ million nurses is $600 per nurse, so the marginal value of labor in nursing is $600 per nurse if 4 million people work as nurses.

PAGE 35—The height of the labor supply curve is $600 per nurse at $L = 1$ million nurses, so the marginal cost of nurses' time is $600 per nurse if 1 million people work as nurses.

PAGE 35—At $w = 900$ in Figure 2.3, quantity demanded is 3.5 million nurses, and quantity supplied is 2 million nurses. The $900 weekly wage generates a shortage of 1.5 (= 3.5 − 2.0) million nurses per week. To illustrate the size of the shortage, draw a horizontal line segment between the labor demand and labor supply curves at $w = 900$.

PAGE 39—Increasing nurses' wage doesn't change the labor demand curve, and it doesn't change the labor supply curve. The wage increase does decrease the *quantity demanded* of nurses and increase the *quantity supplied* of nurses.

PAGE 39—The assembly line certainly increased the supply of cars; that is, the product supply curve shifted right. Despite the fall in the price of cars, employment increased because the marginal value of labor increased.

PAGE 40—The drop in the fertility rate increased the supply of labor. The number of women who wanted to work at each wage increased over the 50 years.

PAGE 43—The minimum-wage line shifts up from $7.25 to $8.00. Employment falls, and the marginal value of labor rises from $7.25 to $8.00 per worker-hour along the labor demand curve. The quantity supplied of labor increases, so the labor surplus also increases.

PAGE 53—The resulting surplus of labor is the length of a horizontal line segment at $w = 400$ between E_0 and a point along the dashed (i.e., $t = 160$) labor demand curve in Figure 2.10a. The length of the line segment is 88.9 workers per week, although the question doesn't call for a precise answer.

PAGE 55—The figures below illustrate the two cases. Workers bear a bigger burden of the tax in the top figure where labor demand is more elastic than labor supply.

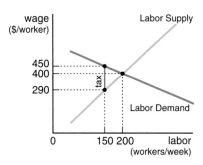

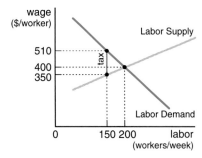

PAGE 57—If the worker receives the wage subsidy, the labor supply curve shifts down by the $160 subsidy. The equilibrium slides down the no-subsidy labor-demand curve to the unlabeled point in Figure 2.12. The weekly wage falls from $400 to $310; with the subsidy, each worker pockets $370. So the subsidy-inclusive wage in this case equals the equilibrium wage if the government subsidizes employers. Also, an employer's cost per worker is the $310 wage, which is the same as the wage net of the subsidy if employers receive the subsidy checks. Employment isn't affect by "who receives the check" either; it's 250 workers per week. Since employment isn't affected, the cost of the subsidy isn't either; it's simply $160 times the number of workers. And the deadweight loss remains the area of the triangle between the labor demand and labor supply curves from 200 to 250 workers per week.

PAGE 62—The labor supply curve in agriculture shifts right by another 10 million worker-hours per week. Employment in agriculture rises from 46 million to 52 million worker-hours per week, and the hourly wage in agriculture falls from $5.40 to $4.80 per worker.

PAGE 65—Increasing employment from 1,100 to 1,200 workers per week increases labor cost by $86,300 ($= \$600,000 - \$513,700$) per week. Since $\Delta L = 100$ and $\Delta C_L = 86,300$, marginal labor cost is $\Delta C_L / \Delta L = \$863$ per worker.

Chapter 3: Labor Supply

PAGE 89—With the 20 percent tax, Gregg's consumption exhausts his income if $c = (1 - .2)10h$. To express this relationship in terms of consumption c and leisure l, replace h with $16 - 1$ and simplify. The result is $c + 8l = 128$. The budget line with the tax is a line from the endowment E on the horizontal axis to 128 on the vertical axis in Figure 3.5b. The slope of the line (in absolute value) is the after-tax real wage, which is 8 units of consumption per hour.

PAGE 94—The indifference curve must slope down, bow toward the origin, and not cross the other indifference curves on the graph.

PAGE 95—Gregg's marginal value of leisure time at X is <u>10</u> units of <u>consumption</u> per <u>hour of leisure</u>.

PAGE 95—An increase in nonlabor income shifts the endowment point <u>up</u> and <u>doesn't change the slope of the budget line</u>.

PAGE 99—Compare points X and Y. The substitution effect of the increase in Gregg's hourly wage from $10 to $14 per hour increases his workday from 10 hours to 12.5 hours and his daily consumption from 100 units to approximately 130 units.

PAGE 101—Beth responds to an increase in nonlabor income by choosing a shorter workday at each wage, so her backward-bending labor supply curve shifts left.

PAGE 105—The point that corresponds to retiring immediately is Olivia's endowment point E. She enjoys 80,000 units of consumption over her 20-year retirement.

PAGE 106—In Figure 3.18a, draw a line that's parallel to the dashed line and tangent to indifference curve I_2. Mark the tangency point, which lies southeast of X and northeast of Y, with a V. The substitution effect from X to V shortens her working life and lengthens her retirement. The income effect from V to Y extends her working life; she retires later and enjoys fewer years of retirement.

PAGE 108—Any budget line through E that's flatter than the thin blue line through E keeps Gregg from working.

PAGE 110—Commuting time subtracts one hour from Gregg's day *if he works*. Commuting time doesn't affect Gregg's endowment at E, but his budget line emerges from an open point one hour left of E, which is (15,40). Find Gregg's reservation wage with commuting time by drawing a line from (15,40) that is tangent to indifference curve I_0. That tangent line is steeper than the indifference curve at E, so the time cost of work raises the reservation wage and lowers the participation rate.

PAGE 113—The arrival of Gregg's first child increases his value of time at home. At each point in Figure 3.10, his marginal rate of substitution of leisure for consumption (i.e., his marginal value of home time) increases, which means the baby steepens Gregg's set of indifference curves. Gregg's budget line doesn't change, so the tangency of the budget line to a new (steeper) indifference curve is

southeast of X. Gregg spends more time at home, works a shorter workday, and consumes less.

PAGE 116—Labor supply curves are <u>more elastic</u> in narrowly defined labor markets. Raising the wage in a small labor market draws workers from many other labor markets. A large labor market has fewer places from which to draw workers. So we expect the labor supply of carpenters to be more elastic than the labor supply of skilled craftsmen and Nashua's labor supply to be more elastic than labor supply in New England.

Chapter 4: Labor Demand

PAGE 130—The average product of labor at $L=7$ is $77/7 = 11$ lawns per worker. The marginal product of labor from $L=6$ to $L=7$ is $(77-63)/(7-6) = 14$ lawns per worker.

PAGE 131—Adding capital increases output at every level of employment, so the new total-product curve is higher than the old total-product curve. The marginal product of labor also rises, so the new total-product curve is steeper than the old total-product curve. Average and marginal products are higher at every L, so labor's average product and marginal product curves shift up.

PAGE 133—Multiply the AP_L in the fourth column and the MP_L in the seventh column by the price of lawn care, $30 per lawn. At $L=7$, the value of the average product of labor is $330 $(= $30 \times 11)$ per worker, and the value of the marginal product of labor is $400 $(= $30 \times 13.33)$ per worker.

PAGE 134—At $L=8$, VMP_L is $350 per worker, which is greater that the $300 wage. Adding one worker increases profit by $VMP_L - w = \$350 - \$300 = \$50$, so increasing employment from 8 to 9 workers per week raises profit by $50 per week.

PAGE 136—Draw a horizontal line halfway between the solid line at $w = 300$ and the dashed line at $w = 200$. This new line intersects VMP_L at 10 workers per week.

PAGE 137—To maximize profit, a firm chooses L to equalize the marginal effects of labor on revenue and cost. The marginal effect of labor on cost is the wage. (We assume the firm operates in a competitive labor market.) The marginal effect of labor on revenue has two parts: (1) The marginal product of labor tells us the effect of the marginal change in labor on output, and (2) marginal revenue tells us the rate at which revenue increases for a marginal increase in output. Therefore, the marginal effect of labor on revenue is $MR \times MP_L$. Recall from your study of monopoly in principles of microeconomics that $MR < p$ if the product market isn't competitive. Therefore, removing or reducing competition in the product market reduces the marginal effect of labor on revenue, which decreases the demand for labor.

PAGE 140—The marginal product of labor is 16 lawns per worker at $(4,3)$, so adding a fifth worker increases output by 16 lawns per week. Since the marginal product of capital is half the marginal product of labor, the 1-worker increase in L pairs with a 2-unit decrease in K to preserve output at 16 lawns per week. The marginal rate of technical substitution is $MP_L/MP_K = 16/8 = 2$ units of capital per worker. Since the slope of the isoquant curve at B is -1.5, the isoquant curve is steeper at $(4,3)$.

PAGE 142—Weekly labor cost is $\$300 \times 4 = \$1200$, and weekly capital cost is $\$200 \times 3 = \$600$, so cost is $\$1,800$ per week. The isocost line through $(4,3)$ is $1800 = 300L + 200K$, which simplifies to $18 = 3L + 2K$. This isocost line runs from 9 on the vertical axis to 6 on the horizontal axis. If the weekly wage falls from $\$300$ to $\$200$ per worker, isocost line $C = 1800$ becomes $1800 = 200L + 200K$, or $9 = L + K$.

PAGE 147—In the context of a payroll tax, the equation of an isocost line is $C = (1+t)wL + rK$ for some value of C. The slope of each isocost line is $-(1+t)w/r$, so the payroll tax steepens the family of isocost lines. (The vertical intercept of each isocost line isn't affected.) Leisure Lawn substitutes out of labor into capital along an isoquant curve, which is the substitution effect. The payroll tax also shifts up Leisure Lawn's marginal cost curve, so the tax reduces Leisure Lawn's supply of lawn care. Leisure Lawn's choice moves to a lower isoquant, and the scale effect reduces labor and capital.

PAGE 148—Leisure Lawn's long-run response to the wage cut leaves it with a new (dashed) short-run labor demand curve in Figure 4.11. From here, the short-run response to a wage increase is to reduce the quantity demanded of labor from 12 to 10 workers per week as a move up along the dashed value-of-marginal-product-of-labor curve, the short-run labor demand curve with $K = 6$. In the long-run, capital falls from 6 to 5 units per week. The short-run labor demand curve shifts down to the original one with $K = 5$, and employment falls by an additional worker (from 10 to 9 workers per week).

PAGE 153—Each lawn-care firm responds to the lower wage by increasing employment, which increases output. Indeed, each firm's supply curve shifts to the right. That increases the market supply of lawn care, and the price of lawn care must fall to clear the lawn-care market. The lower price of lawn care shifts down each firm's VMP_L curve, which shifts down the horizontal summation of firm VMP_L curves. So the sum shifts down because the product price falls to clear the product market.

Chapter 5: Job Attributes

PAGE 166—The quantity supplied of labor to dirty jobs is 1 worker per hour if the hourly wage on dirty jobs is $\$12.50$ per worker. Alan is the only worker to choose a dirty job at that wage.

PAGE 168—At $w_d = 11$, no one wants to work on a dirty job, and every firm wants to employ a worker on a dirty job. The quantity supplied of labor to dirty jobs is 0 workers per hour, and the quantity demanded of labor on dirty jobs is 4 workers per hour. So there's a shortage of 4 workers per hour.

PAGE 171—Sharon's indifference curves are steeper than Sherwin's. She requires a bigger compensating wage differential than Sherwin for any increase in dirt on the job.

PAGE 172—The Big Store's iso-profit curves are flatter than the mining division's iso-profit curves. Cleanup isn't as expensive at the Big Store. The wage associated with a clean work environment at the Big Store doesn't have to be as low to preserve profit along an iso-profit curve. In the mining division, the wage must be much lower to offset the high costs of cleanup, so iso-profit curves are steeper in the mining division.

PAGE 174—A single indifference curve is tangent to a single iso-profit curve, so the equilibrium is a single point. There's only one type of job, so every job pays the same wage.

PAGE 179—The slope of the wage–risk curve is $\Delta w / \Delta r = 8000/80 = 100$ dollars per one-hundred-thousandth of a death. That's $10,000 per one-thousandth of a death, or $10,000,000 per death. So the implied value of a life is $10 million.

PAGE 182—The new point Z is the midpoint between X and Y along the equilibrium consumption–leisure curve. Consumption is halfway between 60 and 88 units per day, which is 74 units per day. Since Gregg has no nonlabor income and the price of consumption is $1 per unit, his daily wage is $74 at Z. His hourly wage on job Z is $12.33 ($= \$74/6$).

PAGE 186—The scale factor is $\frac{1}{1-t} = \frac{1}{.8} = \frac{10}{8} = 1.25$. So the 20 percent tax on wages increases (in absolute value) the slope of each indifference curve by 25 percent.

Chapter 6: Schooling

PAGE 197—The factor is $1.1^{37} = 34$, so the present value of $38,400 in year 37 is $38,400 \div 34 = \$1129$.

PAGE 198—The wage profile for a worker with an associate's degree combines two horizontal line segments. The first segment runs from age 19 to

age 21 at −5,000. The second segment is a line at $38,400 between ages 22 and 65.

PAGE 200—The slope of the wage–schooling curve is $3,200 per grade, and the wage at point D is $51,200. Hence the marginal rate of return at D is $3200/51,200 = .0625$ or 6.25 percent per grade.

PAGE 201—If the interest rate is 10 percent per year, then the present value of $32,000 per year forever is $32,000/.1 = \$320,000$ the year before he begins receiving the wage—that is, in his last year of high school.

PAGE 202—We discount $w/i = \$320,000$ back 12 years. The discount factor is $\frac{1}{(1.1)^{12}} = .3186$, so the present value in the year before little Jacob begins first grade is $101,962 ($= .3186 \times \$320,000$).

PAGE 204—The slope of an iso-wealth curve is $iw(s)$. With $i = .10$, the slope of the iso-wealth curve at B is $.1 \times \$44,800 = \$4,480$ per grade, which exceeds the $3,200-per-grade slope of the wage–schooling curve.

PAGE 210—The solid curve reveals the rate of wage growth at each grade, but the dashed marginal-rate-of-return curve is the schooling demand curve. If $i = .071$, then Edward leaves school with a high school diploma. At $s^* = 12$, Edward's wage grows with schooling 10 percent per grade, which we read off the solid curve at $s = 12$. When Edward leaves school, his wage growth rate exceeds the interest rate by almost 3 percentage points.

PAGE 213—Evaluate Alice's wage–schooling curve at $s = 12$. The height of $w(s, a_1)$ at $s = 12$ is roughly $40,000. Alice's ability advantage at $s = 12$ is worth about $8,000 ($= \$40,000 − \$32,000$), and the return to her college education is $24,000 ($= \$64,000 − \$40,000$).

PAGE 217—In Figure 6.14a, the new, flatter iso-wealth curve through (16, 60,000) runs through (12, 42,000), which is the new point L. The $60,000 college job is comparable to a $42,000 high school job. In this case, Jacob's wealth from a college education exceeds the wealth associated with the $40,000 annual wage on a high-school job. So Jacob goes to college. Since Alice also goes to college, a college education doesn't signal ability in this case.

PAGE 220—On the basis of the reasoning in the previous paragraph, we conclude that Angrist and Krueger's evidence favors the human capital model of schooling. Compelling kids to stay in school doesn't increase productivity and wages in the signaling model.

PAGE 222—In Figure 6.16, draw a line tangent to indifference curve I_1 northwest of point X_{16}. Mark the tangency with X_{18}. The new line is steeper than the dashed line because a graduate degree increases Beth's wage. As a substitution effect from X_{16} to X_{18}, Beth lengthens her workweek, and her consumption and weekly earnings are higher than if she had only a college diploma. But she's not better off. Much of her extra earnings goes to pay for graduate school (i.e., her nonlabor income is lower), and the extra consumption that she enjoys merely compensates her for her longer workweek.

Chapter 7: Training, Turnover, and Migration

PAGE 236—Potential productivity increases with work experience because Gary has accumulated skills through his earlier training. The slope of his potential productivity profile $v_p(x)$ falls with experience x because training falls with experience. Gary trains more at $x = 15$ than at $x = 20$, so the change in v_p from $x = 15$ to $x = 16$ is greater than the change in v_p from $x = 20$ to $x = 21$.

PAGE 237—Foregone productivity at $x = 10$ is $.30 \times \$860 = \$260$ per week. His actual productivity is 600 ($= \$860 - \$260$) per week, and net productivity is 450 ($= \$600 - \$150$).

PAGE 239—The wage profile $w(x)$ splits the difference between the net productivity profile $v_n(x)$ and the productivity profile without training v_0. Here the split is 75 percent record label and 25 percent Gary. So 75 percent of the gap between $v_n(x)$ and v_0 is the distance between $v_n(x)$ and $w(x)$ at each x.

The remaining 25 percent is the distance between $w(x)$ and v_0. Wage profile $w_1(x)$ in Figure 7.3 reflects a 50:50 split, so $w(x)$ with a 75:25 split is flatter than $w_1(x)$.

PAGE 241—The values of the experience expression are $X = .56$ ($= (.04 \times 20) - (.0006 \times 400)$) at $x = 20$ and $X = .66$ ($= (.04 \times 30) - (.0006 \times 900)$) at $x = 30$. The difference is $.10$ or $\underline{10}$ percent.

PAGE 246—If Gary's annual wage is $\underline{\$45,000}$, then Rhythm Records alone invests in Gary. Gary pays for his own MBA if his annual wage is $\underline{\$25,000}$.

PAGE 246—Since the wage can't fall below the minimum wage, training low-skill workers would front-load pay, and these workers would quit before the employer earned a return on its training investment. To avoid losing money, the employer doesn't train minimum-wage workers.

PAGE 249—The difference between $600 and $500 is the weekly [$\underline{\text{cost of}}$, return on] Gary's [general, $\underline{\text{firm-specific}}$] training in year 5.

PAGE 252—The turnover rate is high for workers on tech jobs in Silicon Valley, so their firm-specific training pays a low return. We expect more firm-specific training in the chemical plant in rural Ohio, where the prospects for jumping ship aren't good.

PAGE 254—If Ken stays with his year-4 employer, his year-5 wage would be his year-4 wage, $743 per week. His wage offer from another firm is $784 per week. He accepts the offer and earns $784 per week with the new employer in year 5. His wage in year 4 is greater than his wage offer in year 4 because the wage offer from another firm was less than the $743 wage with his year-3 (and year-2) employer.

PAGE 256—This is a model of learning of match value, so the source of the rising wage is *not* the accumulation of human capital. And workers are *not* moving to better job matches through job shopping. Workers with 15 years of job tenure are more productive on average than workers with 10 years of job tenure because the lowest-match-value workers leave in the intervening five years. That is, the extra information about performance over the five years updates beliefs about match values, and the workers who fare poorly take jobs elsewhere. The workers who remain in year 15 are on average higher-match-value (i.e., more productive) workers in this firm.

PAGE 262—Without the indenture contract, a worker would earn a compensating wage differential for working in the West Indies. The compensating differential in indenture contracts is in terms of the length of the period of service. We expect a shorter indenture period for servants heading to the West Indies to work off the £5 cost of transportation.

PAGE 264—In Figure 7.12a, draw a vertical line segment between the two wage–skill lines at s_0 on the horizontal axis. The length of the line segment is the wage gain to immigration by a Mexican worker with s_0 units of skill. Repeat this process in the right panel to illustrate the wage loss to immigration by a Swede with s_0 units of skill. The gap represents a wage loss because $w_{swe} > w_{us}$ at s_0.

Chapter 8: Discrimination

PAGE 277—The wage ratio is $795 \div 1029 = .773$, or 77.3 percent. The wage gap is $100 - 77.3 = 22.7$ percent.

PAGE 280—The 3-unit skill gap explains $b\Delta x = \$20 \times 3 = \$60$ per week of the wage gap. The residual wage gap is $\$200 - \$60 = \$140$ per week.

PAGE 283—The rate of return to schooling is 6.6 percent, and working women have .42 years more schooling. So the schooling gap explains $.066 \times (-.42) = -.0277$ or -2.8 percent of the male wage premium. The number is less than zero because working women are more educated than working men. That is, we predict that women earn 2.8 percent more than men on the basis of being more educated.

PAGE 289—The Hispanic–non-Hispanic-white gap in the workweek grew .4 hours between 1983 and 2017. We weight this term by the slope of the wage–hours curve, which was 2.6 percent per hour in 1983. The product (1.0 percent) is one element that contributes to the 6.1 entry in the first row of Table 8.4. The increase in the return to schooling is an example of a change in the price of a characteristic. We weight that change (1.3 percent per grade) by the gap in schooling (2.1 grades in 2017), and the result (2.7 percent) contributes to the 2.7 entry in second row of the table. Changing characteristics and changing prices explain 8.8 $(= 6.1 + 2.7)$ percentage points of the widening wage gap. Increasing discrimination against Hispanics might account for the 3.8-percentage-point increase in the residual wage gap.

PAGE 292—$b\Delta x = 26.67 \times 3 = 80$, and $c\Delta y = 25.00 \times 2 = 50$. So the residual wage gap with adjustments for Δx and Δy is $\$200 - \$80 - \$50 = \$70$ per week. If Δy isn't measured in the data, then the residual wage gap is $\$200 - \$80 = \$120$, which overstates wage discrimination by $\$50$ per week.

PAGE 300—The quantity demanded of labor at $w_f = 15$ is 40 workers per hour. Ben, Carl, Dan, and Ed employ women.

PAGE 302—The anti-discrimination campaign raises the lower-right end of the demand for female labor. But that doesn't influence the equilibrium. In particular, the campaign doesn't affect the equilibrium wage gap.

PAGE 302—Shift the supply of blacks to the right, so the equilibrium slides down the demand for black (or female in Figure 8.10) labor. The wage of black workers falls, and the black–white wage gap rises.

PAGE 304—Employers are indifferent between employing men or women if $w_m = (1+d)w_f$, which implies an equilibrium female–male wage ratio $w_f/w_m = 1/(1+d)$. If $d = .25$, then the wage ratio is $w_f/w_m = 1/1.25 = .8$, and the female–male wage gap is 20 percent. If $d = .111$, then the wage ratio is $w_f/w_m = 1/1.111 = .9$, and the female–male wage gap is 10 percent. So the wage gap narrows by 10 percentage points.

PAGE 306—The innovations make it easier to avoid customer discrimination, so we predict that the wage gap shrinks.

PAGE 311—Greenspan's discrimination coefficient was $d = 0$ because he valued men and women equally. He profited by employing less-expensive women rather than more-expensive men to do the same work.

PAGE 312—The sales manager at KOOK hires and promotes less-qualified men over more-qualified women, so his sales team generates less revenue and profit. His wage depends on sales revenue (or profit), so his pay suffers.

Chapter 9: Unions

PAGE 331—After the passage of the Wagner Act in 1935, workers were free to organize a union, organize a second union, join a union, bargain collectively, strike with union approval, strike without union approval, picket, and boycott. Employers were able to bargain with unions, ignore unions, enforce nonunion pledges, pay nonunion workers less than union workers, and dismiss union organizers and union members for their union activities.

PAGE 338—If the union bargains for a $15 wage per worker, then Coalwood's marginal labor cost is $15 per worker from 0 to 1,000 workers per hour. At higher levels of employment, we read marginal labor cost off the marginal-labor-cost curve.

PAGE 341—$MLC = (\$14 \times 120 - \$16 \times 100)/(120 - 100) = (\$1680 - \$1600)/20 = \$4$ per worker-hour.

PAGE 342—At $L = 70$ in Figure 9.6, the marginal wage bill is $7 per worker-hour. (See Table 9.2.) But the nonunion wage is $15 per worker-hour. So cutting employment from 70 to 69 worker-hours per day raises union profit by $8 (= $15 − $7). Since union profit is higher at $L = 69$ than at $L = 70$, employing 70 worker-hours per day doesn't maximize profit.

PAGE 343—The union prefers contracts above iso-profit curve $\pi_u = 500$.

PAGE 344—Each iso-profit curve must slope up left of the labor demand curve and slope down right of the labor demand curve. So each iso-profit curve peaks where it crosses the labor demand curve.

PAGE 346—The union rejects any contract below C because its workers could be paid a higher wage on nonunion jobs. The firm rejects any contract above F because it would lose less by not employing any workers than by employing 100 worker-hours per day at such a high wage.

PAGE 349—$100,000 per week, the area of the triangle defined by B, C, and D. So reducing employment by 2,000 workers per week shrinks the firm's loses from unionization from $800,000 to $700,000 per week.

PAGE 352—The Railway Labor Act cartelized railroads. Mandating collective bargaining at all interstate railroads enabled rail workers to capture a share of cartel profit. The act enabled rail workers to bargain for higher wages with little loss of employment. Railroads couldn't replace union workers with nonunion workers. Bargaining for a high union wage in one railroad didn't shift business to nonunion railroads (because the act unionized all interstate railroads). The act increased labor costs, but the regulated rate hikes passed the higher costs on to shippers.

PAGE 353—Work rules limit substitutability along an isoquant curve, which lowers the elasticity of demand for labor.

PAGE 358—If the labor supply curve in Figure 9.10a pivots through the equilibrium at point E, the new labor supply curve in retail is a steeper line through the gray dot in panel (c). The intersection of this steeper labor supply curve with the labor demand curve is at a lower point along D_n. That is, if the supply of labor is less elastic, then employment in retail grows more and the wage in retail falls more.

Chapter 10: Wage Inequality

PAGE 368—The height of the bar between $1,000 and $1,100 is a little less than 4 percent, and the height of the bar between $1,100 and $1,200 is a little more than 4 percent. So about 8 percent of the workers earn between $1,000 and $1,200 per week.

PAGE 370—The wages of 2̲5̲ percent of workers are at or below $400, and 7̲5̲ percent of workers earn more than $400.

PAGE 371—From Table 10.2, the cumulative wage share at the 90th percentile is 69.5 percent, so the point on the Lorenz curve is (90, 69.5). What does it mean for the Lorenz curve to lie below the 45°? It means that the lowest (in terms of wages) 10 percent of workers earn less than 10 percent of all wages. Since these 10 percent of workers have the lowest wages, their combined wages must be less than 10 percent of all wages. And we could repeat this argument for every percentile p.

PAGE 378—Judy's weekly wage is $w = \$660 \times e^{.03 \times 119.22 - 3} = \$660 \times e^{.5766} = \$660 \times 1.78 = \$1,175$.

PAGE 381—Draw a dashed vertical line from 25 on the horizontal axis. Find the intersections of this line with the three wage–skill curves. Extend a horizontal line from each intersection to the vertical axis to find Picard's wage on each job. Picard's weekly wages would be $675 on a production job, $1,025 on a supervisory job, and $1,200 on a management job. No need to calculate these precisely, but your graph should be consistent with these numbers.

PAGE 382—One possibility is that small differences in skills generate huge differences in corporate bottom lines, so corporate boards (representing the stockholders) compete up the compensation of the most talented top managers. Another possibility is that the lavish compensation of the CEO is the prize in the contest to become CEO, and that contest motivates managers to work hard. But the CEO might also have the board of directors in his or her pocket. In that case, the CEO might

be stealing from the stockholders with the board's help. That's one form of corruption and pull. Another form of corruption and pull is political. Some CEOs are good at lobbying for government handouts and favorable regulation. You probably have an opinion about the relative importance of these possibilities. What do you know about the world that leads you to favor one possibility over another?

PAGE 383—The technology for developing and deploying software applications is a sunset technology. It's expensive to write the code, but it's inexpensive to allow another person to use the application. Your use of an app doesn't preclude me from using the same app. If software applications had a cake technology, Zuckerberg would stop by my house today to get my Facebook updates and stop by your house tomorrow for your updates. While he's at your house, he can show you my Facebook page and anyone else's page. And then he has to return to my house to show me your updated page. Bizarre!

PAGE 388—The entry of young baby boomers in the 1970s and early 1980s shrank the relative supply of experienced workers, which shifted the relative supply of experienced workers left. The equilibrium slid up the relative demand curve. The relative wage of experienced workers w_s/w_u rose. That is, the wage premium associated with skill grew. This steepened the wage profile and increased wage dispersion.

Chapter 11: Compensation Strategies

PAGE 405—Raising the price of the product or service or the marginal product of effort lifts the efficient effort up the marginal-cost-of-effort curve. Increasing the marginal cost of effort—shifting up the $MC(e)$ curve—reduces efficient effort.

PAGE 407—An additional unit of effort increases Katie's output by 1/5 tax returns per week. Partnership revenue rises by the value of the marginal product of her effort $p \times MP_e = 125 \times (1/5) = \$25$

per unit of effort. Since her share of the partnership's profit is 40 percent, her partner earnings rise by $10 per unit of effort, on average. (The solution is at the intersection of the marginal cost curve and a horizontal line at $10 per unit of effort.) Yes, Katie shirks, and she supplies less effort than Julie because Julie's share of profit is greater than Katie's share.

PAGE 408—The equation is $w = 4 + pq/10$.

PAGE 410—Those 55 units of effort deliver $q = 11$ tax returns in a typical week. Since the piece rate is $50 per return, Julie's performance pay is $550 per week. Her guarantee is $75 per week, so her expected pay is $625 per week.

PAGE 410—$a < 0$ is the rental fee that a taxi driver pays to the owner of the cab. b is 100 percent.

PAGE 412—(a) A nurse cares for lots of patients without contributing much to the health of any of the patients. (b) An author writes lots of words (and books) without any literary technique: not much of a plot, superficial characters, muddled theme, etc. (c) A professor produces a stack of unimportant research that has little or no influence on the profession. (d) A web designer creates lots of unattractive and difficult-to-navigate web sites. (e) An illustrator creates lots of unprofessional drawings. (f) A boxer throws lots of weak and ineffective punches.

PAGE 413—Advantages: encourages hard work, attracts talented workers (as well as less risk-averse workers), economizes on the costs of measuring performance, and can reward quality dimensions. Disadvantages: risk associated with wage variability, absence of incentives post-promotion (without another round of promotion), and coasting associated with the standard being too high for some and too low for others.

PAGE 415—Consider Marcia's incentives. Her grade depends on her performance relative to the rest of the class. If the rest of the class does better, Marcia gets a lower grade. Grading on a curve doesn't foster teamwork: if Marcia helps her fellow students, her grade takes a hit. Indeed,

feeding wrong answers and ideas to fellow students improves Marcia's grade. Students do have incentives to collude to reduce study time since lowering performance of the whole class has no effect on grades. Each student, however, has an incentive to cheat on the collusive agreement (by studying), and this incentive is stronger in large classes.

PAGE 418—Increasing the wage w increases effort e and labor L ($= Ne$), which reduces the value of the marginal product of labor.

PAGE 421—Since hiring and training costs are higher at the record label, the increase in the wage that it's willing to pay (to keep profit fixed) for a small reduction in the quit rate is bigger than the wage increase that TaxCrafters is willing to pay. This result implies that the label's iso-profit curves are steeper than TaxCrafters's iso-profit curves. With these steeper iso-profit curves, Rhythm Record's tangency is northwest of J along the wage–quits curve. So the label pays a higher wage, and its workers have a lower quit rate.

PAGE 422—The right side simplifies to $4500 + 9000 + .9 \times w(30) = 13,500 + .9 \times w(30)$.

PAGE 425—At age 65, $R(t) = v$. After age 65, the marginal value of time at home exceeds the value of marginal product at work, so time at home creates more value than time on the job.

PAGE 429—Low-skill CEOs do better in regulated markets, so these markets draw CEOs from the bottom of the skill distribution. In the following figure, CEOs with skills below s' earn more in firms in regulated markets; CEOs with skills above s' lead firms in unregulated markets.

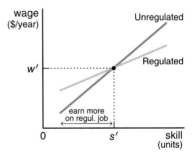

Chapter 12: Unemployment

PAGE 447—1.5 million workers per week are unemployed. Only 500,000 of those workers would be employed without the minimum wage. So the disemployment effect of the minimum wage on unemployment is 500,000 workers per week.

PAGE 449—3.6 (= 2.0 + 1.6) million workers per month exit unemployment. Two million workers find work (i.e., $U \rightarrow E$), and 1.6 million workers leave the labor market (i.e., $U \rightarrow N$). The 3.6 million workers who exit unemployment are 49.3 percent of the 7.5 million unemployed workers.

PAGE 450—The length of time a typical molecule of water stays in the lake depends on the amount of water that escapes from the lake in streams and through evaporation relative to the volume of water in the lake. The length of time a typical worker remains unemployed depends on the number of people who exit from unemployment by finding work or leaving the labor market relative to the number of people who are unemployed.

PAGE 450—The steady-state unemployment rate is 4.88 percent.

$$u^* = \frac{1.4}{27.3 + 1.4} = .0488$$

PAGE 453—2.8 percent of the original group of unemployed workers begin August unemployed. The exit rate from unemployment is 40 percent, so 1.1 (= .4 × 2.8) percent of the original group of unemployed workers exit unemployment in August, and 1.7 percent continue to look for work in September.

PAGE 457—The probability that J.J. accepts an offer falls by the area under the distribution of wage offers between R and 800.

PAGE 459—If J.J.'s reservation wage is $800 per week, then the probability that a job offer is acceptable is .5 because half the wage distribution lies above $800. The probability he receives an acceptable offer in a week is the product of the arrival rate (10 percent) and the probability that an offer is acceptable (50 percent), which is 5 percent. Since the weekly exit rate from unemployment is constant at 5 percent, the expected length of a spell of unemployment is $1/.05 = 20$ weeks.

PAGE 460—The marginal cost curve shifts up, the optimal reservation wage falls, the odds of receiving an acceptable offer increase, spells of unemployment shorten, the unemployment rate falls, and the average accepted wage falls.

PAGE 462—Bruce in PA gets the higher unemployment compensation, so he chooses a higher reservation wage. His spell of unemployment tends to last longer, but the expected value of his wage on an acceptable job is higher. Longer spells of unemployment in PA cause the unemployment rate in PA to be higher.

PAGE 465—We predict that seasonal jobs are more common where the unemployment insurance premium isn't experience rated. If the UI premium isn't experience rated, then firms (and their workers) with low risk of layoff subsidize off-season spells of unemployment in seasonal industries. That is, firms that rarely lay off workers subsidize firms that routinely lay off workers.

PAGE 466—A high minimum wage decreases the employment rate and increases the unemployment rate. Extensive collective bargaining decreases the employment rate in the monopoly-union model; this increases the unemployment rate if displaced workers search for union jobs. Generous unemployment compensation decreases the employment rate and increases the unemployment rate. Ample job-security provisions decrease the employment rate (by increasing the cost of employment) and, if coupled with super-competitive wages (e.g., minimum wage or union wage premium), increase the unemployment rate. High tax rates decrease employment; if coupled with super-competitive wages, high tax rates increase the unemployment rate. (See Problem 12.1.)

PAGE 472—The growth rate of the nominal demand for money is the inflation rate plus the real growth rate. The real growth rate is 3 percent. If the inflation rate were 3 percent, money demand would grow at an annual rate of 6 percent. Money demand would grow 4 percent per year if the inflation rate were 1 percent.

PAGE 474—Shift the aggregate demand curve down from AD_7 to AD_5. The equilibrium slides down a new AS_{SR} through c in the short run. The inflation rate falls from 4 percent to 3 percent, and the real growth rate falls from 3 percent to 2 percent. In the right panel, the equilibrium slides down the short-run Phillips curve with 4 percent expected inflation. The unemployment rate associated with the 3 percent inflation rate is 6 percent. Expectations adjust, and the aggregate equilibrium returns to a in the left panel. In the right panel, the Phillips curve with 2 percent expected inflation replaces the one with 4 percent expected inflation, and the unemployment rate returns to its natural rate of 5 percent at A.

PAGE 476—The new point $(10, 1.8)$ lies between Beveridge Curves 1 and 2 and below Job Creation Curve 2. So the new Beveridge curve lies between the displayed Beveridge curves, and the new job-creation curves is flatter than Job Creation Curve 2. Also, the new Job Creation curve is flatter than the Job Creation curve through point 11/08, so job creation was less profitable in October 2009. Since the new Beveridge curve lies farther from the origin than Beveridge Curve 1, search was less efficient late in 2008.

Glossary

Concepts are defined and described in the context of their use in labor economics.

90–10 PERCENTILE RATIO—wage at the 90th percentile of the wage distribution divided by the wage at the 10th percentile (p. 370)

90–50 AND 50–10 PERCENTILE RATIOS, COMPARISON OF—measure of asymmetry that compares distances to the median wage from the wages at the 10th and 90th percentiles (p. 374)

ABILITY BIAS—overstatement of the rate of return to schooling because more-able people become more educated; attributing the effect of ability on wages to the effect of schooling on wages (p. 213)

ADEQUACY—standard for evaluating hypotheses based on the ability of each hypothesis's assumptions, which are assumed to be true, to imply all aspects of what is to be explained (p. 7)

AGGREGATE DEMAND CURVE—rates of inflation and real growth that clear the market for money; graph of the relationship between the rate of inflation and the growth rate of the real economy such that the growth rate of money demand equals a specified growth rate of money supply (p. 471)

AGGREGATE SUPPLY CURVE—how the growth rate of the real economy depends on the inflation rate; if real growth doesn't depend on inflation in the long run, the long-run aggregate supply curve is vertical (p. 470)

ARGUMENT—form of reasoning that works forward from what is known (in the form of premises) to establish conclusions (p. 7)

ASYMMETRY (OR SKEWNESS)—property of a distribution such that the probability of an outcome d units below the median doesn't equal the probability of an outcome d units above the median; wage distribution is skewed right because its right tail is longer than its left tail (p. 374)

AUDIT STUDY OF HIRING—experimental design that pairs similar black and white job-applicant auditors and compares the hiring rates by race (p. 295)

AVERAGE PRODUCT OF LABOR—output per worker (a.k.a. productivity) (p. 128)

BACK-LOADING PAY—shifting pay, relative to productivity, from early to late in a worker's career (p. 237)

BACKWARD-BENDING LABOR SUPPLY CURVE—graph of the positive relationship between desired hours of work and the wage for low wages and the negative relationship for high wages (p. 100)

BARGAINING WITH A MONOPSONIST—model of unions in which bargaining for a higher wage reduces the underpayment of workers and also increases employment (p. 337)

BEFORE-AND-AFTER COMPARISON—value of some outcome (e.g., average wage) after an event (e.g., a new regulation) minus the value of the outcome before the event (p. 18)

BEVERIDGE CURVE—inverse relationship between unemployment and job-vacancy rates for a search technology (p. 475)

BINDING MINIMUM WAGE—regulated floor on the wage that is set above the market-clearing wage (p. 42)

BIRTH COHORT—see **cohort of workers** (pp. 195, 233)

BLACK–SCHOLES OPTIONS PRICING FORMULA—expression used to calculate the value of the right to buy a share of a stock at a specified price before a specified deadline (p. 430)

BONUS PAY—form of compensation that rewards performance above a production or sales quota with a bonus payment (p. 412)

BUDGET LINE—in the context of labor supply, pairs of consumption and leisure that exhaust income; $pc + wl = y + wT$, where wT is the value of the endowment of time (p. 87)

BUDGET SET—in the context of labor supply, pairs of consumption and leisure that are affordable; points on or inside the budget line (p. 87)

CAKE TECHNOLOGY—standard technology for producing goods and services; cost of production increases with the number of buyers (p. 382)

CASH GRANT—payment from the government to a person who doesn't work (p. 110)

COHORT OF WORKERS—group of workers born or starting careers in the same year (pp. 195, 233)

COLLECTIVE BARGAINING AGREEMENT—outcome of bargaining by a firm and the union representing its workers; union wage and perhaps other conditions of employment (p. 327)

COMMON SHOCK—in the context of production in a firm, a random factor that affects the performance of all workers (p. 413)

COMPENSATING WAGE DIFFERENTIAL—relationship between the wage and the quantity of a job attribute, such as dirt, risk, or an employee benefit (p. 169)

COMPOSITION OF PAY—how compensation is split between wages and in-kind benefits, such as health insurance (p. 184)

CONTEST—form of compensation that pays a prize to the best performer; example of relative performance pay (p. 415)

CONTRACT CURVE—graph of the set of efficient bargains between an employer and its workers (p. 345)

COST MINIMIZATION—choosing the lowest-cost mix of inputs, such as labor and capital, that produces a specified amount of output; tangency of an isocost curve to a specified isoquant curve (p. 142)

COST OF DISCRIMINATING—amount a firm or person foregoes (e.g., in profit) by discriminating (p. 311)

CUMULATIVE WAGE SHARE—for percentile p of the wage distribution, share of total wages earned by the lowest p percent of workers; the sum of wages of all workers up to percentile p divided by total wages of all workers (p. 371)

CURRENT POPULATION SURVEY (CPS)—monthly survey of approximately 60,000 households for the Bureau of Labor Statistics; source of labor force participation, employment, and unemployment rates (p. 10)

CUSTOMER DISCRIMINATION—form of taste discrimination in which customers in one group prefer not to be served by workers in another group (p. 305)

CYCLICAL UNEMPLOYMENT—unemployment associated with cyclical fluctuations in the aggregate economy (p. 469)

DEADWEIGHT LOSS—fall in total surplus that results from a distortion such as a tax or a lack of competition (p. 43)

DIFFERENCE-IN-DIFFERENCE ESTIMATION—for some treatment (e.g., a minimum-wage hike), comparison of the change in the outcome in the treated group with the change in the outcome in a control group (p. 18)

DIMINISHING MARGINAL PRODUCTIVITY—property that the marginal product of labor falls as employment of labor rises, holding other inputs fixed (p. 130)

DISCRIMINATION COEFFICIENT—number that indicates the implicit cost to the firm of employing workers in a discriminated-against group (p. 299)

DISEMPLOYMENT EFFECT OF THE MINIMUM WAGE— reduction in employment relative to the equilibrium (competitive or otherwise) without the minimum wage (p. 42)

DISEQUILIBRIUM UNEMPLOYMENT—unemployment caused by an excess supply of labor (p. 446)

DURATION OF UNEMPLOYMENT—length of time a job searcher remains unemployed (p. 450)

ECONOMIC EFFECTS OF A TAX—effects of a tax on the tax-inclusive wage, the take-home wage, employment, tax revenue, and efficiency (p. 54)

EFFICIENCY WAGE—wage that maximizes profit by trading off higher payroll costs with higher output (from increased effort) or lower training costs (from a lower quit rate) at the margin (p. 417)

EFFICIENT EFFORT—amount of effort that equalizes the value of the marginal product of effort and the marginal cost of effort (p. 405)

EFFICIENT UNION CONTRACT—wage–employment bargain such that no other bargain is preferred by both the union and the employer (p. 345)

EFFICIENT-CONTRACTING MODEL OF UNIONS—model of union bargaining in which the union and employer bargain to an efficient contract (p. 345)

EFFORT SUPPLY CURVE—graph of the relationship between a worker's quantity supplied of effort and a feature of the compensation contract, such as the piece rate; marginal cost of effort (p. 407)

ELASTICITY—unit-free measure of the sensitivity of one variable to variation in another variable; in the context of labor demand (supply), percentage change in quantity demanded (supplied) divided by the percentage change in the wage (p. 21)

ELASTICITY OF SUBSTITUTION—measure of the curvature of an isoquant curve based on percentage changes (p. 143)

EMPLOYEE BENEFITS—compensation in-kind (e.g., health insurance and pensions) and pay for time not worked (e.g., vacations and holidays) (p. 184)

EMPLOYEE DISCRIMINATION—form of taste discrimination in which one group of workers requires a higher wage to work with workers in another group (p. 304)

EMPLOYEE STOCK OPTION—right to buy a share of stock at a specified price within a specified period (p. 429)

EMPLOYER DISCRIMINATION—form of taste discrimination in which an employer acts as if the cost of employing a worker in a group is more than the worker's wage (p. 299)

EMPLOYER MANDATE—government requirement that employers provide a benefit (e.g., health insurance) to their workers (p. 57)

EMPLOYMENT AT WILL—legal doctrine that allows workers to quit and firms to dismiss workers without having to establish cause or to give warning (p. 239)

EMPLOYMENT RATE—ratio of the number of people employed to the population (p. 83)

ENDOGENOUS VARIABLE—variable that is determined by other variables, including random factors, within the model (p. 16)

ENDOWMENT—what a person can consume (including leisure time) without producing or trading with anyone (p. 88)

EQUILIBRIUM—situation in which no buyer or seller (or employer or worker) has any incentive to do anything different; in a competitive labor market, the equilibrium is a wage and a level of employment that equates the quantities demanded and supplied of labor (p. 35)

EXCESS DEMAND—see **shortage** (p. 3)

EXCESS SUPPLY—see **surplus** (p. 3)

EXOGENOUS VARIABLE—variable that is determined by factors outside the model (p. 17)

EXPECTATIONS-AUGMENTED PHILLIPS CURVE—mathematical relationship between the unemployment rate and the unexpected rate of inflation; vertical Phillips curve if inflation is expected; downward-sloping Phillips curve if inflation isn't expected (p. 474)

EXPECTED NET EARNINGS—expected value of earnings minus the cost of effort (p. 406)

EXPLANATION—form of reasoning that works backward from what is known to its cause (p. 7)

FATIGUE EFFECT—decline in the marginal product of labor associated with a longer workday or workweek (p. 180)

FEATHERBEDDING—union practice that requires employers to use too much labor or to pay workers for unnecessary work or for no work at all (p. 351)

FIXED INPUT—input such as capital that is too costly to vary in the short run (p. 127)

FREE AGENCY—in baseball and other sports, system that allows a player to contract with teams other than his or her current team (pp. 68, 247)

FRICTIONAL UNEMPLOYMENT—unemployment associated with job search (p. 448)

FRONT-LOADING PAY—shifting pay, relative to productivity, to early from late in a worker's career (p. 237)

FULL INCOME—nonlabor income y plus the value of the time endowment wT (p. 89)

GAP IN UNMEASURED SKILL—difference across groups in the average value of skill that isn't measured in the data; contaminates an estimate of wage discrimination based on the residual wage gap (p. 291)

GENERAL TRAINING—accumulation of skills on the job that are valued by many or all firms equally (p. 234)

GINI COEFFICIENT—measure of wage inequality based on the area between the 45° line and the Lorenz curve (p. 373)

HIERARCHY OF JOBS—levels of management and other jobs from lowest to highest in terms of responsibilities and required skills (p. 379)

HIRING RATE—number of new hires divided by the number of people unemployed (p. 450)

HISTOGRAM—graph of tabulated frequencies or proportions over discrete intervals (bins); height of each bar is the frequency or proportion of the interval (p. 368)

HOME PRODUCTION FUNCTION—relationship between time engaged in producing values at home and output of those values (p. 113)

HUMAN CAPITAL—knowledge and abilities that influence a worker's productivity; learning in school and on the job combine with innate ability to determine a worker's stock of human capital (p. 195)

HYPOTHETICAL TRUTH—standard for evaluating an hypothesis based on evidence supporting its essential assumptions and testable implications (p. 8)

INCIDENCE OF UNEMPLOYMENT—how often people become unemployed; rate at which employed workers (or people who are not in the labor force) become unemployed (p. 450)

INCOME EFFECT—change in consumption, leisure, or hours of work caused by a change in nonlabor income (p. 96)

INCREASES AT AN INCREASING RATE—in the context of the wage–ability curve, property that the slope of the curve increases as ability increases; generally, that the slope of a function $f(x)$ increases as x increases (p. 378)

INCREASING RETURN TO SKILL—empirical pattern since the 1960s that the rate of return to schooling and the premium for work experience are rising (p. 386)

INCREASING WAGE INEQUALITY—increase in the dispersion of wages since the late 1960s (p. 384)

INDENTURE CONTRACT—legal contract that binds one person to another to work as a servant for a specified period, usually in exchange for transportation to a distant colony (p. 259)

INDIFFERENCE CURVE—in the context of labor supply, pairs of consumption and leisure such that no pair is preferred to any other pair; pairs of consumption and leisure that are equally satisfying to the worker (p. 90)

INPUT-PRICE EFFECT—in the context of a change in the wage, feedback from an input market to the market demand for labor; wage change shifts the demand for capital, which impacts the price of capital unless the supply of capital is perfectly elastic (p. 153)

INSTRUMENTAL VARIABLES ESTIMATION—statistical technique that uses only exogenous variation in the explanatory variables to estimate a causal relationship (p. 17)

ISO-PROFIT CURVE—graph of pairs of wages and quantities of a job attribute with a specific value of profit (pp. 171, 343)

ISO-WEALTH CURVE—in the context of schooling, graph of pairs of wages and schooling with a specific present value of career wages (p. 202)

ISOCOST LINE—pairs of labor and capital that have a specific cost; $C = wL + rK$ for some value of C (p. 141)

ISOQUANT CURVE—graph of pairs of labor and capital that produce a specific amount of output (p. 138)

JIM CROW ERA—period from 1876 to 1965 when racial segregation laws existed in the southern states of the United States (p. 313)

JOB POLARIZATION—change in opportunities that shifts jobs away from workers in the middle of the skill distribution toward low-skill and high-skill workers (p. 393)

JOB SEPARATION RATE—number of workers leaving their employers divided by the number of people employed (p. 450)

JOB SHOPPING—process of searching for a job over a career, especially searching while on the job (p. 253)

JOB TENURE—length of time that a person has worked for his or her employer (p. 250)

JOINT (OR NONRIVALROUS) CONSUMPTION—property in which one person's consumption doesn't preclude another person's consumption of the same unit; property of a sunset technology (p. 382)

LABOR FORCE PARTICIPATION RATE—number of workers employed or unemployed divided by the population (p. 82)

LABOR MARKET MONOPSONY—labor market with one employer or a group of employers colluding to act as a single employer; more generally, any labor market in which an employer faces an upward-sloping labor supply curve (p. 64)

LABOR-MARKET FLOWS—movements of people between labor-market states such as from employment to unemployment and from unemployment to employment (p. 448)

LABOR-MARKET STATE—person's activity related to work: employed, unemployed, or not in the labor force (p. 448)

LEARNING THE MATCH VALUE—learning a worker's productivity with a particular employer by observing his performance over time (p. 256)

LEGAL INCIDENCE OF A TAX—party (i.e., employer or employee) that is legally responsible for a tax obligation (p. 52)

LIFE-CYCLE LABOR SUPPLY CURVE—graph of the relationship between desired hours of work and wages for predictable variation in the wage over a worker's career (p. 242)

LIMITED SUBSTITUTION BETWEEN QUANTITY AND QUALITY—property of preferences such that many low-quality performances substitute poorly for one excellent performance (p. 383)

LOCATIONAL WAGE DIFFERENCES—differences in wages across cities, states, countries, or other locations (p. 60)

LOG-WAGE EQUATION—relationship between wages (expressed in logarithms) and factors that influence wages such as schooling, work experience, and union status (p. 207)

LONG-RUN LABOR DEMAND CURVE—graph of the relationship between the quantity demanded of labor and the wage over the period when all inputs are variable (p. 148)

LORENZ CURVE—graph of the relationship between the share of total wages earned by workers at or below the pth percentile of wages and percentiles of the wage distribution (p. 371)

MARGINAL BENEFIT OF SEARCH—gain from a small increase in the reservation wage; depends on the arrival rate of job offers, the expected length of time on the job, the interest rate, and the expected value of an acceptable wage offer (p. 457)

MARGINAL COST OF EFFORT—change in the worker's implicit cost associated with an additional unit of effort (p. 404)

MARGINAL COST OF SEARCH—increase in the cost of search from a small increase in the reservation wage; out-of-pocket costs (net of unemployment compensation) plus the reservation wage (p. 457)

MARGINAL COST OF WORKERS' TIME—opportunity cost of work for an additional worker; marginal value of workers' time in other activities (p. 34)

MARGINAL INCENTIVES—in the context of bonus pay, a bonus can provide strong incentives to reach the production or sales quota, but marginal incentives vanish beyond the quota; a worker who approaches the quota long before the end of the period (e.g., week or year) coasts the rest of the period (p. 413)

MARGINAL LABOR COST—change in cost associated with an additional unit of labor (pp. 64, 133)

MARGINAL PRODUCT OF LABOR—increase in output that arises from an additional unit of labor, $\Delta q / \Delta L$, holding capital fixed (p. 129)

MARGINAL PRODUCTIVITY THEORY OF DISTRIBUTION—theory that holds labor, as well as other inputs, is paid an amount equal to the value of its contribution to production (i.e., VMP_L) (p. 37)

MARGINAL RATE OF RETURN TO SCHOOLING—wage gain from an additional grade completed Δw divided by the cost of attending a grade of school, which is the foregone wage $w(s)$ plus tuition c; coefficient on the schooling variable in a log-wage regression (p. 200)

MARGINAL RATE OF SUBSTITUTION—rate at which a person is willing to give up consumption to get an additional unit of leisure; absolute value of the slope of an indifference curve (p. 93)

MARGINAL RATE OF TECHNICAL SUBSTITUTION—absolute value of the slope of an isoquant curve; ratio of the marginal products of labor and capital (p. 139)

MARGINAL REVENUE PRODUCT OF LABOR—effect of an additional worker on revenue; same as value of marginal product of labor if the employer operates in a competitive product market (p. 137)

MARGINAL VALUE OF LABOR—effect of an additional worker on revenue; more formally, value of the marginal product of labor (p. 33)

MARGINAL WAGE BILL—change in wage payments to labor associated with an additional worker (p. 339)

MARKET CLEARING—situation in which quantity demanded equals quantity supplied (p. 4)

MARKET LABOR DEMAND CURVE—graph of the relationship between the quantity demanded of labor in the market and the wage; typically includes feedback from changes in the prices of the product and other inputs (p. 150)

MARKET LABOR SUPPLY CURVE—graph of the relationship between the quantity supplied of labor in a market and the wage (p. 115)

MARSHALL'S RULES—four principles laid out by Alfred Marshall that relate the elasticity of demand for labor to the elasticity of substitution between labor and capital, the elasticity of demand for the product, the elasticity of supply of other inputs, and labor's share of costs (p. 153)

MATCH VALUE—value of a worker to an employer that is specific to the employer (p. 253)

MEAN—in the context of the distribution of wages, sum of wages across all workers divided by the number of workers (p. 369)

MEAN–MEDIAN DIFFERENCE—in the context of the wage distribution, mean wage minus median wage;

measure of asymmetry (or skewness) of the wage distribution (p. 374)

MEDIAN—in the context of the distribution of wages, middle of the ordered (from lowest to highest) wages; value of the wage such that half the workers have wages below that value (p. 369)

MIGRATION—movement from one location or area to settle in a distant location or area (pp. 60, 257)

MONEY COST OF WORK—expenses associated with working at all; e.g., monetary cost of commuting to and from work (p. 108)

MONOPOLY MODEL OF UNIONS—model of unions that limits the union's choice to wage–employment pairs along the labor demand curve (p. 339)

MONOPSONY—see **labor market monopsony** (p. 64)

MONOPSONY DISCRIMINATION—form of discrimination that generates wage gaps from differences across groups in labor supply elasticities (p. 307)

MULTI-MARKET EQUILIBRIUM—situation in which every labor market clears and there are no incentives for workers or firms to move across markets (p. 60)

NATURAL RATE OF UNEMPLOYMENT—unemployment rate consistent with no changes in aggregate demand or aggregate supply; unemployment rate generated by frictional unemployment (p. 472)

NET PRESENT VALUE—in the context of migration, present discounted value of wage gains minus the cost of moving (p. 257)

NET PRODUCTIVITY—potential productivity minus foregone productivity (associated with training) and direct costs of training (p. 236)

NONLABOR INCOME—income from sources other than work; e.g., allowances and interest on savings (p. 87)

NONUNION PLEDGE—pledge, required by some employers, not to organize or join a labor union;

rendered unenforceable in federal courts by the Norris–LaGuardia Act in 1932 (p. 329)

NORMAL DISTRIBUTION—bell-shaped curve that graphs the probability associated with each value of a random variable (p. 370)

NORMAL GOOD—good for which higher income increases demand (p. 96)

NORMATIVE STATEMENT—proposition that requires a value judgment (p. 7)

ON-THE-JOB TRAINING—accumulation of job skills (or human capital) while working (p. 234)

OPPORTUNITY COST OF UNION LABOR—nonunion wage times the number of union workers, $w_n L_u$ (p. 339)

PANEL DATA—data that include measurements through time as well as across people (or firms or countries) (p. 257)

PER-WORKER COST—cost of labor that depends on the number of workers but doesn't depend on the length of the workday or workweek (p. 180)

PERCENTILE OF THE WAGE DISTRIBUTION—number from 1 to 100 that indicates the proportion of a sample; e.g., three-quarters of the sample have wages at or below the wage at the 75th percentile (p. 369)

PERFORMANCE BOND—amount held back against satisfactory completion of the job; forfeited if the worker is caught stealing, cheating, or shirking (p. 423)

PERSONAL PERFORMANCE PAY—form of compensation that pays a worker an amount that depends on the worker's own performance (p. 408)

PHILLIPS CURVE—graph of the relationship between the inflation rate and the unemployment rate (p. 469)

PIECE RATE—form of personal performance pay that compensates the worker an amount for each unit produced or sold (p. 408)

POSITIVE STATEMENT—proposition that doesn't depend on value judgments (p. 7)

POTENTIAL PRODUCTIVITY—productivity (based on past training) if the worker receives no current training (p. 235)

PREFERENCE DIRECTION—graphical indicator of whether a person prefers more or less of a good (p. 91)

PRESENT VALUE—value today of a specified amount N periods in the future; size of a deposit today such that the bank balance compounds with interest to the specified future amount in N periods (p. 197)

PRINCIPLE OF PARSIMONY—simplicity of a hypothesis is a virtue; a complicated hypothesis requires more evidence to support its essential assumptions and testable implications (p. 9)

PRODUCT-PRICE EFFECT—in the context of a change in the wage, feedback from the product market to the market demand for labor; wage change shifts the supply of the product, which affects the price of the product unless the demand for the product is perfectly elastic (p. 153)

PRODUCTION FUNCTION—relationship between the quantity of inputs used in production and the quantity of output (p. 127)

PRODUCTIVITY PROFILE—graph that displays the evolution of a worker's productivity over his or her career (p. 235)

PROFILING—popular term for statistical discrimination (p. 308)

PROFIT SHARING—form of compensation that rewards workers with shares of the firm's accounting profit (p. 406)

RACIAL SEGREGATION—result of discrimination, especially employee discrimination, in which black and white workers work in separate firms (p. 313)

RATE-OF-RETURN MAXIMIZATION—in the context of schooling choice, choosing to quit school when the rate of return to schooling is highest, which is sooner than the choice that maximizes wealth (p. 205)

REAL WAGE—rate at which units of time can be traded for units of consumption; wage (in dollars per unit of time) divided by the price of consumption (in dollars per unit of consumption) (p. 88)

REGRESSION ANALYSIS—fitting a line to data points; statistical methods for estimating relationships among variables in data; linear regression involves estimating each explanatory variable's slope coefficient (p. 14)

RELATIVE PERFORMANCE PAY—form of compensation that pays a worker on the basis of personal performance relative to the performance of a reference group of coworkers (p. 414)

RESERVATION WAGE FOR DIRTY WORK—lowest wage that gets the worker to choose a dirty job over a clean job (p. 165)

RESERVATION WAGE IN LABOR SUPPLY—wage that leaves a person indifferent between working and not working (p. 107)

RESERVATION WAGE IN SEARCH—lowest wage offer that a worker would accept while searching sequentially (p. 456)

RESERVE CLAUSE—in baseball and other sports, clause that precludes a player from playing for another team without permission from the owner of the current team (pp. 68, 247)

RESIDUAL (OR ADJUSTED) WAGE GAP—gap in wages between two groups that isn't explained by differences in average skills and other characteristics across the two groups (p. 280)

REVERSE CAUSATION—in the regression context, dependent variable influencing one or more explanatory variables (in addition to the explanatory variables causing the dependent variable) (p. 16)

SABOTAGE—deliberate act of hindering or interfering with the performance of coworkers (p. 414)

SALES QUOTA—minimum performance to qualify for bonus pay (p. 412)

SCALE EFFECT—change in labor and other inputs caused by a change in the price of the product;

movement from a point on one isoquant curve to a point with the same slope on another isoquant curve (p. 149)

SCARRING EFFECT OF UNEMPLOYMENT—deterioration of job opportunities associated with the loss of skills while unemployed (especially for a long period of unemployment) (p. 468)

SCATTER PLOT—graph that displays data as a collection of points; for each point, the value of one variable determines the position of the point on the horizontal axis, and the value of another variable determines the position of the point on the vertical axis (p. 12)

SCHOOLING REQUIREMENT—in the signaling model of schooling, minimal amount of schooling to qualify for the higher wage paid (p. 218)

SCIENTIFIC METHOD—objective procedures to in vestigate phenomena and to acquire knowledge of causes; observe, hypothesize, and test (p. 8)

SELF-SELECTION—sorting into a group (e.g., of workers or immigrants) by personal choice; characteristics of a group formed by self-selection typically don't match the characteristics of the population (p. 263)

SEQUENTIAL SEARCH—accepting or rejecting job offers as they arrive rather than waiting to compare several or many job offers (p. 456)

SEVERANCE PAYMENT—practice of the worker paying the employer to quit or the employer paying the worker to dismiss the worker (p. 246)

SHARING TRAINING COSTS AND RETURNS—worker bearing part of the costs of training by receiving a wage early in his career less than his opportunity wage and the firm bearing the remaining costs by paying a wage early on greater than the value of the worker's productivity net of training costs; late in the career, the wage lies above the opportunity wage (worker's return) and below net productivty (firm's return) (p. 250)

SHIRKING—putting forth less than the efficient amount of effort (p. 407)

SHORT-RUN AGGREGATE SUPPLY CURVE—how the growth rate of the real economy depends on the inflation rate in the short run; mistaken expectations and wage and price rigidities cause the real growth rate to increase with the inflation rate in the short run (p. 473)

SHORT-RUN LABOR DEMAND CURVE—graph of the relationship between the quantity demanded of labor and the wage with the amount of capital fixed (p. 135)

SHORTAGE—situation in which quantity demanded exceeds quantity supplied at a specified price (or wage) (p. 3)

SHUTDOWN WAGE—wage that triggers the firm to shut down; labor cost exceeds revenue at any higher wage (p. 136)

SIGNALING ABILITY—model of wage determination in which employers don't observe ability; high-ability workers distinguish themselves from low-ability workers by getting more education (p. 216)

SKILL GAP—difference in average values of a skill variable between two groups; e.g., average schooling of white workers minus average schooling of black workers (p. 280)

SKILL PRICE—in the method of standardized comparison, slope of the wage–skill line; used to adjust the wage gap for differences in average skills between groups (p. 280)

SKILL-BIASED INNOVATION—change in the production technology that increases the demand for skilled workers relative to the demand for unskilled workers; also known as skill-biased technological progress (p. 387)

SPECIFIC TRAINING—accumulation of job skills that only the current employer values (p. 247)

SPILLOVER TO AN UNCOVERED SECTOR—shift in labor from firms covered by a minimum wage to firms not covered by the minimum wage (p. 61)

STANDARD DEVIATION OF THE LOG OF WAGES— measure of wage dispersion based on the average distance of the log of wages from the mean value (of log wages) (p. 370)

STANDARDIZED COMPARISON—method for comparing wages across groups that adjusts the wages for differences in measured skills (and other measured characteristics) on the basis of market values of the skills (p. 279)

START-UP COST—per-worker cost associated with the time to get started (or become productive) at the beginning of the workday (p. 180)

STATISTICAL DISCRIMINATION—form of discrimination in which employers apply the average characteristics of a group to each member of the group (p. 309)

STEADY STATE—situation in which the number of people in each state doesn't change over time; number of people entering a labor market state (e.g., unemployment) equals the number of people exiting that state (p. 449)

STEADY-STATE UNEMPLOYMENT RATE—unemployment rate that doesn't rise or fall because the flow of people into unemployment equals the flow of people out of unemployment (p. 450)

STEP FUNCTION—graph of a relationship in which the value of y is constant over a range of x and jumps to a higher or lower value of y over another range of x (p. 166)

STRUCTURAL UNEMPLOYMENT—unemployment associated with changes in the structure of the economy (e.g., from manufacturing to services); mismatch between the skills valued by firms and the available skills of workers (p. 447)

SUBSTITUTION AND INCOME EFFECTS—decomposition of the effect of a change in the wage into a movement along the original indifference curve (i.e., substitution effect) and a shift to a new indifference curve (i.e., income effect) (p. 98)

SUBSTITUTION AND SCALE EFFECTS—decomposition of a firm's long-run response to a change in the price of an input into a movement along an isoquant curve (substitution effect) and the scale effect of moving to a new isoquant curve (p. 146)

SUNSET TECHNOLOGY—technology that allows joint or non-rivalrous consumption; special technology in which the cost of providing a service is largely unrelated to the number of people served (p. 382)

SUPERSTAR MARKET—labor market in which a sunset technology (allowing nonrivalrous consumption) combines with limited substitution between quantity and quality of the product or performance to concentrate wages on the most talented workers or performers (p. 382)

SURPLUS—situation in which quantity supplied exceeds quantity demanded at a specified price (or wage) (p. 3)

TASTE DISCRIMINATION—form of discrimination with personal preference as its source (p. 298)

TESTABLE IMPLICATIONS—predictions derived from the essential assumptions of a hypothesis that distinguish it from alternative hypotheses (p. 8)

TOTAL-PRODUCT CURVE—graph of the relationship between output and labor input holding other inputs (e.g., capital) fixed (p. 128)

TOURNAMENT—see **contest** (p. 415)

UI EXPERIENCE RATING—tying an employer's unemployment insurance premium to the historical experience of its workers in claiming unemployment compensation (p. 464)

UI REPLACEMENT RATIO—unemployment compensation divided by the pre-unemployment wage (p. 461)

UNION PROFIT—workers' gain to organizing; union wage bill minus the opportunity cost of union labor, $\pi_u = (w_u - w_n)L_u$; also known as union rents (p. 339)

UNION SPILLOVER EFFECT—depressing effect of the union wage on the nonunion wage caused by workers displaced by shrinking employment in the union sector spilling over to the nonunion sector (p. 356)

UNION THREAT EFFECT—effect of the threat to unionize on nonunion wages (p. 356)

UNION WAGE PREMIUM—union wage w_u relative to the nonunion wage w_n; $(w_u - w_n)/w_n$ (p. 333)

VALUE OF LIFE—market value based on the compensating wage differential associated with small increases in the risk of death on the job (p. 178)

VALUE OF MARGINAL PRODUCT OF LABOR—effect of an additional worker on revenue in a competitive firm; price of the product times the marginal product of labor, $VMP_L \equiv pMP_L$ (p. 133)

VARIABLE INPUT—input in production that can vary in the relevant period; labor is an input that is variable in shorter periods than capital is (p. 127)

WAGE BILL—wage payments to workers wL (p. 339)

WAGE CONVERGENCE—process by which wages across markets converge to a common value through migration of workers and firms (or capital accumulation) (p. 60)

WAGE INEQUALITY—that workers are paid different wages; that wages are spread out over a wide range of values (p. 369)

WAGE GAP—one minus the wage ratio (p. 277)

WAGE PREMIUM—extra amount of pay associated with a skill (e.g., college wage premium) or a bad attribute of the job (wage premium for dirty work); compensating wage differential associated with a discrete difference in a job attribute (e.g., dirty vs. clean) (p. 168)

WAGE PROFILE—graph that displays the evolution of wages over a worker's career (pp. 198, 233)

WAGE RATIO—average (or median) wage of one group divided by the average (or median) wage of another group; e.g., average wage of women divided by the average wage of men (p. 276)

WAGE SUBSIDY—government payment per worker (or as a percentage of earnings) to workers or employers (p. 55)

WAGE–DIRT CURVE—graph of the relationship across jobs between the wage and dirt, an attribute of the job (p. 169)

WAGE–SCHOOLING CURVE—graph of the relationship between the wage and schooling, an attribute of the worker (p. 199)

WEALTH—present value of career wages evaluated in the year before school begins (p. 202)

YELLOW-DOG CONTRACT—see **nonunion pledge** (p. 329)

Index

Note: Page numbers in *italics* indicate figures and charts.

D